CHILDREN'S LANGUAGE

Volume 5

edited by

Keith E. Nelson

CHILDREN'S LANGUAGE

Volume 5

edited by

Keith E. Nelson
The Pennsylvania State University

LEA LAWRENCE ERLBAUM ASSOCIATES, PUBLISHERS
1985   Hillsdale, New Jersey   London

Country Stars is part of William Meredith's set of poems published under the title *The Cheer* by Alfred A. Knopf in New York (1980).

Lawrence Erlbaum Associates, Inc., Publishers
365 Broadway
Hillsdale, New Jersey 07642

ISSN 0163-2809
ISBN 0-89859-346-8

Printed in the United States of America
10   9   8   7   6   5   4   3   2   1

Contents

Preface

The nearsighted child has taken off her glasses
and come downstairs to be kissed goodnight.
She blows on a black windowpane until it's white.
Over the apple trees a great bear passes
but she puts her own construction on the night.

Two cities, a chemical plant, and clotted cars
breathe our distrust of darkness on the air,
clouding the pane between us and the stars.
But have no fear, or only proper fear:
the bright watchers are still there.

In children's language we are in search of the "great bears," the clear solid patterns that hold up after countless angles of view and after many, many lenses have been tried. In the first four volumes of this series, *Children's Language,* there has been coverage of alternative theories and methods in syntax, semantics, discourse, phonology, figurative language, second language learning, the transition to text processing, and story structures, among other topics. In order to present a lively account of development, the authors in the first four volumes were encouraged to each adopt a flexible format—one that best fit their own material rather than sticking to a standard review organization. Exactly the same approach has been taken by the authors of the present volume 5. As we have often seen, one particular lens of theory or method can limit consideration of alternative theories or methods. In this volume the reader will find that there are many ties between the themes and subthemes of the various chapters, not just one organizing theme. There are stimulating accounts on a wide range of topics of keen interest not only to child language specialists, but also cognitive psychologists, developmental psychologists, linguists, anthropologists, and those concerned with preschool language input and remediation of reading, speech and language. In each of the 13 chapters of this volume the authors have shown a particularly fine sense of balanced, critical assessment of current methods and theories in the fields of children's language as well as a sensitivity to the most recent observations and theories. Here there is no turning away from the complex process of integrating the diverse views on children's language development.

In the first chapter MacKain and Stern illustrate well the value of placing a close lens on the input structure of first one language, then another, and still another in order to illuminate the process by which infants in any language come to deal with the speech sound categories that contribute to the meaning of verbal messages. Although prior studies had shown an apparent shift of infant perceptual categories in the direction of the phonetic input provided by adult speakers, a closer look at the actual input available to children shows this input to be much less clear cut and consistent than most investigators had previously recognized. Accordingly, the problem for the infant in learning to deal with the particular sound contrasts that are essential to communication in his or her native language becomes linked from early infancy to the analysis of meaning as well as to the analysis of sound. As MacKain and Stern put it: "Experience listening to the speech of a particular linguistic community will not induce discrimination of a language-specific contrast, shift a boundary to correspond to that of the language user, or attenuate discrimination of a distinction that may be discriminable by virtue of its psychoacoustic characteristics, until infants are aware that certain sounds contrast to convey differences in meaning."

Another consideration of early input arises in Ferrier's discussions of maternal and infant intonation in conversations between 12-month-olds and their mothers. The overall results indicate that infants are in line with their mothers in terms of proportional frequencies of different uses of intonation to convey different communicative functions. These results lead the intriguing open question as to how the child learns uses of intonation. In some infants, however, there is a clear parallel to processes of oversimplification that occur in later semantic and syntactic development: These infants adopted the strategy of using rising intonation almost exclusively to indicate requests for action.

Sara, the child given the most intensive study in chapter 3 by Fein and Moorin, certainly is seen imposing her own constructions on reality. Through the window of pretend play, Fein and Moorin address the always thorny issue of the relation between thought and language. Two observations stand out particularly. First, "pretend actions might be thought of as semantically organized behavior in the sense that objects, actions, and recipients fill open-ended slots defined by abstract relationships among animate and inanimate things and forms of action. If so, the study of particular semantic domains (e.g., feeding someone with something) as these are expressed in language and play might provide the fine tuning required for a theory of the development of representational thinking." Second, as part of a terse review, the authors appropriately note that the understanding of play behavior involving clear pretense requires a thorough look at literal behavior and how literal behavior becomes ritualized and eventually freed from context. One might say that if the observer has one eye on play and the other eye on non-play, then a clearer view of both is bound to emerge.

What do *uncle, dog, jump, talk, kick,* and *float* all have in common? In Chapter 4 Anglin shows that they all can be used in interview studies to give insight into the semantic development of children. Most investigators find it easier to criticize the work of others than to criticize their own. But in this chapter Anglin succeeds in showing the value of the interview method and in critiquing prior work on direct semantic extension of words to pictures, objects, and events, and then turns his critical powers back on the interview studies he and his colleagues have recently completed. His chapter clearly shows the value of seeking convergent views and methods. In addition, there is much fascinating detail on the development of particular nouns and verbs. In very brief summary, it is clear that preschool children express information for noun concepts, such as *dog* and *ball,* that specifies appearance and functions, but for words like *kick* and *float* the information provided much more frequently concerns the participants, objects and locations of the activity. For both nouns and verbs adults supply a much fuller and wider range of information.

In reading words and sentences, children and adults draw upon more complex cognitive, executive skills than most models of reading acknowledge. This is Kleiman's argument in Chapter 5. He also argues that if the processes involved in skilled and not-so-skilled reading are to be understood, then much more rigor than has been typically observed is needed in selection of tasks, in samples of readers, and in analyses. Beyond these reforms, the acceptance of more complex cognitive models of reading will require the introduction of new methods. One essential new goal will be analyses of the ways in which the child manages the multiple cognitive processes that must be integrated and coordinated in order to permit rapid and successful processing of text.

Seven contrasting programs for young children with hearing impairments are assessed by Moores in a longitudinal study presented in Chapter 6. Moores looks at the growth in communication skills of 60 children over four years, from age three to age seven. Programs that emphasized cognitive skills from the early preschool years on, together with socialization and communication, showed great success in facilitating reading and mathematics skills in their pupils. Moores also finds that the use of manual communication along with coordinated use of auditory training in speech contributes to the development of communication ability as well as academic achievement. Further, these gains do not detract from the children's development of oral reception and expression skills. This research thus contributes to the general conclusion that for most deaf children the "bright watchers" of the mind, the essential cognitive mechanisms, are intact, just waiting for the kind of rich, appropriate and consistent input that will lead to a full mastery of skills in verbal communication, reading, and writing.

Related theoretical issues are taken up by Goldin–Meadow in Chapter 7. Here she examines the early language development of profoundly deaf children interacting with hearing parents who have chosen not to use any conventional sign language with their children. Goldin–Meadow argues that under these conditions the profoundly deaf child is not receiving conventional linguistic input in either speech or sign. Nevertheless, the ten deaf children are shown to have developed a structured, gestural communication system comparable in semantic complexity and organization to the early language systems of hearing children. In drawing implications from her research, Goldin–Meadow makes a distinction between resilient language properties and fragile language properties. Fragile properties may include the more complex rules of language and may not develop unless the linguistic input is fairly rich and conventional. In contrast, some of the more basic rules, such as ordering rules in two and three element sentences, may be resilient enough to emerge even when linguistic input is considerably less frequent and less conventionally structured than the usual range of input.

It has become commonplace in discussions about children's language development to stress that the child influences the mother (or any other input source). Unfortunately, it has not become commonplace to see imaginative studies which address the ways in which children may influence what adults say to them. Cross, Nienhaus, and Kirkman (Chapter 8) provide exciting data on how mothers talk to children by looking at a combination of child language measures and mother language measures for groups as diverse as hearing impaired children, language delayed children, dysphasic, autistic, language accelerated children, and the siblings of these groups. To a very large extent the pattern that emerges is that when children's language levels are not in line with their age and social skills, their mothers speak to them not on the basis of their age, but of their demonstrated language level. Of course, the same data also bears on the issue of how differences between mothers concerning input may contribute to relatively slow or delayed pace in language acquisition. As when the child's breath frosts a black cold window white, there are two patterns and each deserves attention. The work by Cross and her colleagues is especially valuable in providing multiple result patterns that point toward clarifying both child–mother and mother–child influences.

In Chapter 9 Leonard and Schwartz approach linguistic input in a somewhat different way, employing techniques of controlled input for development of new lexical items in the child's system. They use this common method, already thoroughly tested with normally developing children, to examine the semantic development of children with specific language impairment. Such children have tested nonverbal intelligence at normal levels and no problems in hearing, but they do have a delay in the development of early stages of language. By studying these children at the one word developmental stage along with younger normally developing children who were also at the one word stage, Leonard and Schwartz find a remarkable similarity in the pace and process of learning new lexical items. They conclude that we need to be cautious when drawing conclusions from language acquisition literature based predominantly on normally developing children. Instead, important lessons about the relationships between play, social development, thinking, and language development must be learned by looking at children with quite varied developmental patterns. How a child sees the world may depend upon a tremendous mix of elements: on apple trees outside the window, eyeglasses, goodnight kisses, travel, and social and linguistic input over extensive periods—a combination of accidental, infrequent events and planned, very frequent events. In building theories and intervention or education programs based upon theory and observations, professionals may also want to actively seek a tremendous mix of observations. As we learn to fill in the picture for atypical and typical learners under typical and varied atypical input conditions, the firm clear patterns that underlie language growth will certainly come into sharper focus.

Longitudinal data is again put to good use in Chapter 10. Hakuta and Diaz examine the relationship between bilingualism and cognitive ability. For sociological and methodological reasons this relationship has often been murky and controversial. With ingenuity and rigor, Hakuta and Diaz garner fundamental new data pointing toward the contribution of increased bilingual skill in cognitive skill development.

In Chapter 11 Hood asks us to look at language development and its research through a different lens. She sees language "not as a window to cognition, a reflection of reality nor as a means of communication; rather, language is a uniquely historical activity...When children learn language they are learning about themselves as historical beings in the sense that they become aware what it means to be a speaker (a producer of speech). In studying how language develops then we are not asking how children acquire mental capacity or develop communicative competence but how children become self-conscious, historical beings."

"Over the apple trees a great bear passes but she puts her own construction on the night." This sentence serves to illustrate in a rough way the kind of complex sentences over which most children have gained productive control during their late preschool years. In addition, it reminds us of the constructions that children formulate on their own even after they appear to have perfected control of certain forms. Bowerman, in Chapter 12, provides many examples of new errors that children introduce at relatively advanced stages of mastery of semantics and syntax. As in recent work by Karmiloff–Smith and by Nelson and Nelson, Bowerman views these seemingly backwards steps as indications of definite steps forward by the child toward achieving reflective, flexible and integrated systems of semantics and syntax. The children's surprising errors point away from too close a tie between form and meaning, too much emphasis on communication pressure and feedback as the impetus for growth, or too much emphasis upon advances in world knowledge as the leading edge that pulls language growth along. As of yet we know virtually nothing about the circumstances or input that promote the child's successful transition to a highly flexible, integrated and self-reflective set of rules for language and for language use.

Steven Pinker also addresses issues of language learning in his concluding chapter. He appropriately argues that a realistic model of language acquisition will take into account both the kinds of input that the child receives and the kinds of mechanisms that the child has available for analyzing input and for analyzing and extending his or her own productive system. Unrealistic models can result from assuming either too much or too little in terms of the structures and skills that the child brings to the language process. Pinker provides an excellent framework for considering the memory, attention, analytic, and rule-making skills that need to be specified and tested before a persuasive model of language acquisition can emerge. Similarly, the actual conditions of input need to be empirically determined rather than assumed.

Given the kinds of refinements in questions and methods that we see in these chapters, there is a clear sense that, despite inevitable obscuring factors, the field of children's language is moving closer to an integrated view of those bright consistent patterns that will maintain stability across both investigator and method.

Jeremy M. Anglin
University of Waterloo, Waterloo, Ontario, Canada

Melissa Bowerman
Max Planck Institute for Psycholinguistics, Nijmegen, The Netherlands

Toni G. Cross
Institute of Early Childhood Development, Melbourne, Australia

Rafael M. Diaz
University of New Mexico, Albuquerque, NM

Greta G. Fein
University of Michigan, Ann Arbor, MI

Linda J. Ferrier
Children's Hospital Medical Center, Boston, MA

Susan Goldin-Meadow
University of Chicago, Chicago, IL

Kenji Hakuta
Yale University, New Haven, CT

Lois Hood Holzman
Empire State College, State University of New York, and Institute for Social Therapy and Research, New York, NY

Maggie Kirkman
Institute of Early Childhood Development, Melbourne, Australia

Glenn M. Kleiman
Teaching Tools: Microcomputer Services, Mountain View, CA

Laurence B. Leonard
Purdue University, West Lafayette, IN

Kristine MacKain
Cornell University Medical College, New York, NY

Donald F. Moores
Gallaudet College, Washington, DC

Elaine R. Moorin
The Merrill–Palmer Institute, Detroit, MI

Terry G. Nienhuys
Department of Education, University of Melbourne, Australia

Steven Pinker
Massachusetts Institute of Technology, Cambridge, MA

Richard G. Schwartz
Purdue University, West Lafayette, IN

Daniel N. Stern
Cornell University Medical College, New York, NY

1 The Concept of Experience in Speech Development

Kristine S. MacKain
Daniel N. Stern
Cornell University Medical College

Essential to language development is the discovery of those sounds that contrast in the target language to convey differences in meaning. In acquiring these oppositions, the language user establishes phonemic categories. The speaker is perceptually sensitive to the acoustic parameters that function to distinguish these categories while remaining relatively insensitive to those parameters that do not distinguish meaning. As a result, a user of a language (L1) may have difficulty discriminating an unfamiliar speech sound pair that users of another language (L2) discriminate easily because, for the speakers of L2, this contrast is used to distinguish meaning. We know some of the sound contrasts, such as r/l, that are particularly difficult to discriminate by language users unfamiliar with them (cf. Miyawaki, Strange, Verbrugge, Liberman, Jenkins, & Fujimura, 1975), and we know that for these particular contrasts, adults learning a new language can eventually come to identify and discriminate them according to the phonetic categories used by native speakers (e.g., MacKain, Best, & Strange, 1981). However, we know very little, if anything, about when and how the infant's perceptual system initially structures the speech heard such that infants' sensitivity to acoustic parameters that potentially can be used to discriminate phonetic categories is significantly altered, be it expressed through an enhancement, attenuation, or shifting of perceptual sensitivity to those parameters.

In this chapter, we review several studies that have tried to demonstrate an effect of experience on the way in which young infants discriminate speech sound categories. First, we critically evaluate these studies while accepting their underlying rationale. In defining linguistic experience, we then argue that discrimination tests are invalid tests of an effect of experience on infants' speech discrimination because they presuppose specific answers to questions concerning the processing capacities of infants about which we presently know very little. Finally, we argue that infants' perceptual boundaries for phonetic categories will not be enhanced, shifted, or attenuated until infants discover which sounds contrast to convey differences in meaning for their language. Without such a "strategy" for perceptually structuring the speech stream, infants' sensitivity to the parameters that distinguish speech sound categories will not be modified. Rather, infants from different linguistic communities will remain equally sensitive to phonetic distinctions that are discriminable by virtue of their psychoacoustic properties.

PRELIMINARIES: PHONEMIC CONTRASTS AND PHONETIC VARIATION IN SPEECH

When individual speech sounds (2 phones) function to convey differences in meaning, they are called *phonemes.* Phonemes are abstract linguistic units that are transcribed between slashes. For example, in English, the words *pin* and *bin* are represented phonemically as /pIn/ and /bIn/.

Certain phones, called *allophones,* represent regularities in the way a phoneme is pronounced in certain contexts. According to a phonological rule in English, when the phoneme /p/ occurs in stressed, syllable-initial position, as in the word *pin,* it is aspirated. This phonetic condition is transcribed in brackets and represented by [pʰ] in [pʰIn]. In *spin,* the /p/ is not aspirated, and the resulting sound is transcribed as [p], as it occurs in [spIn]. In this example, [pʰ] and [p] are allophones or phonetic variants of the phoneme /p/. The phonetic feature that distinguishes these allophones, aspiration, is called a *redundant feature* in this context because its occurrence can be predicted by a phonological rule. When two allophones are conditioned by context, as in the example [pʰIn] and [spIn], they are referred to as *contextual variants.* Sometimes two phones appear in the same context without changing meaning. For example, in English, the word *map* may be produced as [mæp] or [mæpʰ]. In such cases, the phones are said to be in free variation.

Two phones may also represent distinct phonemes. For example, in Hindi, the phoneme /p/ in *pal* (meaning, "take care of") is produced as a voiceless unaspirated stop, transcribed phonetically as [p]. The voiceless aspirated stop [pʰ], which, as noted, is an allophone of the phoneme /p/ in English, is a separate phoneme in Hindi. The Hindi word [pʰal], meaning "edge of knife", is distinguished from [pal] by the phonetic feature, aspiration. Because aspiration distinguishes meaning for these words, it functions as a *distinctive feature* in this linguistic context.

In language, then, phones can function to distinguish meaning (phonemes), or they can occur as variations of the same phoneme. The infant must eventually come to recognize and construct an internal representation of phonetic oppositions with phonemic significance and also assimilate phonologically irrelevant phonetic variations to represent a single phoneme.

VOICING CATEGORIES: ARTICULATORY, ACOUSTIC, AND PHONETIC CONSIDERATIONS

Voice onset time (VOT), defined as the time between the onset of phonation and the release of articulatory closure, is an articulatory dimension that denotes the temporal relationship between glottal adjustments and supraglottal articulation during the production of a stop consonant such as /bdg/ or /ptk/ (Lisker & Abramson, 1964).

For voicing, in most languages, stops may be characterized as produced with *voicing lead* (voice onset precedes stop release), *short voicing lag* (voice onset occurs shortly after stop release), or *long voicing lag* (voice onset occurs a considerable time after stop release). On a VOT scale, the onset of voice and stop release are simultaneous at 0 msec VOT. Negative values correspond to voicing lead, whereas positive values refer to voicing lag. In Fig. 1.1, spectrograms represent each of the three VOT conditions for synthetic labial stops. From top to bottom, the examples are of voicing lead, short lag, and long lag. Voice onset time is represented on the spectrogram as the time between the onset of simulated glottal pulsing and the beginning of the formant pattern for the syllabic vowel at the moment of stop release. (Differences in vocal tract configurations during vowel production result in characteristic resonances called formants.) Note, for example, that in the top spectrogram, the onset of glottal pulsing leads the second formant (F2) by 150 msec, and in the bottom spectrogram, glottal pulsing follows F2 by 100 msec, whereas the upper formants are noise excited.

Lisker and Abramson (1964) found that in most languages, the VOT measure could be used to distinguish the three phonetic categories — prevoiced, voiced, and voiceless — which correspond to voicing lead, short lag, and long lag, respectively.

Figure 1.2 illustrates these three modes in a normalized frequency distribution of VOT values pooled over 11 languages. In this sample, initial prevocalic stops were produced in isolated words for labial, apical, and velar places of articulation.

English employs two phonemic categories, voiced and voiceless, although these category names are not accurate as a phonetic description of English voicing. In phonetic terms, when a stop from the voiced category occurs in stressed syllable-initial position, it is typically devoiced. In articulatory terms, stops from this category are produced with short voicing lag or none, which results in an absence of phonation throughout the stop closure inter-

Three Conditions of Voice Onset Time
Synthetic Labial Stops

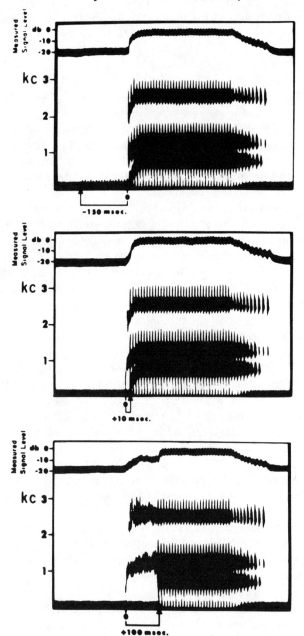

FIG. 1.1 Three conditions of VOT in synthetic labial stops. From top to bottom, spectograms of voicing lead, short lag, and long lag. (From "Voice timing perception in Spanish word-initial stops" by A. S. Abramson and L. Lisker, *Journal of Phonetics,* 1973, *1,* 1–8. Copyright 1973 by Academic Press. Reprinted by permission.)

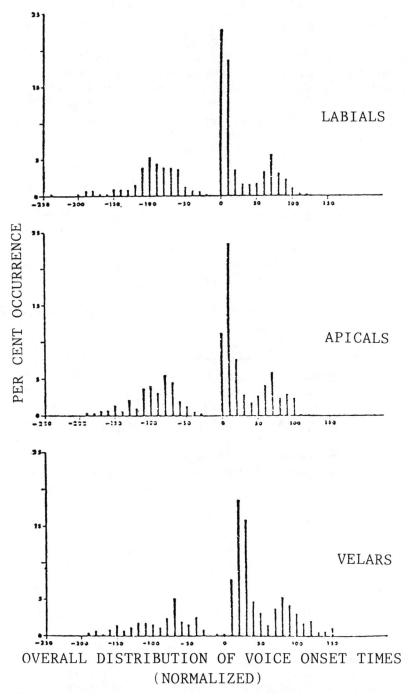

OVERALL DISTRIBUTION OF VOICE ONSET TIMES
(NORMALIZED)

FIG. 1.2 Conglomerate frequency distributions of VOT values for 11 languages, normalized so that all stop categories are equally represented. (From "A cross-language study of voicing in initial stops: Acoustical measurements" by L. Lisker and A. S. Abramson, *Word*, 1964, *20*, 384–422. Copyright 1964 by the Linguistic Circle of New York. Reprinted by permission.)

val, although the stops are not aspirated (Lisker & Abramson, 1964). In stressed syllable-initial position, stops from the voiceless category are produced with long voicing lag and are phonetically described as voiceless and aspirated. However, if such a stop follows an /s/ (e.g., as in *spoon*), the stop is phonetically described as voiceless and unaspirated. Some American speakers consistently produce stops from the voiced category with voicing lead (Lisker & Abramson, 1964, 1967; Williams, 1974), resulting in a stop that is voiced and unaspirated. Lisker and Abramson (1967) also note that when stops from the voiced category are produced in noninitial position in sentences, the stops are usually produced with voicing lead (i.e., unbroken voicing). Table 1.1 provides a description of the phonetic variations for voiced and voiceless stops and examples of some of the positions in which they occur in American English. Also included in this table for purposes of reference are the phonemic and phonetic representations for these stops for each of the three places of production.

The choice of which phonetic feature(s) distinguish(es) voiced from voiceless stops in American English speech therefore depends, in part, on who is speaking and the position in the utterance where the stops to be contrasted occur. The possibilities include the presence versus absence of voicing, aspiration, or these two (binary) features in combination,[1] and intensity of the burst and/or fundamental frequency (Fo) perturbations (Lisker & Abramson, 1964). In stressed syllable-initial position in English, voiced and voiceless stops are distinguished phonetically by the presence versus absence of aspiration. In Spanish and other languages that make a phonemic distinction between stops from prevoiced and voiced categories, but which have no aspirated stops, the presence versus absence of voice pulsing during closure, with resultant acoustic features, distinguishes stops produced at the same place of production.

The acoustic features resulting from stops produced with voicing lead, short voicing lag, and long voicing lag bear no simple relation to the phonetic features used to describe these phonemic distinctions across languages, unless one seeks a physiological mechanism. A focus of research in adult speech perception has been to determine the relative importance of these acoustic features in the perception of stop consonants.

As mentioned earlier, VOT is a simple articulatory dimension that physically distinguishes the three major stop voicing categories.[2] Variations along

---

[1]In final position, an additional phonetic feature, vowel length, may be most important in distinguishing (unreleased) voiced from voiceless stops (cf. Denes, 1955; Raphael, 1972); however, neither this phonetic feature nor its specific acoustic characteristics and potential function as a perceptual cue is discussed as it is not a focus of the experimental work considered in this paper.

[2]There is at least one voicing category, voiced aspiration or "murmur," for which VOT must be combined with another dimension, glottal aperture (A. S. Abramson, personal communication).

TABLE 1.1

English Voiced and Voiceless Phonemic Categories and Phonemic Representations for Stop Consonants in
Three Places of Production and the Corresponding Phonetic Representations and Phonetic Descriptions for
These Phonemes as They Would Appear in Some Positions in American English

Phonemic Category	Phonemic Representation			Phonetic Representation			Phonetic Description	Examples of Position
	Labial	Apical	Velar	Labial	Apical	Velar		
Voiced	/b/	/d/	/g/	[b̥]	[d̥]	[g̥]	devoiced stop	stressed, syllable-initial position; noninitial position (rare)
				[b]	[d]	[g]	voiced unaspirated stop	stressed, syllable-initial position; noninitial position (common)
Voiceless	/p/	/t/	/k/	[pʰ]	[tʰ]	[kʰ]	voiceless aspirated stop	stressed, syllable-initial position; stressed, syllable-final position
				[p]	[t]	[k]	voiceless unaspirated stop	noninitial, stressed or unstressed; following /s/

7

the VOT continuum have a number of acoustic consequences, one of which is variation in the temporal relation between the onset of the first and second formant.[3] Although the timing dimension is regarded as a sufficient cue for the perception of stop consonants, its importance in the context of other (covarying) acoustic features is not clearly understood.

The acoustic effects for stops produced with voicing lead are generally characterized as variations before release in the duration of harmonics that are low in frequency and weak in amplitude. Although this parameter generally is considered to be the primary cue to the perception of voicing lead, Williams (1977) also noted that in Spanish speech, stops produced with voicing lead have a low-amplitude burst or no burst at all, and the low-frequency energy extends through the point of release and immediately following. For stops produced with short voicing lag, there is a relatively strong burst and no glottal pulsing during the lag. Thus, in addition to the presence versus absence of voicing lead, long lead and short lag stops also may be differentiated acoustically by the presence versus absence of a strong release burst and the corresponding presence versus absence of low-frequency periodic energy just following release. Williams suggests that these properties may combine to provide additional perceptual cues to the long lead/short lag distinction. However, in synthetic speech, the release burst typically is omitted. For synthetic speech, voicing lead has been prescribed as being represented by the low-frequency, periodic excitation of the first formant before release (e.g., Abramson & Lisker, 1973; Eilers, Gavin, & Wilson, 1979; Lasky, Syrdal-Lasky, & Klein, 1975; Streeter, 1976).

A number of acoustic effects result when stops are produced with voicing lag.[4] As VOT increases, there are progressive increases in the duration of noise (aspiration) following release and the frequency of F1 onset. As the frequency of F1 increases, the extent and duration of the F1 transition decreases. Stops produced with a long voicing lag are characterized by the attenuation of the F1 transition, traditionally called "F1 cutback" (Liberman, Delattre, & Cooper, 1958) and considerable nonperiodic excitation of the upper formants (i.e., aspiration). Both parameters are represented in the bottom spectrogram of Fig. 1.1. For stops produced with short voicing lag, there is a significant F1 transition following voice onset, and aspiration noise is absent. These observations are represented in the middle spectrogram of Fig. 1.1. In addition to differences in the timing of laryngeal pulsing alone, then, voiced and voiceless stop categories are differentiated acoustically by the

---

[3]It should be noted that in real speech, F1 will be severely attenuated; only in some vowels, however, will it not be excited at all. This situation may be synthesized by not turning on F1 at all during the voicing lag.

[4]See Abramson (1977), Lisker (1975, 1978), and Summerfield and Haggard (1977) for a more detailed discussion of these effects and their potential as perceptual cues.

presence versus absence of an F1 transition following voice onset, differences in fundamental frequency contour, and differences in F1 onset frequency. For adults, the primacy of any one of these parameters associated with laryngeal timing as a perceptual cue in voicing discrimination is currently controversial.[5]

In studies of infants' discrimination of voicing contrasts for stop consonants where VOT is the experimental variable, it is not uncommon for authors to treat VOT as an *acoustic* continuum.[6] In such cases, the simple articulatory dimension of VOT is mistakenly taken also to specify only a simple acoustic parameter, the temporal relation between two acoustic events, thereby ignoring other covarying acoustic parameters. In other instances, VOT is introduced as an articulatory dimension, but in subsequent descriptions of stimulus variation, the timing dimension *alone* is specified as if it is the only parameter that varies. In cases where other acoustic parameters are noted, their potentials as perceptual cues are not. Consequently, the results of experiments such as those testing for discrimination of stop voicing contrasts by infants may mislead the reader into thinking that the only perceptual cue for voicing discrimination is the timing dimension. For example, in the first experiment to test discrimination of systematic variations in VOT with infants, Eimas, Siqueland, Jusczyk, and Vigorito (1971) restricted their definition of VOT to a temporal dimension and referred to VOT as "the" acoustic cue responsible for infants' discrimination of the voiced/voiceless distinction. As we discuss these studies, it is important to keep in mind that although infants' discrimination of voicing distinctions may ultimately be best accounted for in nonlinguistic terms, the basis for infants' discrimination of voicing distinctions is not yet understood.

STUDIES OF THE EFFECT OF EXPERIENCE ON INFANT SPEECH DISCRIMINATION

The question addressed by this research has been whether exposure to a given language during the prelinguistic period affects infants' ability to discriminate voicing contrasts that are phonemic for speakers in the language community studied. If infants from a particular language community discriminated phonemic contrasts as the result of hearing those contrasts, it was assumed that the perceptual boundary (as specified along the VOT con-

---

[5]See Haggard, Ambler, and Callow (1970), Repp (1979), Stevens and Klatt (1974), and Summerfield and Haggard (1977) for experimental results on the effect of these features in perception.

[6]For a reclarification of VOT and discussions of its misapplications, see Abramson (1977) and Lisker (1978).

tinuum) for such infants would coincide with the perceptual boundary that separates two phonemic voicing categories for adults speaking that language.

Some investigators have also attempted to account for infants' discrimination, whether resulting from experience or not, on either phonetic or psychoacoustic grounds. For example, in the seminal work of Eimas et al. (1971), American infants discriminated variations in VOT for labial stops according to voiced and voiceless phonemic categories. Although VOT differences (in msec) were the same for each stimulus pair presented, no evidence for discrimination was found for stimulus pairs that did not cross the phonetic boundary separating voiced and voiceless categories. The infants' discrimination functions approximated those of American English-speaking adults. For adults, discrimination functions can be predicted largely from the way they differentially label the stimuli (as either voiced or voiceless). This phenomenon, called categorical perception, was considered to have a phonetic basis, and consequently, infants' performance on categorical discrimination tasks was thought to reflect an innate predisposition to perceive speech according to linguistic categories. Since then, the view that a linguistic mode of perception underlies categorical discrimination has been eroded by evidence that nonspeech stimuli are perceived categorically by adults (e.g., Miller, Pastore, Wier, Kelly, & Dooling, 1976), and that for speech, non-human mammals discriminate voiced/voiceless categories in the same manner as human infants (Kuhl & Miller, 1975).

An evaluation of the cross-language infant literature first requires a definition of key terms. What does it mean for an infant to have "linguistic experience"? A critical problem in the experimental literature itself and in reviews of this literature is that careful attention has not been given to defining terminology and the consequences of such definitions. The consequences that necessarily follow from a careful definition of linguistic experience debilitate the conclusions that can be drawn from this line of research as it is presently conducted. This point is elaborated in a later section.

For now, we critically review the empirical investigations of the effect of linguistic experience on infant speech discrimination within the experimental frameworks provided. The logic of these studies is that if infants discriminate a contrast used phonemically by speakers in the infants' language community and if infants from a language group where the contrast is *not* used phonemically do *not* show evidence of discrimination, the positive result is due to the one group's previous exposure to the particular contrast in question. The term "linguistic experience," although not rigorously defined in this literature, refers to prelinguistic infants' experience with hearing phonemic contrasts in speech spoken by a given language community. For example, a point explicitly made by Aslin and Pisoni (1980a) is that a speech contrast not used phonemically does not occur in speech at all; thus, "phonologically irrelevant contrasts . . . are obviously not presented to the infant [p. 79]."

Within-Language Studies

Eimas and his colleagues (Eimas, 1975, Experiment 1; Eimas et al., 1971) investigated American infants' discrimination of voicing contrasts that fall into prevoiced, voiced, and voiceless categories as specified by VOT. The infants were presumably reared in a monolingual American English-speaking environment. In these two experiments, the authors' interest was not in the effects of linguistic experience on discrimination but, rather, in whether infants discriminated voiced and voiceless stops categorically. Of interest to this discussion are the within-category conditions of these experiments. In those conditions, discrimination was tested for a phonetic contrast that falls within the phonemic voiced category in English, but which crosses a long lead/short lag boundary phonemic in languages such as Spanish and Thai. For monolingual speakers, the location of the perceptual long lead/short lag crossover for labial stops (Lisker & Abramson, 1970; Williams, 1977) and the crossover for apical stops (Streeter, 1976) appears to vary across languages; however, generally, the perceptual boundary for labial stops falls between -5 and -20 msec VOT, and for apical stops it falls somewhere between -15 and $+10$ msec VOT. In Eimas et al. (1971) and Eimas (1975, Experiment 1), no evidence was found for discrimination of either the labial long lead/short lag contrast (-20, 0 msec VOT) or the apical long lead/short lag contrast (-30, $+20$ msec VOT). These results can be seen in Table 1.2.

In an attempt to demonstrate sensitivity to a long lead/short lag distinction in the purported absence of exposure to this contrast, Eimas (1975, Experiments 2 & 3) increased the VOT difference between apical stimuli that lie on

TABLE 1.2

Eimas and Colleagues' Results of Infants' Discrimination of Speech
Sounds from Prevoiced, Voiced, and Voiceless Speech Sound Categories

Source	Phonemic Categories	Speech Contrasts	VOT Values	Discriminated
Eimas, Siqueland,	voiced/voiceless	p/p^h	+20, +40	yes
Jusczyk, & Vigorito	prevoiced/voiced	b/p	-20, 0	no
(1971)	voiceless only	p^h/p^h	+60, +80	no
Eimas (1975)				
Experiment 1	voiced/voiceless	t/t^h	+10, +60	yes
	prevoiced/voiced	d/t	-30, +20	no
	voiceless only	t^h/t^h	+50, +100	no
Experiment 2	prevoiced only	d/d	-100, -40	no
	prevoiced/voiced	d/t	-40, +20	no
Experiment 3	prevoiced only	d/d	-150, +70	no
	prevoiced/voiced	d/t	-70, +10	equivocal[a]

[a] The (-150, -70) and the (-70, +10) groups did not differ significantly; however, there was a reliable recovery from pre- to postshift for the (-70, +10) group.

either side of the long lead/short lag phonetic boundary by 60 msec (Experiment 2) and 80 msec (Experiment 3).[7] In Experiment 2, no evidence for discrimination was observed for the between-category (-40, $+20$ msec VOT) or the within-category (-100, -40 msec VOT) pairs, although there was a greater recovery for the within-category pair (-100, -40 msec VOT), suggesting that infants may be relatively more sensitive to this contrast. In Experiment 3, there was a reliable recovery from pre- to postshift phases for infants in the between-category condition (-70, $+10$ msec VOT), whereas infants in the within-category condition (-150, -70 msec VOT) showed a nonsignificant increment, suggesting the infants may be sensitive to the -70, $+10$ msec VOT stop contrast. However, the difference between the two groups during the postshift phase was not significant, making the results equivocal (see Table 1.2 for a summary of these results).

Taken together, these studies (Eimas, 1975, Experiments 1, 2, & 3; Eimas et al., 1971) do not provide evidence for discrimination of a long lead/short lag distinction by American infants. The conclusion that many (e.g., Aslin & Pisoni, 1980a; Lasky et al., 1975; Streeter, 1976) have drawn from this is that infants fail to discriminate the long lead/short lag contrast because their linguistic environment does not provide them with the opportunity to hear it. Consequently, the American infants' performance in Eimas' research (1975, Experiments 2 & 3) has been used as a control for experiments (Lasky et al., 1975; Streeter, 1976) designed to test for the effect of linguistic experience on speech discrimination by infants reared in linguistic environments where the long lead/short lag contrast is used phonemically. American infants, however, do not satisfy the requirements of a control group for these cross-language comparisons because, as discussed in the previous section, tokens of the prevoiced category of speech sounds are a common occurrence in American English.

The Occurrence of Stops Produced with Voicing Lead in American English

Figure 1.3 provides an example of the occurrence of the prevoiced category of speech sounds for the three places of production that occur in American English. In this example, prevocalic stops were produced initially in isolated words by four American English-speaking adults. Note that phonemic /b/,

[7]The VOT difference was increased in Experiment 2 to insure that stimuli in the long lead/short lag condition lay on either side of the approximate perceptual boundary (-20 msec VOT) that Eimas reported Lisker and Abramson (1970) found for Thai speakers. From the results of Experiment 2 and some pilot data on American infants' long lead/short lag discrimination provided by Moffitt in a personal communication, Eimas hypothesized that the "real" or universal long lead/short lag boundary was around -50 msec VOT, and in Experiment 3, the VOT difference was increased again to encompass this hypothesized boundary.

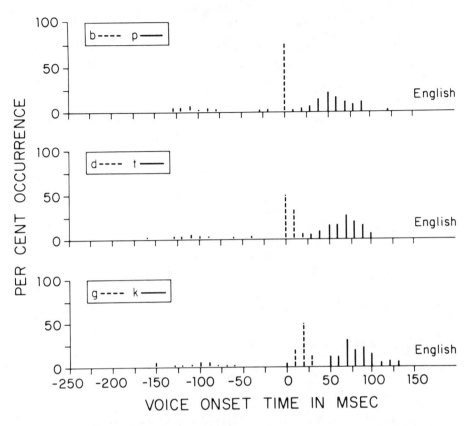

FIG. 1.3   American English: Frequency distributions of VOT values for initial pre-vocalic stops produced in isolated words (four speakers). (From "A cross-language study of voicing in initial stops: Acoustical measurements by L. Lisker and A. S. Abramson, *Word*, 1964, *20*, 384–422. Copyright 1964 by the Linguistic Circle of New York. Reprinted by permission.)

/d/, and /g/ are each bimodally distributed along the VOT continuum. These distributions and their corresponding boundary ranges are not dissimilar to the distributions of prevoiced and voiced categories found in languages that use the long lead/short lag distinction phonemically (see Figs. 1.4 and 1.5). For Fig. 1.3, Lisker and Abramson reported that 95% of the productions of stops (in isolated words) that fall within the prevoiced category were produced by one of the four speakers. This speaker produced all but one of his stops with voicing lead. Another one of the four speakers was responsible for the remaining 5% of the voicing lead productions.

In another study, Zlatin (1974) reported that only 2 out of 20 American English speakers produced initial prevocalic voiced stops in isolated words with no voicing lead. For the remaining 18 subjects, individual analyses showed

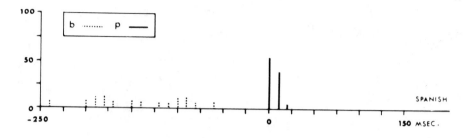

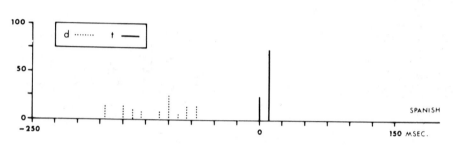

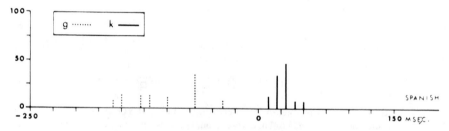

PER CENT OCCURRENCE

FIG. 1.4   Puerto Rican Spanish: Frequency distributions of VOT values for initial prevocalic stops produced in isolated words (two speakers). (From A cross-language study of voicing in initial stops: Acoustical measurements" by L. Lisker and A. S. Abramson, *Word*, 1964, *20*, 384–422. Copyright 1964 by the Linguistic Circle of New York. Reprinted by permission.)

that about 33% of *each* speaker's voiced stop productions occurred with voicing lead. As noted earlier, in noninitial position, voiced stops are usually produced with voicing lead (Lisker & Abramson, 1964, 1967). In American English, then, voiced stops produced with voicing lead are prevalent.[8] These stops are not phonemic for English but, rather, occur in either contextual or free variation.

One might anticipate several objections to the claim that these conditions provide infants with the same kinds of experience that infants might have in a linguistic environment that uses the long lead/short lag contrast phonemi-

---

[8]The occurrence of stops produced with voicing lead in American English has also been noted by Smith and Westbury (1975) and Williams (1974).

cally. First, the majority of occurrences of stops produced with voicing lead are not in initial position. Second, the frequency of occurrence of stops produced with long voicing lead in initial position is considerably lower than in languages for which the long lead/short lag contrast is phonemic. Third, because the contrast is not phonemic for this particular linguistic community, it cannot be experienced as a contrast by infants of that community. With each objection, we must attribute to infants certain abilities in order for linguistic experience to have an effect on speech discrimination. Following the present review section, we consider these prerequisites.

Cross-Language Studies

In Spanish, the voicing lead/short lag distinction is phonemic for labial, apical, and velar places of production. Lasky et al. (1975) used a heart-rate

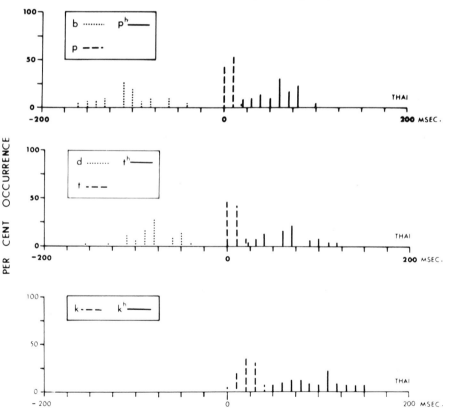

FIG. 1.5   Thai: Frequency distributions of VOT values for initial prevocalic stops produced in isolated words (three speakers). (From "A cross-language study of voicing in initial stops: Acoustical measurements" by L. Lisker and A. S. Abramson, *Word,* 1964, *20,* 384–422. Copyright 1964 by the Linguistic Circle of New York. Reprinted by permission.)

habituation/dishabituation paradigm to investigate the effect of linguistic experience on speech discrimination by 4- to 6 ½-month-old Guatemalan infants reared in a Spanish-speaking community. Samples of speech from Guatemalan Spanish speakers were not obtained. Instead, it was assumed that long lead and short lag productions lie along a range of the VOT continuum similar to the productions of Puerto Rican Spanish speakers obtained by Lisker and Abramson (1964). For these speakers, long lead and short lag stop productions (their values expressed in msec VOT) fell within the appropriate categories (prevoiced and voiced, respectively) as specified along the VOT continuum, and no stop productions fell within the voiceless aspirated, long lag category (see Fig. 1.4).

Lasky et al. (1975) selected three labial stop contrasts straddling three potential perceptual boundaries: (1) the English short lag/long lag distinction (+ 20, + 60 msec VOT); (2) the conventional Spanish/Thai long lead/short lag distinction (− 20, + 20 msec VOT); and (3) a long lead distinction (− 60, − 20 msec VOT) that encompassed a − 50 msec VOT boundary suggested by Eimas (1975) to be the "real" Spanish/Thai boundary (see footnote 7).

The results indicated the infants discriminated the short lag/long lag distinction, suggesting that this discrimination can be made in the absence of experience. The infants did not show evidence of discrimination of the Spanish phonemic long lead/short lag distinction (− 20, + 20 msec VOT), though this distinction crosses an adult Spanish perceptual boundary that separates Spanish voiced and voiceless phonemic categories.[9] However, evidence was found for discrimination of a long lead contrast (− 60, − 20 msec VOT) that is not phonemic for Spanish speakers.

Lasky et al. (1975) interpreted their results as evidence that infants are innately predisposed to perceive three stop voicing categories that vary in VOT with perceptual boundaries lying somewhere between + 20 and + 60 msec VOT for the short lag/long lag distinction and between − 60 and − 20 msec VOT for the long lead/"short lag" distinction. The short lag/long lag distinction was discriminated in the absence of experience, and experience did not result in discrimination of a contrast (− 20, + 20 msec VOT) that encompasses a phonemic boundary for Spanish-speaking adults. They concluded that experience does not affect speech discrimination within the first 4 months of life.

Streeter (1974) examined the contribution of innate and experiential factors to stop voicing discrimination with young Kikuyu infants reared in an environment where Kikuyu, a Bantu language, is spoken. Kikuyu has a pho-

---

[9]This boundary has been estimated at − 5 msec VOT for monolingual Puerto Rican Spanish speakers (Williams, 1977) and at approximately + 14 msec VOT for a dialectally heterogeneous group of bilingual (though native) Latin American Spanish speakers (Abramson & Lisker, 1973).

nemic long lead/short lag distinction for apical and velar stops. There is no labial long lead/short lag distinction although the language employs one prevoiced labial stop, [b]. There is also no short lag/long lag distinction. Voice onset time values obtained from the speech of Kikuyu-speaking adults fell within long lead and short lag categories as specified along the VOT continuum. Productions of labial [b] lay within the range of the Spanish voiced (long lead) category. No productions fell within the category specified as long lag. The discrimination functions obtained from Kikuyu-speaking adults showed a peak at about + 10 msec VOT for apical stops and a peak at about − 15 msec VOT for labial stops. For the infant studies, stimuli were constructed that straddled these perceptual crossover points. A high-amplitude sucking (HAS) paradigm was used to measure discrimination.

Three labial stop (consonant–vowel) contrasts were tested: (1) a long lead/short (no) lag contrast with VOT values of − 30, 0 msec; (2) a short lag/long lag contrast with VOT values of + 10, + 40 msec; and (3) a within-category long lag contrast with VOT values of + 50, + 80 msec. As mentioned, there is no long lead/short lag labial contrast in Kikuyu, although the language employs a prevoiced [b]. The long lead/short lag contrast used in this experiment is phonemic in languages such as English, and the within-category contrast does not cross a phonemic boundary in any known language, although Korean may come close to it (e.g., Lisker & Abramson, 1964).

Infants ranged in age from under 50 days to over 100 days (the precise range was not indicated), with a mean age of 69 days. Each infant received each experimental condition as well as a control condition in which one of the six syllables was repeated throughout the preshift and postshift phases of the procedure.

Results of Streeter's (1974) study indicated that the infants were reliably conditioned before the sound shift and that the response pattern was similar for all conditions. There were no significant differences between the experimental conditions in mean change (increase) of sucking rate from preshift to postshift phases. The short lag/long lag (+ 10, + 40 msec VOT) condition differed from the control condition, but there were no significant differences between the control and the other experimental conditions — long lead/short (no) lag (− 30, 0 msec VOT) and within-category long lag (+ 50, + 80 msec VOT). These results are graphically represented in Fig. 1.6.

To determine whether discrimination performance varied with age, Streeter divided the infants into three age groups (less than 50 days, 50 to 100 days, and greater than 100 days) and analyzed the data for each group separately. She found that discrimination performance decreased with age and subsequently discarded the data from the older age group, claiming that the conditioning procedure was not effective for the older infants. Interestingly, as Streeter herself noted (1974), discrimination performance for the 1- and 4-month-old infants in Eimas et al.'s (1971) experiment using the high-

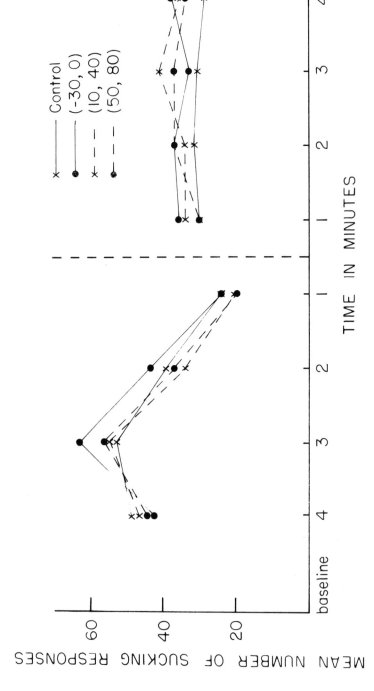

FIG. 1.6   Mean number of sucking responses as a function of time and experimental condition. Time is measured with reference to moment of stimulus shift, indicated by a dashed line. (From "The effects of linguistic experience on phonetic perception" by L. A. Streeter, unpublished doctoral dissertation, Columbia University, 1974.)

amplitude sucking paradigm showed an *increase* in discrimination performance with age. Demonstrating that the conditioning procedure was ineffect-
ive with older infants would require an analysis by age of conditioning
patterns before the shift and before the data analysis.

Nonetheless, the modified data are presented in an account published subsequently (Streeter, 1976). In this account, reliable discrimination was reported for both the long lead/short lag (− 30, 0 msec VOT) and short lag/
long lag (+ 10, + 40 msec VOT) contrasts, but there was no evidence for
discrimination of the within-category long lag (+ 50, + 80 msec VOT) contrast. Figure 1.7 shows the mean change in response rate for each condition.

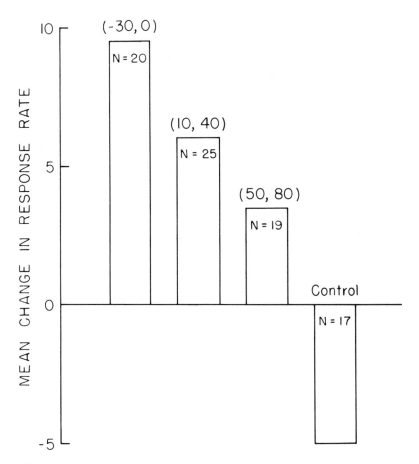

FIG. 1.7   Mean change in response rate per minute as a function of experimental condition. (From "Language perception of 2-month-old infants shows effect of both innate
mechanisms and experience" by L. A. Streeter, *Nature,* 1976, *259,* 39–41. Copyright 1976
by Macmillan Journals Ltd. Reprinted by permission.)

For the sake of argument, let us assume that these data represent the discrimination performance of the younger age groups (i.e., 1 ½ to 2 ½ months). It would appear, then, that discrimination of the English short lag/long lag distinction occurs in the absence of exposure to that contrast. The conclusion that linguistic experience was what accounted for the infants' ability to discriminate the long lead/short lag contrast follows from two faulty premises: (1) that a control group that was not exposed to stops produced with long voicing lead showed no evidence of discrimination of the labial long lead/short lag apical contrast; (2) that because the Kikuyu infants did not have direct experience with a long lead/short lag labial contrast, the experience with a long lead/short lag apical contrast somehow generalized its influence to the labial contrast tested.

Regarding the first premise, Streeter (1974, 1976) compared the discrimination of the long lead/short lag contrast she obtained for infants from the community that employed the long lead/short lag contrast phonemically with the results of Eimas (1975), who found no evidence of discrimination with infants from a community whose speech purportedly lacked stops produced with long voicing lead. However, as indicated earlier, Eimas' infants did have exposure to stops produced with voicing lead, rendering his experiment an inappropriate control. In fact, the American infants were the ones who had *direct* experience with labial stops produced both with long lead and with short (or no) voicing lag.

The second premise for consideration is whether experience with a long lead/short lag contrast at a different place of articulation (apical) can reasonably be assumed to generalize to another place of articulation (labial) such that a demonstration of discrimination of a labial long lead/short lag contrast can be interpreted as evidence for the effect of linguistic experience on the discrimination. Note first that in a preliminary experiment, Streeter (1974) found evidence for discrimination of an apical contrast (0, + 30 msec VOT) by Kikuyu infants that encompasses a perceptual crossover point (estimated at + 10 msec VOT) for Kikuyu adults. However, the premise cannot be accepted until it is independently demonstrated that experience with contrasts at the apical place of articulation generalizes to the labial place of production. Such a demonstration was not carried out for either the Kikuyu infants or the adults. In order to make an argument for an effect of linguistic experience, Streeter (1976) thus relies on a premise established by fiat.

Moreover, it is not clear that such a premise could be demonstrated in any event. Streeter (1974) suggested that either experience with the apical contrast or with the acoustic cues underlying the contrast might generalize to the labial contrast. At the phonetic level, the generalization of experience with long lead/short lag apical stops to the corresponding labials presupposes that the infant has solved the problem of perceptual constancy and has an intuitive grasp of the relationship between contrasts at different places of articulation.

At the auditory level, there is no evidence that the acoustic cues underlying an apical contrast with a perceptual crossover estimated at + 10 msec VOT are the same as those that underlie the long lead/short lag labial contrast (estimated at − 20 msec VOT).

The results of the studies reviewed so far suggest that infants discriminate the short lag/long lag distinction regardless of whether or not their speech environment includes short lag/long lag distinctions. However, infants' discrimination of a long lead/short lag stop contrast has been more difficult to demonstrate. Streeter (1974) found no evidence for discrimination of − 30, 0 msec VOT with Kikuyu infants who had no exposure to this particular contrast. For the studies by Eimas and his colleagues (Eimas, 1975, Experiments 1, 2, & 3; Eimas et al., 1971), American infants who have direct exposure to stops produced with voicing lead and, of course, short voicing lag did not show evidence for discriminating any of the following long lead/short lag contrasts (specified in msec VOT): − 20 and 0; − 30 and + 20; and − 40 and + 20. Results of discrimination for the − 70 and + 10 contrast were equivocal (see Table 1.2). Spanish infants (Lasky et al., 1975) discriminated − 60 and − 20 msec VOT, suggesting sensitivity to a prevoiced contrast; however, their perceptual threshold did not correspond to the phonemic boundary found for Spanish-speaking adults, rendering no effect of "experience."

Eilers et al. (1979) used a head-turning paradigm to investigate discrimination of Spanish long lead/short lag phonemic contrasts and English short lag/long lag phonemic contrasts with 6- to 8-month-old infants. Infants were either members of a Cuban Spanish-speaking or an American English-speaking community. Two pairs of labial stops were compared. For one pair, VOT values were + 10 msec and + 40 msec and were identified by American English-speaking adults as examples of voiced and voiceless phonemic categories, respectively. The other pair (− 20, + 10 msec VOT) were identified by Cuban Spanish-speaking adults as being members of the Spanish voiced (long lead) and Spanish voiceless (short lag) stop categories.

Results indicated that both the Cuban and American infants discriminated the short lag/long lag distinction that is phonemic in English and not in Spanish: + 10, + 40 msec VOT. It should be noted that the voiceless aspirated stops, which fall into the voiceless category on the VOT continuum for English speakers, also appear in the speech productions of some Spanish speakers (Williams, 1974), although Lisker and Abramson (1964) did not find such occurrences in their sample of Spanish speech (see Fig. 1.4). The long lead/short lag distinction that is phonemic in Spanish but not in English (− 20, + 10) was only discriminated by the Cuban infants. Eilers et al. interpreted these results as suggesting that experience with the English short lag/long lag distinction is not necessary for discrimination of that contrast, whereas discrimination of the Spanish long lead/short lag contrast may be dependent on linguistic experience. The authors noted that American infants have experience with stops produced with long voicing lead; however, they did not consider this observation in the discussion of their results.

Aslin and Pisoni (1980b) have criticized this study on a number of counts, to which Eilers (1980) has replied. For the most part, the criticisms seem to be effectively countered by Eilers et al., and we need not discuss these points here except to say that because discrimination of the long lead/short lag stop contrast is notoriously difficult to demonstrate, a within-subjects design would have provided a more robust test on discrimination. A measure of the discrimination performance of each infant could be obtained with substantially more trials than the criterion of five out of six total presentations for each infant that Eilers et al. (1979) used as evidence for discrimination. Eilers et al. (1980) noted they did not present a large number of trials so that infants would not learn to discriminate the contrasts during the course of the experiment.

In any event, let us accept the positive, and correspondingly negative, results of discrimination performance on the long lead/short lag stop contrast by the two cross-language groups, especially in light of Eilers et al.'s (1980) claim that this study has been replicated using more stringent procedures to prevent experimenter bias.

American Infants' Discrimination
of Long Lead/Short Lag Stop Contrasts

The relative difficulty in discriminating long lead/short lag stop contrasts prompted Aslin, Pisoni, Hennessy, and Perey (1981) to devise a method for estimating individual infant's perceptual boundaries for stop contrasts along both the minus and plus regions of the VOT continuum. A major objective of the study was to demonstrate that some American infants could discriminate the long lead/short lag stop distinction, which is not phonemic in English.

Stimuli were synthetic labial stops that varied in 10 msec steps from -70 to $+70$ msec VOT. Infants ranged in age from 5 ½ to 11 months. Each infant was conditioned to respond with a head turn to a change from a repeating background stimulus to a target stimulus. Once a consistent discriminative response was established to two stimuli, which differed (and, presumably, were widely separated) in VOT, a "staircase" phase of the procedure was initiated.

In the staircase phase, a trial consisted of a repeating background stimulus, which changed to a target stimulus. If the infant responded correctly to two consecutive, identical trials, the target stimulus was changed by reducing the VOT difference between the background and target by a specified step size (either by 10 or 20 msec) and a new trial began. For example, a series included a range of VOT values from 0 to -70 msec with a VOT step size of 10 msec. Following two correct responses to a -70 msec VOT background and a 0 msec VOT target, the next trial began with − 70 msec VOT background and − 10 msec VOT target. It should be noted that the background stimulus was selected from one end of the VOT series (e.g., − 70 or 0 msec VOT) and remained the same throughout testing. Any trial in which the infant responded incorrectly resulted in a VOT increase of the specified step size and the initiation of a new trial. A VOT boundary between two voicing categories was estimated by averaging the target VOT value where the infant has attained a criterion level of responding (e.g., target: − 30 msec VOT) and the target value where the infant has not reached criterion (e.g., target: − 20 msec VOT). In this example, the VOT boundary was estimated to be at − 25 msec VOT.

On a − 70, + 70 msec VOT series, results showed that most infants stopped responding to the target stimulus when it was reduced beyond the American English adults' VOT boundary (approximately 20–25 msec VOT) for short lag/long lag labial stop contrasts, suggesting that infants are sensitive to one phonetic boundary along the VOT continuum in accordance with American English speakers. Further tests with other VOT series, including background and target values along the minus region of the continuum (− 20, + 50; − 50; + 20; − 70, 0), resulted in 10 infants showing evidence for boundaries that were less than + 20 msec VOT, although the thresholds across infants were highly variable, ranging from + 19 to − 65 msec VOT.

A reduced number of VOT series (− 70, + 70 and − 70, 0 msec VOT) was presented in a less demanding experiment to a second group of infants. Results from six infants who completed the staircase testing phase for the second VOT series (− 70, 0 msec) corroborated the findings of the first experiment; boundary values were variable but fell short of + 20 msec VOT and, in this case, fell within the minus region of the VOT continuum.

These two studies approximate an auditory training laboratory setting where subjects (human or nonhuman) are trained over a number of sessions and a large number of trials to attend to small differences in an auditory contrast by first maximizing the difference between the two sounds and then progressively reducing that difference until a perceptual threshold is reached. An earlier paper by Aslin, Hennessy, Pisoni, and Perey (1979), which includes Study 1 of the published version, has been criticized by Eilers et al. (1980) as representing unusual sensitivity of a small number of infants under this rigorous testing situation.

To summarize these studies on long lead/short lag stop discrimination, infants from linguistic environments in which the long lead/short lag stop contrast is not phonemic showed either strong evidence for discrimination of this distinction (Aslin et al., 1981) or the results were equivocal (Eimas, 1975). Infants from linguistic environments in which long lead/short lag stop contrasts are phonemic (Lasky et al., 1975) showed evidence of discrimination, but perceptual boundaries did not overlap with those of Spanish-speaking adults. Streeter's (1976) results must be viewed very tentatively because she dropped the data that rendered her results nonsignificant without adequate justification in a post hoc analysis (Streeter, 1974). Finally, Eilers et al. (1980) found group differences in discrimination performance for long lead/short lag stop contrasts between infants from native Spanish and American English environments: Spanish infants discriminated a long lead/short lag VOT contrast that straddled the phonemic boundary for adult speakers, whereas American English infants showed no evidence for discrimination of the same contrast.

The ease with which voicing contrasts that straddle voiced and voiceless categories are discriminated (i.e., stops produced with short voicing lag vs. long voicing lag) has attributed to the marked psychoacoustic changes that occur in the region of the phonetic boundary that separates these categories (e.g., Abramson, 1977; Stevens, 1975). It has also been suggested (Kuhl, 1978) that the difficulty in demonstrating infant discrimination of stops from prevoiced and voiced categories may have to do with the vulnerability of the low-frequency, low-amplitude prevoicing cue to external factors such as ambient noise levels or unsatisfactory signal-to-noise ratios (that attenuate the cue during recording). In addition, there are two acoustic parameters with potential as perceptual cues for the long lead/short lag distinction — the presence versus absence of a strong release burst[10] and the presence versus absence of low-frequency periodic energy at the point of burst release — which may combine to enhance a prevoiced or a voiceless unaspirated percept (Williams, 1977). The addition of the release burst to synthetic tokens that are voiceless and unaspirated might serve to enhance the distinction between stops produced with voicing lead and short voicing lag, making this contrast both more natural and more easily discriminable.

So far, we have critically reviewed the cross-linguistic studies on infants and accepted the logic of using a discrimination paradigm to test the effects of experience on speech sound discrimination. Within this framework, cross-language studies (Eilers et al., 1980; Lasky et al., 1975; Streeter, 1974, 1976) have been flawed in their design: American English speech contains numerous examples of stops produced with voicing lead, making an American English infant group (used as a control in each study cited) an inappropriate control. As we noted earlier, some authors have ignored their own observation that stops produced with voicing lead occur in American English (Eilers et al., 1980), others have dismissed it without theoretical or empirical justification (Eimas, 1975) while others have not indicated any awareness of the occurrence of allophonic variation in speech (Aslin & Pisoni, 1980a). Furthermore, in the experimental literature, the interpretation of findings as an "effect" of linguistic experience on the location of perceptual thresholds (as

---

[10]This is somewhat of an oversimplifiction in that the release burst is not always absent in Spanish stops produced with voicing lead; however, when such a burst occurs, it is characteristically of weak amplitude (Williams, 1977).

expressed in msec VOT) that separate voicing categories for infants has been attributed variously to: (1) generalization from exposure to a phonetic feature contrast (+ prevoice) that appears in the language but does not necessarily occur at the place of articulation used in an experimental test of an effect of experience (Streeter, 1976); (2) experience with the same voicing categories used in testing (Eimas, 1975); (3) experience with the precise categories and corresponding perceptual boundaries experienced by speakers of the language (Aslin et al., 1981; Eilers, 1978; Eilers et al., 1979; Lasky et al., 1975); and/or (4) experience defined in terms of reaching a frequency (of exposure to the contrast) threshold (Aslin & Pisoni, 1980; Eilers et al., 1979). In the next sections, we discuss some important consequences of these definitions and interpretations.

DEFINING LINGUISTIC EXPERIENCE

Let us consider the definition of linguistic experience as experience with speech sound contrasts of the infant's language community. This definition entails that the infant *segments* the speech stream into phonetic units and registers the relation between members of the two phonetic categories such that the two sounds are experienced *as a contrast*. To claim that speech sound contrasts are "experienced" and that such experience enhances sensitivity to the perceptual cues that separate phonetic categories for adults of that community, we must attribute to the infant the processes by which such experience could affect subsequent discrimination performance. That linguistic experience has such an effect presupposes that infants have accomplished at least all of the following:

1. Segmented the speech stream into discrete units.
2. Recognized that the sounds to be contrasted vary along some underlying perceptual continuum(s).
3. Ignored covarying redundant information.
4. Identified variations along certain continuum(s) as perceptually equivalent (perceptual constancy).
5. Recognized that these instances along the continuum(s) separate into contrasting categories.
6. Recognized that these instances have occurred before (such that current experience is identified with previous experience).
7. Accounted for the frequency with which such instances have occurred.

With respect to voicing categories, as yet as we have no independent direct evidence that infants are capable of accomplishing all that would be necessary for "linguistic experience," defined as experience with language–specific contrasts or categories, to have an effect on infants' speech sound discrimination. To conclude an effect of linguistic experience from the most favorable evidence of differing discrimination performance of infants from diverse linguistic communities is to assume, among other things, that prelinguistic infants process speech phonetically. Consequently, it is paradoxical that some of those who have argued *against* a phonetic interpretation of infants' categorical discrimination of speech have argued *for* an effect of experience on infants' speech discrimination.

SPECIFYING PHONETIC INPUT

It may be worthwhile at this point to outline some of the problems and complexities involved in trying to specify phonetic input as it relates to voicing categories infants may experience. The need for prerequisite abilities becomes particularly clear in this context. In addition, those interested in the effect of experience on infants' speech perception must provide systematic descriptions of phonetic input for each linguistic environment studied in order to specify precisely how linguistic environments differ in speech input and to understand how such differences affect speech perception. For example, it has been suggested (Aslin & Pisoni, 1980a; Eilers et al., 1979) that the frequency of occurrence of particular contrasts in the infants' environment might determine whether or not those contrasts are discriminated.

Let us consider the potential categorizations of linguistic experience with respect to sounds that vary along the VOT continuum. This is a complex task both for the researcher, who wishes to provide a systematic description of phonetic input, and for the infant, who has to register phonetic input systematically. The examples to be discussed do not exhaust the problems confronting the researcher or the infant, but they serve to indicate the intricacies involved.

As a result of the process of phonological acquisition, adults can systematically segment the speech stream according to the phonemic categories of their native language. However, the prelinguistic infant is presumably not yet constrained by a phonological system and, consequently, the ways of categorizing discrete speech events are potentially much more numerous.

When we consider the infant's speech environment, we observe that speech sounds most frequently occur in the context of continuous speech. The following excerpt (Stern, personal communication), spoken by a mother to her 2-month-old son, is a typical example:

Is Joseph the best boy?
Yeah, stick that tongue in
Get it in get it in
oops
You put it in

In a passage such as this, stop consonants that fall into prevoiced, voiced, and voiceless categories occur in different positions in the utterance (initial, noninitial, final), are surrounded by various consonantal and vocalic environments, and are produced with varying degrees of stress. These factors pose a number of problems for the researcher and for the infant.

Voicing categories are distributed in the speech environment of the infant across different vocalic and consonantal environments. For adults, the perceptual crossover for the voiced/voiceless distinction shifts as a function of the vocalic environment so that in specifying phonetic input in terms of stop categories for infants, stops cannot be sorted a priori into voiced and voiceless categories. If we define linguistic experience as involving the infant's recognition of phonetic categories in speech, the infant must, for example, isolate a phone from its phonetic environment, recognize it as having occurred before, and recognize instances of a category that occur in the various vocalic and consonantal environments as perceptually equivalent.

Stops from voicing categories also vary with respect to their position — initial, noninitial, and final — in isolated words (and continuous speech). In perception, for initial and noninitial position in isolated words, the acoustic consequences of VOT distinguish voicing categories. But for final position, the duration of the preceding vowel often is the most relevant dimension (e.g., Denes, 1955; Raphael, 1972). In isolated words (or continuous speech), members of the same phonemic category that vary in terms of their position in the word (utterance) may be perceptually equivalent for adults. In this case, the perceptual constancy problem for the infant involves equating phonetic variants of the same phonemic category as the same percept, although the variants are signaled by different acoustic cues. The researcher's decision to include instances that occur in final position as constituting part of the infant's experience with a particular stop voicing category would have to be determined by the infant's performance in a perceptual constancy task that tested for perceptual equivalence across the different positions both in words and, ultimately, in continuous speech.

As we discussed earlier, the same features that specify an allophone in one language (e.g., aspiration) are distinctive features in yet other languages. For instance, Spanish stops produced with long voicing lead in noninitial positions are often fricated (Williams, 1977), Kikuyu labial stops produced with long lead are frequently nasalized (Streeter, 1974), and English stops produced with long lead occur in both free and contextual variation (Lisker & Abramson, 1964). Inasmuch as we are guided by such phonetic considerations as these in defining "phonetic input," sounds with distinctive features such as frication, prevoicing, nasalization, and aspiration should be considered initially as distinct categories, because the infant (unlike the adult) does not know to ignore these nonphonemic distinctions.

In specifying phonetic input, another striking problem arises when we try to identify stops in continuous speech for placement into the appropriate

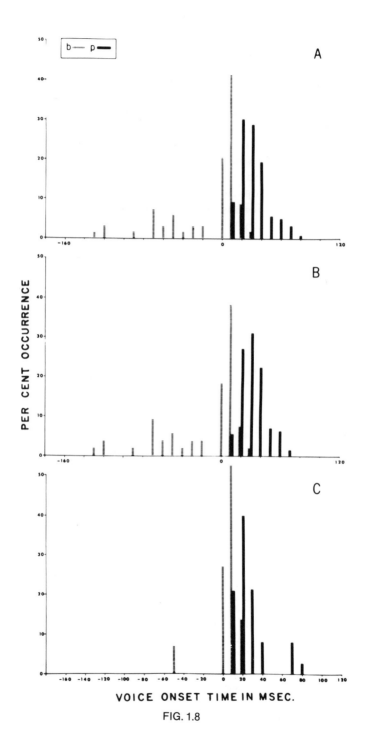

FIG. 1.8

voicing categories. Under such conditions, VOT boundaries become noticeably blurred. Figure 1.8 exemplifies this problem. In this figure, stops produced with both short and long voicing lag are not separated by a well-defined boundary; rather, the VOT tokens overlap and are distributed throughout the boundary range, resulting in tokens that cannot be identified unambiguously by adult listeners from the semantic context of the sentence in which they occur (Lisker & Abramson, 1967). The impact of the blurring of the VOT boundaries in continuous speech for the infant is that the infant could not be "tuning in" to the VOT boundary of a given language (Eilers et al., 1979) because there is no boundary to tune in to. In this description, it appears that a perceptual "boundary" is being regarded as a property that is itself perceived, rather than as the consequence of crossing a perceptual threshold.

RECOGNIZING THE LINGUISTIC FUNCTION OF SPEECH

It has been argued (Aslin et al., 1981; Eilers, 1978; Eilers et al., 1979; Lasky et al., 1975) that for experience to affect discrimination of a stop voicing contrast used phonemically by speakers of the infants' linguistic community, infants' perceptual boundaries for stop voicing contrasts that lie along regions of the VOT continuum must overlap with those of the speakers of the language to be learned. How would such an overlap be achieved? How would Spanish infants, for example, enhance their sensitivity to a phonological long lead/short lag stop contrast and eventually come to ignore those allophonic contrasts (e.g., short lag/long lag stop contrasts) that serve no phonological function in the language? Similarly, how would these infants become sensitive to parameters that result in the -5 msec VOT perceptual boundary separating long lead/short lag labial stops for Spanish speakers rather than those that result in the Thai long lead/short lag labial stop boundary, which lies at about -20 msec VOT? Nothing intrinsic to the speech signal conveys such information. For example, Figs. 1.4 and 1.5 show that the VOT distributions and corresponding boundary ranges for prestressed labial stops produced in isolated words with voicing lead and with short voicing lag are the

FIG. 1.8 *(Opposite page)* American English: Frequency distributions of VOT values for word-initial labial stops produced in sentences in various contexts (10 speakers). Occurrence of voicing lead is notably higher than represented (see text for explanation). Three conditions regarding stress are shown: (A) stressed and unstressed combined; (B) stressed; and (C) unstressed. (From "Some effects of context on voice onset time in English stops" by L. Lisker and A. S. Abramson, *Language and Speech,* 1967, *10,* 1–28. Copyright 1967 by Robert Draper Ltd. Reprinted by permission.)

same in Spanish and in Thai. Furthermore, other perceptually relevant acoustic parameters that covary with the timing dimension during production of sounds with voicing lag and voicing lead are also available in both languages.

For experience to affect infants' discrimination of stop voicing contrasts that are phonemic for the language to be learned, we argue that the infant must have a *strategy* for achieving the primary goal of phonological development. This strategy involves the discovery of those contrasts that convey differences in meaning.[11] The knowledge that certain sounds or sound patterns have particular communicative consequences is used by infants to search for those distinctions that serve a phonological function in their language. In discovering phonological contrasts, infants selectively attend to those parameters that distinguish the contrast. Consequently, sensitivity to these parameters is enhanced. Infants concomitantly screen out or attenuate those parameters that do not inform them about language function (i.e., phonetic variants of the same phoneme). In this way, phonetic categories and their corresponding perceptual boundaries come to overlap with those of the native language speaker.

One major goal for infants is to learn the language of their community. Prerequisite to achieving this goal is to experience the community's language, which is accomplished primarily via the auditory modality by normal language learners. It has been suggested (e.g., Kuhl, 1978) that as language evolved, it may have taken advantage of certain psychoacoustic thresholds, which for example, lay along the VOT continuum for stop consonants, such that those psychoacoustic thresholds corresponded to the phonetic boundaries marking phonological categories, as in the English voiced/voiceless (short lag/long lag) stop distinction. We might further expect that the auditory perceptual mechanism has adapted to the language learning goal, operating on the speech signal in a highly principled fashion in order to facilitate the achievement of this goal. The perceptual mechanism might, for example, naturally segment the speech stream into units the size of a phone, be selectively sensitive to those acoustic parameters that have potential phonetic significance, and/or register the contrastive relation between two sounds from different phonetic categories.

CONCLUSION

In this chapter, we have considered how experience could affect infants' discrimination of speech contrasts that are phonological for their linguistic community by setting out some conditions that must be met before the per-

---

[11]The circumstances that give rise to such a strategy are not known.

ceptual boundaries separating phonetic categories for infants will overlap with those boundaries language speakers use to separate phonological categories for their language. To restate these in brief, the infant must be able to segment the speech stream, recognize that speech sounds vary along a perceptual continuum, ignore redundant covariation, perceive constancy, recognize category contrasts and their recurrences, and be sensitive to the frequency of occurrence of such contrasts. We indicated that these conditions require independent confirmation before we can conclude an effect of experience on infants' speech sound discrimination. Finally, we conclude by arguing that, counter to Aslin and Pisoni (1980a), experience listening to the speech of a particular linguistic community will not induce discrimination of a language-specific contrast, shift a boundary to correspond to that of the language user, or attenuate discrimination of a distinction that may be discriminable by virtue of its psychoacoustic characteristics until infants are aware that certain sounds contrast to convey differences in meaning.

ACKNOWLEDGMENTS

This research was supported by NICHHD (NIH) postdoctoral fellowship grant #HD054707 to the first author. We would like to thank Michael Studdert-Kennedy and Roy D. Pea for their comments and Arthur S. Abramson for his instructive comments on phonetics.

REFERENCES

Abramson, A. S. Laryngeal timing in consonant distinctions. *Phonetica,* 1977, *34,* 295–303.

Abramson, A. S., & Lisker, L. Voice-timing perception in Spanish word-initial stops. *Journal of Phonetics,* 1973, *1,* 1–8.

Aslin, R. N., Hennessy, B. L., Pisoni, D. B., & Perey, A. J. *Individual infants' discrimination of VOT: Evidence for three modes of voicing.* Paper presented at the biennial meetings of the Society for Research in Child Development, San Francisco, March 1979.

Aslin, R. N., & Pisoni, D. B. Some developmental processes in speech perception. In G. H. Yeni-Komshian, J. F. Kavanagh, & C. A. Ferguson (Eds.), *Child Phonology* (Vol. 2). New York: Academic Press, 1980.(a)

Aslin, R. & Pisoni, D. B. Effects of early linguistic experience on speech discrimination by infants: a critique of Eilers, Gavin & Wilson (1979). *Child Development,* 1980, *51,* 107–112.(b)

Aslin, R. N., Pisoni, D. B., Hennessy, B. L., & Perey, A. J. Discrimination of voice-onset-time by human infants: New findings concerning phonetic development. *Child Development,* 1981, *52,* 1135–1145.

Denes, P. Effect of duration on the perception of voicing. *Journal of the Acoustical Society of America,* 1955, *27,* 761–764.

Eilers, R. E. Discussion summary: Development of phonology. In F. D. Minifie & L. L. Lloyd (Eds.), *Communicative and cognitive abilities: Early behavioral assessment.* Baltimore: University Park Press, 1978.

Eilers, R. E. Effects of early linguistic experience on speech discrimination by infants: a reply. *Child Development,* 1980, *51,* 113–117.

Eilers, R. E., Gavin, W., & Wilson, W. R. Linguistic experience and phonemic perception in infancy: A cross-linguistic study. *Child Development,* 1979, *50,* 14–18.

Eimas, P. D. Speech perception in early infancy. In L. B. Cohen & P. Salapatek (Eds.), *Infant perception: from sensation to cognition, Vol. II.* New York: Academic Press, 1975.

Eimas, P. D., Siqueland, E. R., Jusczyk, P., & Vigorito, J. Speech perception in infants. *Science,* 1971, *171,* 303–306.

Haggard, M. S., Ambler, S., & Callow, M. Pitch as a voicing cue. *Journal of the Acoustical Society of America,* 1970, *47,* 613–617.

Kuhl, P. K. Predispositions for the perception of speech-sound categories: A species-specific phenomenon? In F. D. Minifie & L. L. Lloyd (Eds.), *Communicative and cognitive abilities: Early behavioral assessment.* Baltimore: University Park Press, 1978.

Kuhl, P. K., & Miller, J. D. Speech perception in the chinchilla: Voiced–voiceless distinction in alveolar plosive consonants. *Science,* 1975, *190,* 69–72.

Lasky, R. E., Syrdal-Lasky, A., & Klein, R. E. VOT discrimination by four to six and a half month old infants from Spanish environments. *Journal of Experimental Child Psychology,* 1975, *20,* 215–225.

Liberman, A. M., Delattre, P., & Cooper, F. S. Some cues for the distinction between voiced and voiceless stops in initial position. *Language and Speech,* 1958, *1,* 153–167.

Lisker, L. Is it VOT or a first-formant transition detector? *Journal of the Acoustical Society of America,* 1975, *57,* 1547–1551.

Lisker, L. In qualified defense of VOT. *Language and Speech,* 1978, *21,* 375–383.

Lisker, L., & Abramson, A. S. A cross-language study of voicing in initial stops: Acoustical measurements. *Word,* 1964, *20,* 384–422.

Lisker, L., & Abramson, A. S. Some effects of context on voice onset time in English stops. *Language and Speech,* 1967, *10,* 1–28.

Lisker, L., & Abramson, A. S. The voicing dimension: Some experiments in comparative phonetics. In *Proceedings of the Sixth International Congress of Phonetic Sciences.* Prague; Academia, 1970.

MacKain, K. S., Best, C. T., & Strange, W. Categorical perception of /r/ and /l/ by Japanese bilinguals. *Journal of Applied Psycholinguistics,* 1981, *2,* 369–390.

Miller, J. D., Pastore, R. E., Wier, C. C., Kelly, W. F., & Dooling, R. J. Discrimination and labeling of noise-buzz sequences with varying noise-lead times: An example of categorical perception. *Journal of the Acoustical Society of America,* 1976, *60,* 410–417.

Miyawaki, K., Strange, W., Verbrugge, R., Liberman, A. M., Jenkins, J. J., & Fujimura, O. An effect of linguistic experience: The discrimination of [r] and [l] by native speakers of Japanese and English. *Perception & Psychophysics,* 1975, *18,* 331–340.

Raphael, L. J. Preceding vowel duration as a cue to the perception of the voicing characteristic of word-final consonants in American English. *Journal of the Acoustical Society of America,* 1972, *51,* 1296–1303.

Repp, B. H. *Perceptual trading relation between aspiration amplitude and VOT.* Paper presented at the meeting of the Acoustical Society of America, Cambridge, Mass., June 1979.

Smith, B., & Westbury, J. R. *Temporal control of voicing during occlusion in plosives.* Paper presented at the meeting of the Acoustical Society of America, Austin, Tex., April 1975.

Stevens, K. N. The potential role of property detectors in the perception of consonants. In G. Fant & M. Tatham (Eds.), *Auditory analysis and the perception of speech.* London: Academic Press, 1975.

Stevens, K. N., & Klatt, D. H. Role of formant transitions in the voiced–voiceless distinction for stops. *Journal of the Acoustical Society of America,* 1974, *55,* 753–759.

Streeter, L. A. *The effect of linguistic experience on phonetic perception.* Unpublished doctoral dissertation, Columbia University, 1974.

Streeter, L. A. Language perception of 2-month-old infants show effects of both innate mechanisms and experience. *Nature,* 1976, *259,* 39–41.

Summerfield, Q. A., & Haggard, M. P. On the dissociation of spectral and temporal cues to the voicing distinction in initial stop consonants. *Journal of the Acoustical Society of America,* 1977, 62, 435–448.

Williams, L. *Speech perception and production as a function of exposure to a second language.* Unpublished doctoral dissertation, Harvard University, 1974.

Williams, L. The voicing contrast in Spanish. *Journal of Phonetics,* 1977, *5,* 169–184.

Zlatin, M. A. Voicing contrast: Perceptual and productive voice onset time characteristic of adults. *Journal of the Acoustical Society of America,* 1974, *56,* 981–994.

2 Intonation in Discourse: Talk Between 12-Month-Olds and Their Mothers

Linda J. Ferrier
Children's Hospital Medical Center, Boston, Mass.

INTRODUCTION

Intonation, along with other paralinguistic communication systems, is one of the early means by which infants communicate with their caregivers. Before infants can produce many (or indeed any) adult-sounding words, they use intonation in conjunction with gestural systems to communicate a range of functions recognizable to their caregivers. This paper attempts to take a preliminary look at the intentional communications of ten 12-month-old children and their mothers to address the following questions: (1) What speech act functions are distinguished by rising versus nonrising intonation in infants and mothers? (2) What similarities in intonation use exist between mothers and their children? (3) Is intonation use subject to the same processes of simplification of function and overgeneralization of meaning as other areas of language acquisition?

Given the current embattled status of intonation, the controversy over its possible units of analysis, and the nature of its relationship to other aspects of language, it may seem precipitous to begin to look for its origins in development. Intonation has traditionally been related to syntax, a position held by Halliday (1967, 1975a), Crystal (1969), and Ladd (1977). It has variably been tied to speaker attitude (Pike, 1945) and to particular speech act functions (Sag & Lieberman, 1975). A further school (e.g., Brazil, 1975, 1978) sees its relationship to discourse as primary. The most recent movement, spearheaded by Bolinger (1982) and Cruttenden (1981a), demonstrates that any analysis in terms of a relationship between intonation and a single aspect of language can be contradicted by a dozen examples. They posit a more abstract relationship between intonation and language than any advocated thus far. Bolinger (1982) describes intonation in terms of a gestural system that responds to emotional tensions and outbursts in culturally prescribed ways. It is therefore congruent with syntax and lexicon but neither determining nor determined by these other levels of language.

Cruttenden (1981a) sees the distinction between falls and rises as the realization of the more abstract system of *closed* versus *open*. He suggests that there is a basic dichotomy of meaning between falling and rising tones but that this distinction is at a fairly high level of abstraction, which is at different times reflected in meanings that appear at a lower level to be a lexical, grammatical, discoursal, or attitudinal. Conflicts between these various levels are resolved by a hierarchy which, although not formalized explicitly, establishes that grammatical considerations are overruled by lexical, attitudinal, or discoursal considerations.

Cruttenden goes on to survey various dialects of English and other languages to discover how they realize the open versus closed distinction, which in receiving pronunciation and general American English is carried by the rising–falling distinction. He concludes that other dialects and languages utilize different resources to carry this distinction (e.g., pitch range, pitch height, or a distinction between a lax vs. a tense ending). However, in citing examples from various sources (e.g., the pioneering work by Bolinger, 1964) such a distinction appears to be universal.

The question to which this discussion leads is: Given the hypothesized univeral status of these abstract features of intonation, when and how do children learn them? Let us assume for the purposes of this paper that the variables relevant to this question are: (1) receptive processing limitations and strategies; (2) features of the input language in terms of frequency of usage and the functions of use; (3) productive limitations in terms of motor control and the strategies employed to overcome those limitations.

Receptive Processing

The relationship between laboratory assessments of receptive abilities in infants and the use of those abilities in later language is equivocal, but there is some evidence that infants can discriminate differences in pitch in the first year of life (Kaplan & Kaplan, 1971). Kuhl and Miller (1975) found that between 4 and 16 weeks infants could discriminate changes in pitch and vowel quality when other factors were held constant and in vowel quality when the pitch contour changed randomly but not vice versa. This particular finding, however, suggests greater salience of the phonetic content over the intonational contour. Kaplan (1969), using a head-turning paradigm, showed that 8-month-olds can discriminate utterances containing rising versus falling terminal contours, patterns characteristic of American English. Finally, the prosodic theory of phonology acquisition (Waterson, 1971a, 1971b) suggests that each child identifies a schema of phonetic and prosodic features that is shared by productions in the input language. Children then reproduce in their own output features that are "strongly articulated." Although lacking strong evidence, Waterson's theory is attractive in that it accounts for some idiosyncratic speech productions in young children and suggests that the child does not make a distinction between phonetic versus prosodic features, but perceives them as a gestalt.

Features of the Input Language

Ferguson (1964, 1977) was one of the first to draw attention to the systematic simplification and modification of language to small children. Most marked among such features are the increased pitch range and greater use of final rising intonation. Garnica (1977) substantiated these findings by analyzing acoustically the prosodic features of adult talk to children in a variety of controlled settings. Her findings included: "1) the average fundamental pitch of the speaker's voice is higher to the two-year old than to the five-year old. 2) Speech to the two-year old contains instances of rising sentence pitch terminals where the grammatical form would normally dictate a falling pitch, e.g., imperatives. This feature is absent from speech directed to the adult listener and to the five-year old [p. 80]." She concludes that the use of overall higher pitch serves the social function of marking speech intended for the child listener.

The use of rising sentence final terminals serves the regulatory function of maintaining the child's attention. Ryan (1978), in a study involving videotaped sessions between mothers and their 12-month-old infants, found that mothers used final rise when there was a discrepancy between the focus of their attention and that of the child. Evidence for the salience of final rise is suggested by the result that infants were more likely to look at the toy on which mothers were focusing after a rise than a nonrise. A link between the use of final rise and comprehension is indicated in a study by Larson, Ferrier, Chesnick, Liebergott, and Schultz (1982) of the directives addressed by mothers to their infants at 12 and 22 months of age. The mothers of children with good comprehension, as measured by an independent measure of comprehension of two-term relations, used a greater incidence of rise than the mothers of poor comprehenders. By 22 months, the amount of rising intonation addressed to the good comprehenders had dropped to the same level used by the mothers of the poor comprehenders. Stern, Spieker, and MacKain (1982), in a video-tape study of mothers addressing 6-month-old infants, found that the increased use of rising intonation appears to function to achieve the prelinguistic child's visual attention. In addition, these researchers found that particular fundamental frequency contours were associated with particular affective states in the infant. Marked pitch falls were associated with coaxing for more effectively positive behaviors once attention had been achieved. Sinusoidal bell contours were emitted to stimulate a show and sharing of delight.

The burden of this research appears to be that mothers, whether consciously or not, employ the open or rising terminal form, which in adult usage expects a response, to serve an interactive function (i.e., to attract the attention of their infants). There is preliminary evidence that this increased usage is effective in eliciting attention and is moreover associated with good comprehension on the part of the infant. In substantiation of Bolinger's claim of a fundamental link with emotion, mothers of preverbal infants tailor their intonation to the affective states of their infants.

Productive Use

Lieberman (1967) relates rising versus falling intonation to physiological breathing patterns. Falling terminal contour appears to be the physiologically simplest and also the linguistically unmarked form. In English, yes/no questions are typically produced with marked rising terminal contour. On this basis one would predict that falling intonation would precede rising intonation developmentally, and indeed the literature reviewed by Crystal (1979) appears to confirm this. According to this description, only falling tones are present initially. Falling tones are then contrasted with level tones and then falling versus high-rising tones. We are initially concerned with these early contrasts and the functions with which they are typically associated. What little evidence there is (Wells, Montgomery, & MacLure, 1979) suggests that most children at the one- and two-word stage use falling terminal contour on most of their utterances and that even school-age children use final rise less frequently than do adults. Wells et al. found that children mainly used rising intonation for a limited set of social functions such as listing, generally initiated by a parent, elicited politeness markers, attention-getting devices such as "Mummy," and conversational devices such as "mhm" and "uh." Menn (1976) studied the use of rising tones and found that they accomplish a variety of social functions including requesting, attention getting, offering, and registering curiosity. Halliday reports (1975) that his son used a marked rise for all utterances expecting a response and falling intonation only when no response was expected.

This suggests that children first learn final rise to accomplish a narrowly proscribed set of interactive functions and that, as in other areas of language learning, a more abstract notion is not acquired until much later. Cruttenden (1981b) considers that, like other linguistic systems, intonation begins with occasional idiosyncratic contours tied invariantly to a particular communicative function with a particular phonetic content. Only later is this item-learned system supplanted by a rule-governed system in which the child can impose different contours on the same phonetic content to realize different functions.

I assume for present purposes that 12-month-old children are most likely to use rising intonation to accomplish those communicative functions that: (1) are present with high frequency in the input language; (2) can meet their own social and cognitive needs. I also assume that, just as different dialects and languages select different resources from the range of linguistic options available, so will infants make different selections, which at this early stage may be idiosyncratic, and only later will approach the conventional linguistic system (cf. Menn, 1976).

What is lacking is an analysis of infants' use of intonation to communicate speech act functions contrastively, with a simultaneous analysis of the intonational systems to which they are exposed by their parents. Wells, MacLure, and Montgomery (1979) have devised a model of discourse for use with slightly older children, which appears to meet this need. Five pitch levels and five directions of pitch movement are distinguished within the range of each speaker. This system has been modified to suit the purposes of this analysis. And although only rising versus nonrising intonation is distinguished, certain notions central to the discourse analysis are employed.

Discourse Model

Any model that usefully describes mother/infant dialogues must ideally attempt to explain the following features:

1. How two individuals with such different resources, cognitive and linguistic, can yet carry on a successful, continuous dialogue.
2. How each participant can from moment to moment involve the other in meeting his or her needs for information, goods, and services.
3. The organization of turns that allows the participants, in spite of different and sometimes conflicting goals, to maintain the interactions.
4. How infants select from the stream of verbal discourse those items that are salient perceptually and cognitively.
5. How infants put those features to their own uses and how such uses diverge from those of their models, both in the form and the uses to which they are put.

There must, it seems, be some shaping of resources on the part of both parents and child, necessitated by the goal of successful communication. Each participant brings to the interaction a cognitive scheme of the world that includes a history of interactive events with other familiar participants. Each operates on the knowledge of which interactive strategies have been previously successful in getting a response and which therefore can be expected to meet his or her social and cognitive needs in the present. According to the fine-tuning hypothesis (e.g., Cross, 1977), parents restrict their linguistic dialogues to match the competence of the child, continually modifying it in response to the child's growing resources. Parents who most successfully match their output to the cognitive and linguistic level of their children will provide the optimum environment. However, children are, in terms of a hypothesis testing model, consistently selecting from the language to which they are exposed in ongoing conversation. That selection, we must assume, is constrained by their curent cognitive and linguistic state. They then put such information to their own use, which may involve simplification or overgeneralization of the adult system. The set of functions negotiated by each dyad must therefore be a restricted set of the total range of possibilities. Hence, each dyad may specialize in a limited range of functioning, which for that dyad has a felicitous outcome.

The final construct operating within the interaction is the joint activity in which parents and children routinely engage (Bruner, 1975; Bruner, Roy, & Ratner, 1982; Ferrier, 1978; Wells, Montgomery, & MacLure, 1979). The language of parents and their children is closely tied to a gradually expanding set of routine activities. Just as the parents select from their linguistic options to insure communicative success, so too do they select social activities on the basis of what the infant has previously enjoyed and is capable of doing. As the infant engages in physical activity, both constrained and driven by cognitive and motoric abilities, parents translate that activity into linguistic terms by ongoing comments.

I describe some part of the organization of discourse, which allows for the exchange of information and provision of goods and services in the context of joint action. Each discourse turn sets up varying degrees of demand for response. Various speech acts can be aligned on a dimension of strength of expectation of response:

	Initiate	or Continue	Terminate	
Req. Info.	Call	Describe	Reject	Imitate
			Deny	
Req. Action	Offer	Evaluate	Affirm	Acknowledge

Strongest expectation of response ⟷ Weakest expectation of response

In the left-hand category are those speech acts with the strongest expectation of response, such as a request for information or action. These are most often violated by a failure to respond, and such a failure is most likely to be met by a new attempt to elicit a response. In the middle category, functions such as descriptions of states of affairs (e.g., *There is a dog in the garden*) or expressions of internal state (e.g., *I'm chilly*), though they anticipate a response, can more easily be ignored. Finally, in the right-hand category, acknowledgments of affirmations anticipate no further response, and a subsequent turn initiates a new sequence of interaction. The eliciting force of such speech acts organizes the structure of turns throughout the discourse.

Wells et al. (1979) explore the means by which, with limited discourse options, conversation is infinitely expandable. Speech act types may iniate a sequence of interaction by raising the expectation of a response, or they may terminate it by eliminating any further expectation. However, certain speech act types may carry two discourse functions by acting as a response to a previous eliciting utterance while simultaneously signaling the expectation of a further response. This discourse position is referred to as a "continue" by Wells et al., and I employ the same terminology. The following are a variety of continues as used by mothers and infants in our sample:

Daniel: Initiate — /dzae/ (what's that) (touches toy)
Mother: Continue — ʿYou tell mommy
Daniel: Response — φ

Daniel: Initiate — /da/ (that) (turns to look at book)
Mother: Continue — What?
Daniel: Continue — /da/ (that)
Mother: Continue — That aʿsquirrel?
Daniel: Response — φ

Mother: Initiate — Brush your ʿhair. (gives brush to Jessica)
Jessica: Continue — /ae/ (request for action) (puts brush
        to mother's hair)
Mother: Continue — Brush ʿyour hair. (does not bend down
        to have her own hair brushed)
Jessica: Inappropriate response — (sits down)

Mother: Initiate — Look what ʿI found. (holds up beads)
Jessica: Continue — /mae/ (request action) (takes beads)

The dimension of discourse position therefore stipulates the strength of requirement of a response without consideration of the content of the exchange. Particular speech act types specify the content of the exchange in terms of information, goods, services, or simple fun.

As can be seen from these examples, intonation is a major resource used by both infants and their mothers to maintain interaction while at the same time executing their own intentions. Particular prosodic contours are simultaneously a function of the type of speech act, its place in the discourse structure, and the lexical focus realized by the placement of the major stress within the tone group. It is therefore assumed that intonation must be studied in relation to the particular speech act with which it is associated and the discourse position (i.e., initiate, continue, or response) in which it operates.

Perceptual and Cognitive Aspects of the Model

Onto the discourse structure outlined in this model we must add a description of the child's perception of intonation, in contrast with the segmental information of the message, and his or her induction of the meaning. Because there is evidence that infants can discriminate rising versus falling intonation contrasts (Kaplan, 1969) by 8 months and use them productively on babbled strings by 7 months (Tonkova-Yampol'skaya, 1969), prosodic features may be more salient to the infant in the last half of the first year than finer phonetic contrasts. It has yet to be determined whether all infants begin their analysis of language by tuning in to a gestalt or whole word shape to which prosodic features would largely contribute, or whether there is large individual variation. Clearly, there are large individual differences in production in this period. Some infants specialize in jargon strings with sentence-like intonation but minimal phonetic detail, whereas others specialize in babbles with reduplicated phonetic closure and less dramatic prosody. Without experimental evidence, we can only speculate on whether this specialization in babbling is based upon differences in perception or upon production constraints (cf. Macken & Ferguson, 1983).

In the light of evidence to date, it is not unlikely that infants will tune in to the prosodic shapes of utterances to which they are exposed and associate particular communicative intentions with them.

Relations Between Form and Function
in Input Language

The problem that faces the child is one of having to infer the relationship between rising intonation, particular speech act functions, and the English mood system in adult usage. Ryan (1979), in a corpus of maternal utterances to 12-month-old children, found an equal distribution of questions among the three classes of yes/no, tag, and wh- questions. Virtually all questions without a rise were wh- questions, whereas almost all yes/no questions, including tag questions, were spoken with a rise. However, a wh- question was equally likely to be spoken with or without a rise. The strongest association, therefore, from the perspective of the child attempting to break the linguistic code is between yes/no questions and rising intonation. However, yes/no questions are ambiguous as to the function they serve. They are used with equal frequency to request information in the form of a yes or no response or to request action using an indirect polite form. Although the context is generally sufficient to disambiguate the responses required, there are situations in which both a yes/no response and/or action seem appropriate. For example, if A is talking to B on the phone and C is present, A may say to C, "Do you wanna talk to B?" This may truly by a request for information, to which C may respond, "No, I talked to him earlier." But there is an equal chance it may be a request for action for which an appropriate response would be either simply to reach for the phone or accompany such a gesture with an affirmative response. The only inappropriate responses would be to say "yes" but not accept the offered phone, to simply to walk out of the room, or to otherwise fail to show any acknowledgment of the request.

Infants in the face of this ambiguity of intonation functions in input have several options: (1) they may use rising intonations, as did Halliday's son, for all utterances that anticipate a response; (2) they may assume that it is used only to request information; (3) they may assume it is used only to request action; or (4) given this ambiguity, they might ignore rising intonation completely.

In addition to the use of rising intonation to request information, rise serves a variety of other functions. It can signal uncertainty or puzzlement, as in, "Six or seven make twelve?" (where the degree of rise is not quite so acute). Mothers also use it in tags with very high frequency either to reiterate the force of a previous utterance or to request a further turn. For example:

Mother: Can you say something into the 'microphone? Hm?

Or:

Infant: (babbles)
Mother: Yeah?

It is used to make an emphatic contradiction or rejection of a previous statement or act. For example:

Infant: /gʌk/ (points at picture)
Mother: 'That's not a 'duck.

A milder form of this fall–rise contour is used frequently by mothers on the predicate nominal of descriptions. For example:

Mother: That's a 'squirrel.
             (or)
           That's a cookie.

Across all these speech act functions there generally appears to be an expectation of a response associated with a final rise, or else there is an implication that the action accompanying the conversation is open-ended or ongoing.

HYPOTHESES

This model, which sees intonation as playing a role in both the maintenance of discourse and the simultaneous achievement of individual goals through speech act functions, generates the following hypotheses:

1. Both children's and mothers' proportional usage of rising to nonrising terminal contour will be different in the three discourse positions of Initiate, Continue, and Terminate.
2. Each dyad will show a preference for a small set of speech act types, which will have a greater proportional frequency than others practiced by that dyad.
3. Mothers and their infants, given this specialization in particular speech act functions, will show a similar proportional use of rising to nonrising intonation, which will vary from dyad to dyad.
4. However, given the ambiguity of the relationship between rising intonation, the yes/no question form, and the speech act functions of request action and request information: (a) some infants will simplify the meaning of risng intonation, responding to it uniquely as a result for information or a request for action; (b) some infants will use rising intonation in their own productions uniquely as a request for information, as a request for action, or alternatively, for any utterance that expects a response.

METHOD

The subjects were 10 infants drawn from a larger population of 56 subjects taking part in a longitudinal study of language development in matched normal and premature infants. All subjects wer drawn from intact families with English-speaking parents. Audio recordings were made at monthly intervals; video recordings were made at 12 months. In addition, a variety of standardized cognitive measures were administered. Nine of the infants selected for this subpopulation, on the basis of clinical judgment, appeared to be progressing at a normal rate, and one appeared to be developing more slowly. Of the ten infants, five were premature and five were full term.

The children were video taped in their homes when 12 months old. Visits to premature infants were adjusted for full-term gestational age. All infants were video taped using portable Sonymatic Video Recorders for 30 minutes. Mothers were asked to play with their infants during this time. Simultaneous high fidelity audio recordings were made using a Sony TC-D5 cassette recorder and a hand-held unidirectional AKG microphone. The families had already been visited twice and therefore were reasonably at ease with the investigators.

Sample Selection

Video tapes were then scrutinized for clear examples of intentional utterances by the infant. For an utterance to qualify as "intentional" it had to meet at least two of the following criteria:

1. It must be accompanied by a conventional gesture or recognizable social act, such as pointing, reaching, showing, giving, or looking at an object.
2. Eye contact must be made with mother at some point within the sequence in which the utterance occurred.
3. The utterance must be phonetically recognizable as an adult English word.

Each infant utterance was identified, and its accompanying gesture or activity was described. Immediate imitations of a mother's previous utterance were excluded at this stage of analysis. Each infant utterance was then given a broad phonetic transcription, which included the intonation contour and syllable stress where it was marked. Any preceding or following contingently related mother utterances were also transcribed, in addition to any subsequent contingent infant utterances. The prosodic contour was also described for each mother utterance and any accompanying behavior. The motivation behind this sampling procedure was to eliminate infant babbles, which are random accompaniments to action, or practice play. These are of course interesting in their own right, and it is hypothesized that they may in fact by systematically different from socially directed utterances. In addition, by selecting only those maternal utterances that co-occur in sequence with intentional baby utterances, we are describing not the total range to which children are exposed, but only those to which the children make a response or that are responses to their meaningful utterances. Hopefully, we are thereby selecting successful or salient maternal utterances from the infants' perspective and eliminating those which are not salient or at least to which the infant is not attending.

Each series of contingently related utterances was considered a sequence, whose internal structure could be described in terms of the discourse position of each utterance within the sequence. The transcription was done from the high fidelity audio tapes. Each mother and infant utterance was then coded for its discourse position and its speech act function.

Discourse Position

Each utterance was entered in one and only one of the following discourse classes:

1. Initiate: the first utterance in a sequence, which expects a response and begins a new activity.
2. Continue: a noninitiating utterance in a sequence, which although a response to a previous utterance, itself anticipates a response.
3. Terminate: a response that requires no further verbal turn or behavior. (A terminator may in fact be followed by a further terminator, which again expects no response.)

Speech Act Functions

While the set of speech act functions used by adults is open-ended, or at least as large as the set of performative verbs in English (Austin, 1962), mothers interacting with their 12-month-olds clearly are selecting only a small subset of well-practiced functions. The same set of categories was used to describe the utterances of both babies and their mothers, although some categories (e.g., Request for Clarification) were used, as might be expected, almost exclusively by mothers. The categories of speech act functions and their definitions were as follows:

1. *Request for Attention — Call*

    Adult: Kate!

2. *Request for Action:* A request for action or a prohibition realized by a gesture in conjunction with a direct imperative or an indirect form.

    Adult: Play with 'teddy bear? (holds out bear)
    Do you 'wanna take Bu Beans for a 'ride
    with you? (puts Bu Beans on pull toy)
    Push 'Pandy.

    Infant: /ae/ (hands plastic beads to mother, requesting that she pop them together)
    /m̃/ (hands sweater to mother, requesting help to put it on, which in turn is a request to go outside)

3. *Request for Information:* May be a request for affirmation or denial as a response to a yes/no question; also may be a request for a label or other substantive information, using a wh- question form or an equivalent (e.g., "that?").

    Adult: Do you want 'help?
    Do you 'wanna put the 'light on and off?
    Where's the 'clock?

What's 'that? (points at picture in book)

'Jessica, did you go see the monkeys last week?

Infant: /z̆a/ (points at picture in book)

/d̆at/ (points to toy and looks at mother)

4. *Describe:* Includes statements of fact, identity, or clarification.

Adult: No, that's the 'light up there.

It's the 'Celtics.

It's by the 'couch.

Infant: /g͡ɔ/ (points at picture of clock)

5. *Show and Give:* Utterances that accompany showing and giving.

Adult: Look what 'I found. (holds up toy)

Infant: /'d͡ɛde/ (shows object)

6. *Reject:* Rejection of an object or activity.

Adult: Back in the 'living room. (request action)

Infant: /n͡a/ (reject)

Adult: Yes. (reject)

7. *Requests for Performative Play:* Attempts to initiate ritualized games (e.g., nursery rhymes, songs, etc.).

Adult: 'Old Mac'Donald 'had a 'farm . . .

8. *Response to Performative Play*

Infant: jejeje (sings "ee i ee i oh")

9. *Evaluative/Expressive:* Evaluative or expletive responses to objects or events.

Adult: Funny. (looking at picture in book)

Infant: /ɔwai/ (interpret as "all right!") (looking at picture of basketball players)

10. *Affirm:* Positive response to a request for information.

Adult: Yes.

Infant: /jae/

11. *Deny:* Negative response to a request for information.

Adult: That's not a 'duck.

12. *Acknowledge:* Recognition or reinforcement of a previous utterance.

    Adult: Yes.

    Good, terrific.

13. *Request for Clarification:* A request for clarification of a previous utterance.

    Adult: What? (request clarification)

    Mm? (request clarification)

    Where's your 'football? (request action)

    It's by the 'couch. (describe)

    Infant: /m̄/ (looks around) (request clarification)

14. *Conversational Device or Accompaniment to Action:* Social routine and ritual accompaniments to action.

    Adult: See you 'later. (baby crawls away)

    Infant: /dǽ/ (fits in puzzle piece)

The Mood System

Finally, all mothers' utterances were coded for the order and presence of surface structure elements, which distinguish the various moods of English. These decisions were made on the basis of order of constituents, not on intonation.

1. Yes/no question.
2. Wh- question.
3. Imperative.
4. Declarative.
5. Declarative and tag.
6. Wh- questions and tag.
7. Moodless (no verb or not enough surface elements to make a decision as to mood).

RESULTS AND DISCUSSION

The first hypothesis of the study was that the use of rising intonation would reflect the three discourse positions of initiate, continue, and terminate. A comparison of the percentage occurrence of baby versus mother utterances in the three discourse positions reveals group differences between mothers and infants (see Table 2.1). Infants use a higher proportion of their utterances to

TABLE 2.1
Frequency and Percentage Distribution of Utterances
in Three Discourse Positions

	Initiate		Continue		Terminate		
	Freq.	%	Freq.	%	Freq.	%	
Infants	150	45.32	96	29.00	85	25.68	$t = 331$
Mothers	119	28.47	171	40.90	128	30.62	$t = 418$

initiate sequences than to continue or terminate. Mothers, with the highest proportion of their utterances in continue position, are more likely to attempt to elicit in response to a previous utterance by the infant. It seems reasonable that mothers should carry a greater burden of sequence maintenance than their infants at this point in development. All of the infants but one could respond to a previous utterance while simultaneously making a further demand for a response. There was only one infant with no utterances in the continue position, and this may simply be a reflection of the small sample of his utterances.

An examination of the relative use of rising intonation by mothers and infants reveals that mothers use it a greater percentage of time overall: 31.64% versus 20.54%. In addition, mothers and infants use it with different proportional frequencies in the three discourse positions (see Table 2.2). Infants' use of rise is equally distributed between the two eliciting discourse positions of initiate and continue, whereas mothers show a greater proportional use in the continue position. This finding somewhat contradicts that of Ryan (1978), who reported that rising intonation is used to focus attention before the interaction proceeds. However, she did not analyze the proportional frequency of rise in subsequent turns. The high use of rise in the continue position, as shown in these data, is partly a reflection of the frequent use by mothers of requests for clarification, which invariably receive a terminal rise.

Finally, mothers use rise infrequently in the terminate position, and their infants do not use it at all. A closer examination of mothers' use of rise in this position shows that mothers use a fall–rise contour on acknowledgments of their infants' previous utterances. For example:

Infant: Clock.
Mother: Clock.

Alternatively, they may supply it on a filler (e.g., /mhm/). Neither of these forms strongly expects a response in terms of new information or action. However, the intonation alone seems to suggest that the episode is not closed and that a further contribution on the part of the infant is being solicited.

These findings seem to confirm the hypothesis that infants as early as 12 months are sensitive to the requirements of discourse position, reserving the

TABLE 2.2
Percentage Occurrence of Rising to Nonrising Intonation in the
Three Discourse Positions for Group Mothers and Infants

	Initiate		Continue		Terminate	
	% R	% N + R	% R	% N + R	% R	% N + R
Infants	28.95	71.05	24.44	75.56	0	100
Mothers	42.60	57.40	67.64	32.36	10.16	89.84

use of rising intonation for eliciting positions and avoiding it in terminators. (A preliminary examination of data on the same infants at 19 months suggests that by this time they use the fall–rise acknowledge contour used by their mothers in these 12-month data.)

The second hypothesis predicted that infants at this point in development would be involved with their mothers in a limited set of routinely practiced functions. Table 2.3 shows the frequency and percentage of occurrence of the 14 speech act functions for mothers versus infants. Considering only those speech act functions that constitute more than 10% of the total, mothers and infants alike specialize in request for action, request for information, and description. Infants produce slightly more requests for action than do mothers; mothers produce more requests for information than do infants. This finding appears to fit with the cognitive facts: Infants at 12 months are just approaching the stage of reliable representation of the real world. Most of their descriptions and requests for information are the product of naming routines at this age. In addition, infants use more evaluatives than their mothers. At this point, evaluatives are of the following type: routine responses to objects and situations (e.g., "oops" and "uh oh"), which function as accident markers, and a high occurrence of the long vowel /ā/, produced on a low-level pitch, which is used when hugging toys, looking at pictures of babies, and so on. Finally, mothers show a higher proportional use of acknowledgments, which perform both a discourse maintenance and reinforcing function.

These findings are compatible with the hypothesis that to ease the cognitive load and to maintain the conversation infants and mothers at this stage in development specialize in a limited range of speech act functions. Such discrepancies in use as exist between mothers and infants are explainable in terms of the cognitive differences between the conversational partners and the mothers' greater interest in maintaining the discourse.

The third hypothesis predicted that mothers and infants, given a similarity in the use of particular speech act functions, would show a similar proportional use of terminal rise. Table 2.4 shows the percentage use of rising intonation for the four most frequent speech act functions used by mothers and infants. The proportional use of rising intonation for the two groups is remarkably similar, corroborating the hypothesis that infants learn the use of rising intonation via a limited set of speech act functions.

Further evidence for a relationship between the infants' and mothers' use of rising intonation is shown in the ranking of mothers and infants for their proportional use of rising intonation in Table 2.5. A Spearman Rank Order Correlation Coefficient was significant at the .10 level, using a two-tailed test (rho = .564).

The final hypothesis posited that, in spite of the impact of the input language, there would exist individual differences in use of final rise due to strategies of simplification and generalization. Table 2.5 contains evidence that, although all the infants who used a high proportion of final rise had mothers who likewise showed a high proportion of use, there were some infants whose productions did not reflect the impact of their mothers' high use.

Eliza and Michael differed from their mothers in the use of rise by 26.9% and 22.0%, respectively. Both of these infants, although showing accelerated language learning at this point by other project indices, do not seem to be tuning in to intonation as a dominant production strategy. However, three of the infants (Beth, Jessica, and Elizabeth), who are using rising intonation 34.8%, 34.1%, and 33.3% of the time, respectively, are utilizing final rise as a major communicative resource. Jessica and Beth share a common strategy

TABLE 2.3
Frequency and Percentage Use of Speech Act
Functions for Group Mothers and Infants

Functions	Infants		Mothers	
	Freq.	%	Freq.	%
Call	1	.30	4	.96
Request Action	74	22.36	73	17.46
Request Info.	47	14.19	111	26.56
Description	61	18.43	72	17.22
Offer/Show/Give	11	3.32	1	.24
Reject	13	3.92	4	.96
Deny	2	.61	3	.71
Request Performative Play	9	2.72	16	3.83
Request Clarification	6	1.80	31	7.42
Affirm	18	5.44	1	.24
Evaluative	36	10.88	13	3.11
Acknowledge	16	4.83	72	17.22
Conversational Device	17	5.14	13	3.11
Response to Performative Play	20	6.04	4	.96
Total	331		418	

TABLE 2.4
Frequency and Percentage Use of Rising Intonation in the
Four Most Frequent Speech Act Functions for Group Mothers and Infants

	Request for Action		Request for Information		Description		Acknowledge	
	Freq.	%	Freq.	%	Freq.	%	Freq.	%
Infants	33/107	30.84	19/47	40.43	5/61	8.19	0/16	0
Mothers	23/73	31.50	54/111	48.65	6/72	8.33	10/88	11.36

of using final rise mainly to request action (for Jessica, 13 of 14 total uses; for Beth, 11 of 16 total uses). Elizabeth shows a preference for using it to request information (7 of 11 total uses), but she also uses final rise to request action (see Appendix I). This represents some confirmatory evidence that given the ambiguity of the use of rising intonation in adult English between requests for information versus action, children may simplify by limiting the use of final rise to only one function, as Jessica most clearly shows. Elizabeth appears to be approximating the mixed adult system in using rise for both requests for action and information. It must also be remembered that none of these infant utterances are immediate imitations because these were eliminated from the corpus of data.

At this point, Jessica also showed an interesting asymmetry between her responses to her mother's use of rise and her own use in production. As can be seen from Appendix II, which lists the frequency of occurrence of particular speech act functions for individual infants and mothers, Jessica's mother used an equal number of requests for action and requests for information. Jessica at this time was not herself producing requests for information, but she responded to any request for information that included a final rise with an affirmative/jæ/, regardless of the content of the utterance. (This was also

TABLE 2.5
Individual Percentage Use of Rising Intonation

	Infants	Mothers	Difference
Jesse	50.0	42.1	7.9[a]
Beth	34.8	41.3	6.5
Jessica	34.1	37.3	3.2
Elizabeth	33.3	37.8	4.5
Justin	28.6	46.2	17.6
Daniel	22.4	24.3	1.9
Eliza	21.1	48.0	26.9
Lisa	11.1	22.2	11.1
Michael	10.3	32.3	22.0
Caitlin	8.9	16.9	8.0

[a] Jesse was the only baby using a greater proportion of rise than his mother, but this is explained by his small sample of utterances.

tested informally: Jessica would respond to any utterance containing complete nonsense provided it used a final rise.) In addition, the transcript furnished numerous examples of Jessica making affirmative responses to utterances containing a final rise, but whose content was clearly beyond her. Following are a few examples of Jessica's responses to her mother's requests for information which are cued solely by the intonation:

Mother: 'Jessica, did 'you go see the 'monkey last week?
Jessica: /ae/
Mother: Did the 'monkey go off the 'platform on his 'motorcycle?
Jessica: /jae/
Mother: Did he land on a 'baby?
Jessica: /ae/

Jessica appears to represent the extreme case of tuning in to the intonation regardless of the content. In addition, she herself used final rise exclusively to request action, but when her mother used rising intonation on a yes/no question to request action indirectly, Jessica again responded/jae/ (yes) and clearly did not understand the expectation that she should perform the required action. For example:

Mother: 'Jessica, do you wanna 'play with the 'blocks?
Jessica: /jae/ (crawls by, ignoring the offered blocks)

For all the infants and mothers, Appendix III specifies intonation use for the most frequent speech act categories.

Finally, Table 2.6 and Appendix IV show the relationship between intonation contour and the mood system in mothers' speech. Predictably, there is no one-to-one relationship between rising intonation and any one mood type, but the strongest association to a rising intonation is for yes/no questions and tags.

TABLE 2.6
The Relationship Between Rising Intonation and
Mood Types in Mothers' Speech

	Freq.	%
Yes/no questions	62/62	100
Wh- questions	10/74	13.51
Imperatives	11/35	31.43
Declaratives	12/79	15.19
Wh- questions plus tag	3/3	100
Declaratives plus tag	5/12	41.64
Moodless	41/153	26.80
Total rise	144/418	34.45

Ryan (1978) found that wh– questions were equally as likely to have a rising as a nonrising contour. We found a stronger association with nonrise (31.43% rise). As Ryan's research was conducted in Scotland, this may represent a dialect difference.

CONCLUSION

On the basis of these results, we may draw some tentative conclusions. All the infants in the group used rising intonation sometimes, though less than their mothers. They used it as a group with approximately the same proportional frequency as their mothers and generally to perform the same set of speech act functions. Within this broad picture of the impact of maternal input was variance associated with individual strategies. These strategies were clear in the performance of two infants; they simplified the relationship between form, function, and intonation in English by using rise almost invariantly to request action. In these two cases the intonation alone seemed to serve this function because the phonetic content bore no apparent relation to an English word. In addition, one of these two children responded to all uses of rise by her mother as if they were requests for information, supplying an affirmative response. Again, the phonetic content seemed irrelevant to the process.

In a sense, it is easier to explain the learning strategy underlying the production of these two infants than it is to explain the learning mechanism for the others. It is unclear how most of the infants produced "approximately" the same proportional frequency of rise to perform "approximately" the same functions. This research did not test the hypothesis that at this early stage of language production intonation might be item-learned (i.e., that a particular intonation contour must always accompany a particular phonetic content to accomplish the same speech act function). Only a finer analysis of both phonetic content and intonation will provide the answer. The fact that infants used intonation less than their mothers may be accounted for by production factors. Variability in production of segmental information is common until even the early school years; hence, it must also be a factor in the early stage of intonational contrasts.

As in all areas of language acquisition, intonation provides the usual pattern of some clear relationship to input, but it is accompanied by patterns of individual variation. It does not suggest itself as the one clear route to early language use. However, it is perhaps surprising that it should be used by infants so systematically at a stage when many are using only one or even no recognizable adult words.

REFERENCES

Austin, J. L. *How to do things with words.* Oxford: Oxford University Press, 1962.

Bolinger, D. Intonation as a universal. In H. G. Lunt (Ed.), *Proceedings of the ninth international congress of linguistics.* The Hague: Mouton, 1964.

Bolinger, D. Intonation and its parts. *Journal of Child Language,* 1982, *58,* 505–533.

Brazil, D. C. *Discourse intonation: Discourse analysis monographs* (Vol. 1). Birmingham English Language Research, University of Birmingham, England, 1975.

Brazil, D. C. *Discourse intonation: Discourse analysis monographs* (Vol. 2). Birmingham English Language Research, University of Birmingham, England, 1978.

Bruner, J. S. The ontogenesis of speech acts. *Journal of Child Language,* 1975, *2,* 1–19.

Bruner, J. S., Roy, C., & Ratner, N. The beginnings of requests. In K. E. Nelson (Ed.), *Children's Language* (Vol. 3). Hillsdale, N.J.: Erlbaum, 1983.

Cross, T. G. Mothers' speech adjustments: The contribution of selected child listener variables. In C. Snow & C. Ferguson (Eds.), *Talking to children: Language input and acquisition.* Cambridge: Cambridge University Press, 1977.

Cruttenden, A. Falls and rises: Meanings and universals. *Journal of Linguistics,* 1981, *17,* 1–178. (a)

Cruttenden, A. Item-learning and system-learning. *Journal of Psycholinguistic Research,* 1981, *10,* 79–88. (b)

Crystal, D. *Prosodic systems and intonation in English.* Cambridge: Cambridge University Press, 1969.

Crystal, D. Prosodic development in language acquistion. In P. Fletcher & M. Garman (Eds.), *Language Acquisition: Studies in first language development.* Cambridge: Cambridge University Press, 1979.

Ferguson, C. A. Baby talk as a simplified register. In C. Snow & C. Ferguson (Eds.), *Talking to children: Language input and acquisition.* Cambridge: Cambridge University Press, 1977.

Ferguson, C. A. Baby talk in six languages. *American Anthropologist,* 1964, *66,* 103–114.

Ferrier, L. J. Some observations of error in contest. In N. Waterson & C. E. Snow (Eds.), *The development of communication.* Chichester, England: Wiley, 1978.

Garnica, O. K. Some prosodic and paralinguistic features of speech to young children. In C. E. Snow & C. A. Ferguson (Eds.), *Talking to children: Language input and acquisition.* Cambridge: Cambridge University Press, 1977.

Halliday, M. A. K. *Intonation and grammar in British English.* The Hague: Mouton, 1967.

Halliday, M. A. K. Intonation systems in English. In M. A. K. Halliday & A. McIntosh (Eds.), *Patterns of language: Papers in general, descriptive and applied linguistics.* London: Longman, 1975. (a)

Halliday, M. A. K. *Learning how to mean: Explorations in the development of language.* London: E. Arnold, 1975. (b)

Kaplan, E. & Kaplan, G. The prelinguistic child. In J. Eliot (Ed.), *Human development and cognitive processes.* New York: Holt, Rinehart & Winston, 1971.

Kuhl, P. K. & Miller, J. D. Speech perception in early infancy: Discrimination of speech sound categories. *Journal of the Acoustical Society of America,* 1975, *58,* Supplement 1, 556 (Abstract).

Ladd, D. R., Jr. The function of the A-rise accent in English. Paper presented to the University Linguistic Club, University of Indiana, Bloomington, 1977.

Larson, S., Ferrier, L. J., Chesnick, M., Lieborgott, J., & Schultz, M. C. *Tuning infant behaviors: Evolution of mothers' directives.* Paper presented to the American Speech Language and Hearing Association Convention, Toronto, 1982.

Lieberman, P. *Intonation, perception and language.* Cambridge, Mass.: MIT Press, 1967.

Kaplan, E. *The role of intonation in the acquisition of language.* Unpublished doctoral distion, Cornell University, 1969.

Macken, M. A. & Ferguson, C. A. Cognitive aspects of phonological development: Model, evidence, and issues. In K. E. Nelson (Ed.), *Children's Language* (Vol. 4). Hillsdale, N.J.: Erlbaum, 1983.

Menn, L. *Pattern, control and contrast in beginning speech.* Unpublished doctoral dissertation, University of Illinois at Urbana-Champaign, 1976.

Pike, K. L. *Intonation of American English.* Ann Arbor: University of Michigan Press, 1945.

Ryan, M. L. Contour in context. In R. N. Campbell & P. T. Smith (Eds.), *Recent advances in the psychology of language: Language development and mother-child interaction.* London: Plenum Press, 1978.

Sag, J. A., & Lieberman, M. The intonational disambiguation of indirect speech acts. *Chicago Linguistics Society,* 1975, *7,* 487–497.

Stern, S., Speiker, S., & MacKain, K. Intonation contours as signals in maternal speech. *Developmental Psychology,* 1982, *18,* 727–735.

Tonkova-Yampol'skaya, R. Development of speech intonation in infants during the first two years of life. *Soviet Psychology,* 1969, *7,* 48–54.

Waterson, N. Child phonology: A prosodic view. *Journal of Linguistics,* 1971, *7,* 179–211. (a)

Waterson, N. Some views on speech perception. *Journal of the International Phonetic Association,* 1971, *1,* 81–96. (b)

Wells, G., Montgomery, M., & MacLure, M. Adult-child discourse: Outline of a model of analysis. *Journal of Pragmatics,* 1979, *3,* 337–380.

APPENDIX I

Individual Frequency of Use of Rise to Nonrise Intonation in Three Discourse Positions

	Initiate		Continue		Terminate		Total No. Rising Utts.	Total Utts.	% Rising Utts.
	Rise	Nonrise	Rise	Nonrise	Rise	Nonrise			
Jessica	1	6	13	3	0	18	14	41	34.1
Mother	14	9	4	11	1	12	19	51	37.3
Justin	4	4	0	0	0	6	4	14	28.6
Mother	3	2	3	1	0	4	6	13	46.2
Daniel	6	22	5	0	0	16	11	49	22.4
Mother	5	9	8	20	4	24	17	70	24.3
Lisa	2	6	0	2	0	8	2	18	11.1
Mother	3	6	1	3	2	12	6	27	22.2
Caitlin	1	12	3	6	0	23	4	45	8.9
Mother	7	14	4	3	0	37	11	65	16.9
Eliza	1	5	3	10	0	0	4	19	21.1
Mother	2	6	10	4	0	3	12	25	48.0
Elizabeth	11	7	0	12	0	3	11	33	33.3
Mother	6	5	7	13	1	5	14	37	37.8
Beth	11	17	5	7	0	6	16	46	34.8
Mother	2	9	16	12	1	6	19	46	41.3
Michael	4	27	2	20	0	5	6	58	10.34
Mother	5	6	12	29	4	9	19	65	32.3
Jesse	2	1	2	3	0	0	4	8	50.0
Mother	4	2	4	6	0	3	8	19	42.1

APPENDIX II

Individual Frequency of Speech Act Functions

	Call	Req. Action	Req. Info.	Describe	Offer/Show/Give	Reject	Deny	Req. Perf. Play	Req. Clarif.	Affirm	Evaluative	Acknowledge	Convers. Device	Resp. Perf. Play	TOTAL
Jessica	0	14	0	2	5	1	0	3	0	10	0	4	0	2	41
Mother	1	15	15	2	1	0	0	3	2	0	0	11	1	0	51
Justin	0	7	0	0	1	1	0	0	0	1	4	0	0	0	14
Mother	0	5	2	1	0	1	0	0	2	1	0	1	0	0	13
Daniel	0	0	22	10	0	1	0	4	2	0	0	2	3	5	49
Mother	1	11	17	10	0	0	1	5	4	0	5	15	1	0	70
Lisa	0	2	0	5	1	2	1	0	0	1	0	2	1	3	18
Mother	0	4	4	1	0	2	0	1	1	0	0	13	1	0	27
Caitlin	0	0	14	15	2	1	0	0	0	0	11	2	0	0	45
Mother	1	1	21	31	0	0	0	0	4	0	1	6	0	0	65
Eliza	0	3	0	3	0	5	0	0	0	0	4	0	1	3	19
Mother	0	9	2	2	0	0	0	2	2	0	0	3	1	4	25
Michael	0	33	3	13	0	2	1	0	0	2	1	2	1	0	58
Mother	0	10	19	14	0	1	0	0	7	0	0	13	1	0	65
Jesse	0	1	0	1	0	0	0	2	1	0	1	0	1	1	8
Mother	0	1	8	2	0	0	0	2	0	0	0	3	3	0	19
Elizabeth	0	1	8	5	1	0	0	0	0	3	7	0	4	4	33
Mother	0	9	9	6	0	0	2	3	0	0	6	0	2	0	37
Beth	1	13	0	7	1	0	0	0	3	2	8	4	6	1	46
Mother	1	8	14	3	0	0	0	0	9	0	1	7	3	0	46

58

APPENDIX III

Individual Frequency and Percentage Use of Rising Intonation in the
Four Most Frequent Speech Act Functions

	Request Action		Request Info.		Description		Acknowledge	
	Freq.	%	Freq.	%	Freq.	%	Freq.	%
Jessica	13/14	92.86	0/0	0	0/2	0	0/4	0
Mother	5/15	33.33	9/15	60.00	0/2	0	1/11	9.09
Justin	4/7	57.14	0/0	0	0/2	0	0/0	0
Mother	2/5	40.00	2/2	100	0/1	0	0/1	0
Daniel	0/0	0	8/22	36.36	0/10	0	0/2	0
Mother	2/11	18.18	5/17	29.41	2/10	20	0/15	0
Lisa	2/2	100	0/0	0	1/5	20	0/2	0
Mother	1/4	25	3/4	75	0/1	0	2/13	15.38
Caitlin	0/0	0	3/14	21.43	0/15	0	0/2	0
Mother	1/1	100	6/21	28.57	0/31	0	0/6	0
Eliza	1/3	33.33	0/0	0	0/3	0	0/0	0
Mother	4/9	44.40	2/2	100	0/2	0	0/3	0
Elizabeth	1/1	100	7/8	87.50	2/5	40	0/0	0
Mother	4/9	44.40	8/9	88.80	1/6	16.67	2/6	33.30
Beth	11/13	84.62	0/0	0	1/7	14.29	0/4	0
Mother	3/8	37.50	4/14	28.57	1/3	33.30	1/7	14.29
Michael	1/33	3.03	1/3	33.30	1/13	7.69	0/2	0
Mother	1/10	10	11/19	57.89	2/14	14.29	4/13	30.77
Jesse	0/1	0	0/0	0	0/1	0	0/0	0
Mother	0/1	0	4/8	50	0/2	0	0/3	0

APPENDIX IV

Frequency and Percentage of Rising Intonation in Mood Types of Mothers' Speech

	Yes/No		Wh-		Imp.		Decl.		Wh- + tag		Decl. + tag		Moodless	
	Freq.	%	Freq.	%	Freq.	%	Freq.	%	Freq.	%	Freq.	%	Freq.	%
Jessica	12/12	100	0/7	0	0/7	0	0/3	0	1/1	100	1/4	.25	5/17	.29
Justin	2/2	100	0/0	0	1/4	.25	1/2	.50	0/0	0	1/1	100	1/4	.25
Daniel	3/3	100	4/23	.17	0/2	0	4/14	.28	1/1	100	0/0	0	5/27	.18
Lisa	4/4	100	0/1	0	0/3	0	0/1	0	0/0	0	0/0	0	2/18	.11
Caitlin	3/3	100	1/13	.07	1/1	100	1/21	.04	1/1	100	2/6	.33	5/20	.25
Eliza	9/9	100	2/2	100	3/3	100	3/3	100	0/0	0	0/0	0	3/8	.37
Elizabeth	12/12	100	0/4	0	1/4	.25	0/5	0	0/0	0	0/0	0	2/12	.16
Beth	6/6	100	0/11	0	3/5	.60	0/5	0	0/0	0	0/0	0	9/19	.47
Michael	11/11	100	1/7	.14	1/5	.20	3/21	.14	0/0	0	1/1	100	4/20	.20
Jesse	0/0	0	2/6	.33	1/1	100	0/4	0	0/0	0	0/0	0	5/8	.62

3 Confusion, Substitution, and Mastery: Pretend Play During the Second Year of Life[1]

Greta G. Fein
University of Michigan

Elaine R. Moorin
The Merrill-Palmer Institute

The origin, development, and function of pretense have recently become attractive topics of systematic inquiry. Special interest in the early forms of pretense has been stimulated by several factors. One, of course, is curiosity about the origins and unfolding of a striking behavioral form. Another comes from the seeming co-occurrence of pretense and substantial achievements in cognition and language. And finally, the attempt to study pretense during the second year of life nicely confronts us with the need to reckon with what we mean when we identify a behavior as pretense. But this reckoning equally applies to identifying a vocalization as a word or an interpersonal exchange as an instance of aggression, attachment, altruism, or any other behavioral construct. In this chapter, we examine problems associated with the definition of pretense, the concept of context, and the study of pretense in relation to language.

DEFINING PRETENSE

Attempts to classify behavior, regardless of substantive focus, appeal at some level to the intuitive social knowledge of an observer. Classification necessarily requires an intricate set of judgments about the salient contours

[1] Portions of this paper were presented at the meeting of the American Psychological Association, Montreal, September, 1980.

of a behavior as well as attributions about the intention or status of the individual producing the behavior. Such judgments and attributions are present even when seemingly concrete descriptive terms are used. Rather than "aggressive," a behavior might be called "negative physical contact"; rather than "altruistic," "affiliative," or "verbal," behaviors might be called "helping," "proximity-seeking," or "vocal." But these terms are misleading if they are taken to imply greater objectivity. And, if they diminish the theoretical implications of more general terms, they may diminish the importance of the research.

With respect to pretense, the problem of behavioral classification and labeling is nicely illustrated in two recent studies of play during the second year of life. In one study, Zelazo and Kearsley (1980) use the term "functional" to refer to a wide range of behaviors (e.g., rolling a ball, pushing a truck, offering a drink to a doll from an empty cup) in which the child uses objects in an adult-defined manner. However, some of these behaviors are tied to the physical properties of objects as well as their social purposes. Actually, this definition of functional behavior involves two types of inference. One rests upon a historical judgment that the play behavior resembles another behavior that might have occurred previously. The other inference rests upon a judgment concerning the source of the prior behavior (i.e., adults), although it is unclear whether adults shape the child's behavior indirectly as designers and purchasers of play objects or directly as child trainers. Used in this way, the term "functional" misses the theoretically important distinction between the child mouthing the rim of the cup and producing a full-blown drinking motion.

In another study, the concept of pretense was replaced by the notion of "contextual support" (Rocissano, n.d.). In such a scheme, behaviors are coded according to whether they are influenced by the contextual features of objects (e.g., rolling a ball or pushing a truck is contextually constrained, whereas holding a toy bottle to a baby's mouth or lining up silverware is not). However, the central criterion for determining whether actions are contextually or environmentally supported is the judgment that previous modeling is not necessary for the child to perform the action. Thus, environmentally independent action is one in which it is assumed that the child must have observed another person performing a similar action with a similar object. Though germane to the issue, Rocissano does not discuss whether another person might include the child at some earlier time, whether the similar object includes a real baby as well as doll or liquid-containing as well as empty containers, or whether the similar action is dissimilar in some way. And yet, the investigator criticizes the use of pretense as a classifying scheme because an inference about something in the child's mind is required for coding.

The problem, of course, is that inferences *are* made about something in the child's mind when behavior is classified as functional or as environmentally supported. In the former, the inference is embedded in the expression adult-defined; in the latter, it is embedded in the expression previously modeled.

In the classification of a behavior as pretense, there is also an inference, namely that the play behavior simulates another behavior or that there is a resemblance of form and an absence of function. Most certainly, an observer must know how the culture in which the child is reared goes about eating, sleeping, transporting, loving, or fighting in order to perform the proper matching operation. Fortunately, the simulation is often apparent; unfortunately, there may be simulations too subtle to detect.

Perhaps the most disappointing aspect of attempts to avoid the concept of pretense is that findings are presented as if they are new, rather than as replications of earlier work. For example, Zelazo and Kearsley (1980) report that functional play increases between 7 and 15 months, and Rocissano (n.d.) reports that environmentally independent behaviors increase during the second year of life. The vast preponderance of functional or environmentally independent behaviors are what other researchers have referred to as pretense or symbolic, and of course, they also increase during this period (e.g., Fein & Apfel, 1979; Fenson, Kagan, & Kearsley, 1976; Inhelder, Lezine, Sinclair, & Stambak, 1972; Kagan, Kearsley, & Zelazo, 1978; Rosenblatt, 1977). In addition, when environmentally independent actions are separated according to whether they are self-directed or other-directed, the results replicate the findings of investigators using pretense as a descriptive term (e.g. Fein & Apfel, 1979; Fenson & Ramsay, 1980; Watson & Fischer, 1977).

Most certainly, matters of appropriateness and environmental support are central issues in the development of pretense and of a theory that can account for it. But they are central in a way missed by attempts to avoid the concept of pretense. In pretense, the child's behavior is appropriate in one sense, but inappropriate in another (e.g., the cup is empty and the doll is not a baby). Moreover, the cup was designed to hold liquid; its physical design features are in keeping with its functions. To view playful drinking from this object as independent of its physical features or based on social learning obscures the central theoretical issue, namely that the behavior occurs when the cup is empty, at a particular age, and in the absence of adult prompting.

Most important, pretense is a theoretical term, and its value comes from the theoretical notions that govern its use. One of these notions is that early pretense reflects the *decontextualizing* of behavior. Of course, the use of cups to drink from, combs to groom with, and spoons to eat with reflects information about these objects that has been stored and retrieved. But in early pretense, the information is specific to salient physical features of the objects (e.g., the concavity or penetrability of the surface area). Moreover, this information is reflected in nonplay behaviors as well, as when children ask their mother to put milk into the cup or comb their hair. The concept of decontextualized behavior is meant to indicate that in pretense the child's behavior is detached from the motivational, situational, and physical constraints that typically accompany the use of these objects in real life.

CONCEPTUALIZING CONTEXT

As Sutton-Smith (1980) has argued, definitional issues are profoundly embedded in the problem of conceptualizing the meaning of context. To make matters more difficult, there is not just one context, but several, and each serves to shape behavior as well as our interpretation of it.

Three contexts seem especially salient in the study of pretend behavior. One is the immediate behavioral context (i.e., the people and things with which the child is interacting). Another is the child's social history (i.e., those behavioral routines that the child has presumably experienced as observer or participant). Finally, there is the context of the unobserved, interpreting observer, biased by theory and culture to see and value this behavior in a certain way.

It is beyond the scope of this paper to attempt to unravel this contextual web, but the treatment of context in studies of pretend behavior is germane to the question of whether early pretense can be viewed as confusion or mastery and, more important, to our conceptualizaion of the relation between *previous* and *immediate* behavioral contexts.

The Immediate Context

On the surface, the immediate behavioral context is fairly easy to deal with. First, we can record what the child does with people and things. If we vary people and things, we can note how the child's behavior changes. In the case of pretense, we can sort out conditions that optimize the behavior from those that do not. Moreover, we can propose a developmental model detailing how the relation between behavior and circumstances changes with age. For a complex behavior such as pretense, the problem is whether we can say that the simple gestures of the 18-month-old child bear much of a resemblance to the imaginative exuberance of the 48-month-old. If we insist on a linkage, we do so on theoretical grounds. We initially justify our affirmation by the presence of certain criterial properties at these ages. But, the statement and application of criterial properties are interpretive actions imposed on child behavior by the observer according to a theory-based vision of how the child's mind functions.

The paradox is that in order to study the role of context in modulating pretense as it develops, our core definition of pretense must be pegged to its presumably least mature form. For example, if we include productive language as a criterion, we preclude the appearance of pretense in preverbal or nonverbal children and restrict our analysis to children who can and do talk when playing (Ungerer, Zelazo, Kearsley, & O'Leary, 1981). It may appear that such a criterion reduces some of the ambiguity inherent in the classification of behavior as pretense, but actually the ambiguity persists because the classification of words and word combinations in early language presents comparable difficulties.

Moreover, it is a strategic mistake to require effective communication with a partner, whether verbal or nonverbal, as a defining characteristic of pretend behavior (e.g., Bateson, 1955). In doing so, the study of pretense becomes the study of what children can talk about, a focus more in keeping with the study of productive linguistic forms than the study of pretend behavior. By definition, then, pretense cannot be fruitfully studied in prelinguistic children and in nonverbal handicapped children. More seriously, by making productive language a criterion of pretense, the study of the relation between pretense and language becomes the study of the pretend use of language (e.g., Garvey, 1974). And, in the study of individual differences, taciturn children may be viewed as unimaginative or representationally deficient (Smilansky, 1968), a problem that has recently received critical scrutiny (Fein, 1981; Fein & Stork, 1981).

Substitute Objects

Issues related to the immediate context are illustrated in studies of the substitute object. In one of the early studies, the investigators presented children between the ages of 20 and 26 months with two sets of play materials (Fein & Robertson, 1975). One set consisted of highly prototypical materials—a truck-like truck, a cup-like cup, or a doll-like doll. Another consisted of less prototypical materials, matched to those in the prototypical set. Each object in the second set was rated by a group of adults according to its physical similarity to the exemplar used in the first set. Then children's pretense with these objects scaled for prototypicality was examined. The results (Table 3.1) indicate that adults' sense of likeness is rather comparable to the sense children express in their pretense. The rank order correlation between adult ratings and children's pretend activities is .55 ($r < .05$).

These data, then, partially validate the concept of prototypicality. It should be noted, however, that objects in the low-prototypical set were relatively ambiguous objects such as a cardboard box for a truck and a flat piece of metal for a spoon. Pretending with a more-or-less similar ambiguous object most likely involves a different set of operations than pretending with a discrepant, well-structured object. Treating a relatively realistic toy truck as if it were a cup means setting aside some well-established notions about trucks and their functions. Not surprisingly, this ability develops later than the ability to transform a relatively ambiguous object (Elder & Pederson, 1978; Golomb, 1977).

TABLE 3.1
Ratings of Toy Likeness to Prototype Objects

Toy Category	Adult Likeness Scores[a]	Pretend Score[b]
1. cup	1	.07
2. spoon (metal)	2.5	.22
3. fork	2.5	.25
4. bowl	4	.32
5. mug	5	.69
6. spoon (plastic)	6	.44
7. blanket	7	.12
8. doll	8	.28
9. bottle	9	.10
10. crib	10	.40
11. truck	11	.36
12. phone	12	.59
13. comb	13	.77

[a]The less the likeness, the higher the score.
[b]Pretend scores are the difference between a child's pretense with a highly prototypical object and its matched object in the less prototypical set calculated according to the formula: $H - L/H + L$. The proportions thus reflect the performance decrement that occurs for each pairing.

But even though a given less prototypical object may resemble an exemplar "more or less" and even though resemblance may vary according to dimensions of form and function (Jackowitz & Watson, 1980), the individual object derives some of its meaning from those other objects with which it is used. Beds, blankets and pillows are objects that are often used together, as are cups, saucers, spoons, and forks. And babies, animals, adults, and toys that resemble these animate objects are the agents that use them. The observation that a seemingly precocious transformation of an individual object may require contextual anchors from functionally related realistic objects serves as a reminder that several elements enter into the sequence of events that characterize the development of pretense. The task of describing these events is more challenging than a pointless debate about whether a child is really pretending or really representing (cf. Huttenlocher & Higgins, 1978).

Social History

Context as social history is peculiarly troublesome in psychological research. One gets the impression from watching the pretense of American children that most parents serve meals, put children to bed, or go shopping in pretty much the same way. And, of course, children feed themselves, put themselves to sleep, and do such things with objects such as dolls and toy animals. At some point in children's development, these activities and the materials associated with them gain special meaning; they are produced seemingly without provocation in increasingly complex combinations. At a later point, these meanings may be shared. Collective symbolism — or socialized social pretending — seems to occur at about 3 years of age. But for it to happen at all, some fairly complex skills or concepts need to have been mastered. These communication modes are but one aspect of the development of an organized system of behavior that can be expressed when alone or with others. Of course, if the message cannot be understood by an adult observer, the behavior cannot be studied by observational methods.

When pretense first appears during the first half of the second year, its behavioral content is not as esoteric as it will be at 3 years of age. Rather, pretend gestures are about universal, life-maintaining activities (e.g., eating and sleeping) that children engage in by themselves surrounded by the nurturing activities of adult caregivers (Fein & Apfel, 1979). A child, even a very young child, is able to control the coordinations required to ingest food or relieve fatigue. One way of understanding the difference between these actions as surviving and as pretending is to argue that in pretending the activities are detached from their survival context. The child seems to explore what it means to do something without having to do it. Once action becomes liberated from biology, it is but a small step for action to become liberated from culture. If one can play with biology, why not play with culture? This liberationist point of view is consistent with the psychoanalytic stress on the symbolization of bodily functions, but it is at odds with Vygotsky's stress on the organizing force of objects on actions. In stressing the tyranny of objects, pretense becomes an expression of the child's social understanding that "a cup is to drink from." Perhaps liberation and tyranny are each involved. To sleep without sleeping amidst the appurtenances of bedtime (e.g., bed, a blanket, a pillow) may express tyranny by default. In pretending to sleep, the child need only juxtapose "really sleeping" with "not really sleeping." The category of action is well defined, and only motivation is varied. But to move from the child's own bed, blanket, or pillow to someone else's bedding, to bedding in general, and then to something like bedding requires the organization of a classification scheme capable of covering the terrain from tangible to mental.

PRETENSE AND REPRESENTATION

Finally, there is the particular theory of the interpreting observer. To say that a child is behaving as if one thing were another (i.e., pretending) is not the same as saying that the child is engaging in a representational act, although representational theorists are more likely than other theorists to identify the "as if" quality of pretense as relevant to the understanding of early representational thinking. There are numerous theoretical reasons for introducing the construct of representation and the allied notion of symbolization. One reason is that the construct helps to classify and compare different types of presumably similar phenomena (e.g., pretense, drawing, storytelling). Another reason is that it helps to assemble a great deal of information that would otherwise fall through the cracks. Most surely, the concept of representation will require finer theoretical tuning if it is to continue to be useful.

As a theoretical construct, representation is comparable to other theoretical constructs (e.g., attachment). Representation may be defined as a process whereby objects, persons, and relations are rendered as mental events, detached from the immediate behavioral or stimulus field. In some sense, the representational event "stands for" something other than itself. The event may be overt (e.g., an observable gesture, drawing, or word), or it may be covert (e.g., a thought-gesture, picture, or word). As Piaget and Inhelder (1971) have noted, the relation between a representational event and that which it stands for might be arbitrary (e.g., a word) or it might be motivated (e.g., a gesture or picture that bears some resemblance to the referent). All representational events involve designation, but not all designation involves representation (e.g., pointing). In a special sense, representations can be instances of a concept, but they are decontextualized instances insofar as the word, gesture, or picture figuratively but not literally belongs to the same class as the real things (Huttenlocher & Higgins, 1978).

To the discussion of the development of representational thinking Piaget added the notion that deferred imitation was the sensorimotor carrier of early representation. For Piaget, deferred imitation illustrated how bodily actions that are retained or stored in some fashion are put to representational use.

Of course, imitation presupposes designation, but imitations become representational only when there is some detachment of the imitative behavior from that which is being imitated. Thus, the process may be evident in a variety of representational behaviors, a subset of which is pretense. But the process does not appear full-blown, at a discrete point in time; rather, it emerges gradually over time. Representational theorists such as Piaget view the progressive elaboration of pretense as but one expression of the development of representational processes. The process is also expressed in labeling, storytelling, or drawing; each medium requires its own set of skills but also offers special opportunities for refinement in the child's representational thinking.

PLAY AND LANGUAGE

Piaget's notion that pretend behavior marks the beginning of representational thinking and the emergence of the semiotic function have led investigators to examine the relation of pretend behavior to language and cognitive development. Unfortunately, studies of the relation between play and language have stressed language production as reflected in communicative, imitative, or referential speech (Bates, Benigni, Bretherton, Camaioni, & Volterra, 1977; Bates, Camaioni, & Volterra, 1975; Folger & Leonard, 1978; Ingram, 1977; Lowe & Costello, 1976; Nicolich & Raph, 1978), a stress that is inconsistent with either Piaget or other theorists (e.g., Hulme & Lunzer, 1966; Vygotsky, 1967). Generally, the findings suggest that particular phases in the development of symbolic play and language tend to occur together (Ingram, 1977; Nicolich & Raph, 1978), but when age is partialed out, the correlation between play and language is considerably reduced or entirely eliminated (Folger & Leonard, 1978; Lowe & Costello, 1976). Symbolic play may be related to the expressive or communicative functions of language, but these relations may be a function of personal style rather than symbolic maturity (Fein, 1979). Because theorists such as Piaget (1962, 1968) and Vygotsky (1967) stress the meaning or the control functions of language, rather than productive quality or quantity, and because productive speech during the second year of life reflects stylistic as well as mastery differences, studies of language meaning (e.g., comprehension or mediation) might have more theoretical significance than studies of language production. For example, children who score high on tests of word and sentence comprehension at 18 months show more cognitively mature levels of pretend play at 18 and 24 months, whereas measures of expressive speech are related to less mature play forms (Fein, 1979). The need for a distinction between language comprehension and language production is reported in a recent study by Bates, Bretherton, Snyder, Shore, and Volterra (1980). But one problem in interpreting the findings of this study is that the 13-month-olds who participated were strikingly precocious in both their language and their play. Another problem found in much research is that comprehension is measured as single vocabulary items rather than as word combinations. Pretend actions involve combinations of actions and objects, and if the relation between pretense and language is to be studied, an attempt must be made to examine the formal features that might be shared by these two domains.

SOME OBSERVATIONS OF EARLY PRETENSE AND LANGUAGE

A central purpose of this paper is to describe several observations that touch some of the dilemmas encountered in studying the pretense of young children. The study was designed to explore three central issues. One was provoked by the psychoanalytic notion that in its earliest form, pretense expresses focal anxieties about body parts and functions. This notion is also embedded in Vygotsky's (1967) proposal that "play is invented at the point where unrealizable tendencies appear in development [p. 7]." The observation that one of the earliest pretend themes involves eating and feeding is certainly consistent with this view. But if real food was available, would these anxieties abate and pretense not occur? Note that by presenting the child with a situation in which food is really available, we may alter the context and thereby modify the message that "this is play." But, a satiated baby will sometimes "play" with the nipple or, put another way, not suck a suckable. Perhaps the issue is what children do with the opportunities provided by context.

A second question concerns the suggestion that these early feeding activities reflect the child's confusion rather than the decontextualizing of familiar routines (Stern, 1924). According to the confusion hypothesis, the child does not distinguish between full and empty cups or between prototypical and less prototypical containers; rather, a well-learned activity is simply overgeneralized. Limited evidence suggests that even at 12 months, the child's choices of things to feed with are selective (Fein & Apfel, 1979). One purpose of the present study was to explore some dimensions of this selectivity.

A third question concerns the relation between pretense and language. In much of the previous research, investigators have examined language production in order to demonstrate that levels of pretense and levels of language are coordinated in development. But language production most likely underestimates children's language proficiency. Hence, in the present study we simply asked whether children understand the words for what they might pretend to do and, if so, whether the verbal understanding precedes, coincides with, or follows the appearance of pretend behavior.

Our observations come from Sara, the first participant in what was intended to be an exploratory longitudinal study. We observed Sara in a laboratory playroom when she was 12, 14, and 18 months of age. Play sessions occurred within 30 minutes of Sara's lunch time. Her mother and one of two familiar experimenters (Eileen or Elisabeth) were present during all sessions. At each age level, we taped eleven 20-minute sessions over a 3-week period. The first two sessions involved spontaneous play with different sets of materials. The materials in the first session consisted of two 8-ounce plastic baby bottles (one containing juice and one empty), two 4-ounce bottles (one full and one empty), and two dolls. The materials in the second session consisted of two training cups (one full and one empty), a plastic coffee mug, and two less realistic cup-like objects (a plastic toy air mask and an oatmeal box). The bottles and the training cups were those Sara used at home.

We monitored Sara's language comprehension at 12, 14, and 18 months. At 12 months, comprehension data came from a record kept by Sara's mother. At 14 months, her comprehension was assessed in 11 sessions over a period of 3 weeks. In these assessments, materials used during the play sessions (except full bottles and cups) were presented to Sara, and she was given 8 to 10 directions, which varied the form of the verb (i.e., give or feed), the direct object (e.g., cup, spoon, bottle), and the recipient (i.e., me, mommy, doll, Eileen, or Elisabeth). In one set of directions using the verb *feed,* she was given two-word combinations consisting of action and recipient (e.g., *feed doll*). Trials in which Sara ignored the directions were excluded from the analyses, and we considered only first responses that were clearly correct or incorrect.

First, consider Sara's behavior with bottles and cups. At 12 months, Sara preferred to drink from full bottles and empty cups. She drank from full bottles 60% of the time and from empty bottles 40% of the time; from empty cups 64% of the time and from full cups 36% of the time. She used large bottles rather than small ones 74% of the time, but by the end of the bottle session, she had consumed less than half an ounce of the juice in the bottle. Moreover, when she drank from empty cups she chose her own training cup, using the realistic cup only once and the less realistic cups not at all. At this age, she never fed her mother, the experimenter, or the doll.

At 14 months, Sara still preferred to drink from the full bottle, but now she preferred the full cup to the empty one. Although 70% of her drinking motions were from full containers, she still consumed little liquid. And she continued to ignore cups other than her own training cup. But at this age, a new behavior appeared: Sara fed her mother and the experimenter as well as herself. She fed others in about 40% of her bottle feedings and in about 14% of her cup feedings. About half of these other-referenced feedings were with empty containers, and all of them were incorporated in what Piaget calls multischeme patterns. With bottles, all of Sara's other feedings involved recipient runs in which she might feed everyone (e.g., herself, mother, or experimenter), two persons (e.g., herself and the experimenter), or another person more than once. But at this age, she never fed the doll.

By 18 months, self-feeding with full containers became the governing rule. At this age, 82% of her self-feedings were with full bottles and cups. But, feeding other people with full containers dropped to 0 with cups and to 9% with bottles. In the 18-month sessions, Sara for the first time fed the doll, always with an empty bottle. Two of the three feedings were embedded in a sequence of doll-self-doll, and one occurred as a single behavior.

These observations are consistent with previous research (e.g., Fein & Apfel, 1979; Watson & Fischer, 1977). When only *empty* containers are considered, self-feeding declines, feeding others shows an inverted U-shaped function, and doll feeding first appears at about 18 months (e.g., Fein & Apfel, 1979). But, a strikingly different pattern occurs with full containers. Between 14 and 18 months, *full* containers are used predominantly for self-feeding, with feeding others appearing only fleetingly at 14 months.

With respect to language, Sara's productive speech at 12 and 14 months was limited to a few standard expressions, but her language comprehension was fairly extensive. According to her mother's report at 12 months, Sara had a comprehension vocabulary of 37 single words, 23 of which were nominals. Among these, were the words *bottle* and *cup,* but not *doll* or *spoon.* By 14 months, 42 new words had been added, 32 of which were nominals. The words *doll* and *spoon* were among the new additions, as well as verbs such as *give, feed, put on, take off,* and *drink.* What Sara knew about the referents of these words was examined in our language assessments. Note that we were especially interested in whether her understanding of the verb *feed* was congruent with the play behavior likely to occur in children of this age.

In our assessment sessions at 14 months, Sara responded correctly to 67% of the two-word combinations and to 72% of the three-word combinations. She responded slightly better to three-word combinations when the verb was *feed* (78%) than when it was *give* (69%). Of her errors, 78% were in distinguishing recipients (e.g., when asked to give an object to someone other than the speaker, she often gave it to the speaker rather than to the person designated). But when asked to feed the speaker (i.e., me), she often fed the other person. She was less likely to err when asked to feed the doll, especially when the utensil was specified in the request. At 18 months, she made even fewer errors (8%) in response to these directions. In sum, Sara's receptive language at 14 months seemed to outstrip her spontaneous pretense. At this age, the verbal expression *feed the doll* could be translated into the appropriate behavior, but there seemed to be no inclination to engage in this behavior in the absence of specific direction.

Moreover, there was a striking qualitative difference that is not captured in an analysis of correct and incorrect first responses. At 14 months, Sara did not simply respond to the feeding direction and stop there. When asked to feed her mother, she might feed her mother, the experimenter, her mother again, and then herself. These elaborated recipient routines occurred following 54% of her correct responses to the verb *feed,* but following only 14% of her correct responses to the verb *give.* At 18 months, elaborated recipient responses occurred on 4% of her correct trials. But in these sessions, a new type of elaboration appeared. On 33% of the feeding trials in which she responded correctly, she fed the recipient with more than one object, and on 28% of the giving trials, she fed the recipient in addition to giving her the object. At 14 and 18 months, Sara complied with the verbal request and then went beyond it, converting our language comprehension test situation into a playful exchange.

These playful spinoffs were related to the complexity of the direction and to the particular object and recipient involved. At 14 months, elaborations occurred infrequently when the objects were bottles (20%) and more often when the objects were cups and spoons (98%). They occurred 90% of the time when the recipient was the other, 71% of the time when the recipient was me (i.e., the person making the request), and only 17% of the time when the recipient was the doll. Moreover, the doll was never included as a recipient when person-feeding directions were elaborated.

CONCLUSIONS

In this section, we first summarize what Sara taught us about pretense and then comment on the role of theory, definition, and taxonomy in the study of behavioral development.

At 12 months, there was little evidence of overgeneralization or confusion in Sara's behavior. Large bottles and her own training cup were clearly things to drink from. A differential preference for full bottles and empty cups is also indicated in the data. Evidence for deliberate decontextualization in a context that permits, but does not require, contextualized behavior is therefore limited. Of course, Sara did not consume the liquid in the bottles she drank from. Her feeding behavior at 12 months with full bottles was clearly not appetitive; in this sense, it was detached from its ordinary outcome. But, can we label this behavior as pretense? As understood by the child, non-literalness may originate in part from experiences in which the child establishes sufficient control over well-mastered behavior to detach it from consummatory outcomes; sucking (or mouthing) on a full nipple without drawing liquid seems a dramatic illustration of such control. If, as Piaget (1962) claims, pretense is preceded by a transitional period in which well-learned behaviors become ritualized, it may be as important to study changes in literal behavior as it is to study changes in nonliteral behavior. Ritualization can be thought of as the beginnings of behavioral autonomy, by which we mean the ability to create context out-of-context. We would add that psychoanalytic notions are not helpful in understanding Sara's behavior. Wishes, desires, or unsatisfied needs seem to have little bearing upon the pretense examined in this study.

The first real indication of playfulness appears at 14 months. Again, we need more evidence, but when bottles (not cups) were used in playful exchanges with others, it did not seem to matter whether they were full or empty. One might argue that these exchanges with adults are transitional, that they facilitate a separation between the contexts of play and those of reality. On the one hand, Sara seemed to be verifying that others could drink without drinking, just as she had done, as if "doing but not doing" was an intriguing idea worthy of elaboration. On the other hand and in keeping with previous findings, at 18 months, Sara seemed to abandon these exchanges with adults when the doll was discovered as a play object. The new idea seems to be that persons who are not persons can do but not do.

But of course, we observed Sara in a context in which two adults were amicably chatting with one another and uninvolved with her. If children at this age are sensitive to arrangements indicating that conversing adults are not to be disturbed (Fein, 1975), mastery in one domain, the social, is confounded in our observations with mastery in another, the symbolic. As we indicated earlier, developmental change cannot be understood independently of context, but it is a mistake to assume that contexts (even "naturalistic" contexts) do not contribute an independent source of variation to the behavior we observe.

The context changed when we asked Sara to respond to verbal requests. If we use correct and incorrect responses as a unit of analysis, we find substantial mastery of verbal symbols. But if we use response sequence as our unit, we find that Sara's responses were playful as well as correct. Moreover, the verbal requests evoked behavior that did not appear when she was left to her own devices. And yet, even though she could feed the doll when asked, playful elaborations were less likely to occur when the doll was the recipient in the verbal request. In sum, Sara understood the words *feed doll,* or more conservatively, she responded appropriately and discriminatively to statements combining the verb *feed* with different objects and recipients. Word-reference relations seem to have been well established. Sara seemed to know that these words designated particular actions and objects, but when it came to the doll, this knowledge was not generative in the sense that she was less likely to put the doll in the appropriate recipient slots. Person placements (self, mother, experimenter) seemed easier than inanimate object placements, as if the notion of doll as a kind of person, rather than as an object to act upon, was less firmly established. And of course, the persons and objects referred to by the words were presented in the immediate environment. Whether Sara would have responded to the verbal directions with substitutions spontaneously generated in play cannot be determined by our data. The issue, of course, is whether these play elaborations can be viewed as substitutions (i.e., mother as experimenter) or as an expression of her less sophisticated mastery of general categories of action, object, and recipient.

With respect to context, one might argue that asking Sara to feed an adult or the doll constitutes an invitation to pretend. But these requests constitute such an invitation only insofar as a child recognizes them as signifying a departure from the ordinary. If such invitations mark the child's introduction to the language of pretense, we must bear in mind that the pretense is in the child's interpretation of the message as nonliteral and not in the message itself. The surprising thing is that Sara seemed to understand the message long before she could produce it. Our mistake was to assume that she would not understand the message at 12 months, and so we did not test her comprehension at this age.

The foregoing observations pertain to problems of definition and interpretation. It may be useful to classify Sara's feeding behavior at 12 months as pretense, but to interpret the behavior as presymbolic. The classification reminds us that sucking or drinking can be playful and simulative, if the infant wishes it to be, but the sense in which a behavior might be viewed as symbolic or representational requires further specification. Representational thinking develops gradually, and the task is to clarify how prior or primitive forms become more sophisticated over time. The present study suggests that the representational functions of words and pretend actions might converge at an early age. Moreover, pretend actions might be thought of as semantically organized behavior in the sense that objects, actions, and recipients fill open-ended slots defined by abstract relationships among animate and inanimate things and forms of action. If so, the study of particular semantic domains (e.g., feeding someone with something) as these are expressed in language and play might provide the fine tuning required for a theory of the development of representational thinking.

REFERENCES

Bates, E., Benigni, L., Bretherton, I., Camaioni, L., & Volterra, V. From gesture to the first word: On cognitive and social prerequisites. In M. Lewis & L. A. Rosenblum (Eds.), *Interaction, conversation, and the development of language*. New York: Wiley, 1977.

Bates, E., Bretherton, I., Snyder, L., Shore, C., & Volterra, V. Vocal and gestural symbols at 13 months. *Merrill-Palmer Quarterly, 1980, 26,* 407-425.

Bates, E., Camaioni, L., & Volterra. V. The acquisition of performatives prior to speech. *Merrill-Palmer Quarterly, 1975, 21,* 205-226.

Bateson, G. A theory of play and fantasy. *Psychiatric Research Reports,* 1955, *2,* 39-51.

Elder, J. L., & Pederson, D. R. Preschool children's use of objects in symbolic play. *Child Development,* 1978, *49,* 500-504.

Fein, G. G. Children's sensitivity to social contexts at 18 months of age. *Developmental Psychology,* 1975, *11,* 853-854.

Fein, G. G. Echoes from the nursery: Piaget, Vygotsky and the relation between language and play. *New Directions in Child Development,* 1979, *6,* 1-14.

Fein, G. G. Pretend play: An integrative review. *Child Development,* 1981, *52,* 1095-1118.

Fein, G. G., & Apfel, N. Some preliminary observations on knowing and pretending. In M. Smith & M. B. Franklin (Eds.), *Symbolic functioning in childhood*. Hillsdale, N.J.: Lawrence Erlbaum Associates, 1979.

Fein, G. G., & Robertson, A. R. Cognitive and social dimensions of pretending in two year olds. Educational Resources Information Center, ERIC #ED 119 806, 1975.

Fein G. G., & Stork, L. Sociodramatic play: Social class effects in integrated preschool classrooms. *Journal of Applied Developmental Psychology,* 1981, *2,* 267-279.

Fenson, L., Kagan, J., Kearsley, R. B., & Zelazo, P. R. The developmental progression of manipulative play in the first two years. *Child Development,* 1976, *47,* 232-235.

Fenson, L., & Ramsay, D. S. Decentration and integration of the child's play in the second year. *Child Development,* 1980, *51,* 171-178.

Folger, K. M., & Leonard, L. B. Language and sensorimotor behavior during the early period of referential speech. *Journal of Speech and Hearing Research,* 1978, *21,* 519-527.

Garvey, C. Some properties of social play. *Merrill-Palmer Quarterly,* 1974, *20,* 163-180.

Golomb, C. Symbolic play: The role of substitutions in pretense and puzzle games. *British Journal of Educational Psychology,* 1977, *47,* 175-186.

Hulme, I., & Lunzer, E. A. Play, language and reasoning in subnormal children. *Journal of Child Psychology and Psychiatry,* 1966, *7,* 107-123.

Huttenlocher, J., & Higgins, E. T. Issues in the study of symbolic development. In C. Collins (Ed.), *Minnesota Symposia on Child Psychology* (Vol. 10). Hillsdale, N.J.: Lawrence Erlbaum Associates, 1978.

Ingram, D. Sensorimotor intelligence and language development. In A. L. Lock (Ed.), *Action, gesture and symbol: The emergence of language*. New York: Academic Press, 1977.

Inhelder, B., Lezine, I., Sinclair, H., & Stambak, M. Les debut de la function symbolique. *Archives de Psychologie,* 1972, *41,* 187–243.
Jackowitz, E. R., & Watson, M. W. The development of object transformations in early pretend play. *Developmental Psychology,* 1980, *16,* 543–549.
Kagan, J., Kearsley, R. B., & Zelazo, P. R. *Infancy: Its place in human development.* Cambridge, Mass.: Harvard University Press, 1978.
Lowe, M., & Costello, A. *Manual for the symbolic play test.* London: NPER, 1976.
Nicolich, L., & Raph, J. The relation of symbolic maturity as observed in play to spontaneous vocal imitation in early language development. Journal of Psycholinguistic Research, 1978, *7,* 401–417.
Piaget, J. *Play, dreams, and imitation in childhood.* New York: Norton, 1962.
Piaget, J., *Six psychological studies.* New York: Vintage, 1968.
Piaget, J., & Inhelder, B. *Mental imagery in the child.* New York: Basic Books, 1971.
Rocissano, L. *Escape from context.* Mimeographed paper, University of Michigan, n.d.
Rosenblatt, D. Developmental trends in infant play. In B. Tizard & D. Harvey (Eds.), *Biology of play.* London: William Heineman, 1977.
Smilansky, S. *The effects of sociodramatic play on disadvantaged children.* New York: Wiley, 1968.
Stern, W. *Psychology of early childhood.* New York: Holt, 1924.
Sutton-Smith. B. *Expressive styles in fantasy play.* Paper presented at the meeting of the American Psychological Association, Montreal, Canada, September 1980.
Ungerer, J. A., Zelazo, P. R., Kearsley, R. B., & O'Leary, K. Developmental changes in the representation of objects in symbolic play from 18 to 34 months of age. *Child Development,* 1981, *52,* 186–195.
Vygotsky, L. S. Play and its role in the mental development of the child. *Soviet Psychology,* 1967, *5*(3), 6¡8.
Watson, M. W., & Fischer, K. W. A developmental sequence of agent use in late infancy. *Child Development,* 1977, *48,* 828–836.
Zelazo, P. R., & Kearsley, R. B. The emergence of functional play in infants: Evidence for a major cognitive transition. *Journal of Applied Developmental Psychology,* 1980, *1,* 95–117.

4 The Child's Expressi Knowledge of Wor(What Preschoolers About the Meanin{ Nouns and Verbs

Jeremy M. Anglin
University of Waterloo

In this chapter I summarize the results of some studies in which my students and I have interviewed preschool children and asked them to express what they know about certain word concepts and, more specifically, certain nouns and verbs. Following this summary I will compare and contrast the kinds of results we have obtained with this procedure for certain nouns versus certain verbs and discuss some general findings that seem to hold for most domains of words that we have studied. I also attempt to summarize some of the uses to which the interview method described here can be put as well as some of the problems associated with it.

By a *word concept* I mean the knowledge possessed by an individual about a category of objects or events when that category is denoted by a word in the language of that individual (cf. Anglin, 1977, 1983). This includes both knowledge of the category's *extension* (i.e., what objects or events are instances of the category) and knowledge of its *intension* or *meaning* (i.e., what properties are true of the category).

In my recent research on children's word concepts and word meanings I have focused, though not exclusively, on studies of the extension or denotative scope of children's words, and in particular of object names such as *dog, flower, money,* and so on, as a means of illuminating their conceptual and semantic structure (e.g., Anglin, 1977, 1979, 1983; Kay & Anglin, 1982). Extensional or referential methods have also been the proposed method of some, but not all, philosophers both for establishing the extensions of words for a speaker of a given language and for developing hypotheses regarding their intensions as well (e.g., Carnap, 1947). For these reasons, before I con-

77

the interview method, which is the focus of this paper, I would like to consider some of the problems and limitations associated with extensional or referential methods, because my gradual realization of these problems and limitations has led me and my students to supplement extensional tests with other methods, particularly interview studies, for investigating the conceptual and semantic structure underlying the child's words.

PROBLEMS WITH EXTENSIONAL STUDIES

One basically extensional method that has often been used in the study of the semantic development of the child's first words, and especially his or her first object names, has relied upon diaries of the spontaneous speech production of children in naturalistic settings. Such diaries have been kept by numerous students of early language development (e.g., Bloom, 1973; Bower man, 1977; Chamberlain & Chamberlain, 1904a, 1904b; Leopold, 1939; Lewis, 1959; Moore, 1896; Piaget, 1962; Stern, 1930), and one use to which the resulting observations have been put has been to examine the child's natural tendency to extend and "overextend" words (again, usually object names) to refer to various objects in or aspects of the environment. On the basis of the resulting patterns of word generalization observed in such diaries, a number of justifiably influential theories or hypotheses concerning semantic and/or conceptual development have been set forth (e.g., Bloom, 1973, chap. 4; Bowerman, 1977; Brown, 1958; Clark, 1973).

However, there are serious problems with using only spontaneous speech of the kind recorded in such diaries to derive such theories. For example, such speech is biased to show overextension of the child's words but does not reveal nearly so clearly cases of underextension and overlap (Anglin, 1977, 1979, 1983; Kay & Anglin, 1982; Nelson, Rescorla, Gruendel, & Benedict, 1978; Reich, 1976; Saltz, Dixon, Klein, & Becker, 1977), even though other methods show that such cases can and frequently do occur (e.g., Anglin, 1977, 1979, 1983; Kay & Anglin, 1982; Nelson et al., 1978; Nelson & Bonvillian, 1978; Saltz et al., 1977; White, 1982). Also, if overextensions in children's spontaneous speech really imply that their word meanings are different from those of adults, such overextensions should also occur with equal frequency in comprehension. However, a number of studies have reported an asymmetry between the frequency of overextensions in production versus comprehension (e.g., Gruendel, 1977; Huttenlocher, 1974; Rescorla, 1981; Thomson & Chapman, 1977; see also Kay & Anglin, 1982). Moreover, it has been noted by a number of authors that preschool children in the naturalistic setting frequently engage in symbolic play and pretense, which is often accompanied by pretend talk (e.g., Bates, 1976; Fein, 1975; Piaget, 1962; Winner, 1979). This observation is very interesting in its own right, but it can make the assessment of the extension of the child's words difficult (Anglin, 1983). Perhaps the most general problem with using spontaneous speech to infer the conceptual and/or semantic structure underlying the child's words is that such studies are rarely systematic or controlled enough, because the child, in such spontaneous speech, will rarely attempt to name a wide enough range of referents and nonreferents by means of a given word to allow a confident assessment of the denotative scope, or extension, of that word, let alone its intension or meaning for him or her (Anglin, 1983).

These kinds of problems have led me to argue that one should supplement diaries of spontaneous speech, as rich and interesting as they are, with more controlled systematic studies of the extension of the child's words, with testing conducted on a fairly wide range of referents and nonreferents preferrably in comprehension (e.g., by asking the child for each of a set of stimuli "Is this a _____?") as well as in production (e.g., by asking the child for each of a set of stimuli "What's that?"). Some such studies have been conducted (e.g., Kay & Anglin, 1982; see also Anglin, 1977, 1983; Fremgen & Fay, 1980; Macnamara, 1982; Nelson, 1973; Nelson & Bonvillian, 1978; Saltz et al., 1977; Thomson & Chapman, 1977; White, 1982), and taken together, they allow both certain conclusions about the extension of the child's words and some tentative hypotheses about their intensions or meanings (Anglin, 1983).

Thus, controlled tests of the denotative scope of the child's words in comprehension and production are of relevance to the developmental psycholinguist concerned with semantic and/or conceptual development. Systematic tests of the extension of words have been the proposed method of some philosophers for deriving hypotheses concerning the intension of those words for speakers of a given language (e.g., Carnap, 1947). And for very young children just beginning to talk (e.g., for 1- to 3-year-olds), such extensional tests seem to be possibly the best method for deriving hypotheses about meanings for at least some domains of words. Such tests certainly have advantages over simply recording the vocabulary acquired by children and studying the extension of their words as revealed in their spontaneous speech production.

However, there are certain problems even with controlled extensional tests of the denotative scope of the child's words in comprehension and/or production, especially with regard to drawing conclusions about intension or meaning on the basis of such tests. Four of these can be mentioned here. One of the deepest problems, as philosophers such as Goodman (1972) have pointed out, is that even if one establishes for a large but finite number of objects those that are included in the extension of a word versus those that are not, there is always an indefinitely large number of rules or properties which could have been the basis for classifying those objects in that particular way. Thus, the intension of a word for a particular individual will always be underdetermined by extensional tests without resort to additional considerations such as simplicity, which may or may not be justified psychologically. Carnap (1947) acknowledged this problem but maintained that one could at least formulate hypotheses about intensions on the basis of systematic extensional tests, hypotheses which he noted could be reinforced or disconfirmed by means of further careful extensional tasks. Carnap's (1947) position is less nihilistic than that of some philosophers and, I think, justifies the use of extensional tests for studying intensions. But notice that, even after a series of such carefully planned tests, one's conclusions regarding intensions or meanings will always be in the form of more or less tenable hypotheses rather than in the form of established facts.

A second problem is that different methods of testing the extension of the child's word concepts often yield somewhat different assessments of their denotative scope. As noted earlier, a number of studies have revealed an asymmetry in the referential scope of the child's word concepts as suggested by tests of comprehension versus tests of production. A reasonable approach to such asymmetries is to require that the child extend a given word in both production and comprehension before viewing such behavior as truly indicative of the extension of his or her word concepts and reflective of their meanings (e.g., Clark, 1975, 1978, 1979; Thomson & Chapman, 1977). However, the problem is still somewhat complicated because the tendency to extend a word in comprehension particularly and the apparent resulting asymmetry between comprehension and production often seem to depend on the particular test of comprehension being administered (e.g., contrast Kay & Anglin, 1982, vs. Thomson & Chapman, 1977, or Fremgen & Fay, 1980, vs. Kuczaj, 1979). This variability in estimates of the denotative scope of the child's words depending on the particular test being used makes the precise establishment of the extension of those words somewhat difficult. This in turn complicates any inferences about the meanings of those words that might be attempted.

A third and somewhat related type of problem with inferring intension from extensional aspects of the child's words was suggested by a previous study (Anglin, 1977, 1978) in which a group of preschool children was asked: (1) to define a set of common nouns (specifically *animal, food, clothing* and *bird*); and then (2) to classify pictures of objects as referents or nonreferents of the words they had just defined by showing them pictures of instances and noninstances of the categories and asking: "Is this an animal?", "Is this food?" and so on. One analysis of the resulting data revealed that the children (unlike the adults we tested) were most often inconsistent in their classification of the pictures with the definitions they had provided. The child's definitions were, in some cases at least, quite apt in that they mentioned an essential function of the category (e.g., *Food is to eat. You wear clothing.*) or a characteristic action of referents of the category (e.g., *Birds fly.*). However, when classifying pictures of objects into the corresponding categories, these same children would often seemingly disregard the definitions they had given. For example, one child who had defined *food* with the reasonable definition *eat it* in the classification task denied that certain edible objects, which he could correctly identify (e.g., a piece of bread, a lollipop, and ketchup), were *food*. Thus, this study suggested a discrepancy between the same children's classification of objects into verbal categories and their definitions of those categories. And in at least some such cases, their definitions suggested their appreciation of certain aspects of the meaning (especially functional aspects) of the categories, which was not as clearly revealed by their classification behavior. Thus, it seems that studies of classification (i.e., extension) do not always reveal all that children may know about the meanings of some word concepts. In this regard it is worth noting that a number of authors have distinguished between the *core* of a concept (its essential meaning) and the *identification procedure* (which enables classification or naming) (e.g., Anglin, 1977; Miller & Johnson-Laird, 1976; Nelson, 1974, 1978; Smith & Medin, 1981), a distinction which is similar in some respects to that made earlier by Bruner, Goodnow, and Austin (1956) between concept formation and concept attainment. It can be argued that extensional, categorization, or classification studies are more revealing of the concept-identification procedure than they are of the conceptual core because such studies merely consist of having subjects identify objects as either belonging or not belonging to a given concept or to the denotative scope of a given word (Anglin, 1982).

A final limitation on extensional methods concerns the domains of words to which the simple naming and comprehension procedures described earlier can be applied. These extensional methods can be applied to object names and to other domains of words (e.g., proper nouns, color terms, verbs of motion, etc.) for which it is possible to show the child exemplars and nonexemplars of the class in question. But it is harder to conceive of how one would study the semantic aspects of other types of words (e.g., abstract nouns such as *idea,* kin terms such as *mother,* abstract verbs such as *think,* functors such as *and,* etc.) using the simple extensional procedures discussed thus far because it is harder to show children in a clear and simple fashion referents (and nonreferents) of such words for testing purposes.

REVIEW OF PRIOR DEFINITIONAL AND INTERVIEW STUDIES

Given the problems with extensional methods that have been discussed, it seems clear that the developmental psycholinguist concerned with semantic development could benefit from other empirical methods for studying the meanings of words for young children. The purpose of this chapter is to describe the results of studies that have used another method—an interview procedure in which children are asked to express all that they know about the meanings of certain words. In these studies, this is accomplished by asking children standard definitional questions—"What is a(n) _____?" (for nouns); "What does to _____ mean?" and "What is _____ing?" (for verbs)—and these are supplemented by a variety of other follow-up questions to probe further the child's knowledge of the words. This is a method that can be used for studying some domains of words for which the aforementioned extensional procedures are not appropriate. Moreover, the other problems associated with the previously described extensional methods do not really directly apply to the interview method, although this procedure has its own problems and limitations to be considered toward the end of this chapter.

The interview method is obviously akin to the clinical method used by Piaget (e.g., 1928, 1929) in his earlier work on the child's cognitive development. Perhaps even more relevant to the research to be described in this chapter are studies of definitions produced by children of different ages for different vocabulary items (e.g., Al-Issa, 1969; Feifel & Lorge, 1950; Litowitz, 1977; Nelson, 1978; Norlin, 1980; Watson, 1982; Wolman & Barker, 1965). Indeed, a few of these studies (e.g., Nelson, 1978; Norlin, 1980; Watson, 1982) have employed other questions in addition to the basic definitional question "What is a(n) _____?" or "What does _____ mean?" and therefore are quite similar in method to those described later. There have also been a number of definitional or interview studies that have examined the meaning of kin terms to children (e.g., Danziger, 1957; Elkind, 1962; Haviland & Clark, 1974; Piaget, 1928; Swartz & Hall, 1972), although I will postpone my review of these findings until my treatment of a related study by N. Benson and me on the acquisition of kin terms. Apart from the studies of kin terms, those studies that have used the definitional or interview method have either focused exclusively on concrete nouns such as *straw, puddle, tiger, car, book, table,* and so forth (Al-Issa 1969; Norlin, 1980; Watson, 1981; Wolman & Barker, 1965) or have focused primarily on such concrete nouns with little separate analysis of words from other parts of speech (e.g., verbs or adjectives) (Feifel & Lorge, 1950; Litowitz, 1977; Nelson, 1978). Although some of these studies (e.g., Feifel & Lorge, 1950) have investigated school children of different ages, others have extended the procedure to preschool children as young as 3 and 4 years of age (Litowitz, 1977; Nelson, 1978; Norlin, 1980; Wolman & Barker, 1965).

In spite of differences across definitional and interview studies, certain findings have emerged consistently. Perhaps the most commonly reported finding across all studies is the tendency of younger children to define concrete nouns, at least, in terms of use (Al-Issa, 1969; Feifel & Lorge, 1950; Litowitz, 1977, Nelson, 1978; Norlin, 1980; Watson, 1982; Wolman & Barker, 1965; see also Krauss, 1952). Examples are *a gown is to wear, you eat them* for "apple," and *a hole is to dig.* A number of studies have also reported a greater tendency in younger children as compared with older children to define words in term of concrete descriptions (e.g., *straw is yellow*), which often includes mentioning action (e.g., *a bird flies*), in terms of personal experience (e.g., *when you're cutting carrots* for "knife"), or by way of illustration (e.g., *a gem* for "priceless"), association (e.g., *head* for "hat"), or nonverbal behavioral demonstration (e.g., for words like *eyelash* or *"tap"*) (e.g., Al-Issa, 1969; Feifel & Lorge, 1950; Litowitz, 1977; Norlin, 1980, Watson, 1982). Also, not surprisingly, studies that have included relatively difficult words have reported a greater number of irrelevant, semantically empty, or incorrect responses including more repetitions of the word in younger as compared to older children (e.g., Feifel & Lorge, 1950; Litowitz, 1977).

None of these studies has used adults as subjects, but those that have included children aged 7 years and older have consistently reported an increase with age in the tendency of children to produce superordinates in their definitions, which are usually accompanied by differentiating properties as well (e.g., Al-Issa, 1969; Feifel & Lorge, 1950; Litowitz, 1977; Norlin, 1980; Watson, 1982), a tendency which is largely though not completely absent in preschool children (Al-Issa, 1969; Nelson, 1978; Norlin, 1980; Watson, 1982). Examples of such more mature kinds of definitions are: *hay that cattle eat* for "straw"; *a long dress that women wear* for "gown"; *hair over the eye that protects you* for "eyelash"; *citrus fruit* for "orange."

Thus, many studies have supported the notion that there is qualitative change in the structure of definitions with development described as a transition from definitions in terms of use to definitions superior to use, or from concrete definitions based on personal experience to abstract definitions in terms of genus and differentia. Although this transition has often been characterized as being from definitions in terms of use to definitions superior to use, it should be noted that use (or function) is often incorporated implicitly or explicitly in those definitions described as superior to use (cf. Anglin, 1977; Nelson, 1978). Thus, a young child might define a "gown" as *you wear it,* whereas an older one might define it as *a long dress that women wear* (Feifel & Lorge, 1950). It also should be noted that although there are changes with age in the tendency to produce certain types of definitions, the change seems gradual and a child of a given age is likely to produce different types of definitions. In other words, the different types of definitions are not produced exclusively by any given child or age group, even though the relative frequencies of the definitional types change with age as has been outlined (Al-Issa, 1969; Feifel & Lorge, 1950; Nelson, 1978; Norlin, 1980; Watson, 1982; Wolman & Barker, 1965).

Two of the more recent studies (Litowitz, 1977; Watson, 1982) have made explicit a point that is implicit in much of this literature, namely that the development of definitions actually involves two separate though related kinds of change: change in content and change in form. In terms of content, there is a conceptual shift from definitions based on use, description, and personal experience to more general, abstract, and socially shared definitions. In terms of form, there are changes in the grammatical structure of the definitional response. Although there are actually a number of syntactic constructions by means of which definitions can be expressed (Bierwisch & Kiefer, 1969), the standard or prototypical form — and the one that adults tend to use, for nouns at least — is "NP_1 is NP_2" where NP_1 (the definiendum) restates the word to be defined, and NP_2 (the definiens) is cast in terms of a superordinate and defining properties. As children grow up they go through a number of steps in mastering this form (Litowitz, 1977; Watson, 1982), strongly suggesting that the definition is a response that is gradually learned and not completely mastered, if ever, until well after the child has gone to school. A related point made by a number of authors is that the task of defining words is essentially metalinguistic in nature and involves making explicit in definitions meanings that are implicit in language use (Anglin, 1977; Nelson, 1978; Norlin, 1980; Watson, 1982).

The investigations to be described in this paper are clearly related to these studies, and the findings from the latter are consistent with those of the former in certain ways. There are, however, certain differences in the method of the interview studies to be described, and, three will be mentioned now. First, the interview studies have generally used a greater number of questions to elicit from children their expressible knowledge of words. Second, in each of the studies to be described, an adult group was interviewed in the same way as children so as to provide a basis for comparing the children's responses with more highly developed responses. Third, in addition to a study of concrete nouns, two studies of verbs and one of kin terms will also be presented to help clarify similarities and differences across different domains of words. As previously noted, earlier definitional and interview studies have often focussed primarily, and in a number of cases exclusively, on concrete nouns.

STUDIES OF NOUNS

Object Names

The first research summarized here is a study of object names, which I have reported before (Anglin, 1977, 1978). I review it now partly because it was the first study I conducted using the interview method, partly because it was done on the same type of words that I have also studied using extensional methods, and most importantly because I wish eventually to contrast our findings with this type of word with those which have resulted from similar studies of other kinds of words — kin terms and especially verbs. In this study, we interviewed preschool children individually and encouraged them to describe their knowledge of 12 object names in as much detail as possible (see Ack.). The words were: *collie, dog, animal; rose, flower, plant; Volkswagen, car, vehicle; apple, fruit, food.* Fourteen children who ranged in age from 2 years 8 months (2;8) to 6 years 7 months (6;7) were included in the study. A few adults (Harvard undergraduates) were interviewed in the same way as the children. In general we tried to probe the child's knowledge by means of the following five questions or requests for each word.

1. What is a _____?
2. Tell me everything you can about _____s.
3. What kinds of _____s are there?
4. What kind of a thing is a _____?
5. Tell me a story about a _____.

We also asked other questions to follow up on the responses of the children because we wanted to be guided to some extent by the kinds of statements made by the child.

Analyses of the conversations revealed that even 3-year-old children could express some rudimentary knowledge of most of the words except for *collie* and *vehicle.* The adults interviewed clearly could express more knowledge of every kind about each verbal concept, but it is important to give the children credit for the considerable knowledge they are capable of expressing. Before describing this knowledge, I should make a distinction among the kinds of words studied. Previous research had established that certain terms within the hierarchies of words used in this study tend to be acquired first by children (see Anglin, 1977, 1979; also see Brown, 1958; Rosch, 1978; Rosch, Mervis, Gray, Johnson, & Boyes-Braem, 1976). Specifically, *dog* tends to be acquired before *collie* or *animal; flower* before *rose* or *plant; car* before *Volkswagen* or *vehicle;* and *apple* before *fruit* or *food.* In general, four kinds of properties were most frequently mentioned by young children for such basic word concepts: (1) properties that describe what referents of the word or instances of the concept look like (e.g., *round* or *red* for "apple"; *brown and white* for "dog"); (2) properties that describe what referents of the word do (e.g., *an apple grows; dogs bark*); (3) properties that describe the uses to which referents of the word are put (e.g., *I eat apples; you pat dogs*); and (4) properties that describe where referents of the word are found (e.g., *apples are in the fridge; dogs are in pet stores*). Thus, this study suggested that the preschool child's expressible knowledge of such words often includes knowledge of the *form* (or *appearance*), the *activity,* the *use,* and the *location* of the referents of the word.

The most dramatic advances in the child's expressible knowledge beyond this rudimentary base for basic object names included the ability to assign the word to a superordinate class (e.g., *a car is a vehicle that . . .; a flower is a plant with . . .*) and the ability to describe properties of referents of the word other than the four basic concrete ones just mentioned. These other properties included mention of the relation of referents of the word to other things in the world (e.g., *a dog has a brain which is bigger than a fish's but smaller than a human's*), their internal constituents (e.g., *an apple has white stuff and a core and seeds inside it*), their origins (e.g., *flowers grow from seeds*), and also metaphorical extensions or derivative senses of some of the words (e.g., *used in a derogatory sense to refer to someone held in low esteem* for "dog"). The youngest children in the study were less likely than older children and adults to provide the names of subordinates for the basic object names, although even some 3-year-olds could do this, and in general the children appeared to be considerably more adept at providing the names of subordinates than at providing the names of superordinates.

For concepts superordinate to the basic level in this study, children were most adept at providing the names of referents of the word (e.g., *a horsie* for "animal"; *cookies, cereal, dessert, potatoes* for "food") although properties of the referents of the word were also sometimes mentioned (e.g., *plants are green*), including functional properties, in the sense of use (e.g., *you eat food*). In this study, such functional properties were most often mentioned for the superordinate concept "food," although other studies have shown that young children often mention functional properties for certain other superordinate concepts like "clothing," often those which classify human artifacts (e.g., Anglin, 1977; Nelson, 1978). For word concepts subordinate to basic concepts, properties were most often mentioned and these again tended to be descriptions of appearance, use, action, or location of referents of the word. Not surprisingly, subordinates were rarely mentioned for such terms, and more interestingly, children were able to provide the names of superordinates for such terms (e.g., *a Volkswagen is a car; a rose is a flower*) earlier than they were for higher level terms. Broadly speaking, although superordination by preschool children was generally infrequent, the ability to superordinate appeared to decrease as the level of generality of the term within a hierarchy increased.

To a degree and relative to older children and adults, this study suggested that the younger child's expressible knowledge of these verbal concepts was "instance oriented" and at times seemed to be based on his or her ability to recollect specific encounters with particular referents of the word. For example, it was observed that in discussing superordinate words such as *animal* and *food*, younger children would often simply rattle off the names of instances, sometimes exclusively. Also, this tendency to think in terms of particulars may be why the properties younger children came up with for basic word concepts were often not even close to *defining* in the sense of being true of all and only the referents of those words. For example, one child (3;4) when discussing the word *dog* insisted that dogs were *brown and white,* properties which are true neither of all nor of only dogs. Toward the end of the conversation, it became clear that he had recently encountered a brown and white dog at a park, suggesting that his initial response to our questions about *dog* was based primarily on his recollection of that particular experience.

Although a number of the properties mentioned by the younger children were of this nature and therefore not defining, many of the properties they mentioned did in fact specify the essential function (e.g., *eat it* for "food") or an almost defining action (e.g., *bark* for "dog") — the kinds of properties adults mention when they are asked to define such words. Thus, this study showed that for some object names (e.g., *food*) young children did, in fact, know certain properties that are important to adults in defining the terms, in particular, properties that specify the uses and/or actions of referents of these terms. On the other hand, there was evidence from this and a related study (cf. Anglin, 1977, 1978) that even in such cases the children may not have realized that these properties were defining in the sense of being necessary and/or sufficient criteria for inclusion of instances within the word concept. For other terms (e.g., *animal*), it was found that the preschool children had great difficulty in expressing anything like a general definition when discussing them.

On the basis of these results, we constructed schematic representations of the knowledge as it was expressed by each child and each adult for each word. Figure 4.1 shows the representations of the knowledge expressed by four children for the word *dog*. In this figure (and subsequent ones), subordinates are presented below the word discussed, properties are presented to the right, and superordinates are presented above. Also, the question or statement made by the experimenter, which was followed by a given item of expressed knowledge by the child, is indicated below the schematic representations. Figure 4.2 shows a comparable schematic representation of the knowledge expressed by one adult (in this case, a Harvard undergraduate), also for the word *dog*. These schematic representations are presented to provide the reader with some concrete examples of the knowledge displayed in this task by subjects of different ages.

Kin Terms

Kin terms are a kind of noun, but they are very different from the object names, which were the focus of the study just summarized. Whereas most object names are ill-defined (Rosch, 1973; Smith & Medin, 1981), kin terms can be precisely defined as the componential analyses of Wallace and Atkins (1960), Romney and D'Andrade (1964), and Bierwisch (1970) have each elegantly shown. Moreover, whereas perceptual information can often provide useful clues in establishing whether a given object name is appropriate or not,

Miller and Johnson-Laird (1976) note that kin terms "have about as little perceptual basis as any semantic field in the lexicon [p. 360]." And whereas object names are *referential* words, which denote objects or categories of objects, kin terms are *relational* words, which describe people's position within the nuclear or extended family. The nonperceptual and relational quality of the semantics of kin terms makes it difficult to study their meanings for children using the simple referential or extensional methods described in the in-

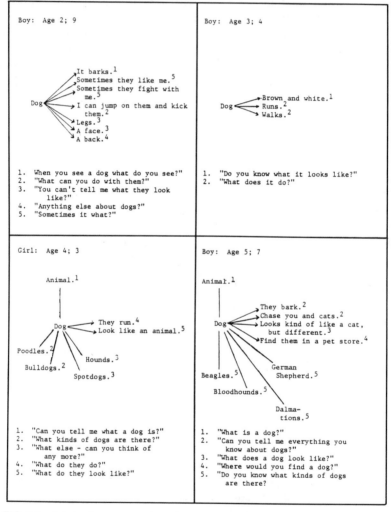

FIG. 4.1   Schematic representation of the expressible knowledge of the word *dog* for four children. Questions that elicited the responses from the children are indicated below the schematic representations (data from Anglin, 1977).

troduction to this chapter. However, it is possible to interview children about their understanding of such terms, and a number of such studies have been conducted (e.g., Danziger, 1957; Elkind 1962; Haviland & Clark, 1974; Piaget, 1928; Swartz & Hall, 1972; see also Chambers & Tavuchis, 1976).

These developmental studies have all consistently shown that as children get older the quality of their definitions of kin terms changes. Piaget (1928) studied definitions of the terms *brother* and *sister* in children aged 4 to 12 years and identified three "stages" in the development of such definitions. In the first stage, children would simply say that a brother is a boy or a sister is a girl. In the second stage, the child would realize that there had to be at least two children with the same parents in order for there to be a brother or a sister. Thus, children in this stage appreciated to some extent the relational nature of the terms, but Piaget emphasized that they did not appreciate the reciprocal nature of this relation. In particular, Stage 2 children did not seem to realize that having a brother or a sister necessarily implies that one is oneself a brother or a sister. In Stage 3, which was reached when the children were about 9 years of age, definitions were both relational and reciprocal. Piaget's findings were essentially replicated by Elkind (1962) and by Swartz and Hall (1972).

Danziger (1957) interviewed children from 5 to 8 years about their understanding of five different kin terms: *brother* and *sister,* which had been studied by Piaget, but also *daughter, cousin,* and *uncle.* For each kin term he asked the children "What is a _____?" and then an additional set of questions depending on the kin term and also how the child responded. He identified four stages in the development of these concepts, which he called precategorical, categorical, concrete relational, and abstract relational. The last three stages were quite similar to Piaget's stages, but in the case of the last two in particular, they were not identical. Specifically, children who gave responses categorized by Danziger as concrete relational mentioned certain concrete bonds such as living in the same house, having the same name, and so on, but not involving another kinship relation. Only in what Danziger called abstract relational definitions did the children respond in terms of the kinship system, which he took as evidence that they now appreciated the relation as part of a system of relations. Danziger (1957) also argued that reciprocity was sometimes partially appreciated by children using concrete relational definitions but that this appreciation broke down "as soon as the child's own relationship is involved [p. 221]." Piaget, in contrast, had attributed reciprocity only to the highest stage. Danziger's first stage, precategorical (not mentioned by Piaget), involved some of the youngest children in his study who simply gave the name of a specific person when asked to define a given kin term.

Haviland and Clark (1974) interviewed 50 children from 3;0 to 8;0 and asked each of them to define 15 kin terms: *mother, father, grandmother, grandfather, son, daughter, grandson, granddaughter, brother, sister, aunt, uncle, niece, nephew,* and *cousin.* For each of these terms the children were asked "What is a(n)_____?" as well as additional questions whenever possible. They classified the children's responses into four categories of definitions. Definitions were classified into Category 1, which corresponded roughly to Danziger's precategorical stage, if children simply named a spe-

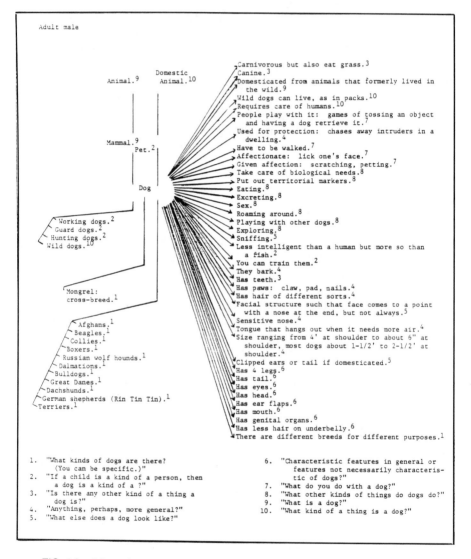

FIG. 4.2   Schematic representation of the expressible knowledge of the word *dog* for one adult (data from Anglin, 1977).

cific person, if they said they did not know what the term meant, or if they gave an irrelevant or incorrect response. Category 2 definitions, which corresponded to Piaget's Stage 1 and to Danziger's categorical stage, were characterized by the child's use of "property" features such as sex and age to define the terms. Category 3 definitions (similar to Piaget's Stage 2) were relational but not yet reciprocal. Finally, Category 4 definitions, like Piaget's Stage 3, were both relational and reciprocal. Thus the child's definitions showed an appreciation that being a grandmother meant having a grandchild, that being an aunt meant having a niece or nephew, or that being a brother meant having a brother or sister, and so on. Consistent with previous studies, Haviland and Clark showed that as children got older their definitions shifted from Category 1 definitions to increasingly higher categories, although even their oldest children (7;0 to 8;10) produced Category 3 definitions more frequently than Category 4 definitions.

In addition to these general developmental trends, Danziger (1957) and Haviland and Clark (1974) both reported that the level of definition achieved by a given child varied with the particular kin term. Danziger did not rank order the five kin terms he studied according to their level of definition or their order of acquisition, but he did conclude that these differences across terms indicate that "the level of conceptualization depends to a large extent on the child's *experience* in handling the different types of content [p. 230]."

Haviland and Clark explicitly ranked the kin terms according to their mean level of definition, which they took as a measure of their order of acquisition. Contrary to Danziger, they found that experience was not very predictive of this order. On the other hand, two metrics of semantic complexity derived from Bierwisch's (1970) analysis of kin terms into relational components were found to be predictive of the mean level of definition produced by the children for the kin terms and their order of acquisition, thus supporting a tenet of Clark's (1973) earlier theory of the acquisition of word meaning.

In our investigation of the child's knowledge of English kin terms, Nancy Benson and I (in preparation) were guided by these previous developmental studies (see Acknowledgments). The 12 terms we used were: *mother, father, sister, brother, son, daughter, wife, husband*—terms describing the relations within the nuclear family (Miller & Johnson-Laird, 1976)—as well as *aunt, uncle, grandmother,* and *grandfather.* Five groups of subjects were interviewed with four males and four females per group. The age groups were 3-year-olds, 4-year-olds, 5-year-olds, 6-year-olds, and an adult group consisting of University of Waterloo undergraduates. The kin terms were presented in a different random order for each child, and for each word three questions or requests for knowledge were posed in a constant order. These were:

1. What is a(n) _____?
2. Tell me everything you know about a(n) _____.
3. What kind of a thing is a(n) _____?

When appropriate, supplementary probe questions were asked to follow up on the subjects' responses. The interviews were tape-recorded and transcribed.

In this study, subsequent to the interviews, a questionnaire was used to assess each subject's familiarity with the terms and the concepts underlying them. Parents completed these questionnaires on their children's behalf. The questionnaire required that the 12 terms be rank ordered according to:

1. The amount of time the subject had spent with each of the relations.
2. The number of times subjects had heard the words spoken.
3. The number of times subjects had spoken the words.

Three analyses of the data from this study will be summarized here. The first analysis was in terms of the generality of the subjects' responses. Responses were assigned a score of 0 if children said they did not know the kin term or if they gave an irrelevant or wrong response (e.g., *I don't know* in response to "What is an uncle?"). If children simply named a particular individual or talked about the term only with reference to personal experience, an instance-oriented score (I) was given (e.g., *Uncle Andrew* in response to "What is an uncle?"). The response was scored G if it was general and abstract (e.g., *an uncle is a man who* . . . in response to "What is an uncle?"). Finally, if the subject's response included both general and instance-oriented elements, it was assigned a score of B for "both." After responses had been classified in this way, a second judge scored a complete protocol from each age group. There was 92% agreement between the two rating sets.

The results of this analysis revealed that the percentage of responses classified as 0 and as I decreased with age, whereas those classified as G or B increased with age. When the 3-year-old children indicated some knowledge of the kin terms, it was most often expressed by particular examples. Beyond the age of 3, there was a decrease with age in the tendency to discuss the words in terms of specific instances previously encountered and an increase in the tendency to talk about them in a more general way. The younger children tended to describe the terms without mention of any general class (e.g., *parent, relative, person,* etc.), whereas older children occasionally and adults often did mention such superordinate terms in their responses.

In the second analysis, we developed a categorization scheme for the responses in terms of definitional level. This system of categorization was similar to those of Piaget (1928), Danziger (1957), and Haviland and Clark (1974) but was expanded to include six levels as opposed to the three or four used by previous researchers. Specifically, responses were assigned to Level 0 if children stated that they did not know what the term meant or gave an incorrect or irrelevant definition. They were assigned to Level 1 if the subject named a particular individual, provided we could validate the response. Responses were classified in Level 2 if the child mentioned what Haviland and Clark (1974) called "property features," including those which are criterial (e.g., sex) as well as those which are characteristic (e.g., age). Definitions were placed in Level 3 if there was some, even vague, expression of family relations and/or relations among kin. Relational definitions that were accurate were assigned to Level 4. This required that the subject accurately describe the term's position within the nuclear or extended family. Finally, Level 5 definitions were accurate definitions that stated reciprocity. Such definitions had to include a reciprocal form of the term in the definition. For example, the reciprocal forms of *grandmother* are *grandson, granddaughter,* or *grandchild.* Piaget (1928) and Haviland and Clark (1974) have viewed reciprocal definitions of kin terms as the most sophisticated type and those which presumably represent the end point of development.

The responses of each subject for each word were categorized into one of these six types of definitions. After the responses were classified according to this scheme, a second rater classified the responses for one protocol from each age group. Interrater reliability was found to be 93% agreement.

It was found that as the children got older the average level of their definitions increased (in a way basically consistent with previous studies). The definitions provided by the 3-year-olds were most often classified at Level 0 (about 46%), next at Level 1 (about 27%), and then at Level 2 (about 25%). Just 2% of their definitions were classified at Level 3, and none were at Levels 4 and 5. The responses of the 4- and 5-year-olds were about equally divided among the first three levels, with very few being classified at higher levels. The modal definition type for the 6-year-olds was Level 2, with 36% of their reponses being classified at this level. Level 3 definitions were produced next most frequently by this age group, with 33% of their responses being classified in this way. Finally, the definitions of adults were all classified in the three highest levels. However, contrary to the assumptions of Piaget (1928) and Haviland and Clark (1974), adults did not use Level 5 definitions – those that state reciprocity – most often. Reciprocal definitions were produced by only about 24% of the adults. Instead, the most common type of response given by adults was classified at Level 4, an accurate definition of the kin term. Of adults' responses, 51% were of this type. The remaining 25% were categorized at Level 3.

The fact that Level 4 responses (accurate definitions) were more than twice as numerous as Level 5 responses (reciprocal definitions) is significant because it was formerly believed that the conceptual development of kin terms moved toward reciprocity (Haviland & Clark, 1974; Piaget, 1928). However, adults were not actually tested in these previous studies. Our study, which did test adults, suggests that reciprocity may not always be the crucial end point of definitional development. Rather, an accurate definition employing the ego reference point is the most common. To illustrate this, adults would respond to the term "aunt" considerably more often with a reply like *a female who is your mother's or father's sister* than with a reply like *a female who has nieces or nephews.* This point should not be exaggerated, because even though adults did not respond in our task most often in terms of reciprocity, it seems likely that they did appreciate the reciprocal nature of these terms (e.g., that an aunt has nieces and/or nephews). But apparently, reciprocity was not usually central enough to their conceptions of these terms for them to mention it in their definitions.

As reported by Danziger (1957) and Haviland and Clark (1974), we found that the mean level of definitional response varied across terms independently of age. (An analysis of variance showed a significant word effect as well as a significant age effect, whereas the word-age interaction was not significant.) In the third analysis to be described here, we followed Haviland and Clark's (1974) procedure of ranking the mean level of response for the kin terms based on the children's data. This ranking was assumed to be their order of acquisition. The order with mean levels of definitions shown in parentheses was: *mother* (1.66), *father* (1.59), *brother* (1.56), *sister* (1.53), *grandfather* (1.53), *grandmother* (1.34), *daughter* (1.28), *uncle* (1.19), *son* (1.09) *wife* (1.09), *husband* (1.09), and *aunt* (.94). We also used the three sets of experiential rankings of the children's parents to generate orderings of the 12 terms. Finally, we used the two metrics of semantic complexity, which Haviland and Clark (1974) had derived from Bierwisch's (1970) analysis of kin terms into relational components, to generate two more orderings of the kin terms.

Correlations between order of acquisition and experience were significant (approximately .8) for all three experiential rankings. Thus, the more experience the children had with a referent of the term and the more the children had experienced the term itself, the earlier that term was acquired. And contrary to the findings of Haviland and Clark (1974), there was not a significant correlation between either of the two metrics of semantic complexity and order of acquisition. In addition, semantic complexity and experience were not found to be correlated significantly.

Because the kin terms examined in this study were not identical to those studied by Haviland and Clark (1974), analyses were conducted for just the 10 words common to both. Results that favored experience over semantic complexity as a predictor of order of acquisition were also obtained in this further analysis (specifically, for our data the three measures of experience were significantly correlated with order of acquisition whereas neither metric of complexity was).

We also analyzed the kin terms according to a measure of cumulative complexity, analogous to Brown's (1973) notion of cumulative complexity, which he applied to grammatical morphemes. This is an analysis whereby a term is considered more complex than another only if it is defined by the same components that define the less complex term, plus one or more other additional components. Bierwisch's (1970) analysis of kin terms into relational components was used for this purpose. Assuming that a less complex term is acquired earlier than a more complex term, cumulative complexity makes 14 specific and not entirely independent predictions about the order of acquisiton of the kin terms in the study by Benson and Anglin (in preparation). These predictions as well as predictions that could be made by the experiential ratings were compared with the actual order of acquisition suggested by our study. The results indicated that cumulative complexity predicted correctly in 11 out of 14 cases and that experience predicted correctly in 13 out of 14 cases for all three measures of experience. Thus, the predictive power of experience is slightly better than that of cumulative complexity, and in addition, the former is less restricted in terms of the number of predictions potentially made.

Thus, overall, this study suggests that experience may predict the quality of definition and the order of acquisition of kin terms more successfully than measures of semantic complexity, although both factors may be of some importance. As a source of concrete examples, Figs. 4.3 and 4.4 are included. They show schematic representations of the knowledge expressed in this study by four children and one adult, respectively, for the word *uncle*.

STUDIES OF VERBS

I now turn to the description of two interview studies in which preschoolers were interrogated about their understanding of sets of verbs as opposed to nouns. As has been noted, especially in Gentner's work (1978, 1981, 1982), verbs differ in many ways from nouns in general and the simple object names considered in the first study summarized in this chapter in particular. With respect to development, verbs are slower to be acquired than are nouns, a finding which appears to hold for both production and comprehension (Goldin-Meadow, Seligman, & Gelman, 1976) and for a variety of different languages (Gentner, 1978, 1981, 1982). In a recent paper, Gentner (1982) has argued that these differences in acquisition rates for nouns versus verbs cannot be completely accounted for in terms of strictly linguistic or other nonconceptual differences but must be at least partly related to deep conceptual representational differences between simple nouns and verbs.

In addition to the acquisition differences, Gentner (1981, 1982) has summarized a number of other differences between simple nouns and verbs: verbs are not remembered as well as nouns in tests of recall and recognition; verbs tend to be associated with more different senses than nouns and therefore have greater breadth of meaning; verb meanings are more altered in paraphrase than are noun meanings; verb meanings appear to vary more cross-

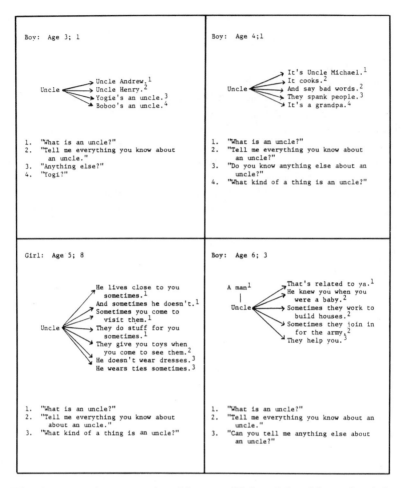

FIG. 4.3 Schematic representation of the expressible knowledge of the word *uncle* for four children (data from Benson & Anglin, in preparation).

linguistically than do the meanings of simple nouns; and, verbs are less directly translatable from one language to another than are simple nouns. These differences again suggest important conceptual differences between the two types of words.

In her earlier work, Gentner (e.g., 1978) suggested that a number of these differences might result from the fact that simple nouns are basically referential in nature, whereas verbs are fundamentally relational. In her recent papers she still maintains the referential-relational distinction, but has emphasized that simple nouns refer to concepts that are to a considerable degree given by the individual's, even the prelinguistic infant's, natural propensity to classify the world perceptually and conceptually into coherent, stable objects independently of language. Verb concepts, on the other hand, have to be invented or discovered to a greater degree than do noun concepts. In any event, Gentner's work makes it clear that there are probably important differences in the conceptual structure underlying simple nouns versus simple verbs, a point which is reinforced by attempts to construct componential representations of words within specific semantic fields from the two domains (e.g., Miller & Johnson-Laird, 1976). For a developmental psycholinguist, such differences suggest a need for the systematic study of the acquisition of verb meaning as well as noun meaning.

A modest number of studies have focused on the development of verb meaning (e.g., Clark & Garnica, 1974; Gentner, 1975, 1978, 1981, 1982; Long, 1975; Macrae, 1976; Richards, 1976), but none of these has employed the interview or definitional procedure with which I am primarily concerned in this chapter. Only a few of the definitional studies reviewed in the introduction to this chapter included verbs as stimuli, and with one exception that I am aware of (Nelson, 1978), no separate analysis for findings for the verbs alone was presented, although the point has occasionally been made that verbs appear to be more difficult to define than nouns (e.g., Litowitz, 1977).

Nelson (1978) asked 17 preschoolers between 3½ and 4½ years of age either to "tell me what x is" (or "what x means") or to "tell me what you know

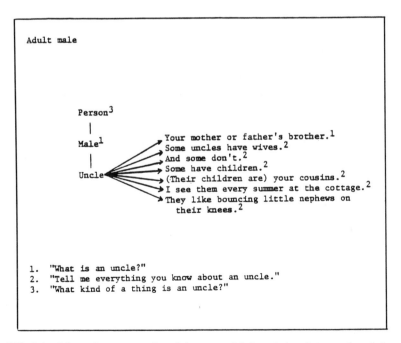

FIG. 4.4   Schematic representation of the expressible knowledge of the word *uncle* for one adult (data from Benson & Anglin, in preparation).

about x" for each of 25 words. Of these 25 words, 4 were verbs: *drive, run, eat,* and *sleep.* These words, which she called "function terms," were not the primary focus of the study, but Nelson (1978) did summarize the kinds of responses preschoolers produced when they were queried about them as follows:

> Responses to function terms in Study 1 were those that fit the questions who? what? when? and where? In response to "drive" one finds "you drive" (who) and "car" (what) as well as experiential relationships such as "drive means be careful" and "learn how to drive". . . . "Eat" elicits a variety of responses "food", "fork", "spoon", "meat", "corn", "fish", (all what or with what); "lunch", "supper", (when); and some more complicated relations: a negative "hay you don't eat"; "mothers cook animals" (!); "maybe rabbits eat gerbils" (!?). "Run" gives primarily footwear ("sneakers"), where you run and where you don't run ("you walk on the rug"), people ("you and someone") and some evaluations: "settle down", "it's a naughty thing because you run too fast." Obviously, "fun" is primarily related to the self as are the other functions. "Sleep" yielded where ("bed"), when ("night"), who ("person", "someone", a list of people) and related objects ("sheet", "blanket", "moon"). *Thus when the term to be defined is an action or function it elicits people, places, and things which are related through that action or function to the self. When the term to be defined is, however, an object or category, the functional aspect of the relation is central and the people, places, and things are peripheral* [p. 64].

It is interesting that although the children in Nelson's study produced responses regarding the verb concepts that answered the questions "who? what? when? and where?" they apparently did not answer the questions "how?" or "why?" That is to say, although the children provided the names of agents and objects of the actions denoted by the verbs as well as temporal and locational information concerning when and where those actions take place, they did not describe the processes by means of which those actions are performed nor the functions or purposes they serve. It seems quite possible that information regarding process and function is often an important part of the meaning of many verbs for adults, as is often the case in dictionary definitions. Adults were not interviewed in Nelson's study, but it seems likely that adults would view process and function as at least as important to the meanings of verbs as agents, objects, temporal contexts, and locations. For example, it seems that the verb "eat" would be defined at least as much in terms of process (e.g., *biting, chewing, swallowing,* etc.) and in terms of function or purpose (e.g., *to nourish one's body*) as in terms of who eats, what is eaten, and when and where the eating occurs. In order to test such speculation, however, it is necessary to test adults as well as children. Thus, unlike in Nelson's study, in the two studies on verbs to be described in this chapter adults were tested as well as preschool children.

Verbs for Physical Activities, Social Activities, and Processes

In the first study on verbs, which was designed and conducted by Lois Campbell and myself (in preparation), preschool children and adults were interviewed and questioned on their knowledge of nine verbs (see Acknowledgments). The words in this study (unlike the following study) were taken from different semantic fields. The verbs fell into three categories that we thought of as physical activities (*eat, play, walk*), social activities (*help, kiss, talk*), and processes (*grow, like, think*). We chose words that we felt would be known at least to some extent by the preschool children. All of the words except one fall within the 500 most frequently occurring words in the speech of Grade 1 children according to Rinsland (1945). The one exception (*kiss*) falls within the 1500 most frequently occurring words.

In this study, we interviewed four groups of seven. There were 3-year-olds (with a mean age of 3;6), 4-year-olds (with a mean age of 4;6), 5-year-olds (with a mean age of 5;5), and a group of adults (with a mean age of 27;9). The children all attended a preschool or a day-care center. Five of the adults were undergraduate students at the University of Waterloo and the remaining two were from the Waterloo community. Each subject was interviewed individually.

In the case of the children, the interviewer began each session by saying: "I want you to play a game with me now and it would really help me if you would try as hard as you can. This game is about different words. I am going to say a word and then I would like you to tell me all you know about it." A tape recorder was turned on at this point, and the words were presented, one at a time, in the following order: *eat, help, grow, play, kiss, like, walk, talk,* and *think*. For each word the subject was asked questions in the following order:

1. What does to _____ mean?
2. What is _____ing?
3. Tell me everything you know about the word _____.
4. Who or what _____s?
5. How do you _____?

These five questions were always asked of each child for each word, except that if the child indicated no knowledge of the word by the second question, the interviewer went to the fourth question. If the child still could not express any knowledge about the word, the interviewer moved on to the next word. Other questions were also asked depending on the child's answers when it was thought that such questions might shed light on the child's knowledge of the words. At the end of the conversation for each verb, the child was asked to act out the verb with the request "Show me how to _____."

The interviews took between 20 and 40 minutes. In the case of a few of the younger preschool children, it was necessary to break the interview into two sessions conducted on different days.

All conversations were transcribed and subsequently coded into responses which were then classified as to whether they were appropriate or inappropriate. The decision was made to be quite lenient in classifying responses as appropriate. The response did not have to be true of all cases of the activity or process denoted by the verb, just true of some such cases. Responses were coded as inappropriate only if they were completely false or unrealistic. For example, if a child said that a chair walked, the response would be coded as inappropriate. A second rater classified the responses as appropriate or inappropriate for one complete transcript from each of the four groups of subjects. Interrater agreement was 96%. It was found that inappropriate responses were relatively infrequent, ranging from 10% for 3-year-olds to no inappropriate responses at all for adults.

In further analyses of the data, only the appropriate responses were considered. On studying the data, Campbell and I gradually devised a set of 13 categories in terms of which we coded the appropriate responses:

1. Participant answered the question "who or what does it?" The participant is the person or object of whom or of which the activity or process is predicated. Examples would be: "*People* walk"; "*Adults* kiss"; but also "A *plant* grows"; "*John* likes." Often these participants would be agents according to Fillmore (1968, 1969), but sometimes they would be treated within case grammar as objects or as experiencers (Fillmore, 1969).

2. Object included responses that answered the question "to whom or to what is the action done?" Examples would be: "I eat *food*"; "You kiss *people*"; "Mommy helps *me*. . . ."

3. Locative (cf. Fillmore, 1968) included responses that answered the question "where does it happen?" and told of the location in which the activity or process takes place. Examples are: "I eat *at the dinner table*"; "You play *in the park.*"

4. Situational Context answered the question "when?" and explained in what situation the action is used. Examples are: "You help someone *when they are hurt*"; "You kiss someone *good night.*"

5. Temporal also answered the question "when?" but told specifically of the time of day or year that the action or process is carried out. Examples are: "You eat *at noon*"; "You kiss *at night.*"

6. Instrumental (cf. Fillmore, 1968) answered the question "with what?" and told of the object or force by means of which the action (or process) is performed. Examples are: "You eat *with a fork*"; "I talk *with my voice.*"

7. Behavioral Manifestation answered the question "how is it shown?" and referred to any statement that expresses how the activity or process is demonstrated or manifested. An example is: "*You hug someone* that you like." for "like."

8. Coordinate answered the question "what similar actions or processes are there?" and included any verb mentioned by a subject that was similar to the verb being discussed but was not subordinate or superordinate to it. Examples would include mentioning *run* when discussing "walk" or mentioning *hug* when discussing "kiss."

9. Subordinate answered the question "what subcategories of the action or process are there?" and included mention of particular types of the action or process being discussed. There were few such cases in the present study, but *hop walking* was mentioned by one child as a type of walking and exemplifies this category.

10. Superordinate answered the question "what kind of an event is it?" and included mention of a general class of which the action or process denoted by the verb being discussed was an instance. For example, if subjects gave a response of *activity* for the word "eat' or *feeling* for the word "like," they were given credit for a superordinate.

11. Process referred to responses that answered the question "how is it done?" and included mention of how the action or process named by the verb is executed and also mention of subcomponents of the action or process. Examples would be: "Eating involves *biting, chewing and swallowing*", "When I play with my friends we *jump and hop and run.*"

12. Function referred to responses that answered the question "why is it done?" and included statements expressing the purpose or use of the activity or process denoted by the verb. Examples would be: "You eat *to nourish your body*", "You talk *in order to communicate.*"

13. Other included any statements that did not fit into any of the foregoing 12 categories. Examples would be: "Thinking is an activity *which cannot be observed*", "You can grow *emotionally.*"

To check for scoring reliability a second judge classified each response from an entire transcript for each age level into the 13 categories, and 83% agreement was found.

In general it was found that adults produced significantly more responses for the words than any of the three groups of children. The 4- and 5-year-old children, although they did not differ significantly from one another, each produced significantly more responses for all words than the 3-year-olds. This same pattern of results was found when responses to verbs denoting physical activities, social activities, and processes were examined separately. Also comparisons of the mean number of responses across these three types of verbs revealed significant differences in just one age group. The 3-year-olds produced significantly more responses to physical activities and social activities than to processes.

What I would like to concentrate on here, however, are the numbers and percentages of responses that were classified into the 13 categories just outlined. Table 4.1 shows for each age group the mean number of appropriate responses per subject across all nine verbs and the percentage of such responses for each of these categories. Although adults produced more responses to each of the 13 types than did each of the three younger groups (except for the locative and situational context categories), they only produced *significantly more* responses than each of these groups in the process, function, superordinate, behavioral manifestation, and other categories. In the situational context, instrumental, and locative categories, there were no significant differences among the age groups. This was also true for the temporal, coordinate, and subordinate categories, but these three response types were very infrequent at all age levels.

For the participant and object categories (which were the most and second most frequent types of responses, respectively, for each of the three groups of

TABLE 4.1
Mean Number and Percentage of Appropriate Responses Across All Verbs in Each Category for Each Age Group

	3 yrs		4 yrs		5 yrs		Adults	
	$\bar{x}$	%	$\bar{x}$	%	$\bar{x}$	%	$\bar{x}$	%
Participant	21.6	40.9	36.9	39.4	34.8	37.1	38.6	19.8
Object	9.7	18.4	18.3	19.5	18.4	19.6	25.4	13.0
Locative	4.3	8.1	4.4	4.7	5.6	6.0	3.7	1.9
Situational Context	3.1	5.9	5.3	5.7	6.6	7.0	6.4	3.3
Temporal	1.4	2.7	1.1	1.2	1.0	1.1	2.7	1.4
Instrumental	5.1	9.7	9.6	10.2	10.6	11.3	12.3	6.3
Behavioral Manifestation	.9	1.7	2.3	2.5	3.4	3.6	8.6	4.4
Coordinate	1.1	2.1	2.0	2.1	.7	.7	1.6	.8
Subordinate	0	0	.3	.3	.3	.3	0	0
Superordinate	0	0	0	0	0	0	5.7	2.9
Process	4.6	8.7	11.3	12.1	9.7	10.3	44.4	22.7
Function	0	0	.3	.3	.4	.4	15.6	8.0
Other	1.0	1.9	1.9	2.0	2.4	2.6	30.4	15.6

children), adults produced significantly more responses than the 3-year-olds, but not significantly more than the 4- and 5-year-olds, who in turn produced significantly more of these responses than did the youngest group. Even still, the 3-year-olds produced more responses that were classified as participant and object than any other type. Thus, children's responses tended to be classified as participants, objects, instrumentals, locatives, and situational contexts, in that order. They also mentioned processes at times, but not nearly as often as adults. Processes were the most frequent single type of response produced by adults. Adults also often produced responses classified as function, superordinate, and other, but such responses were rarely, if ever, mentioned by the children.

When we calculated the percentage of each type of response out of all the responses produced by each age group, a similar picture emerged. There were decreases in these percentages as a function of age from the youngest group to the adults in the participant, object, situational context, locative, and instrumental categories. On the other hand, there were increases in these percentages as a function of age for the process, function, other, superordinate, and behavioral manifestation categories. The percentages for the temporal, coordinate, and subordinate categories were quite low for all age levels.

Thus, this study suggests that, when discussing an activity or process denoted by the verbs we studied, preschool children are fairly adept at stating who or what does it, to what or whom it is done, where it is done, when it is done, and with what it is done. However, although they occasionally mention how it is done, they do not do so nearly as often as adults. And they rarely mention why it is done, what kind of activity or process it is, how it is manifested behaviorally, or other statements about it.

Two other aspects of our findings from this study can be briefly mentioned. The first is that as had been found in other related studies we noted a tendency for children to think in terms of particulars and to be more "instance oriented" in their descriptions of the verbs than were adults. Adults often, though not always, mentioned a more general superordinate category to which the activity or process being discussed belonged, whereas children never did. Young children would often restrict their comments about a verb to a few of the things that can do the activity or process (e.g., *flowers, a frog* when discussing the word "grow") or to a few of the objects that they can do the activity to (e.g., *carrot, popcorn, chicken* when discussing the word "eat"). On the other hand, adults would usually define the verbs in a more general way, including some mention of process and often function, and when they described who or what does the activity or process and to what or whom it is done, they again would usually respond in more general terms (e.g., *"Everything that is alive* grows"; "You eat *food"*).

Second, it should also be noted that although children only occasionally described the processes in terms of which a given activity is performed, they nonetheless showed knowledge at some level of these processes more often for some of the verbs because when we asked them to show how to _____, they often did it actually or in pretense. Thus, there were cases when the children could show how to eat, play, walk, kiss, talk, and grow, even though they did not mention a process in response to our interview question: "How do you _____?" Hence, children appear to possess more of this knowledge at some level than they verbally express.

Figures 4.5 and 4.6 show schematic representations of the knowledge expressed in this study by four children and by one adult, respectively, for the

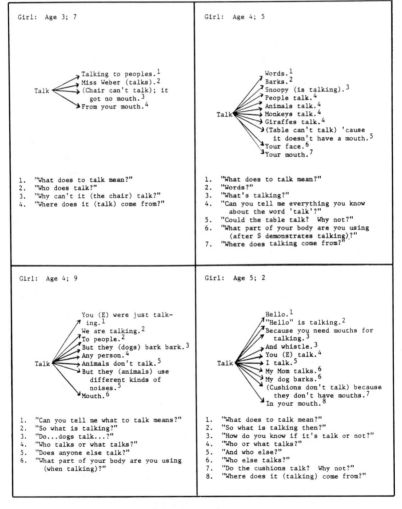

FIG. 4.5   Schematic representation of the expressible knowledge of the word *talk* for four children (data from Campbell & Anglin, in preparation).

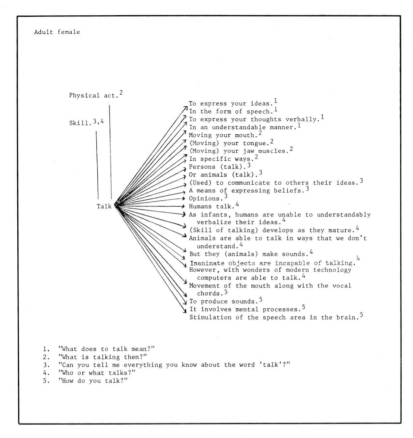

FIG. 4.6   Schematic representation of the expressible knowledge of the word *talk* for one adult (data from Campbell & Anglin, in preparation).

verb *talk*. These figures have been constructed like the previous ones and again are presented to provide the reader with specific examples of the kinds of knowledge expressed by subjects of different ages.

Motion Verbs

The second interview study with verbs (see Acknowledgments) was done by J. Gallivan (1981) who queried preschool children regarding their knowledge of the following verbs of motion: *jump, bounce, drop, float, hop, lift, kick, pull, push,* and *shake.* This set had been selected from a larger set of 217 motion verbs previously studied by Miller (1972) for which he developed a componential analysis according to which the verbs could be understood as being organized in terms of a set of 12 semantic components (see also Miller & Johnson-Laird, 1976, chap. 7). Thus Gallivan's motion verbs, unlike Campbell and Anglin's more heterogeneous set, belonged to a single semantic field. Moreover, it has been noted that verbs describing movement are among the first verbs learned by children (Brown, 1958), and it can be argued that such verbs may be among the "purest and most prototypical" of verbs in general (Miller & Johnson-Laird, 1976).

Apart from the differences in the sets of words chosen, the method used by Gallivan in her interview study was very similar to that of Campbell and Anglin (in preparation). Four groups, each containing 15 subjects, interviewed: 3-year-olds (with a mean age of 3;7), 4-year-olds (with a mean age of 4;6), 5-year-olds (with a mean age of 5;5), and adults (with a mean age of 31;10). Gallivan had generated 15 different random orders of the verbs and used one of these different random orders for each subject within each age group. Each subject was interviewed individually by Gallivan. For each of the 10 motion verbs the following questions or requests were presented with follow-ups like those used by Campbell and Anglin:

1. What does to _____ mean?
2. What is _____ing?
3. Tell me everything you know about the word _____.
4. Who or what _____s?
5. How do you _____?

The interview conversations were transcribed and then analyzed. Gallivan began by judging whether each subject's response was appropriate or not. An appropriate response did not have to express a necessary property of the verb under question; it only had to be true of the action in some situations. Only responses that were clearly incorrect or irrelevant were counted as inappropriate. To assess scoring reliability, Gallivan had a second judge classify each of the responses from eight transcripts, two at each age level, with respect to whether it was appropriate or not. It was found that there was 98% agreement between the second judge and Gallivan in terms of their classifications vis à vis appropriateness. Gallivan found that the adults produced significantly more appropriate responses than did any of the groups of children and that the 5-year-olds produced such responses significantly more than the 3-year-olds. The 4-year-olds did not differ significantly from the 3- or 5-year-olds. Although the number of inappropriate responses was relatively small at all age levels, adults produced significantly fewer inappropriate responses than either the 4- or 3-year-olds. Moreover, 5-year-olds gave such responses significantly less often than did the 4- and 3-year-olds.

To shed some light on the more interesting issue of the kinds of information about the verbs provided by the children and adults, Gallivan adapted the coding scheme developed by Campbell and me to classify appropriate responses. Of the 13 categories used by Campbell and Anglin, Gallivan found that 11 were relevant for her data and that only subordinate and behavioral manifestation were not used by any subject. Gallivan also used four other categories that had not been used by Campbell and Anglin:

1. Directional answers the question "in what direction is the action performed?" An example would be: "You jump *up and down.*"
2. Descriptive Modifier answers the question "in what way(s) may the action be performed?" and was typically expressed in terms of an adverbial phrase. Examples are: "Jump up *high*"; "You can lift something *just a short distance.*"
3. Result answers the question "what is the outcome of the action?" where the outcome would not be construed as the purpose of the action and, therefore, would not be classified as Function. An example is: "If you do it (hop) long enough, *you get tired.*"
4. Sequential Action answers the question "what action(s) might occur subsequent to the action (denoted by the verb)?" An example is: "Kick it (a ball) up to the sky *and then you try to catch it.*"

Both result and sequential action describe things that might occur following a particular action, but in the case of the result response, the subsequent event appears to be a direct result of the action, whereas it is not in the case of sequential action. For example, a 5-year-old subject in discussing the verb "drop" said: *Then you drop it and it's broken and then you have to buy another one.* In this case, Gallivan classified *and it's broken* as a result but *then you have to buy another one* as a sequential action.

An independent rater scored eight of the transcripts, two from each of the age groups, with respect to this classification scheme. It was found that there was 76% agreement on assignment of the responses to Gallivan's 15 response categories.

Because there were significant differences in the number of responses produced by the different age groups, Gallivan analyzed the category data primarily in terms of the proportion of responses falling into each of the 15 categories for each age group. In terms of these proportions, it was found that there were no significant differences across age groups for the categories situational context (e.g., "You kick something *when you're angry*"), temporal (e.g., "You're lifting *all the time*"), locative (e.g., "I bounce *on my bed*"; "You float *in water*"), or directional (e.g., "Lift something *up*"; "You jump *up and down*"). For four other categories the differences across age groups were not large or systematic: instrumental (e.g., "Bounce a ball *with your hands*"; "You kick *with your foot*"), coordinate (e.g., "Push is really the opposite of *pull*"; mention of the word *swim* in discussing the verb "float"), sequential action (e.g., "Kick it [a ball] up to the sky *and then you try to catch it*"), and descriptive modifier (e.g., "Shake something *fast*"; "Jump up *high*"). (Notice that inasmuch as the proportions for these eight categories did not change much as a function age, adults and 5-year-olds did produce more such responses in terms of absolute numbers than the 3- and 4-year-olds because, as noted previously, adults produced significantly more appropriate responses than did any other age group, and 5-year-olds produced significantly more such responses than 3- or 4-year-olds.)

Thus, for eight categories the proportions of responses did not change much as a function of age group. However, for the remaining seven categories there were large and significant differences across age groups. For each group of children, participants (e.g., "*All my friends,* they could bounce"; "*Some people* jump"; "*Leaves* drop") was by far the most frequent response type, and each group of chldren produced a significantly higher proportion of such responses ($\bar{x}$ = 41.5%) than did adults ($\bar{x}$ = 17.4%). There were no significant differences among the three groups of children in the proportion of participant responses. The second most frequent type of response for each group of children was objects (e.g., "You kick *a ball*"; "Pushing *a swing*"), and each group of children produced a significantly higher proportion of such responses ($\bar{x}$ = 20.8%) than did adults ($\bar{x}$ = 14.5%). Again, there were no significant differences among the three groups of children in the proportion of such responses. Although they were not nearly as frequent as participant or object responses, result responses (e.g., "[Push a button] and *the [garage] door goes down*"; "[Can pull glass down from the counter] and *they could break*") showed the same pattern with each group of children, producing a significantly higher proportion of such responses than adults but not differing significantly from each other (The children averaged 1.8%; the adults averaged .2%).

For the remaining four categories, on the other hand, adults produced many more responses and a significantly higher proportion of responses than each group of children in each category. In the process category (e.g., *move from side to side sort of rapidly, but not very large lateral movements* for "shake"; *having an object leave one position perhaps hit a surface and rebound off that surface* for "bounce"; *paddle your arms, kick your feet* for "float"), the proportion of such responses produced by adults was significantly higher than that produced by any of the groups of children. Moreover, 5-year-olds produced a significantly higher proportion of such responses than did 3- or 4-year-olds, between whom there was no significant difference.

Adults also produced a significantly higher proportion of responses that were classified into the function category (e.g., *to dislodge something, to mix something, to get something out* for "shake"; *to get an object closer to you* for "pull"; *it's their [rabbits] normal means of locomotion* for "hop") than did any of the groups of children, who did not differ significantly among themselves. Function responses were not mentioned by adults as frequently as they had been in the experiment by Campbell and Anglin. On the average, in Gallivan's study function was mentioned 4.20 times for the 10 verbs by the adults, whereas in the study by Campbell and Anglin the purposes of actions were usually mentioned by most adults for most verbs. Nonetheless, even in this study, function responses were mentioned considerably and significantly more often than they were by children (who rarely produced them, $\bar{x}$ = .33 for the 10 verbs).

Similarly, superordinate responses (e.g., "jumping is *an action* that . . ." "shaking is *a movement* which . . ."; "Lifting is a *physical process* by means of which . . .") were produced much more frequently by adults than by any of the groups of children. Adults did not always produce a superordinate for every verb (the average number of superordinates produced by the adults for the 10 verbs was 7.47), but all but one of the adults produced some superordinate responses. On the other hand, only one child (a 5-year-old) produced a superordinate response in Gallivan's study.

Finally, other responses (e.g., *it hurts* for "kick"; *you take a drink of liquor and they say it has a real kick to it* for "kick"; *sometimes people say they're floating and it's the feeling of being in a certain position above everything else, being on top of the world, a happy feeling* for "float"; *a check can bounce* for "bounce"; *an elevator is called a lift* for "lift"; *it's used in a slang sense like you'd boost a car, they call it jumping a car* for "jump"; *it's not good to do it* for "push") were produced far more frequently by adults than by any group of children, and the proportion of other responses produced by the adults was significantly greater than it was for each group of children, who did not differ significantly from one another on this measure. Recall that any response that could not be classified into any of the preceding 14 categories was classified as other. In this study, roughly 5% of the responses of each group of children were classified in this way, whereas about 95% of their responses fit into the 14 specific categories. For adults, on the other hand, about 14% of their responses were classified as other, whereas about 86% fell into the specific categories. A greater proportion of such other responses for adults as compared to children had also been observed in the study of object names (Anglin, 1977, 1978) and the study by Campbell and Anglin (in preparation).

Gallivan noted that several of these other responses mentioned by adults were related to the basic action meanings but were derivative senses or metaphorical extensions of them. Examples were *lifting someone's spirits* for "lift" or *a check can bounce* for "bounce". When she analysed the other responses of adults and children specifically for derivative or metaphorical extensions, she found that none of the children had ever talked about the verbs in this way, whereas 11 of the 15 adults had. For the 11 adults who had, the average number of words for which they produced such metaphorical extensions or derivative senses was 5.55. According to Gallivan, one possible reason for this outcome is that the meanings of these words were more general and abstract for the adults than for the children.

Gallivan did another analysis of her data which also suggested that the children conceived of the verbs in more specific terms than did the adults. Recall that the most frequent type of response given by the children was participants. Gallivan examined the participant responses produced by all subjects according to whether they referred to particular individuals or not. Participant responses were classified as having referred to specific individuals if they were expressed as proper names (e.g., *Johnny* including words like *Mommy* and *Daddy*), if they were used in the singular (e.g., *Mommy* vs. *Mommies*), if they were expressed in terms of the personal pronouns (e.g., *I, me,* and *you* if "you" was in reference to the experimenter), or if they were expressed by means of a possessive pronoun followed by a singular noun (e.g., *my brother,* but not *my friends*). Overall she found that 39.62% of the participant responses of the 3-year-olds referred to specific individuals, a figure that dropped to 27.29% for the 4-year-olds, to 11.94% for the 5-year-olds, and finally to .01% for the adults. Similarly when she looked at just the participant responses that were produced in response to the question "Who or what _____s?" she found that 56% of these responses by the 3-year-olds referred to specific individuals, a figure that dropped monotonically to 32.98%, 15.85%, and 0.46% for the 4-year-olds, 5-year-olds, and adults, respectively. Gallivan found for each of these analyses that adults produced a significantly smaller proportion of specific responses than did each of the groups of children and that the 5-year-olds produced a significantly smaller proportion than the 3-year-olds.

At this point it would be instructive to compare the results from these analyses by Gallivan on her set of motion verbs with those obtained by Campbell and Anglin summarized earlier on a more heterogeneous set of verbs. Overall the results from the two studies were strikingly similar, although there were certainly differences worthy of mention. In both studies, the youngest children most often talked in terms of participants and objects, often exclusively. In both studies, each of the groups of children produced a larger proportion of these two types of responses than did the adults. Both studies also showed the children to be able at times to mention situational context, locative, and instrumental responses, and there were no large differences in the tendency to produce such responses by children as compared to adults. Nor were there large differences with age in the tendency to produce temporal or coordinate responses, although these categories were relativly infrequent at all age levels in both studies. On the other hand, in both studies it was found that adults produced a strikingly greater number and higher proportion of process, function, superordinate, and other responses.

With respect to the differences between the two studies, the following two seem most important. First, Campbell and Anglin used two categories (behavioral manifestation and subordinate) that were not relevant to Gallivan's data, and Gallivan used four categories (directional, descriptive modifier, result, and sequential action) that had not been used by Campbell and Anglin. Nonetheless, the vast majority of responses (about 90% in Gallivan's study; about 95% in Campbell & Anglin's study) could be classified into the 11 categories that were common to both studies. Second, even though the adults in both studies produced function responses significantly more often than any group of children, who almost never produced such responses, the adults in Gallivan's study did not produce function responses (mean per subject per verb = .42) as often as did the adults in Campbell and Anglin's study (mean per subject per verb = 1.73).

Thus, there were differences across the two studies that are probably attributable largely to the different domains of verbs investigated. Nonetheless, the similarities described earlier are more striking. There was an additional similarity in the findings of the two studies beyond those that have been mentioned which pertains not to the verbal responses provided in the interview task, but rather to the relation between these verbal responses and the child's ability to demonstrate the actions denoted by the verbs behaviorally. As had been the case in study by Campbell and Anglin, children were often observed by Gallivan to be able to demonstrate a given action behaviorally either spontaneously or when requested to "show me how to _____," even though in such cases they often did not describe how the action is done verbally in terms of process responses. Thus, for example, one girl (3;11) could show in reasonable fashion how to shake, push, jump, kick, pull, and even float, and a boy (4;7) showed how to pull, shake, push, kick, bounce, hop, drop, and jump, but they did not describe how to do these things verbally when requested. Such observations suggest that even though these children did not usually describe the processes involved in executing the actions denoted by the verbs, they did at some level appreciate these processes more than their verbal behavior revealed.

A last analysis by Gallivan will complete my summary of her study. The analyses just described did not directly assess the extent to which subjects produced descriptions that were *defining* of the concepts being discussed. In order to get at this, Gallivan performed an analysis similar to the one by Benson and Anglin in terms of level of definitions, described earlier. Gallivan began by postulating for each of the motion verbs a set of criterial properties, which she felt should be expressed in an accurate definition of the verb. For example, for the verb *jump* the criterial properties were postulated to be: (1) motion/movement, (2) into the air/off a surface, (3) caused by muscular force/effort/action, and (4) by legs/feet. For the verb *pull* the criterial properties were postulated to be: (1) to move (or tend to move) something, (2) by force/effort/physical action, (3) in a direction toward the source/agent. Each subject's descriptions of each verb were then classified into one of six categories according to how well they defined the verb in view of these criterial properties. Any description that included an accurate general definition was classified into the highest level (Category 5). This description must have included mention of all of the criterial properties postulated by Gallivan, and it must have been stated generally enough to apply to all concept instances. Any description that included all the criterial properties but stated so that they did not apply to all concept instances was classified in the next level (Category 4). For example, one description of "pull" was *it's involving your muscles and moving the object toward you,* which was classified into Category 4. In this description the three criterial properties were alluded to, but because the force involved in pulling does not always involve muscles (e.g., a boxcar on a train, which is pulled by the engine), this definition was not considered to be general enough to apply to all concept instances. A description that included mention of one or more of the postulated criterial properties, but not the entire set, was assigned to Category 3. Descriptions that included mention of properties that are characteristic, but not criterial or defining, of the action denoted by the verb were assigned to Category 2. For example, if a subject talked about "jumping *up and down,*" this was considered to be a characteristic property because jumping is often, but not always, done in an up and down direction; therefore, it is probably characteristic of this motion pattern for many people. Descriptions were assigned to Category 1 if they referred only to specific instances of the concept. If descriptions included only examples of the action denoted by the verb (e.g., *pulling a string*) or references to personal experience (e.g., *Steven pushed me home*), they were classified at this level. Finally, descriptions were classified into the lowest level (Category 0) if no appropriate responses at all were mentioned for a verb.

Each subject's descriptions for each verb were classified according to this system. When subjects produced responses in their descriptions that could be classified at different levels, the highest category was assigned. To assess scoring reliability, Gallivan asked a second judge to classify the descriptions produced by two subjects from each age group into this classification scheme. Overall, 79% agreement was obtained.

Gallivan then averaged the scores (from 0 to 5 according to category level) for each subject across the 10 words. These scores were then averaged across all 15 subjects for each age group, and she found that the mean level of definitional scores increased as a function of age group with the 3-year-olds achieving a mean score of 1.35, the 4-year-olds 1.44, the 5-year-olds 1.96, and the adults 3.19. Mann-Whitney U tests revealed that adults scored significantly higher on this measure than did any of the groups of children and that the 5-year-olds scored higher than the 4- and 3-year-olds, between whom there was no significant difference. Thus, the aptness of the descriptions as definitions generally increased with age.

When the distribution of the 150 verb descriptions produced by each age group across the six category levels was examined, it was found that the 3-

and 4-year-olds' modal type of definition fell into Category 1 with about 2/3 of their descriptions being of this type. Next most frequent for these groups were Category 2 followed by Category 3. None of their descriptions were classified as Category 4 or 5. For the five-year-olds the most frequent types were Categories 2 and 3, with a roughly equal number of their descriptions being classified at these two levels. For adults the most frequent level was Category 3, with 2/3 of their descriptions being classified at this level. The next most frequent type was Category 4. Only 5 (out of 150) of the adults' definitions were classified as Category 5, and these were the only definitions provided by any subjects in any age group to be classified at this level. None of the adults' descriptions were classified into either of the two lowest levels, although a relatively small number of them (13 out of 150) were classified into Category 2.

It is possible to rank order the 10 motion verbs studied by Gallivan in terms of the mean definitional level achieved by the children. Such a ranking has sometimes been used as a measure of order of acquisition of a set of words (e.g., Benson & Anglin, in preparation; Haviland & Clark, 1974). Gallivan did this and arrived at the following order in which the first verb has the highest definitional level: (1) *kick*; (2) *hop*; (3) *lift*; (4–5) *jump* and *float* (a tie); (6) *push*; (7–8) *bounce* and *drop*; (9–10) *shake* and *pull*.

One might be tempted to use this ranking as an estimate of the order of acquisition of these words. However, Gallivan found that this ranking was not correlated with other estimates of the order of acquisition of the words based on production and comprehension, which led her to conclude that referential and definitional tasks assess different aspects of word knowledge. It is also of some interest that none of the rankings provided by Gallivan's three tasks were well predicted by a measure of semantic complexity of the verbs that Gallivan derived from Miller's (1972) componential analysis. However, it should be noted that Miller's (1972) componential analysis was based on the method of incomplete definitions, and the components he identified were of a general nature and only those which seemed to be shared by a reasonably large number of the motion verbs he studied. For this and other reasons, Miller's (1972) componential analysis may not provide a measure of "cumulative semantic complexity" (cf. Brown, 1973) for the motion verbs, and therefore, the conclusion that complexity is a poor predictor of the order of acquisition of Gallivan's motion verbs should be regarded as tentative. Nonetheless, it is interesting that as Miller (1972) had anticipated the most complicated verbs in terms of shared semantic components according to his analysis (e.g., *hop* and *jump*) were not found by Gallivan to be acquired relatively late according to any of her measures. Nor were the simpler verbs in terms of shared semantic components according to Miller (1972) found to be acquired relatively early. For example, the word *float* was the simplest of the verbs studied by Gallivan in terms of Miller's (1972) componential analysis, but in terms of definitional level, it was ranked as being tied with *jump* at fourth place; in terms of Gallivan's production and comprehension measures, it was ranked as being acquired last in each case.

Figure 4.7 shows four schematic representations of the knowledge expressed in Gallivan's study of motion verbs by three children and one adult for the verb *jump*.

DISCUSSION

In view of the studies that have been summarized, I shall conclude this chapter by discussing some of the uses to which the interview method can be put, some of the differences that result from this method when different domains

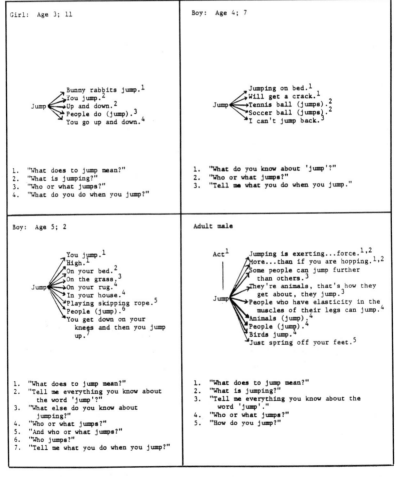

FIG. 4.7   Schematic representation of the expressible knowledge of the word *jump* for three children and one adult (data from Gallivan, 1981).

of words are studied, some general developmental trends that seem to hold across the various domains investigated, and finally, some limitations and qualifications regarding inferences that might be drawn from interview studies about the nature of semantic development.

The interview procedure can be used to study what children and adults are able to express about their knowledge of a variety of domains of words, some of which could not be studied easily using extensional methods of the type discussed in the introduction to this chapter. Of the words investigated in the four studies that have been summarized, the kin terms and a few of the verbs (especially *like* and *think*) would have been difficult to study using referential paradigms. However, there is no reason to believe that the interview method could not also be adapted to investigate various other domains such as abstract nouns (e.g., *dream, feeling*), abstract verbs (e.g., *wish, imagine*), abstract adjectives (e.g., *good, generous, intelligent*), adverbs (e.g., *very, happily*), and probably certain prepositions (e.g., *above*), conjunctions (e.g., *or*), and others for which simple referential methods would not be suitable. The technique can be used with preschool children as young as 3 years for at least some domains of words as well as with older children, adolescents, and adults. Our experience has indicated that it is not an appropriate procedure for children younger than 3, but even 3-year-olds can express a considerable amount of knowledge about some words in spite of the seemingly metalinguistic nature of the task, and what they do express is often rich, fascinating, and does provide at least some insight into what the words mean to them and their knowledge of them.

Comparisons of the knowledge expressed by children of different ages and by adults for a given word or domain of words reveal some interesting developmental trends in what individuals articulate about the words as a function of age. Further, comparisons of such trends across different domains reveal interesting differences as a function of different types of lexical items. By comparing the knowledge expressed by children of different ages about certain words, or types of words, with either idealized definitions of those words or with the corresponding knowledge expressed by adults about them, one can get a fairly precise feeling for which of the components of knowledge included in idealized or relatively advanced definitions or descriptions children express and which they do not. By means of such comparisons, it is also possible to rank a set of words in terms of mean level of definition achieved by children, and such a ranking might be used as an estimate of the order of acquisition of the words (e.g., as was done in the previously summarized study of kin terms; see also Haviland & Clark, 1974). It is possible, moreover, to compare such a ranking with various metrics (e.g., of complexity, of familiarity, etc.) to test hypotheses about predictors of the order of acquisition of vocabulary.

The study of different semantic domains with the interview procedure has led me to the feeling that it is difficult to overestimate the importance of differences across different domains of words. Of course, each different word will be defined by adults and often by children in terms of different specific properties. However, for fairly homogeneous domains of words or semantic fields, words are often described or defined, to some extent at least, in terms of the same general types of properties. Thus, concrete nouns or basic level object terms (cf. Rosch,1978; Rosch et al., 1976) such as *dog, apple,* and *book* are often described by preschool children in terms of use, activity, appearance, and location (Anglin, 1977, 1978; Norlin, 1981). However, preschool children describe domains such as kin terms less frequently and domains such as motion verbs much less frequently in terms of these types of properties. Many previous studies of children's definitions (e.g., Al-Issa, 1969; Feifel & Lorge, 1950; Nelson, 1978; Norlin, 1980; Watson, 1982; Wolman & Barker, 1965) including my own studies (Anglin, 1977, 1978) have consistently reported that children often define words in terms of use or function. However, all of these studies focused primarily, and in many cases exclusively, on concrete nouns. In our study of kin terms, we found that use or function was not mentioned quite as frequently by children or by adults. And in the two studies of verbs described in this paper, it was found that although function (in the sense of purpose) was often mentioned by adults (although less often in the case of motion verbs), it was rarely mentioned by children for any of the verbs. Thus, the tendency in preschool children to define words in terms of use or function seems to apply especially to concrete nouns. The types of knowledge expressed by adults also varied dramatically across different domains (cf. theoretical analyses by Miller & Johnson-Laird, 1976).

In this regard it is interesting to contrast the kinds of information produced by preschool children and by adults for some simple concrete nouns, which are among the earliest nouns to be learned by children (e.g., *dog, apple, car, flower,* etc.), versus some relatively simple verbs, which are among the first verbs to be learned by children (e.g., *eat, play, jump,* *kick,* etc.). For simple concrete nouns in the interview situation, preschool children provide information that tends to answer the questions: (1) What do referents of the word look like? (2) What do they do? (3) What can you do with them? and, (4) Where do you find them? Thus, they tend to supply information about the appearances (or forms), the activities, the uses, and the locations of referents of such words. Adults, when discussing such nouns, provide information that answers these questions as well but also information that answers questions such as the following: (5) What kinds of things are they? (6) What kinds of them are there? (7) Where do they come from? (8) What are their internal constituents? (9) What are their relations with other things in the world? Thus, in addition to the four basic or concrete properties most often mentioned by children, adults also often provide information regarding superordinates, subordinates, origins, internal constituents, relations with other things, and others, including metaphorical extensions or derivative senses for some of the words.

In contrast, for some simple verbs, preschool children most often provide information that answers the questions: (1) Who or what does it? (2) To what or whom is it done? They also answer, though somewhat less frequently: (3) Where is it done? (4) When is it done? and (5) With what is it done? (cf. Nelson, 1978). Thus, they most often provide information about the participants and objects of the activities denoted by such verbs as well as information about the locations and situational contexts in which these activities are done and the instruments with which they are performed. Adults are quite capable of supplying these kinds of information, but they supply other kinds as well. Although children occasionally provide information that answers the question: (6) How is it done? they do not do so nearly to the extent that adults do, for whom description of process seems to be very important in their definitions and discussions of such simple verbs. Moreover, adults often provide information that answers the questions: (7) Why is it done? and (8) What kind of an activity or process is it? which preschool children rarely provide. Moreover, adults express other kinds of information about such verbs including metaphorical extensions or derivative senses, which preschoolers infrequently do. Thus, in addition to describing participants, objects, locational information, situational contexts, and instruments, adults also mention processes, functions (or purposes), superordinates, and various other kinds of information including metaphorical extensions or derivative senses for these verbs much more frequently than do young children.

Figure 4.8 roughly illustrates the general kinds of knowledge expressed by preschool children and by adults for some concrete nouns and for some relatively simple verbs in terms of schematic representations. The two long horizontal arrows in the center of Fig. 4.8 are meant to indicate the direction of developmental change. Naturally, for any given concrete noun or simple verb a given child or adult may not always express all of the general types of information indicated in the schematic representations, and sometimes he or she might express other general types of information not shown in the figure. For example, objects would not be expressed by children or by adults for intransitive verbs. In the two studies of verbs described earlier, almost all of the verbs had at least one transitive or objective sense, although verbs such as *jump, walk, grow,* and *hop* were often discussed by some adults and by many children without mention of objects. Similarly, as previously noted, certain kinds of information were expressed in Gallivan's study of motion verbs (e.g., directional information), which did not occur in Campbell and Anglin's study of a more heterogeneous set of verbs frequently enough to induce us to use such categories in our coding scheme. I have not included such categories in Fig. 4.8, but their occurrence in the study of motion verbs illustrates the fact that certain kinds of fairly simple verbs evoke types of information

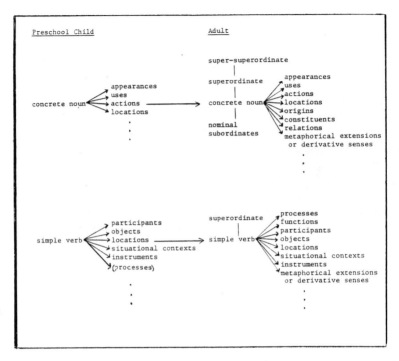

FIG. 4.8   Schematic representation of the general kinds of knowledge expressed by pre-school children and by adults for some concrete nouns and for some relatively simple verbs. The two long horizontal arrows in the center of the figure indicate the direction of developmental change.

that other fairly simple verbs do not. Indeed, such differences arise even within a fairly homogeneous semantic field such as motion verbs (cf. Miller, 1972), and they certainly occur across different semantic fields within the same part of speech. Similar points could be made about the schematic representations for concrete nouns. Of course, I have not attempted to represent superordinates or kin terms and some other kinds of nouns (e.g., abstract nouns) in Fig. 4.8 because the knowledge expressed by children and by adults about them is quite different from the knowledge expressed about concrete or basic-level object names. Even within the domain of concrete nouns, there are differences. For example, use tends to be mentioned more often for names of human artifacts (e.g., *ball, car*) than for some natural kind terms (e.g., *tree, lion*). And of course, as mentioned earlier, even different words from the same homogeneous semantic field (e.g., *cat* and *dog*) will be shown to elicit different kinds of information from both children and adults if a fairly specific scheme is used to code such information. Thus, Fig. 4.8 is simplified and general and is presented primarily to provide a rough contrast of the different kinds of knowledge often expressed by children and by adults for some concrete nouns versus some relatively simple verbs.

Although there are a few similarities in terms of the general kinds of information provided by children and adults for simple nouns versus relatively simple verbs (e.g., mention of locational information by children in both cases; production of superordinates and of metaphorical extensions or derivative senses by adults but not by children in both cases), the differences are more numerous and more striking. There were differences even in the case of the apparent similarities. For example, metaphorical extensions and derivative senses were mentioned by adults (for whatever reason) more frequently for the verbs than for the nouns (cf. Gentner, 1981, 1982). With respect to the production of superordinates, preschool children, though not adept at producing superordinates in either case, were sometimes observed to produce them for simple nouns but virtually never for relatively simple verbs. Adults who usually produced superordinates for nouns and often a number of them (e.g., *pet, mammal, animal, living thing* for "dog") only occasionally produced more than one superordinate for the verbs and sometimes none at all. Adults also produced subordinates infrequently for the verbs, whereas they usually mentioned many for the nouns, suggesting that verbs do not have the hierarchical depth that nouns do.

Thus, simple nouns appear to be semantically quite different from simple verbs in adults as well as children, as Gentner (1978, 1981, 1982) has suggested (at least insofar as interview data are relevant to inferences about semantics, to be discussed shortly). Also, inconsistent with arguments put forward by Gentner, it is my impression that preschool children have a better appreciation of the meanings of simple nouns than of simple verbs, at least as indicated by their descriptions and definitions, because they sometimes mention almost-defining properties for the former, such as use and action, whereas for the latter they infrequently mention almost-defining properties, such as process and function or purpose (see Litowitz, 1977). For similar reasons, my impression is that preschool children also have a better appreciation of the meanings of concrete nouns then they do of kin terms, again to the extent that interview data are relevant to inferences about meanings.

In spite of these differences and others across the different domains of words studied, there are some very general and quite related similarities in the developmental trends that emerged from the different interview studies. Four of these similarities can be described here. First, to a degree, younger preschool children appear to base their responses upon their recollection of personal experiences. It is possible that I have overemphasized this tendency in young children in the past (cf. Nelson, 1978), but relative to older children and especially to adults, this seems to be the case. Each of the four studies summarized in this chapter suggested this, and each suggested that increasingly with age, responses in the interview task become somewhat less tied to personal experience.

Second, young children tend to mention more perceptually observable or concrete properties of the words. Increasingly with age, they mention, in addition, more subtle, more relational, and more abstract kinds of properties. Again, each study suggested this in one way or another.

Third, young preschool children infrequently assign the words to a superordinate class. Increasingly with age and especially by adulthood, they do so more frequently. This was also suggested by each of the studies.

Fourth, increasingly with age, children's descriptions of words approximate definitions, by which I mean that increasingly they tend to supply the kinds of properties included in dictionary definitions of the words, which tend to specify all and only the referents of the words. One can postulate a continuum of word descriptions in terms of the extent to which they approximate definitions from not known, to responses based on personal experience, to characteristic properties, to some defining properties, to all or most defining properties. As children get older, their responses tend to move up this kind of scale. Of course, even adults do not always produce definitions of the most advanced type on such a scale, and a given child's descriptions often fit at different levels on such a scale depending on the words he or she has discussed (cf. Keil and Batterman, in press). Moreover, it is not necessarily the case, and indeed it seems unlikely, that for any given word, children's descriptions would always move up such a scale step by step in an invariant sequence. (Longitudinal investigations would appear to be necessary to shed light conclusively on this.) However, children's responses about the words seemed generally to move up this kind of scale as they got older. This was explicitly shown in the studies of kin terms and motion verbs, and it seemed to be the case for the other studies as well (see also Keil and Batterman, in press; Litowitz, 1977).

Progress in terms of each of these developmental trends seemed more rapid for the object names than for the kin terms or verbs. Nonetheless, each of the studies tended to suggest each of these progressions in spite of differences in rate across the domains of words studied.

I would like to conclude this chapter by mentioning and, in what I see as the most important case, discussing some of the limitations and problems associated with interview studies of the kind described in this chapter vis à vis inferences that can be drawn from them regarding semantic development. First, as noted earlier, my experience has been that this procedure is not suitable for children less than 3 years of age. For reasons that may include linguistic constraints in the child, the metalinguistic nature of the task, and/or factors of interest and attention, children younger than about 3 years do not often produce much meaningful information in this kind of interview setting, even though it is clear that children between 1 and 3 years of age do learn many words that do have meaning for them. For such children, different methods are necessary to illuminate their appreciation of the semantic and conceptual structure underlying their words.

Second, in retrospect, certain interesting issues could have been examined in the studies that have been described with certain modifications in the methods or analyses employed. For example, many words are polysemous, and it would be interesting to study the child's understanding of the different senses of a given word or set of words (Miller, 1978). The interview procedure can be used to study the acquisition of the different senses of polysemous words as a study by one of my students, Colin Clark, is showing. But this study is not far enough along yet to be described here. The studies described in this chapter do suggest that the number of derivative senses or metaphorical extensions mentioned for words increases with development, but they were not designed or analyzed to shed much light on the issue of polysemy directly. It has also occurred to me in retrospect that it would have been interesting to ask certain other questions about the words. For example, an interesting finding from the studies of verbs was that adults tended to describe why actions denoted by the verbs are performed in terms of their functions or purposes, whereas preschool children did not. In view of this, it might have been interesting to ask subjects a question like "Why do people _____?" to see if children might describe this sort of information when directly asked for it. As a final example, it might have been interesting to analyze responses to the first definitional question ("What is a _____?"; "What does _____ mean?") separately from the other subsequent questions (cf. Nelson, 1978; Watson, 1982) as a possible way of trying to distinguish definitional meaning from encyclopedic knowledge or core meaning from peripheral meaning (even though I should add that I would anticipate problems with operationally defining core meaning vs. encyclopedic knowledge in this way). These are examples of some interesting things to do in studies like those described in this paper. Although they were not done in these studies, it is encouraging to note that they could be done in future studies or analyses.

Third, in each of the studies summarized in this paper, in addition to the basic sets of questions about the words, additional probe questions were also asked on occasion to follow up on subjects' responses and to clarify what knowledge they seemed to be trying to express. This kind of flexibility in the questioning was introduced in the hopes of helping subjects express their knowledge as well as possible. Such follow-up questions have been used by Piaget in his clinical interviews (e.g., Piaget, 1928, 1929) and by many others who have used the interview procedure (e.g., Danziger, 1957; Haviland & Clark, 1974; Norlin, 1981). However, care must be taken when asking such additional questions to assure that the interviewer does not supply the subject with relevant information. Actually, in the studies described in this chapter (and in many other interview studies), I believe this was rarely a problem because a deliberate attempt was made to use general probes which did not supply specific relevant information. Nonetheless, it should be mentioned that such care should be taken lest one overestimate what the child knows.

Fourth, and finally, there is the opposite and much more serious possibility of underestimating what the child knows on the basis of interview data. The interview task assesses what knowledge children can articulate or express verbally about the words they attempt to describe. It is quite possible, indeed probable, that because of the metalinguistic nature of the task and/or constraints in children's capacity to express themselves verbally, they may not always reveal all that they know implicitly about the words (cf. Anglin, 1977, 1978; Litowitz, 1977; Nelson, 1978; Norlin, 1980; Watson, 1982). Indeed, in at least two important cases in the studies described in this chapter, it is fairly clear that the preschool children were not always expressing important items of knowledge about some of the words, which in some sense they may have appreciated tacitly or implicitly.

The first example is that in both studies of verbs children only occasionally *described* how to perform or enact the actions denoted by the verbs in terms of processes, whereas adults almost always described processes in their discussions of the verbs. However, when children were asked to *show* how to act out the verbs with specific requests for a behavioral demonstration (e.g., "Show me how to jump"; "Show me how to eat"), they could in fact often perform reasonably appropriate actions. Sometimes they demonstrated these actions spontaneously. They did not always give appropriate behavioral demonstrations for all of the verbs, and some of their demonstrations were not always perfectly accurate, but they could often do this to such an extent that it seemed clear that at some level they appreciated the processes involved in the actions denoted by the verbs to a greater degree than they revealed in their verbal descriptions.

Second, even in the case of concrete-object names, it was found that preschool children only infrequently produced superordinate terms such as *animal* for "dog," *fruit* or *food* for "apple," and so on. However, other studies using different methods have indicated that even most 3-year-olds appreciate that various animals are called *animals,* that various foods are called *food,* that various toys are called *toys* and so forth (e.g., Anglin, 1977; Macnamara, 1982). Similarly, in a recent study of the child's definitions of certain concrete nouns, Watson (1982) found that although 5-year-old children infrequently produced superordinates in response to the standard definition question "What is a _____?" they produced more such responses when the question was asked again with emphasis on the copula ("What *is* a _____?"). Moreover, in a test of comprehension, these same children showed a still greater degree of appreciation of superordinates. As Watson (1982) and Litowitz (1977) have pointed out, younger children may not yet have learned that in defining a noun, part of the standard form of the response is to begin the definiens with a superordinate, even though they may at some level appreciate the superordinate categories to which at least some of the words they attempt to define belong (see also Nelson & Earl, 1973).

These two examples illustrate the clearest and most important cases for which there is fairly convincing independent evidence that children do not always express all they know about words in the interview situation. They do, however, raise the possibility that this may be true in other cases as well. For example, it may be that at some tacit level preschool children sometimes appreciated the functions of verbs or the superordinate categories to which they belonged even though they virtually never expressed this understanding verbally. However, I have no independent evidence that this was the case, and therefore, it is difficult to decide one way or the other. Thus, in drawing inferences about the meanings of words for children on the basis of interview data, I now feel that one can be fairly safe in attributing what children express about words to their understanding of their meanings, provided this knowledge was not suggested by leading questions. However, I also feel that it is not safe to assume that children do not appreciate aspects of their meanings or of the concepts they signify only because they have not expressed such aspects in the interview task. To decide about aspects of meaning and knowledge that the child has not expressed, it would seem prudent to withold judgment until other methods, perhaps especially tests of comprehension, were administered as well.

Therefore, as indicated by the title of this chapter, the interview method tells us what children can *express* about their word meanings and word concepts. This may well be what is most accessible and salient for them about, these meanings and concepts and, therefore, is of considerable relevance for our understanding of the growth of word meanings and the development of semantic memory. But the interview method may not tell us everything children understand implicitly or tacitly about their words. Thus, just as I argued in the introduction to this chapter that it is necessary for the developmental psycholinguist concerned with semantic development to supplement referential tests with other methods, so I am now arguing that it is necessary to supplement interview and definitional tasks with other methods as well. Indeed, it seems unlikely that any single task will provide all or even most of the answers to questions about semantic development. Rather, it seems that a variety of different but complementary methods will ultimately be necessary to unravel the mysteries about this aspect of the child's language development.

ACKNOWLEDGMENTS

This chapter was written while I was a Visiting Fellow at Princeton University during a sabbatical. I would like to take this opportunity to thank Dr. George Miller, mentor and colleague, for constructive suggestions and criticisms concerning this work and more generally for helping to make my sabbatical a most rewarding experience. I am also grateful to Dr. Juan Pascual-Leone for useful discussions concerning the distinction between extension and intension, to Drs. David Olson and Rita Watson for enlightening me about children's definitions, and to Drs. Susan Carey and Wolfgang Wannenmacher for their helpful comments regarding the implications of interview data for inferences about semantic development. I would also like to thank the excellent students who have worked with me on the studies reported in this chapter. Marc Fiedler and Sophia Cohen helped immensely with the analysis of the results from the study on object names. Nancy Benson conducted the study of kin terms with great care, and the study by Benson and Anglin (in preparation) summarized in this chapter grew out of her undergraduate honors thesis, which I supervised. She was a joy to work with. Similarly, the first study of verbs by Campbell and Anglin (in preparation) grew out of Lois Campbell's undergraduate honors thesis, which I supervised. I enjoyed working with her very much. I would also like to thank Dr. Joanne Gallivan who conducted the study of motion verbs. This was the third study of her interesting doctoral dissertation, which I supervised, and I am most grateful to her for providing me with examples from her data illustrating the various types of responses made by children and by adults when discussing the motion verbs. Finally, I would like to express my appreciation to Drs. Leslie Rescorla, Dedre Gentner, Sam Glucksberg, and Keith Nelson for helpful comments on an earlier version of this chapter.

REFERENCES

Al-Issa, I. The development of word definitions in children. *Journal of Genetic Psychology,* 1969, *114,* 25–28.

Anglin, J. M. *Word, object, and conceptual development.* New York: Norton, 1977.

Anglin, J. M. From reference to meaning. *Child Development,* 1978, *49,* 969–976.

Anglin, J. M. The child's first terms of reference. In N. R. Smith & M. B. Franklin (Eds.), *Symbolic functioning in childhood.* Hillsdale, N.J.: Lawrence Erlbaum Associates, 1979.

Anglin, J. M. Modeling conceptual structure. Review of E. Smith & D. Medin, *Categories and concepts. Canadian Journal of Psychology,* 1982, *9,* 554–558.

Anglin, J. M. Extensional aspects of the preschool child's word concepts. In T. Seiler & W. Wannenmacher (Eds.), *Concept development and the development of word meaning.* New York: Springer-Verlag, 1983.

Bates, E. *Language and context.* New York: Academic Press, 1976.

Benson, N., & Anglin, J. M. *The child's knowledge of English kin terms.* In preparation. (A preliminary report was presented at the meeting of the Society for Research in Child Development, Boston, April 1981.)

Bierwisch, M. Semantics. In J. Lyons (Ed.), *New horizons in linguistics.* Baltimore: Penguin, 1970.

Bierwisch, M., & Kiefer, F. Remarks on definitions in natural languages. In F. Kiefer (Ed.), *Studies in syntax and semantics.* Dordrecht, Holland: Reidel, 1969.

Bloom, L. M. *One word at a time.* The Hague: Mouton, 1973.

Bowerman, M. The acquisition of word meaning: An investigation of some current conflicts. In N. Waterson & C. Snow (Eds.), *Procedings of the Third International Child Language Symposium.* New York: Wiley, 1977.

Brown, R. How shall a thing be called? *Psychological Review,* 1958, *65,* 14–21.

Brown, R. *A first language.* Cambridge, Mass.: Harvard University Press, 1973.

Bruner, J. S., Goodnow, J., & Austin, G. *A study of thinking.* New York: Wiley, 1956.

Campbell, L., & Anglin, J. M. What children can say about the meanings of verbs. In preparation.

Carnap, R. *Meaning and necessity.* Chicago: University of Chicago Press, 1947.

Chamberlain, A. F., & Chamberlain, J. Studies of a child I. *Pedagogical Seminary,* 1904, *11,* 264–291. (a)

Chamberlain, A. F., & Chamberlain, J. Studies of a child II. *Pedagogical Seminary,* 1904, *11,* 452–483. (b)

Chambers, J. C., & Tavuchis, N. Kids and kin: Children's understanding of American kin terms. *Journal of Child Language,* 1976, *3,* 63–80.

Clark, E. V. What's in a word? On the child's acquisition of semantics in his first language. In T. E. Moore (Ed.), *Cognitive development and the acquisition of language.* New York: Academic Press, 1973.

Clark, E. V. Knowledge, context, and strategy in the acquisition of word meaning. In D. P. Dato (Ed.), *Georgetown University Round Table on Language and Linguistics.* Washington, D.C.: Georgetown University Press, 1975.

Clark, E. V. Strategies for communicating. *Child Development,* 1978, *49,* 953–959.

Clark, E. V. Building a vocabulary: Words for objects, actions, and relations. In P. Fletcher & M. Garman (Eds.), *Studies in language acquisition.* Cambridge: Cambridge University Press, 1979.

Clark, E. V., & Garnica, O. K. Is he coming or going? On the acquisition of deictic verbs. *Journal of Verbal Learning and Verbal Behavior,* 1974, *13,* 559–572.

Danziger, K. The child's understanding of kinship terms: A study in the development of relational concepts. *Journal of Genetic Psychology,* 1957, *91,* 213–232.

Elkind, D. Child's conceptions of brother and sister: Piaget replication study V. *Journal of Genetic Psychology,* 1962, *100,* 129–136.

Feifel, H., & Lorge, I. Qualitative differences in the vocabulary responses of children. *Journal of Educational Psychology,* 1950, *41,* 1–18.

Fein, G. A transformational analysis of pretending. *Developmental Psychology,* 1975, *11,* 291–296.

Fillmore, C. The case for case. In E. Bach & T. Harms (Eds.), *Universals in linguistic theory.* New York: Holt, Rinehart & Winston, 1968.

Fillmore, C. Types of lexical information. In F. Kiefer (Ed.), *Studies in syntax and semantics.* Dordrecht, Holland: Reidel, 1969.

Fremgen, A., & Fay, D. Overextensions in production and comprehension: A methodological clarification. *Journal of Child Language,* 1980, *7,* 205–211.

Gallivan, J. *The acquisition of English motion verbs.* Unpublished doctoral dissertation, University of Waterloo, 1981.

Gentner, D. Evidence for the psychological reality of semantic components: The verbs of possession. In D. A. Norman & D. E. Rumelhart (Eds.), *Explorations in cognition.* San Francisco: Freeman, 1975.

Genter, D. On relational meaning: The acquisition of verb meaning. *Child Development,* 1978, *49,* 988–998.

Gentner, D. Some interesting differences between verbs and nouns. *Cognition and Brain Theory,* 1981, *4*(2), 161–178.

Gentner, D. Why nouns are learned before verbs: Linguistic relativity versus natural partitioning. In S. Kuczaj (Ed.), *Language development: Language, cognition and culture.* Hillsdale, N.J.: Lawrence Erlbaum Associates, 1982.

Goldin-Meadow, S., Seligman, M., & Gelman, R. Language in the two-year-old. *Cognition,* 1976, *4,* 189–202.

Goodman, N. On likeness of meaning. In N. Goodman (Ed.), *Problems and projects.* Indianapolis, Ind.: Bobbs-Merrill, 1972.

Gruendel, J. M. Referential extension in early child language. *Child Development,* 1977, *42,* 1567–1576.

Haviland, S., & Clark, E. This man's father is my father's son: A study of the acquisition of English kin terms. *Journal of Child Language,* 1974, *1,* 23–47.

Huttenlocher, J. The origins of language comprehension. In R. L. Solso (Ed.), *Theories in cognitive psychology.* Hillsdale, N.J.: Lawrence Erlbaum Associates, 1974.

Kay, D., & Anglin, J. M. Overextension and underextension in the child's expressive and receptive speech. *Journal of Child Language,* 1982, *9,* 83–98.

Keil, F. C. and Batterman, N. A characteristic-to-defining shift in the development of word meaning. *Journal of Verbal Learning and Verbal Behavior,* in press.

Krauss, R. *A hole is to dig.* New York: Harper & Row, 1952.

Kuczaj, S. A. *Young children's overextensions of object words in comprehension and/or production: Support for a prototype theory of early word meaning.* Paper presented at the meeting of the Society for Research in Child Development, San Francisco, April, 1979.

Leopold, W. F. *Speech development of a bilingual child: A linguist's record, vol. 1. Vocabulary growth in the first two years.* Evanston, Ill.: Northwestern University Press, 1939.

Lewis, M. M. *How children learn to speak.* New York: Basic Books, 1959.

Litowitz, B. Learning to make definitions. *Journal of Child Language,* 1977, *4,* 289–304.

Long, B. S. The development of features: How children learn verbs of motion (Doctoral dissertation, Cornell University, 1975). *Dissertation Abstracts International,* 1975, *36,* 945B. (University Microfilms No. 75-17, 316)

Macnamara, J. *Names for things: A study of human learning.* Cambridge, Mass.: MIT Press, 1982.

Macrae, A. J. Movement and location in the acquisition of deictic verbs. *Journal of Child Language,* 1976, *3,* 191–204.

Miller, G. A. English verbs of motion: A case study in semantics and lexical memory. In A. W. Melton & E. Martin (Eds.), *Coding processes in human memory.* Washington, D.C.: Winston, 1972.

Miller, G. A. The acquisition of word meaning. *Child Development,* 1978, *49,* 999–1004.

Miller, G. A., & Johnson-Laird, P. N. *Language and perception.* Cambridge, Mass.: Harvard University Press, 1976.

Moore, K. C. The mental development of the child. *Psychological Review Monograph Supplements,* 1896, *1.*

Nelson, K. *Some evidence for the cognitive primacy of categorization and its functional basis. Merrill-Palmer Quarterly of Behavior and Development,* 1973, *19,* 21–39.

Nelson, K. Concept, word and sentence: Interrelations in acquisition and development. *Psychological Review,* 1974, *81,* 267–285.

Nelson, K. Semantic development and the development of semantic memory. In K. E. Nelson (Ed.), *Children's language* (Vol. 1). New York: Gardner Press, 1978.

Nelson, K., Rescorla, L., Gruendel, J., & Benedict, H. Early lexicons: What do they mean? *Child Development,* 1978, *49,* 960–968.

Nelson, K. E., & Bonvillian, J. D. Early language development: Conceptual growth and related processes between 2 and 4½ years of age. In K. E. Nelson (Ed.), *Children's language* (Vol. 1). New York: Gardner Press, 1978.

Nelson, K. E. and Earl, N. Information search by preschool children: Induced use of categories and category hierarchies. *Child Development,* 1973, *44,* 682–685.

Norlin, P. F. The development of relational arcs in the lexical semantic memory structures of young children. *Journal of Child Language,* 1980, *8,* 385–402.

Piaget, J. *Judgment and reasoning in the child.* London: Routledge & Kegan Paul, 1928.

Piaget, J. *The child's conception of the world.* London: Routledge & Kegan Paul, 1929.

Piaget, J. *Play, dreams, and imitation in childhood.* New York: Norton, 1962.

Reich, P. A. The early acquisition of word meaning. *Journal of Child Language,* 1976, *3,* 117–123.

Rescorla, L. Category development in early language. *Journal of Child Language,* 1981, *8,* 225–238.

Richards, M. M. Come and go reconsidered: Children's use of deictic verbs in contrived situations. *Journal of Verbal Learning and Verbal Behavior,* 1976, *15,* 655–665.

Rinsland, H. D. *A basic vocabulary of elementary school children.* New York: Macmillan, 1945.

Romney, K., & D'Andrade, R. G. Cognitive aspects of English kin terms. *American Anthropologist,* 1964, *66,* 146–170.

Rosch, E. On the internal structure of perceptual and semantic categories. In T. E. Moore (Ed.), *Cognitive development and the acquisition of language.* New York: Academic Press, 1973.

Rosch, E. Principles of categorization. In E. Rosch & B. Lloyd (Eds.), *Cognition and categorization.* Hillsdale, N.J.: Lawrence Erlbaum Associates, 1978.

Rosch, E. H., Mervis, C. B., Gray, W., Johnson, D., & Boyes-Braem, P. Basic objects in natural categories. *Cognitive Psychology,* 1976, *8,* 382–439.

Saltz, E., Dixon, D., Klein, S., & Becker, G. Studies of natural language concepts III. Concept overdiscrimination in comprehension between two and four years of age. *Child Development,* 1977, *48,* 1682–1685.

Smith, E. E., & Medin, D. *Categories and concepts.* Cambridge, Mass.: Harvard University Press, 1981.

Stern, W. *Psychology of early childhood up to the sixth year of age.* New York: Holt, 1930.

Swartz, K., & Hall, A. E. Development of relational concepts and word definitions in children five through eleven. *Child Development,* 1972, *43,* 239–244.

Thomson, J. R., & Chapman, R. S. Who is 'daddy' revisited: The status of two-year-olds' overextended words in use and comprehension. *Journal of Child Language,* 1977, *4,* 359–375.

Wallace, A. F. C., & Atkins, J. The meaning of kinship terms. *American Anthropologist,* 1960, *62,* 58–79.

Watson, R. *From meaning to definition: The development of word meaning in the school-aged child.* Unpublished doctoral dissertation, University of Toronto, 1982.

White, T. G. Naming practices, typicality, and underextension in child language. *Journal of Experimental Child Psychology,* 1982, *33,* 324–346.

Winner, E. New names for old things: The emergence of metaphoric language. *Journal of Child Language,* 1979, *6,* 469–491.

Wolman, R. N., & Barker, E. N. A developmental study of word definitions. *Journal of Genetic Psychology,* 1965, *107,* 159–166.

5 Comparing Good and Poor Readers: A Critique of the Research

Glenn M. Kleiman
Teaching Tools Software, Inc.
Mountain View, CA

Many studies of children's reading have compared reading ability groups on measures of cognitive performance. The primary aim of this work has been to identify the underlying causes of children's reading problems. A large variety of measures have been used, including tests of perceptual discrimination, visual scanning, within-modality and between-modality matching, vocabulary knowledge, decoding, whole word recognition, short-term memory, memory for sentences, deductive and inductive reasoning, verbal and nonverbal IQ, and many more. The population of main interest has been children who have reading problems that are not attributable to neurological, physiological, emotional, general cognitive, or environmental factors. These children are often said to be dyslexic or to have specific reading disabilities. Because the definitions of these terms are subject to debate (Rutter, 1978; Rutter & Yule, 1975), labels such as below average, disabled, poor, problem, or retarded readers are used in many studies. The comparison children who do not have reading problems are typically called normal, good, superior, or skilled readers.

Studies comparing good and poor readers can be divided into three general categories according to the dependent measures used. One category consists of studies using measures of reading performance, such as number of comprehension questions correctly answered, number of errors in oral reading, or speed of reading. Studies using these measures fall into two subtypes. One subtype involves manipulations of aspects of the text, such as vocabulary difficulty, syntactic complexity, presence of illustrations, or use of adjunct questions. The other involves comparisons of reading performance before and after a training program. Some training studies look at poor readers only, but many include comparisons of reading ability groups.

The second category consists of studies measuring performance on sub-processes of reading, such as letter discrimination, word recognition, knowledge of letter-sound correspondences, or sentence parsing. Most of the studies in this category have focused on processes of word recognition. Many of these studies have simply tested for absolute differences between good and poor readers. Such differences are generally found: Poor readers score lower than good readers on most measures of cognitive performance. The more interesting studies in this category have been concerned with interactions between reading ability and two or more measures of performance. That is, they look for patterns of differences — not only are poor readers' scores typically lower than good readers' scores on measure X, but the difference is greater than on measure Y.

The third category consists of studies measuring performance on cognitive processes that are not specific to reading. These studies are based on the view that poor readers' problems are not reading specific, but stem from a more basic or general cognitive deficit. Examples in this category are studies comparing good and poor readers on tests of visual discrimination, short-term memory span, or IQ. As in the previous category, there are studies that test for absolute differences between good and poor readers and studies that test for interactions or patterns of differences.

Reviews of subsets of the extensive literature comparing good and poor readers can be found in many places, including a book by Vellutino (1979), volumes edited by Benton and Pearl (1978), Knights and Bakkar (1976), and Waller and MacKinnon (in press), and *Reading Research Quarterly* articles by Golinkoff (1975–1976), Samuels (1973–1974), and Torgeson (1978–1979). I do not re-review this literature here. Rather, I focus on some problems that severely limit the interpretability and generalizability of much of this research.

In any of the types of studies just described, the researcher must: (1) decide on what tasks or tests good and poor readers should be compared; (2) obtain samples of good and poor readers and measure their performance; and (3) interpret the results. Problems arise at each of these steps, and they have often been neglected or answered simplistically. These problems are considered in the three main sections of this chapter.

PROBLEMS IN CHOOSING THE TASKS OR TESTS

A researcher's choice of the tasks to use in a study comparing good and poor readers rests on the assumed answers to two questions: (1) what types of knowledge and cognitive processes are required for skilled reading? (2) on which type of knowledge or processes are poor readers likely to be most deficient? That is, the choice is based on the researcher's views of skilled reading and reading disability.

A View of Skilled Reading

The view of skilled reading adapted in this chapter is well characterized by the following three quotes, all over 60 years old:

> Understanding a paragraph is like solving a problem. . . . The mind is assailed as it were by every word in the paragraph. It must select, repress, soften, emphasize, correlate and organize, all under the influence of the right mental set or purpose or demand [Thorndike, 1917].

> To completely analyze what we do when we read would almost be the acme of a psychologist's achievements, for it would be to describe very many of the most intricate workings of the human mind [Huey, 1908/1968, p. 6].

> A reader or listener has at each moment but a limited amount of mental power available. To recognize and interpret the symbols presented to him requires part of this power; to arrange and combine the images suggested by them requires a further part; and only that part which remains can be used for realizing the thought conveyed. Hence the more time and attention it takes to receive and understand each sentence, the less time and attention can be given to the contained idea; and the less vividly will that idea be conceived [Spencer, 1852/1881, p. 11].

The three main characteristics of skilled reading captured by these quotes are: (1) it is a goal-directed, flexible, cognitive skill; (2) it is complex, requiring the coordination of multiple processes and the use of knowledge of the language and the world in general; (3) like all cognitive skills, it is constrained by limits of the human information-processing system, such as short-term memory span and attentional capacity. These points require elaboration.

Reading is goal directed and flexible in that good readers can use written texts in many ways. They can skim for main points or scan for particular information. They can read quickly or slowly, carefully or cursorily, silently or aloud. They can read for gist or for detail, to proofread or to memorize. They can read many types of materials, from comic books to technical journals, from recipes to novels, from students' essays to Shakespeare's plays.

The many intricate workings of the human mind required for reading include general cognitive processes, such as perceptual discrimination, short-term memory storage and retrieval, serial order encoding, attention allocation and direction, long-term memory encoding and retrieval, and inferential processing. Also included are language comprehension processes, such as retrieving word meanings, parsing sentences, integrating word meanings, determining anaphoric references, and analyzing discourse structures. Reading-specific processes (e.g., using letter-sound correspondences and recognizing the visual forms of words) are also necessary. These processes interact in many ways. For example, the retrieval of appropriate world knowledge can facilitate meaning retrieval and sentence parsing (see Rumelhart, 1977).

According to this view, reading comprehension is not a passive accumulation of word or sentence meanings, nor is it simply an active attempt to reconstruct the meaning intended by the author. Rather, the reader has certain goals — either implicit or explicit, specific or general — and these goals influence the reading process. For example, when rapidly skimming text, readers rely on prior knowledge of the topic and a sample of the words in the text. They do not carefully process each word nor carefully parse each sentence. That is, they depend heavily on top-down or knowledge-driven processes. Alternatively, when reading carefully, each word and sentence is processed, and there is greater dependence on bottom-up or text-driven processing (Rumelhart, 1977).

This flexibility requires the inclusion of executive or control processes in an analysis of reading (Brown, 1980). These serve to determine the overall goal of reading, divide it into manageable or local subgoals, choose and integrate the processes to be used, and continually monitor their success, making adjustments in processing when necessary.

The human information-processing system is limited in a number of ways (Newell & Simon, 1972), and the many subprocesses of reading must be coordinated to operate within these limits. For example, there are limits on how much can be perceived in a single fixation, how quickly the eyes can move, how many chunks of information can be held in short-term memory, and how quickly information can be retrieved from long-term memory. There is also a general limit in attentional capacity or cognitive resources. As Spencer (1852/1881) pointed out over 130 years ago, if we attend to the individual pieces, we cannot attend to the meaning of the whole. In order to read well, the lower level processes (e.g., word recognition) must function automatically (i.e., without requiring attention), so that attention can be directed to higher order meanings (LaBerge & Samuels, 1974).

Where Might Poor Readers' Problems Lie?

Given this view of reading, the next question is: On what aspects of reading might poor readers be most deficient? There are many possibilities. They might be deficient in one or more of the general cognitive processes, such as perceptual discrimination, short-term memory storage, or long-term memory access. Or they might be deficient in reading- or language-specific processes, such as word recognition, meaning retrieval, or sentence parsing. Or perhaps poor readers lack the requisite knowledge — they may not know the words or the concepts found in the texts they are expected to read. Or they may be adequate in all the necessary knowledge and individual processes, but deficient in applying and integrating them — that is, in the executive processes. Poor readers may, for example, overrely on knowledge-driven or text-driven processes (Spiro, 1979).

A large proportion of the studies comparing good and poor readers have focused on word recognition and decoding (for reviews see Barron, in press; Golinkoff, 1975–1976; Vellutino, 1979).[1] This emphasis on word level processing is based on two assumptions. One is that, except for word recognition, reading and listening comprehension require identical cognitive processing (see Danks, 1974). The second is that most children are fairly competent at listening comprehension by the time reading instruction begins. These assumptions lead to the view that reading problems most frequently stem from difficulty in recognizing written words or decoding written words to their spoken equivalents (cf. Wolf, 1982).

The assumption that listening and reading comprehension require identical cognitive processing (once word recognition is accomplished) is challenged later in this chapter. It is argued that there are important differences in the cognitive demands of naturalistic reading and listening tasks, and that reading is more demanding than listening on several higher order cognitive processes that are not well developed in many children. These processes warrant consideration in attempts to identify the causes of reading problems.

Differences Between Written and Spoken Language

Consideration of the differences between written and spoken language has a long and respectable history, although these differences have generally been neglected in recent psychological, educational, and linguistic research. Plato, in the dialogue *Phraedrus,* pointed out that speakers can modify their communications to fit individual listeners, and listeners can influence the communication, but these options are not available to authors and readers. Aristotle, in the *Art of Rhetoric* (Book III, Chap. XII), pointed out that writing and speech differ in both function and style. His discussion included the greater precision and detail typically found in writing, the greater amount of repetition found in speech, and the availability of intonation in speech but not writing.

The Russian psychologist Vygotsky (1933/1962) described many of the differences between writing and speech. He considered differences in sentence structure, precision, and detail: "In writing . . . we are obliged to use many more words, and to use them more exactly" [p. 144]. He discussed the effects of prosody and gestures on spoken communication, citing a passage from Dostoyevsky in which the same spoken word is said to be used with six different meanings. Vygotsky's (1933/1962) description of the uses of the two modes of language is especially worth considering:

---

[1]See Ryan (in press) for a review of the studies that have compared good and poor readers on higher order linguistic processes and on executive processes.

> Writing is . . . addressed to an absent or an imaginary person or to no one in particular — a situation new and strange to the child. . . . In conversation, every sentence is prompted by a motive. Desire or need lead to request, question to answer, bewilderment to explanation. The changing motives of the interlocutors determine at every moment the turn oral speech will take. It does not have to be consciously directed — the dynamic situation takes care of that. The motives for writing are more abstract, more intellectualized, further removed from immediate needs. In written language, we are obliged to create the situation, to represent it to ourselves. This demands detachment from the actual situation [p. 99].

More recently, Olson (1976, 1977) and Rubin (1980) have discussed differences between the spoken language preschool children have mastered and the language children encounter in school. Olson emphasizes a distinction (similar to Vygotsky's) between interpersonal language and ideational language. Interpersonal language, the language of conversation, is familiar to young children. It is the language of action, used for requesting, questioning, and responding. It is closely tied to the immediate situation and to the desires and interests of the communicators. Ideational language, on the other hand, is not very familiar to children before they begin reading. It functions to communicate ideas, to describe, and to explain. It tends to be much more abstract and to have less immediate relevance than interpersonal language.

Rubin (1980) presents a taxonomy of language experiences and a set of dimensions on which these experiences differ. The language experiences include conversation, listening to a radio, watching a play, reading a letter, reading a story, and a variety of others. The dimensions on which these differ are divided into two types: medium-related and message-related. Medium-related dimensions include whether the message is written or spoken, whether the communicators can interact, whether they share a spatial and temporal context, whether the receiver is directly involved in the communication, and whether the referents of the message are physically present. The medium dimensions are structure (vocabulary, syntax, and discourse organization), topic, and function.

One main thrust of both Olson's and Rubin's papers is that the cognitive processes mastered by preschool children in their language experiences may be qualitatively different from those required to understand much of the language encountered in school. In this chapter, I limit consideration to "school language" and, more specifically, to language that presents information to be learned. I argue that even when the goal of listening and reading is restricted in this way, important differences remain in the cognitive demands of understanding the two modes of language. First, I consider differences due to the availability of prosodic information (intonation, rhythm, and stress or accent) in speech but not in writing. Then, I discuss some of the advantages teachers have over textbooks in making their presentations of information easily understood by children.

Prosody.   Prosodic information is conveyed by patterns of pitch, loudness, and duration, and therefore cannot be directly represented in writing. As the linguist Bolinger (1975) has stated: "The convergence of writing and speech virtually stops at the level of morphemes. . . . Writing never really got around to providing a regular way of marking accent. . . . Punctuation and capitalization serve as a rough guide to some of the rhythmic and intonation contrasts in speech, but much is left out [pp. 471–472]."

Linguistic and acoustic analyses have shown that certain prosodic patterns tend to co-occur with certain aspects of speech. Prosody provides information that may be useful to listeners in determining:

1. Changes in the topic of discourse (Bolinger, 1975).
2. The ends of sentences and whether they are statements, questions, or commands (Bolinger, 1975; Lefevre, 1970).
3. Whether sentences convey direct or indirect speech acts (Sag & Liberman, 1975.
4. The ends of clauses within sentences and, in many cases, phrases within clauses (Cooper & Sorenson, 1977; Grosjean, Grosjean, & Lane, 1979; Kleiman, Winograd, & Humphrey, 1979; Scholes, 1971; Sorenson, Cooper, & Paccia, 1978).
5. The words a speaker wants to make prominent because they convey new or contrastive information (Bolinger 1972; Chafe, 1974, 1976; Hornby, 1972; Lieberman, 1963).
6. The referents of some pronouns (Maratsos, 1973).

Written language can be understood without prosody because prosodic information is usually redundant with syntactic, lexical, or semantic information, or is replaced by punctuation. Although language without prosody can be understood, the redundancy that prosody provides may facilitate comprehension, and the lack of prosody in written language may contribute to reading problems (Kleiman et al., 1979; Read, Schreiber, & Walia, 1983). The possibility that children have difficulty compensating for the lack of prosody in written text is supported by evidence that children tend to rely more than adults on prosodic cues and are less able to use syntactic, lexical, and semantic cues (Hornby, 1971; Hornby & Hass, 1970; Read et al., 1983). The strongest evidence for a role of prosody in understanding speech is in the use of prosodic cues for sentence parsing and in determining the words the speaker intends to mark as focal. Some of this evidence is reviewed next in this chapter.

Parsing sentences into meaningful phrases and clauses is an essential step in language comprehension. According to current models (e.g., Clark & Clark, 1977; Kleiman, 1975), language comprehension involves a limited-capacity working memory, which holds surface representations of input words. Various processes operate upon the words in working memory to parse them into constituents (phrases and clauses) and to determine the meanings expressed. In the comprehension of both written and spoken language, lexical, syntactic, and semantic information can be useful in parsing sentences (see Clark & Clark, 1977, Chap. 2). Speech also contains useful prosodic information.

Once the meaning of a constituent has been determined, the individual words no longer need to be held in working memory, thereby freeing some of its capacity for new input. If one fails to parse sentences appropriately, comprehension will be impaired. In fact, there is evidence that parsing difficulty is often an aspect of reading comprehension failure. A common reading problem is that of reading "word-by-word," rather than chunking the words into meaningful phrases and clauses (Clay & Imlach, 1971; Golinkoff, 1975–1976). This may be due in part to the children having difficulties compensating for the lack of prosodic cues in parsing written sentences (Kleiman et al., 1979; Read et al., 1983).

Several types of prosodic cues to phrase and clause boundaries have been identified in acoustic studies. Cooper and Sorenson (1977) found evidence that these boundaries tend to be marked by a specific pattern of pitch change. Klatt (1976) and Sorenson et al. (1978) found that phrases are marked by an increase in the duration of their final syllables. Scholes (1971) argued that the relative peaks in loudness provide the most reliable cues to syntactic boundaries. In addition, pauses in speech provide information of potential use in parsing (Grosjean et al., 1979). These studies suggest that pitch, duration, loudness, and pauses can all provide useful information. Which dimension dominates may vary according to the speaker and the structure of the sentence.

The usefulness of prosodic cues in parsing is most apparent in cases of surface structure ambiguity. For example, the sentence *I fed her dog biscuits* has two possible readings; either she was fed dog biscuits or her dog was fed biscuits. In speech, these two readings would be reflected in different prosodic patterns which would enable the listener to determine whether the appropriate parsing is *I fed her / dog biscuits* or *I fed / her dog / biscuits.* Lehiste (1973) provides evidence that listeners can use prosodic information to determine the intended meanings of such sentences.

Prosodic cues to sentence structure are also available in sentences that are not ambiguous. In a study by Scholes (1971), pairs of words were used that, when placed in different contexts, either were within the same clause or had a clause boundary between them. For example, the word pair *spotted plants* appeared in the following two sentences:

If you find your flowers spotted plant them in the sun.
If you find your spotted plant let me know.

Tape-recordings were made of speakers reading each of the sentences aloud. The word pairs were then excised from the sentences and played to subjects who were asked to judge which sentence each word pair was in when it had been recorded. Subjects did significantly better than chance.

Several other studies have provided evidence for the use of prosody in sentence parsing by creating sentences in which there is a mismatch between prosodic and syntactic information. This is done by using sentence pairs that have a string of words in common, but different constituent boundaries within the string, as in the *spotted plant* example. Both sentences are recorded with normal intonation, and then the common word string is spliced from one context to the other. These studies have yielded three main findings. One is that subjects' recall errors generally consisted of changes in wording such that the syntactic structure of the reported sentence fit the prosodic pattern that was actually presented (Darwin, 1975; Wingfield, 1975; Wingfield & Klein, 1971). That is, subjects resolved the discrepancies between intonation and syntax by altering the syntactic structures of the sentences. This may be related to Garnes and Bond's (1975) finding that misperceptions of natural speech occur on phonemes, syllables, words, and phrases, but stress and intonation patterns are rarely misperceived.

The second result is based on the finding that, with normal spoken sentences, subjects tend to report the location of interrupting stimuli (e.g., clicks) accurately when they occur at syntactic boundaries, but inaccurately when they occur within syntactic units (Fodor & Bever, 1965). In sentences in which syntax and prosody mismatched, interrupting stimuli that occurred at the boundary marked by prosody were reported most accurately (Wingfield & Klein, 1971; see also Geers, 1978).

The third relevant finding on the effects of misleading prosody has been recently reported by Read et al. (1983). They trained 7-year-old children to listen to sentences and then repeat the subject-noun phrase only. When presented with normal sentences, in which prosody and syntax match, the children correctly repeated the subject-noun phrase 83% of the time. When prosody and syntax mismatched, the children were correct on only 30% of the sentences. Moreover, 78% of the errors in children's repetitions ended at the misleading prosodic cue. In the same task, adults were much less affected by misleading prosody.

Prosody also provides cues to the topic of the sentence (Hornby, 1971), the new information (Clark & Haviland, 1977), and information the speaker believes contrasts with the listener's expectations or prior information (Chafe, 1976). These cues take the form of sentence stress or accent. In an acoustic analysis, Lieberman (1960) found that fundamental frequency, relative amplitude, and duration are all correlates of stress. Lieberman (1963) demonstrated that speakers produce the more informative (i.e., less predictable) words with more stress than other words.

A clear case of sentence stress is found in question answering. Consider the following sentences spoken with the italicized word stressed:

A. *John* stole the picture.
B. John *stole* the picture.
C. John stole the *picture*.

In each case, the stressed word would be the one carrying the new information, while the rest of the sentence specifies the given information. That is, sentences A, B, and C could be answers to questions A', B', and C', respectively.

A'. Who stole the picture?
B'. What did John do with the picture?
C'. What did John steal?

Hornby (1971) studied children's use of stress and syntactic cues in determining the topic of sentences. He presented children with active, passive, cleft and pseudocleft sentences, and sentences with contrastive stress. The children's task was to select a picture that shows the action described in the sentence. The sentences and pictures were designed so that the choices would reflect the children's views of the topic of the sentence. The results led Hornby to conclude that stress is the primary device children use in determining the topic of sentences (see also Hornby & Hass, 1970).

Teachers Versus Textbooks.   In addition to the use of prosody, two other aspects of teachers' presentations make them very different from textbook presentations: (1) teachers and students interact during the presentation; (2) teachers have some knowledge of what the students already know, do not know, and how easily they can understand new material. Both of these aspects of speech were contrasted with writing by Plato in the dialogue phraedrus (see Fowler, 1914):

> Written words seem to talk to you as though they were intelligent, but if you ask them anything about what they say, from a desire to be instructed, they go on telling you just the same thing forever . . .

> Speech can be varied so that it is appropriate to each nature . . . addressing a variegated soul in a variegated style . . . and a simple soul in a simple style.

The French novelist Sartre (1964) provides an analysis from a very different perspective, but points out the same distinctions between natural spoken language and the language of books. Recalling his shock the first time his mother read him a story, he writes:

> I was bewildered: who was telling what and to whom? My mother had gone off: . . . I didn't recognize her speech . . . A moment later, I realized: it was the book that was speaking. Frightening sentences emerged from it: they were real centipedes, they swarmed with syllables and letters. . . . Rich in unknown words, they were enchanted with themselves and their meanderings without bothering about me. Sometimes they disappeared before I was able to understand them; at other times I understood in advance; and they continued to roll nobly to their end without sparing me a single comma. That discourse was certainly not meant for me [p. 46].

It is well documented that speakers modify their language to suite their listeners (e.g, Snow & Ferguson, 1977) and that, in interactive situations, listeners provide a great deal of feedback to speakers (Wilkinson, 1971). In classrooms a very common "teaching cycle" consists of the teacher asking a question, one or more students responding, and the teacher then evaulating or modifying the response (Bellack, Davitz, Kliebard, & Hyman, 1963; Sinclair & Coulthard, 1975).

In a study of differences between listening-to-learn and reading-to-learn, Schallert and Kleiman (1979) obtained samples of expository texts written for children and tape-recordings and observations of teachers presenting comparable material to their classes. The children's reading materials had been adapted from materials originally intended for adults. The teachers used the adult materials as a basis for preparing their presentations. These language samples have been used to identify some of the ways teachers use their knowledge of the children and of the flexibility of oral presentations to make their lessons easier to understand than comparable material presented in textbooks. Teachers can adjust the amount and complexity of the material covered and the vocabulary and sentence structures used. In addition, teachers can provide external aids to help children with three processes, each critical to comprehension and learning. Schallert and Kleiman (1979) refer to these processes as activating relevant prior knowledge, focusing attention on main ideas, and monitoring comprehension.

Children with reading difficulties may lack adequate background knowledge (Anderson, 1977) or fail to make use of the knowledge they do have (Spiro, 1979). When teachers orally present lessons, they often guide the students in retrieving and using relevant prior knowledge. Teachers can check the students' prior knowledge to fill in missing information, correct erroneous information, and relate new information to things the students already know. For example, in Schallert and Kleiman's language samples, one of the teachers began her presentation of a lesson on sequoia trees as follows:

T: Today we are going to learn about something that's the oldest and the biggest living thing that we know of. The oldest and the biggest. Now think just a minute before you get your hand up. The *oldest* and the *biggest*. What do you think it is — Jeff?
S: Dinosaur.
T: Why is dinosaur not a good answer?
S: Not living.

This type of interchange continues with students suggesting elephant, whale, shark, and the earth, until:

S: Trees. Trees are living.
T: All right. Say it again. Listen again. Heidi's got the answer over here. Say it again.
S: Sequoia tree.
T: Sequoia trees. How many of you've ever heard of a sequoia tree?;

With this brief introduction to the lesson, the teacher has done several things that may help her students understand and learn the material. First, she began by finding out about the children's prior knowledge. This provided an opportunity to correct their initial responses and, in so doing, to make clear the characteristics that are central to the discussion. Moreover, it enabled her to remind the children of information they already possessed and to contrast the new information with what they already knew. When one student gave the correct answer, the teacher directed the class' attention to that child, had the child repeat it, and then repeated the answer herself. The teacher then went on to find out more about the students' prior knowledge by asking how many have heard of sequoia trees.

Another aspect of skilled reading that is difficult for many children is determining the main ideas of a passage. In studies with subjects from third grade through college, Brown and Smiley (1977a, 1977b) found large developmental differences in the ability to determine the importance of structural units of prose passages. When given time to study the passage, subjects who were able to determine which parts were important focused their attention on those parts, but subjects who were unable to pick out the main ideas distributed their study time over all the information in the passage. Eamon (1978–1979) also presented evidence that distinguishing main ideas from peripheral information can be difficult for poor readers. In presenting information, teachers explicitly point out main ideas and provide cues to importance by intonation patterns, repetition, and phrasing. All of this may make the task of determining main ideas much easier when listening to a teacher's presentation than when reading.

Effective monitoring of one's own comprehension (i.e., determining whether or not one has understood the information) is another critical process in language comprehension. Recent studies have shown that children are often poor at comprehension monitoring. For example, in a study by Markman (1979), elementary school children were asked to act as consultants to help evaluate essays. Each essay had a blatent contradiction. For example, part of one essay read: "Fish must have light in order to see. There is absolutely no light at the bottom of the ocean. It is pitch black down there. When it is that dark, fish cannot see anything. They cannot even see colors. Some fish that live at the bottom of the ocean can see the color of their food." Children often judged these essays as making sense and being easy to understand. Further evidence is provided by studies of referential communication in which children serving as listeners were instructed to ask questions if they needed more information (Cosgrove & Patterson, 1977; Ironsmith & Whitehurst, 1978; Patterson, Massad, & Cosgrove, 1978). The children, particularly those below the fourth grade, often failed to request further information, even when the original message was completely uninformative.

When presenting information, teachers frequently monitor the students comprehension by asking questions. They also note looks of puzzlement and drifts of attention. When students are not adequately comprehending, the teacher will repeat and rephrase information or fill in necessary background information. This external monitoring, repetition, and further information makes the need for children to monitor their own comprehension much less in listening-to-learn than in reading-to-learn.

Determining main ideas and monitoring comprehension are relevant to one advantage that writing has over speech. Writing is permanent, and therefore, readers control how they sample information from the text. Readers can preview the material, choose to read some parts slowly and carefully and to skim others, and reread at will.

There is evidence that good readers take advantage of the options afforded by the permanence of written texts. Tinker (1958) reports that the rate of reading decreases as the text becomes more difficult. Furthermore, the pace is not simply set and then maintained throughout the text. Skilled readers slow down for important or confusing passages and speed up for easy or unimportant ones. Taylor (1957) reports that 15% of all eye movements in college level readers are regressive. The use of this rereading option may be crucial for skilled reading. Skilled readers proceed rapidly, hypothesizing about what will come next, and integrating what is read with previous parts of the text. The rereading option enables them to do this without taking too large a risk of misinterpreting or failing to comprehend, because they can go back and reread when necessary. Wanat (1971) demonstrated that regressive eye movements are likely to occur when the text does not match readers' expectations. He compared adults' eye movements while they read two types of sentences: agentive passives (e.g., *The ball was hit by the boy*) and locative passives (e.g., *The ball was hit by the park*). Because passive sentences usually specify the agent at the end, readers are more likely to expect an agent (e.g., *boy*) than a location (e.g., *park*). Wanat found more regressions and longer regression durations with the locative passives than with the agentive passives. Also, the regressions usually occurred after the locative and were directed back to the word *by*. Further evidence that the nature of the text influences eye fixation patterns is provided by Rayner and McConkie (1976), Carpenter and Just (1978), and Just and Carpenter (1980).

The ability to sample the text efficiently is an important reading skill that differs from any skills used in listening. A study by Neville and Pugh (1976–1977) provides evidence that some readers in the middle grades do not make good use of the potential to sample information. They tested fifth graders on three types of cloze tests: a regular reading test, a restricted reading test, and a listening test. On the listening and restricted reading tests, information about the words following the missing one was not available. On the regular reading cloze test, this information was available. However, only the better readers seemed to make use of it. The poor readers' performance was equivalent on all three types of tests, and their errors on the regular reading test were consistent with the preceding context, although sometimes inconsistent with the words that followed. The good readers' performance on the regular reading test was superior to the other two tests, and their errors were consistent with both the preceding and following context.

In order to sample information from written texts efficiently, readers must continuously evaluate what they are reading to determine if it is important and needs to be read carefully, and they must constantly monitor their own comprehension to determine if they are understanding the text sufficiently. The evaluating and monitoring processes are often difficult for children, and the demands for these processes are much greater in reading than in listening.

Choosing Tasks or Tests: Summary

To summarize the main argument presented in this section, there are many differences in the cognitive demands of reading and listening tasks children encounter in school. In listening, prosodic cues facilitate sentence analysis, and teachers provide external aids in retrieving relevant prior knowledge, focusing attention on main ideas, and monitoring comprehension. Determining main ideas and monitoring attention are especially important in taking advantage of the permanence of written language. There is evidence that each of these aspects of reading presents difficulties for children. As psychologists and educators turn their attention to reading comprehension, rather than individual word recognition and decoding, the differences between listening and reading warrant careful study. It is likely that the causes of many reading problems will be found in the skills necessary in reading that differ from the skills children have mastered in listening.

PROBLEMS IN SUBJECT SAMPLING AND MEASUREMENT

There are serious sampling and measurement problems in many of the techniques used in studies comparing good and poor readers. These problems have long been known, and excellent discussions can be found in Campbell and Stanley (1963) and Thorndike (1963). However, these methodological faults continue to appear frequently in published studies. In this section, some of the most frequent and critical problems are discussed briefly. The reader interested in more extensive and technical discussions is referred to Applebee (1971), Campbell and Stanley (1963), Chapman and Chapman (1973, 1974), Cronbach and Snow (1977), and Thorndike (1963).

The most frequent and critical problems in studies comparing reading ability groups include: (1) lack of comparability across studies and restricted generalizability of findings; (2) misguided procedures for matching good and poor readers on IQ and other variables; (3) low reliability of measures and neglect of statistical regression; and (4) neglect of effects attributable to the scale of measurement used. Each of these is discussed further in the following subsections.

Lack of Comparability and Generalizability of Findings

Samples of poor readers in different studies are often not comparable because they were obtained from different populations or because different selection criteria were used. Poor readers selected from regular classes may not be as severely disabled as those selected from remedial reading classes. Both of these groups may differ from poor readers referred to clinics, and different types of clinics (e.g., psychological vs. neurological) tend to receive children with different types of problems.

In most studies, samples of poor readers are obtained from schools, and poor readers are identified on the basis of standardized reading test scores. Unfortunately, the fact that different reading tests emphasize different types of materials and questions is usually neglected. For example, some tests heavily weight individual-word reading, others weight literal comprehension questions, and others weight inferential questions (i.e., questions requiring information beyond that stated in the text). Some tests require a great deal of oral reading; others require no oral reading at all (see Farr, 1969; MacGinitie, 1973). Jerrolds, Calloway, and Gwaltney (1971) showed that different tests yield different numbers of children classified as disabled readers. They also found that the groups of children identified as disabled according to different reading tests showed different patterns of performance on verbal and performance IQ tests. That is, different reading tests did not just alter the number of children classified as poor readers; the poor readers' patterns of performance on other cognitive tests were also altered.

Differences among tests are particularly critical when cross-age comparisons are made. Even when tests from the same series are used, the skills measured at different grades are not the same. For example, the Stanford Diagnostic Reading Test has four levels, one each for Grades 1-2, 3-4, 5-8, and 9-12. The test for Grades 1-2 heavily weights measures of auditory discrimination and auditory vocabulary. The test for Grades 3-4 heavily weights phonetic and structural analyses of written words and word parts. The tests for the older children heavily weight literal comprehension, inferential comprehension, and rate of reading. Children classified as having reading problems on the basis of one level of a test should not be assumed to have problems with the same aspects of reading as children classified as having reading problems on the basis of a different test, even if it is another level from the same test series.

The criteria used to classify children as poor readers also affect the nature of the sample obtained. The most common procedure is to classify children as poor readers if their reading test scores are 2 or more years below their age-appropriate grade placement. The criterion makes interpreting patterns across grades difficult. The percentage of children fitting this criterion increases with grade level, ranging from less than 2% at the beginning of third grade to nearly 30% by the end of ninth grade (Applebee, 1971). By most standards, a ninth-grade child reading at the seventh-grade level is not as severely disabled as the third-grade child reading at the first-grade level. To make samples of poor readers more comparable across grades, criteria have been proposed that would classify as poor readers the same proportion of children at each grade (e.g., Jerrolds et al., 1971).

Problems in Matching Good and Poor Readers

Most researchers try to identify differences between good and poor readers that are specific to reading, not attributable to IQ differences. These researchers have tried to identify children who are reading more poorly than would be expected on the basis of their IQ scores. Rutter and Yule (1973, 1975), in an epidemiological study, obtained strong evidence that reading problems not attributable to IQ occur in an educationally significant proportion of the population. They also found that the populations of children with reading problems attributable to low IQ and children with reading problems not attributable to low IQ differ in many ways, such as male/female ratios, severity of spelling problems, and prognosis for improvement. Despite the demonstrated existence of the population, attempts to limit the sample of poor readers to those whose reading problems are not due to low IQ have resulted in some misguided procedures.

Two procedures have been widely used. One is to use a minimal IQ criterion, often 90. Only children whose reading scores are below a set criterion and whose IQ scores are above the minimal criterion are selected for the study. Alternatively, the subject selection criterion is set as a difference between IQ and reading scores. Typically, both scores are converted to chronological age (i.e., the age at which the obtained score would reflect average performance), and if the reading score is 2 or more years below the IQ score, the child is classified as having a specific reading disability.

The problems with these procedures stem from the fact that IQ and reading scores are highly correlated. IQ tests that emphasize verbal skills overlap in content with reading tests. In fact, factor analyses of both verbal IQ tests and reading tests generally yield vocabulary knowledge as the most heavily weighted factor. Even nonverbal IQ tests show positive and significant correlations with reading tests. Yule, Rutter, Berger, and Thompson (1974) report correlations between nonverbal IQ and reading scores for five populations. The five correlations, each based on scores from over 1100 subjects, are all greater than .6.

Because IQ and reading scores are positively correlated, children with low reading scores but not low IQ scores do not comprise a representative sample of poor readers. Therefore, the generality of findings from such a sample is restricted. More critically, when two measures are highly correlated, selecting a sample low on one measure but not low on the other results in selecting subjects with scores that have large errors of measurement (Calfee, 1976; Campbell & Stanley, 1963). In the case of children with low reading scores but not low IQ scores, retesting will result, on average, in higher reading scores and lower IQ scores than on the initial test. If, as is often done, the good or average readers are selected to match the poor readers on IQ, the match will not be as good as it appears; the poor readers' IQ scores will have large errors of measurement, and on retesting the average IQ of these poor readers will be found to be lower. Similar problems occur when good and poor readers are matched on other variables, such as decoding ability or vocabulary knowledge (see Calfee, 1976).

Using a criterion based on differences between IQ and reading test scores is not a satisfactory solution to this problem. The basic problem with this procedure is that difference scores of correlated measures have low reliability. When difference scores are taken, the variability common to the two original measures (reflected in the correlation between the measures) cancels, whereas the errors in measurement (reflected for each measure by 1 minus the reliability coefficient) accumulate. The reliability of a difference score measure can be calculated by:

$$(1) \; r\text{diff} = \frac{\frac{1}{2}(r11 + r22) - r12}{1 - r12}$$

where $r$diff is the reliability of the difference score, $r11$ and $r22$ are the reliabilities of the two original measures, and $r12$ is the correlation of the two original measures (Thorndike & Hagen, 1977, Chap. 3). This formula shows that as the correlation between the two measures approaches their average reliability, the reliability of the difference score approaches 0. To give one example with values typical of those for reading and IQ scores, if the average reliability of the two tests is .8 and the correlation of the two tests is .6, then the reliability of the difference score measure is .5. This is not adequate reliability for most classification purposes, and a large proportion of the children will be incorrectly assigned in a study that uses this procedure.

The best procedure to follow when IQ and reading ability need to be separated is to use an appropriate regression equation to predict children's reading scores on the basis of their IQ scores and select those children whose reading scores are substantially below the predicted score (see Thorndike, 1963; Yule, et al., 1974). This procedure should be used with IQ and reading tests that have minimal content overlap and that are both highly reliable.

Reliability and Regression Problems

Poor readers, by definition, are at the low end of the distribution of reading scores. The extreme scores on any measure have the largest error of measurement. On any test with less than perfect reliability, regression to the mean will occur on retesting. Children with scores above the mean on the initial testing will score, on the average, closer to the mean (but still above it) on retesting. Likewise, children with scores below the mean will tend to score closer to the mean (but still below it) on retesting. The magnitude of the expected regression to the mean is determined by the reliability of the test (the higher the reliability, the smaller the regression effect) and the discrepancy of the initial score from the mean for the population (the larger the discrepancy, the larger the regression effect). More specifically, the best prediction of the change in score on retesting, assuming no other influences besides statistical regression, can be calculated by:

$$(2) \quad C = (M - S)(1 - r)$$

where C is the change from initial test to retest, M is the population mean, S is the score on the initial test, and r is the reliability of the test.

A widely cited study by Cromer (1970) provides examples of both inappropriate matching procedures annd resulting problems due to statistical regression: Cromer's study is used by Gibson and Levin (1975) and Golinkoff (1975–1976) as major support for the claim that there are poor readers whose problems are not in reading individual words, but in sentence organizations. Most of the following discussion of Cromer's study is based on Calfee (1976).

Cromer's subjects were junior college students. He purported to divide the poor readers into two groups that were equally poor in reading comprehension and to match each group with good reading comprehenders. The *deficit* poor readers also scored poorly on a vocabulary test; hence, word reading problems were assumed to be the cause of their comprehension problems. The *difference* poor readers scored as well on the vocabulary test as did their good reader matches; hence, it was assumed their comprehension problems stemmed from word-by-word reading or sentence organization difficulties.

To test the assumptions about deficit and difference types of poor readers, Cromer administered reading tasks to each group. Each task involved reading stories and answering multiple choice questions. The conditions differed in the ways the stories were presented. The two conditions relevant to this discussion were: (1) regular sentence presentation, and (2) phrase presentation, in which the sentences were divided into meaningful phrases.

Inasmuch as the difference poor readers were thought to be poor at sentence organization, one of Cromer's predictions was that the preorganized phrase presentation would facilitate reading comprehension for this group. But as the good readers and the deficit readers were thought to have adequate sentence organizational skills, their comprehension should be the same for the regular sentence and phrase presentation conditions. Cromer claims that the results of his study support these predictions.

Cromer's study is subject to severe problems in the subject selection procedures, much like those that arise when one attempts to match good and poor readers for IQ. The selection procedures used result in regression effects, which were not controlled for in the experimental design.

Reading comprehension and vocabulary measures are highly correlated. Selecting subjects who are high in one and low in the other (Cromer's difference poor readers) results in a high error of measurement. As a result of regression to the mean, on a retest the difference poor readers' vocabulary scores would decrease, whereas their comprehension scores would increase. They would no longer be well matched on vocabulary with their good reader controls, nor well matched on comprehension with the deficit poor readers. In fact, Cromer reports that in the regular sentence condition, six of the sixteen difference poor readers had higher comprehension scores than their matched controls. Because this condition was basically a replication of the original measure used to assigned subjects to groups, it shows that the difference poor readers and their matched controls were not reliably assigned. Cromer ignored this problems and simply reassigned these subjects and reanalyzed the data. Further problems with this study are discussed by Calfee (1976).

The neglect of statistical regression is sufficient to make the drawing of any conclusions from this study questionable. The same serious error can be found in other studies following Cromer's deficit and difference group distinction (e.g., Levin, 1973).

Neglecting statistical regression is a critical flaw in many studies using test-retest designs (see Calfee, 1976 for further discussion). Poor readers should be expected to improve their scores on retesting even without any training or other manipulations. The more extreme the poor readers' initial scores, the larger the regression effect. The best solution to this problem is to divide the poor readers into treatment and control groups randomly. Both should show equal regression effects on retesting. Any differences between the two groups on retesting can then be attributed to the experimental treatment or training procedure (Campbell & Stanley, 1963; Thorndike, 1963).

Scale of Measurement Problems

Studies testing for absolute differences between good and poor readers or for interactions between reading ability and performance on two or more measures are also subject to scale of measurement problems. The simplest and most recognized of these problems are ceiling and floor effects. If the task is very easy or very difficult, so that both good and poor readers score very high or very low, differences between the groups may be obscured. Ceiling and floor problems can also yield spurious interactions. For example, if poor readers perform better on test X than on test Y, but good readers perform at ceiling on both tests and therefore cannot do better on X than on Y, a statistical interaction may appear in the data analysis.

Statistical interactions are also of questionable interpretability when, as is typical in studies comparing good and poor readers, the groups are not equated on any base-line measure. One example of this problem is found in a set of studies on good and poor readers' use of sentence contexts in recognizing words. Some models of reading (e.g., Smith, 1971) claim that good readers make better use of contextual information than do poor readers. In fact, in these models, use of contextual information is viewed as one of the main determinants of reading ability. Stanovich (1980) makes the opposite claim that skilled readers make less use of prior sentence context in recognizing words while reading.

Stanovich's claim rests largely on his interpretation of three experimental studies by Schvaneveldt, Ackerman, and Semelar (1977), West and Stanovich (1978); and Perfetti, Goldman, and Hogaboam (1979). In all three studies, the time it took readers of various ability levels to perform a word recognition task was measured. The main comparison in each study was the time to recognize words with and without potentially helpful contexts. In each case, the absolute decrease in reaction time in the context condition, as compared to the no-context or control condition, was greater for the lower ability readers. However, there are problems in using these data to support the view that poor readers generally make greader use of context than do good readers.

One major difficulty stems from the fact that in all cases the group with larger context effects also took longer to recognize the words both with and without context. For example, in the Schvaneveldt et al. (1978) study, the mean reaction times to recognize words in the relevant conditions were 1164 msec for the younger group and 916 msec for the older group. The context effects (average time with context minus average time in the control condition) were 94 msec and 49 msec for the younger and older groups, respectively. This suggests that the apparently higher context effect may be a function of higher base-line time, which allows more possibility for any facilitative effect.

More technically stated, the problem stems from the fact that interactions may depend on the scale of measurement (Winer, 1971). Of the three research reports just cited, only Perfetti et al. (1979) show any awareness of this problem. In the text of their paper, Perfetti et al. report a significant context by reading ability interaction, with the less able readers showing the larger context effect. However, in a footnote they report a second analysis in which they transformed the data to reduce the inequality of variances between reading ability groups. In this analysis, there was no context by reading ability interaction. More recent work by Perfetti and Roth (personal communication) provides evidence that, given comparable base lines, good and poor readers do not differ in their use of context to facilitate word recognition.

Chapman and Chapman (1973, 1974) provide more technical discussions of problems of developing measures that enable interpretation of interactions involving ability groups. In general, interactions of this sort are not directly interpretable unless the group that is superior on one relevant measure is inferior on another (i.e., a cross-over interaction) or the two groups ar equal on a relevant base-line measure.[2] Because good readers are superior to poor readers on most cognitive measures, these conditions are rarely met in research comparing good and poor readers.

PROBLEMS IN INTERPRETING EMPIRICAL FINDINGS

In the previous section, I discussed some of the most common sampling and measurement problems found in studies comparing good and poor readers. In this section, the question to be considered is: Assuming appropriate meth-

---

[2]This statement rests on certain conditions, such as that the measures are equal in discriminative power and that ceiling or floor effects are not responsible for the groups being equal on the base-line task.

odology has been used, what conclusions can logically be drawn from findings of differences between good and poor readers? That is, once a difference between reading ability groups has been established, what are we to make of it?

The primary aim of the research considered in this chapter is to identify the underlying cognitive causes of reading disability. When poor readers are found to do less well than good readers on a cognitive task that can be related to reading, it is tempting to draw causal inferences. However, such inferences are likely to be erroneous.

A difference between good and poor readers might be a symptom of the actual underlying causal component, but may not provide any useful information about it. A good example of a symptomatic difference is found in eye-movement research. It has long been established that the eye-movement patterns of good and poor readers differ (Tinker, 1958). However, attempts to train poor readers to move their eyes like good readers have not been successful in improving reading skill. Current models view eye movements as reflecting underlying cognitive processes (e.g., Just & Carpenter, 1980). From this current perspective, training eye-movement patterns would not be expected to improve reading; it would be treating the symptom, rather than the cause.

Differences between good and poor readers may also be secondary effects, rather than causes, of reading ability. That is, deficits in poor readers may well be caused by their reading problems, rather than being causes of them. Or the reading problem and the other deficit(s) may cyclically reinforce one another. A good example is vocabulary knowledge. Is lack of an adequate vocabulary a cause of reading problems? Or, do reading problems lead to poor vocabularies? Or is it some of each?

Finally, cognitive deficits may be correlated with reading problems without causal connections in either direction. This is very likely, because reading ability is related to IQ, socioeconomic status, and quality of schooling, and these factors can be expected to have wide-ranging effects.

Comparisons of reading ability groups do not provide a direct way of determining whether an obtained difference stems from a component of reading that causes reading problems, is a symptom of a causal component, is a secondary effect of reading ability, or is due to a process that is correlated with reading ability but not causally related to it. In some cases, causal differences can be separated from the other differences by data from training studies. If poor readers are deficient on cognitive process X (as compared to good readers) and if this causes reading disability, then training poor readers on X should improve reading performance (given certain assumptions). If X is a symptomatic, secondary, or correlated difference, then training on X should not improve reading ability (see Fleisher, Jenkins, & Pany, 1979; Weaver,

1979, for recent applications of this logic). Training studies have been fruit-ful in research on memory development and disabilities (for discussions of this work and methodological suggestions, see Belmont & Butterfield, 1977; Brown & Campione, 1979). Ryan (in press) has also advocated adapting the "instructional method" of studying memory to the study of reading.

The final problem to be discussed is perhaps the most critical, having to do with the basic assumptions about reading disability that underlie compari-sons of reading ability groups. An excellent discussion of this problem can be found in Applebee (1971), who describes the general stimulation as follows:

> Any investigation of the problem of reading disability begins with a set of scores X_1 to X_n on measures the investigator expects will be relevant to reading ability, and with a score Y which indicates performance on a reading criterion. . . . Any analysis carried out on the X's in an attempt to predict Y, or to describe the dif-ferences between groups specified in terms of relative scores on Y, is predicted, consciously or not, on some mathematical model of the functional relationship between the two sets of variables [p. 99].

The problem is that a variety of models are logically possible, and the models assumed for group comparisons may be invalid.

According to the simplest model, one and the same cognitive component is responsible for all reading disabilities. This view underlies searchers for a single cause of all reading problems (that is not attributable to low IQ, envi-ronmental, neurological, or environmental factors). Such searches have typi-cally focused on a basic cognitive process such as visual perception, inter-sensory matching, serial order encoding, or short-term memory functioning (see Vellutino, 1979, for a review and critique of this work). There have also been proposals that the usual cause of reading problems is deficits in language-specific processes (e.g., speed of lexical access), reading-specific processes (e.g., decoding fluency), executive or control processes (e.g., set-ting the goal as word pronunciation and not attending to meanings), or lack of an adequate knowledge base.

If this simplest model held, group comparisons might be able to isolate the causal component; all poor readers would be deficient on it, and no good readers would be. More specifically, the distributions of good and poor read-ers' scores on a measure tapping this component would not overlap (except for measurement error). Scores on tests tapping other components should overlap, and on components that are not affected by the critical causal one, good and poor readers should not differ. Unfortunately, the available data do not take this form. Distributions of good and poor readers' scores gener-ally have a great deal of overlap. The average score of poor readers is lower than the average score of good readers on most measures of cognitive performance. These data, combined with the diversity of the knowledge and cognitive processes required for skilled reading, make it unlikely that there is a single cause of most reading problems.

According to a slightly more complex model, each reading problem is caused by a deficit in a single cognitive component, but the component varies across individuals. This view, coupled with an assumption that there are a small number of different causal components, underlies attempts to develop taxonomies of reading problems. If this model holds, group comparisons will show poor readers to score lower than good readers on a variety of measures. This might lead to the erroneous conclusion that poor readers are typically deficient on multiple components, when each individual is actually deficient on only one.

It is also possible that each reading problem is caused by a deficit on a single component, but that the deficit can be on any of the requisite processes or knowledge bases. If this is the case, it will be difficult to develop a usable taxonomy, and group comparisons will obscure the specific deficits of individuals.

As Applebee (1971) points out, the actual situation may be best characterized by a multiple regression model. According to this model, each of the many cognitive components of reading contribute to determining one's reading level. The various components may be differentially weighted, with certain ones contributing more of the variance in reading ability. In this view, reading disability can be caused by a slight deficit on many components, a moderate deficit on several components, or a large deficit on one or two components. That is very different patterns of performance across cognitive components would be found for different poor readers. Some might have a localizable deficiency, others a global one. Group comparisons would obscure such patterns.

In the final model to be considered, it is not simply the levels of abilities on cognitive components that matter, but patterns of abilities and how they are used by the control processes. For example, someone who is poor in individual-word reading would usually be expected to be a poor reader. However, this may not be the case if the executive processes can use context and prior knowledge to compensate for the deficit in word reading. That is, good and poor readers might be equally capable on many components, but differ in certain key combinations or in the way the control processes use strengths to compensate for weaknesses. Stated differently, there may be many different reading strategies, any of which can be successful for some individuals. Group comparisons will not provide information about the various possible strategies.

Given our current knowledge of the complexity of reading, it is likely that one of the more complex models (i.e., the multiple regression or patterns of abilities models) will be necessary to characterize reading disabilities. If one of these models holds, reading ability group comparisons will obscure rather than elucidate the patterns of reading disabilities. Perhaps so much research effort has yielded so little progress because the assumed simple models are inappropriate.

The apparent solution is to focus on detailed analysis of individual reading problems. Information about many individual cases is necessary to determine which of the possible models of reading disability is most appropriate. This approach of going from the detailed study of individual cases to general principles is the inverse of the nomothetic approach of group comparisons. The detailed study of individuals within a cognitive framework has been very productive in Newell and Simon's (1972) work on problem solving. It is also a central feature of the cognitive-functional approach (Meichenbaum, 1976; Ryan, in press).

SUMMARY

The large number of studies comparing good and poor readers have yielded few conclusive findings. This is due to a variety of serious problems, many of which have been discussed in this chapter. The first set of problems discussed, those haviing to do with the choice of tests or tasks, may be remedied by research within the next few years (see Brown, 1980; Ryan, 1980). Another set of problems has to do with subject sampling and experimental design and measurement. Good discussions of these problems have been available for many years (Campbell & Stanley, 1963; Thorndike, 1963), but inadequate procedures continue to appear in published studies, and results from these studies continue to be accepted in review articles. Properly sampling subjects, establishing the discriminative power of measures, and avoiding confounding due to statistical regression required a large commitment of time and resources.

Even when sampling, design, and measurement procedures are adequate, there are serious problems in interpreting the results of studies comparing good and poor readers. We are interested in differences that provide information about the causes of reading disability, but differences obtained in these studies do not necessarily reflect causal factors. Training studies are the best hope for separating causal from noncausal differences.

Finally, there is a critical problem that cannot be remedied by improvements in studies comparing good and poor readers. Inteptreting the results of these studies requires the assumption that there is homogeneity within each group of readers (i.e., that certain cognitive components are typically responsible for reading difficulties). However, there may well be a great diversity of patterns of reading disability. Group comparisons would obscure this diversity (Applebee, 1971). The homogeneity assumption can be tested only by de-

tailed studies of individual readers. The lack of studies of individual poor
readers, from a cognitive processing point of view of reading, is a critical gap
in research. Such studies may make important contributions to our knowledge of reading disability.

REFERENCES

Anderson, R. C. *Schema-directed processes in language comprehension.* (Tech. Rep. No. 50).
Urbana: University of Illinois, Center for the Study of Reading, 1977.
Applebee, A. N. Research in reading retardation: Two critical problems. *Journal of Child
Psychology and Psychiatry,* 1971, *12,* 91–113.
Barron, R. W. Development of visual word recognition: A review. In T. G. Waller & G. E.
MacKinnon (Eds.), *Reading research: Advances in theory and practice* (Vol. 2). New York:
Academic Press, in press.
Bellack, A. A., Davitz, J. R., Kliebard, H. M., & Hyman, R. T. *The language of the classroom.*
New York: Teachers College Press, 1963.
Belmont, J. M., & Butterfield, E. C. The instructional approach to developmental cognitive
research. In R. V. Kail & J. W. Hagen (Eds.), *Perspectives on the development of memory and
cognition.* Hillsdale, N.J.: Lawrence Erlbaum Associates, 1977.
Benton, A. L., & Pearl, D. (Eds.). *Dyslexia: An appraissl of current knowledge.* New York:
Oxford University Press, 1978.
Bolinger, D. Accent is predictable (If you're a mind reader). *Language,* 1972, *48,* 633–644.
Bolinger, D. *Aspects of language.* New York: Harcourt Brace Jovanovich, 1975.
Brown, A. L. Metacognitive development and reading. In R. J. Spiro, B. C. Bruce, & W. F.
Brewer (Eds.), *Theoretical issues in reading comprehension.* Hillsdale, N.J.: Lawrence Erl-
baum Associates, 1980.
Brown, A. L., & Campione, J. C. Permissible inferences from the outcome of training studies in
cognitive development research. *Quarterly Newsletter of the Institute for Comparative
Human Development,* 1978, *2,* 46–53.
Brown, A. L. & Smiley, S. S. *The development of strategies for studying prose passages* (Tech.
Rep. No. 66). Urbana: University of Illinois, Center for the Study of Reading, 1977. (a)
Brown, A. L., & Smiley, S. S. Rating the importance of structural units of prose passages: A
problem of metacognitive development. *Child Development,* 1977, *48,* 1–8. (b)
Calfee, R. C. Review of Gibson and Levin's "The Psychology of Reading." *Proceedings of the
National Academy of Education,* 1976, *3,* 1–80.
Campbell, D. T., & Stanley, J. C. Experimental and quasi-experimental designs for research in
teaching. In N. L. Gage (Ed.), *Handbook for research in teaching.* Chicago: Rand McNally,
1963.
Carpenter, P. A., & Just, M. A. Reading comprehension as eyes see it. In M. Just & P. Carpen-
ter (Eds.), *Cognitive processes in comprehension.* Hillsdale, N.J.: Lawrence Erlbaum Associ-
ates, 1978.
Chafe, W. L. Language and consciousness. *Language,* 1974, *50,* 111–133.
Chafe, W. Giveness, contrastiveness, definiteness, subjects, topics, and points of view. In C. Li
(Ed.), *Subject and topic.* New York: Academic Press, 1976.
Chapman, L. J., & Chapman, J. P. Problems in the measurement of cognitive deficit. *Psychological Bulletin,* 1973, *79,* 380–385.
Chapman, L. J., & Chapman, J. P. Alternative to the design of manipulating a variable to com-
pare retarded and nonretarded subjects. *American Jourrnal of Mental Deficiency,* 1974, *79,*
404–411.

Clark, H. H., & Clark, E. V. *Psychology and language: An introduction to psycholinguistics.* New York: Harcourt Brace Jovanovich, 1977.

Clark, H. H., & Haviland, S. E. Comprehension and the given-new contract. In R. O. Freedle (Ed.), *Discourse processes and comprehension.* Norwood, N.J.: Ablex, 1977.

Clay, M. M., & Imlach, R. H. Juncture, pitch, and stress as reading behavior variables. *Journal of Verbal Learning and Verbal Behavior,* 1971, *10,* 133-139.

Cooper, W. E., & Sorenson, J. M. Fundamental frequency contours and syntactic boundaries. *Journal of the Acoustical Society of America,* 1977, *62,* 133-139.

Cosgrove, J. M., & Patterson, C. J. Plans and the development of listener skills. *Developmental Psychology,* 1977, *13,* 557-564.

Cromer, W. The difference model: A new explanation for some reading difficulties. *Journal of Educational Psychology,* 1970, *61,* 471-483.

Cronbach, L. J., & Snow, C. E. *Aptitudes and instructional methods: A handbook for research on interactions.* New York: Irvington, 1977.

Danks, J. H. Comprehension in listening and reading: Same or different? In *Proceedings of the Interdisciplinary Institute on Reading and Child Development.* Newark, Delaware: University of Delaware, 1974.

Darwin, C. J. On the dynamic use of prosody in speech perception. In A. Cohen & S. G. Nooteboom (Eds.), *Structure and process in speech perception.* New York: Springer-Verlag, 1975.

Eamon, D. B. Selection and recall of topical information in prose by better and poorer readers. *Reading Research Quarterly,* 1978-1979,*15,* 244-257.

Farr, R. *Reading: What can be measured?* Newark, Del.: International Reading Association, 1969.

Fleisher, L. S., Jenkins, J. R., & Pany, D. Effects on poor readers' comprehension of training in rapid decoding. *Reading Research Quarterly,* 1979, *15,* 30-48.

Fodor, J. A., & Bever, T. G. The psychological reality of linguistic segments. *Journal of Verbal Learning and Verbal Behavior,* 1965, *4,* 414-420.

Fowler, H. N. Plato with an English translation. London: William Heinemann, Ltd.: 1914.

Garnes, S., & Bond, Z. Slips of the ear: Errors in perception of causal speech. In R. E. Grossman, J. J. San, & T. J. Vance (Eds.), *Papers from the eleventh regional meeting of the Chicago Linguistics Society.* Chicago: Chicago Linguistics Society, 1975.

Geers, A. E. Intonation contour and syntactic structure as predictors of apparent segmentation. *Journal of Experimental Psychology: Human Perception and Performance,* 1978, *4,* 273-283.

Gibson, E. J., & Levin, H. *The psychology of reading.* Cambridge, Mass.: MIT Press, 1975.

Golinkoff, R. M. A comparison of reading comprehension processes in good and poor reading. *Reading Research Quarterly,* 1975-1976, *4,* 623-659.

Grosjean, F. Grosjean, L., & Lane, H. The patterns of silence: Performance structures in sentence production. *Cognitive Psychology,* 1979, *11,* 58-81.

Hornby, P. A. Surface structure and the topic-comment distinction: A developmental study. *Child Development,* 1971, *42,* 975-988.

Hornby, P. A. The psychological subject and predicate. *Cognitive Psychology,* 1972, *3,* 632-642.

Hornby, P. A., & Hass, W. A. Use of contrastive stress by preschool children. *Journal of Speech and Hearing Research,* 1970, *13,* 395-399.

Huey, E. D. *The psychology and pedagogy of reading.* Cambridge, Mass.: MIT Press, 1968. (Originally published, 1908).

Ironsmith, M., & Whitehurst, G. J. The development of listener abilities in communication: How children deal with ambiguous information. *Child Development,* 1978, *49,* 348-352.

Jerrolds, B. W., Calloway, B., & Gwaltney, A. A comparative study of three tests of intellectual potential, three tests of reading achievement, and the discrepancy scores between potential and achievement. *Journal of Educational Research,* 1971, *65,* 168–172.

Just, M. A., & Carpenter, P. A. A theory of reading: From eye movements to comprehension. *Psychological Review,* 1980, *87,* 329–354.

Klatt, D. H. Linguistic uses of segmental duration in English: Acoustic and perceptual evidence. *Journal of the Acoustical Society of America,* 1976, *59,* 1208–1221.

Kleiman, G. M. Speech recoding in reading. *Journal of Verbal Learning and Verbal Behavior,* 1975, *14,* 323–339.

Kleiman, G. M., Winograd, P. N., & Humphrey, M. M. *Prosody and children's parsing of sentences* (Tech. Rep. No. 123). Urbana: University of Illinois, Center for the Study of Reading, 1979.

Knights, R., & Bakkar, D. J. (Eds.). *The neuropsychology of learning disabilities.* Baltimore: University Park Press, 1976.

LaBerge, D., & Samuels, S. J. Toward a theory of automatic information processing in reading. *Cognitive Psychology,* 1974, *6,* 293–323.

Lefevre, C. A. *Linguistics, English and the language arts.* New York: Teachers College Press, 1970.

Lehiste, I. Phonetic disambiguation of syntactic ambiguity. *Glossa,* 1973, *7,* 107–122.

Levin, J. R. Inducing comprehension in poor readers: A test of recent model. *Journal of Educational Psychology,* 1973, *65,* 10–24.

Lieberman, P. Some acoustic correlates of word stress in American English. *Journal of the Acoustical Society of America,* 1960, *32,* 451–455.

Lieberman, P. Some effects of semantic and grammatical context on the production and perception of speech. *Language and Speech,* 1963, *6,* 172–187.

MacGinitie, W. H. (Ed.). *Assessment problems in reading.* Newark, Del.: International Reading Association, 1973.

Maratsos, M. The effects of stress on the understanding of pronominal co-reference in children. *Journal of Psycholinguistic Research,* 1973, *2,* 1–8.

Markman, E. M. Realizing that you don't understand: Elementary school children's awareness of inconsistencies. *Child Development,* 1979, *50,* 643–655.

Meichenbaum, D. Cognitive factors as determinates of learning disabilities: A cognitive functional approach. In R. Knight & D. Bakker (Eds.), *The neuropsychology of learning disabilities.* Baltimore: University Park Press, 1976.

Neville, M. H., & Pugh, A. K. Context in reading and listening: Variations in approach to cloze tasks. *Reading Research Quarterly,* 1976–1977, *12,* 13–31.

Newell, A., & Simon, H. A. *Human problem solving.* Englewood Cliffs, N.J.: Prentice-Hall, 1972.

Olson, D. R. The language of instruction: On the literate bias of schooling. In R. C. Anderson, R. J. Spiro, & W. E. Montague (Eds.), *Schooling and the acquisition of knowledge.* Hillsdale, N.J.: Lawrence Erlbaum Associates, 1976.

Olson, D. R. From utterance to text: The bias of language in speech and writing. *Harvard Educational Review,* 1977, *47,* 257–281.

Patterson, C. J., Massad, C. M., & Cosgrove, J. Children's referential communication: Components of plans for effective listening. *Developmental Psychology,* 1978, *14,* 401–406.

Perfetti, C. A., Goldman, S. R., & Hogaboam, T. W. Reading skill and the identification of words in discourse context. *Memory & Cognition,* 1979, *7,* 273–282.

Rayner, K., & McConkie, G. W. What guides a reader's eye movements? *Vision Research,* 1976, *16,* 829–832.

Read, C., Schreiber, P., & Walia, J. Why short subjects are harder to find than long ones. In L. Gleitman & E. Wanner (Eds.), *Language acquisition: The state of the art.* New York: Cambridge University Press, 1983.

Rubin, A. D. Comprehension processes in oral and written language. In R. J. Spiro, B. C. Bruce, & W. F. Brewer (Eds.), *Theoretical issues in reading comprehension.* Hillsdale, N.J.: Lawrence Erlbaum Associates, 1980.

Rumelhart, D. E. Toward an interactive theory of reading. In S. Dornic (Ed.), *Attention and performance* (Vol. VI). Hillsdale, N.J.: Lawrence Erlbaum Associates, 1977.

Rutter, M. Prevalence and types of dyslexia. In A. L. Benton & D. Pearl (Eds.), *Dyslexia: An appraisal of current knowledge.* New York: Oxford University Press, 1978.

Rutter M., & Yule, W. Specific reading retardation. In L. Mann & D. Sabatino (Eds.), *The first review of special education* (Vol. 2). Philadelphia: JSE Publishers, 1973.

Rutter, M., & Yule, W. The concept of specific reading retardation. *Journal of Child Psychology and Psychiatry,* 1975, *16,* 181–197.

Ryan, E. B. Identifying and remediating failures in reading comprehension: Toward an instructional approach for poor comprehenders. In T. G. Waller & G. E. MacKinnon (Eds.), *Reading research: Advances in theory and practice* (Vol. 2). New York: Academic Press, 1980.

Sag, I. & Liberman, M. The intonational disambiguation of indirect speech acts. In R. E. Grossman, L. J. San, & T. J. Vance (Eds.), *Papers from the eleventh regional meeting of the Chicago Linguistics Society.* Chicago: Chicago Linguistics Society, 1975.

Samuels, S. J. Success and failure in learning to read: A critique of the research. *Reading Research Quarterly,* 1973–1974, *8,* 200–239.

Sartre, J. *The words.* (B. Frechtman, trans.). New York: George Braziller, 1964.

Schallert, D. L., & Kleiman, G. M. *Some reasons why teachers are easier to understand than textbooks* (Reading Education Rep. No. 9). Urbana: University of Illinois, Center for the Study of Reading, 1979.

Scholes, R. J. *Acoustic cues for constituent structure.* The Hague: Mouton, 1971.

Schvaneveldt, R., Ackerman, B. P., & Semelar, T. The effect of semantic context on children's word recognition. *Child Development,* 1977, *48,* 612–616.

Sinclair, J. M., & Coulthard, R. M. *Towards an analysis of discourse: The English used by teachers and pupils.* London: Oxford University Press, 1975.

Smith, F. *Psycholinguistics and reading.* New York: Holt, Rinehart & Winston, 1971.

Snow, C. E., & Ferguson, C. A. *Talking to children: Language input and acquisition.* Cambridge: Cambridge University Press, 1977.

Sorenson, J. M., Cooper, W. E., & Paccia, J. M. Speech timing of grammatical categories. *Cognition,* 1978, *6,* 135–153.

Spencer, H. The philosophy of style. In *Essays: Moral, political and aesthetic.* New York: Appleton, 1881. (Originally published, 1852.)

Spiro, R. J. *Etiology of reading comprehension style* (Tech. Rep. No. 124). Urbana: University of Illinois, Center for the Study of Reading, 1979.

Stanovich, K. E. Toward an interactive-compensatory model of individual differences in the development of reading fluency. *Reading Research Quarterly,* 1980, *16,* 32–71.

Taylor, E. A. The spans: Perception, apprehension, and recognition. *American Journal of Ophthalmology,* 1957, *44,* 501–507.

Thorndike, E. L. Reading as reasoning: A study of mistakes in paragraph reading. *Journal of Educational Psychology,* 1917, *8,* 323–332.

Thorndike, R. L. *The concepts of over- and underachievement.* New York: Teachers College Press, 1963.

Thorndike, R. L., & Hagen, E. *Measurement and evaluation in psychology and education.* New York: Wiley, 1977.

Tinker, M. A. Recent studies of eye movements in reading. *Psychological Bulletin,* 1958, *55,* 215–231.

Torgesen, J. K. Performance of reading disabled children on serial memory tasks: A selective review of recent research. *Reading Research Quarterly,* 1978–1979, *14,* 57–87.

Vellutino, F. R. *Dyslexia: Theory and research.* Cambridge, MA: MIT Press, 1979.

Vygotsky, L. S. *Thought and language.* Cambridge, MA: MIT Press, 1962. (Originally published, 1933.)

Waller, T. G., & MacKinnon, G. E. (Eds.). *Reading research: Advances in theory and practice* (Vol. 2). New York: Academic Press, 1981.

Wanat, S. F. *Linguistic structure and visual attention in reading.* Newark, DE: International Reading Association, 1971.

Weaver, P. A. Improving reading comprehension: Effects of sentence organization on instruction. *Reading Research Quarterly,* 1979, *15,* 129–146.

West, R. F., & Stanovich, K. E. Automatic contextual facilitation in readers of three ages. *Child Development,* 1978, *49,* 717–727.

Wilkinson, A. *The foundations of language: Talking and reading in young children.* London: Oxford University Press, 1971.

Winer, B. J. *Statistical principles in experimental design.* New York: McGraw-Hill, 1971.

Wingfield, A. The intonation-syntax interaction. In A. Cohen & S. G. Nooteboom (Eds.), *Structure and process in speech perception.* New York: Springer-Verlag, 1975.

Wingfield, A., & Klein, J. F. Syntactic structure and acoustic pattern in speech perception. *Perception & Psychophysics,* 1971, *9,* 23–25.

Wolf, M. The word-retrieval process and reading in children and aphasics. In K. E. Nelson (Ed.), *Children's language* (Vol. 3). Hillsdale, NJ: Lawrence Erlbaum Associates, 1982.

Yule, W., Rutter, M., Berger, M., & Thompson, J. Over- and under-achievement in reading: Distribution in the general population. *British Journal of Educational Psychology,* 1974, *44,* 1–12.

6 Early Intervention Programs for Hearing Impaired Children: A Longitudinal Assessment

Donald F. Moores
Gallaudet College
Washington, D.C.

This chapter presents the results of a longitudinal evaluation of preschool programs for hearing impaired children. The purpose of the evaluation was to assess the effectiveness of various early intervention strategies being employed in the education of hearing impaired children. The evaluation was designed to identify and isolate variables that would be predictive of success in educational achievement and development of communicative skills.

The initial year of the evaluation project was devoted to organizing and planning. Formal commitments were given to and received from participating programs following visitations and/or discussions with administrators and personnel. The majority of time during the first year was spent in the development and pilot study of assessment techniques.

Because deafness is a low-incidence handicap, the study extended over a wide geographical area in order to encompass the desired variety of programs. The seven programs that participated in the evaluation project represent a diversity of educational methodologies, organizational structures, and philosophies. Methodologies of communication among the seven programs included oral-aural, total communication, and the Rochester method.

When possible, existing standardized scales were utilized. During the course of the evaluation project, instruments were constructed and revised to assess the children's communicative abilities, receptive and expressive language development, speech skills, academic achievement, level of cognitive functioning, and psycholinguistics abilities. Additional scales to evaluate parental attitude, classroom structure, and methods of communication within the classroom (between students as well as between student and teacher) also were developed and adapted for use in the evaluation. An advisory committee representing the disciplines of audiology, psychology, psycholinguistics, and deaf education was convened to provide professional assistance.

In the subsequent 4 years, test data were collected on the longitudinal sample of subjects. Visits to the seven programs were made each spring (March through May) by a team of investigators who tested the students and observed in their classrooms. Fall visits were made to administer the Leiter International Performance Scale in the first year of testing and the Performance section of the Weschler Intelligence Scale for Children (WISC) in the fourth year. Following the collection and analyses of each year's data, an annual research progress report was published. These annual reports emphasized methodological, ethological, and programmatic comparisons. After data gathering was completed, a report was published which concentrated on an analysis of the sample as a whole (Weiss, Goodwin, & Moores, 1975). A final report (Moores, Weiss, & Goodwin, 1976) consisted of a series of recommended policies and procedures for preschool programs for hearing impaired children. I believe that the diversity of the subjects and the programs they were attending have provided a generally representative corpus of data relative to education of profoundly hearing impaired preschool children. Thus, those data seem to give a suitable basis from which to address issues of practical importance in educating the young hearing impaired child.

REVIEW OF THE LITERATURE

The study was predicated on the belief that there are extremely important and complex issues in the education of preschool deaf children which should be empirically investigated. These include questions of methodology, placement, program orientation, structure, and emphasis.

Although the need for such information is apparent, to date relatively few investigations pertaining to these issues have been undertaken. Yet, decisions are made daily regarding education of hearing impaired children. The necessity for sound, empirically based information to assist in the educational decision-making process becomes even more urgent in light of the recent proliferation of preschool programs for the hearing impaired.

The apparent lack of comprehensive data may be traced to two primary sources. First, the numerous problems in evaluating the effectiveness of preschool programs are compounded by the added dimension of deafness. The difficulty in assembling a sufficiently large sample, the overriding factor of effectively communicating with young deaf children, and the lack of available instruments that are appropriate for evaluation of a population of preschool deaf children are some of the difficulties encountered in the collection of empirical data.

The second, and perhaps even more, inhibiting factor is the highly emotional nature of the question of educational methodology with young deaf children. In a report to the Secretary of Health, Education and Welfare (Babbidge, 1965), it was noted that for more than 100 years emotion had served as a substitute for research in the education of the deaf. For example, the issue of manual communication is emotionally charged. Some educators firmly believe that the use of any kind of manual communication with a deaf child will prevent the development of speech and language, and the result will be a mute subculture. Others believe just as firmly that depriving a deaf child of manual communication will cause irreparable linguistic, educational, and emotional damage. Given such a climate, most researchers prefer to investigate other questions in the area of deafness or to concentrate on issues in other areas.

Evaluations of the effectiveness of preschool programs for the deaf generally have been restricted to those conducted by individuals closely affiliated with the program they are assessing (Craig, Craig, & DiJohnson, 1972; Hester, 1963; McConnell & Horton, 1970; McCroskey, 1968; Simmons, 1967). In many cases, reports of these evaluations are basically explanations and justifications of certain procedures. The value of such evaluations is usually limited because they assess only on program. Also, it is difficult to be objective about a program with which one has been intimately involved. Furthermore, such evaluations usually have a number of inherent problems, the greatest of which has been designating children to serve as a control group (i.e., children who do not receive the educational treatment being evaluated).

With the exception of the present preschool evaluation project by Moores and associates (see Moores & McIntyre, 1971; Moores, McIntyre, & Weiss, 1972; Moores, Weiss, & Goodwin, 1973, 1974; Weiss et al., 1975, for prior progress reports), very few investigations directly comparing the efficiency of methodologies have been undertaken. One such study was conducted by Quigley (1969) who reported that preschool children taught by the Rochester method (the simultaneous use of speech and fingerspelling) were superior to children taught by the oral-only approach in measures of speechreading, reading, and written language.

Research on the relative academic and linguistic superiority of deaf children of deaf parents has had a great and growing influence on the field of deaf education. These findings suggest that deaf children of deaf parents tend to be better adjusted, to achieve at a higher academic level, to have better language abilities, and to have speech development equivalent to deaf children of hearing parents (Best, 1972; Brasel, 1975; Meadow, 1967; Quigley & Frisina, 1961; Stevenson, 1964; Stuckless & Birch, 1966; Vernon & Koh, 1970). Of great importance is the evidence that deaf children of deaf parents increase their relative advantage with age so that by late adolescence their superiority is much more pronounced.

A number of studies focusing on evaluation of preschool programs report few or no differences between deaf children with preschool training and those who have not been involved in preschool programs. Craig (1964) found no differences between speechreading skills of children with preschool experiences and those with no such experience. In a comparison between children who received preschool training and those who did not, Phillips (1963) found that by age 9 no differences existed between preschool and nonpreschool groups in the areas of language arts, arithmetic, and socialization. Mc-Croskey (1968) found some differences between children who participated in a home-centered program with an auditory emphasis and a control group of children who received no preschool training. Differences favored the control group; however, because the hearing losses of the control group were less severe and the IQ scores of that group were somewhat higher, it is difficult to generalize from these results. As part of a follow-up study of graduates of the Tracy Clinic from 1944–1968, Vernon and Koh (1971) matched those graduates on age, IQ, and sex with deaf children who had no preschool experience. There were no differences found between the subjects trained at the Tracy Clinic and those with no preschool experience in speech, speechreading, and academic programs, including reading instruction.

The research efforts just cited, which were conducted by investigators who were not affiliated with their subjects' programs, compared children trained in oral-only preschools with those who received no preschool training (Craig, 1964; McCroskey, 1968; Phillips, 1963; Vernon & Koh, 1970). These inquiries illustrate the absence of consistent findings.

In view of the findings in favor of deaf children of deaf parents, which suggest the benefits of exposure to signs from birth, it has been argued that many traditional preschool programs have failed because they have been restricted to oral-only instruction (Vernon & Koh, 1971). Thus, it has been hypothesized that perhaps the addition of manual communication would improve results. Such reasoning has led to the development of many recent preschool programs utilizing a system known as *total communication,* which involves the use of signs, fingerspelling, and oral-aural communication.

Although the evidence of academic and linguistic superiority of deaf children of deaf parents is substantial, it does not necessarily follow that the use of manual communication in preschool programs will produce better results. For example, deaf parents may be better equipped emotionally to deal with deafness in their children. Maestas y Moores (1979, 1980) has found that deaf parents utilize a variety of strategies involving vocal, manual, and tactile means of communicating with their children from the first week after birth and during the first 2 years of life. Ten sets of deaf parents with a variety of educational, ethnic, and linguistic backgrounds all signed *and* spoke to their children. They would also make signs on the babies' bodies, physically guide the babies through signs, stimulate vocalization by manipulation of the babies' mouths, and monitor vocal production by noting mouth movements and by placing their hands on the babies' chests.

During the first months of a child's life, deaf parents typically do not know their child's hearing status. Although the majority of children of deaf parents have normal hearing, the incidence of hearing loss in this group is greater than in the general population (Moores, 1982). Most deaf parents are aware of the possibility of having deaf children and usually are able to accept deafness in a child more readily than hearing parents can. The impact is not overwhelming, as it may be for parents with normal hearing who typically have had little knowledge of the effect of deafness on linguistic, social, and academic development (Moores, 1973). Hence, deaf children of deaf parents may have a number of advantages over deaf children of hearing parents, only one of which would be early manual communication.

PROCEDURES

Program Descriptions

As has been noted, the seven programs participating in the preschool evaluation were specifically selected to provide a diverse representation of approaches to educating the preschool deaf child. I am aware of differences that exist in the definitions of various methods of instruction, especially in reference to the term "total communication." Hence, for purposes of the study, the methodologies were defined as follows:

1. *Oral-aural method.* In this method, the child receives input through speechreading (lipreading) and amplification of sound. Expression is through speech alone. The use of signs and fingerspelling are not part of the educational process.

2. *Rochester method.* This method is a combination of the oral-aural method plus fingerspelling. Children receive information through speechreading, amplification, and fingerspelling. The use of signs is not permitted.

3. *Total communication.* This approach, also known in this context as the simultaneous method, is a combination of the oral-aural method plus fingerspelling and signs. The child receives input through speechreading, amplification, signs, and fingerspelling. A proficient teacher will sign in coordination with the spoken word. In some programs, teachers use fingerspelling to illustrate function words and bound morphemes.

The administrators of the programs that participated in this study were not obligated to maintain any particular aspect of their program for the duration of the research. They were simply requested to continue to provide what they considered to be the most effective program possible for hearing impaired children. This has presented some difficulty in methodological classification of the programs because some were in transition from the use of one method or philosophy to another during the course of the evaluation. However, this transition has enabled the investigators to assess the effects of change.

Table 6.1 summarizes the methodological approaches employed in the various programs during the evaluation. Some programs have been classified as transitional to indicate that although a new methodology had been implemented in a particular program, teachers and staff were in the process of developing and refining their proficiency in the use of the newly adopted approach. Two oral-aural programs incorporated total-communication components into their educational structure during the evaluation to provide an additional manual supplement to those students diagnosed as requiring such a supplement. These programs are indicated in Table 6.1 by the notion Oral-Aural (TC). In the program employing the individualized approach, students were instructed in either the total-communication or oral-aural approach, as determined by the program's staff.

Subject Descriptions

Of the total sample population ($n = 89$), complete data were obtained for 60 children who comprised the 4-year longitudinal sample. These subjects possessed the following characteristics:

1. Chronological age from 2 years 6 months to 4 years 6 months in September of the first year of data gathering.
2. Sensorineural hearing loss of 70 dB or greater in the better ear across the speech range.
3. Leiter International Performance Scale IQ of 80 or better.

TABLE 6.1
Methodologies Employed by Programs
During the 4 Years of Data Gathering

Program	Years			
	1	2	3	4
A	Oral-Aural	Transitional (TC)	TC	TC
B	Oral-Aural	Oral	Oral-Aural (TC)	Transitional (TC)
C	—	TC	TC	TC
D	Oral-Aural	Oral-Aural	Oral-Aural (TC)	Oral-Aural (TC)
E	TC[a]	TC	TC	TC
F	Transitional (Rochester)	Rochester	Rochester	Rochester
G	Rochester	Individualized (TC, Oral-Aural)	Individualized (TC, Oral-Aural)	Individualized (TC, Oral-Aural)

[a]TC = Total Communication.

TABLE 6.2
Chronological Age, Leiter IQ, Sex, and Hearing Loss of
Longitudinal Subject Group
(as of Completion of Testing)

Program	Number of Subjects	Male	Female	CA Mean in Months	Leiter IQ Mean	Hearing Loss Mean (dB)
A	6	5	1	83.18	114.17	97.67
B	12	8	4	82.83	124.33	95.83
C	8	5	3	87.88	107.29	103.50
D	13	11	2	83.69	112.54	96.08
E	7	2	5	84.57	132.00	101.12
F	8	3	5	89.25	104.00	102.00
G	6	3	3	84.50	123.33	93.67
Total/Means	60	37	23	85.16	116.57	98.55

4. Age of onset of hearing loss of 2 years or younger.
5. No other severe handicap in addition to the hearing loss.

Data were gathered on the children for 4 years in all of the programs except for eight subjects in Program C, which became affiliated with the study in September 1971, 1 year after it began.

Table 6.2 summarizes the ages, severity of hearing impairments, and Leiter IQ scores for the longitudinal subject group ($n = 60$) as of the testing period of the final year.

The chronological ages of the 60 subjects in the longitudinal sample at the time of the final testing period ranged from 74–97 months, with a mean age of 85 months. The IQ measure employed at the onset of this project was the Leiter International Performance Scale (Arthur, 1952). Because it is designed for, and had normative information for, lower chronological age levels than other scales and because it is designed to test the ability to learn rather than skills already learned, it was deemed appropriate. An additional measure of intellectual functioning, the performance scale of the Wechscer Intelligence Scale for Children (WISC), was administered to the entire sample population in the fall of the fourth year. Table 6.3 summarizes by program the mean scaled score for each of the WISC Performance Scale subtests as well as the mean Performance IQ score and the Leiter IQ scores. For the WISC, scaled subtest scores are derivations of raw scores such that at each age and for each subtest the mean scaled score for the standardization sample is 10 with a standard deviation of 3.

The mean Performance IQ for the 60 children in the longitudinal group was 110 for the WISC and 117 for the Leiter Scale. WISC scaled subtest scores ranged from 13.62 (picture completion) to 9.85 (picture arrangement) with intermediate scores at 10.03 (coding), 11.93 (block design), and 12.02 (object assembly).

TABLE 6.3
Mean Wechsler Intelligence Scale for Children (WISC) Scaled
Scores on Performance Subtests, Total WISC Performance
IQ Scores, and Mean IQ Values Obtained by the
Leiter International Performance Scale

Program	n	Picture Completion	Picture Arrangement	Block Design	Object Assembly	Coding	Total WISC Performance IQ	Mean Leiter IQ
A	6	12.50	8.67	11.83	8.67	11.17	103.33	114.17
B	12	14.83	10.00	12.58	13.33	9.67	113.58	124.33
C	8	12.13	9.75	11.63	11.38	9.50	104.38	112.54
D	13	12.85	9.54	11.69	12.92	10.38	110.38	107.25
E	7	13.75	10.75	12.75	12.38	10.13	113.50	132.00
F	8	14.38	10.13	11.06	12.25	8.25	108.50	104.00
G	6	14.83	11.17	11.83	10.83	11.83	114.50	123.33
Totals/Means	60	13.62	9.85	11.93	12.02	10.03	110.09	116.57

For the 60 children in the longitudinal sample, comparisons of the WISC Performance IQ scores and the Leiter Performance IQ scores obtained 4 years earlier reveal a decrease of approximately 6.4 points. This decrease in IQ scores across time is consistent with the findings of Quigley (1969) who reported a difference of 12 points between the Leiter Scale mean score and average scores from the WISC Performance Scale administered 4 years later. From the data of the present study, a significant Pearson product-moment correlation of .54, $p < .001$, was found to exist between the WISC Performance scores and the Leiter scores that were obtained earlier.

Inspection of the WISC scores obtained in 1974 indicates that the subjects were functioning within the normal range. However, the overall WISC Performance IQ of 110 is somewhat above the hearing norm. There are no apparent large differences in the WISC scores among the programs. Therefore, it seems unlikely that the intellectual levels of the children within the programs influenced their performances on other measures.

Audiometric data yielded a mean hearing loss of 98.50 dB (ANSI, 1969) for the sample, with a range of 75–110 dB. Hearing aid usage was high, ranging from 85% of the children in the first year of the study to 92% in the third year. Comparisons on the basis of sex, age, and hearing loss reveal no significant difference between programs. The breakdown of the sample by etiology and age of onset of hearing loss may be found in Tables 6.4 and 6.5, respectively.

By the end of the study, the eight children in Program C, which entered the study at the beginning of the second year, had been in attendance at the program for 3 academic years. The 52 children in the other six programs all had been in attendance for 4 academic years or more. Eighteen pupils were living in residential schools during the final year of the data gathering; the remaining children attended day classes either in public schools, residential schools on a commuting basis, or speech and hearing centers.

Instruments

This project made use of several testing instruments to obtain empirically based results in an attempt to make the evaluation as comprehensive as possible. An attempt was made to identify and employ assessment tools to tap the broad spectrum of abilities generally characteristic of preschool children. The following are brief descriptions of all measures employed during the 4-year evaluation. Throughout, instructions were provided in the mode of communication consistent with the methodologies employed in the various programs. When necessary, adaptations for use with sign systems were made.

Academic Achievement

In an effort to assess the educational development of the subjects, the Metropolitan Readiness Tests (MRT) (Hildreth, Griffiths, & McGauvran, 1969) and the Metropolitan Achievement Tests (MAT-Primer Battery) (Durost, Bixler, Wrightstone, Prescott, & Balow, 1971) were selected for inclusion in the evaluation. Selection of these measures was based on appropriateness of content and format, clarity of wording, and the stated purpose of each instrument. These tests are designed to measure the extent to which children have acquired those abilities that contribute to success in first grade.

On the basis of pilot testing, the following subtests from the MRT were administered in the third year test battery in the evaluation: (1) matching; (2) alphabet; (3) numbers; and (4) copying. The assessment of academic achievement was continued in the spring of the final year when the reading and numbers subunits of the MAT (Primer Battery) were administered.

TABLE 6.4
Diagnosed Etiologies of Deafness for Children by Program

Program	Heredity	Illness	Meningitis	Prematurity	Rh Factor	Maternal Rubella	Trauma at Birth	Unknown	Program Total
A	4	0	1	0	0	0	0	1	6
B	1	0	0	0	0	5	0	6	12
C	4	0	1	0	0	1	1	1	8
D	1	0	1	1	0	5	0	5	13
E	1	1	1	1	0	0	0	3	7
F	2	2	1	0	0	0	0	3	8
G	0	0	2	1	1	0	0	2	6
Totals	13	3	7	3	1	11	1	21	60

TABLE 6.5
Age of Onset of Hearing Loss by Program of Subject Group

Program	Present at Birth	Birth to 12 Mo.	12 to 24 Mo.	Unknown	Program Total
A	4	1	0	1	6
B	10	0	0	2	12
C	7	1	0	0	8
D	11	0	1	1	13
E	3	0	2	2	7
F	2	2	0	4	8
G	3	0	2	1	6
Totals	40	4	5	11	60

Illinois Test of Psycholinguistic Abilities (ITPA)

The following five visual-motor subtests of the ITPA (Kirk, McCarthy, & Kirk, 1969) were administered to the sample population: (1) visual reception; (2) visual association; (3) manual expression; (4) visual closure; and (5) visual sequential memory.

Communication Battery

Because of the need for empirical tests of the communication skills of the young deaf children, three scales were developed to assess their receptive communication, expressive communication, and articulation abilities. Vocabulary for all three scales were developed from lists of words the children knew (provided by the teachers in the programs).

Receptive Communication Scale.   The Receptive Communication Scale was developed to assess five different, but not mutually exclusive, modes of communication: (1) sound-alone; (2) sound plus speechreading; (3) sound and speechreading plus fingerspelling; (4) sound and speechreading plus signs; and (5) the printed word. The first is similar to an auditory-only method; the second is comparable to the oral-aural method; the third resembles the Rochester method; and the fourth corresponds to total communication. Reception of speechreading, fingerspelling, or signs alone was not investigated. The object was to test the children under close to normal pedagogical conditions used wth the deaf (i.e., conditions which always included the spoken word).

At this point, perhaps it is important to note that technically none of the programs used American Sign Language (ASL). The programs used manual codes on English, which represent modifications of ASL vocabulary, syntax, and morphology, to conform to English to the extent that messages can be signed and spoken in coordination following English word order. Thus, Jordan, Gustason, and Rosen (1979) reported that approximately 65% of programs for the deaf in the United States used total communication as the primary mode of communication. Not one reported using ASL as the primary mode. Complete discussions of the issues are provided by Moores (1980, 1982) and Wilbur (1979).

In the second year, 20 items representing four levels of difficulty were developed. For each item, pictures showed the correct choice and three additional multiple choice foils; the alternate choices were balanced in matrix form. For example, the correct choice "red ball" was accompanied on the page by the blue ball, red top, and blue top. Therefore, in order to respond correctly the child must understand the entire phrase rather than part of it. This Receptive Scale was expanded in 1973 to include 5 items of noun-verb construction, increasing the total number of items to 25.

Receptive Communication Supplement.   In the final year, additional items consisting of five negative and five reversible passive voice forms adapted from Schmitt (1969) were randomized into the existing Receptive Scale. These additions increased the number of items for each mode of communication from 5 to 7, for a total of 35 items. In addition, for assessment of comprehension of verb tenses, 15 items were developed incorporating vocabulary and tense from Thorndike (1932).

The two oral programs requested that neither sign language nor fingerspelling be used in testing their oral students. With the exception of the children enrolled in total-communication classes within these oral programs, these modes were not employed with either group. The request by the Rochester method program not to employ signs was also honored. Children in oral clases were given three sound plus speechreading tests. Children in the Rochester method program received two sound plus fingerspelling administrations in place of the sign tests, which were ordinarily used in these portions of the measure.

Expressive Communication Scale.   A communication scale was also developed to assess expressive language abilities. In the third year, stimuli for the expressive scale consisted of 25 pictures selected from the false foils of the Receptive Communication Scale representing the five levels of linguistic difficulty. Pilot testing at the beginning of the final year showed that more complex stimuli provided a greater opportunity for subjects to use connected language in their expressive attempts. Therefore, in the final evaluation, eight sequenced picture stories were used as stimulus items. Each consisted of four to five pictures selected from the Developmental Learning Material (DLM) Sequential Cards. The children were free to say as much or as little about each picture as they chose, in the communication mode of their preference.

Word Intelligibility. This portion of the communication battery was comprised of the following 10 one- and two-syllable words:

apple	top
bird	fish
cat	milk
dog	red
eye	shoe

Each word was presented individually by means of a colored, 5 × 7 inch illustration, and the subjects were instructed to repeat each word after the examiner until it was determined that their best attempts at that word had been audio-recorded.

Responses of children from all programs were mixed randomly. The resulting tapes were then played for two groups of raters, most of whom were unfamiliar with the speech of the deaf. The raters were presented with a list of 25 words and instructed to select from this list the words uttered by the subjects.

Matching Familiar Figures Test (MFF)

The (MFF) is a series of visual discrimination tasks designed to measure reflection-impulsivity. This dimension describes a tendency to display slow or fast decision times consistently in problem-solving situations with high response uncertainty. Reflective children are those whose response time is above the median and whose error score is below the median. Those children classified as impulsive score above the median on errors but below it on response time. This measure has been used to predict success or failure in the acquisition of reading skills (Kagan, 1965).

The test is comprised of twelve items, each consisting of a picture of a familiar object (the standard) and six similar alternate choices, one of which is identical to the standard. The scores are: (1) the total number of errors and (2) the average response time, in tenths of a second, for the first selection.

TABLE 6.6
Metropolitan Readiness Tests: Significant t–Test Comparisons Between
Sample Mean and Population Mean by Tests

Test	*Hearing Impaired* *Sample Mean*	*Standardization* *Population Mean*	*t*	*df*
Matching	9.57	7.49	5.65**	56
Alphabet	12.95	9.39	6.84**	56
Numbers	9.47	12.02	-5.01**	56
Copying	8.49	6.82	3.43	56

$*p < .01$
$**p < .001$

Communication Analysis for Classrooms

During visits to the preschool programs, observations were made in the three classes containing the largest number of children in each of the seven programs. This chapter reports only on the segment of the form entitled Communication Analysis. The mode(s) of communication employed in the classroom by the teacher and child (child to child, child to teacher, teacher to child) were rated on the same 7-point scale, ranging from never to frequently observed.

RESULTS

Academic Achievement

Metropolitan Readiness Tests (MRT)

In their discussion of the standardization for the MRT, Hildreth et al. (1969) do not provide ages of the standardization subjects. The sample consisted of over 6500 beginning first grade students, and therefore, a chronological age for those subjects of somewhat greater than 6.0 seems reasonable. If that is a reasonable assumption, the mean age of the standardization sample was similar to that of the children in the present study at the time of testing.

The performance of the 57 children in the third year of the study on the individual tests was different from that of the standardization sampe (Table 6.6). Raw scores of deaf children were significantly higher on matching, $p < .001$, alphabet, $p < .001$, and copying, $p < .01$. However, their performance on the numbers test was significantly lower than that of the standardization sample, $p < .001$. The relatively poor performance on the numbers test may be due in part to the fact that all questions on this test were presented vocally. In all schools, including those where signs and fingerspelling were added to the vocal presentation, the present author's subjective opinion is that it is possible the results were influenced by the receptive communication abilities of the children.

Metropolitan Achievement Test (MAT)

The two subtests of the MAT were administered in the final year of the 60 subjects in the present sample. The authors of the MAT do not provide age-adjusted scaled scores, hence statistical analyses were computed on the subject group's raw scores by subtest. Raw score means for the sample were as follows: reading, 25.85; numbers, 19.95; and total score, 45.50. Inasmuch as the mean chronological age of the current sample is approximately 7 years, the percentile rank for the middle of first grade appeared to be the most appropriate for comparison with the present subjects. That comparison showed the present sample of 60 children to have achieved a mean percentile rank of 62 on the reading subtest, which is, of course, above the average performance of hearing first graders. However, the present sample fell to a mean percentile rank of 35 on the arithmetic subtest, which is below the typical score of the hearing group.

These findings are similar to those of the MRTs in which the sample of deaf children scored significantly higher on the reading-related matching and alphabet subtests, and their performance on the numbers test was significantly lower than that of the standardization sample. As with the results of the MRT, the verbal nature of the arithmetic subtest may account in part for the relatively poor performance of the deaf subjects on computational tasks. Nevertheless, these data lend further support to indications that these children may have been functioning below their hearing counterparts in the area of arithmetic.

The range of mean raw scores *by program* for the MAT was from 39.85 to 51.87, with the low score obtained by children in an oral-aural program and the high score obtained by the children in a Rochester method program (Table 6.7). The difference was significant at the .05 level.

Illinois Test of Psycholinguistic Abilities (ITPA)

The comparison of the present subjects' performance on the ITPA was to the scaled scores on five ITPA subtests over 4 years. The transformation of raw scores at each age and for each subtest is such that the mean of the standardization sample is 36, with a standard deviation of 6. Table 6.8, giving the means of the ITPA subtest and total scaled scores for the sample for the 4 years, shows that the means of the subtests fluctuate around the means of the standardization sample of hearing children. The mean of the total scale score across the 4-year period (180.68) is almost identical to the mean of that standardization sample of hearing children (180).

TABLE 6.7
Metropolitan Achievement Test (Primer Battery):
Mean Raw Scores by Program and Subtest, Fourth Year

	n	Reading		Arithmetic		Combined	
		X	SD	X	SD	X	SD
A	6	26.00	3.35	20.17	5.85	46.17	7.63
B	12	23.92	6.80	17.50	6.79	41.42	12.37
C	8	27.13	6.81	23.25	9.98	50.38	15.77
D	13	22.69	7.65	17.15	6.94	39.85	13.02
E	7	27.86	4.26	21.14	6.57	49.00	9.68
F	8	29.50	3.07	22.38	5.80	51.87	7.33
G	6	27.50	6.06	21.67	7.71	49.17	12.94
Total	60	25.85	6.23	19.95	7.23	45.50	12.23

TABLE 6.8
Longitudinal Sample ITPA Mean Scaled Scores by Year

Year	n	Visual Reception	Visual Sequential Memory	Visual Association	Visual Closure	Manual Expression	Total Score
1	48	36.46	40.73	32.91	30.50	38.68	179.21
2	56	36.28	37.95	34.59	34.12	41.00	183.95
3	59	34.32	36.32	35.00	33.44	39.88	178.90
4	60	35.16	36.76	34.48	34.31	40.50	180.65
Mean Scores		35.56	37.94	34.25	33.09	40.02	180.68

Communication Battery

Receptive Communication Scale

The data from the Receptive Communication Scale that were analyzed consisted of the percentage correct for each of the five modes of stimulus presentation (communication) as well as the total percentage correct on all 25 items for each subject in years 2, 3, and 4. Tables 6.9, 6.10, and 6.11 present the average scores for mode of stimulus presentation within each program, as well as the total subject group. Arcsin transformations (Winer, 1962) were applied before the statistical analysis to minimize difficulties inherent in the use of proportional data.

Examination of Tables 6.9, 6.10, and 6.11, suggests that for each year scores improve as modalities of stimulus presentation are added to the modes of communication. Because they do not involve direct person-to-person communication, printed word scores are considered separately. For the remaining four modes of communication, in the second year scores improve from sound alone (34%), to sound plus speechreading (56%), to sound and speechreading plus fingerspelling (61%), to sound and speechreading plus

TABLE 6.9
Percentage Correct on Receptive Communication Scale by Program
and Mode of Communication, Second Year

Program	n	Printed Word	Sound Alone	Sound & Speechreading SR	Sound, SR, & Fingerspelling	Sound, SR, & Signs	Total % Correct
A	11	32	25	50	48	61	43
B	18	37	32	52	—	—	45
C	7	54	39	57	79	75	59
D	15	32	40	63	—	—	52
E	6	42	33	67	71	75	57
F	11	36	34	48	51	—	44
G	6	45	37	75	75	87	60
Totals n	74	74	74	74	41	30	74
X̄		38	34	56	61	72	50
SD		28	25	29	30	30	20

TABLE 6.10
Percentage Correct on Receptive Communication Scale by
Program and Mode of Communication, Third Year

Program	n	Printed Word	Sound Alone	Sound & Speechreading SR	Sound, SR, & Fingerspelling	Sound, SR, & Signs	Total % Correct
A	9	64	31	62	76	91	65
B	13	48	38	73	—	—	61
C	8	63	38	65	63	85	63
D	14	47	59	65	—	—	61
E	9	69	31	62	67	87	64
F	8	60	45	48	68	—	59
G	6	47	63	67	80	80	69
Totals *n*	67	67	67	67	40	32	67
X̄		56	43	63	72	86	62
SD		28	25	29	30	30	20

signs (72%). The overall accuracy is 50%. By the fourth year the scores were: sound alone, 44%; sound plus speechreading, 68%; sound and speech-reading plus fingerspelling, 75%; sound and speechreading plus signs, 88%. The overall accuracy increased to 69%. Despite continued improvement in the children's receptive communication skills, the hierarchy of difficulty for these four modes of communication has remained constant across the 3-year period.

As all person-to-person modes of communication involved some degree of auditory input, it was decided to analyze the results of the communication scale by hearing loss to determine its relationship to communication ability

TABLE 6.11
Percentage Correct on Receptive Communication Scale
(Core Items) by Program and Mode of Communication,
Fourth Year

Program	n	Printed Word	Sound Alone	Sound & Speechreading SR	Sound, SR, & Fingerspelling	Sound, SR, & Signs	Total % Correct
A	6	90	40	53	77	83	68
B	12	67	40	65	51	80	63
C	8	77	37	65	75	93	69
D	13	65	58	67	55	85	64
E	7	80	34	51	80	94	68
F	8	90	35	83	89	—	75
G	6	77	53	90	97	93	82
Totals *n*	60	60	60	60	48	40	60
X̄		76	44	68	75	88	69
SD		29	27	31	28	21	19

Source: Moores, D. *Educating the deaf: Psychology, principles and practices.* Boston: Houghton Mifflin, 1982, p. 249.

TABLE 6.12

Correlation Between Hearing Loss and Receptive Communication
Scale Scores (Core Items) by Mode of Communication

	Year of Testing		
	Two	Three	Four
Printed word	.03	.14	-.03
Sound alone	-.31*	-.18	-.50**
Speechreading	-.40**	-.44**	-.46**
Fingerspelling	-.14	-.15	-.30
Sign language	.09	.02	.09
Total score	-.45**	-.27	-.36*

*p <.01
**p <.001

by mode and total score. Table 6.12 gives these results. Degree of hearing loss
was not highly correlated with scores on the printed word, fingerspelling, or
sign language for years 2 through 4, but the scores for sound alone and
speedreading indicate a significant relationship with hearing acuity. Correlation coefficients were statistically significant for sound alone in years 2 and 4,
and for speechreading in all 3 years of testing. Although hearing loss correlated significantly with total receptive communication scores for years 2 and
4, a level of statistical significance was not reached for the third year.

Passive Voice

For passives, the overall percentage of correct responses was 29% with
subjects choosing the reverse interpretation of the passive phrases 47% of the
time (Table 6.13). It therefore appears that deaf subjects frequently employ
the active interpretation of passive phrases and ignore the passive marker *by*.
In separate investigations of deaf children's acquisition of the passive voice,
both Power (1971) and Schmitt (1969) observed deaf individuals between the
ages of 8 and 18 making similar types of errors in the comprehension of
passives. They suggest that this incorrect interpretation occurs because of the
student's failure to reverse the subject-object order of passive sentences.
Thus, the deaf child not only fails to interpret passive sentences but frequently derives information that is the opposite of what is intended (cf.
younger hearing children; e.g., Strohner & Nelson, 1974).

Examination of the passive scores by mode of communication indicates
that deaf children received a considerably higher percentage of correct responses (50%) when items were presented using the printed word. Scores for
the remaining modes of communication cluster around the chance level with
sign language at 38%, fingerspelling at 25%, speechreading at 24%, and
sound alone at 22%. Initial *t*- test comparisons revealed no significant differences for passive scores by program.

TABLE 6.13
Receptive Communication Scores (Passives)
by Program, Fourth Year

Program	n	Percentage Correct	Percentage of Reversed Passives Chosen	Range of Individual Subject Scores (Percentage Score)
A	6	40	47	70-60
B	12	25	45	0-60
C	8	28	53	0-60
D	13	31	49	0-80
E	7	37	40	0-60
F	8	23	58	0-60
G	6	37	37	20-60
Total	60	29	47	0-80

Expressive Communicaton Scale

There are a total of 56 subjects in this subsection's analysis. Due to mechanical failure, distortion of the audio and visual portion of the tape for four subjects in Program F rendered the tape uninterpretable. As might be expected, interpreters made more correct identifications (56.66%) than deaf adults (31.41%) and graduate students (19.54%). It is of interest to note that, although the interpreters were processing information both auditorily and visually, little more than half of the subjects' expressive attempts were correctly identified. These results, detailed in Table 6.14 for year 4, seem to suggest a lack of effectiveness in the children's overall communication abilities.

The following criteria for identification of a subject's preferred mode of communication were developed:

1. *Total communication* — 70% of all units of expression conveyed via simultaneous verbalization and signing or fingerspelling.
2. *Rochester method* — 70% of all units of expression conveyed via simultaneous verbalization and fingerspelling.
3. *Sign* — 70% of all units of expression conveyed via signs. Signs were not consistently accompanied by spoken words.
4. *Fingerspelling* — 70% of all units of expression conveyed via fingerspelling. Fingerspelling was not consistently accompanied by spoken words.
5. *Gesture* — 70% of all units of expression conveyed via gestures.
6. *Manual* — 70% of all units of expression conveyed via gestures, signs, or fingerspelling, which were not necessarily accompanied by verbalization.
7. *Oral* — 70% of all units of expression conveyed via vocalization only.

Analysis of the preferred mode of communication by children indicates that the most commonly employed mode was total communication (simultaneous oral-manual), $n = 18$, followed by oral, $n = 17$. The variation across subjects was extensive. Distribution of preferred mode of communication within programs has indicated that, although each participating program implements a particular methodological approach to instruction, students seem to have developed personal communicative styles that often are not limited to the given philosophy of communication employed by particular programs.

Word Intelligibility

Although the use of different recording systems and raters across the 3 years may have had some effect on the word-intelligibility scores, this variation probably does not account for the consistently low scores obtained for each year. Scores on this measure consist of the percentage of correct identifications by raters for each of the children. The word most readily identified was *apple* (71%), followed by *eye* (48%) and *bird* (48%). The words *cat* (17%) and *red* (25%) were identified with the greatest difficulty. The overall accuracy across all seven programs was 37%. Program D (65%) and Program G (60%) received the highest scores; the remaining five programs scored considerably lower with scores ranging from 21% to 29%. Scores for children in these programs were higher than for those in other programs over the 4 years of data gathering. It should be noted that Program D was primarily oral-only, and Program G used both total communication and oral-only modes. Program comparisons employing the *t* test revealed that word in-

TABLE 6.14
Expressive Communication Scale:
Intelligibility Scores by Program, Fourth Year

Program	n	Graduate Students Mean Percentage	Interpreters Mean Percentage	Deaf Adults Mean Percentage	Total % Intelligible	Range of Individual Scores[a]
A	6	14.27	43.54	42.23	33.36	29-41%
B	12	18.10	42.43	29.18	29.90	21-42%
C	8	14.23	59.89	61.23	45.11	27-57%
D	13	29.30	46.56	15.99	30.61	10-48%
E	7	11.68	48.86	42.98	34.50	8-51%
F	4	7.84	17.81	17.18	14.28	10-21%
G	6	30.62	48.10	14.73	31.15	15-55%
Total	56	19.54[b]	56.66[b]	31.41[b]	32.21[b]	8-57%

[a] Each individual score computed as average of 24 raters.
[b] Weighted mean.

telligiblity scores from Program D and Program G were significantly higher than those of the remaining five programs.

It was hypothesized that there would be a relationship between word-intelligibility scores and hearing loss. Pearson product-moment correlations of .43, $p < .001$, in the second year, .58, $p < .001$ in the third year and .60, $p < .001$, in the fourth year between word-intelligibility scores and hearing loss confirmed this hypothesis and indicated a moderate relationship.

Matching Familiar Figures Test (MFF)

The MFF was administered only once to the children in the spring of the third year. A significant Pearson product-moment correlation between average time and errors of $- 31, p < .01$, was obtained. This is within the range of correlations reported by Kagan (1965).

Using Kagan's criteria, 22 reflective and 22 impulsive children were identified. These two groups did not differ significantly on the basis of sex, IQ, age, etiology, hearing loss, or program. Because the MFF has been used previously in reading research, t-test comparisons were made between the scores of the reflective and impulsive children for those measures designed to evaluate prereading or reading skills (i.e., the copying, matching, and alphabet portions of the MRT and the printed word subtest of the Receptive Communication Scale). Significantly higher scores were achieved by the reflective children on the matching test, $t = 4.61, p < .001$, and copying test, $t = 3.66$, $p < .001$. However, scores did not differ significantly on the alphabet test or the printed word subtest of the MAT.

Communication Analysis

The degree and mode in which children communicated with each other and with their teachers were rated on a 7-point scale from "never" to "frequently." Means of the rating were computed. In order to assess the consistency of classroom communication patterns with the official program methodology, program ratings were combined according to methodology by year (see Table 6.1 for a summary of the methods of communication used in each program for each year of the study).

For the oral programs from years 2 through 4, the children's most frequently employed mode of communication was oral-aural, followed closely by gestural communication. In the first year, gestures were the most frequently noted mode of communication among children, and the oral-aural mode was the next most frequently employed.

Within combined programs in the first year, gestural communication among children was the most commonly used modality, followed closely by the oral-aural and sign categories. However, in combined programs from years 2 through 4, children employed signs without accompanying verbalizations most frequently when conversing among themselves. The second most frequently used modes of communication were oral-aural and gestural in year 2 and combined and gestural in year 3. By the final year, scores in the combined category dominated the secondary position.

It is interesting to note that scores in the combined category exhibited the greatest increase across the 4-year period. Although ratings in the gestural category are relatively high for the children in combined programs, they do not approximate the magnitude of those for children in oral programs (Table 6.15).

No written communication between children was observed in either oral or combined programs.

Table 6.16 summarizes interaction scores from child to teacher. In oral programs for all 4 years, the oral-aural model was the most frequently noted type of communication from child to teacher, followed by gestures.

The ratings of communication modes from child to teacher in the combined programs exhibited a less stable pattern across years. In year 1, scores for three modes were relatively close; the most frequently observed mode was gestures, followed by fingerspelling and oral-aural communication. The oral-aural style of communication was the most frequently noted in year 2, followed by signs. Scores in years 3 and 4 are somewhat similar to each other in that the category most often employed was signs. The greatest increase in scores occurred in the combined category where scores rose from 1.17 in year 1 to 4.28 in year 4.

Table 6.17 indicates that, again, modes of communication in the oral classrooms did not differ across years. For teachers the most frequently employed method of communication each year was oral-aural, followed by gestures.

For combined programs, the patterns of teacher communicative mode use are less clearly defined. For the years 1 and 2, oral-aural communication was

TABLE 6.15
Communication Analysis by Year (Child to Child)

Programs		Fingerspelling	Sign	Oral-Aural	Combined	Written	Gestures
	Year						
Oral	1	1.00	1.83	2.21	1.00	1.00	3.17
	2	1.00	1.00	3.50	1.00	1.00	4.09
	3	1.00	1.75	4.38	1.00	1.00	4.21
	4	1.00	1.25	5.25	1.00	1.00	4.50
	Year						
Combined	1	1.58	1.79	1.92	1.17	1.00	3.33
	2	2.33	3.62	2.98	1.58	1.00	2.93
	3	2.17	5.05	3.03	3.72	1.00	3.72
	4	2.71	4.91	3.24	3.74	1.00	2.93

TABLE 6.16
Communication Analysis by Year (Child to Teacher)

Programs		Fingerspelling	Sign	Oral-Aural	Combined	Written	Gestures
Oral	Year						
	1	1.00	2.00	3.33	1.00	1.00	2.76
	2	1.00	1.09	4.91	1.00	1.00	3.42
	3	1.00	1.13	5.25	1.00	1.00	3.54
	4	1.00	1.00	5.50	1.00	1.00	3.50
Combined	Year						
	1	2.50	2.25	2.42	1.17	1.25	2.67
	2	2.32	3.57	3.87	2.00	1.33	2.83
	3	2.41	4.75	3.86	3.75	1.36	3.19
	4	3.26	4.91	4.00	4.28	1.12	2.64

the most commonly employed mode. In years 3 and 4, the high scores cluster in three categories — sign, oral-aural, and combined — with the highest score occurring in the sign category in year 3 and the combined category in year 4. The amount of combined oral-manual communication used by teachers increased dramatically from 1.67 in the first year (1971) to 5.24 in 1974.

Regular Class Subjects

In recent years, there has been an increasing trend toward the intersection of the typical child into mainstream education. In the area of deaf education, it appears that the mainstreaming effect has often been applied to the child with the greatest potential to succeed (i.e., with articulate skill and hearing acuity sufficient to support him or her in the integrative mode). Seemingly, this effort has been facilitated by evaluation and preparation for entering the major educational network along with supportive service in speech habilitation and auditory training. It was believed that the importance of successfully integrating the hearing impaired child in the regular classroom environment was an issue deserving of further investigating, thus its inclusion in this reseach effort.

During the 4 years of the evaluation, fourteen of the children in the longitudinal sample and three other children, who had moved from their original programs and received unique placement outside of the seven programs participating in this evaluation, had been placed in integrated settings. The placement of these seventeen children was as follows:

Three children participated in a regular first grade class on a full-time basis assisted by a teacher of the deaf within the classroom,

Five children participated in regular and hearing impaired kindergarten, each on a half-day basis,

Nine children participated in regular classes within their home districts and received supplemental speech instruction.

In an attempt to identify characteristics of children functioning in regular class settings that were different from those who remained in class for the deaf, statistical comparisons were made between these groups in the following areas: academic achievement (MAT), receptive communication, expressive communication, word intelligibility, age, and hearing loss. In addition, the distributions of children within the two groups by sex, etiology, age of onset of hearing loss, and preferred mode of communication for the expressive communication scale were examined.

The two groups did not differ significantly on the basis of Metropolitan Achievement Test scores, receptive communication, expressive communication, sex, age, etiology, or age of onset of hearing loss. The group of children integrated into classes for the hearing had significantly better hearing acuity, $t = 5.01$, $p < .001$, and achieved significantly higher scores on the word-intelligibility measure, $t = 9.03$, $p < .001$. All integrated children chose oral communication as their preferred mode during expressive communication scale video-taped sessions.

Longitudinal scores of two groups were further examined in an effort to trace the development of the word-intelligibility scores in the integrated group. It was found that in year 2, the integrated group scored significantly higher than the nonintegrated children, $t = 5.98$, $p < .001$. This suggests that word intelligibility of the integrated group was superior to that of the children who remained in self-contained situations prior to the integration effort.

TABLE 6.17
Communication Analysis by Year (Teacher to Child)

Programs		Fingerspelling	Sign	Oral-Aural	Combined	Written	Gestures
	Year						
Oral	1	1.00	1.17	6.92	1.00	2.00	2.50
	2	1.00	1.00	6.50	1.00	2.33	3.50
	3	1.00	1.00	6.37	1.00	1.00	4.00
	4	1.00	1.00	6.75	1.00	1.75	4.00
	Year						
Combined	1	5.33	2.42	6.00	1.67	2.00	2.33
	2	3.57	3.98	6.28	3.12	2.63	2.20
	3	4.03	5.17	4.75	4.95	1.75	3.33
	4	4.52	5.19	5.02	5.24	1.56	2.36

DISCUSSION

Academic Achievement

Academic achievement of the sample, as assessed by the MAT Primer Battery, reading and arithmetic subjects, was comparable to that of the hearing children of approximately the same age in the area of reading and below that of their hearing counterparts in the area of arithmetic. Results of a nationwide survey of hearing impaired children and youth conducted by the Office of Demographic Studies (ODS) at Gallaudet College (Gentile, 1972) produced similar trends. Using the Stanford Achievement Test to assess the achievement level of 16,680 deaf children and young adults, it was found that between 6–8 years (the age of the sample in the current inquiry), reading scores were higher than arithmetic scores. For all older age groups (9–21 years), reading scores were exceeded by those of arithmetic.

Different measures were employed in the studies, hence a direct comparison of results cannot be made. The results of the Gallaudet study, however, lend support to the conclusion that development of arithmetic skills is not emphasized adequately in programs for the deaf until after age 8. It is my conclusion that inadequate attention was paid to the development of arithmetic skills. In their efforts to attack what is perceived as the major problem facing deaf children — the acquisition of English — the programs neglect to some degree the teaching of arithmetic at an early age.

Although the children in the present study appeared to be developing reading skills comparable to hearing children, it must be reemphasized that none of the programs succeeded in assisting the children to develop English language skills comparable to those of hearing children. Results of tests of expressive and receptive communication in the investigation indicated that the children in the sample experience difficulty with complex grammatical structures. Even though the present data suggests they possessed adequate prereading skills, it seems likely that as they become older and as reading content includes more complex linguistic structures (e.g., passive, negative, interrogative constructions), the reading ability of these children, relative to hearing children, will decline due to their delayed English development unless exceptional new interventions are provided.

Illinois Test of Psycholinguistic Abilities

The overall mean scaled scores of 179.21, 183.95, 178.90, and 180.65 in years 1 through 4 indicate that the functioning of young deaf children in the study on visual motor subtests of the ITPA was essentially normal. The predicted mean scaled score for children with normal hearing would be 180. These scores seem to indicate strong stability over a period of years. The finding suggests that deaf children function at normal levels on the abilities tapped by ITPA visual motor subtests. Because the subjects of this study maintained scores equivalent to their hearing age group over the period of 2 calendar years, there is evidence to suggest that the rate of growth is also normal.

The ITPA scaled subtest scores present graphic evidence of the lack of differences between the deaf subjects and the hearing standardization population on four of five subtests. During 4 years, the only statistically significant difference showed the deaf students to be superior in manual expression, which was the only subtest in which the average score of children in each of seven programs was above the hearing average of 36. The consistency of the results lends credence to the hypothesis (Moores et al., 1972) that deaf children, in developing mechanisms to cope with the environment, may acquire superior skills in this area.

Communication Battery

Receptive Communication Scale

In terms of relative efficiency across modes of communication, excluding the printed word, the children in this study understood communication most efficiently in the final year of testing when presented simultaneously through speech and signs (88%), followed by simultaneous speech and fingerspelling (75%). The most inefficient method of communication was sound alone (44%), that is, when the child had to rely on hearing alone, without the benefit of visual clues. The addition of speechreading improved scores to 68%. It appears that the addition of each mode of communication (i.e., sound plus speechreading plus fingerspelling plus signs) adds to the ability of the profoundly hearing impaired preschool child to understand communication. It is also apparent that the use of manual communication does not detract from oral receptive skills.

Tables 6.9, 6.10, and 6.11 indicate an increase in receptive communication scores from year to year. The smallest gains were in the sound alone subtest. Given the severity of hearing loss in the subject group, it is not surprising that reliance on sound alone would be relatively inefficient. Scores approached ceiling when signs were used, especially in Programs C, E, and G, where scores were above 90% correct.

The greatest improvement was noted in the printed word subtest in which scores increased from 38% in year 2, to 56% in year 3, and 76% in year 4. This finding probably reflects continued emphasis on the development of prereading and reading skills among the educational programs, and it supports the original decisions to treat understanding of the printed word separately from the other four subtests, which are more measures of person-to-person interaction.

Program scores on the printed word subtest cluster in exactly the same way as reading and arithmetic scores on the MAT: The top five programs (A, C, E, F, and G) earned average scores ranging from 90% down to 77% correct. The lower cluster, as in the MAT scores, is comprised of Program D (65%) and Program B with (64%). Programs D and B had less academic orientation than the others. Again, the results suggest that programs with little initial academic orientation face difficulties in the future achievements of their children.

Examination of Table 6.11 for year 4 reveals a number of interesting patterns across programs and the four person-to-person modes of communication. The patterns suggest that the relationship between methodology and communication effectiveness is highly complex. Beginning with the sound alone subtest, it may be seen that children in Program D (mean of 58% correct) and Program G (mean of 53% correct) scored far higher than those in the other five programs, where mean scores ranged from 34% to 40% correct. A similar pattern was reported in year 3, when children in Program G ranked first, children in Program D ranked second, and children in the other five programs were clustered at a much lower level. The reasons for the consistent superiority of the children from these two programs in use of residual hearing are not readily apparent because the programs differ in methodology, philosophy, and orientation. Aside from geographic propinquity, their only shared characteristic is that they are the only two public school programs in the study. The differences cannot be explained by integration or placement continguous to hearing peers because the majority of the Program D children and half of the Program G children are in self-contained classes. Also, methodology is not a factor because all of the Program G children started with the Rochester method and later were exposed to signs. All of the Program D children started with an oral-aural method. The author concludes that the superiority is explained by more intensive attention to auditory training and aural rehabilitation in these programs.

The addition of speechreading to sound presents a completely different rank in program effectiveness. In terms of the often repeated goal of "communication with the hearing world," the measurement of speechreading combined with sound is the most significant indicator because it approximates the task typically facing a deaf individual attempting to understand the message of a hearing individual (i.e., the deaf person directly faces the hearing person and makes use of residual hearing and speechreading simultaneously). In this context, the sound alone subtest provides little information on actual person-to-person communication abilities.

Although the overall average mean scores rose from 44% for sound alone to 68% for sound and speechreading, there was great diversity in the amount of improvement from program to program. In terms of efficiency, there appear to be three groupings: Program G (90%) and Program F (83%) were at the top; Program D (67%), Program B (65%), and Program C (65%) were in the middle; Program A (52%) and Program E (51%) were at the bottom. One immediate and obvious conclusion is that early manual communication per se does not hinder oral receptive skills, because children in the two top programs used manual communication — the children in Program G from the beginning of the study and children in Program F for the last 2½ years of the study. Conversely, it is obvious that early manual communication per se does not automatically facilitate oral receptive skills, because children in the bottom two programs also used manual communication.

Analysis of scores program by program suggests that much more is involved than just oral-manual considerations. For example, the greatest improvement from sound alone to sound and speechreading was registered by children in Program F from year 2 to 4. Those children's mean scores rose from 35% to 83% correct, an increment of 48%. The smallest improvement of only 9% was found in the Program D group, whose mean scores rose from 58% to 67%. The scores of the Program F children suggest a strong visual orientation in the program which, to some extent, may have compensated for insufficient attention to auditory processes. The scores of the Program D children, conversely, reflect a strong auditory orientation and an inadequate visual one. The second largest program increment was recorded by the Program G children, whose mean scores improved by 37%, from 53% for sound alone to 90% for sound and speechreading. In this case, the scores appear to reflect strength in both auditory and visual components.

The addition of fingerspelling reflects further patterns and interrelationships. The overall improvement of 7% of sound and speechreading (68%) with the addition of fingerspelling (75%) may be an underestimate because of two factors. This subtest contained a greater range of scores than any of the others. The score of 97% correct was the highest for any program on any subtest. The fact that even integrated children scored high on this test — and higher than they had in year 3 — suggests that they may continue to utilize simultaneous oral-manual communication in some situations. The mean score of 55% for children in Program D reflects performance of a small number of children who were exposed to manual communication in the classroom during the last year of the study. There were children who were judged as not progressing satisfactorily in an oral-only class and who had scored below norms consistently during the survey. The children in Program B were switched to a total communication system with a year and a half to go in the study. The program utilized a Seeing Essential English (SEE) system of signing, which placed little reliance on fingerspelling. An additional consideration is the near perfect score of Program G children (97%), indicating they reached the ceiling for the test.

The addition of fingerspelling resulted in the greatest proportional increases in mean scores in Program E (51% to 80%, for a 29% increase) and

Program A (53% to 77%, for a 24% increase). However, the children's scores in both programs remained below those of Programs F and G. Inasmuch as the children in Programs A and E scored lowest on sound and speechreading, it appears that less emphasis is given to oral-aural skills than to manual communication in those two programs.

As noted previously, the simultaneous use of sound and speechreading and signs was the most efficient method of communication, with an overall score of 88% correct. Program E (94%), Program C (93%), and Program G (93%) approached the ceiling for the test and even the "nonaural" children in Program D scored at 85%, although they were only recently exposed to signs in the classroom. The lowest scores, 83% for Program A and 80% for Program B, were still high relative to other modes.

During the 3-year period, correlations of hearing loss to the various modes of communication revealed highly significant relationships of hearing loss to the sound alone and speechreading subtests. The relationship of hearing acuity to sound alone is an obvious one in that as the degree of hearing decreases, so too does one's ability to receive information auditorily. Again, the importance of auditory input to information received in the sound plus speechreading condition is noted in the hearing loss to speechreading correlation. The lower correlations of hearing loss to fingerspelling and sign language modes indicated that children are less dependent on residual hearing for success in these tasks. Given the consistently higher scores for these modes across 3 years, I conclude that the traditional auditory-only and oral-aural methods are inappropriate for children with profound hearing losses. Combined oral-aural-manual input appears to be much more effective. Whether the manual component should involve fingerspelling alone or signs plus fingerspelling is unclear at present.

The results indicate that reliance on a unisensory auditory-based approach with young deaf children is inadequate. The development of auditory receptive skills is unrelated to methodology. The early use of manual communication has no effect, either positive or negative, on the effective use of residual hearing. The implications are clear. It is a mistake to wait for a child to "fail" before employing manual communication. By then, it may be too late. Any time there is a question about a child's ability to process information auditorily, manual communication should be added.

Receptive Communication Supplement

Although scores on the receptive communication core items suggest consistent improvement in program functioning over a 3-year period, the most difficult linguistic constructions tapped were of the subject-verb-object or subject-verb-prepositional phrase types that are active declarative sentences addressed to the present. In view of the extensive literature documenting the difficulties that most deaf children encounter in the comprehension of verb tense, passive voice, and other complex constructions, the present study also included measures of this type. The results are less promising than those found for the core items and suggest that all programs need to devote more attention to mastery of various English structures.

Analysis of error patterns reveals the discouraging finding that deaf children choose the *reverse* interpretation of negatives and passives more frequently than they chose the correct one. For example, the overall percentage of correct responses for passives was 29%, with subjects choosing the reverse (incorrect) interpretation of passive sentences 47% of the time (Table 6.13). It appears that deaf children frequently employ the active interpretation of passive phrases and ignore the passive marker *by*. Similarly, the overall percentage of correct responses for negatives was 36%, with subjects choosing the incorrect positive interpretation 46% of the time. The children tended to ignore negative cues and selected the opposite meaning more frequently than the correct one.

The results obtained are similar to those reported by Power (1971) and Schmitt (1969), who found deaf children tended to ignore linguistic markers and typically processed sentences as active declaratives. This situation is doubly serious. Not only do deaf children commonly fail to interpret passive sentences and negative sentences, but they frequently derive information that is the opposite of what was intended. This pattern can be interpreted as one sort of language delay, in that hearing children of 3 or 4 years of age often apply similar interpretive strategies (cf. Strohner & Nelson, 1974).

The printed word tended to facilitate recognition of both negatives and passives. It appears that complex constructions are introduced to the children primarily through print and that they are employed consistently in face-to-face communication whether it be oral-only or combined oral-manual. The results lead the author to believe that adequate mastery of these components of the English language will not be achieved unless the programs consciously address themselves to developing specific activities in which the children have the opportunity to practice different basic constructions of English. This statement holds regardless of the communication method (oral-only, etc.) utilized.

Although the potential benefits of manual communication can be great, it must be emphasized that the use of simultaneous oral/manual English communication is a skill that requires a great amount of training and practice. For beginning teachers, the tendency is to eliminate word endings and function words, the very elements which are also most difficult to perceive aurally or through speechreading.

Expressive Communication

Results on intelligibility are discouraging thus far. For example, only 51% of the children (28 of 55) met a criterion that at least two thirds of the morphemes contained in utterances must be eligible for calculation of T-units. A T-unit is defined as an utterance containing at least a noun phrase and a predication on the noun phrase. Several children had less than 10% of their morphemes contained in T-units. Data analysis has progressed to the stage at which it may be stated that, in spite of great strides in the effectiveness of early intervention programs, a significant number of hearing impaired children who have gone through these programs are unable to express basic grammatical and semantic relationships in an intelligible manner.

Word Intelligibility

The authors must emphasize that scores on this test do not represent measures of language per se. They are ratings of recognitiion of single words uttered in isolation by the children, and the authors are unwilling to project these scores to spoken, written, fingerspelled, and/or signed language.

Children in Program D (65%) and Program G (60%) scored higher than children in the other five programs (with from 21% to 29% of the words understandable). The situation is similar to that of the sound alone subtest of the Receptive Communication Scale in which children from these two programs were superior, suggesting again that the two programs have superior speech and aural rehabilitation components.

There is a moderate correlation between word intelligibility and hearing loss. Aside from that, scores seem to reflect the amount of attention programs pay to speech per se. It should also be noted that the range of scores within programs was great. In each program, including Programs D and G, there were children who were almost completely unintelligible, leading to the conclusion that no program is developing adequate speech skills in all children.

Matching Familiar Figures Test (MFF)

Because no differences existed between programs on the MFF, the authors conclude that program differences have no discernible effects on the "perceptual tempo" (Kagan, 1965) of children within the programs. In terms of etiology, it was of particular interest to determine if a proportionately larger number of children classified as rubella might appear in the impulsive category. The lack of differences by etiology suggests that rubella children with no handicaps other than deafness are not more "impulsive." Whether or not this is true of multiply handicapped rubella children is a different matter and cannot be addressed here.

Inasmuch as reflective children were superior only on those subtests of the ITPA (visual closure) and MRT (copying and matching) that are timed, it is possible that "impulsive" children in this sample may not be inferior on prereading skills but rather that, when facing a task with time constraints, they tend to use inappropriate strategies under pressure.

Communication Analysis

Examination of Tables 6.15, 6.16, and 6.17 reveals great variety in the amount and type of communication that takes place. This is explained by the different modes of communication employed and by differences between programs regarding their philosophy concerning personal interaction.

For the period of the study, children in oral programs employed oral communication most consistently. However, considerable use of gestures and signs was also observed. This finding suggests that when children do not have formal signs freely at their disposal, they still resort to gestural communication to some extent and perhaps must do so to be effective.

Communication performance in combined programs was somewhat erratic and basically manual for the initial years of the evaluation, but it appears that during the later years a more combined oral-manual approach to communication was employed as well.

Although some signing was noted in child-to-teacher communication, children generally tended to employ an oral-aural communication style supplemented by gestures. Again, as in child-to-child communication, the reliance on gestures appears to be substantial. Despite some instability in child-to-teacher communication for combined programs in the first 2 years, it appears that children used signs as a communication tool. An increase in signing accompanied with verbalization was more frequently observed during the latter 2 years of the study.

Oral-aural communication followed by gestural communication from teacher to child seems to have predominated in oral classrooms across the 4 years. Similarly, written communication was observed for 3 of the 4 years, while in the first year some signing was demonstrated. Again, a strong gestural component was noted in the communication process within the oral classrooms. The initial years of the evaluation illustrate that in combined programs, the oral-aural approach was most commonly employed by teachers. Sign, oral-aural, and the combined modes of communication were most frequently noted in the last 2 years. Therefore, the teachers probably were moving toward more effective utilization of simultaneous oral-manual communication. By the final year, teachers were employing the combined methodology most frequently.

Examination of teacher-to-child communication patterns reveals that there are no "pure" programs; perhaps there should not be. The combined category of communication tended to be most frequent for programs endorsing simultaneous oral-manual communication in years 3 and 4, followed closely by oral-aural communication. Obviously, even teachers in those programs did not sign and spell everything they said.

Other discrepancies may be noted in children's modes of communication. First, children in both the Rochester method school and oral programs were observed signing to each other and, in some cases, to teachers. Second, in no program was there a direct one-to-one relationship between oral communication and its manual counterpart. In all cases, spoken communication without an accompanying sign or fingerspelled word or, less frequently, manual communication without verbalization were observed. In this context, the flexibility of the children is impressive. They appear to have three modes of communication at their disposal: oral-aural, simultaneous oral-aural-manual, and manual. Although there is more of a tendency to use the oral-aural with teachers (most of whom hear) and the manual with classmates, the children apparently adapt with little or no difficulty.

The evidence over 4 years strongly indicates that reliance on an oral-only system can greatly limit all aspects of communication — child-to-child, child-to-teacher, and even teacher-to-child. Both children and teachers are forced to develop a gesture system to the extent that the program, much as it may be denied, evolves into an oral-gestural system.

It is clear that a program label such as acoupedic, oral-aural, Rochester-method, or total communication does not necessarily reflect the reality of classroom interaction. All programs have a manual component. It is just that in the "oral-only" programs gestures are used instead of signs and fingerspelling. On the other hand, it was not until the latter part of the study that "combined" programs consistently used combination oral-manual communication. This was probably due to the fact that most of the programs were in stages of transition from oral-only instruction and the teachers' use of manual communication initially was inconsistent.

Regular Class Subjects

The question of integration has received growing attention because of the widespread trend toward the "mainstreaming" of handicapped children. On the basis of the information available from the present study, integration seems to be an administrative device that has little impact on the children served.

For the children studied, integration does not appear to promote or hinder academic achievement, nor is there a visible relationship to academic performance or achievement as measured by MAT scores. Speech is one of the most tangible physical abilities, and the integrated children more closely approximated hearing children in that respect. Unfortnately, there is little evidence that regular classrooms make any effort to accommodate deaf children with less intelligible speech, even if they are high achievers academically.

It is interesting to note that the only difference between integrated deaf children and those in self-contained classes was word intelligibility. It appears that integration decisions for the programs under study were made solely on the basis of hearing loss and speech abilities. Those children who were integrated were speaking more clearly prior to integration than were their classmates in the programs for the hearing impaired. Thus, it must be emphasized that children do not speak better because they are integrated, but rather, they are integrated because they speak better.

CONCLUSIONS

In academic achievement, the deaf children exhibited beginning reading skills comparable to hearing peers. Math scores were below those of their hearing counterparts, indicating that computational skills receive less emphasis within preschool programs for the deaf.

Subjects continue to approximate the hearing norms on four of the five ITPA visual motor subtests (visual reception, visual-motor association, visual sequential memory, visual closure). Relatively higher scores have been illustrated in the area of manual expression, indicating that deaf children may develop superior skills in this area.

Results of the Receptive Communication Scale reveal a hierarchy of intelligibility across the modes of communication tested. The least efficient receptive mode was sound alone. Performance improved with the addition of speechreading. Further improvement was noted in the sound and speechreading plus sign language mode, which was proven to be the most efficient mode of receptive communication for these young deaf children.

It appears that although manual communication facilitates the reception of information, when more highly complex grammatical structures (i.e., passives, negatives, and verb tenses) are introduced, the reception of such information is inefficient regardless of the mode of communication used.

The overall lack of improvement in articulation scores across the 3 years raises questions as to the effectiveness of present rehabilitative techniques employed in improving the speaking ability of those children who have scored consistently at the lower range on the measure of articulation.

Those children who have been selected by their respective programs for placement in regular classroom situations have illustrated no superiority in academic achievement, communication, or psycholinguistic abilities. Integration into mainstream education appears neither to hinder nor promote academic success. Mainstreamed subjects differ from those who have remained in classrooms for the hearing impaired only in degree of hearing loss and articulation ability. Integrated children possessed greater hearing acuity and better articulation skills prior to integration, suggesting that integration is not a causal element in the enhancement of articulation ability. It appears that children do not speak better because of integration, but rather are integrated because they speak better.

In summary, as the participants of this investigation progress through the educational process it has become increasingly evident that there exists within programs a complex interaction among program emphasis, structure, orientation, and methodology. Hence, it is this complex interaction rather than specification of any particular methodological approach to education that seems critical to success.

The programs in which children functioned most effectively had a number of characteristics in common, two of which deserve special mention. First is an emphasis on cognitive/academic as well as on a socialization component from the beginning of training. Children in programs with an emphasis on "communication" or socialization alone were behind in academic achievement, with the retardation progressively increasing as they entered primary grades.

The second characteristic predictive of success is an intensive, coordinated use of auditory training, speech, and manual communication from the start. Children receiving such training were superior in communication ability and academic achievement. The results indicate that the use of manual communication at an early age has no effect on oral reception and expression skills, but it does facilitate academic achievement and the development of English skills. The tendency of educators of the deaf to wait for a child to "fail" orally before introducing manual communication is misguided. Manual communication should be introduced at a very early age. If a child does not need it, it can be withdrawn.

As an illustration, the program in which children across the 4 years consistently scored high on the largest number of measures utilized combined oral-manual communicaton at the time of entrance to the program, and the program had a heavy academic/cognitive emphasis. The program in which children consistently scored lowest on the largest number of measures may be classified as having a unisensory "acoupedic" socialization orientation.

The evidence gathered during the study suggests that the programs participating in the longitudinal evaluation in general were more effective than those involved in previous studies. Obviously, great improvements and advances have been made in recent years. However, as those affiliated with the programs acknowledge, the education of young children with severe hearing impairment still constitutes a difficult and frustrating process, and there seem to be no major breakthroughs in sight. Academic achievement and English proficiency remain below the norms for children with normal hearing. Although much progress has been made, there is still a long way to go. It is hoped that the information generated by this study will help close the gap between where we are now and where we hope to be in providing service to hearing impaired children and their families.

REFERENCES

ANSI (American National Standards Institute). *Specifications for audiometers* (ANSI 53.6). New York: American National Standards Institute, 1969.

Arthur, G. *The Arthur adaptation of the Leiter International Performance Scale.* Washington, D.C.: The Psychological Service Center Press, 1952.

Babbidge, H. *Education of the deaf in the United States* (The Report of the Advisory Committee on Education of the Deaf). Washington, D.C.: U.S. Government Printing Office, 1965.

Best, B. *Development of classification skills in deaf children with and without early manual communication.* Unpublished doctoral dissertation, University of California, 1972.

Brasel, K. *The influence of early language and communication environments on the development of language in deaf children.* Unpublished doctoral dissertation, University of Illinois, 1975.

Craig, W. R. Effects of preschool training on the development of reading and lipreading skills of deaf children. *American Annals of the Deaf,* 1964, *109,* 280–296.

Craig, W., & Craig, H. (Eds.). Director of services for the deaf. *American Annals of the Deaf,* 1975, *120*(2).

Craig, W., Craig, H., & DiJohnson, A. Preschool verbotonal instruction for deaf children. *Volta Review,* 1972, *74,* 236–246.

Durost, W. N., Bixler, H. H., Wrightstone, J. M., Prescott, G. A., & Balow, I. H. *Metropolitan achievement tests.* New York: Harcourt Brace Jovanovich, 1971.

Gentile, A. *Academic achievement test results of a national testing program for hearing impaired students.* United States: Spring, 1971. Washington, D.C.: Office of Demographic Studies, Gallaudet College, 1972.

Hester, M. *Manual communication.* Paper presented at the International Conference on the Education of the Deaf, Washington, D.C., June 1963.

Hildreth, G., Griffiths, N. L., & McGauvran, M. E. *Manual of directions Metropolitan Readiness Tests.* New York: Harcourt Brace & World, 1969.

Jordan, I., Gustason, G., & Rosen, R. An update on communication trends in programs for the deaf. *American Annals of the Deaf,* 1979, *125*(3), 350–357.

Kagan, J. Reflection impulsivity and reading ability in primary grade children. *Child Development,* 1965, *36,* 609–628.

Kirk, S. A., McCarthy, J. J., & Kirk, W. D. *Examiner's manual: Illinois Test of Psycholinguistic Abilities* (Rev. ed.). Board of Trustees of the University of Illinois, 1969.

Maestas y Moores, J. *Communication strategies of deaf parents with children from birth to 18 months.* Paper presented at NATO Advanced Study Institute on Sign Language, Copenhagen, Denmark, August 1979.

Maestas y Moores, J. Early linguistic environment: Interactions of deaf parents with their infants. *Sign Language Studies,* 1980, *26,* 1–13.

McConnell, D., & Horton, K. *A home teaching program for parents of very young deaf children* (Final Rep. USOE Grant No. OEG–32–520450–6007). Nashville, Tenn.: Vanderbilt University, 1970.

McCroskey, R. *Final report of four-year training program.* Paper presented at the Alexander Graham Bell National Convention, San Francisco, July 1968.

Meadow, K. M. *The effect of early manual communication and family climate on the deaf child's development.* Unpublished doctoral dissertation, University of California, Berkeley, 1967.

Moores, D. *Recent research on manual communication.* University of Minnesota Research, Development and Demonstration Center in Education of Handicapped Children, Occasional Paper #7, April 1971.

Moores, D. Families and deafness In A. Norris (Ed.), *Deafness annual* (Vol. 3). Silver Spring, MD: Professional Rehabilitation Workers with the Adult Deaf, 1973.

Moores, D. Non vocal systems of verbal behavior. In R. Schiefelbusch & L. Lloyd (Eds.), *Language perspectives — Acquisition, retardation and intervention.* Baltimore: University Park Press, 1974.

Moores, D. American Sign Language. In R. Schiefelbusch (Ed.), *Non-Speech Language and Communication.* Baltimore: University Park Press, 1980, pp. 93–100.

Moores, D. *Educating the deaf: Psychology, principles and practices.* Boston: Houghton Mifflin, 1982.

Moores, D., & McIntyre, C. *Evaluation of programs for hearing impaired children: Progress report 1970-71* (University of Minnesota Research, Development and Demonstration Center in Education of Handicapped Children, Research Report No. 27). December 1971.

Moores, D., McIntyre, C., & Weiss, K. *Evaluation of programs for hearing impaired children: Progress report 1971-72* (University of Minnesota Research, Development and Demonstration Center, Research Report #39). December 1972.

Moores, D., Weiss, K., & Goodwin, M. *Evaluation of programs for hearing impaired children: Progress report 1972-73.* (University of Minnesota Research, Development and Demonstration Center, Research Report #57, December 1973.

Moores, D., Weiss, K., & Goodwin, M. *Evaluation of programs for hearing impaired children: Programs report 1973-74.* University of Minnesota Research, Development and Demonstration Center, Research Report #81, December 1974.

Moores, D., Weiss, K.., & Goodwin, M. *Recommended policies and procedures: Preschool programs for hearing impaired children.* University of Minnesota Research, Development and Demonstration Center in Education of Handicapped Children, Research Report #104, November 1976.

Phillips, W. D. *Influence of preschool training on achievement in language arts, arithmetic concepts and socialization of young deaf children.* Unpublished doctoral dissertation, Columbia University, 1963.

Power, D. J. *Deaf children's acquisition of the passive voice* (Doctoral dissertation, University of Illinois, 1971). University Microfilms No. 72-12, 342.

Quigley, S. P. *The influence of fingerspelling on the development of language, communication, and educational achievement in deaf children.* Urbana: University of Illinois Press, 1969.

Quigley, S. P., & Frisina, D. R. *Institutionalization and psychoeducational development of deaf children.* Washington, D.C.: Council for Exceptional Children Research Monograph, 1961.

Schmitt, P.J. *Deaf children's comprehension and production of sentence transformations and verb tenses.*Unpublished doctoral dissertation, University of Illinois, 1969.

Simmons, A. Home Demonstration Teaching for Parents and Infants in Central Institute for the Deaf. *Procedures of International Conference on Oral Education of the Deaf.* Washington, D.C.: A. G. Bell Association, 1967, pp. 1862-1873.

Stevenson, E. A study of the educational achievement of deaf children of deaf parents. *California News,* 1964, 80-143.

Strohner, H., & Nelson, K. E. The young child's development of sentence comprehension: Influence of event probability, nonverbal context, syntactic form, and strategies. *Child Development,* 1974, *45,* 567-576.

Stuckless, E. R. & Birch, J. W. The influence of early manual communication on the linguistic development of deaf children. *American Annals of the Deaf,* 1966, *111,* 452-560.

Thorndike, I. L. *A teacher's word book of the twenty thousand words found more frequently and widely in general reading for children and young people.* New York: Columbia University Press, 1932.

Vernon, M., & Koh, S. Effects of manual communication on deaf children's educational achievement, linguistic competence, oral skills, and psychological development. *American Annals of the Deaf,* 1970, *116,* 527–536.

Vernon, M., & Koh, S. Effects on oral preschool compared to manual communication on education and communication in deaf children. In E. Mindel & M. Vernon (Eds.), *They grow in silence.* Silver Spring, Md.: National Association of the Deaf, 1971.

Weiss, K., Goodwin, M., & Moores, D. *Characteristics of young deaf children and early intervention programs.* University of Minnesota Research, Development and Demonstration Center in Education of Handicapped Children, Research Report #91, August 1975.

Wilbur, R. *American Sign Language and Sign Systems Research and Applications.* Baltimore: University Park Press, 1979.

Winer, B. J. *Statistical principles in experimental design.* New York: McGraw-Hill, 1962.

7 Language Development Under Atypical Learning Conditions: Replication and Implications of a Study of Deaf Children of Hearing Parents

Susan Goldin-Meadow
University of Chicago

We have shown that deaf children, whose severe hearing losses have prevented them from making use of the oral language input that surrounds them and whose hearing parents (having chosen to educate their children under the oral method) have not yet exposed them to conventional manual language input, can develop spontaneous gestural communication systems which are structured as natural child language systems are (Feldman, Goldin-Meadow, & Gleitman, 1978; Goldin-Meadow, 1979, 1982; Goldin-Meadow & Feldman, 1977). Thus, a child deprived of the rich linguistic input children typically receive can nevertheless develop a communication system which is language-like in many structural respects. This phenomenon suggests that the child has strong biases to communicate in language-like ways.

The phenomenon of gesture creation in deaf children has powerful implications for the nature–nurture question with respect to language acquisition. Accordingly, it would be important if this phenomenon were shown to be a robust one, not tied to any one population in any one locale, nor an artifact of any one method of data analysis. We have, up until this point, studied the phenomenon in six deaf children of hearing parents, ranging in age from 1;5 to 4;1 at the first interview, all living in the Philadelphia area. I present data in the next three sections that replicate this phenomenon on a second sample of four deaf children of hearing parents, ranging in age from 1;4 to 3;1 at the first interview and residing in a different region of the United States (the Chicago area). Further, I address the methodological and theoretical difficulties that have been raised in conjunction with this work, in particular, with our notions of underlying structure. Finally, I consider the implications of this phenomenon for developmental theories of language acquisition.

REPLICATION

Purpose and Rationale

As in our previous work, this replication study focuses on three primary questions. I first ask whether the deaf children in the second sample use gestures to communicate in the same way as our original subjects did. I then proceed to determine whether each child uses those gestures in a structured fashion; that is, can consistent patterns of production be found *within* each child's set of gestures? Finally, I ask whether those structured regularities are language-like; that is, are they regularities that can be found in natural human languages?

It is, of course, unlikely in the extreme that any one of our deaf subjects can develop a gesture system as complex as a naturally occurring language spoken by adults. After all, young children, even when exposed to language models, do not develop languages as complex as adult languages during their early stages. Consequently, the heuristic I have adopted in this study is to compare the gestures developed by my deaf subjects to naturally occurring *child* languages. I use the tools researchers have developed to study natural child languages to determine whether my deaf subjects' gestures are structured, and I use descriptions of the structural properties of natural child language as the framework within which to evaluate whether my deaf subjects' gestures are language-like.

It should be noted, however, that researchers within the field of child language are not in total agreement over which particular classification system should be used to describe the language of young children (see, e.g., Bowerman, 1978, for discussion). Here I adopt one widely used technique to describe my deaf children's gestures — the method of rich interpretation originally proposed by Bloom (1970) (see the sections on Underlying Structure for further discussion). I first show that this technique, with some additional assumptions, can be used to describe the deaf children's gestures. In the section on Coding Categories, I detail the assumptions and criteria I have used in applying the method of rich interpretation to my deaf subjects' gestures, showing where my procedures follow those standardly used in child language descriptions and where my procedures necessarily differ as a result of the idiosyncratic nature of the deaf child's gestures. I then show that when this descriptive system is applied to the deaf children's gestures, each child's gestures appear to be structured as were the gestures of our original deaf subjects (see the section on The Deaf Child's Communication System). We have shown elsewhere (see Goldin-Meadow, 1979; Goldin-Meadow & Mylander, 1984) that the *types* of structures (not necessarily the particular structures themselves) found in all of the deaf children's gestures can be found in the hearing child's early word sentences as well.

In sum, my goal in this study is to show that the gesture systems developed by both my old and new deaf subjects *without* the benefit of a conventional language model, when described using the tools of the field of child language, contain the structural properties of the language systems developed by young children who *have been* exposed to conventional language models.

Methods and Procedures

Subjects

The four children in this study, two girls and two boys, ranged in age from 1;4 to 3;1 at the time of the first interview and 3;8 to 4;2 at the time of the final interview (see Table 7.1, which also presents comparable information in summary form on the six Philadelphia subjects;[1] the names of all subjects have been changed in this report). Each of the four Chicago children came from white, middle-class families. At the time of these observations, Marvin had no siblings, Karen one younger hearing sibling, Abe one older hearing sibling, and Mildred three older hearing siblings. All had two parents living in the home, with mother as primary caregiver.

Each child was congenitally deaf with no other known cognitive or physical disabilities. Each had a severe to profound (greater than 90 dB) hearing loss and, even when wearing hearing aids (which the children wore continuously at school and often at home), was unable to acquire speech naturally.

All four children were being educated by the oral method of deaf education, a method which advocates early and intense sound training for the deaf child and which discourages the use of conventional sign language. Mildred, Karen, and Marvin all attended one oral preschool for the deaf in the Chicago area, and Abe attended a second oral preschool. When first observed, each of the children was receiving private sound sensitivity lessons 1 or 2 days a week and was not yet enrolled in daily group classes. Part way through the study, the children graduated first to half-day and then to full-day group sessions. At the time of these interviews, the children had made little progress in acquiring spoken English.

In addition, none of the four children was exposed to conventional sign language (e.g., Signed English or American Sign Language). Consistent with the oral education philosophy, sign language was not used in either of the oral schools these children attended. Moreover, neither the children's hearing parents nor their hearing siblings knew sign language. Thus, these children, who at the time of the study had made little use of oral linguistic input, were also not exposed to conventional manual linguistic input.

It is, of course, possible that, in an effort to communicate, the hearing caregivers of these deaf children spontaneously generated a structured ges-

---

[1]See Goldin-Meadow (1979) for further details on the six Philadelphia subjects.

TABLE 7.1
Summary Description of Gesture Samples

Chicago Subjects			Mean Length of Gesture Sequence	Longest Gesture Sequence Produced	Number of Gesture Sequences Per Hour
Child	Session	Age(yrs;mos)	(MLG)	(Upper Bound)	(Rate)
Mildred	I	1;4	1.07	2	52.5
	II	1;6	1.12	4	72.4
	III	1;10	1.14	3	24.7
	IV	1;11	1.31	3	47.3
	V	2;2	1.13	3	40.6
	VI	2;4	1.11	2	50.6
	VII	2;8	1.07	2	83.6
	VIII	2;11	1.25	5	72.4
	IX	2;12	1.17	4	40.6
	X	3;2	1.15	3	49.1
	XI	3;5	1.25	4	102.4
	XII	3;8	1.31	5	94.5
Abe	I	2;3	1.00	1	24.6
	II	2;5	1.19	2	60.0
	III	2;9	1.17	2	54.6
	IV	2;10	1.17	4	111.6
	V	3;0	1.19	6	100.2
	VI	3;4	1.22	4	109.2
	VII	3;5	1.28	3	51.0
	VIII	3;7	1.17	3	120.0
	IX	3;9	1.30	8	158.4
Marvin	I	2;11	1.33	3	91.8
	II	3;1	1.35	3	85.5
	III	3;4	1.26	3	87.3
	IV	3;7	1.37	8	156.4
	V	3;9	1.22	3	180.0
	VI	4;2	1.41	7	187.5
Karen	I	3;1	1.23	3	67.5
	II	3;4	1.08	3	71.3
	III	3;7	1.29	6	127.5
	IV	3;11	1.38	4	110.6
	V	4;0	1.36	5	140.6
	VI	4;2	1.39	4	133.1

Philadelphia Subjects

Child	Number of Sessions	Age Range	MLG Range	Upper Bound Range	Rate Per Hour Range
David	8	2;10-3;10	1.14-1.80	2-9	36.0-384.0
Donald	11	2;5 -4;6½	1.04-1.25	2-4	6.6-198.3
Kathy	9	1;5 -2;8	1.00-1.27	1-6	40.0- 93.0
Dennis	4	2;2 -2;6	1.04-1.21	2-3	50.9-102.0
Chris	3	3;2 -3;6	1.15-1.20	4	92.2-120.9
Tracy	2	4;1 -4;3	1.22-1.30	4-6	119.1-142.1

ture system, which their children then learned, or that the caregivers unconsciously shaped the structure of their children's gestures by patterning their responses to those gestures. Both of these hypotheses have been shown to be false in an analysis of the communications of six hearing mother-deaf child pairs (the four subjects described here and two others from our original Philadelphia sample; see Goldin-Meadow & Mylander, 1983, 1984).

Procedure

Each child was video taped at home during play sessions approximately once every 2 to 4 months (see Table 7.1). The primary caregiver, the mother in every instance, was asked to interact with her child for at least ½ hour of each session. Either the mother then continued to play with the child, or an experimenter or one of the child's siblings played with the child for the remainder of the session. A large bag of toys, books, and puzzles (described in Goldin-Meadow, 1979) served to facilitate interaction. Each session lasted from 1 to 2 hours, depending on the child's attention span.

Each child's video tapes were coded for both vocalizations and gestures. Because the coding system is central to the interpretation of results, I review and justify the coding decisions and criteria in some detail in the next section.

CODING CATEGORIES

How does one begin a description of the deaf child's gesture system? The problem lies, in some sense, in entering the system. After all, there is no established language model toward which the deaf child's system is developing. Consequently, there are no hints from a conventional system that might guide initial descriptions. As a result, the description procedure necessarily becomes a bootstrap operation. It begins with preliminary decisions on how to categorize the gestures produced by deaf subjects (e.g., how to isolate gestures from the stream of motor behavior, how to segment those gestures, how to describe them and assign them meanings).

Our preliminary coding categories were based on two sources. The first was the descriptions of spoken language, particularly child language, and the growing number of descriptions of conventional sign languages. The second, and perhaps more important, source was our intuitions about the motoric forms and the semantic meanings of the gestures produced by deaf subjects.

Having established preliminary coding categories, we began to utilize them while transcribing video tapes. We tested the utility of our tentative categories in two ways. We first asked if the coding categories were reliable and established reliability by comparison of judgments between one experimenter and a second coder who was not at the original taping sessions. The agree-

ment scores between two coders were found to be quite high (between 83%
and 100% depending on the coding category), confirming category reliability.

The second and more important test of our category definitions was to ask
if these particular categories resulted in coherent descriptions of the deaf
child's gesture system. The claim made here is that if a description based on
these particular coding categories turns out to be coherent, this fact is substantial evidence for the usefulness of the categories themselves. Consider the
following example. Suppose we applied the semantic categories *patient* (object acted upon) and *act* to the deaf child's gestures. If we then discover a pattern based on those categories (e.g., a sign-ordering rule following, say, a
patient-act pattern), a pattern which has both retrospective validity and predictive value, we have some evidence that those particular categories are useful descriptions of the deaf child's system. The very existence of the pattern
confirms the utility of the categories, because the former is formulated in
terms of the latter.

There is, of course, the possibility that these patterns and categories are
products of the experimenter's mind rather than the child's. However, our
study is no more vulnerable to this possibility than are studies investigating
spoken child language. Although this problem can never be completely
avoided, the following assumption allows us to proceed: A coherent description of the deaf child's gestures is more likely to be accurate than is an incoherent description. That is, if a category turns out to "make sense of," or organize, the child's communications (e.g., by forming the basic unit of a
pattern), we are then justified in isolating that category as a unit of the system
and in attributing that category to the child. In sum, the consistency of the results described here and in our previous work justifies the establishment of
the coding categories described herein.

Identifying a Gesture

In attempting to describe the features of the deaf child's gestured communications, the first task is to isolate communicative gestures from the stream of
ongoing motor behavior. The problem here is to discriminate acts that communicate indirectly (e.g., pushing a plate away, which in some sense indicates
that the eater has had enough) from those acts whose sole purpose seems to
be to communicate (e.g., a "stop-like" movement of the hands produced in
order to suggest that another helping is not necessary). Inasmuch as we do
not consider every nudge or facial expression produced by the deaf subjects
to be a communicative gesture (no matter how much information is conveyed), we are forced to develop a procedure that isolates only those acts used
for deliberate communication.

Lacking a generally accepted behavioral index of deliberate or intentional communication (see MacKay, 1972, for an illuminating discussion of this problem), we have decided that a communicative gesture must meet both of the following criteria. First, the motion must be directed to another individual. This criterion is satisfied if the subject makes an attempt to establish eye contact with the communication partner (the criterion was strictly enforced unless there had been recent previous communication with eye contact such that the child could assume the continued attention of his or her partner). Second, the gesture must *not* be a direct motor act on the partner or on some relevant object. As an example, if subjects attempt to twist open a jar, they are not considered to have made a gesture for *jar* or *open,* even if in some sense they, by this act, are trying to communicate to the experimenter to do something (i.e., to help open the jar). But if subjects make a twisting motion in the air, with their eyes first on the experimenter's eyes to establish contact, we consider a communicative gesture to have been made.

Once isolated, the children's gestures were recorded in terms of the three dimensions commonly used to describe signs in American Sign Language (ASL) (see Stokoe, 1960): the shape of the hand, the location of the hands with respect to places on the body or in space, and the movement of the hand or body.

Segmenting Signs and Sentences

After determining how to isolate gestures from the surrounding motor context, we next determined the units appropriate for describing combinations of gestures. We faced two segmentation decisions. First, are there grounds for dividing one long complicated gesture into more than one word-like or *sign* unit? Second, are there grounds for parsing sequences of these sign units into larger organizations? That is, can these signs be said to be concatenated into *sentences*?

Defining a Sign

We employed distributional criteria for sign segmentation whenever possible (cf. Bloomfield, 1933; Harris, 1951). Specifically, a gesture was considered to be composed of two signs if each of those signs occurred separately in other communication contexts. However, distributional criteria alone were insufficient for segmenting signs, primarily because there was no corpus extensive enough for these purposes. Therefore, an intuitive criterion based on the motor organization of the gesture was also used. A sign was defined as a continuous, uninterrupted gestural flow or a single motor unit. This motor flow, though difficult to describe (particularly without an established descriptive system of motor organization), was nevertheless easy to note, especially because of the change or break in the flow of movement preceding and following the sign. For example, a child might produce a twisting movement and then, breaking the twist, point to the table. The twist movement is, in some unformalizable sense, self-contained, as is the pointing movement; these movements, therefore, comprise two units, each of which is called a sign. The results described later in this paper suggest that the segmentation criteria chosen to isolate sign units feed into a coherent structural description of the deaf child's gesture system; that is, the criteria chosen allow us to isolate units that seem to be appropriate for the deaf child's system.

Defining a Sentence

The most obvious determinant of sentence boundaries was timing: If two signs were uninterrupted by an appreciable time interval, they were candidates for being "within a sentence." Conversely, if two signs were interrupted by an appreciable pause, they were likely to belong to separate sentences. However, sequential signs were judged by an additional criterion in order to be considered within or outside of a single sentence: the return of hands to neutral signing space. If present, the relaxation of the hands in front of the body after a gesture or series of gestures was taken to signal the end of a sentence. For example, if a child pointed to a toy and then, without bringing his hands to his chest or lap, pointed to the table, the two pointings were considered within a sentence. The same pointings, interrupted by a relaxation of the hands, would be classified as two isolated signs. This second criterion was chosen initially because "return to neutral position" is recognized to mark sentence boundaries in ASL (see Stokoe, 1960). We have continued to use these criteria for our deaf children's gestures because, using our bootstrap heuristic, when these criteria are employed to define sign sentences, a coherent description of the deaf children's gestures is produced.

Assigning Lexical Meanings to Signs

Our subjects produced three types of signs, which differed in form. *Deictic* signs were typically pointing gestures that maintained a constant kinesic form in all contexts. These deictics were used predominantly to single out objects, people, places, and the like in the surroundings. In contrast, *characterizing* signs were noted to be stylized pantomimes whose iconic forms varied with the intended meaning of each sign. For example, a fist pounded in the air as someone was hammering or two hands flapping in the presence of a pet bird both were considered characterizing signs. Finally, *marker* signs were typically head or hand gestures (e.g., nods and side-to-side shakes, one finger held in the air signifying *wait*) which tend to be conventional in our culture and which the children used as modulators (e.g., to negate, affirm, doubt).

We next attempted to devise a system to assign lexical meanings to both deictic and characterizing signs. The problems we faced were in many ways comparable to those that arise in assigning meanings to a young hearing child's words. Consider an English-speaking child who utters the sentence *duck walk,* as a toy Donald Duck waddles by. Adult listeners assume that because the child has used two distinct phonological forms, *duck* and *walk,* she intends to convey two different meanings, that is, to talk about two semantic aspects of the event in front of her, the feathered object and the walking action. Specifically, it is assumed that the child's noun *duck* refers to the object and that the verb *walk* refers to the action of that object.

Note that in attributing lexical meanings to the young hearing child, it is assumed that the child's particular lexical meanings for the words *duck* and *walk* coincide with adult meanings for these words. In general, we assume that nouns refer to objects, people, places, and the like and that verbs refer to actions, processes, and so forth. This decision, although difficult to justify (for discussion, see Braine, 1976), is bolstered by data from the child's language system taken as a whole. To the extent that children have mastered other aspects of the adult system that are based on the noun-verb distinction (e.g., verb agreement), they can plausibly be said to have mastered the distinction in the instance of lexical meanings.

At this same stage of the lexical meaning assignment procedure for the deaf subjects, we must also make assumptions. However, this time there is no adult language model to guide us. The decision criteria behind the inferential assumptions for the deaf subjects therefore must differ from those for the hearing child. For the deaf child's gesture system, we chose to use sign form as a basis for lexical assignment decisions. We assumed, in general, that deictic signs (e.g., point at the duck) refer to objects, people, and places and that characterizing signs (e.g., walking motions produced by the hands) refer to actions and attributes (see the following discussion). This decision is motivated and justified by a number of lines of argument.

Glossing Deictic Signs

The assumption made in assigning lexical meanings to deictic signs was that the child's pointing sign was, in fact, intended to make reference and that the referent of that deictic sign was a person, place, or thing (and not an action or an attribute). This assumption is motivated as follows. When pointings are included in analyses as nominal lexical items, the deaf children's sign systems look remarkably similar, both semantically and syntactically, to the hearing child's early spoken language. Semantically, the referents of the deaf children's deictic signs can be described in terms of precisely those categories that can be used to describe the referents of the hearing child's nouns (see Feldman et al., 1978). Syntactically, as has been previously shown (Feldman et al., 1978; Goldin-Meadow, 1979) and as is shown later here, deictic signs appear to play the same role in the deaf children's sign sentences as nominals play in the hearing child's spoken sentences. For these reasons, we feel justified in including pointing signs as nominal lexical items in our analyses.

Note that these deictic signs, like pro-forms (e.g., in English, *this* or *there*), effectively allow the child to make reference to any person, place, or thing in the present (remarkably, the deaf child appears to be incapable of taking full advantage of this latitude and instead acquires only as limited a nominal vocabulary as the hearing child at a comparable stage; see Feldman et al., 1978; Goldin-Meadow & Morford, 1984). Further, as with the hearing child's pro-forms, context is essential for the interpretation of the deaf children's deictic signs.

It should be recognized that the relationship between the pointing sign and its referent is, at some level, quite different from the relationship between a word and its referent. The pointing sign, unlike a word, serves to direct a communication partner's gaze toward a particular person, place, or thing; thus, the sign explicitly specifies the location of its referent in a way that a word (even a pro-form) never can. The pointing does not, however, specify what the object is; it merely indicates *where* the object is. That is, the pointing is location-specific, but not identity-specific, with respect to its referent. Single words, on the other hand, are often identity-specific (e.g., *cat* and *ball* serve to classify their respective referents into different sets), but not location-specific unless the word is accompanied by a pointing gesture.

Glossing Characterizing Signs

In contrast to their location-specific points, the deaf child's characterizing signs were identity-specific. Recall that the characterizing sign is an iconic sign whose form is related to its referent by apparent physical similarity (e.g., a fist pounded in the air referring to the act of hammering). Through its iconicity, the characterizing sign can specify the identity of its referent, but like words and unlike pointing, the sign cannot specify its referent's location.

Using both sign form and context as a guide to lexical meaning assignment, it was easily established that subjects could gesture about actions with their characterizing signs. For example, one child held a fist near his mouth and made chewing movements while someone was eating lunch (eat); another twisted his hand over an imaginary jar in order to request that his mother twist open the jar lid (twist). Similarly, sign form and context allowed us to establish that the children could gesture about perceptual attributes with their characterizing signs. For example, one child distinguished between a large and a small kangaroo by holding his flat palms parallel to each other and wide apart (big).

Occasionally, sign form and context did not lead to the same lexical meaning assignments. For example, one child gestured the characterizing twist to identify a picture of a jar, whereas another indicated round, stubby appendages on the head to identify Mickey Mouse's ears. Sign form suggests that the twist sign refers to an action and that the round sign refers to an attribute; context, however, suggests that the two signs are both nominals, referring to the jar and to the ears, respectively. The decision in these situations was to assume that the form of the sign gives its lexical meaning (i.e., twist, round) and that context provides information about the way the sign is used (i.e., identification of an object in each instance). Thus, in the example of the twist used with the picture of the jar, although the child is indeed identifying an object with his characterizing sign, he is nevertheless using an action feature to identify that object. It is, therefore, assumed that he is conveying an action characteristic of that object (i.e., that it can be *twisted* by someone, or that one can *twist* it). Consequently, an action lexical meaning was assigned to the twisting sign. In general, we attribute to the child the lexical meaning related most closely to the form of the sign.

This assumption requires further justification. In conventional languages such as ASL or English, signs and words are (metaphor aside) handed down to us ready-made. We as sign users or word users may therefore not always be aware of the etymological history of a name and thus may not realize, for example, that the sign for a girl in ASL, "thumb drawn along the chin," was originally chosen because it represented the ribbon on a young girl's bonnet (Frishberg, 1975). Similarly, we may be quite surprised to discover the underlying justification for some common English words. For example, skyscrapers are so named for their literally sky-scraping characteristics. Names such as *girl* in ASL or *skyscraper* in English each have some nonarbitrary relationship to their respective referents. But how are we to know when to attribute knowledge of this relationship to an individual? After all, any given individual may or may not have had the "eureka" experience resulting in insight into a particular word's origin.

However, we can be quite confident that we are rightfully attributing such derivational knowledge to an individual when that individual is the inventor of the name. The first user of *skyscraper* was undoubtedly aware of the relationship between the celestial aspiring object and its name. Indeed, the inventor selected the name to emphasize just that relationship. Similarly, on these grounds we feel justified in attributing to our deaf subjects knowledge of the relationship between action and attribute sign forms and their respective referents, precisely because these children are themselves the sign inventors. The young children themselves choose to identify, or name if you will, a particular object in terms of either its action features or its perceptual attributes (see Feldman et al., 1978, for further discussion).

One consequence of this attention to sign form as the basis for lexical meanings is that we are able to extract more information from our deaf children's sign sentences than one could ever possibly hope to infer from an equally long string of a hearing child's words. For example, when the hearing child identifies an object by saying *that ball* (glossed, "that is a ball"), the adult listener might infer several things from the word *ball*: that it is *round,* that it is *thrown,* that it *rolls,* or indeed any aspect at all of ballness, including some aspects which, though second nature to adult users of *ball,* may be totally foreign to the speaking child's experiences. Adults cannot determine what, if anything, the speaking child means about the ball from these words alone. In contrast, the forms of the deaf child's characterizing signs, if taken literally, allow us readily to discriminate among the several meanings. For example, deaf children might point at the ball and then draw a circle in the air (the sign *round*) to convey "that is round"; they might point at the ball, then make a throwing motion in the air (*throw*) to convey "that can be thrown by someone"; or they might point at the ball, then trace with their hands the forward motion of the ball as it would roll along the ground (*roll*) to convey "that can roll."

Assigning Relational Meanings to Signs and Sentences

In the final coding decision we classified gesture sequences according to the semantic relations conveyed. Gesture sequences that contained single markers and/or deictic signs used only to point out the existence of an object, person, place, and the like ("deictic indicators") were not coded any further and were not assigned relational meanings. All other gesture sequences—those containing deictic and characterizing signs alone or in combination—were assigned one (or more in the case of multiproposition, i.e., complex, sentences) of the relational meanings defined in the following examples. For each relation, in addition to presenting an example from our deaf children's gesture corpus, we present examples of spoken sentences produced by young hearing children, which have been interpreted as conveying these same relations (examples and coding from Bloom, Lightbown, & Hood, 1975).

Action Relations

a. Transfer. An act by an actor on a patient which results in the patient's transfer to a new location or person.

1. TRANSFER-puzzle board   (I/Marvin *transfer* piece to *puzzle board*) [Marvin IIIb.2].[2]

---

[2]The following conventions are used in describing examples:
   a. The examples should be read from left to right; the sign that occurs first in the temporal sequence is the first entry on the left.
   b. The referents of deictic signs are in lower-case letters (e.g., puzzle board); capitalized words (e.g., TRANSFER) are glosses for the referents of characterizing signs.
   c. The sentence in parentheses is an English gloss of the sign sentence. The italicized

As an example of a transfer relation in a young hearing child's speech, Kathryn said *put in box* (p. 11) as she was throwing a car and a truck into a box. Bloom, Lightbown, and Hood code sentences of this type either as conveying (transitive) Locative Action relations (Agent-Locative Action-Object-Place) or, if the recipient of the transferred patient is animate (*bring Jeffrey book,* Appendix), as conveying Dative relations.

  b. Transform.   An act by an actor on a patient which affects the state of that patient.

  2. Bubbles-TWIST   (you/Marolyn *twist bubbles*)   [Karen IIc.8].

As an example of a transform relation in a hearing child's speech, Kathryn said *open drawer* (p. 10) while she herself was opening the drawer (coded as conveying an [transitive] Action relation [Agent-Action-Object]).

  c. Transport.   An act by an actor which results in the actor's relocation.

  3. COME-mother   (*you/mother come* to my side)   [Marvin Ic.8].

As an example of a transport relation in a hearing child's speech, Eric said *you come here* (Appendix) while looking out a window and shouting to a man who had walked away. Sentences of this type are coded as conveying (intransitive) Locative Action relations (Mover-Locative Action-Place).

  d. Perform.   An act by an actor which affects the actor's own state and not the state of an external patient.

  4. Train-CIRCLE   (*train circles*)   [Marvin IVa.89].

As an example of a perform relation in a hearing child's speech, Peter said *tape go round* (p. 11) while watching the reels of a tape-recorder. Or, Kathryn said *Kathryn jumps* (p. 11) after she had just jumped. Bloom, Lightbown, and Hood code sentences of this type as conveying (intransitive) Action relations (Actor-Action).

Attribute Relations

  a. Description.   A description of the size, shape, posture, etc. of an entity.

---

  words stand for those referents which are explicitly signed in the sentence; the remaining words stand for referents which are omitted from the sentence and must be inferred from context.
  d. The information in brackets indicates the name of the child who produced the sentence (e.g., Marvin), the session in which he or she produced the sentence (e.g., IIIb), and the transcription number of the sentence (e.g., 2).

5. Ketchup bottle-LITTLE   (*ketchup bottle is little*)   [Karen Va.49].

As an example of a description relation in a hearing child's speech, Eric said *little that* (Appendix) while holding up a sheep (coded as conveying an Attribute relation).

b. Similarity.   A similarity relation between two entities.

6. Elephant's back-Abe's back   (*elephant's back* is like *Abe's back*) [Abe IXd.56].

The function of the similarity relation for the deaf child seems to be to classify an entity as one of a set, without necessarily specifying the criterial attributes of that set. If deaf children use a description relation to classify an entity as a Mickey Mouse, for example, they specify (with their characterizing sign) an attribute which that entity shares with all instances of Mickey Mouse (e.g., round ears). In contrast, deaf children can use the similarity relation to indicate the likeness of an entity to other entities without specifying the basis of similarity between the two entities, that is, without specifying the dimension(s) on which the two entities share attributes. A hearing child learning English can achieve this function by naming an entity (rather than by describing the entity with an adjective, which would be comparable to our description relation) and thereby by classifying it as one of a set of entities. Thus, when Kathryn says, *that ə mirror* (Appendix) while picking up a mirror, her spoken sentence seems to be functioning as does the deaf children's similarity sentence. Bloom, Lightbown, and Hood code sentences of this type as conveying Existence relations.

c. Picture Identification.   A likeness relation between an entity and a picture representing that entity.

7. Picture of potato chip-potato chip   (*potato chip picture* is like *potato chip*)   [Abe IXb.25].

The picture identification relation is, in fact, a subset of the similarity relation: The deaf child is classifying an entity represented in a picture as one of a set of entities (again without specifying the criterial attributes of the set). As an example of a picture-identification relation in a hearing child's speech, Kathryn said *that dogs* (Appendix) looking at a picture of dogs (coded as conveying an Existence relation).

d. Location.   A location relation between an entity and its place of location.

8. Picture of bandaid-Mildred's finger   (*bandaid* belongs on *finger*) [Mildred XIIc.40].

As an example of a location relation in a hearing child's speech, Peter said *light ə hall* (p. 12) while pointing to the overhead light in the hallway (coded as Locative State).

    e. Possession.   A possession relation between an entity and its possessor.

9. Picture-Abe   (*picture* belongs to *me/Abe*)   [Abe IXb.37].

As an example of a possession relation in a hearing child's speech, Gia said *mommy scarf* (Appendix) after walking into the kitchen, seeing her mother's scarf, and reaching for it (Possession relation coding).

    Following Bloom (1970), we used the context in which a sequence was produced as the primary basis for assigning these relations. In Bloom's system, if a hearing child said *mommy sock* while mother was putting on the child's own sock, Bloom would assign that sentence an Action (in our system, a transform) relational meaning, "you/mother are putting on my sock." If, however, the child said *mommy sock* while mother was holding her own sock, Bloom would assign the sentence a Possession relational meaning, "mommy's sock" or "the sock is mommy's." Similarly, in our study, if a child pointed first at a jar, then at mother, and context indicated that he wanted mother to move the jar to the table, that gesture sequence would be assigned a *transfer* relational meaning, "you/mother move the jar to the table." If, however, the child pointed at that same jar, then at mother, but this time context indicated that he wanted mother to open the jar, the gesture sequence would be assigned a *transform* relational meaning, "you/mother open the jar."

Case and Predicate Semantic Elements

    Afer a relational meaning was assigned to the gesture sequence, deictic signs in all action relations were assigned semantic *case* meanings (actor, patient, or recipient), and characterizing signs in action relations were classified as *act predicates*. The case and predicate semantic elements we used in this study are reminiscent of those proposed by Fillmore (1968) to describe adult case grammars and of those proposed by Brown (1973) to describe the early spoken sentences of hearing children. Our case and predicate terms are defined and exemplified in the following sign sentences from our deaf subjects and spoken sentences from Bloom, Lightbown, and Hood's hearing subjects:

Act Predicate. The act that is carried out to effect a change of either state or location (e.g., *TRANSFER*-puzzle board and "*put* in box" in example 1, bubbles-*TWIST* and "*open* drawer" in example 2, and train-*CIRCLE* and "tape *go round*" in example 4).

Patient Case. The object or person that is acted upon or manipulated (e.g., *bubbles*-TWIST and "open *drawer*" in example 2).

Recipient Case. The locus or person toward which someone or something moves, either by transporting himself/herself/itself or by being transferred by an action (e.g., TRANSFER-*puzzle board* and "put in *box*" in example 1).

Actor Case. The object or person that performs an action in order to change its own state or location, or to change the state or location of an external patient (e.g., COME-*mother* and "*you* come here" in example 3, and *train* CIRCLE and "*tape* go round" in example 4).[3]

Although context typically provided information sufficient to determine relational meanings, occasionally it proved inconclusive. In many of these unclear instances, however, gesture *form* allowed us to decide between two interpretations of a given sentence. Two of the more common instances where gesture form entered our decision-making process follow.

Deciding Between Transitive and Intransitive Action Meanings

Consider a situation in which a child gestures to comment on the actions of a mechanical duck. Mother has just wound the duck (a transitive act on the object), and the duck has moved forward (an intransitive act performed by the object). Context cannot easily tell us where the child is describing the act *on* or *by* the duck, but gesture form of the characterizing sign can help. If the child produces a twisting gesture, pivoting finger and thumb, we can assume that the child is describing the mother's transitive action on the duck, a *transform* relation; the child's point at the duck would then be considered a *patient* case. If, on the other hand, the child produces a movement forward in the gesture, we can assume that the child is describing the duck's intransitive walking action, a *transport* relation; the child's point at the duck would then be an *actor* case.

Deciding Between Directional and Nondirectional Action Meanings

A similar situation arises when we consider a child gesturing to comment on a toy frog moving forward by hopping. The child could either be de-

---

[3]Occasionally, the children produced a fourth case, the *place* case (the locale where an action is carried out, but not the end point of a patient's or actor's change of location, e.g., EAT kitchen, meaning "I eat cookies in the kitchen"). The place case, although produced infrequently, was produced in sentences expressing each of the four action semantic relations.

scribing the fact that the frog is transporting itself across space or the fact that the frog is performing a hopping motion. Again, gesture form might provide guidance where context proves insufficient. If the child produces a forward-moving motion in the gesture, a flat palm crossing space, we can assume the child is describing the directional path of the frog, a *transport* relation. If, on the other hand, the child produces a gesture oscillating vertically in one place, a flat palm "hopping" in one place, we can assume the child is describing the nondirectional action of the frog, a *perform* relation. (Note that a deictic point at the frog would be considered an *actor* case in either situation.)

In the instances when neither context nor gesture form could disambiguate between two interpretations, the gesture sequence was eliminated from the relational and structural analyses.

Vocalization Coding Categories

All of each child's vocalizations were noted, and two coding decisions were made on each vocalization. First, we noted whether or not a vocalization occurred in the same sequence as a gesture. Second, we noted whether a vocalization was meaningful or not. Meaningless vocalizations were either unrecognizable sounds spontaneously produced by the child or sounds elicited by the child's caregiver who, in an attempt to encourage lipreading and vocalization in her child, would often hold an object near her mouth, point to her lips, and mouthe in exaggerated fashion the word for that object. Reliability in coding vocalizations ranged from 88% to 99% agreement between two coders.

The first 30 minutes of every session, the period of intensive mother-child interaction, were coded completely as described. The remaining reels of video tape were coded omitting all single signs and all vocalizations.

THE DEAF CHILD'S COMMUNICATION SYSTEM

All four deaf children in this study were found to use both vocalizations and gestures to communicate. However, in every instance, as I show in the following sections, gestures appeared to be the child's primary means for communicating information.

Gestures: An Overview

The gestures of the four deaf children differed from their vocalizations in two significant respects. First, the children's gestures were interpretable (and thus differed from their predominantly meaningless vocalizations). Second, their gestures were often concatenated into sentences (and thus differed from their few meaningful vocalizations, which were used only as single, unconnected words, and never concatenated).

Each of our four children produced the three types of signs found in the gesture systems of our original six subjects (marker, deictic, and characterizing signs), alone and in sign sentences. Table 7.1 presents each child's rate of production of gesture sequences for each observation session. The table also indicates the mean length of those gesture sequences for each session (MLG), as well as the Upper Bound (the longest gesture sequence produced) for each session. The gesture analysis that follows concentrates on two aspects of the deaf children's gesture systems: *semantic content,* that is, the types of notions conveyed by the children's gestures, and *structural form,* the formal means by which these notions were conveyed.

Semantic Content

Each of the four children conveyed at least eight of the nine types of semantic relations described in our original study of six deaf children. Semantic relations could be conveyed by a sentence of at least two signs (deictic and/or characterizing), as the examples in the section on gesture coding categories indicate, or by a single deictic or characterizing sign taken in context. For example, if the child has made it clear (by gentle nudges and whines) that he wants mother to sit near him and then points at the spot at his side, we assume his point is representing the recipient (end point) case of a transport relation.

Table 7.2 presents the proportions of single signs and of simple sign sentences (those conveying only one semantic relation) for the four Chicago subjects and the proportions of simple sign sentences for the six Philadelphia subjects (single signs were not coded for these subjects) which convey each of the nine relations. It can be seen that the children tended to convey the same relations in the same proportions. The transitive action relations (transfer and transform) were most often conveyed, whereas the intransitive action relations (transport and perform) and the five attribute relations were conveyed far less frequently by all but one (Tracy) of the ten children. Furthermore, the four Chicago children tended to convey each of the semantic relations in roughly the same proportions in both their single signs and their simple sign sentences.

In all natural languages, when word-like units are strung together to create sentences, those units are strung together in a structured and rule-governed fashion. We now attempt to determine whether the deaf subjects' simple sign sentences possess this most important of all properties of language — structure.

We have previously shown that the simple sentences of our original six subjects were indeed structured at both underlying and surface levels. I begin by

TABLE 7.2
Semantic Relations[a]

		Action Relations				Attribute Relations					Total (n)
		Transfer	Transform	Transport	Perform	Description	Similarity	Picture Identification	Location	Possession	
Chicago Subjects											
Mildred	Single Signs	.26	.32	.02	.17	.02	.06	.11	.04	.00	53
	Sign Sentences	.25	.35	.10	.10	.05	.00	.15	.00	.00	20
Abe	Single Signs	.40	.40	.12	.02	.00	.00	.00	.02	.04	52
	Sign Sentences	.32	.20	.12	.00	.08	.20	.08	.00	.00	25
Marvin	Single Signs	.44	.29	.07	.06	.02	.01	.06	.04	.00	134
	Sign Sentences	.45	.29	.03	.08	.11	.03	.00	.03	.00	38
Karen	Single Signs	.44	.24	.02	.04	.08	.00	.02	.10	.06	50
	Sign Sentences	.28	.24	.08	.12	.08	.00	.04	.08	.08	25
Philadelphia Subjects											
Dennis	Sign Sentences	.51	.32	.03	.00	.00	.10	.00	.03[b]		31
Kathy	Sign Sentences	.46	.27	.07	.07	.02	.05	.02	.05		42
Chris	Sign Sentences	.40	.16	.05	.09	.02	.14	.09	.04		43
Donald	Sign Sentences	.30	.22	.06	.04	.14	.13	.09	.01		138
David	Sign Sentences	.22	.23	.09	.04	.16	.07	.14	.05		437
Tracy	Sign Sentences	.03	.21	.05	.09	.20	.09	.28	.05		65

[a]Each entry is the total number of single signs (or the total number of simple sign sentences) conveying a particular semantic relation produced during the first half hours of all observation sessions for the Chicago subjects and produced during the entirety of all sessions for the Philadelphia subjects, over the total number of single signs (or simple sign sentences) conveying semantic relations produced during those periods.

[b]Location and possessions relations were not distinguished in our original study of the six Philadelphia subjects. These two relations were called static relations in Goldin-Meadow (1979).

considering data from the four new subjects on underlying structure and then turn to data on surface structure, including both ordering and production probability surface rules.

Simple Sentences: Underlying Structure

Bloom (1970), in her analyses of the early sentences of young English speakers, was the first to suggest that the hearing child's two-word sentences could be characterized by an underlying structure richer than the surface structure actually produced by the child (see pages 230–238, Underlying Structure, for further discussion). I follow Bloom in arguing that the early sign sentences of both my old and new deaf subjects can also be characterized by underlying structures (in fact, the same underlying structures as are found in the sentences Bloom's subjects produce, see the section on Underlying Structure). As in Bloom's data, the deaf children's underlying structures also turn out to be richer than the surface structures of their sign sentences.

The first evidence for this appears in the particular arrays of two-sign sentences the children produced to convey a given relation. Though few of the subjects ever explicitly gestured in one sentence all of the semantic elements posited for a four-element relation such as *give,* they did sign each of these posited elements at one time or another when describing a "giving" event. For example, Mildred exhibited knowledge that *actor, patient,* and *recipient* are associated with the *act* of transfer by overtly expressing each of these four elements in describing "transferring": *patient-act* (point at cowboy-GIVE, meaning "you/mother *give cowboy* to me/Mildred," VIb.10); *act-recipient* (GIVE-point at own chest, meaning "you/Susan *give* apple bank to *me/ Mildred,*" IXc.28); *recipient-actor* (point at own eyes-point at Marolyn, "*you/Marolyn* put glasses on *eyes,*" XIc.11); and *patient-recipient-actor* (point at glasses-point at own eyes-point at mother-point at glasses-point at mother," "*you/mother* put *glasses* on *eyes,*" Xc.12). Thus, Mildred, as well as the other three children, conveyed transfer relations by concatenating any two, and occasionally three, of the four case and predicate elements — patient, act, recipient, and actor. It is these four elements that we posit as the underlying structure of transfer sentences.

Transform relations, notions about an actor affecting the state of an object, were also conveyed as concatenations of different cases and predicates (examples from Karen): *patient-act* (point at bubbles-TWIST, "you/Susan *twist bubbles,*" IC.21); *actor-patient* (point at Marolyn-point at bubbles, "*you/Marolyn* twist *bubbles,*" Ic.4); and *act-actor* (TWIST-point at own chest, "*I/Karen twist* robot," VIa.3). Thus, transform relations appear to be conveyed by concatenating any two of three elements — patient, act, and actor — and it is these three elements that we posit as the underlying structure for transform sentences.

Transport relations, notions about an actor (object or person) relocating himself/herself/itself, were conveyed in sentences of the following types (examples from Abe): *recipient-actor* (point outside-point at own chest, "*I/Abe* move *outside,*" IXc.4); *actor-act* (point at train-GO, "*train goes* to end of path," IXa.77); *act-recipient* (GO-point at bottle slot, "coin *goes* to *bottle slot,*" VIIc.8); and *recipient-actor-act* (point at candles-point at friend-MOVE, "*you/friend move* to *candles,*" VIIIb.18). Transport relations thus are posited to have three-element underlying structures containing actor, recipient, and act elements.

Finally, perform relations, notions about an actor's (object or person) movements that affect only himself/herself/itself, tend to be conveyed by one surface form: *actor-act* (point at train-CIRCLE, "*train circles,*" Marvin IVa.128; this sentence was produced to describe a battery powered train which can circle on its own). Perform relations consequently are posited to have two-element underlying structures containing actor and act elements.

The two-, three-, and four-element underlying structures we have posited for the deaf children's gesture systems receive further empirical support from the distributional patterns of these subjects' two-sign sentences. As the foregoing examples suggest, the deaf children were producing primarily two-sign sentences (just as in a comparable period of development, the hearing child produces primarily two-word sentences, e.g., Bloom, 1970; Brown, 1973). The two-sign child will clearly not be able to explicitly sign *in one sentence* all four of the elements we posit as part of the underlying structure of transfer relations. *Production probability* is the measure that reflects this surface structure limitation, and it is defined as the likelihood that a case or predicate will be explicitly signed in a sentence of a certain length, conveying a given relation (see Fig. 7.1). We take production probability as an index of underlying structure on the basis of the following chain of logic. If, for example,

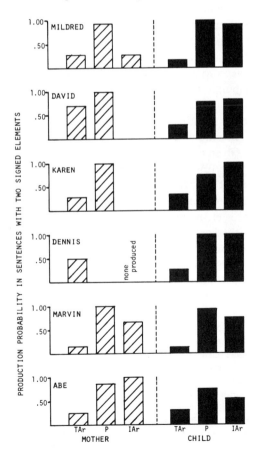

FIG. 7.1 Production probability patterns in mother and child simple sign sentences. Production probability was calculated on the following number of sign sentences with two explicit elements: Mildred, mother 14 for the transitive actor and patient, 4 for the intransitive actor, child 22, 2; David, mother 10, 1, child 54, 16; Karen, mother 7, 1, child 23, 4; Dennis, mother 2, 0, child 10, 1; Marvin, mother 6, 8, child 30, 4; Abe, mother 8, 2, child 29, 19. (*TAr* = Transitive Actor, *P* = Patient, *IAr* = Intransitive Actor.)

transfer relations were in truth to have an underlying structure of only two elements (e.g., actor and act elements), we would then expect the actor case to be explicitly signed in 100% of the child's two-sign sentences conveying transfer relations. If, however, transfer relations were to have three elements in underlying structure (e.g., combinations of actor, act, and patient elements), we would now expect the actor case to be signed in less than 100% of the child's two-sign transfer sentences simply because three elements would be competing for the limited number of slots (two) in surface structure. Following the same logic, if transfer relations were to have four elements in underlying structure, we would expect the actor case to be explicitly signed even less frequently in two-sign transfer sentences, again because of the increased competition for the limited number of surface slots. Thus, actor production probability in surface structure ought to vary depending on the number of elements in underlying structure.

In short, if we find that actor production probability does vary across types of semantic relations in the direction we predict, we then have evidence supporting the notions of underlying structure in the deaf children's gesture systems. After all, if there were no underlying structure affecting the surface structure of the deaf children's sign sentences, there would be absolutely no reason to expect actor production probability to vary at all across different semantic relations (see the section on Underlying Structure for further discussion). Thus, we look to determine whether the probability of producing actors remains constant or varies across the four action semantic relations we have isolated in the deaf children's gesture systems.

Given our observations of the range of two-sign sentences conveying each of the four relations, we would expect actor production probability to be lowest in transfer sentences hypothesized to have four-element underlying structures, higher in transform and transport sentences hypothesized to have three-element underlying structures, and highest in perform sentences hypothesized to have two-element underlying structures. The data in Table 7.3, production probability as a function of hypothetical underlying structures in sentences with two signed elements, conform to this pattern for each of the four Chicago children.[4]

---

[4]Actor production probability in perform sentences hypothesized to have two-element underlying structures was not 100% simply because occasionally the *place* case (representing the place where the action occurs) was concatenated with either the actor or the act. Note that the *place* case can and does tend to occur with each of the four relations (each action must occur in a place). I have not included the *place* case as part of the underlying structures for each of the four relations primarily because the case was signed relatively infrequently. It is important to note that adding one element to each of the hypothetical underlying structures would not change the structure of the argument presented here, simply because the addition would not change the relative positions the underlying structures hold to one another.

When production probability is calculated for the patient case and the act predicate, similar patterns are observed. Table 7.3 also presents act production probability in sentences with two signed elements for all four Chicago children, as well as comparable data on the patient (note that patients cannot occur in intransitive perform and transport relations assumed to have two-element and three-element underlying structures, respectively). In three out of four instances for the act and in all four instances for the patient, production probability increases systematically as the number of elements hypothesized in underlying structure decreases. Thus, the distributional facts of the deaf children's sign sentences suggest that the gesture systems developed by these four subjects possess underlying structure, as do the gesture systems of our original six deaf subjects (see also Table 7.3) and the speech systems of young hearing children (Bloom, Miller, & Hood, 1975; see also the section on Underlying Structure).

It is important to note that a priori there is no reason to expect different types of actors, patients or acts to be signed with different probabilities, as is the case in our deaf subjects' sign sentences and in Bloom, Miller, and Hood's (1975) hearing children's spoken sentences. For actors, there is no obvious reason to expect *dancers* to be more likely signed than *goers* or *eaters,* nor is there reason to expect *goers* or *eaters* to be more likely signed than *givers.* It is only when a *dancer* is considered a member of a two-element underlying configuration, a *goer* a member of a three-element configuration, and so on that these variations in surface probabilities become coherent. Similarly, for patients, there is no a priori reason to expect an *eaten apple* to be more likely signed than a *given apple.* Yet in nine of the ten children's sign sentences, we find this to be the pattern. Finally, for acts, there is no reason to expect dancing acts to be more likely signed than going or eating acts, nor going or eating acts to be more likely signed than giving acts. It is only when actors, patients, and acts are classified as members of differently sized underlying configurations that these surface variations become predictable and interpretable.

Up to this point, I have mounted evidence for an organized level of representation that underlies the surface level of a sentence and affects the probability with which a semantic element will appear in this level. I now turn to a description of the surface level itself, looking first at the ordering and then at the likelihood of occurrence of particular elements in surface structure.

Simple Sentences: Surface Structure

Construction Order Patterns

The four children in this study (like the Philadelphia children) showed a tendency to order patients, acts, and recipients in their two-sign sentences. Table 7.4 presents the data for the Chicago children's two-sign sentences con-

TABLE 7.3

Underlying Structure in Simple Sentences with Two Signed Elements[a]

	Actor Production Probability			Act Production Probability			Patient Production Probability	
Chicago Subjects	4-element	3-element	2-element	4-element	3-element	2-element	4-element	3-element
Mildred	.05	.25	1.00	.85 √	.79	1.00	.85	.91
Abe	.03	.40	1.00	.65	.77	1.00	.65	.76
Marvin	.00	.21	.75	.59	.91	1.00	.68	.93
Karen	.03	.44	.67	.71	.85	1.00	.69	.74
Philadelphia Subjects								
David	.02	.43	1.00	.47	.87	1.00	.78	.83
Donald	.08	.24	1.00	.75	.94	1.00	.53	.90
Kathy	.13	.50	1.00	.81 √	.75	1.00	.63	.87
Dennis	.08	.27	—	.46	.73	—	.85	1.00
Tracy	.00	.38	1.00	1.00 √	.80	1.00	1.00 √	.85
Chris	.00	.13	1.00	.71	1.00 √	1.00	.64	1.00

√ = Violation of the underlying structure pattern.

[a] Production probability was calculated on the following number of sentences with two signed elements: Mildred for the actor and act 4-element 20, 3-element 24, 2-element 5 and for the patient 4-element 20, 3-element 22; Abe for the actor and act 34, 8, 1 and for the patient 34, 29; Marvin for the actor and act 41, 34, 5 and for the patient 41, 30; Karen for the actor and act 35, 27, 6 and for the patient 35, 23; David for the actor and act 88, 123, 17 and for the patient 88, 88; Donald for the actor and act 40, 37, 5 and for the patient 40, 29; Kathy for the actor and act 16, 12, 3 and for the patient 16, 9; Dennis for the actor and act 13, 11, 0 and for the patient 13, 10; Tracy for the actor and act 2, 16, 6 and for the patient 2, 13; Chris for the actor and act 14, 8, 4 and for the patient 14, 7.

TABLE 7.4
Sign Order Patterns in Simple Sentences[a]

	PA	AP[a]	PR	RP	AR	RA
Chicago Subjects						
Mildred	19	8*	2	0	1	0
Abe	11	12	6	2	10	4
Marvin	21	12	13	2**	10	4
Karen	17	8+	6	1++	6	1++
Philadelphia Subjects						
David	44	18***	36	1***	11	2*
Donald	26	15*	7	0*	10	1**
Kathy	8	4	2	0	4	2
Dennis	10	1**	4	0++	1	1
Chris	6	4	2	1	4	1
Tracy	7	1+	0	0	0	0

[a] P = patient, A = act, R = recipient. Each entry is the number of two-sign sentences following a particular sign order pattern (e.g., PA, patient precedes act) produced by each child.
++ p = .13
+ $p < .10$
* $p < .05$
** $p < .01$
*** $p < .001$

taining concatenations of patients, acts, and recipients, as well as comparable data for the Philadelphia children. We find that if a Chicago child used a consistent construction sign order when concatenating two of these semantic elements, the construction order turned out to be one of the several construction order patterns described in our original study: Signs for the patient tended to precede signs for the act (Mildred $p < .05$, Karen $p < .10$, trend, Binomial Test, two-tailed); signs for the patient tended to precede signs for the recipient (Marvin $p < .01$, Karen p = .13, trend); and signs for the act tended to precede signs for the recipient (Karen p = .13, trend). Only Abe showed no strong tendency to order patients, recipients, and acts. Abe, however, did show the only construction order pattern involving the actor case; he produced 10 sentences with signs for the actor before signs for the act and none in the reverse order, p = .002. Tracy, in our original sample, also showed an actor-act construction order (ArA 9 vs. AAr 0, p = .004). Thus, the same ordering patterns observed in the data of our original six subjects are found in the data of these four new subjects.

It should be noted, however, that although the children tended to generate the same preferred construction order for a given pair of semantic elements, there was at least one idiosyncratic exception. Table 7.4 indicates that Chris has no patient-act ordering tendency: He produced six PA sentences and four

AP sentences. However, if the types of relations of these sentences are examined more closely, two consistent construction order patterns emerge. Chris tended to adhere to a PA construction order in producing sentences conveying transfer relations (e.g., "apple-GIVE," 6 PA vs. 0 AP) but tended to adhere to an AP construction order in producing sentences conveying transform relations (e.g., "EAT-apple," 0 PA vs. 4 AP). Thus, patients and acts were ordered differently in Chris' sentences conveying transfer and transform relations (Fisher Exact, p = .005, one-tailed).

Production Probability Patterns

We defined production probability as the likelihood that a particular case (or predicate) will be signed in a sentence when that case (or predicate) can be signed in that sentence (a determination made on contextual grounds, see Coding Categories). In our study of the six Philadelphia deaf children, we found a tendency for the production probability of certain cases to vary even when the structure of the relation underlying a sentence was held constant. In particular, we found that in transform sentences (transitive sentences which appear to have three elements at an underlying level—actor, act, patient), the patient case was very likely to be signed when it could be (i.e., the patient had a high production probability), whereas the transitive actor case was relatively unlikely to be signed (i.e., the transitive actor had a low production probability). Table 7.5 shows that this same pattern was found in the four Chicago subjects' sign sentences (and presents the original data for the six Philadelphia subjects).

An interesting point arises from extending this production probability analysis of surface structure to the intransitive relation, transport (also a relation with three elements in underlying structure—actor, act, recipient).[5] Table 7.5 also reveals that, in three of the four Chicago children (Abe's data are less clear-cut) and in all six Philadelphia children, production probability of the intransitive actor case in transport sentences resembled production probability of the patient case in transform sentences; it was also much higher

---

[5]We limit our analysis to transitive and intransitive relations which have the same number of elements in underlying structure (two arguments and one predicate) simply because we have found (as reported in the preceding section) that production probability of a given element in two-sign sentences is affected by the number of elements hypothesized to be in underlying structure. For example, within the transitive relations, the actor in transfer relations hypothesized to have four elements in underlying structure is less likely to be produced in two-sign sentences than the actor in transform relations hypothesized to have three elements in underlying structure (.03 vs. .24 for the Chicago subjects, and .05 vs. .24 for the Philadelphia subjects). Similarly for intransitive relations, the actor in transport relations hypothesized to have three elements in underlying structure is less likely to be produced in two-sign sentences than the actor in perform relations hypothesized to have two elements in underlying structure (.66 vs. .82 for the Chicago subjects, and .80 vs. 1.00 for the Philadelphia subjects).

TABLE 7.5
Production Probability Patterns in Transform and Transport Sentences[a]

Chicago Subjects	Transitive Actor	Transitive Patient	Intransitive Actor
Mildred	.18	.91	1.00
Abe	.31	.76	.53
Marvin	.13	.93	.75
Karen	.35	.74	1.00
Philadelphia Subjects			
David	.28	.83	.80
Donald	.10	.90	.75
Dennis	.20	1.00	1.00
Chris	.00	1.00	1.00
Kathy	.44	.77	.67
Tracy	.30	.85	1.00

[a] Production probability was calculated on the following number of sentences with two signed elements: Mildred for the transitive actor and patient in transform sentences 22, and for the intransitive actor in transport sentences 2; Abe 29, 19; Marvin 30, 4; Karen 23, 4; David 88, 35; Donald 29, 8; Dennis 10, 1; Chris 7, 1; Kathy 9, 3; Tracy 13, 2.

than the relative probability of production of the transitive actor in transform sentences. Comparing transport and transform — two relations with underlying structures of equal size — it is apparent that the transitive actor and the intransitive actor are clearly distinguished by the deaf children. The children consistently treat the intransitive actor like the patient, not like the transitive actor.

This production probability pattern in which the intransitive actor (e.g., "*boy* run [to W]") resembles the patient (e.g., "[X] open *jar*") but not the transitive actor (e.g., "*boy* open [Y]") is a probabilistic analogue of the structural case-marking patterns of ergative languages (Dixon, 1979; Silverstein, 1976) and is, in fact, distinct from the accusative case-marking pattern seen in English. The hallmark of the distinction between ergative and accusative languages is the manner in which the intransitive actor is treated (Fillmore, 1968). Consider the intransitive sentence *you go to the table*. In this sentence, the intransitive actor, "you," in some sense has a double meaning. On the one hand, "you" refers to the goer, the actor, the effector of the going action. On the other hand, "you" refers to the gone, the patient, the affectee of the going action. At the end of the action, "you" both "have gone" and "are gone," and the decision to emphasize one aspect of the actor's condition over the other is to a certain extent arbitrary.

In English, the effector properties of the intransitive actor "you" are emphasized by treating it like other effectors. For example, the intransitive actor "you" in *you go to the table* is treated just like the transitive actor "you" in *you eat grapes*; that is, both actors precede the verb. In contrast, ergative languages emphasize the affectee properties of the intransitive actor by treating it like other affectees (i.e., patients). Thus, the intransitive actor of a going relation (you) is treated just like the transitive patient of an eating relation (grapes). In sum, accusative languages such as English highlight the effector properties of the intransitive actor by treating it like transitive actors, whereas ergative languages, with which the deaf child's gesture system appears to share certain characteristics, highlight the affectee properties of the intransitive actor by treating it like transitive patients.

Concordance Between Production Probability and Construction Order Patterns

To summarize, we have found that the deaf child's probability-of-production pattern appears to be a probabilistic analogue of the structural case-marking patterns of ergative languages. This ergative-like pattern, if a characteristic of the deaf child's entire gesture system, might also be expected to appear in the second formal property of the deaf child's system — construction order patterns. If so, intransitive actors should be ordered in a similar construction position to that of patients (which tend to occur just before signs for acts) and in a different construction position from that of transitive actors (which should then occur in some differentiable position, e.g., after signs for acts). Only David produced a sufficient number of sentences with transitive and intransitive actors to address this question (50 such sentences compared to 11, the maximum number of actor plus act sentences any of the other children produced). David tended to produce signs for intransitive actors before signs for acts (32 Ar_I A vs. 7 AAr_I) and signs for transitive actors after signs for acts (3 Ar_T A vs. 8 AAr_T). The construction order for intransitive actors and acts (Ar_I A), which was reliably different from the construction order for transitive actors and acts (AAr_T), $X^2 = 9.6$, $df = 1$, $p < .01$, was precisely the same as the construction order for patients and acts (PA) in David's system. David's gesture system thus appears to follow ergative patterns with respect to two formal aspects of the system — construction order and production probability patterns.

The only other reliable actor construction orders found in the data were those already mentioned for Abe and Tracy. Both tended to produce signs for actors — transitive as well as intransitive — before signs for acts (Ar_T A vs. AAr_T, 2 vs. 0 for Tracy, 4 vs. 0 for Abe; Ar_I A vs. AAr_I, 7 vs. 0 for Tracy, 6 vs. 0 for Abe.). This pattern would be considered analogous to the accusative pattern of a language such as English if intransitive actors in the system, in addition to being treated like transitive actors, were also treated differently from patients. Recall that signs for patients in Tracy's system tended to precede signs for acts; thus, patients were not distinct from intransitive actors in terms of construction order in Tracy's system. Abe, however, had no patient-act ordering preference in his system; thus, patients were distinct from intransitive actors, and Abe's system was analogous to accusative systems when considered in terms of construction orders. Note that, with respect to production probability patterns, Abe's gesture system was the only system not found to have ergative properties. Thus, it is possible that Abe's gesture system is organized around a different set of principles from those that structure the gesture system of David and possibly the other children as well.

Complex Sentences: Rules of Recursion

In addition to their simple sign sentences, each of the four deaf children in the replication produced a number of complex sentences in which they conveyed at least two semantic relations (or propositions) before they relaxed their hands or returned them to neutral positions. Mildred, Abe, Karen, and Marvin produced 11, 45, 31, and 38 complex sentences containing two or more semantic relations, accounting for 12%, 25%, 22%, and 23% of each child's sentences, respectively. In our original study, David, Donald, Dennis, Chris, Kathy, and Tracy produced 240, 12, 4, 8, 11, and 10 complex sentences, accounting for 31%, 7%, 11%, 14%, 17%, and 12% of each child's sentences, respectively.

Two of the four children in our Chicago study were producing complex sentences during the first sessions they were observed: Marvin at 2;11 and Karen at 3;1. The other two children began producing complex sentences over the course of our observations: Mildred at 2;2 and Abe at 2;5. These onset times are, in general, comparable to those observed in the original study: Four of the six Philadelphia subjects were producing complex sentences during the first sessions they were observed (Dennis at 2;2, David at 2;10, Chris at 3;2, and Tracy at 4;1), and the other two children began producing complex sentences during our study (Kathy at 2;2, an age comparable to the onset ages of our Chicago subjects, and Donald at 3;11, an age later than those of our Chicago subjects; it should be noted, however, that Donald was not observed between 3;1 and 3;11, and therefore he might have begun producing complex sentences as early as 3;2).

The most common type of complex sentence observed in the children's gestures concatenated two actions. For example:

10. Susan-WAVE-Susan-CLOSE (*you/Susan wave* then *you/Susan close door*) [Abe IX.256].

Mildred, Abe, Marvin, and Karen produced 6, 28, 28, and 15 of these action-plus-action sentences, accounting for 55%, 62%, 76%, and 71% of their complex sentences with just two relations, respectively. The four children also concatenated two attribute relations (example 11) and three of the four concatenated an action-plus-attribute relation (example 12):

11. Wrist-picture of watch-ROUND   (*watch* belongs on *wrist* and *watch* is *round*)   [Marvin Vb.12].
12. GIVE-ROUND-Abe-GIVE   (you/Susan *give me/Abe* cookie which is *round*)   [Abe VIc.12].

Mildred, Abe, Marvin, and Karen produced 5, 5, 4, and 5 attribute-plus-attribute sentences (accounting for 45%, 11%, 11%, and 24% of their two-relation complex sentences) and 0, 12, 5, and 1 action-plus-attribute sentences (accounting for 0%, 27%, 14%, and 5% of their two-relation complex sentences), respectively. Each of our six original subjects produced action-plus-action sentences (David 85, Donald 4, Kathy 2, Tracy 5, Chris 7, and Dennis, 3, accounting for 57%, 36%, 33%, 50%, 100%, and 100% of their two-relation complex sentences, respectively), but only three of these subjects produced attribute-plus-attribute sentences (David 37, Donald 7, and Tracy, 1, accounting for 25%, 64%, and 10% of their two-relation complex sentences, respectively), and three produced attribute-plus-action sentences (David 27, Kathy 4, and Tracy, 4 accounting for 18%, 67%, and 40% of their two-relation complex sentences, respectively).

Although none of the children created explicit lexical signs for the conjunctive links between the relations of a complex sentence, it was usually easy to infer these links from the nonlinguistic context. For example, a complex sentence that described a sequence of events which, from the adult's point of view, were temporally but not causally linked, was inferred to have a "then" conjoining link (e.g., Susan-WAVE-Susan-CLOSE, meaning "you/Susan wave *then* you/Susan close the door"). Or, if the complex sentence described two coordinate relations that in some way contrasted with one another, a "but" link was inferred (e.g., pear-banana-[side-to-side head shake]-ROLL, meaning "the pear *but* not the banana rolls to my leg"). As a final example, if the complex sentences described a relation that was restricted, qualified, or elaborated on by a second relation in the sentence, a "which" link was inferred (e.g., GIVE-ROUND-Abe-GIVE, meaning "you/Susan give me/ Abe cookie *which* is round"). Note that the deaf children did not produce explicit signs for the conjoining links we inferred. Our heuristic was to infer a given link, for example, "then" whenever a "then" link could plausibly be inferred for that situation by an adult. It is worth noting that in studies of the hearing child's early complex sentences, experimenters are also at times forced to use context to infer a particular conjoining link. For example, Clark (1973) reports that *and* was often used by her young hearing subjects to mean "then" (i.e., to imply temporal sequence, e.g., *I want to look at them and* [then] *come back*), a coding decision not made on the basis of the actual conjunction expressed, but rather on the basis of an adult's view of the relationship between the two events mentioned in the sentence.

Table 7.6 presents the number of complex sentences produced by each child as a function of the type of conjunctive link each sentence was inferred to have. These types of links resemble those inferred in the complex sentences of our original deaf subjects (also presented in Table 7.6) as well as those explicitly produced in the complex sentences of comparably aged hearing children (Brown, 1973; Clark, 1973; Gvozdev, as reported by El'konin, 1973; Menyuk, 1971; Miller, 1973; Smith, 1970).

Moreover, all of the children who produced "which" complex sentences tended to use the subordinate semantic relation in sentences of this type to elaborate on the patient rather than the actor of the primary semantic relation (see, e.g., sentence 12 in which Abe used the second semantic relation *cookie is round* to further describe the characteristics of the patient [cookie] of the primary semantic relation *"you give me cookie*). Of all the "which" complex sentences Marvin produced, 80% (4/5) were of this patient-elaborating type; 73% of Abe's (8/11), 59% of David's (10/17), and 100% of Kathy's (5/5), Karen's (9/9), Tracy's (4/4), and Chris' (2/2) "which" complex sentences were of the patient-elaborating type. Hearing children learning English also tend to produce "which" complex sentences of the patient-elaborating type (Limber, 1973; Menyuk, 1969).

Vocalizations

Table 7.7 presents the proportions of each child's communications that contained gestures alone, vocalizations alone and gesture and vocalizations com-

TABLE 7.6
Conjunctive Links in Complex Sentences[a]

Chicago Subjects	And	Then	Which	But	Or	While	Cause
Mildred	10	1	0	0	0	0	0
Abe	8	21	11	1	1	1	2
Marvin	12	12	5	2	3	1	2
Karen	15	4	9	1	0	1	1
Philadelphia Subjects							
David	52	43	17	21	5	0	9
Dennis	0	3	0	0	0	0	0
Tracy	0	2	4	1	1	0	2
Chris	4	1	2	0	0	0	0
Donald	10	1	0	0	0	0	0
Kathy	0	0	5	0	0	0	1

[a] Each entry is the number of complex sentences with conjunctive links of each type produced by the children over the total interview sessions.

TABLE 7.7
Distribution of Gestures and Vocalizations

| | | Gesture + Vocalization | | Vocalization Alone | | |
	Gesture Alone	Meaningless Vocalization	Meaningful Vocalization	Meaningless Vocalization	Meaningful Vocalization	Total[a]
Abe	.12	.20	.02	.64	.01	1242
Mildred	.34	.18	.02	.44	.02	807
Marvin	.58	.15	–	.26	.01	574
Karen	.72	.14	.01	.11	.02	469

[a]Total = total number of communications produced by each child during the first half hour of each of his or her observation sessions.

bined for the four Chicago subjects (vocalizations were not coded in our original study of the Philadelphia subjects and, therefore, are not presented here). The children varied tremendously in their production of meaningless vocalizations alone (recall that meaningless vocalizations were either unrecognizable sounds spontaneously produced by the child or imitated sounds elicited by the child's caregiver). Moreover, this variability across subjects in meaningless vocalizations alone appeared to be systematically related to the children's production of gestures alone: The more meaningless vocalizations alone a child produced, the fewer gestures alone that child produced.

Despite the great variability with respect to meaningless vocalizations, the children were quite consistent in the minimal amount of meaningful vocalizations each produced: From 1% to 4% (1 to 36 utterances) of all of the communications produced by each child contained meaningful vocalizations. Moreover, meaningful vocalizations comprised a small subset of the vocalizations each produced: From 1% to 10% of the four children's vocalizations were meaningful.

In addition, all of each child's meaningful vocalizations were single words (either nouns, verbs, adjectives, or modulators such as *no, yes, uh-oh*). Almost half (43%, 36/82) of all of the meaningful words produced by the four children were accompanied by a gesture, and in 69% (25/36) of those gesture-plus-vocalization sequences, the word conveyed the same meaning as the gesture.

In sum, although the children were indeed producing vocalizations, and thus were making progress in their oral education, their vocalizations were by and large meaningless in a referential, although perhaps not in a communicative, sense. Furthermore, at the time of these observations there was no evidence that the children could combine their few meaningful words into sentences and therefore no evidence that the children had at this point learned any of the rules of English syntax.

Summary

To summarize, I have replicated in every detail on four new subjects our basic findings on the gesture systems of six previously observed subjects: All of the children's systems were used to convey the same types of semantic notions (conveyed in both simple and complex sentences), all appeared to have underlying structure, and all appeared to have surface structure. It is important to note that the underlying and surface patterns described in this study were not based on a small number of lexical items. The children produced a relatively large number of different types of characterizing signs (Mildred 55, Abe 59, Marvin 63, Karen 45), many of which appeared in sign sentences (Mildred 29, Abe 36, Marvin 34, Karen, 24). Moreover, these lexical items tended not to occur in only one sentence combination; rather, the children produced a number of tokens of these lexical types in sign sentences (Mildred 52, Abe 69, Marvin 73, Karen, 62).[6] Thus, the rules that we have isolated to describe the deaf children's sign sentences do not appear to be tied to a small number of particular lexical items (as Braine, 1976, has suggested some of the hearing child's earliest ordering rules might be; see Goldin-Meadow & Mylander, 1984, for further discussion of this issue with respect to both the deaf children's data and data on chimpanzees learning sign language). The rules consequently appear to be general statements about sign sentences in the deaf children's gesture systems.

In terms of the relevance of this phenomenon to normal language acquisition, it is important to stress that the gesture systems developed by these deaf children are comparable in semantic content and structure to the spoken systems acquired by hearing children under typical learning conditions (also see Goldin-Meadow, 1979, and Goldin-Meadow & Mylander, 1984).[7] The deaf children, however, developed their structured communication systems without the benefit of conventional linguistic input.

I turn now to a discussion of the implications of this phenomenon. First I discuss its implications for descriptive issues in child language, specifically,

---

[6]It should be noted that we were rarely forced to infer a lexical item which could not be found somewhere in the child's corpus. Only two lexical types not signed anywhere in the corpus were inferred for Mildred. Comparable numbers for Abe, Marvin, and Karen were one, four, and one, respectively.

[7]There were noticeable differences in the communication systems developed by our ten deaf subjects and by hearing children in terms of the kinds of information certain lexical items could convey (e.g., the deictic point vs. the noun), the children's mean length of sentences, and their average rate of production (see Goldin-Meadow & Mylander, 1984, for details). However, the important point is that despite these differences both the deaf and hearing children were found to convey the same topics using comparable formal structures.

the issue of underlying structure, and then I discuss its implications for acquisition mechanisms in child language, specifically, environmental effects and noneffects on the development of subsets of language properties.

UNDERLYING STRUCTURE: HOW RICH
SHOULD RICH INTERPRETATION BE?

In 1963 and 1964, three studies on the early stages of the hearing child's language acquisition were published (Braine, 1963; Brown & Fraser, 1963; Miller & Ervin, 1964), each of which concentrated solely on the distribution of forms in the child's spoken output, completely ignoring any meaning that these forms might have had for the child. It was not until 1970 that Lois Bloom first suggested that the forms produced by the child should be interpreted in context; in other words, that the sound-meaning pairings rather than the sound forms alone should comprise the data base for language acquisition studies. Bloom's data interpretation procedure became known as the "method of rich interpretation" and has been widely accepted as standard procedure within the field (but see Bloom, Capatides, & Tackeff, 1981; Duchan & Lund, 1979; Golinkoff, 1981; Howe, 1976, 1981, for discussion).

However, there has been ongoing debate within the field focusing on exactly how rich "rich interpretation" ought to be. If one of Bloom's subjects produced the sentence *mommy sock* while mother was putting on the child's sock, Bloom inferred that the child was conveying an agent-action-object relation, with the agent (mommy) and the object (sock) explicitly mentioned in the sentence and the action (put on) inferred from the nonlinguistic context. Bloom consequently was suggesting that at some underlying level the child could control three elements (mommy, put on, and sock), even though only two of those elements actually appeared in the surface form of the sentence.

Bloom mounted several different lines of evidence for her rich underlying structure claim. First, she found that the child is able to produce, at times, two-word utterances with all three of these types of elements: agent-action (*mommy push*), action-object (*helping mommy*), as well as agent-object (*mommy sock*). In fact, the child can produce all three elements in two consecutive (but still separate) utterances, such as *baby touch* (agent-action) *touch milk* (action-object), said when touching mother's milk glass. In addition, Bloom observed the child producing an occasional three-element utterance (agent-action-object, e.g., *baby touch milk*), suggesting that the child has control of all three elements at some underlying level, but cannot consistently produce these three elements in the surface forms of utterances. Finally, Bloom showed that the child's affirmative sentences are more likely to have fully expressed surface forms than are negative sentences, presumably because negative sentences have one more element in underlying structure (the negative marker) than do affirmative sentences. For example, the child would be more likely to say the agent in an affirmative utterance such as *Kathryn ə making house* than to say the agent in a negative utterance such as *no make a truck,* both utterances said while Kathryn was doing the building. Thus, Kathryn appears to have control of the agent at some underlying level — she can produce it when the number of elements in underlying structure (three in the previous affirmative sentence: agent, action, object) does not exceed her surface structure length limitation (three at this stage). But she fails to produce the agent when the number of elements in underlying structure (four in the negative sentence: agent, action, object, negative) goes beyond her three-word surface limitation.

Bloom's original underlying structure hypothesis entailed two claims, one which has been rejected by even Bloom herself, and a second which not only has not been refuted, but for which we find strong evidence in our data. The first claim attributed to the child a set of transformational rules (specifically, deletion rules), which transformed the child's rich underlying structure into more sparse surface structures. Under this hypothesis, in order for children to advance to the next stage of development, they had to *unlearn* this set of deletion rules — hardly a parsimonious description of development. Rather than attribute transformational rules to the young child, it is now generally accepted that the child has output constraints operating on speech-processing faculties (the most likely candidate being memorial limits), constraints which could lead naturally to omission in surface structure.

Bloom's second claim — the fact of surface structure omission in the young child's two-word sentences — although accepted by many, has not been hailed by all. For example, Brown (1973) maintains that children should be credited in underlying structure with no more than actually appears in their speech (i.e., that there is no underlying structure/surface structure distinction). The sentence *mommy sock* is described as a two-term agent-object relation, the sentence *put-on sock* as a *totally unrelated* two-term action-object relation. Brown thus attributes no more to children than they actually produce. But note that Brown's hypothesis, although seemingly more parsimonious than the underlying structure hypothesis, actually fails to account for a large number of facts about child language. In Brown's system, it is merely a coincidence that the child produces both *baby touch* and *touch milk;* moreover, it is only an accident that the child produces *baby milk* when "touch" is the understood action but fails to produce *baby milk* when, say, "sleep" is understood. Both facts are predicted by an underlying structure account that considers "touch" part of a three-term underlying structure and "sleep" part of a two-term underlying structure. Furthermore, although said to be a theory about development, Brown's hypothesis fails to account for the fact that, as children get older, they begin producing sentences like *baby touch milk* but fail to produce sentences like *baby sleep milk.* Thus, by not attributing a rich underlying structure to the young child's sentences, Brown will be forced to posit an additional set of rules or constraints to account for the sentences the two-word child does and does not produce and for the sentences the child will produce as he or she develops.

We have argued, relying on evidence comparable to Bloom's, that the deaf children in our studies also be credited with an underlying structure richer than the surface forms they actually produce. We find that the deaf children simultaneously produce gesture sentences that are two and three terms in length. For example, the child signs an occasional three-term sequence "food-EAT-Susan" (which we categorize as patient-act-actor) during the same developmental time period that he signs the two-term sequence "food-EAT" (which we categorize as patient-act with an inferred actor). Moreover, we also find situations in which the child first produces a sentence with two of the three terms hypothesized to be in the underlying structure of that sentence followed by another containing the omitted third term. For example, the child first signs the sentence "food-EAT" (patient-act) and immediately thereafter signs "EAT-Susan" (act-actor). Finally, we have distributional evidence based on the surface phenomenon of production probability for underlying structure in the deaf child's sentences: Givers (actors of four-element underlying structures) are less likely to be explicitly signed than eaters or goers (actors of three-element underlying structures), which in turn are less likely to be explicitly signed than dancers (actors of two-element underlying structures). It should be noted that evidence for at least some of these particular underlying structures can also be found in the hearing child's early two-word sentences (see Table 7.8, which provides actor, act, and patient production probability data on four hearing children from Bloom, Miller, & Hood, 1975, in our underlying structure format).[8]

In summarizing, it is important to note that Bloom's description of the child's two-word sentences in terms of underlying structures systematically related to surface structures, and Brown's (1973) description of these same sentences solely in terms of surface elements, *both* can adequately describe the particular two-word sentences the child actually produces. However, Bloom's description can also predict which particular semantic elements are likely to appear in the longer sentences children will produce during their next developmental stage. Brown's surface-oriented description will not. More-

---

[8]In Bloom, Miller, and Hood's (1975) terminology, sentences with four-elements underlying structure convey *agent-locative action-object-place* relations (comparable to our transfer relation); their sentences with three-element underlying structure convey *agent-action-object* relations (comparable to our transform relation) and *mover-locative action-place* and *patient-locative action-place* relations (comparable to our transport relation). Intransitive sentences (*agent-action*) which could have had two-element underlying structures (comparable to our perform relation) were not included in the analyses presented in Bloom et al. Our action is comparable to three different cases in Bloom et al., terminology: (1) Agent (in the four-element agent-locative action-object-place and in the three-element agent-action-object relations); (2) Mover (in the three-element mover-locative action-place relation); and (3) Patient (in the three-element patient-locative action-place relation). In addition, our Patient is comparable to their Object, and our Act comparable to their Action or Locative Action (labeled "Verb" in Bloom et al.'s tables).

TABLE 7.8

Underlying Structure in Simple Sentences with Two Spoken
Elements Produced by Four Hearing Children[a]

	Actor Production Probability		Act Production Probability		Patient Production Probability	
Subjects	4-element	3-element	4-element	3-element	4-element	3-element
Gia	.24	.51	.78	.88	.68	.74
Peter	.10	.16	.82	.99	.55	.90
Eric	.32	.42	.87	.97	.52	.87
Kathryn	.14	.30	.83	.97	.89 √	.87

Note: The data for this analysis are from Bloom, Miller, Hood (1975); from Table 5 for Gia II through VI; Table 7 for Peter IV through IX; Table 4 for Eric II through VI; and Table 6 for Kathryn I through IV.

√ Violation of the underlying structure pattern.

[a]Production probability was calculated on the basis of the following number of sentences with two spoken elements: Gia for the actor and act 4-element 88, 3-element 456, and for the patient 88, 334; Peter for the actor and act 83, 401, and for the patient 83, 311; Eric for the actor and act 69, 400, and for the patient 69, 218; Kathryn for the actor and act 152, 656, and for the patient 152, 447.

over, and perhaps more importantly in terms of a synchronic grammatical description of the child's sentences, Bloom's description can account for the particular distributional facts found in the set of two-word sentences the child produces; in particular, her description can account for the production probability patterns in the hearing child data, patterns which we have found to characterize our deaf children's two-sign sentences as well. Again, Brown's description, taking only surface elements into account, fails to capture these facts. Thus, in order to account not only for the particular two-word sentences the child produces, but also for the relationships among those sentences (i.e., for the system which appears to underlie the sentences taken as a set), we are forced to describe both underlying and surface levels for the hearing child's two-word sentences and for the deaf child's two-sign sentences.

The need to posit an underlying structure for the young child's two-sign and two-word sentences is motivated in large part by the production probability patterns found across the deaf and hearing children's sentences. Several objections might be raised to the production probability data and to the arguments for underlying structure based on these data.[9] Below we review some of the more central objections to the production probability measure and its relation to the underlying structure argument.

---

[9]Brown (1978) has objected to the underlying structure hypothesis by arguing that the surface variation we find in the deaf child's sentences is totally attributable to a particular type of sentence — sentences in which I inferred "one" as the implicit actor or "(t)here" as the implicit recipient — a sentence type which he feels I have overinterpreted and which therefore should not be included in the data base at all. I have since reanalyzed the data, omitting all sentences of this type, and found the same surface phenomenon for all six children in the original study, as well as for the later sessions of the three children still accessible (Goldin-Meadow, 1980). Thus, the phenomenon under discussion does not appear to be an artifact of a particular sentence type.

Production Probability
as a Measure of Underlying Structure

The first objection to the underlying structure argument concerns the production probability measure itself: It might be suggested that the production probability data we call upon to argue for underlying structure cannot fail to support the underlying structure hypothesis; that is, the analysis is tautological and production probability will unavoidably decrease as the number of elements hypothesized in underlying structure increases because of the procedure we use to calculate production probability. It is worth emphasizing that the argument we have mounted for underlying structure is not circular: Our procedure for calculating production probability does not prevent the unpredicted outcome (i.e., the procedure does not itself prevent production probability from increasing as the number of elements in underlying structure increases). For example, in describing a situation in which an actor gives a patient to a recipient, the child might (for reasons known best to him, e.g., salience) only produce sentences that contain patients (e.g., actor-patient, act-patient, recipient-patient). This hypothetical child would therefore be producing patients in 100% of his change-of-location transfer sentences, which are hypothesized to have four elements in underlying structure. Further, in describing a situation in which an actor eats a patient, the child might produce only actor-patient and act-patient sentences — the patient would therefore also occur in 100% of the child's change-of-state sentences, which are hypothesized to have three elements in underlying structure. Thus, in this not unreasonable hypothetical system, the eaten apple (the patient hypothesized as part of a three-element underlying structure) would be just as likely to be expressed as the given apple (the patient hypothesized as part of a four-element underlying structure). In the sign systems produced by each of the 10 children we have studied thus far, this situation is not observed.

A second set of objections to the underlying structure hypothesis might assume that the production probability pattern we observe is real, but would argue that this pattern could be explained more simply, relying on a description that credits children with no more in underlying structure than they explicitly produce in surface structure.

The Redundancy Hypothesis

It has been suggested (Brown, 1978) that the pattern of surface variation we observe in the deaf child's sign sentences can be accounted for by assuming simply that the child will fail to express explicitly that which is most obvious, or redundant, in the nonlinguistic situation. For example, in a request situation, the person who is being asked to be the actor is usually obvious from the nonlinguistic context. In contrast, the actor described in a statement is not as likely to be obvious from the nonlinguistic context. Thus, if actors are often requested to transfer the location of objects or to change the state of objects (a not unlikely event in parent-child interactions), actors of transfer and transform relations might be infrequently expressed simply because they are redundant with the nonlinguistic context (and not because they are components of underlying structures with a large number of elements).

To test the possibility that the actor production probability pattern we observe reflects sentence functions and not underlying structure, I have divided the sign sentences produced by each of the four Chicago subjects into those making requests and those making statements or asking questions. Table 7.9 presents the same actor production probability data found in Table 7.3 for these four subjects divided into request and statement/question sentences. Although there do appear to be very few request sentences hypothesized to have two-element underlying structures, where the data do exist the production probability pattern observed previously can be seen for all children in request sentences and for three out of the four children for statement/question sentences. Even when the function of a sentence is held constant, actor production probability increases systematically as the number of elements hypothesized in underlying structure decreases. Thus, the surface structure variation we observe, which can be accounted for by an underlying structure hypothesis, cannot be accounted for by this particular application of the redundancy hypothesis.

Brown himself applied this redundancy hypothesis to our data by suggesting that first and second persons should be infrequently expressed because they are often obvious from the nonlinguistic context, whereas third persons should be frequently expressed because they are, in general, less obvious. Thus, first and second persons should have low production probabilities, whereas third persons should have relatively high production probabili-

TABLE 7.9
Underlying Structure in Request and Statement/Question
Simple Sentences

| | Actor Production Probability[a] | | | | | |
| | Request Sentences | | | Statement/Question Sentences | | |
	4-element	3-element	2-element	4-element	3-element	2-element
Mildred	.05	.67	—	.00	.00 √	1.00
Abe	.00	.40	—	.20	.42	1.00
Marvin	.00	.35	1.00	.00	.11	.67
Karen	.03	.20	—	.00	.50	.67

√ = Violation of the underlying structure pattern.

[a]Actor production probability was calculated on the following number of sentences with two signed elements: Mildred for requests 4-element 19, 3-element 9, 2-element 0, and for statement/questions 1, 16, 5; Abe for requests 29, 20, 0, and for statement/questions 5, 26, 1; Marvin for requests 27, 14, 2, and for statement/questions 12, 18, 3; Karen for requests 34, 10, 0, and for statement/questions 1, 14, 6.

ties regardless of relation type (i.e., regardless of the number of elements hypothesized in underlying structure). This version of the redundancy hypothesis is also not supported by our data. We have analyzed first, second, and third persons separately in the data from our original six subjects (see Table 7.10, which presents actor production probabilities in sentences with two signed elements). Although the number of sentences in certain cells is small, where the data are available it is clear that as the underlying structure hypothesis predicts, actor production probability varies systematically with the number of elements hypothesized in underlying structure for first, second, and third person actors. Thus, within each person category, production probability increases as the number of elements hypothesized in underlying structure decreases (see Goldin-Meadow, 1980, for further details). It is not the case that, as the redundancy hypothesis would have predicted, third person actors are likely to be signed regardless of relation type, nor does it appear to be true that first and second person actors are unlikely to be signed across all relation types. The underlying structure hypothesis consequently appears to explain surface structure variation in the deaf children's sign sentences more adequately than does the redundancy hypothesis.[10]

The Lexicalization Hypothesis

It might be suggested that the underlying structures hypothesized for the young children reflect their lexicalization of the aspects of the world they attend to (in particular, the aspects of the world that are salient for them; see Braine, 1974; Schlesinger, 1974). For example, the two-word child attends to four aspects of a change-of-location transfer situation—the actor, act, patient, and recipient—and, at any given time, lexicalizes the salient two of those four aspects. He or she attends to three aspects of a change-of-state situation—the actor, act, and patient—and, at any given time, lexicalizes the salient two of those three aspects. This lexicalization hypothesis essentially boils down to a restatement of the underlying structure hypothesis: Aspects

---

[10]Greenfield and Zukow (1978) propose the informativeness principle, a hypothesis similar to the redundancy hypothesis we have entertained, to account for variation in the particular semantic elements conveyed by the one-word speaker. They suggest, as does the redundancy hypothesis, that the child is more likely to express information which is situationally the least redundant. To account for the production probability data we have presented, the informativeness principle would have to predict that a semantic element, say, the patient, in a "giving" relation (a relation we hypothesize to have four elements in underlying structure) tends to be less informative in context than does the patient of an "eating" relation (hypothesized to have three elements in underlying structure). The child would then tend to produce signs for the less informative given apple less often than for the more informative eaten apple. Although possible, at present we have no evidence to suggest that the informativeness principle can account for the production probability phenomenon. However, it should be noted that perhaps some sort of informativeness principle might be able to account for the fact that actors in general tend to have lower production probabilities than do patients.

TABLE 7.10
Underlying Structure in Simple Sentences with 1st, 2nd, and 3rd Person Actors[a]

Actor Production Probability[b]

	1st Person Actors			2nd Person Actors			3rd Person Actors		
	4-element	3-element	2-element	4-element	3-element	2-element	4-element	3-element	2-element
David	.06	.43	1.00	.03	.46	—	.00	.51	.88
Donald	.00	.20	1.00	.06	.10	—	.00	.40	.88
Kathy	.00	.25	—	.06	.57	—	—	.50	1.00
Dennis, Tracy, and Chris	.00	.50	—	.03	.29	—	—	.50	1.00

[a] The data are from David sessions I-XIII, Donald I-XVI, Kathy I-XII, Dennis I-IV, Tracy I-II, and Chris I-III.

[b] Production probability was calculated on the following number of sentences with two signed elements: David for 1st person 4-element 18, 3-element 35, 2-element 3, for 2nd person 136, 48, 0, and for 3rd person 4, 70, 17; Donald for 1st person 2, 5, 1, for 2nd person 51, 10, 0, and for 3rd person 1, 25, 8; Kathy for 1st person 1, 4, 0, for 2nd person 31, 7, 0, and for 3rd person 0, 6, 5; Dennis, Tracy, and Chris for 1st person 5, 4, 0, for 2nd person 34, 14, 0, and for 3rd person 0, 8, 4.

237

of change-of-location situations are less likely to be lexicalized than aspects of change-of-state situations because there are four change-of-location aspects competing for lexicalization but only three change-of-state aspects.

The lexicalization hypothesis, however, does differ from the underlying structure hypothesis in one respect: Rather than call the four aspects of a change-of-location situation an "underlying structure," which the child is assumed to bring to the situation, the lexicalization hypothesis attributes the four-part structure to the situation itself. I find no persuasive reason to believe that a priori a change-of-location situation must be viewed as a four-part event. After all, the change-of-location event moves the object from a *source*, occurs in a *time* and *place*, and might even involve an *instrument* or a nonacting *observer*; each of these units could conceivably be considered integral to the change-of-location situation, making at least a five-part event. Or alternatively, perhaps for the young child, the actor transferring an object is not at all integral to the change-of-location situation; change-of-location would then be a three-part event. Cognitive psychologists have successfully demonstrated precisely this point: Events do not necessarily come packaged into irreducible units. Rather, we appear to interpret situations by imposing our own structures on them (e.g., the Piagetian liquid conservation situation is seen differently by a 5-year-old child and by an adult). Thus, the change-of-location situation itself does not *require* a four-part interpretation, and if we find (as we do) that the child interprets change-of-location as a four-part event, that interpretation cannot easily be attributed to the external situation.

In sum, our data suggest that children do interpret change-of-location transfer as a four-part event, an interpretative structure I suggest they themselves must bring to the transfer situation. Moreover, this four-element structure (along with the three- and two-element structures we have described) was found to influence the distributional patterns in the surface structures of the child's two-sign sentences and, in this sense, can be considered a rich structure that underlies those sentences.[11]

THE RESILIENCE OF LANGUAGE

Replication: Deaf Children of Hearing Parents

One purpose of this study was to replicate the phenomenon of gesture development on a second sample of deaf children. I have shown that the four deaf children in the Chicago sample developed gesture systems comparable in se-

---

[11]There remains a crucial question about whether the type of underlying structure we have described can be distinguished from the meaning of the sentence, from what we might call semantic structure. In simple one-proposition sentences there are no grounds for such a distinction. However, when complex, two-proposition sentences are considered, an argument can be made for an underlying structure distinct from semantic structure (see Goldin-Meadow, 1982).

mantic content and structural properties (particularly, construction order patterns, production probability patterns, and rules of recursion) to the gesture systems developed by the six original deaf subjects in the Philadelphia sample. The ten deaf children we have observed over the course of our two studies share the two characteristics necessary for inclusion in the studies: (1) each child was congenitally deaf and unable to acquire spoken language naturally even with a hearing aid; (2) each child had not yet been exposed to a conventional sign language. Thus, all of the children in our studies experienced the same atypical language learning conditions, but none was prevented by these atypical conditions from developing a structured communication system.

Apart from their shared lack of conventional linguistic input, the ten deaf children varied on a number of sociological dimensions: race (two of our subjects were black, eight were white), socioeconomic status (two were lower class, eight were middle class), siblings (three had none, seven had at least one), number of parents in the home (two had one parent in the home for most or all of the study, eight had both parents), and educational setting (one did not start oral preschool until after our observations began, two attended the same oral preschool, three attended a second oral preschool, and four attended a different oral preschool). Despite this great variability, all ten of the children developed structured gesture systems.

The phenomenon of gesture development in deaf children lacking a conventional language model has been replicated by an independent investigator studying deaf children of hearing parents in Australia. Mohay (1982) completed a study comparable to ours of two deaf children, ranging in age from 1;6 to 2;6 and from 1;9 to 3;2, whose severe hearing losses prevented them from acquiring speech naturally and whose hearing parents chose not to expose them to conventional manual language. Mohay found that both of her deaf subjects used their gestures to convey the same semantic relations expressed by our deaf subjects and by hearing children at a similar stage of language development.

Moreover, Mohay found that both of her subjects combined gestures with other gestures, occasionally producing sequences three and four gestures long. In terms of structural properties, however, Mohay looked only at ordering tendencies of pointing gestures and found that points did not occupy privileged positions of occurrence in one of her subject's gesture sentences and that, although points occupied first position of the two-gesture sentences of her second subject up to 28 months (excluding point plus point sentences), on later tapes the point gesture ceased to occupy its privileged position.

In considering construction order in our subjects' gestures, we did not analyze our subjects' sign sentences at the level of *sign form* as did Mohay (i.e., in terms of deictic pointing forms). When such an analysis is performed, only three of our ten subjects are found to display ordering tendencies based on the deictic pointing form: Tracy (Binomial test, $p < .002$), Dennis (Binomial

Test, $p = .02$), and Mildred ($X^2 = 2.9$, $df = 1$, $p < .10$, trend) tended to produce deictic pointing signs in first position of their action sentences with one deictic and one characterizing sign. A comparable analysis for the hearing child's word sentences might presumably focus on the child's tendency to produce certain *word forms* before others (e.g., the tendency to produce nouns in first position of two-word sentences). Note that such ordering tendencies based on word form have not been reported for the hearing child. Thus, there is no particular reason to expect the deaf subjects (either ours or Mohay's) to display ordering tendencies based on the form of signs in their two-sign sentences.

However, for all of our deaf subjects we did find construction order tendencies in their two-sign sentences when these sentences were analyzed in terms of *semantic elements* (acts, patients, recipients, etc.). It is possible that Mohay would also find construction order tendencies in her subjects' sign sentences (as we did in ours and as researchers do in hearing children's spoken sentences) were she to analyze her data in terms of semantic elements.

The Resilient and Fragile Properties of Language

We have just seen that the phenomenon of gesture creation in deaf children of hearing parents is indeed replicable. Despite this robustness, we do not wish to claim that all deaf children of hearing parents will necessarily develop structured gesture systems. It is quite possible that certain types of deafness or certain types of social situations might prevent a child from communicating in a structured fashion. We have made no attempt to discover the internal and external limits of the child's propensity to develop structured language; that is, to determine which kinds of children under which kinds of circumstances will fail to exhibit this propensity.

Rather than explore the conditions that do not allow the child's language learning propensity to appear, our studies of deaf children of hearing parents have provided evidence that even under less-than-perfect language learning conditions, the child's propensity to develop language finds expression. We have shown that ten deaf children lacking conventional linguistic input can develop communication systems that have many of the structural properties of natural child language. I have called these properties of language "resilient." They are properties whose development can proceed under extreme variations in language learning conditions (Goldin-Meadow, 1978, 1982).

If the notion of resilient properties of language is to be of general value, it should predict that some set of properties of language will be developed in spite of extreme language learning conditions, whereas another set of properties of language (called "fragile") will tend not to appear. In fact, precisely those properties of language that do appear under linguistic hardship are the properties which must be called resilient. Those properties that do not appear must a priori be fragile. Each individual variation in the language learning environment in effect sets up a kind of experiment of nature, allowing one to determine subsets of resilient and fragile language properties with respect to each particular language learning environmental manipulation.

A seminal study by Newport, Gleitman, and Gleitman (1977) on the effects and noneffects the relatively small variations in natural mother speech have on the rate of the hearing child's acquisition of English adds support to this notion of resilient and fragile properties of language. Newport et al. correlated mother speech at Time 1 with the changes in child speech from Time 1 to Time 2 and found the acquisition rate of properties we have called resilient (e.g., recursion) to be unaffected by (or insensitive to) variation in mother speech. The acquisition rate of properties we have called "fragile" (e.g., the auxiliary) was found to be correlated with (or sensitive to) variations in mother speech. Thus, resilient properties of language appear to be unaffected by variations in linguistic input (variations both large and small), whereas fragile properties of language appear to be quite sensitive to even relatively small variations in linguistic input.

The notion of resilient and fragile properties of language is further refined by the results of other studies of language learning under atypical conditions, some of which do explore the limits that external factors place on the child's propensity to develop structured language. For example, Brown (1958) in a review of the literature on children raised by wolves and bears reports that these wild children do not spontaneously begin to speak. Moreover, Curtiss (1977) has studied a modern-day "wild child," Genie, who was deprived of linguistic, social, and perceptual stimulation for the first 13 years of her life. During this time, Genie failed to develop any sort of communication system. Thus, there do appear to be limits to the human child's ability to develop even the resilient properties of language. The extreme environmental conditions of wild children such as Genie, not surprisingly, surpass those limits.

Although Genie did not generate her own communication system during her long period of isolation, when her social situation improved and she finally was exposed to spoken English (after the age of 13, the age often considered to be the end point of a critical period for language acquisition in humans, Lenneberg, 1967), she did make linguistic progress. However, Genie did not succeed in acquiring all of the properties of spoken English even after she was exposed to linguistic input. Rather, she acquired many of the same language properties we have found in the deaf child's spontaneous gesture systems (e.g., ordering rules, recursion); that is, she acquired some of the properties of language which we have called resilient. Thus, the development of some resilient properites of language not only appears to be resistant to wide (and small) variations in quality of linguistic input, but also appears to be resistant to wide variations in time of initial exposure to linguistic input.

Further, even after intervention, Genie failed to develop certain properties of English (e.g., the auxiliary, movement rules). These properties of language were also found to be absent from the deaf child's gesture system.

Thus, these properties do indeed appear to be fragile — properties of language whose development appears to require the conditions under which language is typically learned.

Sachs and her co-workers (Sachs, Bard, & Johnson, 1981; Sachs & Johnson, 1976) provide further evidence for resilient and fragile subsets of language properties in their studies of a hearing child, Jim, whose deaf parents exposed him neither to conventional oral nor to conventional manual linguistic input and who had heard English only from the television and briefly at nursery school. During his period of limited exposure to conventional language, Jim was found to develop many of the resilient properties of language (e.g., the expression and concatenation of semantic relations), but was not observed to develop the fragile properties (e.g., the auxiliary and certain movement rules). (After intervention at 3;9, Jim began to acquire the properties of English he lacked and went on to become a normal English speaker.)

It is particularly gratifying (but need not necessarily have been the case) that the subsets of resilient and fragile properties defined for one particular linguistic deprivation (our deaf children developing their communication systems without rich linguistic input) tend to coincide with the resilient and fragile subsets defined by other environmental manipulations (Genie developing English after age 13, Jim developing English with restricted linguistic input, and even language learning children facing the relatively small variations found in natural mother speech). An entire spectrum of severity of language learning deprivations might eventually be established in this manner, environments which would empirically define a spectrum of language properties running from the most resilient (developed virtually everywhere) to the most fragile (needing the most finely tuned support to find expression).

In sum, the study of the structured gesture systems developed by deaf children of hearing parents suggests that certain resilient properties of language can be developed even without the rich linguistic input children typically receive, but other fragile properties of language cannot. Moreover, data from other studies of language learning under atypical environmental conditions converge with our own, suggesting that resilient properties of language are those whose development is *resistant* to variations in time of initial exposure to linguistic input, as well as to variations in the richness of linguistic input. Conversely, fragile properties of language are those whose development is *sensitive* not only to variations in richness of linguistic input, but also to variations in time of initial language exposure. Thus, there appears to be a distinction in language properties based on the effects and noneffects of linguistic environments on the development of those properties: Resilient properties of language, resembling hardy weeds, crop up under even markedly atypical conditions, whereas fragile properties of language, more like hothouse orchids, flourish only in a restricted environmental range.

ACKNOWLEDGMENTS

I am most grateful to Lila Gleitman, Martha McClintock, Elissa Newport, William Meadow, and Carolyn Mylander for their particularly insightful comments on various versions of this manuscript. I thank Breckie Church, Ellen Eichen, Carolyn Mylander, Marolyn Morford, and Denise Unora for the many long hours of video tape transcription they have contributed to this study, and my subjects and their families for their continued cooperation. This work was supported by NSF Grant BNS 77-05990, by a grant from the Spencer Foundation, and by a Biomedical Sciences Support Grant PHS 5 507 PR-07029 to the University of Chicago.

REFERENCES

Bloom, L. *Language development: Form and function in emerging grammars.* Cambridge, Mass.: MIT Press, 1970.

Bloom, L. *One word at a time.* The Hague: Mouton, 1973.

Bloom, L., Capatides, J. B., & Tackeff, J. Further remarks on interpretive analysis in response to Christine Howe. *Journal of Child Language,* 1981, *8,* 403–412.

Bloom, L., Lightbown, P., & Hood, L. Structure and variation in child language. *Monographs of the Society for Research in Child Development,* 1975, *40*(2, Serial No. 160).

Bloom, L., Miller, P., & Hood, L. Variation and reduction as aspects of competence in language development. In A. Pick (Ed.), *The 1974 Minnesota Symposium on Child Psychology.* Minneapolis: University of Minnesota Press, 1975.

Bloomfield, L. *Language.* New York: Holt, 1933.

Bowerman, M. Semantic and syntactic development: A review of what, when and how in language acquisition. In R. Schiefelbusch (Ed.), *The bases of language intervention.* Baltimore: University Park Press, 1978.

Braine, M. The ontogeny of English phrase structure: The first phase. *Language,* 1963, *39,* 1–13.

Braine, M. Length constraints, reduction rules, and holophrastic processes in children's word combinations. *Journal of Verbal Learning and Verbal Behavior,* 1974, *13,* 448–456.

Braine, M. Children's first word combinations. *Monographs of the Society for Research in Child Development,* 1976, *41*(Serial No. 164).

Brown, R. *Words and things.* New York: The Free Press, 1958.

Brown, R. *A first language.* Cambridge, Mass.: Harvard University Press, 1973.

Brown, R. *It may not be Phrygian but it is not Ergative either.* Unpublished manuscript, Harvard University, 1978.

Brown, R., & Fraser, C. The acquisition of syntax. In C. N. Cofer & B. Musgrave (Eds.), *Verbal behavior and verbal learning: Problems and processes.* New York: McGraw-Hill, 1963.

Clark, E. How children describe time and order. In C. A. Ferguson & D. I. Slobin (Eds.). *Studies in child language development.* New York: Holt, Rinehart & Winston, 1973.

Curtiss, S. *Genie: A psycholinguistic study of a modern-day "wild-child."* New York: Academic Press, 1977.

Dixon, R. M. W. Ergativity. *Language,* 1979, *55*(1), 59–138.

Duchan, J., & Lund, N. J. Why not semantic relations? *Journal of Child Language,* 1979, *6,* 243–252.

El'konin, D. B. General course of development in the child of the grammatical structure of the

Russian language (according to A. N. Gvozdev). In C. A. Ferguson & D. I. Slobin (Eds.), *Studies in child language development*. New York: Holt, Rinehart & Winston, 1973.

Feldman, H., Goldin-Meadow, S., & Gleitman, L. Beyond Herodotus: The creation of language by linguistically deprived deaf children. In A. Lock (Ed.), *Action, symbol, and gesture: The emergence of language*. New York: Academic Press, 1978.

Fillmore, C. J. The case for case. In E. Bach & R. T. Harms (Eds.), *Universals of linguistic theory*. New York: Holt, Rinehart & Winton, 1968.

Frishberg, N. Arbitrariness and iconicity: Historical change in American Sign Language. *Language*, 1975, *51*(3), 696–719.

Goldin-Meadow, S. A study in human capacities. *Science*, 1978, *200*, 649–651.

Goldin-Meadow, S. Structure in a manual communication system developed without a conventional language model: Language without a helping hand. In H. Whitaker & H. A. Whitaker (Eds.), *Studies in neurolinguistics* (Vol. 4). New York: Academic Press, 1979.

Goldin-Meadow, S. *An unpragmatic view of underlying structure in child language*. Unpublished manuscript, University of Chicago, 1980.

Goldin-Meadow, S. The resilience of recursion: A study of a communication system developed without a conventional language model. In L. R. Gleitman & E. Wanner (Eds.), *Language acquisition: The state of the art*. New York: Cambridge University Press, 1982.

Goldin-Meadow, S., & Feldman, H. The development of language-like communication without a language model. *Science*, 1977, *197*, 401–403.

Goldin-Meadow, S., & Morford, M. Gesture in early child language: Studies of deaf and hearing children. To appear in *Merrill-Palmer Quarterly*, 1984.

Goldin-Meadow, S., & Mylander, C. Gestural communication in deaf children: The effects and non-effects of parental input on early language development. To appear in *Monographs of the Society for Research in Child Development*, 1984.

Goldin-Meadow, S., & Mylander, C. Gestural communication in deaf children: Noneffect of parental input on language development. *Science*, 1983, *221*, 372–374.

Golinkoff, R. M. The case for semantic relations: Evidence from the verbal and nonverbal domains. *Journal of Child Language*, 1981, *8*, 413–438.

Greenfield, P. M., & Zukow, P. G. Why do children say what they say when they say it? An experimental approach to the psychogenesis of presupposition. In K. Nelson (Ed.), *Children's language* (Vol. 1). New York: Gardner Press, 1978.

Harris, Z. S. *Methods in structural linguistics*. Chicago: University of Chicago Press, 1951.

Howe, C. The meanings of two-word utterances in the speech of young children. *Journal of Child Language*, 1976, *3*, 29–47.

Howe, C. Interpretive analysis and role semantics: A ten-year mesalliance? *Journal of Child Language*, 1981, *8*, 439–456.

Lenneberg, E. H. *Biological foundations of language*. New York: Wiley, 1967.

Limber, J. The genesis of complex sentences. In T. E. Moore (Ed.), *Cognitive development and the acquisition of language*. New York: Academic Press, 1973.

MacKay, D. M. Formal analysis of communicative processes. In R. A. Hinde (Ed.), *Non-verbal communication*. New York: Cambridge University Press, 1972.

Menyuk, P. *Sentences children use*. Cambridge, Mass.: MIT Press, 1969.

Menyuk, P. *The acquisition and development of language*. Englewood Cliffs, N.J.: Prentice-Hall, 1971.

Miller, W. R. The acquisition of grammatical rules by children. In C. A. Ferguson & D. I. Slobin (Eds.), *Studies of child language development*. New York: Holt, Rinehart & Winston, 1973.

Miller, W. R., & Ervin, S. The development of grammar in child language In U. Bellugi & R. Brown (Eds.), The acquisition of language. *Monographs of the Society for Research in Child Development*, 1964, *29*(Serial No. 92).

Mohay, H. A. A preliminary description of the communication systems evolved by two deaf children in the absense of a sign language model. *Sign Language Studies,* 1982, *34,* 73–90.

Newport, E. L., Gleitman, H., & Gleitman, L. Mother I'd rather do it myself: Some effects and non-effects of maternal speech style. In C. E. Snow & C. A. Ferguson (Eds.), *Talking to children: Language input and acquisition.* New York: Cambridge University Press, 1977.

Sachs, J., Bard, B., & Johnson, M. L. Language learning with restricted input: Case studies of two hearing children of deaf parents. *Applied Psycholinguistics,* 1981, *2,* 33–54.

Sachs, J., & Johnson, M. L. Language development in a hearing child of deaf parents. In W. von Raffler-Engel & Y. Lebrun (Eds.), *Baby talk and infant speech.* Lisse, Netherlands: Swets & Zeitlinger, 1976.

Schlesinger, I. M. Relational concepts underlying language. In R. L. Schiefelbusch & L. L. Lloyd (Eds.), *Language perspectives: Acquisition, retardation and intervention.* Baltimore: University Park Press, 1974.

Silverstein, M. Hierarchy of features and ergativity. In R. M. W. Dixon (Ed.), *Grammatical categories in Australian languages.* Canberra: Australian Institute of Aboriginal Studies, 1976.

Smith, C. S. An exprimental approach to children's linguistic competence. In J. R. Hayes (Ed.), *Cognition and the development of language.* New York: Wiley, 1970.

Stokoe, W. C. Sign language structure: An outline of the visual communications systems. *Studies in linguistics,* Occasional papers 1960, *8,* 3–78.

Parent-Child Interaction with Receptively Disabled Children: Some Determinants of Maternal Speech Style

8

Toni G. Cross
Institute of Early Childhood Development
Melbourne, Australia

Terry G. Nienhuys
Department of Education
University of Melbourne, Australia

Maggie Kirkman
Institute of Early Childhood Development
Melbourne, Australia

Research into the context of language development has become common-place in recent years. This is in sharp contrast to the focus of previous years, which emphasized the autonomy and uniqueness of language development and the endogenous determination of the developmental process. Context-based research, however, reflects a renewed concern with seeking fuller explanations, especially with probing the general hypothesis that factors external to the child can account for nontrivial aspects of the process.

In keeping with this approach, research on caregiver-child interaction has reached a stage where the initial concern to identify features that are common across individual interaction styles is giving way to an interest in the extent and causes of variation. At the same time, a related shift in the study of language development can be detected. In an important paper on differences in language development, K. Nelson (1981) argues that a "new consensus" is emerging that nontrivial differences exist in the language development patterns of individual children, the study of which will be uniquely informative in attempts to explain the process of development. She also points out that the existence of such differences will require explanation in terms of both variation in individual children's makeups and in their characteristic learning contexts.

Recent results of cross-cultural research into the contexts of language development are adding impetus to such shifts in perspective. Researchers who have been accustomed to working with data gathered from the relatively homogeneous contexts of Western middle-class societies now face the challenge of assimilating the findings of ethnographic investigations of non-Western communities (e.g., Ochs, in press; Schieffelin, 1979). Although it is probably too early to evaluate the impact of this type of work, it should at least serve to alert us to the scope of variation possible in patterns of caregiver-child interaction and in the process of language learning. It is becoming apparent that to ignore the issue of variation on either side of the interaction between child and context is to risk remaining ignorant of essential factors in the development process.

Although it is probable that innovations in cross-cultural research will extend our understanding of the global limits and consequences of sociocultural variation, the contribution of intracultural research will continue to be that of definition, refinement, and detail in investigation. For researchers concerned with the context of development, it is a priority that we understand the nature, extent, and causes of variation in children's linguistic experiences. A full description of parental or caregiver speech, studied as input to language learning, is as essential to our understanding of the process as is the achievement of similar detail in the description of child speech and comprehension as output. It now seems obvious that in order to frame significant statements about the developmental process, we will need to have marshaled sufficient detail on both sides of the interaction to perceive those patterns which hold not only over sociocultural differences but also over development within a given culture.

It is from this empirical perspective that the data on variation in styles of mother-child interaction are presented in this chapter. In general terms, the basic questions at issue are perceived to be:

> To what extent is there variation in the linguistic context provided by different mothers?
> What are the primary determinants of variation in mother-child interaction styles?
> What roles do children themselves play in affecting stylistic differences in the ways their parents interact with them?

In addressing these questions, we seek not to deal directly with the effect of input variation on child language development, but rather to investigate the limits of variability in parental speech styles as they occur in spontaneous interactions between mother and child.

In general, three sources of influence affecting maternal speech style have been identified. The most obvious are social factors that influence the mother herself in approaching her interactions with her child, such as her socio-economic status, educational background, size of family, marital status, employment, personal makeup, and so forth. Although undoubtedly important and, regrettably, little researched, such factors are also not our direct concern but, where possible, are held constant in our studies (by homogeneity of socioeconomic status, educational level, place of residence, etc.) across experimental groups.

Of special interest to us are a second group of factors — those salient characteristics of the child as a conversational partner which may create variations in maternal speech style and which, we have argued previously, require careful experimental control if their influences on maternal speech style are to be evaluated. Cross (1979, 1981b) has discussed the range of separate and possibly interacting child variables that need to be considered and the consequent methodological implications. Child characteristics which may influence maternal speech style in direct ways include chronological age, level of cognitive development, and communicative ability, the last encompassing both spontaneous speech and receptive abilities. However, it is also known that some features of maternal speech alter according to the developmental level of the child, and thus, the various child characteristics may have differential effects at different stages of development (e.g., Cross, 1977; Cross & Morris, 1980; Ellis & Wells, 1980). When assessing the respective effects of child age, cognitive level, or linguistic abilities on maternal speech style, experimental designs need to control, or examine separately, these stage-dependent effects. Only then can the child's influence on maternal speech features, rather than the converse, be experimentally evaluated.

A third group of factors are those that may be associated with special characteristics of individual mother-child dyads; they are factors which have influence even after children are equated for age, language, or cognitive development and which relate to more specific influences operating on mother-child interactions in particular circumstances or for particular dyads. We have investigated such factors by comparing mothers addressing normal children with mothers addressing children who, although equated for the more general factors, have specific forms of communicative disabilities such as deafness, developmental dysphasia, or childhood autism.

To define our approach further, we should stress that our focus is directed to understanding the extent of children's influence on parental speech style and, hence, on the nature of their own linguistic experiences. This chapter brings together several lines of research that have been conducted to explore this question. The unifying theme in the work is that each study had concentrated on conditions of communication within the mother-child dyad which were selected to produce extremes of naturally occurring variation in the adult's style of interaction. We are concerned with identifying the aspects of the adult's conversation that can be altered by communicative and behavioral characteristics of children. In so doing, our aim is to empirically disentangle the cause–effect relationships between child and linguistic experience which interact in the language development process. To this end, we report six comparative studies which investigate the similarities and differences in a large number of maternal speech features to normal and communicatively impaired children.

COMPARISONS OF RAPIDLY DEVELOPING AND NORMAL GROUPS

A number of studies have suggested that differences among children in either course or rate of development are associated with differences in their parents' style of interaction. However, previous analyses have interpreted the direction of cause and effect as operating from parental variation to effects on child language development. For instance, Newport, Gleitman, and Gleitman (1977) showed that children who spontaneously use certain grammatical constructions more often than other children have mothers who 6 months earlier used different proportions of certain syntactic forms and expansions in their speech to them. Furrow, Nelson, and Benedict (1979) have shown stronger and more numerous correlations between maternal speech style and measures of child language after a 9-month developmental period. Both studies used a method of correlating mothers' speech at an early child age with measures of child speech at a later point in development.

Two studies adopted the method of selecting groups of children to contrast in terms of rates of development and then examining differences in their mothers' speech. Cross (1978) attempted to control the effects of child linguistic ability on mothers' speech by selecting two groups of 2-year-old children at the same level of linguistic development who were either accelerated or normal in rate of development. Ten children in the Accelerated Group (AC) were linguistically matched with ten children in the Normal Child Group (NC) who were on the average 7 months older in chronological age. The range of mean length of utterance (MLU) for all children was 1.5–3.4, and both groups had a mean of 2.2 morphemes.

Table 8.1 summarizes the relatively few maternal speech features (of the 70 compared) that significantly differentiated the groups. The majority of differences between the AC and NC mothers were found in measures of the degree of semantic relationship between the mothers' responses and the content of the children's preceding utterances. This result was consistent with Newport et al.'s findings of a positive association between maternal expansions and children's rates of development. More recent studies (e.g., Ellis &

Wells, 1980; K. E. Nelson, 1977, 1981; Nelson, Carskaddon, & Bonvillian, 1973; Nelson, Denninger, Bonvillian, Kaplan, & Baker, 1983) have obtained similar results for various measures of the semantic contingency of adult upon child speech in adult and child conversation. In Cross's comparison, however, higher degrees of maternal fluency were also associated with more rapid child growth, which is consistent with a finding by Newport et al. (1977). Further associations were found between child rate and higher proportions of maternal partial repetitions and pronoun usage, and lower proportions of self-answers and maternal utterances per turn (for details and a discussion of these results, see Cross, 1978).

However, many of the features that differentiated the AC and NC mothers' speech styles were the same as those we had shown, in a study conducted at about the same time, to be implicated in a causal relationship whose direction appeared to be from the child's stage of development to the mother's conversational adjustment. The semantic contingency of maternal utterances on preceding child utterances, maternal repetitions and self-answers, and measures of maternal fluency had all been shown by Cross (1977) to be correlated with simultaneously measured aspects of child language development. The design of this study, as well as the specific patterns of association between variables, indicated that these correlations were attributable to the child's influence on the mother's speech rather than the reciprocal direction.

A later study by Ellis and Wells (1980), using children of similar ages, found associations between child language development and maternal speech style that were not in accord with the results just mentioned. This study, too, highlights the difficulty inherent in disentangling the cause–effect relationship. Ellis and Wells adopted a retrospective rather than a concurrent approach. They selected a subsample of preschool children from longitudinal data and divided them into groups of fast and slow developers. The fast developers achieved a gain of two morphemes in MLU within 6 months of a given developmental point, but the slow developers took 12 months or longer from the same starting point. The differences in maternal speech for each child group showed that faster development was associated chiefly with larger amounts of parental speech. Further, whereas semantic contingency did not emerge as a significant factor, a number of functional categories did: questions, prohibitions, commands, and acknowledgments. Imitations and repetitions were also associated with more rapid development, as were the proportions of utterances related to children's actions, a finding which contrasted with Cross' (1978) study which included an identical category.

Probable reasons for the discrepancies in the results of studies attempting to correlate features of parental speech style with measures of rate of child language development have been discussed in some detail by Cross (1979, 1981b). It is likely that a major reason is the different methods used to measure rate of development. Both Newport et al. and Furrow et al. used prospec-

TABLE 8.1

Summary of the Patterns of Differences in the Accelerated (AC)
and the Normal Child (NC1) Comparison and Delayed (DC)
and Normal Child (NC2) Comparison

Mothers' Speech Measures	AC Means	NC1 Means	DC Means	NC2 Means
Discourse Features				
Exact Imitations	3.71	2.58*	3.89	3.50*
Complete Expansions	7.46	5.79*	6.05	9.05*
Partial Expansions	7.00	5.67	5.50	7.78*
Elaborated Expansions	5.67	3.39**	4.33	5.22
Interpretations (total)	23.83	18.54**	20.44	26.06
Predictate Extension	.91	.25**	2.33	.94
Interprets + NP Extensions	36.17	29.92**	27.72	40.61
Interprets + Tot. Extensions	59.37	50.92**	51.00	55.12
Interprets x Repetitions	7.96	5.75*	6.94	7.39
Extensions x Repetitions	17.00	12.16**	13.61	12.89
Synergistic Sequences (total)	24.96	17.92***	22.61	26.17
Semantic Unique Responses	3.71	5.42*	4.61	3.33
Theme-Related Responses	9.04	12.92*	9.05	9.00
Noncontingent Responses (total)	12.71	18.37*	13.66	12.33
Exact Repetitions	1.79	1.42	4.55	2.17**
Partial Repetitions	8.25	6.54**	6.78	8.94*
Self-Answers	.71	1.25**	8.17	2.33**
Stock Expressions	1.90	2.21	4.11	2.78**
Syntax				
Questions (total)	35.04	31.42	49.22	37.39**
Wh- Questions	15.92	15.38	26.17	18.44**
Imperatives (total)	7.29	6.50	9.50	5.55**
Regular Imperatives	5.92	5.04	6.89	4.28**
Pronouns	.63	.44*	.56	.67
Referentiality				
Attentionals	3.46	3.88	4.89	3.40*
Remote References	11.13	13.88	22.33	8.00**
Speech Style				
Amount of Speech (M/C Utts)	1.26	1.47	.93	1.12*
Rate of Speech (WPM)	71.94	71.06	76.96	68.08*
Disfluent Utterances	2.96	4.00*	5.63	3.00**
Unintelligible	.87	1.94***	3.72	1.72***
Total Degraded Utterances	5.00	7.25**	10.00	5.28**
Run-On Sentences	8.46	10.46	15.39	8.17*
Conversational Measures				
Mother Utterances per Turn	1.88	1.78*	1.42	1.86**
Null Responses	13.20	14.12	15.61	11.61**
Token Responses	12.04	13.63	18.17	13.72**
Non-informative Responses	35.25	37.79	42.05	25.33**
Simultaneous Talk	3.33	3.59	2.27	4.16*
Child Overtalk	1.71	1.67	.67	1.94*

TABLE 8.1 (continued)

Mothers' Speech Measures	AC Means	NC1 Means	DC Means	NC2 Means
Tutorial Features				
Quiz Questions	14.54	13.87	18.02	15.77*
"What's That?" Questions	4.83	5.67	9.39	6.94**
Prods	.50	.96	1.50	.88*

* $p < .05$ (two-tailed test).
** $p < .01$.
*** $p < .001$.

tively designed follow-up studies (as did K. E. Nelson, 1981, Table 1, and Nelson et al., 1983), but Cross used a concurrent design, and Ellis and Wells adopted a retrospective design. However, there were also crucial differences between the two prospective studies. Furrow et al. initially equated children for age and linguistic ability and then chose a 9-month follow-up period over which to measure child growth, whereas Newport et al. chose a 6-month period and used a partial correlational technique at the outset of their study to attempt to control the effect of children's differing ages and linguistic stages on their mothers' speech styles. Furthermore, the follow-up periods chosen by Ellis and Wells varied across groups and across individual children, and in the concurrent design by Cross it was not possible to determine the period during which the differences in maternal speech had influenced the child's development. If, as each of the authors acknowledge, it is methodologically difficult to determine the direction of cause and effect, then this variation in the length of time during which each partner can affect the other's language usage could have caused the discrepancies in results.

In Furrow et al.'s study, the confounding of cause–effect relationships was not overcome even though explicit attention was given to this problem. Their 9-month follow-up period, which was taken over very early stages of development, still provided ample time for increments in child language ability to have altered parental speech features over the observation period. Equating children at the beginning of this period for age and stage of development was not a sufficient measure to allow confidence in inferring (after what was a fairly substantial period of development) that it was the initial pattern of parental speech features which accounted for the correlations with subsequent child speech, rather than the patterns which held at points later in the follow-up period. Their design did not guarantee that the causal direction was not, in reality, from the rapidly developing child to the parent's speech style. Contrary to the authors' claim, they have not eliminated the possibility that the sets of features which differentiate the adults' interactions with rapidly developing children from those with more slowly developing children are primarily responses to inherent differences in the styles of interaction of the children themselves.

As a further point in attempting to explain the discrepancies, it is relevant that the ages, stages, and ranges of child development at the outset of each study were different. If children's linguistic abilities affect parental speech style, then those styles will alter with developments in the child. If a further possibility is admitted, namely that *effects* of different parental speech features will alter according to changes in child language maturity and learning strategies, then one would not reasonably expect the same patterns of correlations between children's rates of growth and parental speech features for children at different stages of development (see also K. E. Nelson, 1981).

COMPARISON OF SLOWLY DEVELOPING AND NORMAL CHILDREN

In an attempt to replicate the patterns of association between mothers and children found in Cross' (1978) comparison of accelerated and normal children, we recently undertook a comparison of language-delayed and normal children (Cross, 1981a). In order to ameliorate the problems posed by the influence of the children's linguistic maturity on maternal speech, two controls were adopted. First, all children selected were equated as closely as possible for level of linguistic ability by restricting the range of child abilities within the samples and also by matching pairs across the child groups for M.L.U., mean length of their longest utterances, and linguistic comprehension. Second, we reproduced the simultaneous comparative design of the accelerated-normal comparison.

Although a different set of subjects was used, all aspects of the study were designed to be comparable with the first comparison. Thus, the second comparison was based on 10 pairs of children matched for measures of language ability (e.g., MLU range for both groups was 1.8–2.6), but permitted to vary in age. However, in this case, the mean age difference, 27:8 (range 22–35 months difference), was much larger than in the AC–NC comparison, 6:3 (range 4–10 months difference). The delayed group of children was contacted through speech therapists who had diagnosed each child as specifically and markedly language delayed with no additional developmental complications. The normal group was selected to match the delayed group, pair by pair, in terms of family socioeconomic status, maternal education, birth order, sex, as well as language level. Spontaneous conversations between mother and child were recorded in the home in the same way as in the AC–NC comparison, and the measures of maternal speech were coded in precisely the same manner.

Table 8.1 presents the results of the comparisons of maternal speech to delayed and normal children (DC–NC2) beside the results of the accelerated and normal child (AC–NC1) comparison. Overall, as in the AC–NC1 comparison, we found relatively few maternal speech features discriminated the groups (27 of the 70 features compared). However, there was a larger number of differences in the DC–NC2 comparison, presumably because of the larger differences in rate of development between the children.

In broad terms, the pattern of DC–NC2 differences retained some of the elements of the AC–NC1 comparison (e.g., differences in the appropriate directions for complete expansions, partial self-repetitions, degraded speech, and proportion of utterance per turn), but there were also some marked discrepancies. Of particular interest was the result that many more measures of conversational structure reached significance, which generally indicated a stronger tendency for mothers to provide more informative and progressive conversation for the normal children, and for the DC dyads to produce a smaller degree of conversation overlap between partners. Also discrepant was the group of findings showing differences in sentence types and the use of several tutorial devices that had not reached significance in the previous comparison. Further, the latter comparison produced results reflecting Ellis and Wells' finding of a positive association between more rapid (i.e., normal) development and mothers' tendency to avoid the use of remote (nonpresent) references in their utterances, although direct reference to child actions was again not significantly different.

Discussion of the patterns of results that were similar for the two comparisons, their relationships to other similar findings in the literature, and their implications for the question of what factors in parental speech are associated with rate of language development is provided in Cross (1978, 1981a). Of relevance to our present concerns are the maternal features that were shown to alter according to whether the comparison was between mothers addressing normal and accelerated developers or between normal and delayed developers. If one takes the position that maternal speech is *directly* implicated in rate of language development, there are several plausible explanations for these discrepancies. Three invoke general methodological or conceptual rationales, which have been put forward previously (see Cross 1979, 1981b), and one hinges on the specific nature of the discrepant differences in the maternal features.

On the first point, it has been argued that it is unlikely that all features of parental speech will have uniform effects on child acquisition at all stages of development. Several researchers have previously contended that aspects of parental speech will have stage-contingent effects (e.g., Brown 1973; Cross 1975, 1979, 1981b; Ervin-Tripp 1977; Moerk 1977; K. E. Nelson 1981). If, as we argued earlier, some features of parental speech are effective only at a particular stage of development, whereas others have effect at other times, then different results can be expected as a direct consequence of variation in the stage and span of development represented by the children. This argument has been used previously to explain discrepancies in the results of studies using different designs, but it may also be used to explain the discrepancies between the AC–NC1 and DC–NC2 comparisons. Because the range of linguistic abilities represented by the DC–NC pairings was much narrower across the group (i.e., spanning only child MLUs of 1.8 to 2.6) relative to the AC–NC comparison (which contained matched child pairs ranging from 1.5–3.4), it is probable that the comparisons were being made for a number of child pairs that were at different stages of development in each study.

However, the discrepancies also encourage the hypothesis that the external factors inhibiting development (i.e., causing *delay* in development) are in some degree different from (or more numerous than) those that accelerate development. To be consistent with the present results, one could posit that, although certain concentrations of specific features in the input may be necessary to produce an enhanced rate of normal development, it may require not only deficiencies in this set of features (i.e., those that were reliable and consistent in direction across the comparisons) but also deficiencies in other aspects of parent-child interaction in order to decelerate language acquisition.

A third possibility is that there are co-relationships between the different levels of analyses used that produce a package of interaction between parental features. In this case, one could argue that the consistent features only are implicated crucially in affecting rate of development, but at certain (high) levels of differences between the groups in these features, other noncausal features in the package are incidentally picked up and carried into reliable differences by their correlation with the causal features. For instance, it may be that disfluency in maternal speech has a negative effect on rate of development but that rate of speech with which it is positively correlated in our samples is associated negatively with rate of child development only because it is implicated in producing degradation in maternal speech. Depending on the *extent* of the differences in rate of children, or in the ranges of their abilities in comparative studies, such associated features would be expected to vary in the extent to which they reached criterion for statistical reliability in differences across the groups of mothers.

However, there are indications in the present sets of results, at the level of the directions of differences in the specific features that were discrepant across the two comparisons, that the nonconsistent features may be associated with an effect *on parents* produced by the accelerated or delayed children themselves. This seemed likely in the case of the conversational measures, which gave a clear picture of breakdown in the progressive conversational structure of the mothers addressing the delayed child group. It was noted by the observers that the children in this group were much less talkative than those in the normal groups and appeared to be much less willing to engage in extended conversations with others. They tended to produce less than half the number of utterances in the same time period and responded to significantly fewer maternal utterances. The reduced levels of responding by their mothers were reflected in lower amounts of speech and a lower ratio of mother over child utterances. Similarly, the higher incidence of non-informative or token responses could be argued to be a direct consequence of the child's conversational reluctance. The lower proportions of simultaneous talk and child overtalk can also be interpreted as reflecting a reduced level of child participation in the conversation. If this direction of cause and effect is pursued, several other discrepancies can be explained. The DC mothers' greater usage of questions, particularly wh- questions and quiz questions, can be seen as reflecting a heavier reliance on conversation elicitation techniques, the much higher proportion of self-answers as a response to the child's failure to respond to questions, and the higher use of stock expressions, imperatives, attentionals, and prods as devices to keep a reluctant child engaged in conversation. Even the heightened incidence of remote references and run-on sentences, as well as the more rapid rate of speech, can be viewed as responses to the child's failure to participate adequately. These last features seemed to reflect monologic moments in the conversation; that is, when the DC mothers tended to give up their endeavors to include the child in genuine dialogue and resorted to a strategy of talking to themselves.

Thus, the discrepancies between the two sets of results provided prima facie grounds for hypothesizing a major role not only for the specific linguistic abilities of children in affecting details of their parents' speech styles, but also for an overlaid effect of conversational cooperation (or noncooperation) which, in the case of the child with slower language development, can further confuse the picture of the forward effect of parental language on child development.

That a similar explanation can account for the features that were significantly different in the AC–NC comparison and not in the DC–NC comparison is suggested also by the nature of the differences. All of them were contained under the heading Discourse Features and coded the degree of semantic, or content, relationship between child utterance and immediately succeeding maternal utterance. All of them also indicated a direction of association showing a greater degree of semantic contingency of maternal on child utterance for the accelerated child group. Comparisons between the children's contributions to the conversation showed clearly that the accelerated children asked significantly more questions of their mothers. It is thus likely that their mothers' more frequent use of semantically related utterances directly reflected the AC children's greater conversational demands for adult participation.

On these grounds, we designed a further study to clarify the relationship between the child as a major determinant of mothers' speech style and mothers' speech as a causal factor in the rate of child language development.

COMPARISON OF THE DELAYED GROUP'S SIBLINGS AND THE NORMAL CHILD GROUPS

To test the hypothesis that it was the special influence of the language disabled children that caused their mothers to differ from the NC mothers, we selected a group of seven linguistically delayed children who had normally developing younger siblings (DCS) of the same ages and stages as most of the children in our normal groups. We were thus able to match each of these younger siblings with a child from one of our NC groups (forming a NC3 group) and to compare their mothers' speech. Our simplest prediction was that, when the DC mothers were addressing their younger normal children, they would not differ significantly from the NC3 group.

The results are presented in Table 8.2. It can be seen that well over half of the reliable differences between the NC and DC mothers fell below significance when the DC mothers were recorded in interaction with their younger, more normal children (DCS). Many of these features were argued previously to reflect compensatory techniques the mothers were using with their delayed children to impose a conversational style of interaction on a reluctant, communicatively inhibited conversational partner, such as, exact self-repetitions, questions (especially quiz questions), prods, attentionals, imperatives, token responses, and so forth. Moreover, the incidence of simultaneous talk and overtalking by the child were reduced to almost the same level as that found in the NC groups. This result supported our observation that the delayed children were more reluctant to make contributions to the conversation than the normal groups and that this reluctance was influencing the two-way conversational structure.

Eleven features, however, showed reliable differences that were consistent with those found in the DC–NC2 comparison, but only two sets of features were also consistent with the differences found in the AC–NC1 comparison. One set, maternal expansions, particularly partial expansions (which reached significance in the DC–NC2 and DCS–NC3 comparison and fell just below significance in the AC–NC1 comparison), reinforced indications in the recent literature that the semantic matching of maternal replies and child speech is a crucial factor in aiding language learning (e.g., Cross, 1978, K. E. Nelson, 1977, 1981; Nelson et al., 1973; Newport et al., 1977; Snow, 1977). The other set, the proportion of degraded speech, has also been found elsewhere to be associated with rate of development (Newport et al., 1977), supporting the conclusion that clarity and fluency in the input assist the child, at

TABLE 8.2
Summary of Significant Differences for the Comparison of Maternal
Speech to the Normal Siblings of the Delayed Children (DCS)
and to Matched Normal Children (NC3)

Mothers' Speech Measures	Means for Siblings of Delayed Group	Means for Matched Normal Group
Discourse Features		
Partial Expansions	5.27	7.27*
Syntax		
Imperatives (negative)	.93	.02**
Speech Style		
Amount of Speech (M/C Utts.)	1.32	1.12**
Rate of Speech (WPM)	87.00	69.60**
Disfluent Utterances	5.67	4.00*
Unintelligible Utterances	4.54	2.60***
Total Degraded Utterances	10.07	6.80**
Run-On Sentences	12.20	8.33**
Conversational Measures		
Mother Utterances per Turn	1.41	1.71**
Null Responses	16.80	13.30*
Noninformative Responses	39.53	27.53*

$*p < .05$ (two-tailed test).
$**p < .01$.
$***p < .001$.

least in the early stages, to process and learn from parental speech. That is, the direction of effects suggested by the consistencies across comparisons is toward a positive relationship between rate of language development in children and the frequency of maternal expansions by their mothers, and toward a negative relationship between the proportions of degraded speech in the mothers' samples and rate of development.

Consistent results from all three comparisons, in terms of implications for the direction of cause and effect, encourage the framing of some specific causal statements; that is, features which have been consistently associated with rate of child language development across all our comparisons, and which also find support in other studies, deserve very close experimental attention as probably robust general influences on rate of development in the early stages. These are the degree of semantic relationship between the child's and mother's utterances and the characteristic amount of disfluency and unintelligibility in mothers' speech. The first is an aspect of discourse style that makes it possible for children to relate meaning and structure on the basis of predictably close correspondence between their own utterances and their mothers' immediately succeeding responses; the second is an aspect of speech style that may serve to increase or reduce confusion in the language the child is attempting to use as primary data.

On the other hand, features that have been found to covary with child rate in some studies but not others should probably be retained as candidates for the role of influencing development, with the proviso that they be investigated further (perhaps at first naturalistically) in terms of the possibility that they may have only limited and stage-specific effects on child growth.

However, for those maternal speech features that have been found to depend on the communicative proficiency and interactional behavior of children — those that no longer differentiated the mothers of normal children from the mothers of the delayed children when addressing their younger normal siblings — it can be argued that they would be unlikely to directly influence child language learning. They must be regarded as caveats on the interpretation of research results designed to show causal effects of mother upon child. This is not to suggest that they are not relevant to language development but rather to argue that we must address the issue of the extent to which communicative and behavioral differences in children are directly responsible for the incidence of features of maternal speech at specific stages of development. Further, this must be done before drawing any conclusions as to the role of such features in acceleration or delay in development.

COMPARISONS OF HEARING AND HEARING IMPAIRED CHILD GROUPS

In order to further disentangle the two-way cause–effect interaction in mother-child dyads, we have recently completed a series of studies comparing the speech of hearing mothers of hearing and severely hearing impaired children equated variously for language development and chronological age. These comparisons were designed either to control, or to manipulate experimentally, the effects of differences in children's attention, language, and general maturation on their mothers' spontaneous conversations.

Four groups of eight middle-class hearing children were selected: infants (Group HO) with a mean age of 4 months (range 3–6 months); 1-year-olds (Group H1) with a mean age of 11 months (range 10–13 months); 2-year-olds (Group H2) with a mean age of 26 months (range 23–29 months); and 5-year-olds (Group H5) with a mean age of 63 months (range 61–66 months). Two further samples of eight deaf children were selected: 2-year-old deaf children (Group D2) with a mean age of 30 months (range 25–34 months) and 5-year-old deaf children (D5) with a mean age of 66 months (range 61–70 months). All hearing children had been tested using free-field audiometry at 7 and 9 months, and none had demonstrated a significant hearing loss. All children in Groups D2 and D5, however, suffered unaided prelingual hearing losses in the better ear exceeding 70 db SPL across the speech range of frequencies

(250, 500, 1000, 2000 HZ). All aided hearing losses in the better ear were in excess of 40 dB SPL, and all children wore aids (either of the radio frequency or conventional types) during the data-gathering sessions. No additional handicapping conditions were known to be present in any hearing impaired child; their siblings and parents could all hear normally. The mothers, with their deaf children, were all attending educational programs in which only oral-aural methods of communication were employed. (The subjects of this study are described more fully in Cross, Johnson-Morris, & Nienhuys, 1980.)

Group H2, the hearing 2-year-olds, was selected so that the children's mean lengths of utterance (group MLU = 1.94, range 1.61–2.94) were similar to those of the D5 group, the deaf 5-year-olds (group MLU = 1.59, range 1.43–2.34). Groups H2 and D5 were also matched on the basis of the average length of their longest utterances (H2 = 3.8, and D = 3.17), similar scores for the Peabody Picture Vocabulary Test (H2 = 21.8, D5 = 26.6), and similar scores on a sentence comprehension test (H2 = 32.9, D5 = 36.1). On the other hand, the hearing infants (HO), the hearing 1-year-olds (H1), and the deaf 2-year-olds (D2) were all prelingual and could not yet be scored on any of the foregoing tests.

In the design of this study, therefore, it was possible to equate the child groups for those variables that have most often been argued to influence the nature of maternal speech adjustment – child linguistic ability (in terms of both spontaneoous speech and receptive language measures), chronological age, and general attentional abilities. Thus, if child age uniquely influences maternal speech, no differences would be predicted between the 2-year-old groups or between the two 5-year-old groups, but differences would be expected between the 2- and 5-year-old groups. Similarly, child linguistic ability, for which groups D5 and H2 on the one hand, and D2, H1, and H0 on the other hand, were equated, would not be expected to reveal differences between matched groups if this were the primary source of speech and adjustments. If, however, the receptive-attentional disability associated with child deafness influences maternal speech, differences between hearing and deaf groups should emerge irrespective of matching for other child variables.

The measures of maternal speech used in this investigation encompassed several levels of analysis and a broad range of specific measures within each level. The major levels of analysis included utterance and sentence complexity, the propositional content of utterances, selected utterance and sentence types, maternal repetitions and expansions, sentence acceptability, and speech fluency. Brief definitions are provided in Table 8.3, and the full code has been defined in a report of a smaller scale study of several of the groups by Cross et al. (1980), where the recording and coding procedures are also outlined.

The data were based on 200 sequential, intelligible maternal utterances recorded in spontaneous conversations between mothers and their children in their homes and were thus comparable with the data of the previous compari-

TABLE 8.3

Brief Definitions of Mothers' Language Measures

Mean Length of Utterance was calculated according to Brown's (1973) procedure for 200 maternal utterances.

Mean Length of Longest Utterances calculated the mean length of the longest 10% of maternal utterances.

Standard Measure of Propositional Complexity calculated the proportion of sentence nodes underlying 200 maternal utterances.

Sentence Propositional Complexity used the standard procedure above, except that it was based only on complete major or elliptical sentences.

Rich Propositional Complexity was similar to the standard measure above, except that attributive adjectives were treated as propositional.

Propositional Content of Utterances

Proposition-Present Utterances included all fully propositional creatively used (nonidiomatic) major and elliptical sentences.

Proposition-Opaque Utterances had no *direct* relationship between the utterance and the underlying proposition and contained either no verb or a verb which did not realize its literal meaning (e.g., *That's my girl!*).

Creative P-O Utterances included isolated complement phrases, prepositional phrases, and noun phrases used nonidiomatically.

Stereotyped Utterances included social stereotypes (e.g., *Thank you*), idioms (*There you go"*), Yes/No words, and single 'WW'/words.

Proposition-Free Utterances were utterances where no explicit proposition appeared to be intended, as in vocatives, interjections, etc.

Vocatives were instances where the child's name was used to gain attention.

Greetings were utterances like *Hi, Hello,* or *How d'y do?*

Interjections were utterances that expressed only feelings or attitudes, such as *Oh, Dear me,* or *Goodness.*

Action Routines were utterances like *Hop hop hop* as the mother made a top hop, or *Ring ring* as she dialed a toy phone.

Selected Sentence Types

Declaratives were defined syntactically as either regular declaratives or as subject deleted declaratives, e.g., *Put dolly on the chair* as the mother performed this action.

Labeling Forms were all sentences of the forms $\triangle$ be NP.

Deictic Statements were of the form Pronoun be NP.

Imperatives included standard subject-deleted imperatives, "Let's" imperatives, and subject-present imperatives, e.g., *You do it.*

Interrogatives were Wh- questions, Yes/No questions, tag questions, and utterances spoken with questioning intonation.

Acceptability and Fluency

Acceptability was a measure of the proportion of total utterances that were considered to conform to acceptable standards in adult discourse.

Disfluent Utterances were the number of utterances which contained within-utterance revisions, hesitations, repetitions, etc.

Degraded Utterances were the total of the proportion of utterances that were either unacceptable or disfluent or both.

TABLE 8.3 *(continued)*

Discourse Interactional Features

Repetitions included all occasions on which a mother repeated her preceding utterance, and included Exact Repetitions, repetitions with new elements added (Plus Repetitions), partial repetitions (Part Repetitions) and repetitions where some transformation of the repeated utterance occurred (Transformed Repetitions).

Paraphrases were utterances that altered the contentives of the previous utterance but conveyed the same meaning.

Self-Answers were utterances which were immediate responses to the mother's own preceding question.

Expansions included all occasions on which the mother expanded the child's foregoing utterance and included Regular Expansions, partial or Incomplete Expansions, expansions with new elements added (Plus Expansions), and expansions which transformed the child's utterance (Transformed Expansions).

Imitations were all utterances that imitated exactly (Exact Imitations) or partly (Part Imitations) the child's foregoing utterance.

---

sons. Table 8.4 presents the results of the planned analysis of variance comparisons across eight pairings of groups designed specifically to test the significance of the difference between the groups matched for child language ability, hearing status, or age. A number of interesting overall patterns emerged from these comparisons, as can be seen in the right-hand columns in Table 8.4. The differences between the mothers addressing the hearing groups (H0, H1, H2, H5) were most marked between the points in development representing child addressees who were prelingual (the 1-year-olds) and those who had commenced to use and comprehend spoken language (the 2-year-olds). In this comparison (H1–H2), 21 (i.e., half) of the 42 features showed significant differences beyond the .05 level (two-tailed test). This strong influence of linguistic feedback from the child is highlighted by the fact that 12 significant differences were found between mothers addressing the hearing 2- and 5-year olds (H2–H5) and only 5 between the two prelingual hearing groups, the infants and 1-year-olds (HO–H1). This pattern is paralleled, though in weaker fashion, in the deaf child groups where there were 12 differences between the hearing mothers of the prelingual and language-using deaf children (D2–D5). The weaker pattern supports a conclusion drawn by Cross et al. (1980), based on their smaller scale comparison, that hearing mothers of deaf children adjust their language less closely to their children's linguistic abilities than do hearing mothers of hearing children.

A pattern that attests further to the importance of the child's language abilities is evident when one compares the number of differences between deaf and hearing children equated for age with those of children equated for lan-

TABLE 8.4

Means and Planned Comparisons of Measures of Maternal Language
to Hearing and Hearing Impaired Child Groups

Child Groups	Means of Groups						Planned Comparisons							
							Age-Matched		Language-Matched		Hearing Groups			Deaf Groups
	HO	H1	H2	H5	D2	D5	H2-D2	H5-D5	H1-D2	H2-D5	H0-H1	H1-H2	H2-H5	D2-D5
1. MATERNAL COMPLEXITY (Scores)														
M.L.U.	3.96	4.13	5.01	5.66	3.69	4.22	***	**					*	*
M.M.L.U.	10.04	9.74	11.20	13.16	8.50	9.80	***	**					*	*
Standard Complexity	.93	1.01	1.15	1.15	.99	.98	**	***		*		*		
Rich Complexity	.83	.80	.98	1.10	.78	.80	**						*	
Sentence Complexity	1.23	1.21	1.28	1.39	1.14	1.14	**			*				
2. PROPOSITIONAL CONTENT (percentages)														
(i) Proposition-Present Utterances	66.7	60.4	71.7	72.1	64.9	65.6						**		
Major Sentences	60.9	60.3	70.1	71.2	60.9	65.3	*					*		
Elliptical Sentences	3.1	0.8	1.3	2.2	1.6	1.0		*		*				
(ii) Proposition-Present Utterances	24.2	28.2	27.9	26.9	28.8	38.0								
Proposition-Opaque Creative	3.0	8.8	12.4	7.9	9.9	16.5		**			***			*
Proposition-Opaque Stereotyped	21.1	19.5	15.6	19.0	18.8	21.5								
(iii) Proposition-Free Utterances	10.7	10.8	1.1	1.3	7.2	2.5	**	*				***		**
Vocatives	4.2	2.8	.3	.1	5.1	1.6	**	*				*		*
Greetings	3.6	5.2	.1	0	1.3	.2						**		*
Interjections	1.0	.6	.5	1.1	.6	.4			*				*	
Action Routines	1.9	2.3	.3	0	.1	.3								

3. SENTENCE TYPES (percentages)

Declaratives	18.0	15.6	21.8	26.8	16.1	18.7						**	**
Deictic Statements	1.6	4.0	5.3	4.2	7.4	4.8					*	*	
Labels (△ be NP forms)	1.7	5.2	8.9	5.1	6.4	11.3			**				
Imperatives	10.2	15.4	9.4	5.9	17.7	9.3	*						
Interrogatives	29.0	18.3	27.7	24.7	17.9	28.9	*		*				*
"Wh- Questions"	12.7	9.4	17.3	13.6	8.6	17.5	**			**		*	**
Yes/No Questions	16.3	8.9	10.4	11.1	9.4	11.4			*	*		*	**

4. MATERNAL ACCEPTABILITY AND FLUENCY (percentages)

(i)

Total Degraded Speech	1.0	1.6	4.2	5.8	3.7	4.2	*		*		*	
Disfluent Utterances	.7	1.0	3.9	4.1	1.4	2.4					*	
Run-On Utterances	.3	.6	.3	1.7	2.3	1.8						*

(ii)

Unacceptable Sentences	2.1	2.1	2.1	2.1	1.7	.8	*

5. DISCOURSE INTERACTIONAL FEATURES (percentages)

(i)

Repetitions	22.5	21.3	8.8	3.3	21.3	13.4	**	***			**	*
Total Repetitions	13.2	12.5	1.6	.5	9.6	4.3	**	**			***	*
Exact Repetitions	2.5	2.4	1.8	.9	3.4	2.2		*				*
Plus Repetitions	3.6	3.5	1.1	.8	4.6	2.9	**	*			**	*
Part Repetitions	2.3	2.4	3.6	.7	2.7	3.6		*				*
Transformed Repetitions	.9	.4	.9	.4	1.0	.4				*		
Paraphrase								*				
Self-Answers	1.5	1.0	.9	.8	2.1	2.2						
Self-Corrections	.1	0	0	.6	.1	.1				*		

(ii)

Expansions								*			*
Total Expansions	0	0	10.8	2.1	.8	4.5	**				**	***
Expansions	0	0	4.4	.6	.3	1.6	*				**	*
Incomplete Expansions	0	0	4.4	.8	.3	2.3	*				*	

265

TABLE 8.4 (continued)

		Means of Groups					Age-Matched		Language-Matched		Hearing Groups			Deaf Groups
Child Groups	H0	H1	H2	H5	D2	D5	H2-D2	H5-D5	H1-D2	H2-D5	H0-H1	H1-H2	H2-H5	D2-D5
Plus Expansions	0	0	.8	.3	.1	.4	*						**	
Transformed Expansions	0	0	1.3	.4	.1	.3								
(iii) Imitations														
Total Imitations	0	.3	4.6	2.1	.2	3.5	**					**		*
Full Imitations	0	.3	3.9	1.6	.2	2.8	**					*		*
Part Imitations	0	0	.8	.6	0	.8	*					*		

* *p* < .05 (two-tailed test).
** *p* < .01.
***p < .001.

DEAF CHILD GROUPS (n=8)

D2 = 2-year-olds.
D5 = 5-year-olds.

HEARING CHILD GROUPS (n=8)

H0 = Infants 3-6 months.
H1 = 1-year-olds.
H2 = 2-year-olds.
H5 = 5-year-olds.

guage. For the age-matched younger groups (H2–D2), 21 differences reached significance, in contrast to only 1 when prelinguistic status was equated (H1–D2). This pattern persists, though less strongly, for the older groups in which there were 16 differences when age was equated (H5–D5) and only 7 in the language-equated comparison (H2–D5). The specific patterns of results for those comparisons are summarized in the five sections that follow.

Maternal Utterance Complexity

For the complexity of maternal speech, three clear patterns of results are evident. First, most measures of complexity to the hearing children increased consistently with the children's ages. Second, when hearing and deaf children were matched for age, as in the H2–D2 and H5–D5 comparisons, four out of the five measures showed highly significant differences in maternal complexity for both comparisons in favor of more complex speech to both hearing groups. But when the groups were matched for linguistic ability (H2–D5 and H1–D2), the differences were much less striking, although two favoring the hearing children in the H2–D5 comparison remained. Third, whereas maternal speech complexity increased in tune with the hearing children's general increase in development, this was only slight for the deaf groups. Indeed, along some complexity dimensions, maternal speech to both prelingual and verbal deaf children approximated the complexity levels directed to the youngest hearing children, the prelingual infants (HO). This is one of a number of features where child deafness seems to have an additional effect on maternal speech beyond that attributable directly to the child's linguistic ability (Cross et al., 1980).

Propositional Content of Maternal Speech

In terms of the propositional content of maternal speech, Table 8.4 shows that, when the dyads were matched for child age at 2 years, the deaf children received significantly fewer major sentences and more proposition-free utterances, especially vocatives. By 5 years, the numbers of differences in the propositional content were similar: Hearing 5-year-olds received more elliptical sentences, more creative but propositionally opaque utterances, and again more vocatives.

When maternal speech for the groups matched for linguistic ability was compared, the differences decreased to the point where the language-using match (H2–D5) produced no significant maternal differences, and the prelingual match (H1–D2) produced a difference only in a higher incidence of greetings to the hearing toddlers. Thus, again there is a pattern of decreasing difference in maternal speech style when the children's linguistic ability is similar. However, particularly in the higher incidence of vocatives for both deaf groups, we have a further indication of a special effect of child deafness on maternal adjustments beyond that attributable directly to the children's respective levels of language development. Data suggesting that these differences are related to differences in the children's behavior in the conversational context is discussed later.

Selected Sentence Types

In the age-equated comparisons for the 2-year-old groups, with regard to the types of sentence forms, the mothers of the deaf children used significantly more imperative forms. They also used significantly fewer questions, particularly wh– questions. At the 5-year-old level, the D5 mothers used significantly fewer declaratives but more labeling forms (Δ be NP).

In striking contrast, no significant differences were found for the mothers when their deaf and hearing children were equated for linguistic ability at either the prelingual or the language-using stages of development. To emphasize further the central role of the children's level of linguistic ability in influencing maternal conversation style, one can point to the four differences that occurred between the two deaf groups: The D5 mothers used significantly more labeling forms, interrogatives, and wh– questions, but fewer imperatives.

Sentence Acceptability and Speech Fluency

When child age was held constant for both age groups on the measures of acceptability and fluency, the only significant difference was found for disfluent utterances, where the D2 mothers produced fewer than the H2 mothers. However, when maternal groups were matched for the linguistic ability of their children, two significant differences emerged: The D5 mothers produced fewer unacceptable sentences and run-on utterances than did the H2 mothers. However, inspection of this section of Table 8.4 again suggests a specific effect of child deafness on maternal conversations. In general, the pattern for the hearing groups indicates decreases in maternal disfluency and degradation as the children advance in age and linguistic ability. This pattern, though, is interrupted by the inclusion of the deaf child groups, whose mothers provide less degraded, more fluent speech to their children. This is most clearly noticeable for the greater acceptability and fluency of the language-using D5 group. In addition, this category provided the only case in which the language-matched comparisons produced as many differences as the age-matched comparison. It is of interest to note that in previous analyses (Cross, 1975, 1977), these features of disfluency and degradation in maternal speech have been shown to be more highly correlated with the age of hearing children than with any of the five measures of child linguistic ability.

Discourse-Interactional Features

The pattern for the discourse-interactional features again supported the linguistic hypothesis of the determination of maternal speech. Maternal self-repetitions were significantly different — three for the 2-year-old and six for the 5-year-old comparisons. In both comparisons, the deaf children's mothers used higher rates of self-repetitions. Notice also that seven of the eight measures of expansion and initiation showed significant differences in the 2-year-old comparison, with the D2 mothers using fewer expansions and imitations. However, when the groups were matched for language ability, the numbers of differences decreased substantially to a point where there were no significant differences between any of the prelingual groups in the incidence of maternal repetition or expansions. For the language-using child groups, only two significant differences emerged in self-repetitions: The D5 mothers used more partial self-repetitions and self-answers. One significant difference, in the frequency of expansions, was apparent for the expansion-imitation measures (H2 > D5).

The pattern of differences within the language match for the more mature children should again be understood as a specific effect of child deafness on parent speech. Where child deafness and lack of language coincide, as in the prelingual deaf 2-year-old group, only a slight difference is apparent between their mothers' repetitions and expansions and those of the mothers of either hearing prelingual group. However, once deaf children are older and capable of language use and comprehension, their mothers still use large numbers of repetitive utterances at a significantly greater rate than do the mothers of their hearing peers, but they fail to use expansions as frequently. This again suggests an overriding adjustment to the specific nature of the children's attentional-receptive disability — their severe hearing impairment.

Referential characteristics of maternal utterances have also been shown to reflect child deafness, especially for the younger deaf children. In their smaller scale analysis, Cross et al. (1980) showed that mothers addressing the deaf 2-year-olds used fewer references to the children's own activities or focus of attention than did mothers addressing any of the hearing groups, including the infants. Instead, as for the delayed children, the mothers of the deaf groups were found to refer significantly more frequently to their own activities. This difference was particularly striking for the mothers of the youngest deaf children and supports the authors' argument that severe communicative impairment in the child depresses the dialogic nature of mother-child conversations. Because this tendency was so marked with the younger deaf children — even in comparison with the mothers of the prelingual hearing infants — it is argued later that it reflects maternal *beliefs* about the conversational competence of deaf children rather than direct feedback from the child's actual participation in the conversation.

In sum, the results of these comparisons provide some answers to our questions about the determinants of variation in maternal speech style. First, there is a recurrent pattern in many features indicating that child-directed talk is influenced strongly by the linguistic capacities of the child. Moreover, differences occur far more often when the ages of the children are equated than when their receptive and productive language abilities are equated. In fact, differences between the language-matched groups are nearly nonexistent for the earliest stages examined and only infrequent for the older comparison, despite the severity of the deaf children's hearing disability and large differences in the ages, maturity, and cognitive abilities of the language matched hearing and deaf child groups. However, when differences do occur between these deaf and hearing groups, most are explicable in terms of specific maternal adjustments to the deaf children's attentional-receptive disadvantages in comparison with their hearing peers.

The Deaf Children's Contribution

The children's data, from the same transcripts, provide some clues to the factors within the conversational interaction that may have produced these results. In the first instance, the results provide evidence that the linguistic matching of the deaf and hearing groups reflected certain aspects of the children's conversational ability. Kirkman and Cross (1981) show that the children's participation in the conversation, as measured by their failure to respond verbally to maternal questions, was similar for deaf and hearing children at the same language levels. Table 8.5 shows little difference in either nonresponses or nonverbal responses to maternal questions between language-matched groups (H1-D2 and H2-D5 comparisons). The H5 group, by contrast, showed predictably smaller frequencies on these measures than did the other groups. On the other hand, Table 8.5 also shows that the deaf 5-year-olds produced far fewer conversational acts in total and in type than

TABLE 8.5
Means for Hearing and Hearing-Impaired Children's Measures

Child Measures	H1	H2	H5	D2	D5
Nonresponses (to maternal questions)	53.7	25.0	17.1	52.2	25.9
Nonverbal responses (to maternal questions)	27.6	18.2	9.9	20.4	19.8
No conversational acts (to mother's 200 acts)	0	140	156	0	82
Types of conversational acts	0	17	22	0	13

either of the other language-using groups, which accords with observers' impressions of less active participation by the deaf children.

Nienhuys, Horsborough, and Cross (in prep.), again using the same transcripts, have found further that the language-using, hearing children (H2 and H5) used many more conversational initiatives, verbal or nonverbal (32.3% and 35.8%, respectively), than the D2 and D5 children (8.0% and 20.2%, respectively). The hearing groups were also found to respond more adequately to their mothers' conversational initiatives. These patterns in child dialogue were generally reflected by the mothers' rates of conversational initiatives (roughly interrogatives, requests, and imperatives) and by their response rates to the children's verbal and nonverbal communicative acts.

These data provide support for the hypothesis that a number of features of mothers' speech to deaf children may reflect not only their children's receptive deficits but also their reduced and less active participation overall in the conversations. The following functional analysis of maternal speech was undertaken to elucidate this hypothesis.

FUNCTIONAL COMPARISONS OF MATERNAL SPEECH TO DEAF AND HEARING CHILDREN

In a recent investigation of functional parameters of maternal speech to normal hearing children, Kirkman (1980) has shown a large number of differences in specific speech acts and in the range of conversational acts produced by mothers with children at three different ages. In this study, the most marked differences occurred once again between mothers of prelingual 1-year-olds and mothers of language-using 2-year-olds, suggesting that the acquisition of language in the second group also had a marked effect at this level of analysis.

A similar analysis was undertaken, therefore, to discover whether mothers of deaf children use a similar conversational style when compared with mothers of hearing children, again equated either for age for stage of language development. In order to make comparisons between the adjustments found in the structural and discourse aspects of maternal speech reported earlier, the present study was conducted using the conversational data from five of the groups described previously. (The hearing infants, H0, were excluded).

This analysis used a version of the functional coding scheme devised by Dore (1979), a summary of which is presented in Table 8.6. This scheme was modified by the addition of five types of particular conversational acts at the finest level of analysis and by the omission of one. We also recorded each occasion on which a maternal act was contingent upon an action by the child

TABLE 8.6
Code Definitions (Adapted from Dore, 1979)

Requestives: solicit information or action.
　Choice Questions seek either/or judgments relative to propositions.
　Product Questions seek information relative to most wh- interrogative pronouns.
　Process Questions seek extended descriptions or explanations.
　Action Requests seek the performance of an action by the hearer.
　Permission Requests seek permission to perform an action.
　Suggestions recommend the performance of an action by hearer or speaker or both.

Assertives: report facts, state rules, convey attitudes, etc.
　Identifications label objects, events, people, etc.
　Descriptions predicate events, properties, locations, etc. of objects or people.
　Internal Reports express emotions, sensations, intents, and other mental events.
　Evaluations express personal judgments or attitudes.
　Evaluations of Partner express personal judgments of the conversational partner.
　Attributions report beliefs about another's internal state.
　Rules state procedures, definitions, 'social rules,' etc.
　Explanations state reasons, causes, justifications, and predictions.

Performatives: accomplish acts and establish facts by being said.
　Enactives speak for imaginary characters, things, or animals in fantasy play or sound effects.
　Routines consist of songs, rhymes, peekaboo games, and action routines.
　Claims establish rights for the speaker.
　Jokes cause humorous effects by stating incongruous information, usually patently false.
　Teases annoy, taunt, or playfully provoke a hearer.
　Protests express objections to a hearer's behavior.
　Warnings alert hearer of impending harm.

Responsives: supply solicited information or acknowledge remarks.
　Choice Answers provide solicited judgments of propositions.
　Product Answers provide wh- information.
　Process Answers provide solicited explanations etc.
　Compliances express acceptance, denial, or acknowledgment of requests.
　Self-Answers provide information etc. in response to a question asked by the same speaker.
　Clarification Responses provide solicited confirmations or clarifications.
　Qualifications provide unsolicited information to requestive.
　Agreements agree or disagree with a prior nonrequestive act.
　Acknowledgments recognize prior nonrequestives.

Regulatives: control personal contact and conversational flow.
　Attention-Getters solicit attention.
　Speaker Selections label the speaker of the next turn.
　Rhetorical Questions seek acknowledgment to continue.
　Clarification Questions seek clarification of a prior remark.
　Partner's Turns occur when one partner in the conversation takes the turn of the other.
　Boundary Markers indicate openings, closings, and shifts in the conversation.
　Politeness Markers indicate ostensible politeness.

TABLE 8.6 *(continued)*

Expressives: nonpropositionally convey attitudes.
   Exclamations express surprise, delight, or other attitudes.
   Accompaniments maintain contact by supplying information redundant with respect
   to some contextual feature.

Miscellaneous Codes
   Uncodable utterances are incomplete utterances and those whose role in the conver-
   sation is unclear.
   Unintelligible utterances.

and subdivided this category into child behavior which seemed deliberately communicative or was merely read by the mother as informative of the child's intention or state.

In all respects the design and procedure of this study were the same as those in the previous investigation of the same groups, with the important exception that statistical analyses were redesigned to provide more demanding tests of the comparisons based on the age and linguistic ability of the child addressee. An additional comparison was included to test a hypothesis, derived from previous analyses (Cross et al., 1980; Morris 1978), that the adjustments of mothers of deaf children over given ages and stages of development were not as marked as mothers of hearing children over the same ages and stages. These alterations resulted in three planned comparisons of the groups based on the following combinations.

The first two comparisons tested the alternative hypotheses of the relative influences of child age and child language ability on maternal conversations:

1. *H1 + H2 vs. D2 + D5:* This comparison was based on matched *language* and yielded statistically significant differences where the language of the child was a factor secondary to age in influencing maternal speech functions.
2. *H2 + H5 vs. D2 + D5;* This comparison was based on matched *ages* and yielded statistically significant differences where the age of the child was of minor importance but language levels mattered.

The third hypothesis was that the difference between H1 and H2 was *not* equivalent to that between D2 and D5. To test this hypothesis the appropriate contrast was:

3. *H2 + D2 vs. H1 + D5:* This third planned comparison was designed to test whether the difference between mothers conversing with deaf 2- and 5-year-olds is as great as the difference between mothers conversing

with hearing 1- and 2-year-olds (assuming that child *language* is the significant factor in maternal speech adjustments). The prediction derived from the previous study was that there would be less difference for the deaf groups.

The algebraic sequence necessary to justify this third planned comparison is as follows:

The change from H1 to H2 is H2 − H1, and the change from D2 to D5 is D5 − D2. The null hypothesis (of no difference) is then the equivalent of the differences between the changes being 0.
i.e., (H2 − H1) − (D5 − D2) = 0
which is   H2 − H1 − D5 + D2 = 0
or   H2 + D2 − H1 − D5 = 0
which is   H2 + D2 = H1 + D5
The appropriate contrast is, therefore: H2 + D2 vs. H1 + D5

Failure to achieve statistical significance (on the basis of a directional test with alpha set at .05) would have indicated comparable differences between the two deaf groups and between the two hearing groups.

As shown in Table 8.7, the general results for these contrasts were clear-cut. Comparisons using Dore's broad classes, when based on similar language abilities (1) revealed only one significant difference (perceivable phenomena), regardless of the differences in age or hearing status of the children. In contrast, comparisons based on similar ages (2) revealed significantly greater differences than those based on language for 6 of the 12 overall categories. Similarly, for the 33 subcategories tested, 26 showed greater differences for the comparisons based on age and 12 of these reached significance. There were significant differences in only 3 of the comparisons based on the children's linguistic levels, but groups matched for age revealed greater differences in each case.

It may be concluded, therefore, that for mothers' performance of conversational acts, the linguistic ability of the child is of greater importance than the child's age or general cognitive ability. In this respect, it is clear that the functional level of maternal speech corresponds with the structural and discourse levels in being primarily adjusted to the child's linguistic ability. A similar conclusion was warranted by results for the 4 new measures of mothers' conversation — as the last 4 rows of Table 8.7 document.

The final hypothesis — that there would not be an equivalent difference between mothers addressing deaf 2-year-olds and deaf 5-year-olds when compared with the appropriate hearing groups — was tested using language ability of the children as the criterion. To this end, the mothers were compared using the algebraically derived third comparison, H2 + D2 versus H1 + D5 on both levels of conversational acts and the additional measures. One significant difference was found in the 12 broad categories of conversational acts and 1 in the 33 subcategories tested. With these minor exceptions, it must be concluded that the hypothesis has not been supported; the difference between conversational acts of mothers of deaf 2- and 5-year-olds is as great as that between mothers of the linguistically matched hearing 1- and 2-year-olds. This confirms the previous conclusion that the major determinant is the linguistic development of the child and contrasts with the interpretations of previous analyses (e.g., Cross et al., 1980) of noncomparable sensitivity for mothers of deaf and hearing children.

Having drawn this conclusion, it is important to consider those features that were shown *not* to be fully accounted for by either the children's ages or their linguistic abilities. Of particular interest are those features on which the mothers of the deaf child groups were shown to differ significantly from their linguistically matched hearing peers. As with the delayed-language child groups, these maternal features are likely to reflect the special characteristics of communicatively impaired children as conversational partners. In the case of the present comparisons we were concerned with the more frequent use by the mothers of the younger deaf children of protests, attention-getters, and references to perceivable phenomena, and the reduced use of suggestions, acknowledgments, and responses to nonverbal child acts.

The use of fewer suggestions (RQSU) by the mothers of both deaf groups can be explained on the grounds of differences in the conversational quality of the mother-deaf child interactions. The outstanding feature of suggestions is that they convey a sense of equality between speaker and hearer because a request is made in such a way that it is acceptable to dispute it and implies that each participant is capable of influencing the conversation (Kirkman, 1980). The low rate of suggestions for the deaf child groups can be seen to indicate a more dominant role of the mother in these conversations. Kirkman suggests that it also reflects a tendency for mothers of deaf children to use their verbal interchanges more often to try to improve their children's language use than do mothers of hearing children. Mothers of deaf children, she argues, use conversations more frequently and more explicitly for this purpose. This conclusion is also drawn by Morris (1978) in an analysis of the syntactic aspects of the same mothers' speech.

The younger deaf children also received significantly fewer acknowledgments (RSAK) than their hearing peers. Kirkman argues that two factors probably contribute jointly to this reduced score. According to Kirkman, the fact that the deaf children themselves contributed fewer initiatives (even when nonverbal communicative acts were scored) may have a minor influence in reducing maternal acknowledgments; the children provided their mothers with fewer opportunities to acknowledge their contributions. She argues more confidently, however, that mothers of hearing children are more likely to treat noncommunicative acts as communicative; that is, they construe information from the child's behavior as if it were communicative and respond accordingly. The low acknowledgment score for deaf 2-year-olds,

TABLE 8.7

Mean Scores and Results of Comparisons for Types of Conversational Acts in Mothers' Speech

Mothers' Speech Measures		Mean Scores						Planned Comparisons for Hypotheses		
								(1) H1 + H2 vs D2 + D5	(2) H2 + H5 vs D2 + D5	(3) H1 + D5 vs H2 + D2
		H1	H2	H5	D2	D5	overall			
Requestive										
1. Solicit Information		41.3	59.0	58.0	41.5	59.3	*			
Choice Questions	RQCH	25.6	25.8	31.5	25.1	21.5				
Product Questions	RQPR	15.4	32.3	24.8	15.1	36.0	***			
Process Questions	RQPC	0.3	1.0	1.8	0.9	1.8				
2. Solicit Action		29.4	17.6	11.9	23.6	13.3	***			
Action Requests	RQAC	26.3	12.1	5.5	22.3	9.8	***		*	
Permission Requests	RQPM	0	0	0	0.1	0.3				
Suggestions	RQSU	3.1	5.5	6.4	1.3	3.3	**	*	**	
Assertive										
3. Perceivable Phenomena		26.3	21.8	32.4	47.4	26.0	***	**		**
Identifications	ASID	13.8	8.0	11.6	25.3	10.6	*			
Descriptions	ASDC	12.5	13.8	20.8	22.1	15.4				
4. Internal Phenomena		14.4	6.4	9.6	5.9	8.9	*			**
Internal Reports	ASIR	0.4	0.6	1.6	0.9	1.5				
Evaluations	ASEV	4.0	2.6	6.4	1.5	4.5	*			*
Evaluation of Partner	ASEP	8.5	2.6	1.4	2.5	2.6				
Attributions	ASAT	1.5	0.5	0.3	1.0	0.3				
5. Social Phenomena		4.1	5.3	10.0	2.3	4.8	**		**	
Rules	ASRU	1.8	1.5	1.9	1.1	1.4				
Explanations	ASEX	2.4	3.8	8.1	1.1	3.4	**		**	

		1	2	3	4	5			
Performative									
6. Initial		18.6	0.8	0	8.6	7.0		***	***
Enactives	PFEN	9.3	0.6	0	6.8	5.0		***	**
Routines	PFSR	9.3	0.1	0	1.9	1.8		***	**
Claims	PFCL	0.1	0	0	0	0		**	
Jokes	PFJO	0	0	0	0	0.1			
Teases	PETE	0	0	0	0	0.1			
7. Reactive		1.8	1.3	0.4	3.3	2.0		*	
Protests	PFPR	1.4	1.3	0.3	3.1	1.9	*	*	**
Warnings	PFWA	0.4	0	0.1	0.1	0.1	*	*	**
Responsive									
8. Supply Solicited Information		3.1	6.4	11.0	5.3	6.0		***	**
Choice Answers	RSCH	0	1.3	2.4	0	0.3		**	**
Product Answers	RSPR	0	1.6	3.8	0.3	1.1		***	*
Process Answers	RSPC	0	0	0.1	0	0			
Compliances	RSCO	0.4	0.9	2.3	0.3	0.3		*	**
(RSCH + RSPR + RSPC + RSCO)		0.4	3.8	8.5	0.5	1.6		***	**
Self Answers	RSAS	2.8	2.6	2.5	4.8	4.4			
9. Supply Additional Information		13.1	39.1	36.1	6.0	28.6		***	***
Clarification Responses	RSCL	0	0.4	1.6	0	2.1			
Qualifications	RSQL	0	0.8	1.6	0.1	0.4		**	*
Agreements	RSAG	4.0	15.0	21.3	3.4	12.6		***	**
Acknowledgements	RSAK	9.1	23.0	14.9	2.5	13.5	*	***	***
Regulative									
10. Solicit Other		25.4	32.0	9.0	38.9	33.3		***	***
Attention-getters	ODAG	17.3	7.6	4.9	31.8	9.5	*	***	***
Speaker Selections	ODSS	0	0.4	0	0	0.1			
Rhetorical Questions	ODRQ	0	0	0.3	0	0.1		***	
Clarification Questions	ODCQ	0.6	4.4	1.8	0.9	4.0		***	***
Partner's Turns	ODPR	7.5	19.6	2.1	6.3	19.5			

TABLE 8.7 (continued)

Mothers' Speech Measures		Mean Scores						Planned Comparisons for Hypotheses		
								(1) H1 + H2 vs D2 + D5	(2) H2 + H5 vs D2 + D5	(3) H1 + D5 vs H2 + D2
		H1	H2	H5	D2	D5	overall			
11. Mark Content		3.3	1.1	3.1	3.4	3.4				
Boundary Markers	ODBM	1.1	0.5	3.0	2.1	2.8				
Politeness Markers	ODPM	2.1	0.5	0.1	1.3	0.6				
12. Express Attitudes		17.9	7.6	8.6	11.5	4.4	**			
Exclamations	EXCL	11.5	3.5	3.3	7.5	2.3	**			
Accompaniments	EXAC	6.0	4.1	5.4	3.9	2.1				
Uncodable		1.3	1.4	3.5	1.9	2.6				
Unintelligible		0.5	0.5	4.6	0.6	0.6	*			
Other Measures										
13. Response to Non Verb. Acts	RNV	57.3	7.4	2.9	39.5	21.5	***		***	*
Communicative	RNVC	31.6	4.1	1.4	20.8	15.1	***		***	
Informative	RNVU	25.7	3.3	1.5	18.8	6.4	***		***	
14. Diversity		21.1	23.6	23.5	21.1	22.8				

Significance Levels: *p < .05 (two-tailed test) **p < .01 ***p < .001

together with the relatively low score for maternal responses to nonverbal informative acts (RNVU), are indications that there may be something inherent in expectations about a child's deafness that leads parents to doubt either the child's capacity for intentional behavior or the likelihood that the child will communicate particular intentions, or both.

The greater incidence of protests and attention-getters in maternal speech to the younger deaf group may also reflect mothers' beliefs about their deaf children's communicative limitations and conversational potential. Such a claim could incorporate the finding of a heightened use of vocatives to this group in the previous comparison. Each of these speech acts can be seen as attempts by the mother to keep the child engaged in the conversational task. However, Kirkman (1980) argues for the possibility that the mother (particularly if she is unfamiliar with the effects of deafness, as would be probable for the mothers of the younger deaf children) will find her own communicative competence challenged by a partner in whom the normal avenues for communication appear to be barred. The frequent use of attention-getting and similar devices, as well as reference to maternal rather than child behavior, may indicate such a lack of confidence: The mother may be seeking reassurance from the child that her communicative abilities are adequate for the situation that confronts her, and this tends to override the need to provide language for the child's focus of attention.

The closer match between the mothers of the deaf 5-year-olds and mothers of their hearing peers possibly reflects the development of maternal confidence as the mother becomes familiar both with the effects of deafness and the evidence of the child's language development. Nonetheless, in the previous study of formal and discourse features, the fact that more differences occurred between the language-matched deaf and hearing comparison than in the equivalent prelingual comparison provides a strong indication that at later ages child deafness can still override overt linguistic ability in influencing certain aspects of maternal speech.

However, although Table 8.7 shows clearly that the *distribution* of maternal speech functions (at both the broad and more differentiated levels of analysis) is strongly determined by the children's language ability, the *range* of functions used by the mothers (using a measure of functional diversity) was found by Kirkman and Cross (1981) to be much less related to child language. They found at all stages of development (for both hearing and hearing impaired groups) that the mothers tended to use much the same types of speech acts, although the proportions were altered according to the children's communicative abilities. This stability in the diversity of adult speech acts, despite variation in child maturity, is consistent with the results of other analyses (e.g., Dale, 1980; Juchnowski & Cross, in press), which show only weak correlations between maternal differentiation of functions and increases in children's linguistic maturity.

In all, however, the primary pattern of adjustment to child language ability is apparent in each of the preceding analyses. The secondary pattern of occasional specific adjustment to communicative impairment in children has also been found in each study. This was evident in the analysis involving language delay, which showed some differences in adjustment of the same mothers according to whether they were addressing their normal or language-delayed children, despite equivalence of the children's linguistic levels. It was also evident in several aspects of the results for the deaf and hearing comparisons and in the finding that some adjustments to deaf 2- and 5-year-olds were less marked, in terms of either age or language changes, than for the equivalent hearing child groups.

That there may be a unique influence of child deafness, which overrides the child's actual language abilities, was clearly suggested by the differences in specific maternal features between mothers addressing the language-using deaf and hearing child groups. This result gives rise to the possibility that different types of receptive disorders in children (i.e., disorders that are known to have different etiologies) may have specialized effects on their parents' conversational styles. Inspection of the features that distinguished mothers addressing language-delayed and normal children at the same stages of development from mothers addressing matched deaf and hearing children at a similar stage indicated to us that it would be profitable to investigate this possibility directly.

COMPARISON OF NORMAL, DYSPHASIC, AND AUTISTIC CHILD GROUPS

The hypothesis that specific communicative disorders in children have unique, distinguishable effects on maternal speech was tested in a final comparison of mothers — in this case, mothers conversing with normal, developmentally dysphasic, and autistic children, once again equated for stage of language development. Details of this comparison are reported in Horsborough, Cross and Ball (in press). Essentially, the clinical children (the developmental dysphasics and childhood autistics) were differentially diagnosed according to strict clinical and research criteria and were considered to be derived from discrete clinical populations. They were selected, as far as possible, to represent diagnostically distinct cases of each syndrome. All the autistic children had been diagnosed by clinical psychologists as Class I autistics using a taxonomic system devised by Prior, Boulton, Gajzago, and Perry (1975). All dysphasic children were diagnosed by both a clinical psychologist and a speech therapist as suffering from specific developmental receptive dysphasia. This screening process yielded eight autistic and eight receptively dysphasic children matched in pairs on several linguistic measures. Eight normal children were then selected to match, individually, each autistic-dysphasic child pair on the same measures of language development. Table 8.8 contains the relevant subject data.

The mothers' speech, collected as in the previous studies, was then compared across all three child groups using many of the same features. These results are presented in Tables 8.9 and 8.10.

It is again evident that the child's *linguistic level* exercises the primary constraint on maternal speech style, despite extreme differences in the clinical groups' communicative disabilities and social skills. Of the 73 variables compared, only 29 were found to differentiate the child groups significantly. Over half of these features significantly distinguished both clinical groups from the matched normal group, but only 4 features were significantly different when the mothers addressing the autistic and dysphasic groups were compared. These few differences underscore the secondary role of the specific disabilities of the children in influencing maternal speech adjustments.

This result was surprising because in a previous comparison of the discourse and functional abilities of the *children themselves,* using many of the measures used for the mothers' speech, we found marked differences between the dysphasic and autistic children's use of language in the same observational context (Ball, Cross, & Horsborough, 1981). At this pragmatic level of analysis, the dysphasic children showed only 9 differences from their normal language peers out of 39 measures, whereas the autistic pattern was consistently deviant (25 measures were significantly different from the normal sample). In particular, the functional analysis revealed that the autistic children rarely used speech for informative or regulatory functions, but uttered instead a much higher proportion of labeling forms, repetitions, nonsensical utterances, and inappropriate responses than their normal or dysphasic counterparts.

Since we had matched the children precisely on several measures of their formal language abilities, we must conclude that the similarity of their mothers' speech—even in comparable functional and discourse measures—

TABLE 8.8
Mean Ages and Language Measures for Normal,
Autistic, and Dysphasic Children

| | | Means | |
Child Measures	Normal	Autistic	Dysphasic
Age	3-6	9-11	5-8
Peabody Vocabulary Mental Age	3-10	4-3	4-2
Mean Length of Utterance	3.24	3.36	3.16
Mean Longest Utterances	8.09	8.32	8.07
Reynell Comprehension	4.23	3.98	3.88
Reynell Expression	3.41	3.86	3.76
Leiter Performance Scale	-	71,50	88.63

TABLE 8.9
Means and Comparisons of Mothers Language to Normal,
Autistic, and Dysphasic Children

	Means			Planned Comparisons		
Mothers' Speech Measures	Normal	Autistic	Dysphasic	Normal vs. Autistic	Normal vs. Dysphasic	Autistic vs. Dysphasic
1. LENGTH AND COMPLEXITY						
MLU	5.31	5.49	5.52			
Standard Complexity	1.01	1.02	1.05			
Sentence Complexity	1.29	1.21	1.23			
Rich Complexity	1.15	1.11	1.10			
Single Word Utterances	15.00	10.00	7.50	*	**	
2. PROPOSITIONAL CONTENT						
(i) Sentence Types						
Yes/No Questions	10.25	11.13	10.63			
Wh- Questions	14.50	36.00	35.25	***	***	
Declarative + Tag	4.87	3.38	4.25			
Declaratives	30.50	20.75	19.75			
Deictic Statements	1.75	2.75	2.13			
Imperatives	7.38	5.75	9.88			
Elliptical Utterances	3.75	6.63	5.88			
(ii) Sentence Fragments						
Wh- Phrases	1.50	3.38	3.38			
Wh- Words	.50	1.38	.78			
Idiomatic Constructions	1.88	.75	0		*	
Attentionals	2.38	1.50	3.38			
Declarative Labels (△ be NP)	6.75	6.75	6.25			
Question Labels (△ be NP?)	.88	1.50	.38			*
Prepositional Phrases	2.00	2.25	.63			*
Yes/No Words	10.13	6.25	5.63	*		
(iii) Proposition-Free Utterances						
Vocatives	.63	1.38	.25			
Greetings	.25	.13	.25			
Interjections	1.13	.13	.38			
Action Routines	.25	0	0			
3. DISCOURSE INTERACTIONAL FEATURES						
(i) Repetitions						
Exact Repetitions	.88	2.50	1.75	*		
Plus Repetitions	1.00	1.38	2.13			
Part Repetitions	.38	1.38	1.38		**	
Transformed	.63	5.13	3.13	*	*	

TABLE 8.9 *(continued)*

Mothers' Speech Measures	Means			Planned Comparisons		
	Normal	Autistic	Dysphasic	Normal vs. Autistic	Normal vs. Dysphasic	Autistic vs. Dysphasic
Repetitions						
Total Repetitions	2.88	10.38	8.38	*	**	
Paraphrase	.63	2.88	1.75	**		
Self-Answers	.50	1.50	.25			
(ii) Expansions						
Expansions	1.13	1.38	1.63			
Incomplete Expansions	.63	1.25	1.25			
Plus Expansions	.13	.38	.13			
Transformed Expansions	.75	.75	1.63			
Total Expansions	2.63	3.75	4.63			
(iii) Imitations						
Imitations	.75	2.38	4.50	*	**	
Part Imitations	1.50	3.63	5.63	*	**	

*$p < .05$ (two-tailed test).
**$p < .01$.
***$p < .001$.

indicates that the major influence on maternal speech style, is the formal linguistic ability of the children and not their general communicative competence as measured by their functional or conversational styles. Neither does it appear that behavioral characteristics distinguishing the child groups — characteristics which are used in differential diagnosis — are a potent source of influence. On the contrary, such results are highly consistent with previous findings for mothers of normal children which show that measures of children's abilities in comprehending the language addressed to them produce the strongest correlations with most aspects of maternal speech style (Cross, 1977).

Tables 8.9 and 8.10 also show that in both comparisons of maternal speech to the clinical children with maternal speech to their normal language matches, 15 significant differences were found in the normal-autistic comparison and 14 in the normal-dysphasic comparison. Twelve of these differences were for the same features; the remainder were specific to each comparison.

The differences that were specific to the normal-autistic comparison indicated that mothers of autistic children used reliably more wh– questions, yes/no words, exact self-repetitions, and paraphrases. In the functional analysis, they used more commentative functions expressing the location of ob-

TABLE 8.10

Means and Comparisons of Mothers Functional Language Measures to
Normal, Autistic and Dysphasic Children

| | | Means | | | Planned Comparisons | | |
Functional Code	Normal	Austistic	Dysphasic		Normal vs. Austistic	Normal vs. Dysphasic	Autistic vs. Dysphasic
A. PERFORMATIVE ASPECTS							
I. Informative Functions	10.37	5.75	8.75				
Statement of Knowledge	3.75	2.12	3.00				
Statement of Affect	2.50	1.75	1.75				
Statement of Intent	.62	.62	.37				
Report	2.12	1.00	3.00				
Hypothetical Statement	1.87	.25	.62		*	*	
II. Regulatory Functions	10.25	9.50	13.87				
Request	.25	.37	.12				
Command	4.25	5.12	7.62				
Rejection	.12	.25	1.37				
Attention-Directing	5.00	3.75	4.12				
Suggestions	.12	0	.62				
III. Interrogative Functions	27.50	50.12	46.62		***	**	
Information Question	20.00	14.75	22.50				
Clarification Question	.37	.50	2.25				
Quiz Question	7.12	34.87	21.87		***	**	*

IV. Commentative Functions	20.50	7.62	9.75	**
Self-Actions	1.12	.25	.37	
Labeling	2.37	1.62	2.25	*
Description of Object	8.00	3.37	3.00	*
Description of Event	1.87	1.12	1.50	
Description of Location	3.75	.37	1.62	**
Enactment	3.37	.87	1.00	
V. Other	5.12	3.25	2.75	
Exclamation	.50	.12	0	
Salute	.25	0	.50	
Repetition on Request	1.87	2.12	1.37	
Request for Repetition	.12	.12	.25	
Stock Utterances	2.37	.87	.62	*
B. DISCOURSE ASPECTS				
I. Responses	21.62	22.37	12.87	
Content Response	7.12	5.62	3.37	
Yes-No Answer	.87	1.25	.12	
Acknowledgment	11.25	12.87	7.00	
Contradiction	2.37	2.62	2.37	*

*p < .05 (two-tailed test).
**p < .01.
***p < .001

jects. On the other hand, the normal-dysphasic comparison showed that the mothers of the dysphasic children used more idiomatic constructions and more partial self-repetitions. The functional analysis revealed that they also used fewer stock utterances.

The mothers of both clinical groups were alike, however, in reliably deviating from the normal group by using fewer single words, much larger numbers of wh- questions (a result similar to the mothers of the language delayed), and more self-repetitions and imitations of their children's utterances (similar to the mothers of the deaf children). In the functional analysis, they were also alike in using fewer hypothetical statements, a great many more interrogative functions (especially quiz questions), and markedly fewer commentative functions (particularly descriptions of objects).

In the comparison of the mothers of the clinical children, the autistics' mothers used more labeling forms and more isolated prepositional phrases than did the mothers of the dysphasic children. Functionally, they used more quiz questions and fewer acknowledgments. These few differences provided only slight support for the hypothesis that mothers' speech would reflect the specific nature of their children's communicative impairment. In contrast, the more general hypothesis that maternal speech is primarily adjusted to child language ability has received convincing support. The large majority of features examined did not reliably differentiate children whose ages, cognitive abilities, and communicative styles differed radically but whose formal language abilities were similar. Nevertheless, roughly the same proportion of features as differentiated the mothers addressing deaf and language-delayed children from mothers addressing their normal language peers (approximately one third) also differentiated the mothers of both groups of hearing children with the clinical syndromes of developmental dysphasia and autism from those conversing with their normal linguistic peers.

CONCLUSIONS

It remains in conclusion to gather together the similarities and discrepancies across six investigations reported in this chapter. With regard to the impressive degree of common adjustment in maternal speech to children at similar stages of language development, two conclusions can be drawn. First, it can be claimed that the language ability of the child is a powerful determinant of variation in many aspects of maternal speech and conversation style. It is thus essential, in defining the effective input to the language development process, that we specify this potent cause of systematic variation in adult-child interaction and acknowledge that development in the child can produce substantial alterations in the nature of the input.

Second, and more precisely now, we can suggest that aspects of the formal linguistic ability of children (probably their ability to comprehend maternal speech) seem to be the most salient source of cues for appropriate maternal adjustment. There was a strong (but not unassailable) indication in the latter studies that functional differences in children's conversation, or even marked deviations in their conversational competencies, only occasionally overrode the mothers' ability to "tune in" to their children's formal linguistic levels. This appeared to be true in cases such as deaf, dysphasic, and autistic children in which the children's ages, cognitive, receptive, and social abilities were not synchronized normally with their language levels. The mothers of these children, for the most part, addressed them as if they were younger normal children of appropriate linguistic abilities. These results lend strong support to a number of previous studies that have shown correlations between measures of adult speech style and certain formal measures of the language development of the children they are addressing (e.g., Cross, 1977; Ellis & Wells, 1980; Moerk, 1977; Newport et al., 1977). Although there has been some contention in the literature about the extent and interpretation of such correlations (e.g., see Nelson et al., 1983; Wells, 1980), the present series of studies tip the balance in favor of maternal sensitivity to the child's linguistic ability. It thus seems that at least in middle-class Western communities, and in contexts in which young children are able to engage in relatively uninterrupted one-to-one conversations about matters of interest to the child, the primary input to the language learning process will generally keep pace with the output of that process.

Discussion of the discrepancies observed in maternal adjustments across the groups is impeded by the fact that not all the maternal speech features examined in each case were included in all comparisons, and a few were measured in incompatible ways. The drawing of direct comparisons is also restricted by the fact that across the groups not all children were at the same linguistic stages. (The last three groups — the normal, autistic, and dysphasic children — were more linguistically advanced than the preceding deaf, language-delayed, and normal groups.) Although these differences may cause us to underestimate the general influence of a communicative disorder on maternal speech, we can conclude there was only limited evidence that the precise pathognomic features of each communicative impairment were reflected in maternal conversational style. From our present patterns of results, it is unlikely that we could predict the nature of the child's disorder (with the possible exception of severely hearing impaired children) from the mothers' speech profile alone. However, this is a challenge we plan to pursue by comparing all maternal groups once we can equate all children precisely for linguistic level.

An initial comparison of the tables presented in this chapter, however, suggested a number of characteristics of maternal conversation styles that were persistently associated with the presence of a severe communicative impairment in the child. Selecting only the children who had begun to use language, we can provide a summary of the maternal speech features that consistently discriminated the mothers talking with the groups of communicatively impaired children: the language-delayed 4-year-olds, the deaf 5-year-olds, the dysphasic 6-year-olds, and the autistic 9-year-olds. An increased use of the discourse device of self-repetition (usually, though not always, exact self-repetition) was a statistically reliable characteristic of all their mothers. No other feature (or set of features) held across all impaired-child groups. The mothers of the language-delayed, autistic, and dysphasic children also resorted to significantly more frequent use of questions, particularly wh– and quiz questions, but the mothers of the deaf children used fewer of these questions. The mothers of the autistic and dysphasic groups, as we have seen, shared a number of discrepant features including imitating their children more often, using fewer single words and commentative functions, and making fewer hypothetical statements. The mothers of the language-delayed and deaf children used increased numbers of self-answers and attentionals, but fewer expansions and less degraded speech.

At this stage of our research, we cannot derive any further evidence of common adjustments to communicative impairment in children. However, we can draw attention to the fact that many of these special maternal adjustments were argued earlier in this paper to be evidence of maternal compensation for the child's current or anticipated inadequacy as a conversational partner. This has repercussions for our thinking about adjustments to developmentally normal children: It reinforces the conclusion that mothers adjust their conversation not only to the linguistic skill of their children, but also in accordance with their beliefs (which perhaps could also be directly assessed) about the child's current and potential communicative abilities. However, because the autistic and dysphasic children were uniformly superior in language ability to the language-delayed and deaf children, it is likely that we will find further common adjustments when we have equated all child-impaired groups for stage of language development. Our delay in taking this step has, of course, left us vulnerable to the implications of our own findings: Apparent discrepancies between results derived from different types of communicative disorders may be resolved once we have, ourselves, taken account of the primary role played by the child's language ability in influencing maternal speech.

ACKNOWLEDGMENTS

The research reported in this chapter was funded by grants from the Australian Research Grants Scheme to Toni Cross and Terry Nienhuys. The authors gratefully acknowledge the major contribution to data analyses made by the project's senior research assistant, Kim Horsborough.

REFERENCES

Brown, R. *A first language: The early stages.* Cambridge, Mass.: Harvard University Press, 1973.

Ball, J., Cross, T. G., & Horsborough, K. M. *A comparative study of the linguistic abilities of autistic, dysphasic and normal children.* Proceedings of the Second International Congress on the Study of Child Language, Vancouver, Canada, August 1981.

Cross, T. G. Some relationships between motherese and linguistic level in accelerated children. *Papers and Reports on Child Language Development* (No. 10). Stanford University, 1975.

Cross, T. G. Mothers' speech adjustments: The contribution of selected child listener variables. In C. E. Snow & C. A. Ferguson (Eds.), *Talking to children: Language input and acquisition.* Cambridge: Cambridge University Press, 1977.

Cross, T. G. Mother's speech and its association with rate of linguistic development in young children. In N. Waterson & C. E. Snow (Eds.), *The Development of Communication.* London: Wiley, 1978.

Cross, T. G. Mothers' speech adjustments and child language learning: Some methodological considerations. *Language Sciences,* 1979, *1,* 3–25.

Cross, T. G. The linguistic experience of slow language learners. In A. R. Nesdale, C. Pratt, R. Grieve, J. Field, D. Illingworth, & J. Hogben (Eds.), *Advances in child development: Theory and research.* Nedlands, Western Australia: NCCD, 1981. (a)

Cross, T. G. Parental speech as primary linguistic data: Some complexities in the study of the effect of the input in language acquisition. In P. S. Dale & D. Ingram (Eds.), *Child language —An international perspective.* Baltimore: University Park Press, 1981. (b)

Cross, T. G., Johnson-Morris, J. E., & Nienhuys, T. G. Linguistic feedback and maternal speech: Comparisons of mothers addressing hearing and hearing-impaired children. *First Language,* 1980, *1,* 163–189.

Cross, T. G., & Morris, J. E. Linguistic feedback and maternal speech: Comparisons of mothers addressing infants, one-year-olds and two-year-olds. *First Language,* 1980, *1,* 98–121.

Dale, P. Is early pragmatic development measurable? *Journal of Child Language,* 1980, *7,* 1–12.

Dore, J. Conversations and pre-school language development. In P. Fletcher & M. Garman (Eds.), *Language Acquisition.* Cambridge: C.U.P., 1979.

Ellis, R., & Wells, G. Enabling factors in adult-child language discourse. *First Language,* 1980, *1,* 1–16.

Ervin-Tripp, S. A psychologist's perspective. In C. E. Snow & C. A. Ferguson (Eds.), *Talking to children: Language input and acquisition.* Cambridge: Cambridge University Press, 1977.

Furrow, D., Nelson, K., & Benedict, H. Mothers' speech to children and syntactic development: Some simple relationships. *Journal of Child Language,* 1979, *6,* 423–442.

Horsborough, K. M., Cross, T. G., & Ball, J. *Conversational interaction between mothers and their autistic, dysphasic and normal children.* Proceedings of the Second National Child Development Conference, Melbourne, Australia, August 1982 (in press).

Juchnowski, M., & Cross, T. G. *Some characteristics of employed mothers.* Proceedings of the Second National Child Development Conference, Melbourne, Australia, August 1982 (in press).

Kirkman, M. *A conversational analysis of mothers' speech to their deaf and hearing children.* Unpublished honors thesis, Department of Psychology, University of Melbourne, 1980.

Kirkman, M., & Cross, T. G. *Functional diversity as a developmental phenomenon in child and parent conversation.* Proceedings of the Second International Congress on the Study of Child Language, Vancouver, Canada, August 1981.

Moerk, E. L. *Pragmatic and semantic aspects of early language development.* Baltimore: University Park Press, 1977.

Morris, J. E. *An investigation of the nature and determinants of mothers' speech adjustments.* Unpublished honors thesis, University of Melbourne, 1978.

Nienhuys, T. G., Horsborough, K., & Cross, T. G. *A dialogic analysis of interaction between mothers and their deaf or hearing pre-schoolers.* Manuscript in preparation.

Nelson, K. E. Facilitating children's syntax. *Developmental Psychology,* 1977, *13,* 101–197.

Nelson, K. E. Toward a rare-event cognitive comparison theory of syntax acquisition. In P. Dale & D. Ingram (Eds.), *Child language — An international perspective.* Baltimore: University Park Press, 1981.

Nelson, K. E., Carskaddon, G., & Bonvillian, J. Syntax acquisition: Impact of experimental variation in adult verbal interaction with children. *Child Development,* 1973, *44,* 497–504.

Nelson, K. E., Denninger, M., Bonvillian, J., Kaplan, B., & Baker, N. Maternal input adjustments and nonadjustments as related to children's linguistic awareness and to language acquisition theories. In A. D. Pellegrini & T. D. Yawkey (Eds.), *The development of oral and written languages: Readings in developmental and applied linguistics.* Norwood, N.J.: Ablex, 1983.

Nelson, K. Individual differences in language development: Implications for development and language. *Developmental Psychology,* 1981, *17,* 170–187.

Newport, E. L., Gleitman, L., & Gleitman, H. Mother I'd rather do it myself: Some effects and non-effects of maternal speech style. In C. E. Snow & C. A. Ferguson (Eds.), *Talking to children: Language input and acquisition.* Cambridge: Cambridge University Press, 1977.

Ochs, E. Variation and error: A sociolinguistic approach to language acquisition in Samoa. In D. Slobin (Ed.), *The cross cultural study of language acquisition.* Hillsdale, N.J.: Lawrence Erlbaum Associates, in press.

Prior, M., Boulton, D., Gajzago, C., & Perry, D. The classification of childhood psychoses by numerical taxonomy. *Journal of Child Psychology and Psychiatry,* 1975, *16,* 321–330.

Schieffelin, B. Getting it together: An ethnographic approach to the study of the development of communicative competence. In E. Ochs & B. Schieffelin (Eds.), *Developmental pragmatics.* New York: Academic Press, 1979.

Snow, C. E. The development of conversation between mothers and babies. *Journal of Child Language,* 1977, *4,* 1–22.

Wells, G. Apprenticeship in Meaning. In K. E. Nelson (Ed.), *Childrens Language, Volume 2,* Gardner Press Inc.: New York, 1980.

9 Early Linguistic Development of Children with Specific Language Impairment

Laurence B. Leonard
Richard G. Schwartz
Purdue University

Although most children acquire the language spoken around them with considerable ease, a significant minority acquires language slowly and with great effort. Children experiencing these language learning difficulties often exhibit other types of handicaps that may relate or contribute to their problems with language. However, there is one group of language deficient children for whom this is not so clearly the case. These children exhibit what has been termed *specific language impairment,* a condition seen in approximately 1 of every 1000 children.[1] Although children with specific language impairment (or "language impaired children") constitute a heterogeneous group, they share several key characteristics. These children show significant deficits in linguistic functioning in the face of adequate auditory acuity, age-appropriate performance on nonverbal tests of intelligence, and the absence of gross neurological disability.

Since the 1960s a great deal of research has focused on the syntactic, morphological, semantic relation, phonological, and pragmatic abilities of language impaired children (see reviews in Johnston, 1982; Leonard, 1979, 1982; Rice, 1978). However, surprisingly little work has been devoted to a

---

[1] A number of other terms have been used in the literature to refer to children with specific language impairment. These include: "delayed language," "infantile speech," "deviant language," "language disorder," and "congenital," "developmental," or "childhood aphasia." With the exception of "language disorder," each term carries a connotation of the nature of the language impairment. The first two terms imply that the linguistic system of the children is like that of younger normal children. The third implies that the linguistic system of language impaired children is different from that of normal children of any age. Finally, terms that include the word "aphasia" imply that the language impairment may have a pre- or perinatal neurological basis.

study of the lexical abilities of these children. In fact, only a few case studies have appeared that document what has been in clinical practice a hallmark of language impairment — the late emergence of first words (e.g., Bender, 1940; Nice, 1925; Werner, 1945). In this chapter, we provide a progress report of an investigation of the lexical acquisition of language impaired children in the early stages of learning how to speak. The investigation has been selective, focusing only on certain aspects of lexical acquisition. However, given how little we knew about the nature of lexical acquisition in language impaired children, it served as an important first step toward an understanding of this process.

SOME CHARACTERISTICS OF EARLY LEXICAL ACQUISITION

The major purpose of the investigation was to determine whether certain characteristics seen in normally developing children's acquisition of words are exhibited as well in the early lexical development of children with specific language impairment. A brief review of these characteristics follows.

Selection Constraints

A number of child phonologists (Ferguson & Farwell, 1975; Ingram, 1974; Kiparsky & Menn, 1977) have observed that young children tend to be select-ive in terms of the adult words they attempt. This selectivity in production seems to be independent of comprehension. They appear to select words with certain phonological characteristics and fail to select others, following a vari-ety of individual patterns. This selection seems to be based largely upon ini-tial consonants (Shibamoto & Olmsted, 1978). It has been presumed that this selectivity initially simplifies the task of phonological acquisition by permitting the child to concentrate on only a few lexical types. Additionally, it has been suggested that these patterns are reflective of children's early lexi-cal and phonological representation and organizations (Schwartz & Leon-ard, 1982).

Because the foregoing investigations only involved observation of the child, they did not rule out differences in *input* as the basis for the origin and continuation of these patterns. More recently, though, two investigations have demonstrated that even with balance in input, patterns of selectivity continue to be manifested. In an investigation by Schwartz and Leonard (1982), children with productive lexicons of 5 or fewer words acquired more nonsense words that were phonologically consistent with their existing lexi-cons than words that were inconsistent. Leonard, Schwartz, Morris, and

Chapman (1981) yielded similar results for unfamiliar words with children who were slightly more advanced, having vocabularies of 30 to 50 words.

To date, only one investigation has indicated the existence of phonological selection in older children with specific language impairment (Schwartz, Leonard, Folger, & Wilcox, 1980). However, as with the earlier investigations of young normal children, this finding was based only upon informal observation of the children. Further investigation of this factor in the lexical acquisition of language impaired children is of interest for two reasons. First, such an examination will reveal whether this variable plays a significant role in the determination of lexical production for these children, as it does for normally developing children. Second, study of the role of phonological selection in these older children may shed some light on the role of perceptual experience in phonological selectivity.

Lexical Types

One of the most consistent observations concerning normal children's early lexical acquisition is the relative frequency of different lexical types. In particular, Nelson (1973) noted that within the first 50 words produced by children, words for objects represented the largest category. For some children, as much as 50% of their lexicons at this point in development took the form of object words, whereas words for actions represented approximately 15%. More recently, Benedict (1979) reported similar percentages in production, but a somewhat smaller gap in the percentages of object and action words comprehended. These findings were all based upon parental report and some systematic observation. Thus, although they indicate a bias toward object words, they do not provide any information concerning the basis of this bias. Additionally, these findings fail to reveal whether this bias is simply quantitative or whether children more readily and rapidly acquire object words.

In a more direct assessment of 2-year-old children's comprehension of nouns and verbs, Goldin-Meadow, Seligman, and Gelman (1976) found that children appeared to be at one of two points in development: receptive or productive. In the receptive phase, the children understood many more nouns than they produced, and produced no verbs but understood many. The children in the productive phase produced almost as many nouns as they comprehended. They also produced a number of verbs, though not as many as they understood. This investigation indicated that at least some nouns are produced earlier than verbs, but it left a number of other questions unanswered. The subjects' experience with the stimuli may have varied significantly, leaving the role of such experience an open question. Additionally, the apparent bias toward object words may still have simply reflected relative frequency in the environment rather than inherent differences in the relative ease and rapidity with which children acquire different word types. Finally, the distribution of stimuli may have influenced the results. Only 30 verbs were tested, whereas 70 nouns were tested.

More recently, experimental paradigms involving the use of unfamiliar referents and either contrived or unfamiliar words have been employed in examining the children's acquisition of object and action words (Leonard et al., 1981; Schwartz & Leonard, 1980). Even with their relative frequency in input controlled, object words were acquired earlier, more rapidly, and in greater numbers than action words. This was found to be true for children at the outset of lexical acquisition (Schwartz & Leonard, 1980) as well as for children who had acquired between 30 and 50 words (Leonard et al., 1981). The object bias was consistent both in production and in comprehension but in the latter case was smaller in magnitude, a pattern consistent with Benedict's (1979) findings.

A number of potential explanations for this gap between object and action words have been proposed. It may simply be the case, as Benedict (1979) suggested, that children view objects as things to be named and actions as things to be done. Additionally, there may be some inherent difference in the relative representational complexity of objects, which tend to be perceptually more constant and typically present, and actions, which are more transitory. Gentner (1978) has argued that actions are inherently more complex than objects in that they are relational, whereas objects are not. Alternative explanations have also included proposals concerning asymmetries in input (Gentner, 1982; Tanouye, 1979) and the syntactic role of verbs (Bloom, 1981). Specifically it has been suggested that differences in the sentential positions of nouns and verbs in adults' speech to children influence early lexical acquisition. An examination of this possibility in observational, cross-linguistic data indicated no sentence position effects were noted (Gentner, 1982). Furthermore, experimental investigations involving control of input frequency and sentential position also reveal an object bias in the lexicons of young normally developing children (Leonard et at. 1981; Schwartz & Leonard, 1980). Consequently, the most viable explanations seem to be the hypotheses of some difference in the underlying basis or complexity of object and action words.

This object bias becomes a particularly interesting factor in an examination of the lexical acquisition of children with specific language impairment. Given the apparent developmental change in this gap reported by Goldin-Meadow et al. (1976), it is possible that because language impaired children are older than normally developing children at a comparable point in language development, the object-action gap may be different in magnitude. In any case, results on this question may indicate the role of chronological age and consequently general experiential factors in the lexical bias toward object words.

Relationship Between Comprehension and Production

There are two issues in the relationship between comprehension and production in early lexical acquisition. The first concerns the developmental sequence of comprehension and production for any given unit of language. The second concerns the specific characteristics of comprehension abilities as compared with those of production abilities.

It has long been a commonplace in the child language literature that comprehension precedes and is necessary for the production of any unit of language. In a broad logical sense this must be the case. It is difficult to imagine any meaningful or communicative use of language without some degree of understanding of the language structures involved. However, what has been ignored is the fact that the demonstration of comprehension and the demonstration of production abilities involve very different task requirements, perhaps strategies (Chapman, 1978), and possibly early in development, largely separate linguistic systems. This initial separation of productive and receptive systems has been posited for phonological behavior (Schwartz & Leonard, 1982; Straight, 1980) as well as for the early use of word order (Chapman & Miller, 1975).

In the area of lexical acquisition, there have been a number of reported instances of production without prior evidence of comprehension (Leonard, Newhoff, & Fey, 1980; Nelson & Bonvillian, 1978; Rice, 1980). Leonard et al. observed three types of word usage without prior evidence of comprehension: play, acknowledgment, and what they termed "phonological triggering." In play, the children appeared to use the word itself as an object of play without any apparent relationship to the object. Acknowledgment, also noted by Keenan (1974), involved confirming the relationship between a word and its referent. Finally, in phonological triggering, the production of an unfamiliar word without any relation to its referent seemed to lead to the production of a phonologically similar but more familiar word. Not all of the children studied produced words in this way.

Nelson and Bonvillian (1978) reported similar individual differences in the demonstration of production and comprehension abilities, both across children and within children across words. In an investigation of concept acquisition, they found seven children who demonstrated a comprehension bias. These children comprehended a large proportion of concepts that they gave no evidence of producing. In addition, there were sixteen children who appeared to have a production bias, only producing a number of concept words but producing and comprehending the remainder. Finally, there were two children who seemed to have equal comprehension and production. Within children there also seemed to be significant variation in that some concept words were produced in the presence of the appropriate referent without ever being identified in response to the phrase "Find me a _____." Other concept words were comprehended yet not produced, and others were produced and comprehended simultaneously.

Similarly, children without prior nonlinguistic knowledge of color categories learned correct production of these terms in reference to object attributes, but in some cases did not demonstrate comprehension of these terms (Rice, 1980). In this investigation, comprehension and production may have involved different conceptual requirements. For the production task the children had to recognize that a color term was associated with a given referent and recall that word. However, the comprehension task seemed to require that the child be more generally aware of the categorical boundaries of color terms. Thus, in general, the assumption of comprehension performance as a prerequisite to production seems unwarranted for normally developing children.

The second issue regarding comprehension and production concerns differences in these two domains. As mentioned earlier, Benedict (1979) observed differences in the magnitude of the object-action gap in production and in comprehension. Additionally, Thomson and Chapman (1977) found different patterns of word overextension in production and comprehension for some of the children they studied. Such findings suggest that these two domains of language performance have different organizations and may in some respect be initially quite separate.

As specified in the later section on subject description, children with specific language impairment seem to be significantly more impaired in their production abilities than in their comprehension abilities. The fact that the comprehension abilities of these children are somewhat more consistent than production abilities with their chronological age may lead to some differences between language impaired and normal children in the comprehension-production gaps observed. The lack of or presence of such differences in extended observation will shed light on the relationship between lexical comprehension and production in language impaired children, and perhaps more generally on the nature of these two domains.

Imitation

One aspect of normal children's speech that has received considerable attention is characterized by the immediate, unsolicited repetition or part of all of an adult's utterance. The tendency to engage in imitation varies from child to child, ranging from the absence of imitation (Bloom, 1973) to a proportion of over half of the child's utterances (Ryan, 1973). Although imitation does not appear to be a process necessary for the acquisition of language, investigators have sought to explain its occurrence in the speech of the children who do exhibit this behavior.

Investigations focusing on young children's unsolicited imitations of adult utterances have identified at least two major functions that such imitations may serve. One is to facilitate the child's acquisition of new linguistic material, such as lexical items and syntactic forms (e.g., Bloom, Hood, & Lightbown, 1974; Moerk, 1977). The second, more recently proposed, function is to increase the child's ability to serve as a co-conversationalist by providing him or her with a means for turn-taking (e.g., Keenan, 1974; Mayer & Valian, 1977).

The greatest amount of research has dealt with whether imitation facilitates children's acquisition of new linguistic material, with the most compelling evidence pertaining to lexical acquisition. Bloom et al. (1974) and Ramer (1976) observed that young children were more likely to imitate lexical items not yet established in their expressive vocabularies. These investigations noted that as imitation of a particular lexical item decreased across time, the spontaneous use of the lexical item increased. These findings have been interpreted as evidence that imitation could serve as a vehicle through which new words are introduced into the lexicon. Similar conclusions were drawn by Rodgon and Kurdek (1977) in a correlational study in which a positive relationship was observed between young children's tendency to imitate words and the size of their expressive lexicons.

The hypothesis explored in the studies just noted is that imitated words are acquired more readily as a result of the imitation process. Bloom et al. (1974) and Ramer (1976) may have provided the only test of this hypothesis that can be performed, as there is no way of determining how easily imitated words would have been acquired if they had not been imitated. However, a related and equally important testable hypothesis is that, for imitating children, words that are imitated are acquired more readily than those that are not. An investigation by Leonard, Schwartz, Folger, Newhoff, and Wilcox (1979) indicated that imitated words appeared no earlier in spontaneous speech than words to which the children received equal exposure but did not imitate. In the present study, we adopted the methodology of Leonard et al., but modified it in order to increase its sensitivity in detecting lexical advancement attributable to imitation. Leonard et al. (1979) exposed each of a set of contrived words for five sessions and employed spontaneous production as their only gauge of lexical acquisition. In the present study, each word was exposed over a greater number of sessions, a formal assessment of production was made upon completion of these sessions, and a comprehension measure was added.

The Need for Controlled Input and Observation

All of the main issues that have been discussed fed into the present investigation of language impaired children's lexical acquisition. Language impaired and younger normal children were compared with respect to: (1) the tendency to acquire words according to their initial consonant composition; (2) the tendency to acquire a greater number of object names than action names; (3)

the tendency for word comprehension to outpace production; and (4) the contribution of unsolicited imitation to lexical acquisition.

The initial identification of these characteristics of early lexical acquisition has been, for the most part, based upon careful observation of normally developing children, the examination of diary data, and parental report. Unfortunately, such methodologies have inherent limitations for the explication of lexical development. Observations of young children is invariably subject to sampling limitations. Obviously, in any one situation, children may demonstrate far less than they know. Even with periodic observation, if such observation is limited to spontaneous behavior, a good deal of the child's knowledge concerning various words and referents may go untapped. Most problematic, though, is the fact that with periodic observation it is difficult to accurately chronicle a child's experience with a given word and its referents prior to the first observation and between observations.

Longitudinal diary data ameliorate some, but not all, of these problems. Sampling limitations may be less of a problem. However, the use of informal observation or observation of only spontaneous behavior may yield an incomplete picture of the child's knowledge. In addition, certain types of words (e.g., object words) typically have a close correspondence between surface form and use and may be accurately reported and categorized. For other types of words, however, this is not always the case. For example, *thank you,* which superficially is a personal-social word (Nelson, 1973), can be used by the child as an action word. Parental report of any type is potentially subject to this kind of error.

Of the earlier investigations cited, only one has involved a more formal methodology (Goldin-Meadow et al., 1976), in which children's abilities to produce and comprehend a preselected set of nouns and verbs were assessed. However, this methodology also has some limitations. First, the stimuli were biased in the direction of greater noun usage and comprehension because far more nouns than verbs were tested. Second, given individual variations in normal children's early lexicons (Nelson, 1973), it is possible that a set of preselected stimuli will not be totally appropriate for a particular child. Finally, this approach engenders the same limitation that observational paradigms entail in that it does not allow control over the child's experience with the word or referent. In order to examine the characteritics of lexical acquisition identified, a paradigm was needed that would allow control over input and exposure and permit easier determination of production and comprehension abilities.

One such paradigm involves the use of unfamiliar referents and either unfamiliar or contrived words. Experimental stimuli such as these have been successfully employed in examining children's abilities to infer word meaning within sentence contexts (Werner & Kaplan, 1952) as well as their abilities to apply morphophonological rules to new words (Berko, 1958). More recently,

Nelson and Bonvillian (1973, 1978) and Nelson and Nelson (1978) demon-strated the ability of yonger normal children to acquire unfamiliar words for unfamiliar object referents as well as contrived words for such referents. The paradigm has also been employed by Schwartz and Leonard (1980, 1982) in demonstrating that phonological selection and differential acquisition of ob-ject and action words occur when input and exposure are controlled. Thus, it affords an opportunity to similarly examine these factors in the lexical acqui-sition of children with specific language impairment. Because the children are exposed to these referents only in the presence of the investigators, it also permits closer examination of relationships among imitation, comprehen-sion, and production. Finally, it may serve to reduce the experimental advan-tage that the language impaired children hold over the language-matched but younger normal children, because neither would have had prior exposure to the experimental words or referents.

METHOD OF THE PRESENT STUDY

Subjects

Of the 44 children participating in the experimental activities discussed in this chapter, 22 had been diagnosed as language impaired. The remaining children performed within normal limits in linguistic functioning. The speech of the children in both groups was limited to single-word utterances, with ex-pressive vocabularies ranging from 25 to 75 words ($\bar{x}$ for language im-paired = 44.10, s.d. = 13.81; $\bar{x}$ for normal = 39.93, s.d. = 13.45) ac-cording to an examination of their speech supplemented by a parental interview.

The language impaired children ranged in age from 2;8 to 3;4. There were 16 males and 6 females. Each language impaired child showed a performance IQ of at least 85 on the Leiter International Performance Scale (Arthur, 1952). Each scored from 6 months to 1 year below performance mental age level on the Test for Auditory Comprehension of Language (Carrow, 1973) or, for the children under 3;0, the Auditory Comprehension subtest of the Preschool Language Scale (Zimmerman, Steiner, & Evatt, 1969). For all but one child, comprehension deficits were not marked; these children's compre-hension performance was 6 to 9 months below mental age level. All of the children exhibited production deficits that were more severe than those seen for comprehension. The degree of each child's single-word utterance usage (100%) represented a level exceeding 1 year below performance mental age level according to the normative data for single-word usage provided by De-velopmental Sentence Types (Lee, 1974). In addition, each child performed at least 1 year below mental age level on the Verbal Ability subtest of the Preschool Language Scale. For 20 children, expressive language performance was 12 to 16 months below mental age level. The remaining language impaired children performed 18 and 29 months below mental age level. The difference between comprehension and production performance did not exceed 10 months for 21 of the 22 children. For the remaining child, however, a difference of 21 months was observed.

Each child passed both a hearing screening and an examination of oral structure and function adapted from Yoss and Darley (1974). None of the children had a history of recurring otitis media, although individual episodes had been reported for several. No child exhibited any apparent disturbances in the capacity to relate appropriately to persons and objects. During the period of the study, none of the children had been under medication for the prevention of seizures. However, one child had been under such medication prior to this period. No child had experienced a seizure within a year prior to the commencement of the study.

The criteria used to select the language impaired children for this project were adapted from those used by Tallal and Stark (1980). The characteristics of the children meeting these criteria are consistent with the traditional definition of expressive language impairment. According to Benton (1978), for example, an expressively language impaired child's "understanding of oral speech may be mildly or moderately subnormal but the expressive speech disorder, which is his primary problem, is always more severe [p. 43]." Importantly, these criteria insured at least some degree of homogeneity in the subject group studied.

The 22 normally developing children (10 males, 12 females) ranged in age from 1;5 to 2;0. The particular tests administered to the language impaired children could not be used with these children due to their young ages. However, each of these children scored within 6 months of age level on both the Language and Cognitive subtests of the Lexington Developmental Scale (1974) and had achieved each of the major milestones for motor and social development on schedule according to parental report. As can be noted from the foregoing, the level of these children's linguistic development, as measured by utterance length and expressive vocabulary size, matched that of the language impaired children. The majority of the children in both groups came from middle-income homes. However, the education level of the parents of the normally developing children was somewhat higher. Although females represented only slightly more than half of the normally developing group, there was a larger number of females in this group than in the group of language impaired children. Males typically represent a larger percentage of the language impaired population than do females (with ratios varying from 2:1 to 5:1 across different studies, see Ingram, 1975). Thus, although not matched according to sex, the children selected were quite representative of the normally developing and language impaired populations in terms of sex distribution.

Speech Sample and Mother-Child Interaction

The initial session with each child was devoted to obtaining a representative sample of the child's speech as well as his or her level of play. For most of the children it was also possible to obtain a sample of interaction between the child and his or her mother during this session.

During each sample, one investigator interacted with the child, a second operated a video-camera, and a third transcribed the child's utterances and made notes about relevant context. Separate audio-recordings were also made for each session to insure a more sensitive record of the child's speech. In cases where the referent of a child's word was unclear, the video-recording of the session was reviewed. The audio-recording of the session was reviewed when the investigator was unsure of the transcription. Much of the speech of the mother and investigator interacting with the child was transcribed from the audio- and/or video-recordings, as their output could not be adequately captured in the live situation. The adults' speech was transcribed orthographically. The children's speech was transcribed using the IPA transcription system, supplemented by diacritics suggested by Bush, Edwards, Luckau, Stoel, Macken, and Peterson (1973).

The child's utterances during the entire session constituted the speech sample. The samples ranged from 108 to 311 intelligible, interpretable, nonimitative utterances. In order to insure that the sample was representative, the child's mother was asked to provide a list of words used by the child. These words were probed (e.g., by asking the child to name an object) toward the end of the session if they had not been noted during the sample. In a few cases, words were reported for a child whose referents were unavailable or inappropriate to present in the session. These were simply noted, but not probed.

Experimental Words

Sixteen experimental words were selected for each child by the investigator who transcribed the speech samples. Based on the speech sample and parental report, the child showed no evidence of comprehending or producing any of the experimental words. Eight of the experimental words were object names (e.g., *latch, gourd*), and the remaining eight were action names (e.g., *crouch, whirl*). All of the words selected were relatively infrequent in their occurrence in general usage. The experimental words were individually selected for each child, based on the phonological characteristics of his or her speech. Four of the eight object names and four of the eight action names contained word-initial consonants or consonantal clusters deemed absent from the child's speech ("out-of-phonology" words). A consonant or cluster was considered absent from a child's speech if it: (1) was not produced by the child during the speech sample; (2) was not characteristic of the adult words attempted by the child during the speech sample; and (3) was not characteristic of the adult words reported to be in the child's lexicon but not observed during the speech sample. The remaining four experimental words of each type contained word-initial consonants or clusters that the child was observed to produce accurately in over 50% of his or her attempts at adult words containing these consonants ("in-phonology" words). All sixteen experimental words were monosyllabic. For the out-of-phonology words, the word-final consonants were either absent from the child's phonology or attempted but never produced accurately. For the in-phonology words, the word-final consonants had been attempted but produced with varying percentages of accuracy.

Pretesting

In order to insure that the children were unfamiliar with the experimental words, pretests were administered prior to the experimental sessions. Each child was presented with a 16-item test for the production of the 16 experimental words and a 16-item test of the child's comprehension of these words. The investigator administering these tests was not provided with information concerning which words had been classified as in-phonology and out-of-phonology for a particular child. The following procedure was used for the production test. For those test items involving experimental words referring to objects, the investigator held up the object and asked "What's this?" For those test items involving experimental words referring to actions, the investigator maneuvered a doll to perform the action and asked "What's the baby doing?" The following procedure was used for the comprehension test. For those test items involving object names, the eight referent objects were placed in front of the child and he or she was instructed "Give me the _____." After each object was picked up by the child, it was returned so that the child was always choosing from among eight objects. The child's comprehension of the action names was assessed by handing the child a doll and instructing him or her to "Make the baby _____." Audio-recordings were made of all pretests.

Experimental Procedure

Following pretesting, 14 normal and 14 language disordered children were assigned to the experimmental condition. The remaining children were assigned to the control condition. Each child in the experimental condition participated in 10 experimental sessions. Approximately three sessions were conducted per week. Each session lasted approximately 45 minutes. The investigator conducting these sessions was not the same investigator who administered the pretests. The sessions were designed to simulate informal play sessions. During the course of each session, the investigator produced each experimental word five times. For experimental words referring to objects, these exposures occupied sentence-final position in sentences (e.g., *Here's the badge*) that accompanied some act that the investigator directed toward the referent object (e.g., placing it in a toy truck). For experimental words referring to actions, the exposures occupied sentence-final position in sentences (e.g., *Watch the baby kneel*) accompanying the investigator's manipulation of a doll to perform the action. Every fifth exposure of each experimental word took the form of a comprehension probe, following the procedure used in the comprehension pretest. However, in this case if the child did not select the appropriate object within 5 seconds, the investigator picked it up and said "Here it is." The child was never asked to produce or imitate the experimental words. However, any spontaneous or imitative use of the experimental words on his or her part was noted. The children in the control condition participated in 10 sessions that were identical to those of the children in the experimental condition with the exception that the names of the experimental objects and actions were never provided by the investigator. The experimental and control sessions were audio-recorded. The investigator who conducted the experimental and control sessions had no knowledge of which words had been classified as in-phonology and which as out-of-phonology.

Posttesting

Following the 10 experimental or control sessions, each child was given posttests for production and comprehension that were identical to the pretests. Audio-recordings were made of each of the posttest administrations. The posttests were administered by the same investigator involved in pretesting. This investigator had no knowledge of the experimental word usage or comprehension shown by the child during the experimental sessions.

Scoring for Comprehension, Production, and Imitation of Experimental Words

A child was credited with the use of an experimental word on the production test if such usage contained at least a recognizable consonant and vowel to permit identification that the production was the name of the object or action being tested. The same criterion was applied in crediting the child with spontaneous use of an experimental word during the experimental sessions. However, in these cases, additional criteria were applied. First, the child's usage had to occur while he or she was pointing to, playing, and/or looking at the appropriate referent object or action. Second, the child's use of the word could not immediately follow an utterance produced by the investigator that contained the word, unless the child had also produced an intervening word not used in the investigator's utterance. If the child's use of an experimental word followed the investigator's use of the word with no intervening utterance on the child's part, the production was classified as an imitation.

A child was credited with comprehending an object name on the comprehension test or probe if he or she selected only the appropriate referent object. Credit for comprehending an action name was given if the child performed only the appropriate action with the doll. For the comprehension probes administered during the experimental sessions, the child was credited with comprehending an experimental word only if he or she made no incorrect selections on that item during subsequent probes. Refusals to respond were not counted as incorrect responses.

LEXICAL ACQUISITION: ANALYSES BASED ON THE CHILDREN'S EXPERIMENTAL TASK PERFORMANCE

In this section, the children's comprehension, production, and imitation of the experimental words are examined. Additional details of the comprehension and production data appear in Leonard et al. (1982).

The mean number of experimental words comprehended on the posttest by the children assigned to the experimental condition was 7.14. The corresponding mean for the children assigned to the control condition was .02. The mean number of experimental words produced on the posttest by the children in the experimental condition was 3.50. For the children assigned to the control condition, the corresponding mean was .01. These findings suggest that the posttest comprehension and production of the experimental words by the children in the experimental condition could not be attributed to factors such as maturation and/or extraexperimental exposure to the words. The remaining comparisons in this section pertain to the performance characteristics of these children.

Comprehension

The children's performance on the comprehension posttest was the focus of the first analysis. The data were analyzed by means of a mixed model analysis of variance with subject type (normal vs. language impaired) serving as a between-subjects variable and lexical type (object word vs. action word) and phonological composition (in-phonology word vs. out-of-phonology word) serving as within-subjects variables. A greater number of object words (mean = 4.89) was comprehended on the posttest than action words (mean = 2.25), $F(1, 26) = 55.57$, $p < .001$. No other main effects or interactions achieved statistical significance. A summary of the children's performance on the comprehension posttest appears in Table 9.1

TABLE 9.1
Mean Number of Experimental Words Comprehended on the Posttest

Subject Group	Object Words		Action Words	
	In-Phonology	Out-of-Phonology	In-Phonology	Out-of-Phonology
Normal	2.64	2.50	0.79	1.14
Language Impaired	2.43	2.21	1.64	0.93

Note. Adapted from Leonard et al. (1982).

A second analysis of the children's comprehension performance focused on the experimental words comprehended on the probes administered during the experimental sessions. A significant difference according to lexical type was again observed, $F(1, 26) = 66.01$, $p < .001$. The children comprehended a greater number of object words (meant = 5.75) than action words (mean = 2.43) on the comprehension probes. A three-way interaction was also noted, $F(1, 26) = 9.67$, $p < .01$. A least significant difference test revealed that both the normal and the language impaired children comprehended a greater number of in-phonology and out-of-phonology object words than in-phonology and out-of-phonology action words. In addition, the language impaired children comprehended a greater number of in-phonology action words than did the normal children. No other main effects or interactions were observed. Table 9.2 gives a summary of the children's comprehension on the probes administered during the experimental sessions.

Production

An analysis of the children's performance on the production posttest revealed several significant differences. As was seen in the analysis of the children's comprehension performance, a greater number of object words (mean = 2.79) was produced on the posttest than action words (mean = 0.72), $F(1, 26) = 34.14$, $p < .001$. However, unlike the case for comprehension, a significant difference was also seen according to the phonological composition of the experimental words, $F(1, 26) = 23.61$, $p < .001$. A greater number of in-phonology words (mean = 2.57) was produced on the posttest than out-of-phonology words (mean = .93). A subject type × lexical type interaction was also observed, $F(1, 26) = 5.84$, $p < .05$. For each group of children, a greater number of object words was produced on the posttest than action words. However, the language impaired children produced a greater number of action words than did the normal children. A lexical type × phonological composition of word interaction was also seen, $F(1, 26) = 38.24$, $p < .001$. A greater number of in-phonology object and action words was produced on the posttest than out-of-phonology object and action words. For both in-phonology and out-of-phonology words, a greater number of words referring to objects was produced on the

TABLE 9.2

Mean Number of Experimental Words Comprehended on the Probes
Administered During the Experimental Sessions

Subject Group	Object Words		Action Words	
	In-Phonology	Out-of-Phonology	In-Phonology	Out-of-Phonology
Normal	3.07	2.57	0.86	1.36
Language Impaired	2.86	3.00	1.57	1.07

Note.   Adapted from Leonard et al. (1982).

posttest than words referring to actions. This difference was greater for in-phonology words, $p < .001$, than out-of-phonology words, $p < .05$. No other main effect or interactions were observed. A summary of the children's performance on the production posttest is presented in Table 9.3.

Another analysis dealt with the number of experimental words produced spontaneously during the experimental sessions. A greater number of object words (mean = 4.00) was used spontaneously than action words (mean = 1.93), $F (1, 26) = 52.68$, $p < .001$. In addition, a greater number of in-phonology words (mean = 3.72) was produced than out-of-phonology words (mean = 2.21), $F (1, 26) = 27.63$, $p < .001$. A lexical type × phonological composition of word interaction was also observed, $F (1, 26) = 10.32$, $p < .001$. A greater number of in-phonology object words was produced spontaneously than out-of-phonology object words, and a greater number of in-phonology action words was produced than out-of-phonology action words. However, although the number of out-of-phonology object words exceeded the number of out-of-phonology action words produced, no difference was seen between the number of out-of-phonology object words and the number of in-phonology action words produced spontaneously. No other main effects or interactions were noted. Table 9.4 summarizes the number of experimental words used by the children during the experimental sessions.

Relationship Between Comprehension and Production

It did not seem safe to assume comparability of correct response probability on the comprehension and production tasks. Therefore, direct comparisons

TABLE 9.3

Mean Number of Experimental Words Produced on the Posttest

Subject Group	Object Words		Action Words	
	In-Phonology	Out-of-Phonology	In-Phonology	Out-of-Phonology
Normal	2.21	.93	.07	.14
Language Impaired	1.93	.50	.93	.29

Note.   Adapted from Leonard et al. (1982).

TABLE 9.4
Mean Number of Experimental Words Used Spontaneously
During the Experimental Sessions

Subject Group	Object Words		Action Words	
	In-Phonology	*Out-of-Phonology*	*In-Phonology*	*Out-of-Phonology*
Normal	2.79	1.71	1.29	.86
Language Impaired	2.29	1.21	1.07	.64

Note.   Adapted from Leonard et al. (1982).

of the children's performance on the two tasks were not made. However, it was possible to compare the normal and language impaired children in terms of the relationship between their comprehension and production of the experimental words. Specifically, the normal and language impaired children were compared in terms of the percentages of comprehended words that were produced. The two groups were quite similar on this measure, and no significant differences were observed. The mean percentage of comprehended words produced by the normal children was 33.00. The corresponding percentage was 27.86 for the language impaired children.

The normal and language impaired children were somewhat different in the distribution of action and object words in production versus comprehension. Only 7% of the experimental words produced on the posttest by the normal children were action words, whereas 20% of the experimental words comprehended on the posttest represented names of actions. For the language impaired children, action words represented approximately 30% of the experimental words produced as well as comprehended.

An interesting finding was that children in both groups produced experimental words, either during the experimental sessions or on the posttest, that they had not given evidence of comprehending during the comprehension probes or posttest. Seven normal children produced a total of 26 words of this type, whereas nine language impaired children produced a total of 14 such words.

Production Constraints

Although fewer out-of-phonology words were attempted than in-phonology words, it seemed important to examine how those attempted were actually produced by the children. As a first step, we compared the percentage of accurate word-initial consonant productions of the in-phonology and out-of-phonology words by the normal and language impaired children. The data for object and action words were collapsed. For these analyses, only those children who attempted both in-phonology and out-of-phonology words were included. Seven language impaired and nine normal children attempted both types of words on the posttest. During the experimental sessions, twelve language impaired and ten normal children attempted the two types of experimental words. The posttest analysis revealed greater word-initial consonant accuracy for in-phonology words (mean = 78.44% accuracy) than out-of-phonology words (mean = 3.12%), F (1, 14) = 130.98, $p < .001$.

Neither a difference between the normal and language impaired children nor an interaction was observed. The experimental session analysis dealt only with the children's first attempts at each in-phonology and out-of-phonology word. Again, a main effect favoring in-phonology words was seen, F (1, 20) = 93.25, $p < .001$. In-phonology and out-of-phonology words were produced with 72.05% and 8.50% accuracy, respectively. No other differences were observed. An inspection of the children's inaccurate attempts at the out-of-phonology words revealed use of the same simplification processes observed in the children's initial speech samples.

Imitation

Although all children in the study engaged in some unsolicited imitative behavior, the analyses of the effects of imitation on the acquisition of the experimental words were confined to those children who could be safely regarded as "imitators" (Bloom et al., 1974; Boskey & Nelson, 1980). We included only those children for whom at leat 12% of the lexical types produced during the initial sample were immediate imitations of prior adult utterances. All 14 normal and 13 language impaired children met this criterion. The first analysis was an attempt to determine if the number of exposures required prior to the child's spontaneous use of the experimental words varied as a function of whether or not the words were first imitated. Because relatively few action words were used by the children, object and action words were combined in the analysis. No main effects or interactions were observed. For both groups of children, words that had been imitated emerged no sooner in spontaneous speech than those that had not been first imitated.

It seemed possible that our measure of lexical acquisition, spontaneous production, was insensitive to changes that may have been occurring in the children's knowledge of the experimental words as a function of imitation. Given the available evidence that comprehension of new lexical items usually precedes spontaneous usage (e.g., Benedict, 1979), it seemed plausible that the contribution of imitation to the acquisition of words might be evidenced first in the children's comprehension rather than production of these words. In order to explore this possibility, an analysis like the one just described was performed, using the number of experimental word exposures prior to the children's comprehension of the words on the probes as the dependent measure. Again, however, no interaction or main effects were observed.

Finally, we attempted to determine whether facilitative effects of imitation might be noted on a production measure that was less susceptible to sampling error than spontaneous usage of the experimental words during the experimental sessions. Therefore, we examined the children's posttest productions of the experimental words in terms of those that had and had not been first imitated. For both groups, the percentage of first-imitated words produced on the posttest was no higher than the percentage for words that had not been first imitated. When the data were examined from a different perspective, it was found that of the words produced on the posttest, there was no difference in the number that had and had not been first imitated for either subject group. Somewhat different results emerged when imitations were considered without regard to whether or not they had preceded spontaneous usage. For both groups, imitated words were more likely to be produced on the posttest than nonimitated words, and a greater number of the words produced on the posttest had been imitated than had not, $ps < .05$, sign tests. A close inspection of the data revealed that production of a word on the posttest was more closely related to prior imitation coupled with prior spontaneous production (regardless of their order of occurrence) than with either prior imitation or spontaneous production alone.

DISCUSSION

It appears that the controlled input employed in this study allows us to draw a number of conclusions concerning the nature of the children's lexical acquisition. The normal and language impaired children in this study acquired the experimental words in a highly similar manner. Although the similar patterns of performance in the two groups came as no surprise, the finding that they acquired the same number of experimental words was quite unexpected. Previous investigations have suggested that language is not only slow to emerge in language impaired children, but that subsequent development of language progresses at a slower pace than is seen in normal children (e.g., Johnston & Schery, 1976; Morehead & Ingram, 1973). Thus, it was anticipated that the language impaired children in our study would acquire fewer experimental words than the normal children.

The reason for the performance similarities between the normal and language impaired children may be that, except for the late emergence of first words, lexical development may not have presented much difficulty for the language impaired children, at least when concentrated linguistic stimulation was provided as in the present study. Some support for this interpretation is provided by the relatively few studies that have focused on the acquisition of words in language impaired children. Whitehurst, Novak, and Zorn (1972), for example, found that during a 3-month period in which a language impaired child (age 3;4) received language stimulation in the form of object names and descriptions of daily activities, the child showed an increase in his lexicon from 5 to 110 words. This rate of lexical growth is quite high, exceeding that reported for normal children at the same level of linguistic development (see Nelson, 1973).

One important qualification must be added to the conclusion that lexical development through stimulation may not be particularly troublesome for language impaired children. The tasks used in the present study required the children to associate each experimental word with a single referent. No assessment was made of the children's ability to extend the experimental word, either in comprehension or production, to appropriate but novel referent exemplars. Whether or not language impaired and normal children show similar abilities in this regard is a question we are currently investigating.

Selection Constraints

One important outcome of our study was the finding that the language impaired children, like the normal children, were more likely to produce words containing sounds already in their repertoires than words whose sounds were absent. Although this tendency is well documented in the normal child language literature, only one other study of which we are aware has noted similar findings for language impaired children. In an analysis of naturalistic speech samples from three language impaired children, Schwartz et al. (1980) observed a prevalence of attempted words containing certain sounds and a notable absence of words composed of other types of sounds. The results of the present study suggest that such selection and avoidance tendencies can be seen even when controls are placed on the frequency with which words containing these sounds occur.

The children's tendency to produce in-phonology words was not absolute, however. Several words attempted by the children were inconsistent with their phonologies. Some of this usage may have been due to sampling errors on our part. That is, we may have regarded a particular consonant or cluster as out of the child's phonology when in fact the child possessed a word with the consonant but was not observed using it. However, it seems that much of this usage may have reflected the child's willingness to attempt the word in spite of its phonological characteristics. Ingram (1976) has noted that when children begin to show a spurt in lexical development, shortly after acquiring a lexicon of 50 words, they show a marked decrease in their tendency to avoid the use of certain sounds. The children in our study were approaching, and in a few cases had reached, this point in development. This change in the children's approach to complex words seems to have had its price. As was seen in the analysis of the children's attempts at the out-of-phonology words, these productions were rarely accurate.

The use of a comprehension task enabled us to gain considerable insight into the children's tendency to produce a greater number of in-phonology words than out-of-phonology words. Both the normal and language impaired children comprehended as many out-of-phonology words as in-phonology words. The comprehension task required the children to search for and select the appropriate object or act out the appropriate action with a doll. Given that the children were equally likely to perform such behaviors regardless of the experimental word tested in comprehension, it seems reasonable to conclude that the children's production biases could not be due to factors such as the relative attractiveness of the referents involved.

The children's performance on the comprehension task also leads us to doubt that their selection tendencies were attributable to an inability to perceive the out-of-phonology sounds. That is, the children could evidently discriminate the out-of-phonology words from one another and from the in-phonology words. It is possible that the children were not able to perceive every detail of the out-of-phonology words. This issue could be resolved only with a comprehension test with more carefully selected foils than the one used here, including words forming minimal pairs with the out-of-phonology words.

Lexical Types

The object and action word performances of the normal children was highly similar to that of the normal children studied by other investigators. The children both comprehended and produced a greater number of object words than action words. An examination of the language impaired children's performance revealed the same pattern. The relative ease of learning object words has often been attributed to the nature and complexity of their referents. For example, Gentner (1978; 1982) has pointed out that the difference between object and action words can be traced to differences between referential and relational meaning. In order to learn the referent of an object word, the child often can rely on perceptual information. However, the referents of action words are integrally related to the agents who perform these actions, and in many cases, the objects or persons that are the recipients of the actions.

An additional factor may have influenced the comprehension performance differences seen for object and action words. The object word comprehension task required the children to select from among eight objects placed in front of them. For action words, however, the children's responses were not limited in this way. Thus, the probability of a correct response may have been different in the two tasks. This possibility seems particularly likely in light of Oviatt's (1980) finding that young children could learn new action words quite readily when learning was assessed by means of a recognitory comprehension task.

In spite of the higher performance associated with object words in both the normal and language impaired children, the two groups were not identical in their object and action word performance. The language impaired children produced a greater number of action words on the posttest than did the normal children. The two groups differed in one other respect. Like the children studied by Benedict (1979), the normal children in the present study showed less of a bias against action words in comprehension than in production. Only 7% of the experimental words produced on the posttest by the normal children were action words. However, 20% of the experimental words comprehended on the posttest represented names of actions. The language impaired children did not show the same tendency. For these children, action words represented approximately 30% of the experimental words produced as well as comprehended. The language impaired children were older and were operating at somewhat higher levels of intellectual functioning than the normal children. For this reason, they may have had less difficulty dealing with both the relational properties of the actions and the comprehension task employed to assess their understanding of these actions.

Relationship Between Comprehension and Production

A greater number of experimental words was comprehended than produced by both the normal and language impaired children. However, because correct response probability was not the same on the production and comprehension tasks, the children's performance on the two tasks could not be directly compared. Instead, the relationship between comprehension and production was examined by computing the percentage of comprehended words that was produced. On this measure, the normal and language impaired children were highly similar.

It was not the case that the children in the two groups produced only those experimental words that they had comprehended. At least half of the children in each group produced experimental words that they never comprehended on the comprehension probes or posttest. Such a finding is inconsistent with data reported by Goldin-Meadow et al. (1976). These investigators tested 12 2-year-old children on 70 different object words and 30 different action words. No child who was correct on any item on the production task was reported to have failed the same item on the comprehension task. However, other studies of normally developing children are more consistent with our findings. Nelson and Bonvillian (1978) exposed experimental words to a group of 25 2-year-olds and found that 24 of the children produced at least 1 and as many as 11 of these words without having comprehended them. Similarly, Leonard et al. (1980) reported on four children (ages 1;6 to 1;9) who each produced several experimental words (out of 12 exposed) prior to demonstrating comprehension.

The discrepancy between the Goldin-Meadow et al. (1976) findings and those of Nelson and Bonvillian (1978), Leonard et al. (1980), and the present study may be due to the fact that the former simply tested the children on common words expected to be known by 2-year-old children, whereas each of the latter studies presented uncommon or nonsense words for a number of experimental sessions, enabling the children's pattern of acquisition of these words to be carefully monitored (see Nelson, Rescorla, Gruendel, & Benedict, 1978). It is possible that some of the subjects in Goldin-Meadow et al.'s cross-sectional study may have, at a prior point in time, shown the same pattern of producing words before exhibiting comprehension of these words on a comprehension task. In fact, Huttenlocher's (1974) investigation of three young children (ages 0;10 to 1;2 at the outset of the study) yielded results that are consistent with this possibility. Huttenlocher observed that the first words produced by the children were not always those to which the children responded systematically on a comprehension task.

How is it possible for words to be produced without the child showing evidence of comprehension? One possible explanation has been provided by Rice (1980). She trained ten children (ages 2;3 to 3;4) to produce appropriate color terms for objects. Of the eight children who were administered a color comprehension task following training, four demonstrated comprehension difficulties even though they exhibited correct production. Although all of the children could match identical objects by color, the four children with comprehension difficulty had problems placing assorted objects into groups according to their color. The children who demonstrated appropriate comprehension as well as production either displayed this color sorting ability from the outset or acquired the ability during the period in which training was being provided. The ability to perform correctly on the sorting task was dependent on the knowledge that color is not only an attribute that can be used to discriminate objects, but also one that can be used as the basis for grouping objects as equivalent. According to Rice, the comprehension task, but not the production task, may also have required the knowledge that color could serve as a critical attribute for categorical equivalence. For the comprehension task, the child was required to choose from among assorted multi-attribute objects (e.g., three red pigs, three yellow dogs, three green goats, one black cow) when asked, for example, "Give me a red one." Thus, it may have been necessary for the child to have coded the relationship between color terms and color properties of objects as that of "criterial attribute for categorical equivalence (Rice, 1980, p. 102)." In the production task, on the other hand, the child was required to name the color of an object when asked "What color is this?" According to Rice, this task may have required only recognition of the color of the object and recall of the color term corresponding to this color.

If this proposal is correct, it allows for the possibility that, in the present study, words that were produced but not comprehended were coded differently from words that were both produced and comprehended. Such coding differences seemed to be word- rather than child-specific, because the children who produced but did not exhibit comprehension for certain words were seen to both produce and comprehend other words. The semantic complexity of a referent can influence how the word is coded, which in turn can affect comprehension but not production (see Daneman & Case, 1981). However, if such complexity served as a factor in our study, it was not a complexity inherent in the referents themselves. That is, words such as *sheath* and *pipe* that were produced but not comprehended by some children were both produced and comprehended by others.

However, there is another possibility. Although careful controls were placed on the sentence contexts in which the words were exposed and the frequency of these exposures, the nonlinguistic context of the exposures may have varied from session to session on occasion and, more probably, from child to child. This variation may have occurred in one of two ways. First, the play themes into which the experimenter incorporated the objects and actions may have varied sufficiently as to create different episodic information to be associated with each referent, some being more facilitative for certain types of retrieval (comprehension vs. production). Alternatively, the children may have been the source of this variation by performing or not performing the referent actions and by performing either various actions or no actions on the referent objects (cf. Schwartz, 1980). This seems to be a useful topic for future research.

Imitation

Consistent with previously reported findings (Leonard et al., 1979), we found no evidence that imitation affected the rate of lexical acquisition by the children in this study, when acquisition is defined as a single spontaneous production, or as correct selection on a comprehension probe. However, when it co-occurred with spontaneous production, imitation did appear to increase the likelihood of acquisition as measured by posttest production.

These findings, based on a paradigm involving controlled input, provide somewhat more convincing evidence for the facilitative effects of imitation than previously reported findings. In addition, the results suggest that this facilitating effect may depend on the co-occurrence of imitation and spontaneous production. This suggests the possibility that imitation in conjunction with spontaneous production may serve as some type of overt rehearsal, facilitating subsequent productions.

Contribution of the Study of Specific Language Impairment to an Understanding of the Language Acquisition Process

The findings of this study have important implications for the clinical management of children with specific language impairment. However, as with the study of other atypical populations, some useful insights into the language acquisition process itself are also gained. Children with specific language impairment serve as test cases for the extent to which a number of linguistic behaviors are linked to general developmental level.

There seems to be little doubt that many of the early linguistic characteristics under exploration here are more closely tied to the language level of the child than to factors such as motor, social, or general intellectual ability. Specifically, the language impaired children exhibited phonological selection constraints and simplification processes, and engaged in unsolicited imitation in a manner similar to the normal children operating at the same productive language level but considerably less developed in motor, social, and some aspects of general intellectual level. Like younger normal chidlren, the language impaired children acquired object names more readily than action names. The relationship between lexical comprehension and production was also highly similar in the two groups. Findings such as these indicate that great caution should be taken in assuming that such linguistic characteristics are integrally tied to factors such as the child's world knowledge or his or her knowledge of social relationships. It seems that many of these linguistic characteristics are natural products of the linguistic ability of the child, apart from the skills he or she exhibits in other developmental areas.

Some linguists have ardently maintained their focus on the ideal adult speaker-hearer and continued to evaluate linguistic theories exclusively on the basis of formal grounds (e.g., Postal, 1972). But with the growth of psycholinguistics, other linguists have recognized and argued for the importance of the real adult speaker-hearer in providing data that can distinguish among models of language. More recently, a few linguists (Ferguson, 1975; Menn, 1979, 1982) have maintained that rather than linguistics forming our views of child language, the reverse should be true. Menn took this one step further in arguing that other types of exceptional language, such as the language of aphasics, second language learners, and psychotics, may provide similarly valuable information.

As developmental psycholinguists, we have clearly taken the first step in employing data from real as opposed to idealized speakers in our attempts to construct and evaluate theories of acquisition. It seems equally important that we take the second step and recognize the value of data from exceptional language learners in such endeavors. As we have attempted to demonstrate, children with specific language impairment are of interest in their own right in understanding this impairment and developing clinical strategies. Of equal importance, though, is the fact that such children provide a means of answering some questions that cannot be answered by examining normally developing children alone. If we are ultimately able to construct theories of acquisition that account not only for normal language development but also for deviations such as specific language impairment, our theories will be that much stronger.

ACKNOWLEDGMENTS

The research reported in this paper was supported by NINCDS Grant NS 16154. Appreciation is extended to Kathy Chapman, Cheryl Messick, Patricia Prelock, Lynne Rowan, Brenda Terrell, and Amy Weiss for their contributions to the research reported in this chapter.

REFERENCES

Arthur, G. *The Arthur adaptation of the Leiter International Performance Scale.* Chicago: Stoelting, 1952.

Bender, J. A case of delayed speech. *Journal of Speech Disorders,* 140, *5,* 363.

Benedict, H. Early lexical development: Comprehension and production. *Journal of Child Language,* 1979, *6,* 183–200.

Benton, A. The cognitive functioning of children with developmental dysphasia. In M. Wyke (Ed.), *Developmental dysphasia.* New York: Academic Press, 1978.

Berko, J. The child's learning of English morphology. *Word,* 1958, *14,* 150–177.

Bloom, L. The importance of language development: Linguistic determinism in the 1980's. In H. Winitz (Ed.), *Native language and foreign language acquisition. Annals of the New York Academy of Sciences, Vol. 379.* New York: New York Academy of Sciences, 1981.

Bloom, L. *One word at a time.* The Hague: Mouton, 1973.

Bloom, L., Hood, L., & Lightbown, P. Imitation in language development: If, when and why. *Cognitive Psychology,* 1974, *6,* 380–420.

Boskey, M., & Nelson, K. *Answering unanswerable questions: The role of imitation.* Paper presented at the Boston University Conference on Language Development, Boston, 1980.

Bush, C., Edwards, M., Luckau, J., Stoel, C., Macken, M., & Peterson, J. *On specifying a system for transcribing consonants in child language* (Child Language Project). Unpublished manuscript, Stanford University, 1973.

Carrow, E. *Test for auditory comprehension of language.* Austin, Tex.: Teaching Resources Corporation, 1973.

Chapman, R. Comprehension strategies in children. In J. Kavanaugh & W. Strange (Eds.), *Speech and language in the laboratory, school, and clinic.* Cambridge, Mass.: MIT Press, 1978.

Chapman, R., & Miller, J. Word order in early two and three word utterances: Does production precede comprehension? *Journal of Speech and Hearing Research,* 1975, *18,* 355–371.

Daneman, M., & Case, R. Syntactic form, semantic complexity, and short term memory: Influences on children's acquisition of new linguistic structures. *Developmental Psychology,* 1981, *17,* 367–378.

Ferguson, C. *New directions in phonological theory: Language acquisition and universals research.* Address delivered to the Linguistic Institute of the Linguistic Society of America, Tampa, Fl., 1975.

Ferguson, C., & Farwell, C. Words and sounds in early language acquisition: English initial consonants in the first 50 words. *Language,* 1975, *51,* 419–439.

Gentner, D. On relational meaning: The acquisition of verb meaning. *Child Development,* 1978, *48,* 988–998.

Gentner, D. Why nouns are learned before verbs: Linguistic relativity versus natural partitioning. In S. Kuczaj (Ed.), *Language development: Language, thought and culture Vol. II.* Hillsdale, NJ: Lawrence Erlbaum Associates, 1982.

Goldin-Meadow, S., Seligman, M., & Gelman, R. Language in the two-year-old. *Cognition,* 1976, *4,* 189–202.

Huttenlocher, J. The origins of language comprehension. In R. Solso (Ed.), *Theories of cognitive psychology*. New York: Halsted Press, 1974.

Ingram, D. Phonological rules in young children. *Journal of Child Language*, 1974, *1*, 49-64.

Ingram, D. *Phonological disability in children*. London: Edward Arnold, 1976.

Ingram, T. Speech disorders in childhood. In E. H. Lenneberg & E. Lenneberg (Eds.), *Foundations of language development* (Vol. 2). New York: Academic Press, 1975.

Johnston, J. The language disordered child. In N. Lass, J. Northern, D. Yoder, & L. McReynolds (Eds.), *Speech, language and hearing*. Philadelphia: Saunders, 1982.

Johnston, J., & Schery, T. The use of grammatical morphemes by children with communication disorders. In D. Morehead & A. Morehead (Eds.), *Normal and deficient child language*. Baltimore: University Park Press, 1976.

Keenan, E. Conversational competence in children. *Journal of Child Language*, 1974, *1*, 163-184.

Kiparsky, P., & Menn, L. On the acquisition of phonology. In J. Macnamara (Ed.), *Language learning and thought*. New York: Academic Press, 1977.

Lee, L. *Developmental sentence analysis*. Evanston, Ill.: Northwestern University Press, 1974.

Leonard, L. Language impairment in children. *Merrill-Palmer Quarterly*, 1979, *25*, 205-232.

Leonard, L. The nature of specific language impairment. In S. Rosenberg (Ed.), *Handbook of applied psycholinguistics*. Hillsdale, N.J.: Lawrence Erlbaum Assoicates, 1982.

Leonard, L., Newhoff, M., & Fey, M. Some instances of word usage in the absence of comprehension. *Journal of Child Language*, 1980, *7*, 189-196.

Leonard, L., Schwartz, R., Morris, B., & Chapman, K. Factors influencing early lexical acquisition: Lexical orientation and phonological composition. *Child Development*, 1981, *52*, 882-887.

Leonard, L., Schwartz, R., Chapman, K., Rowan, L., Prelock, P., Terrell, B., Weiss, A., & Messick, C. Early lexical acquisition in children with specific language impairment. *Journal of Speech and Hearing Research*, 1982, *25*, 554-564.

Leonard, L., Schwartz, R., Folger, M., Newhoff, M., & Wilcox, M. Children's imitations of lexical items. *Child Development*, 1979, *50*, 19-27.

Lexington developmental scale. Lexington, Ky.: United Cerebral Palsy of the Bluegrass, 1974.

Mayer, J., & Valian, V. *When do children imitate? When imitate? When necessary*. Paper presented at the Boston University Conference on Language Development, Boston, 1977.

Menn, L. *Towards a psychology of phonology: Child phonology as a first step*. Paper presented to the Michigan State University Conference on Metatheory: Applications of Linguistic Theory in the Human Sciences, East Lansing, 1979.

Menn, L. Child language as a source of constraints for linguistic theory. In L. K. Obler & L. Menn (Ed.), *Exceptional language and linguistics*. New York: Academic Press, 1982.

Moerk, E. Processes and products of imitation: Evidence that imitation is progressive. *Journal of Psycholinguistic Research*, 1977, *6*, 187-202.

Morehead, D., & Ingram, D. The development of base syntax in normal and linguistically deviant children. *Journal of Speech and Hearing Research*, 1973, *16*, 330-352.

Nelson, K. Structure and strategy in learning to talk. *Monographs for the Society for Research in Child Development*, 1973, *38*(1-2, Serial No. 149).

Nelson, K., Rescorla, L., Gruendel, J., & Benedict, H. Early lexicons: what do they mean? *Child Development*, 1978, *49*, 960-968.

Nelson, K. E., & Bonvillian, J. Concepts and words in the two-year-old: Acquisition of concept names under controlled conditions. *Cognition*, 1973, *2*, 435-450.

Nelson, K. E., & Bonvillian, J. Early language development: Conceptual growth and related processes between 2 and 4½ years of age. In K. E. Nelson (Ed.), *Children's language* (Vol. 1).

Nelson, K. E., & Nelson, K. Cognitive pendulums and their linguistic realization. In K. E. Nelson (Ed.), *Children's language* (Vol. 1). New York: Gardner Press, 1978.

Nice, M. A child who would not talk. *Pedagogical Seminary*, 1925, *32*, 105-144.

Olmsted, D. *Out of the mouths of babes*. The Hague: Mouton, 1971.

Oviatt, S. The emerging ability to comprehend language: An experimental approach. *Child Development*, 1980, *51*, 97–106.

Postal, P. The best theory. In S. Peters (Ed.), *Goals of linguistic theory*. Englewood Cliffs, NJ: Prentice-Hall, 1972.

Ramer, A. The function of imitation in child language. *Journal of Speech and Hearing Research*, 1976, *19*, 700–717.

Rice, M. Identification of children with language disorders. In R. Schiefelbusch (Ed.), *Language intervention strategies*. Baltimore: University Park Press, 1978.

Rice, M. *Cognition to language: Categories, word meanings, and training*. Baltimore: University Park Press, 1980.

Rodgon, M., & Kurdek, L. Vocal and gestural imitation in children under two years old. *Journal of Genetic Psychology*, 1977, *131*, 115–123.

Ryan, J. Interpretation and imitation in early language development. In R. Hinde & R. Stevenson-Hinde (Eds.), *Constraints on learning*. New York: Academic Press, 1973.

Schwartz, R. *The role of action in early lexical acquisition*. Paper presented to the American Speech-Language-Hearing Association, Detroit, 1980.

Schwartz, R., & Leonard, L. *Words, objects and actions in early lexical acquisition*. Paper presented at the Child Language Research Forum, Stanford, Calif., 1980.

Schwartz, R., & Leonard, L. Do children pick and choose? Phonological selection and avoidance in early lexical acquisition. *Journal of Child Language*, 1982, *9*, 319–336.

Schwartz, R., Leonard, L., Folger, M., & Wilcox, M. Evidence for a synergistic view of language disorders: Early phonological behavior in normal and language disordered children. *Journal of Speech and Hearing Disorders*, 1980, *45*, 357–377.

Shibamoto, J., & Olmsted, D. Lexical and syllabic patterns in phonological acquisition. *Journal of Child Language*, 1978, *5*, 417–456.

Straight, H. Auditory versus articulatory phonological processes and their development in children. In G. Yeni-Komshian, J. Kavanaugh, & C. Ferguson (Eds.), *Child phonology, Volume 1: Production*. New York: Academic Press, 1980.

Tallal, P., & Stark, R. Speech perception of language-delayed children. In G. Yeni-Komshian, J. Kavanaugh, & C. Ferguson (Eds.), *Child phonology, Vol. 2*. New York: Academic Press, 1980.

Tanouye, E. The acquisition of verbs in Japanese children. *Papers and Reports on Child Language Development*, 1979, *17*, 49–56.

Thomson, J. R., & Chapman, R. S. Who is "Daddy" revisited: The status of two-year-olds' overextended words in use and comprehension. *Journal of Child Language*, 1977, *4*, 359–375.

Werner, H., & Kaplan, E. The acquisition of word meanings: A developmental study. *Monographs of the Society for Research in Child Development*, 1952, *15*(1, Serial No. 51).

Werner, L. Treatment of a child with delayed speech. *Journal of Speech Disorders*, 1945, *10*, 329–334.

Whitehurst, G., Novak, G., & Zorn, G. Delayed speech studied in the home. *Developmental Psychology*, 1972, *7*, 169–177.

Yoss, K., & Darley, F. Developmental apraxia of speech in children with defective articulation. *Journal of Speech and Hearing Research*, 1974, *17*, 399–416.

Zimmerman, I., Steiner, V., & Evatt, R. *Preschool language scale*. Columbus, OH: Merrill, 1969.

10

The Relationship Between Degree of Bilingualism and Cognitive Ability: A Critical Discussion and Some New Longitudinal Data

Kenji Hakuta
Yale University

Rafael M. Diaz
University of New Mexico

In 1962, Elizabeth Peal and Wallace Lambert of McGill University published a monograph entitled "The Relation of Bilingualism to Intelligence." The research, conducted in Montreal with 10-year-old children, compared the performance of monolinguals to that of bilingual, French/English-speaking subjects on a variety of standard tests of intelligence. In contrast to previous research on bilingualism and intelligence, Peal and Lambert (1962) discovered that their bilingual sample showed superior performance on measures of verbal intelligence and on nonverbal tests "involving concept-formation or symbolic flexibility [p. 14]." What differentiated the study from its ancestral relatives was the care with which Peal and Lambert exercised control over sample selection. They drew a distinction between true, "balanced bilinguals" who are proficient in both their first (L1) and second language (L2) and "pseudo-bilinguals" who, for various reasons, have not yet attained age-appropriate abilities in their second language. According to Peal and Lambert (1962): "The pseudo-bilingual knows one language much better than the other, and does not use his second language in communication. The true (or balanced) bilingual masters both at an early age and has facility with both as means of communication [p. 6]." Into their sample of bilinguals, only those considered "balanced" were admitted.

Peal and Lambert's study had substantial impact on two fronts. First, it raised the consciousness of researchers on the problem of selecting appropriate bilingual samples to an extent such that the prototype of subsequent studies on bilingualism became group comparisons of balanced bilinguals to monolingual counterparts matched on appropriate variables. Second, the results served to allay commonly held fears concerning the products of bilingual education, namely, that it would produce retarded, poorly educated, anomic individuals without affiliation to either ethnolinguistic group and incapable of functioning in either language (Tucker & d'Anglejan, 1971). Bilingual education would not create, the study assured, a social or cognitive Frankenstein.

In this chapter, we provide a brief review of research prior to Peal and Lambert's study and more recent studies on bilingualism and intelligence (for an earlier review with a linguistic focus, see Lindholm, 1980; for an expanded and detailed review of the first 6 decades of research, see Diaz, 1983). In the course of the review, we point out both theoretical and methodological weaknesses inherent in the typical bilingual-monolingual comparison. In addition, we stress the paucity of longitudinal investigations that allow for the assessment of statements concerning the cause–effect relations between bilingualism and cognitive abilities. Then, we report preliminary results from our own study, which attempts to correct for these weaknesses. We conclude with some theoretical speculations regarding the nature of the relationship between bilingualism and thought.

THE FIRST 4 DECADES OF RESEARCH

Psychological studies of the relation between bilingualism and cognitive abilities began in the early 1920s out of concern raised by the flourishing of psychometric tests of intelligence. The concern was that bilingual children would suffer from some linguistic disadvantages, which could, in turn, prevent fair assessment of their intellectual abilities and potential. The fact that the measurement of intelligence is heavily dependent on verbal abilities made psychologists and educators deeply concerned (and rightfully so!) about the validity of such tests for bilingual children. As expected, the majority of studies prior to Peal and Lambert's (1962) study found that bilinguals were linguistically deficient in comparison to their monolingual counterparts. Among other things, bilinguals were shown to have deficient articulation (Carrow, 1957), lower standards in written composition, more grammatical errors (Harris, 1948; Saer, 1924), and a considerably reduced vocabulary (Barke & Williams, 1938; Grabo, 1931; Saer, 1924). The consistent finding was that bilinguals suffered from a so-called "language handicap" (see reviews by Arsenian, 1937; Darcy, 1953, 1963; Macnamara, 1966).

Unfortunately, consistent findings about bilinguals' "language handicap" led too quickly to statements regarding the negative effects of bilingualism rather than to a serious questioning of the validity of psychometric tests of intelligence for this population. Negative, and rather harsh, statements condemning bilingualism as a social plague (Epstein, 1905) or as "a hardship devoid of apparent advantage" (Yoshioka, 1929) were common in the early literature. In short, the measured language handicap of bilinguals was interpreted as a linguistic confusion that deeply affected children's intellectual development and academic performance up to the college years (Saer, 1940).

The majority of early studies in the area, however, suffered from a wide range of methodological problems, and as a result, most current investigators in the field regard the findings of early studies as totally unreliable (see Cummins, 1976). A good number of early studies, for example, failed to control for group differences in socioeconomic status between bilingual and monolingual samples. As early as 1930, McCarthy pointed out that bilingualism in the US was seriously confounded with low socioeconomic status. She found that more than half of the bilingual school children could be classified as belonging to families from the unskilled labor occupational group. Along the same lines, Fukuda (1925) alerted researchers to the fact that high-scoring English-speaking subjects were mostly in the occupational and executive classes; he reported a correlation of .53 between the Whittier (socioeconomic) Scale and the Binet IQ in his sample. Nevertheless, prior to the early 1960s, most studies investigating the effects of bilingualism on children's intelligence did not take into account group differences in socioeconomic status.

A second major methodological flaw of early studies is that it was often questionable whether the "bilingual" subjects were in fact fluent in both languages. Brunner (1929), for example, assumed that children's bilingualism would be estimated by the foreignness of their parents. Brunner divided his bilingual sample into three categories: (1) both parents born in this country; (2) one parent born here and the other abroad; and (3) both parents born abroad. The classification was simply assumed to represent various degrees of children's bilingualism. In other studies, the sample's bilingualism was assessed through family names or even place of residence (see Darcy, 1953, for a review). As present investigators have repeatedly stated, it is impossible to ascertain whether the bilingual subjects of many studies were indeed bilingual or just monolingual of a minority language.

Toward the end of the 1950s, research on the effects of bilingualism showed the following consistent findings. Monolinguals performed significantly higher than bilinguals on measures of verbal intelligence. On measures of nonverbal ability, some studies showed that monolinguals were also at an advantage, but group differences on this variable were not consistent across studies. However, because of the serious methodological flaws just mentioned, none of the results, even if they were statistically significant in either direction, can be easily interpreted. Peal and Lambert's (1962) study, described briefly in the introduction, took steps to assure the selection of true, balanced bilinguals. In addition, it recruited wisdom from previous studies in controlling for socioeconomic level.

PEAL AND LAMBERT (1962): THE PUNCTUATION POINT IN RESEARCH

Both bilingual and monolingual samples for the Peal and Lambert study were selected from the same school system in Montreal. All 10-year-old children in the system were included in the initial screening by four measures, the composite of which was used to determine whether the child should be considered monolingual or balanced bilingual. The measures were: (1) the relative frequency of words provided in a word association task in L1 and L2; (2) the relative frequency of words in L1 and L2 detected in a series of letters; (3) the frequency of words recognized in L2 (English) from a subset chosen from the Peabody Picture Vocabulary Test; and (4) subjective self-ratings on ability in speaking, understanding, reading, and writing in L2. Children who fell in the extremes of these scales were determined to be monolingual or balanced bilingual. The final sample consisted of 75 monolinguals and 89 bilinguals; all children were administered a modified version of the Lavoie-Larendeau Group Test of General Intelligence (Lavoie & Laurendeau, 1960), the Raven's Coloured Progressive Matrices (Raven, 1956; Raven, Court, & Raven, 1976), and a French version of selected subtests of the Thurstone Primary Mental Abilities Test (Thurstone & Thurstone, 1954).

Contrary to the findings of earlier studies, the results of the Peal and Lambert study showed that bilinguals performed significantly better than monolinguals on most of the cognitive tests and subtests, even when group differences in sex, age, and socioeconomic status were appropriately controlled. Bilingual children performed significantly higher than monolinguals on tests of both verbal and nonverbal abilities; the bilinguals' superiority in nonverbal tests was more clearly evident in those subtests that required mental manipulation and reorganization of visual stimuli, rather than mere perceptual abilities. A factor analysis of test scores indicated that bilinguals were superior to monolinguals in concept formation and in tasks that required a certain mental or symbolic flexibility. Overall, bilinguals were found to have a more diversified pattern of abilities than their monolingual peers.

Peal and Lambert's (1962) findings must be considered with a certain degree of caution, however. First, as Macnamara (1966) has pointed out, the process of subject selection might have introduced a bias in favor of the bilingual sample. Peal and Lambert's bilingual sample included only children who scored above a certain determined level in the English Peabody Picture Vocabulary Test, a test commonly used to measure intelligence in monolinguals.

It is possible that the intelligence of French-Canadian children might be reflected in a measure of English (the second language) vocabulary. Second, the bilingual sample, on the average, belonged to a higher grade than the monolingual sample; perhaps the superiority observed in bilinguals was the result of their having longer exposure to formal education. And third, the frequency distribution of the Raven's test scores was very different for the two groups of children; it was negatively skewed for bilinguals, whereas the opposite was true for monolinguals. In short, the cognitive advantages observed in Peal and Lambert's balanced bilingual sample could have been inflated by several artifacts in their subject selection procedures. As Peal and Lambert (1962) admitted:

> A partial explanation of this [the results] may lie in our method of choosing the bilingual sample. Those suffering from a language handicap may unintentionally have been eliminated. We attempted to select bilinguals who were balanced, that is, equally fluent in both languages. However, when the balance measures did not give a clear indication of whether or not a given child was bilingual, more weight was attached to his score on the English vocabulary tests. Thus some bilinguals who might be balanced, but whose vocabulary in English and French might be small, would be omitted from our sample. The less intelligent bilinguals, those who have not acquired as large an English vocabulary, would not be considered bilingual enough for our study [p. 15].

Nevertheless, Peal and Lambert's (1962) empirical distinction between bilinguals and pseudobilinguals made a significant (and much needed) methodological contribution to the field. Their distinction has forced recent investigators to select their bilingual sample with greater care and measure the sample's actual knowledge of the two languages.

RECENT STUDIES

Since Peal and Lambert (1962), a variety of studies have been reported in which monolingual children are compared to balanced bilingual children. In most of these studies, balanced bilinguals have shown advantages in several cognitive abilities, such as concept formation (Liedtke & Nelson, 1968) and metalinguistic awareness (Cummins, 1978). In addition, many studies suggest that balanced bilinguals demonstrate a greater flexibility than monolinguals in their performance on different cognitive tasks (Balkan, 1970). Above all, recent research not only has replicated Peal and Lambert's positive findings regarding balanced bilingualism, but also has given empirical support for linguists' statements regarding the cognitive and linguistic advantages of raising a child bilingually.

In contrast to early psychological studies of childhood bilingualism, individual case studies by linguists (Leopold, 1939, 1947, 1949a, 1949b; Ronjat, 1913) had concluded that early bilingualism was advantageous to children's cognitive and linguistic development. In particular, Leopold (1961), based on observations of his bilingually raised daughter, suggested that bilingualism promoted an early separation of the word sound from the word meaning: "a noticeable looseness of the link between the phonetic word and its meaning [p. 358]." Furthermore, Leopold postulated a fascinating connection between the semantic and cognitive development of bilingual children, namely that the separation of sound and meaning leads to an early awareness of the conventionality of words and the arbitrariness of language. This awareness could promote, in turn, more abstract levels of thinking. Vygotsky (1935/1975) saw the cognitive advantages of bilingualism along the same lines; in his own words (as cited in Cummins, 1976), bilingualism frees the mind "from the prison of concrete language and phenomena [p. 34]."

Leopold's observations have been tested empiricaly by Ianco-Worrall (1972) in a remarkable well-designed and controlled study of English-Afrikaans bilingual children in South Africa. The bilingual sample consisted of nursery school children who had been raised in a one person-one language environment, similar to the situation of Leopold's daughter Hildegard. The sample's degree of bilingualism was determined by several measures, including detailed interviews with parents and teachers as well as a direct test of the children's vocabulary in both languages. Two comparable monolingual samples, one English and one Afrikaans, were included in the study.

In a first experiment, children were administered a semantic-phonetic preferences test. The test consisted of eight sets of three words each. A typical set contained the words *cap, can,* and *hat.* Children were asked questions such as: "Which word is more like *cap, can* or *hat?*" Choosing the word *can* or *hat* indicated the child's phonetic preference or semantic preference, respectively, in analyzing word similarities. The capacity to compare words on the basis of a semantic dimension is regarded as more advanced developmentally than comparing words along a phonetic dimension.

The results of this experiment showed not only that semantic preferences increased with age, but also that bilinguals outranked monolinguals in choosing words along a semantic rather than a phonetic dimension. As Ianco-Worrall (1972) reported: "of the young 4–6 year old bilinguals, 54% consistently chose to interpret similarity between words in terms of the semantic dimension. Of the unilingual groups of the same age, not one Afrikaans speaker and only one English speaker showed similar choice behavior [p. 1398]." Ianco-Worrall concluded that bilingual children raised in a one person-one language environment reach a stage of semantic development 2–3 years earlier than monolingual children.

In a second experiment, using Vygotsky's (1962) interviewing techniques, Ianco-Worrall (1972) asked her subjects to explain the names of different things (e.g., why is a dog called "dog"?). She also asked children whether or not the names of things could be arbitrarily interchanged. Children's responses to the first question were assigned to different categories such as perceptible attributes, functional attributes, social convention, and so forth. The results of this second experiment showed no reliable differences between bilingual and monolingual children in the types of explanations offered. For the second question, however, the differences favored the bilingual children; bilinguals replied that names of objects could in principle be changed, whereas the opposite was true for monolingual children.

Lindholm (1980) reports a study by Sandoval (1976) in which a replication of Ianco-Worrall's results was attempted with a Spanish/Enlish sample of kindergartners and third graders. Although there was a trend favoring the bilinguals, it did not reach statistical significance. However, it is not clear whether the bilingual subjects were truly balanced or simply enrolled in bilingual schools.

More recently, Bain and Yu (1980) investigated the cognitive consequences of raising children according to Ronjat's (1913) one person-one language principle. Bain and Yu studied German-French, English-French, and Chinese-English bilinguals with monolinguals from the respective languages in three different geographical locations. The dependent cognitive variables concerned children's developing awareness of the functions of language as postulated by Luria and examined in tasks such as the ability to follow a set of increasingly complex directions in hide-and-seek situations. In particular, Bain and Yu hypothesized that bilingualism would promote the use of language as a self-directive tool in cognitive tasks. Using a modified version of Luria's (1961) experimental procedures, the results showed that, at about age 4, children raised bilingually in one person-one language environment were better able to use both overt and covert language as a guide and control in their cognitive functioning. The data also favored younger bilingual children, but this trend failed to reach statistical significance. More importantly, the findings were consistent across different language groups and geographical situations.

Several investigators have explored the effects of bilingualism on the development of metalinguistic awareness. Metalinguistic awareness refers to the ability to analyze linguistic output objectively; that is, according to Cummins (1978), "to look *at* language rather than *through* it to the intended meaning [p. 127]." Indeed, as children develop, they become more capable of looking at language as an objective set of rules, as an objective tool for communication. Because bilingualism induces an early separation of word and referent, it is possible that bilingual children also develop an early capacity to focus on and analyze the structural properties of language. Vygotsky (1935/1962) suggested that, because bilinguals could express the same thought in different languages, a bilingual child would tend to "see his language as one particular system among many, to view its phenomena under more general categories, and this leads to an awareness of his linguistic operations [1962, p. 110]." More recently, Ben-Zeev (1977b) hypothesized that bilinguals develop an analytic strategy toward language in order to fight interference between their two languages. Lambert and Tucker (1972) noted that children in the St. Lambert bilingual experiment engaged in some sort of "contrastive linguistics" by comparing similarities and differences between their two languages.

Cummins (1978) investigated the metalinguistic development of third- and sixth-grade Irish-English bilinguals. Children in the sample came from homes where both Irish and English were spoken; all children received formal school instruction in Irish. An appropriate monolingual comparison group was selected that was equivalent to the bilingual group on measures of IQ and socioeconomic status. A first task investigated children's awareness of the arbitrariness of language. Similar to the measure used by Ianco-Worrall (1972), children were asked whether names of objects could be interchanged; they were then asked to explain or justify their responses. The results indicated that, at both third- and sixth-grade levels, bilinguals showed a greater awareness of the arbitrary nature of linguistic reference.

In a second task, children were presented with several contradictory and tautological sentences about some poker chips that were either visible or hidden. The sentences varied in two additional dimensions: true versus false and empirical versus nonempirical. According to Cummins (1978), nonempirical statements refer to sentences that "are true or false by virtue of their linguistic form rather than deriving their truth value from any extralinguistic state of affairs [p. 129]." The task was chosen as a measure of metalinguistic awareness because previous researchers had shown that, in order to evaluate contradictions and tautologies correctly, it is necessary to examine language in an objective manner. Although the performance on this evaluation task was not clear-cut in favor of the bilinguals, sixth-grade bilingual children showed a marked superiority in correctly evaluating hidden nonempirical sentences. But Cummins (1978) notes that the monolinguals "analyzed linguistic input less closely, being more content to give the obvious 'can't tell' response to the hidden nonempirical items [p. 133]."

In a second experiment with balanced Ukranian-English bilinguals, Cummins (1978) investigated children's metalinguistic awareness using a wide variety of measures, including analysis of ambiguous sentences and a class inclusion task. Contrary to previous findings, the bilinguals in this study did not show advantages on the Semantic-Phonetic Preference Test or on an arbitrariness of language task. However, Cummins (1978) reports that "the results of the Class Inclusion and Ambiguities tasks are consistent with previous findings in that they suggest that bilingualism promotes an analytic orientation to linguistic input [p. 135]."

In the studies that have been described, bilinguals exceeded monolinguals in a wide range of linguistic and metalinguistic abilities. Bilinguals showed a greater capacity to analyze the similarity of words along semantic rather than acoustic dimensions, a greater use of language as a self-directing tool in cognitive tasks, and a greater overall awareness of the conventional nature of words and language. Also, in a different study (Feldman & Shen, 1971), bilingual 5-year-olds were better than their monolingual peers at relabeling objects and expressing relations between objects in simple sentences. This awareness or flexibility with respect to the use of language seems to play an important role in the cognitive functioning of bilingual children. In fact, several investigators have claimed that bilinguals are more "cognitively flexible" than monolinguals when performing on both verbal and nonverbal tasks. Although the notion of cognitive flexibility has never been adequately explained (see Cummins, 1976), it is possible that bilinguals' unusual use and awareness of language contributes to a greater flexibility in the manipulation of both verbal and nonverbal symbols.

One of the most frequently cited studies of bilinguals' cognitive flexibility was conducted in Switzerland by Balkan (1970). Balkan administered several tests of nonverbal abilities that purportedly measured cognitive flexibility. The bilingual group, as expected, performed significantly higher than the control monolingual group in two of these measures. One task, Figures Cachees, involved the ability to reorganize a perceptual situation, similar to the familiar Embedded Figures Test. The other task, Histoires, involved sensitivity to the different meanings of a word. Interestingly enough, the positive effects of bilingualsm on these measures were much stronger for children who had become bilingual before the age of 4. The differences between monolinguals and children who had become bilingual at a later age were in favor of the latter but did not reach statistical significance.

Balkan's study implies, as earlier individual case studies by linguists had suggested, that bilingualism might have the most beneficial cognitive effects for those children who learn their two languages simultaneously. Because balanced bilinguals have two different words for most referents, it is not surprising that they show a greater sensitivity than monolinguals to the possible different meanings of a single word, as shown in the Histoires task. On the other hand, Balkan's study offers no clue as to how or why bilingualism should contribute to a greater ability to reorganize and reconstruct perceptual arrays, as shown in the Figures Cachees task. As recent research suggests, the clue might be in bilinguals' greater awareness and flexibility with respect to the use of language, as well as in their greater use of both overt and covert speech in the monitoring of their cognitive functioning (Bain & Yu, 1980).

Further evidence of bilinguals' so-called cognitive flexibility has been offered by Ben-Zeev's (1977) study with Hebrew-English bilingual children. When compared to monolinguals, the bilingual children in the study showed a marked superiority in symbol substitution and verbal transformation tasks. The symbol substitution task involved children's ability to substitute words in a sentence according to the experimenter's instructions. In a typical instance, children were asked to replace the word *I* with the word *spaghetti*. Children were given correct scores when they were able to say sentences like "Spaghetti *am* cold," rather than "Spaghetti *is* cold" or a similar sentence that, although grammatically correct, violated the rules of the game. The bilinguals' higher performance on the verbal transformation task involved better detection of changes in a spoken stimulus that is repeated continuously by means of a tape loop. Warren and Warren (1966) have reported that when a spoken stimulus is presented in such a way, subjects older than 6 years report hearing frequent changes in what the taped voice says. The authors attributed this illusion to the development of a reorganization mechanism that aids in the perception of ongoing speech.

The bilingual children in Ben-Zeev's study also outperformed the monolingual group on certain aspects of a matrix transposition task. Bilinguals were better at isolating and specifying the underlying dimensions of the matrix, but no group differences were found on the rearrangement of figures in the matrix. The two comparison groups also performed similarly on Raven's progressive matrices. It should be noted that the bilinguals in Ben-Zeev's study showed cognitive advantages only on measures that were directly related to linguistic ability and on the verbal aspects of the matrix transformation task.

Ben-Zeev (1977) noted that throughout the study bilingual children seemed to approach the cognitive tasks in a truly analytic way. They also seemed more attentive to both the structure and details of the tasks administered, as well as more sensitive to feedback from the tasks and the experimenter. Ben-Zeev explained these improved abilities in terms of bilinguals' confrontation with their two languages. She argued that, in order to avoid linguistic interference, bilinguals must develop a keen awareness of the structural similarities and differences between their two languages as well as a special sensitivity to linguistic feedback from the environment. Supposedly, this more developed analytic strategy toward linguistic structures is transferred to other structures and patterns associated with different cognitive tasks. Ben-Zeev (1977) summarized her results as follows:

> Two strategies characterized the thinking patterns of the bilinguals in relation
> to verbal material: readiness to impute structure and readiness to reorganize.
> The patterns they seek are primarily linguistic, but this process also operates
> with visual patterns, as in their aptness at isolating the dimensions of a matrix.

With visual material the spatial reorganizational skill did not appear, however [p. 1017].

In conclusion, the nature or meaning of cognitive flexibility is far from being fully understood; however, the studies just reviewed suggest that the flexibility noted in bilinguals could stem from language-related abilities, such as the use of language in monitoring cognitive functioning or an early awareness of the conventionality and structural properties of language.

OBSERVATIONS ON THE STATE OF THE ART

The recent studies suggest that if one compares bilinguals who are approximately equivalent in their abilities in L1 and L2 with a monolingual group matched for age, socioeconomic level, and other relevant variables and administers a measure of cognitive flexibility to both groups, the bilinguals will do better. Now, consider an ideal (from the viewpoint of good experimental science) research design. You would begin by taking a random sample of individuals and assigning them randomly to either an experimental group or control group, thereby controlling for any background error in sampling. The experimental group is placed in an environment that fosters bilingualism, whereas the control group remains in a monolingual environment. Once the treatment has had time to take effect (i.e., once the subjects in the condition have become balanced bilinguals), you administer your dependent measure, making sure that the person who administers the dependent measure is blind to whether the subject being tested is in the treatment or control condition. And, lo and behold, you find a difference in favor of bilinguals. Under this ideal situation, one can reasonably conclude that bilingualism causes cognitive flexibility, or whatever cognitive advantage this flexibility stands for. You could also go on to speculate about why this result came about and construe various other experimental conditions to test your hypotheses.

In what ways is the ideal research design unlike the circumstances under which current studies of bilingualism are conducted? We would point out at least two. First, in the real world, there is no such thing as random assignment to a bilingual or monolingual group. Most often, bilingualism or monolingualism is determined by sociolinguistic facts that are, as would be true of most sociolinguistic facts, related to a wide range of social variables. What this really means is that there will be a large number of variables that differentiate the bilingual from the monolingual other than simply that the bilingual speaks two languages and the monolingual one. It is possible, of course, to match the two groups with respect to some variables (e.g., ethnicity) or to control them statistically (e.g., by partialing out the effects of socioeconomic level). But at what point can we be satisfied that *all* the relevant variables have been controlled for, such that the difference between the two groups can be attributed to the number of languages that the person knows? So, the skeptic could argue, "While you have controlled for *a,b,c,d,e,* and *f,* you haven't controlled for *g.*"

The second way in which the ideal situation is unlike the reality of the studies is more methodological and has to do with the adoption of a blind procedure (a double-blind is impossible, because presumably the subjects would know whether they are bilingual or monolingual). In none of the studies reviewed have we seen evidence of attempts by the researchers to keep the identity of the subject blind to the experimenter. If the experimenter is keen on the hypothesis of the study and in addition knows whether the subject is a bilingual or a monolingual child, one cannot rule out unintended experimenter bias effects (Rosenthal, 1976). In practice, it may be quite difficult to attempt to maintain a blind procedure. Bilingual and monolingual children are most often found in different schools, different neighborhoods, and would probably show some behavioral manifestations of their linguality. It is, however, an effect that one must bear in mind when interpreting the results of studies using the prototype design.

The methodological problems stemming from the reality of actual bilingual situations lend difficulty to supporting empirically the claim that bilingualism is associated with greater cognitive flexibility. One partial solution to both of these problems can be achieved in a rarely used design of looking at effects *within* a bilingual sample (Duncan & DeAvila, 1979). If *degree* of bilingualism can be reliably measured within a sample of children becoming bilingual and if this measure of degree can be shown to be related to cognitive flexibility, then one would have come one step closer to finding a pure relationship between bilingualism and cognitive flexibility. Using a within-bilingual sample, it is also possible to control for experimenter bias. Inasmuch as the subjects could come from the same schools, if the L1 and L2 abilities were kept blind to the experimenter, it would minimize bias effects.

In addition to the foregoing problems, there is the implied but untested statement about direction of causality. As Peal and Lambert (1962) put it: "one may ask whether the more intelligent children, as measured by nonverbal intelligence tests, are the ones who become bilingual, or whether bilingualism itself has a favorable effect on nonverbal intelligence [p. 13]." One handle on this problem would be through a longitudinal study in which both variables are measured repeatedly over time. We are aware of just one study (Barik & Swain, 1976) in which longitudinal data were available. Barik and Swain compared 32 low L2 achievers with 32 high achievers in a French immersion program in Ottawa over a 3-year period (Grades K–3). They report that the high achievers performed better on subtests of analogies and following verbal directions even when initial IQ scores at Time 1 were controlled.

The study we report in the remainder of the chapter addresses the foregoing concerns with previous studies of the relationship between bilingualism
and cognitive flexibility. We are interested in assessing the relative abilities in
both L1 and L2 of children in the process of becoming bilingual and in following them on a longitudinal basis to determine whether degree of bilingualism is related to cognitive flexibility and to assess the direction of causality
between linguistic and cognitive variables.

THE PRESENT LONGITUDINAL STUDY

The two-dimensional space created by relative abilities in L1 and L2 is pictured in Fig. 10.1 (a), marked by a line with a slope of 1 along which ideally
balanced bilinguals will cluster. This two-space is, of course, an ideal situation that is unmeasured, and we presently have no way of locating any given
sample of bilingual individuals in absolute terms. Thus, depending on sample
characteristics, the two-space defined by a set of L1 and L2 measures can
vary. Figure 10.1 (b) shows two hypothetical samples, A and B, where B represents a group of individuals that is more "balanced" than A. The point is
that although we cannot determine the two-space location of a group of bilinguals in any particular study using a particular measure, the effects of degree
of bilingualism can be studied by looking at the variation in the L2 measure
while controlling for variation in the L1 measure. As can be seen in Fig. 10.1
(c), individual A2 is more bilingual than individual A1, and B2 is more bilingual than B1. We hypothesize that the variation in L2 controlling for variation in L1 is attributable to the degree of bilingualism, and this variation
should be related in a positive way to cognitive ability.

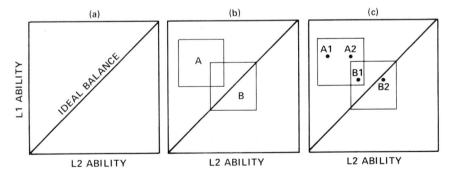

FIG. 10.1   Conceptualization of balanced bilingualism, how different bilingual samples
are embedded within it, and how individuals are embedded within samples. Panel a shows
ideal balance line between L1 and L2 abilities. Panel b shows placement of two different
samples (A and B) within idealized space. Panel c shows individuals within the sample
spaces.

Description of the Project

The subjects in our study are currently enrolled in classes from the Bilingual Education Program in the New Haven, Connecticut, public schools. Children who are enrolled in the program are dominant in Spanish. Placement in the bilingual program for the subjects is determined primarily on the basis of information provided by the parents and by the teachers of the classrooms to which they are initially assigned. Children who are reported as being exclusively Spanish-speaking or mainly Spanish-speaking are channeled into the bilingual classes, while those reported as predominantly or exclusively English-speaking are placed in monolingual, mainstream classrooms. Those children who reportedly use both languages are further assessed for dominance through the Language Assessment Battery, and Spanish-dominant children are placed in the bilingual classrooms.

The director of the bilingual program estimates that of the 165,000 residents in New Haven, there are 18,000 Hispanics, primarily Puerto Ricans. There are at present roughly 2700 Hispanic students in the school system between Grades K–12, of which roughly 45% are in bilingual classes.

All bilingual classes are conducted on a 50:50 ratio of Spanish and English as languages of instruction. Based on teacher recommendation, when the children approach equivalence between their English and Spanish ability, they are placed into the mainstream, English monolingual classes. Thus, like most bilingual education programs in the United States, the New Haven program is transitional in nature, as opposed to the maintenance or immersion programs found in Canada (see Swain, 1974).

Subjects

At Time 1 (the beginning of the Fall Semester), we began by screening all children in the kindergarten and first-grade classes in three schools in the New Haven public school system. We wanted to exclude from the study children who showed evidence of general language impairment. All 180 children were administered a Spanish adaptation of the Peabody Picture Vocabulary Test (SPVT), which is described in more detail later. On the basis of the distribution of the SPVT scores, subjects whose score was more than 1 standard deviation below the mean were eliminated. Our test-based evaluations were consistent with the reports of classroom teachers. In sum, out of the initial 180, we were left with 154 subjects, who were further tested with the remainder of the Time 1 measures.

By Time 2, approximately 6 months later, 30 of the 154 subjects had moved away from the school system, leaving us with 124 subjects. In addition (or, more accurately, in subtraction), a remaining subject at Time 2 was so exceedingly dominant in English at both times that she was eliminated from the study as being quite different from the rest of our sample. Thus, our final sample for the first year of the study consisted of 123 subjects, and we leave out of further discussion the remainder of the subjects.

The sample of 123 subjects contained 56 (45%) kindergartners and 67 (55%) first graders, with 55 (45%) girls and 68 (55%) boys. All of these children were of Puerto Rican descent. The mean age was 6 years 0 months, with a range from 4.1 to 8.3.

Aside from this general information, which was available for all subjects, we obtained more specific demographic information through a questionnaire sent to the parents. The questionnaires were distributed at Time 1, and of our sample, 88 (72%) responded, some after a second request. We have done some analyses to see whether the estimates obtained from the questionnaire responses would be reasonable estimates for the total sample. We compared all available variables in the study between responders and nonresponders and did not find any significant differences in the means. Thus, we assume the 88 responses to be a reasonably unbiased representation of the population sampled.

The questionnaire data indicate that 42% of the subjects were born in the United States, the remainder in Puerto Rico. The parents have lived in the continental United States for a mean of 2 years (SD = 6 years), ranging from 5 months to 26 years. They have lived at their reported address for an average of 2 years (SD = 1 year, 10 months), with the range extending from 1 month to 8 years. There is a mean of .91 rooms per occupant in the household (SD = .60). Of the heads of household, 37% are employed and 63% are unemployed.

Employment is directly related to the number of adults in the household. Of all questionnaire respondents, 55% were single-parent heads of household, and 32% had two adults in the household. Of the two-adult households, 64% (18/28) had the head employed, whereas only 14% (6/42) of single-adult household heads reportedly were employed. The significant association between number of adults and employment, $\chi^2(1)$ = 18.64, p = .001, is consonant with the understanding that single parents in general have low rates of employment, presumably due in part to the fact that a caretaker would be required at home. Only a small minority of the subjects are without siblings (7%). The median number of siblings is 2.

In the questionnaire, we also asked the parents to rate the extent to which Spanish and English are used between various individuals at home. We provided a 5-point scale, with 1 corresponding to "only Spanish," 3 to "both Spanish and English," and 5 to "only English." In all three possible discourse combinations (adult-child, child-sibling, adult-adult), the responses were heavily skewed toward Spanish (for adult-child, 1 = 42%, 2 = 23%, 3 = 33%, 4 = 2%, 5 = 0%; for child-sibling, 1 = 32%, 2 = 21%, 3 = 43%, 4 = 2%, 5 = 2%; for adult-adult, 1 = 50%, 2 = 32%, 3 = 17%,

$4 = 2\%$, $5 = 1\%$. These three ratings of the extent of use of Spanish and English at home are highly correlated, $r = +.52$ to $r = +.61$, and when combined, related negatively with the years of residence the United States mainland mentioned earlier, $r = +.34$. It appears that the longer the stay (and the earlier the year of arrival) in the United States, the more the dominant language permeates the home.

Measures

The ability in Spanish (L1) was assessed by administering an adaption of the Peabody Picture Vocabulary Test reported and distributed by Wiener, Simond, and Weiss (1978). Like the English version of the Peabody Picture Vocabulary Test (Dunn, 1965), the test is individually administered and consists of the child choosing a series of vocabulary items (ordered by increasing age-normed difficulty) out of four pictured alternatives. Wiener et al. standardized their Spanish version on Puerto Rican children in New York City. English (L2) ability was assessed through Form A of the vocabulary test. We refer to the Spanish test as SPVT and the English test as EPVT; when they are followed by a number (EPVT1, EPVT2, SPVT1, SPVT2), the number refers to the Time (1 = fall or 2 = spring) variable.

We should make it clear at this point that we did not intend to use these vocabulary tests as a measure of intelligence, as is commonly used (and misused) in monolingual populations. Rather, they were meant to be a measure of the relative abilities within each of the two languages for our bilingual sample. It should be noted here that the numerical raw scores for the two tests are not comparable. That is to say, a child who receives a score of 20 on both the EPVT and SPVT cannot be considered equivalent in his or her relative abilities in English and Spanish. On the other hand, the SPVT and EPVT have demonstrated the ability to rank children reliably along the respective Spanish and English language proficiency dimensions.

In order to validate the SPVT and EPVT as measures of language, a group of 40 children within our sample was given a story-retelling task in the two languages. Both the Spanish and English stories consisted of 14 sentences, paired with cartoon pictures. The experimenter first told the story while flipping through a picture book and, immediately upon completion, asked the child to tell the story cued by the pictures. The child's utterances were tape recorded and subsequently transcribed. The protocols were rated in a 5-point scale, with 1 being minimal use of the language and 5 being full fluency, by two independent raters. Only fluency was judged; accuracy of the retelling was ignored for this study. Interrater reliablities were .96 (Spearman-Brown) for English and .89 (Spearman-Brown) for Spanish. The mean ratings for both English and Spanish were significantly correlated with the EPVT1 and SPVT1 scores, $r = +.82$ for English rating with EPVT1, $r = +.36$ for

Spanish. The lower Spanish correlation most likely reflects the fact that the range of SPVT1 scores was more restricted than the EPVT1 scores for this particular subsample and also the possibility that the children are more Spanish-dominant and a simple story-retelling task may not reflect differences at higher levels of linguistic ability. We are currently pursuing further validation of the vocabularly measures, but for the moment believe that the tests do mirror quite accurately our subjects' variation in ability in both languages.

As a measure of nonverbal cognitive ability, we chose the Raven's Coloured Progressive Matrices Test (Raven, 1956; Raven et al., 1976), a measure on which the most robust differences were found between bilinguals and monolinguals in the Peal and Lambert study. Raw scores rather than percentiles were used because the test has not been standardized on populations comparable to ours. The Raven scores at Time 1 and Time 2 are hereafter referred to as Raven1 and Raven2.

In addition to these measures, we administered a test of metalinguistic ability (to judge the grammaticality of Spanish sentences and to detect English words embedded in Spanish sentences) and a measure of social perpective-taking (Chandler's "bystander cartoons"), but these data are still in the process of being analyzed and are not reported in this chapter.

Procedures

All measures were administered individually at the schools in empty rooms or quiet hallway corners by Spanish-English (balanced) bilingual experimenters. Except for presentation of the EPVT items, all testing was conducted in Spanish. Each measure was administered twice, once during the fall semester (Time 1) and again in the spring (Time 2). The average time lag between the two times was 6 months. Except for the constraint that SPVT1 was administered first at the very beginning of the study for initial screening, as mentioned earlier with reference to sample selection, order of tests was counterbalanced. At each time, each child was tested in three sessions, one with the SPVT, second with the EPVT, and third with the cognitive tests. In order that the experimenter remain blind to the child's ability in both languages, the same experimenter never tested any particular child in both EPVT and SPVT; hence, the subject's degree of bilingualism was not known to the experimenters until after completion of the data collection.

Results

There are two separate questions we ask of the data. First, is degree of bilingualism related to cognitive ability at any one time? This can be answered by looking within Time 1 and within Time 2 separately. Second, does degree of bilingualism at Time 1 predict cognitive ability at Time 2, or alternatively, does cognitive ability at Time 1 predict degree of bilingualism at Time 2?

Within-Time Analysis: Time 1.   The means and standard deviations for Time 1 and Time 2 measures can be found in Table 10.1. The first analysis divided subjects into groups on the bases of their abilities in each language. We grouped subjects into three levels of EPVT scores and three levels of SPVT scores, the crossing of which produces nine groups. EPVT1 raw scores ranged from 3 to 55, $M = 26.24$, $SD = 14.86$, and SPVT1 raw scores ranged from 21 to 81, $M = 44.32$, $SD = 13.26$. Upon inspection of the data, we felt that 20-point intervals for both EPVT and SPVT raw scores would represent reasonable layering of subjects with respect to their abilities, recognizing of course that the division is arbitrary and conducted solely for purposes of inspecting differences described in means. The following were divisions, imposed both on the Time 1 and Time 2 data: Spanish Layer 1: SPVT 1–40; Spanish Layer 2: SPVT 41–60; Spanish Layer 3: SPVT greater than 60; English Layer 1: EPVT 1–20; English Layer 2: EPVT 21–40; English Layer 3: EPVT greater than 40. Means and standard deviations for Raven1 scores for each of the nine groups composed of the crossing of the Spanish and English layers can be found in Table 10.2 (a). Inspection of the means suggests strongly that Raven1 means increase with increasing levels of English layering. However, this is confounded with the ages of the subjects in the groups, as can be observed in Table 10.2 (b).

The next step was to assess the strength of the relationship between degree of bilingualism and cognitive ability through partial correlation, where EPVT1 is correlated with Raven1, controlling for age and SPVT1. The partial correlation coefficient is $.267$ $p = .002$, indicating a significant relationship between degree of bilingualism and nonverbal cognitive ability.

TABLE 10.1
Means and Standard Deviations of Basic Measures
for the Bilingual Sample ($w = 123$)

Variable	Mean	SD
Time 1 Measures		
Age in months	71.89	10.15
EPVT1	26.24	14.86
SPVT1	44.33	13.26
Raven1	15.34	3.17
Time 2 Measures		
Age in months	77.89	10.15
EPVT2	33.99	16.94
SPVT2	52.69	13.56
Raven2	16.16	3.72

TABLE 10.2(a)
Raven1 Means for Bilingual Groups

		English		
		Layer 1 EPVT (1-20)	Layer 2 EPVT (21-40)	Layer 3 EPVT (>40)
Spanish	Layer 3 SPVT (>60)	$M = 11.0$ $SD = 0$ $n = 1$	$M = 13.5$ $SD = 2.1$ $n = 2$	$M = 18.3$ $SD = 5.7$ $n = 7$
	Layer 2 SPVT (41-60)	$M = 14.4$ $SD = 3.0$ $n = 15$	$M = 15.5$ $SD = 2.6$ $n = 38$	$M = 16.5$ $SD = 3.5$ $n = 14$
	Layer 1 SPVT (1-40)	$M = 14.3$ $SD = 2.5$ $n = 30$	$M = 16.4$ $SD = 3.2$ $n = 14$	$M = 13.5$ $SD = .8$ $n = 2$

TABLE 10.2(b)
Mean Age for Bilingual Groups at Time 1

		English		
		Layer 1 EPVT (1-20)	Layer 2 EPVT (21-40)	Layer 3 EPVT (>40)
Spanish	Layer 3 SPVT (>60)	$M = 74.0$ $SD = 0$ $n = 1$	$M = 82.0$ $SD = 8.485$ $n = 2$	$M = 79.0$ $SD = 5.8$ $n = 7$
	Layer 2 SPVT (41-60)	$M = 71.4$ $SD = 11.5$ $n = 15$	$M = 77.8$ $SD = 8.1$ $n = 38$	$M = 79.4$ $SD = 7.1$ $n = 14$
	Layer 1 SPVT (1-40)	$M = 61.9$ $SD = 3.4$ $n = 30$	$M = 66.4$ $SD = 7.3$ $n = 14$	$M = 63$ $SD = 7.071$ $n = 2$

From the parent questionnaires, we included two measures of the socio-economic levels of the subjects. One was simply whether the head of household was employed (coded 1) or unemployed (coded 0). The other was the number of rooms in their residence, divided by the number of occupants. Although the two measures were not related, $r = .09$, *ns,* both were correlated with EPVT1, for employment, $r = .20$, $p < .05$; for home space, $r = .18$, $p < .05$. When EPVT1 is correlated with Raven1 controlling for these socioeconomic variables in addition to age and SPVT1, the relationship is still significantly different from 0, partial correlation $= .201$, $p < .05$. Thus, even controlling for socioeconomic level, degree of bilingualism is related to nonverbal cognitive ability.

Within-Time Analysis: Time 2.   The overall means for the measures at Time 2 can be found in Table 10.1. The detailed means shown in Table 10.3 specify Raven's levels and age levels when the subjects were divided into groups by Spanish and English layerings using the same criteria as in Time 1.

The partial correlation of EPVT2 and Raven2, controlling for age and SPV2 is .357, $p < .001$. Controlling for the socioeconomic variables, the relationship does not change substantially, partial correlation = .281, $p = .008$. Thus, both Time 1 and Time 2 data indicate that degree of bilingualism is related to performance on the Raven's matrices.

Between-Time Analysis.   We established earlier that degree of bilingualism is positively related to Ravens at both times. However, which of these is

TABLE 10.3(a)
Raven2 Means for Bilingual Groups

		English	
	Layer 1 EPVT (1-20)	Layer 2 EPVT (21-40)	Layer 3 EPVT (>40)
Layer 3 SPVT (>60)	M = 14.8 SD = 2.8 n = 6	M = 17.0 SD = 3.4 n = 11	M = 18.8 SD = 4.1 n = 17
Layer 2 SPVT (41-60)	M = 14.2 SD = 1.6 n = 15	M = 15.1 SD = 3.0 n = 20	M = 17.7 SD = 4.1 n = 31
Layer 1 SPVT (>1-40)	M = 13.9 SD = 1.7 n = 10	M = 13.4 SD = 2.5 n = 10	M = 18.7 SD = 4.2 n = 3

(Spanish label on left margin)

TABLE 10.3(b)
Mean Age for Bilingual Groups at Time 2

		English	
	Layer 1 EPVT (1-20)	Layer 2 EPVT (21-40)	Layer 3 EPVT (>40)
Layer 3 SPVT (>60)	M = 74.0 SD = 11.1 n = 6	M = 85.5 SD = 8.1 n = 11	M = 88.2 SD = 6.3 n = 17
Layer 2 SPVT (41-60)	M = 71.7 SD = 10.1 n = 15	M = 77.8 SD = 9.4 n = 20	M = 79.9 SD = 8.1 n = 31
Layer 1 SPVT (>1-40)	M = 67.3 SD = 2.9 n = 10	M = 71.6 SD = 7.7 n = 10	M = 72.3 SD = 8.5 n = 3

TABLE 10.4
Zero-Order Correlation Matrix for Language and Ravens
at Both Times ($n = 123$)

N	Age	EPVT1	SPVT1	Raven1	EPVT2	SPVT2	Raven 2
Age	--	.476	.658	.166	.446	.522	.351
EPVT1	.476	--	.445	.318	.828	.333	.484
SPVT1	.658	.445	--	.165	.399	.687	.436
Raven1	.166	.318	.165	--	.315	.128	.486
EPVT2	.446	.828	.399	.315	--	.316	.466
SPVT2	.522	.333	.687	.128	.316	--	.331
Raven2	.351	.484	.436	.486	.466	.331	--

the causal factor? Specifically, we need to know whether Raven2 can be predicted by degree of bilingualism at Time 1 while controlling for the appropriate variables (including Raven1), or whether we can explain more variance by predicting degree of bilingualism at Time 2 by Raven1 while controlling for appropriate variables (including degree of bilingualism at Time 1). These alternatives are not mutually exclusive, of course, but statistical rejection of one model makes the alternative model more plausible. The zero-order correlation matrix of age, EPVT1, SPVT1, Raven1, EPTV2, SPVT2, and Raven2 can be found in Table 10.4. From the basic information described, we tested two alternative models using multiple regression.

The first analysis tested the null hypothesis that degree of bilingualism is not predicted by Ravens. In a stepwise multiple regression, EPVT2 was regressed on age, EPVT1, SPVT1, and SPVT2 in Step 1; then Raven1 was entered in Step 2. The important statistic here is the Beta for Raven1 for its F ratio. The results of the analysis show that Raven1 does not add significantly to the variance accounted for when controlling for age, EPVT1, SPVT1, and SPVT2, Beta $= .056$, F (1, 117) $= 1.077$, ns. The multiple R for the final equation was .832. Raven1 contributed only .3% additional variance toward predicting EPVT2. We conclude, then, that the null hypothesis cannot be rejected.

In the second analysis, we tested the null hypothesis that degree of bilingualism does not predict Raven scores. In this stepwise multiple regression, Raven2 was regressed on age, Raven1, SPVT1, and SPVT2 entered in Step 1; then EPVT1 entered in Step 2. The results show a significant Beta for EPVT1, Beta $= .252$, F (1, 117) $= 8.761$, $p < .01$. The multiple R for the final equation was .643. EPVT1 contributed 4.1% additional variance toward predicting Raven2, even when the other variables were entered first. Thus, we reject the null hypothesis in favor of the interpretation that degree of bilingualism affects nonverbal cognitive ability.

To control for socioeconomic level, we decided to test the results controlling for employment and home space for the 77 subjects for whom we had data available. Raven2 was regressed on age, Raven1, SPVT1, SPVT2, employment, and residence in Step 1; then EPVT1 in Step 2. EPVT1 still maintained a significant Beta, .251, $F(1, 69) = 3.89$, $p = .05$. Multiple R was .54, with EPVT adding 4% toward predicting variance in Raven2.

DISCUSSION

We began our study with a concern that studies reported in the literature did not unambiguously show that bilingualism fosters cognitive development. A first difficulty was that most studies involved group comparisons of bilinguals and monolinguals, and therefore, the results could be attributed to group differences other than language ability. Second, most studies involved cross-sectional comparisons where cause–effect relationships could not be appropriately evaluated. The study just reported makes more plausible the claim about the positive effects of bilingualism. First, we were able to show an effect *within* a sample of bilinguals. And second, when two alternative models for the direction of causality were tested on the longitudinal data, the model claiming degree of bilingualism to be the causal link was more consistent with our obtained data than the model claiming cognitive ability to be the causal variable. By the end of the full term of this longitudinal study, in which we will follow up the subjects for an additional 2 years, with the addition of other cognitive measures, we hope to make an even stronger claim regarding the positive effects of bilingualism on cognitive abilities.

The fact that our data support the claim that bilingualism fosters cognitive development is just a first step in understanding the issues at hand. The question remains as to *how* bilingualism affects cognitive ability, especially when cognitive ability is measured by performance in nonverbal tasks. A long time ago, Leopold (1949b) postulated that bilingual children were forced to higher levels of abstract thought by the early need to separate the word from its referent. In a similar vein, Cummins (1976) and Ben-Zeev (1977) have suggested that the cognitive advantages of bilingualism could be explained by bilinguals' need to objectify and manipulate linguistic structures. Ben-Zeev, for example, argues that in order to avoid linguistic interference bilingual children must develop a greater awareness and sensitivity to linguistic cues. Bilinguals' greater sensitivity to linguistic structure and detail is then transferred and generalized to different verbal and nonverbal tasks.

The process by which bilinguals' metalinguistic awareness affects performance in nonverbal tests such as the Ravens has never been adequately explained or understood. Bain and Yu's (1980) study suggests that bilinguals are better able to use language as a tool to monitor cognitive functioning, increasing their capacity to memorize information and control more effectively the different steps in solving a problem. Cognitive-developmental research shows an increasing use of verbal mediation in the performance of nonverbal tasks with increasing age (Conrad, 1971). Furthermore, Hunt's (1974) research suggests that performance on the Raven test would be improved by the use of linguistic, rather than spatial, strategies in the solution of the matrices. It is possible, as Diaz (1983) suggested, that childhood bilingualism fosters a rather precocious use of verbal mediation in the processing of information and this, in turn, explains bilinguals' improved performance on nonverbal tasks.

One of the main difficulties in answering such important questions lies in the fact that most studies in the area have relied on data from psychometric tests. To the best of our knowledge, there are no information-processing studies of young bilingual children, and it is not clear what cognitive processes or cognitive strategies, if any, truly differentiate bilingual from monolingual children. It is almost impossible, with our present knowledge, to develop a process model of how bilingualism affects children's cognitive abilities or accelerates cognitive development. The development (and empirical support) of a detailed model relating bilingualism and cognitive development is still a few years ahead.

Finally, theory developed at the individual level of the child must ultimately be related to the larger picture of bilingualism as it occurs in various forms around the world. An important distinction that must be included in any study of the effects of bilingualism is between additive versus subtractive bilingualism (Lambert, 1978; Lambert & Taylor, 1981), which is related to the distinction between elite versus folk bilingualism (Fishman, 1977; Paulston, 1975, 1980). In an additive situation, children learn their second language in addition to their first, thus creating balanced bilingualism. As Lambert and Taylor (1981) recently put it: "an additive form of bilingualism [implies] that these children, with no fear of ethnic/linguistic erosion, can add one or more foreign languages to their accumulating skills, and profit immensely from the experience, cognitively, socially, and even economically [p. 14]." In a subtractive situation, the second language gradually replaces the first. To quote Lambert and Taylor (1981) once again: "the hyphenated American child, like the French-Canadian child, embarks on a 'subtractive' bilingual route as soon as he/she enters a school where a high prestige, socially powerful, dominant language like English is introduced as the exclusive language of instruction [p. 14]."

As Cummins (1976) pointed out, studies that have shown positive effects of bilingualism invariably are conducted in situations of additive bilingualism. This observation led Cummins to hypothesize that there is a critical threshold level of L1 and L2 ability that must be attained before the positive effects of bilingualism can be observed. In our own study, the children in the sample at the time of observation were definitely in an additive bilingual situation; that is, they were progressing in both L1 and L2, rather than L2 gradually replacing L1. Unfortunately, the policy of limiting bilingual education in the United States to transitional programs translates into the fact that as children are mainstreamed into monolingual classes, the bilingual situation takes a turn toward a subtractive form. We believe that the study of bilinguals' cognitive development is not only a fascinating academic problem with serious theoretical implications, but also an important data base that should influence society's choices regarding the policy of educating children bilingually.

ACKNOWLEDGMENTS

We thank Aida Comulada, Director of the Bilingual Program, New Haven Public Schools, for her cooperation and warm support of the project. We also thank the teachers, children, and parents involved. The assistance of Alicia Fernandez and Juan Perez in data collection is gratefully acknowledged. The research reported here was supported by NSF Grant DAR-8010860 and NIE Grant G-81-0123 to Yale University. The final manuscript was completed while the first author was a Fellow at the Center for Advanced Study in Behavioral Sciences, Stanford, Calif. 94305.

REFERENCES

Arsenian, S. *Bilingualism and mental development.* New York: Columbia University Press, 1967.

Bain, B., & Yu, A. Cognitive consequences of raising children bilingually: "One parent, one language." *Canadian Journal of Psychology,* 1980, *34,* 304–313.

Balkan, L. *Les effets du bilinguisme francais-anglais sur les aptitudes intellectuelles.* Bruxelles: Aimav, 1970.

Barik, H. C., & Swain, M. A longitudinal study of bilingual and cognitive development. *International Journal of Psychology,* 1976, *11,* 251–263.

Barke, E. M., & Williams, D. E. P. A further study of the comparative intelligence of children in certain bilingual and monoglot schools in South Wales. *British Journal of Educational Psychology,* 1938, *8,* 63–77.

Ben-Zeev, S. The influence of bilingualism on cognitive strategy and cognitive development. *Child Development,* 1977, *48,* 1009–1018. (a)

Ben-Zeev, S. Mechanisms by which childhood bilingualism affects understanding of language and cognitive structures. In P. A. Hornby (Ed.), *Bilingualism: Psychological, social, and educational implications.* New York: Academic Press, 1977. (b)

Brunner, E. D. *Immigrant farmers and their children.* New York: Doubleday, Doran, 1929.

Carrow, S. M. A. Linguistic functioning of bilingual and monolingual children. *Journal of Speech and Hearing Disorders,* 1957, *22,* 371–380.

Conrad, R. The chronology of the development of covert speech in children. *Developmental Psychology,* 1971, *5,* 398–405.

Cummins, J. The influence of bilingualism on cognitive growth: A synthesis of research findings and explanatory hypotheses. *Working Papers on Bilingualism,* 1976, *9,* 1–43.

Cummins, J. Cognitive factors associated with the attainment of intermediate levels of bilingual skill. *Modern Language Journal,* 1977, *61,* 3–12.

Cummins, J. Metalinguistic development of children in bilingual education programs: Data from Irish & Canadian Ukranian-English programs. In M. Paradis (Ed.), *The Fourth Lacus Forum 1977*. Columbia, S.C.: Hornbeam Press, 1978.

Darcy, N. T. A review of the literature on the effects of bilingualism upon the measurement of intelligence. *Journal of Genetic Psychology*, 1953, *82*, 21-57.

Darcy, N. T. Bilingualism and the measurement of intelligence: Review of a decade of research. *Journal of Genetic Psychology*, 1963, *103*, 259-282.

Diaz, R. M. Thought and two languages: The impact of bilingualism on cognitive development. *Review of Research in Education*, 1983, *10*, 23-54.

Duncan, S. E., & DeAvila, E. A. Bilingualism and cognition: Some recent findings. *NABE Journal*, 1979, *4*, 15-50.

Dunn, L. *Peabody Picture Vocabulary Test*. Circle Pines, Minn.: American Guidance Service, 1965.

Epstein, I. *La pensee et la poligloise*. Lausanne: Libraire Payot, 1905.

Feldman, C., & Shen, M. Some language-related cognitive advantages of bilingual five-year-olds. *Journal of Genetic Psychology*, 1971, *118*, 235-244.

Fishman, J. A. The social science perspective. In *Bilingual education: Current perspectives* (Vol. 1). Arlington, Va: Center for Applied Linguistics, 1977.

Fukuda, T. A survey of the intelligence and environment of school children. *American Journal of Psychology*, 1925, *36*, 124-139.

Grabo, R. P. *A study of comparative vocabularies of junior high school pupils from English and Italian speaking homes* (Bulletin No. 13). Washington, D.C.: U.S. Office of Education, 1931.

Harris, C. W. An exploration of language skill patterns. *Journal of Educational Psychology*, 1948, *32*, 351-364.

Hunt, E. Quote the Raven? Never more. In L. W. Gregg (Ed.), *Knowledge and cognition*. Hillsdale, N.J.: Lawrence Erlbaum Associates, 1974.

Ianco-Worrall, A. D. Bilingualism and cognitive development. *Child Development*, 1972, *43*, 1390-1400.

Lambert, W. E. Some cognitive and sociocultural consequences of being bilingual. In J. E. Alatis (Ed.), *International dimensions of bilingual education*. Washington, D.C.: Georgetown University Press, 1978.

Lambert, W. E. & Taylor, D. M. *Language in the education of ethnic minority immigrants: Issues, problems and methods*. Paper presented at the conference on The Education of Ethnic Minority Immigrants, Miami, Fla., December 1981.

Lambert, W. E., & Tucker, G. R. *Bilingual education of children: The St. Lambert experiment*. Rowley, Mass.: Newbury House, 1972.

Lavoie, G., & Laurendeau, M. *Tests collectivs d'intelligence generale*. Montreal, Canada: Institut de Recherches Psychologigues, 1960.

Leopold, W. F. *Speech development of a bilingual child: A linguist's record* (4 vols.). Evanston, Ill.: Northwestern University Press, 1939, 1947, 1949a, 1949b.

Leopold, W. F. Patterning in children's language learning. In S. Saporta (Ed.), *Psycholinguistics*. New York: Holt, Rinehart & Winston, 1961.

Liedtke, W. W., & Nelson, L. D. Concept formation and bilingualism. *Alberta Journal of Educational Research*, 1968, *14*, 225-232.

Lindholm, K. Bilingual children: Some interpretations of cognitive and linguistic development. In K. E. Nelson (Ed.), *Children's language* (Vol. 2). New York: Gardner Press, 1980.

Luria, A. R. *The role of speech in the regulation of normal and abnormal behavior*. New York: Liveright, 1961.

Macnamara, J. *Bilingualism and primary education*. Edinburgh: Edinburgh University Press, 1966.

McCarthy, D. A. *The language development of the preschool child.* Minneapolis: Univ. of Minnesota Press, 1930.

Paulston, C. B. Ethnic relations and bilingual education: Accounting for contradictory data. In R. Troike & N. Modiano (Eds.), *Proceedings of the First Inter-American Conference on Bilingual Education.* Arlington, Virginia: Center for Applied Linguistics, 1975.

Paulston, C. B. *Bilingual education: Theories and issues.* Rowley, Mass.: Newbury House, 1980.

Peal, E., & Lambert, M. The relation of bilingualism to intelligence. *Psychological Monographs,* 1962, *76*(546), 1–23.

Raven, J. C. *Coloured Progressive Matrices: Sets A, Ab, B.* London: Lewis, 1956.

Raven, J. C., Court, J. H., & Raven, J. *Manual for Raven's Progressive Matrices and Vocabulary Scales.* London: Lewis, 1976.

Ronjat, J. *Le development du langage observe chez un enfant bilingue.* Paris: Champion, 1913.

Rosenthal, R. *Experimenter effects in behavioral research.* New York: Irvington, 1976.

Saer, D. J. The effects of bilingualism on intelligence. *British Journal of Psychology,* 1924, *14*, 25–38.

Sandoval, J. *Aspects of cognitive development in the bilingual: An exploratory study of the word-object separation.* Unpublished master's thesis, University of California, Los Angeles, 1976.

Swain, M. French immersion programs across Canada: Research findings. *Canadian Modern Language Review,* 1974, *31*, 117–129.

Thurstone, L. L., & Thurstone, T. G. *Primary mental abilities: Ages 7 to 11.* Chicago: Science Research Associates, 1954.

Tucker, G. R., & D'Anglejan, A. Some thoughts concerning bilingual education programs. *Modern Language Journal,* 1971, *55*, 491–493.

Vygotsky, L. S. [Multilingualism in children.] (M. Gulutsan & I. Arki, trans.). Center for East European and Soviet Studies, The University of Alberta, 1975. (Originally published in 1935.)

Vygotsky, L. S. *Thought and language.* Cambridge, Mass.: MIT Press, 1962.

Warren, R. M., & Warren, R. P. A comparison of speech perception in childhood, maturity, and old age by means of the verbal transformation effect. *Journal of Verbal Learning and Verbal Behavior,* 1966, *5*, 142–146.

Wiener, F. D., Simond, A. J., & Weiss, F. L. *Spanish picture vocabulary test.* New York: Marymount Manhattan College, 1978.

Yoshioka, J. G. A study of bilingualism. *Journal of Genetic Psychology,* 1929, *36*, 473–479.

11 Pragmatism and Dialectical Materialism in Language Development

Lois Hood Holzman
Empire State College
State University of New York

New York Institute for
Social Therapy and Research

The field of language development has undergone several major changes in the course of its brief existence as a discipline. Among these are changes in the focus of study (from syntax, to semantics, to pragmatics), changes in the methods employed and subjects of study (adult intuitions, experiments with children, observations of children, experiments and observations of children with their caregivers), and changes in the training and background of the researchers active in this work (from people who identify themselves as linguists and psychologists to people who identify themselves as linguists, psychologists, anthropologists, philosophers, sociologists, and others). Such changes have been well documented, along with some of the changes in the prevalent theoretical viewpoints on such issues as: Is there a biological basis for language? How much, if any, of language is innate? What is the relationship between language and cognition through development?

Many of these changes represent progressive development — a growing recognition of the complexity and interrelatedness of social and developmental factors that play a part in language and an emerging sense of the value of past and contemporary voices in other fields of inquiry and other countries. What I want to address in this paper is another development, which to my knowledge has not yet been discussed. It represents a new direction in language development, although the aforementioned changes are suggestive of the direction of movement. The change I am referring to is a fundamental philosophical and methodological one, a change in the conception of what language and its development are, and a change in what the very enterprise of studying language development is.

This philosophical and methodological change is of great practical concern. I believe that it is of importance not only to students of language and development, and not just as a theoretical issue, but that it has implications for the activities of the scientific community and for the relation between this community and the "rest of society." It concerns the very practical questions of what we, as students of communication and development, are doing. How are we, as a scientific community, advancing knowledge that is relevant to the particular history of our science and the particular problems and conditions of society more generally? Do the very ways in which we attempt to advance our knowledge actually impede the advancement of knowledge? These questions should be kept in mind throughout the paper and are directly returned to at the end.

Since the early 1970s, there has been a growing body of literature that approaches language development as a social process, that emphasizes the primacy of the child's interaction with others, and that refers to the "pragmatics of language" (how language is used) (e.g., Bates, 1976; Bruner, 1976; Dore, 1975, 1978). Much of this work utilizes the same methods and orienting framework as the structuralist approach, with its emphasis on syntax and semantics (e.g., Bloom, 1970; Brown, 1973), and represents a change in emphasis rather than a change in methodology. More recently, there has been an attempt to link this emphasis on language pragmatics with the philosophical tradition of pragmatism associated in the United States with John Dewey, G. H. Mead, and William James.

Only the briefest outline of pragmatism can be presented here, particularly as it relates to psychology and human behavior. In general, the pragmatists reacted against the strictly structural psychology that was developing in the early 1900s and attempted to develop a behavioral science that saw human beings as playing an active role in their development. For example, Mead called his approach "social behaviorism" and took an evolutionary and social perspective in contrast to the mechanical and individualistic conceptions of action and development that were prevalent at the time. For the pragmatists, interaction between people and "effective communication" were the prime determinants of socialization, self-reflexivity, and thought. Among the pragmatists, Mead is the one who has recently been rediscovered by developmental psychologists.

A similar rediscovery has occurred in relation to another important figure of the early 20th century, the Soviet psychologist L. S. Vygotsky. Like Mead, Vygotsky was concerned with the prevailing approaches of the new science of psychology. In the early 1920s, he characterized what he saw as a "crisis in psychology," in which the only alternatives open to psychologists were either behavioristic reductionism or idealism. According to Vygotsky, behavioristic reductionism refused to recognize consciousness as within the realm of psychological investigation, whereas the idealistic, subjective approaches believed consciousness could only be studied through nonobjective methods such as introspection. Refusing to choose between these untenable positions, Vygotsky insisted (Wertsch, 1981) that consciousness should be the focus of psychological investigation and, furthermore, that consciousness was "the objectively observable *organization* of behavior that is imposed on humans through participation in *socio-cultural practices.*" [201]. This premise of the social nature of consciousness stems from Marx, and indeed, Vygotsky and his followers have attempted to develop a science of human development and behavior based on the principles of dialectical materialism.

This rebirth of interest in Mead and Vygotsky is interesting for many reasons, including what it says about the perceived limitations of a strictly cognitive approach to language and the consequent opening up of Western psychology to other disciplines and perspectives. However, what I find fascinating and want to explore is the debt that developmentalists pay to Mead and Vygotsky in the same breath and the accompanying claims that their views are extremely similar, if not identical. A comparison of Mead and Vygotsky is made here briefly, with emphasis placed on the similarities and differences between the work of their acknowledged disciples.

In an article entitled "Social Dialectics and Language," Harris (1975) touches upon some of the issues that Mead and Vygotsky, in their time, were reacting to. In criticizing language development studies up to the mid-1970s, Harris (1975) draws this characterization: "One is often left with the impression that the child in the post-Chomskian universe lies in a world without human communication, an acolyte scientist, armed with epistemological intentions, seeking structure in language and in experience. Mother, when in the language setting, is reduced to the status of informant at the service of the child linguist [p. 82]."

How different the characterization in the *post*-post-Chomskian universe: It is almost as if the child lives in a world that exists solely of human communication, with mother having the awesome status of not only being the one to interpret her child's actions, but also of giving the action of intending *to* the child. Newson (1978) writes: "it is only because he is treated as a communicator that he learns the essential human art of communication [p. 42]." According to Lock (1978b): "Finally, the employment of these gestures leads the child to the possession of sufficient social knowledge and communicative expertise as to provide a basis for the symbolization and conceptual articulation of his experience — language proper [p. 12]." How far we have come — or have we? In what sense is this pragmatic, dynamic, social view of the becoming-verbal child an advance over the infant epistemologist? Does it have its roots equally in the works of Mead, a pragmatist, and Vygotsky, a dialectical materialist? This paper attempts to point the way toward answering these questions by discussing empirical studies that utilize Mead and Vygotsky and by outlining my own view of a dialectical perspective on language development.

The studies to be discussed come from two different traditions and two different countries. One focus is representative of the pragmatic approach, and it acknowledges its debt to Mead. The bulk of this work has been done in England and is represented in two recent collections of articles, Lock's *Action, Gesture and Symbol: The Emergence of Language* (1978a) and Richards' *The Integration of a Child into a Social World* (1974).[1] The second is representative of the dialectical approach, and it acknowledges its debt to Vygotsky and other Soviet psychologists (e.g., A. N. Leont'ev, Luria, Rubinstein). This group is less homogeneous in its focus on emerging language; thus far, Vygotsky has been more influential on workers interested in cognitive activity more generally, not primarily language or development (cf. Cole, Hood, & McDermott, 1978; Hood, McDermott, & Cole, 1980; Scribner & Cole, 1978; Wozniak, 1975). Representatives of language development research explicitly based on Vygotsky are Wertsch and his collaborators, and Zukow, Reilly, and Greenfield (1982).

Representatives of both groups often acknowledge their debt to either Mead or Vygotsky and then point to the similarity in thinking of one to the other. The clearest instance is in Wertsch's (in press) translator's notes to a chapter by Vygotsky:

> It is interesting to note that almost at the exact time that Vygotsky was developing this argument about the social foundation of the individual in the Soviet Union, a very similar argument was being developed in the West by George Herbert Mead. Although Mead wrote many articles during his lifetime, a comprehensive account of his approach only appeared in 1934—the year of Vygotsky's death. There is no evidence that Vygotsky ever read Mead's work, but it almost seems that the following passage from Mead's *Mind, Self and Society* could have been taken from Vygotsky's writings about the transition from the interpsychological plane of functioning:

> We must regard mind, then, as arising and developing within the social process, within the empirical matrix of social interactions. We must, that is, get an inner individual experience from the standpoint of social acts which include the experiences of separate individuals in a social context wherein those individuals interact. The processes of experience which the human brain makes possible are possible only for a group of interacting individuals: only for individual organisms which are members of a society; not for the individual organism in isolation from other individual organisms.

---

[1]The number of studies dealing with the pragmatics of language is steadily growing. Most of that literature is not discussed here, because the focus is on those studies that attempt to link their interest in pragmatics to pragmatism (and especially to Mead).

And from Clark (1978) whose article "could be thought of as an extension of, and a tribute to, the highly original thought of the pragmatist philosopher G. H. Mead (p. 231):" "This approach bears a close relation to Mead's (1934) pragmatic analysis of the nature of language and language derived abilities, and is also related to some extent to Vygotsky's (1966) writings [p. 234]."

The likening of Mead's and Vygotsky's views on language, on communication, and on self or consciousness is surely tempting. As the foregoing quotations show, there are parallels in some of their basic terminology and emphases. Both language and society are key concepts for them. Before examining what they and their disciples mean by the terms language, communication, and social, I briefly summarize the contemporary studies upon which this discussion is based.

VYGOTSKIAN APPLICATIONS

Vygotsky's work has been influential in an emerging line of research on "cognitive activity." The term "activity" is the focal point of Soviet psychology, and it is discussed further later in this chapter. For the moment, it is necessary to briefly describe its origins in Vygotsky's writings and illustrate its applications. Vygotsky's concern was that "higher mental functions" such as memory, perception, and attention be studied not as isolated psychological functions but in terms of how they are organized in concrete human activity, and further, how this organization changes as a function of social conditions and development. Vygotsky believed that both consciousness and self-regulation are dependent on "psychological tools," such as language. For the contemporary disciples of Vygotsky, cognitive activity is viewed as a social activity. Thus, instead of focusing on the very beginnings of language or communication, the role of language and/or social interaction in how children come to plan and monitor their activities in various everyday task settings is the central question. This work includes explorations of "metacognitive" skills in young children (Flavell, 1976; Kreutzer, Leonard, & Flavell, 1975), applications of this to performance deficits among those children labeled mentally retarded and learning disabled (especially the work of Brown and her associates), studies of the various ways adults "tutor" children and "scaffold" their learning (Wood, Bruner, & Ross, 1976), and recent Soviet work on joint cognitive activity of many different types including memory, problem solving, and concept formation (Kol'tsova, 1978; Lomov, 1978). These studies are fascinating but a bit peripheral to the topic at hand. For purposes of this discussion, the work of Wertsch has been singled out because it is more relevant to child language research and is most purposefully an attempt to develop a research tactic based on Vygotskian theory.

In a series of articles (Wertsch, 1979, 1980a, 1980b; Wertsch, Dowley, Budwig, & McLane, in press), Wertsch and his colleagues have explored the form and function of social interaction between mother and child as it relates to the child's developing cognitive processes. Their concern has been the nature of the communicative mechanisms that make joint cognitive activity possible. Perhaps the term "cognitive activity" is an unfortunate one because Wertsch, following Vygotsky, does not begin with the assumption that some of the things human beings do are social and others are cognitive. Rather, that dichotomy does not exist if one begins with the concept of human activity. This social/cognitive split is closely related to another dichotomy prevalent in psychology, the separation between intellect and affect. We seem to have made little progress since Vygotsky (1956) noted that:

> The separation of the intellectual side of our consciousness from its affective, volitional side is one of the fundamental defects of all traditional psychology. Because of it thinking is inevitably transformed into an autonomous flow of thoughts thinking themselves. It is separated from all the fullness of real life, from the living motives, interests, and attractions of the thinking human [p. 53].

It is interesting to note that, having made this criticism, Vygotsky neglected the "affective," as does Wertsch in his emphasis.

Wertsch takes both the problem he studied and the methodology he employed from Soviet psychology. The well-known (but no less profound) claim of Vygotsky's—that all higher psychological processes appear on the interpersonal level first and then on the intrapersonal level—is taken seriously by these researchers: They ask, how? What is the process by which the child comes to "internalize"? Also from Soviet psychology comes the procedure, the "microgenetic" approach. For Vygotsky, the way to discover what something is is to study its history. As Soviet psychology has developed, this has become the "genetic" approach, the study of process. One form of the genetic approach is the microgenetic one, where the transition from inter- to intrapersonal can be charted over the course of a relatively brief interaction.

In one study (Wertsch, 1979), the importance of Wittgenstein's notion of a "language-game" is posited as having important implications for understanding this transition. The specific language-game that is the subject of these studies is a puzzle-construction task situation that mothers and their 2½-, 3½-, or 4½-year-old children were to do together. They were given two identical puzzles, the model and an intact copy. They were told that the copy would be taken apart and their task was to make the copy look just like the model. Mothers were instructed simply to help their children whenever they thought it was necessary. All sessions were of individual mother-child pairs, and they were video taped, transcribed, and coded for various nonverbal behaviors as well as all verbal communication.

In successively finer analyses, Wertsch has discussed how the communicative situation becomes one in which the mother's utterances are used to regulate the child's performance in the task to the point where the child takes over much of the regulatory function and comes to share the mother's definition of situation and goal. For example, Wertsch (1979) identifies four levels in the transition from other- to self-regulation:

1. The child fails to interpret the adult's utterances in terms of the goal of putting the puzzle together.
2. The child understands that the adult's utterances are connected to the task in some way but does not have the same understanding of the task and communicative situation to make full use of these utterances.
3. The child has taken over some of the responsibility in the task (e.g., asks "Where does the black one go?") and can follow rather implicit directives that the adult uses (e.g., after the child asks, "Where does the black one go?" the mother says, "Where's the black one go on *this* one?").
4. The child is able to complete the puzzle without any assistance from the adult.

In the next study (Wertsch, 1980a), the specific semiotic mechanism of referential perspective was chosen for analysis, that is, the kinds of expressions used to point out objects (e.g., *the wheel, the blue one, this one*). Changes in the mother's use of these expressions were noted relative to the points in the transition from other- to self-regulation. Very often, mothers would start out using referential expressions that *assumed* a shared task understanding that did not exist (*the wheel*). Mothers would immediately switch to expressions that enabled the child to take part in the task (e.g., *this one,* accompanied by pointing).

In the latest analysis (1980b), Wertsch discusses how such referring expressions are related to the degree of "intersubjectivity" of the mother and child. Effective communication, he claims, comes about through partial, not complete, intersubjectivity; the tension of the incompleteness is a factor that leads to successful joint cognitive activity. The degree of intersubjectivity that is established, maintained, and re-established through referring expressions was found to be a key factor in the joint activity of the mothers and children.

Wertsch shows the importance of language as a vehicle for both increasing coherence between the mother's and the child's understanding of the task situation and for developing self-regulation. In addition, language is also seen as a result of such interaction; for example, in the fourth level of transition from other- to self-regulation, the child's utterances are similar to those that the mother had used previously. Wertsch (1979) states this clearly: "it becomes apparent that what the child has mastered as a result of functioning in other-regulation communicative contexts at the various levels is all the procedures in a language-game. That is, she/he has not simply mastered the ability to carry out one side of the communicative interaction by responding to the directives of others. She/he has taken over the rules and responsibilities of both participants in the language-game [p. 18]."

In a study of kindergarten children's narrative skills, McNamee (1979) followed a similar line of reasoning and analysis. She explored the hypothesis that children's understanding of a particular story, as well as their understanding of the particular task being used to tap their understanding of the story, emerges first in social interaction. McNamee observed kindergarten teachers and found that they used an informal and indirect method of guiding children through narrative and dramatic activities, a method similar to the mothers in Wertsch's studies. Through an analysis of transcribed interaction between a teacher and a 5-year-old-girl, McNamee traced the progression from other- to self-regulation, identifying patterns in the teacher's questioning strategy that fostered this transition.

THE COMMUNICATIONISTS

The second group of studies is concerned with the pragmatics of communication and especially with how language originates. The authors vary in the extent to which they themselves identify their position as pragmatic (or their debt to Mead), but that is one unifying characteristic of their work. They identify themselves as anti-cognitive, emphasizing the social nature of language over its logical nature, anti-innatist for the most part, and uniformly take communication as the essence of humankind. The meaning of this last statement and its consequences are discussed later; let us simply identify them as "communicationists" and proceed to a summary of their work.

Lock (1978b) begins his discussion by raising the possibility that recent experiments and observations of primates are heralding the beginnings of an evolution of primate language and culture. He is critical of the typical way this issue is ignored, namely, by identifying the crucial difference between human and primate language as being that we *gave* primates language (i.e., primates did not discover it themselves). Lock disagrees and claims that we have only provided them with the conditions that enable them to discover language for themselves. The same situation applies to human infants; they discover language through the conditions provided by their interactions in the social world. Lock (1978b) summarizes his argument as follows: "Children discover language through a process of guided reinvention [p. 4]." Using examples from video-taped interactions between three mothers and their 9–14-month-old children, Lock provides evidence for his argument through an analysis of how the child and mother accomplish "being picked up."

Lock's main point is that both mother and child create intentions in one another, for example, the child by anticipating the mother's actions and raising his arms when she enters the room, thus creating the intention and subsequent action of her picking him up, thus creating anticipation of her moves. Lock proceeds to show the development of such interactions. Soon the child is not simply anticipating being picked up, but actively pursuing that as a goal, as when 10-month-old Paul crawled to his mother, scratched her leg, and in response to her asking what he wanted, raised his arms.

The combinations of various actions, such as crying, arm raising, and pointing, are seen as the fundamentals of language; they are the transitions between affective and referential communication. Reference, gesture, and communication are intertwined. Lock (1978b) writes: "Through looking at the emergence of language in this way the evolutionary perspective is opened up. Gestures arise in the interactions between people, in the communicative acts they share. At the height of their development these gestures show all the rudiments of language and at least in some cases, patterned speech results from the internalization of the structure of these shared acts [p. 10]." Lock concludes by likening his position to those of Piaget, Mead, and Vygotsky. Unfortunately, he does not open *this* up. For example, Vygotsky (1956) also discussed the relationship between actions and gestures and, in fact, used the same kind of example whereby the infant's action comes to take on communicative meaning because of how it fits into the social interaction that is going on between adult and child. However, there is a major difference between his view and Lock's. Vygotsky differentiated between the transformation of actions on the social plane and on the individual plane. The specific point here is the difference between the transformation whereby the child's reaching becomes a gesture *in the social situation,* that is, it takes on communicative meaning by virtue of its occurrence and whether the reaching action has been transformed *for the child* into a gesture. This distinction appears to be blurred by Lock and the other communicationists as well, but within Vygotsky's framework the distinction is crucial.

Studies by Newson, Clark, and Travarthan and Hubley follow a similar line of argument. They analyze a particular type of interaction between mother and child to make the point that many of the infant's actions are effective only due to the monitoring and completion of them by another person. In his introduction to *Action, Gesture and Symbol,* Lock (1978b) states the logic of these studies in this way:

> . . . those actions come to be used by the infant in the knowledge that they are effective through the efforts of that other person: thus actions become transformed via interaction into gestures. Finally, the employment of these gestures leads the child to the possession of sufficient social knowledge and communicative expertise as to provide a basis for the symbolization and conceptual articu-

lation of his experience — language proper. Thus language is seen as very much predicated on gesture: reliant as much on social knowledge as on sensorimotor knowledge of the physical world [p. 12].

Clark's article (1978), "The Transition from Action to Gesture," also presents an alternative to cognitive theories of language. His starting proposition is that "communication is that which is involved in the co-ordination of the separate activities of two or more individuals into a single social activity [p. 233]." He analyzes "primitive communication structures" between mothers and infants under 1 year of age, structures that involve the giving and taking of objects. He concludes that the course of development of communication structure proceeds in this way: Action leads to gesture, which implies action; gesture leads to sounds, which imply both gesture and action. "Talking about" is verbally equivalent to "pointing to." The child progresses from communicating incidentally (before gesture) to communicating intentionally. According to Clark (1978), "language can be seen as a complication of the basic notion of communication; whatever it is that enables the activities of individuals to be coordinated with one another [p. 257]."

Newson (1978) calls for an intersubjective as opposed to the prevalent objective approach to explain the development of communication or of socially shared understandings. He believes we cannot describe the development of shared understandings with the terminology of the neutral, detached scientist; rather, we must adopt the point of view of the participant observer. In longitudinal studies of infants 4 to 11 months old and their mothers, he has observed patterns of "displays" that are conversation-like. This comes about in part because, in the mother's desire to establish shared understanding with her infant, she treats him or her as if the infant was like any other communicating person. Newson (1978) writes:

It is only because mothers impute meaning to 'behaviours' elicited from infants that these eventually do come to constitute meaningful actions so far as the child himself is concerned. Actions achieve this status to the extent that they are capable of being used as communication gestures which he knows how to produce, on cue, in the context of a social exchange between himself and someone else. In a real sense, therefore, gestures only acquire their significance insofar as they can be utilized as currency within social dialogues [p. 37].

Trevarthen and Hubley (1978) present data from one infant-mother pair to show that an important change occurs at around 9 months in the way the infant relates to persons. Previous to this, the infant's attention to objects and to people is separate. At this time, however, objects and people become joined, and a new type of social interaction, which the authors call "secondary intersubjectivity," is created. The major characteristic of this new intersubjectivity, according to Trevarthen and Hubley (1978), is that the infant "develops a will to share the foci of interest in situations and to define objects of use within acts of meaning [p. 226]."

Trevarthen and Hubley represent somewhat of a departure from the other communicationists in their view of how such communicative skills develop. Their explanation is innatist; they refer to a "need for sharing" that is intrinsic in human beings and to changes in the brain to explain the infant's changing behavior. Indeed, Trevarthen and Hubley (1978) believe that the mother plays a reactive role: "The intrinsic pattern of infant initiatives and responses is as much a creator of the mother's play, baby talk or instruction as any pattern of intention, inherent or acquired, in the mother [p. 226]." The mother is unconsciously tutored by the infant. Trevarthen and Hubley go even further and say that all cultural artifacts (e.g., language, games, toys) enhance the infant's growth because they meet the infant's "habits of intersubjectivity," habits which are due to changes triggered by maturation.

The Trevarthen and Hubley article is included as an instance of the communicationist view in spite of the authors' explicitly innatist interpretation. First, the data do not support such an explanation to the exclusion of a pragmatic interpretation. The authors may feel this at times, likening their work to that of Habermas and Vygotsky, but their interpretation certainly is at odds with those positions. Second, and more important, they are primarily concerned with the social and affective aspects of language, not the logical. Although the communicationist position developed in part as a critique and corrective of innatist and cognitive views, it is not inconsistent with innatism.

Indeed, it appears that there is an implicit premise of many of the pragmatic language studies that human beings are born with a shared understanding, a need for sharing, or a need to communicate. There seems to be an assumption that the human infant in some gross way divides the world up the way adults do, for if that was not the case, how could the socialization that begins at birth and continues through life ever get underway? The dialectical view is different. In studying development, the focus is not on what is innate or what must be present for socialization to proceed, but on how it does proceed. In a report on the impressive work that has been done in the Soviet Union with children who are born deaf and blind, Levitan (1979) discusses the philosophical and very practical questions that have been engaged by the people doing this work. Beginning with Meshcheryakov, who pioneered work with deaf-blind children, the approach has been to find ways to make such children human, not to "unlock" the humanity and spirituality lying dormant within them, as presented in "The Miracle Worker" story of Helen Keller. Meshcheryakov (in Levitan, 1979) states:

> Man is not born a human being: he becomes one. He has within him as much of the human being as he has assimilated of what is human, as much as he has seen, heard, and smelled around him, as much as things made by social labor have come into his hands and into his language [pp. 11–12].

And what of the children who have neither seen nor heard anything?

> A child deprived of any means of obtaining information about the external world — that is the raw stuff that has the possibility of becoming a human being. To what extent this process is successful depends on the joint activity of teacher and child. Together they must resolve an almost irresolvable problem, namely, to create a human personality [p. 14].

In other words, the concern is not with what makes humans human, but with the precise form of humanness possible for a given individual at a given historical point.

LANGUAGE AS SOCIAL/SOCIAL AS HISTORICAL

The work of the communicationists and the Vygotskians has certain characteristics in common. Both are concerned with how language functions in, and is a function of, social interaction. Both view the child as having an active role in her or his socialization and development. In this section, I point out more clearly the differences between these approaches and how these differences have their roots in Mead and Vygotsky. In the final section, suggestions for a new approach are presented.

As mentioned previously, a striking parallelism can be found in the writings of Mead and Vygotsky if one takes sentences in isolation. However, the crucial step in determining the similarity between them comes from a deeper analysis — an examination of what they each mean by social and what their overall goal in developing a science of mind was. The seemingly similar sentences take on different meaning in light of this.

For example, both Vygotsky and Mead make the point that social interaction is the basis of an individual's development ("psychological processes" for Vygotsky; "mind" for Mead). Yet, this has different meanings and implications for them. Mead's (1964) goal of developing a theory of social behaviorism stems from and influences his opinion of what is uniquely social about human beings:

> The peculiar character possessed by our human social environment belongs to it by virtue of the peculiar character of human social activity. That character is found in the process of communication, and more particularly in the triadic relation on which the existence of meaning is based. That is the relation of the gesture of one organism, in its indicative capacity as pointing to the completion or resultant of the act it initiates (the meaning of the gesture being thus the response of the second organism to it as such, or as a gesture) [pp. 209–210].

For Mead, the process of communication, of interpersonal interaction, is what social activity is all about.

Vygotsky's conception of social is different, emphasizing its historical and cultural nature, two characteristics that are lacking in the communicationists (who, following Mead, reduce social to interpersonal interaction). Just how far-reaching Vygotsky's conception is can be seen in a few quotations:

> The word "social" when applied to our subject [the genesis of higher mental functions] has great significance. Above all, in the widest sense of the word, it means that everything which is cultural is social [1960, p. 22].

> Verbal thought is not an innate, natural form of behavior but is determined by a historical-cultural process and has specific properties and laws that cannot be found in the natural forms of thought and speech. Once we acknowledge the historical character of verbal thought, *we must consider it subject to all the premises of historical materialism,* which are valid for any historical phenomenon in human society. It is only to be expected that on this level the development of behavior will be governed essentially by the general laws of the historical development of human society [1962, p. 51, italics added].

For Vygotsky, social does not mean interpersonal; social interaction is not what the child has to learn, nor is social interaction all there is in the world or all that is possible to know about. For Vygotsky, the activities of human beings, at all stages of development and organization, are social products and must be seen as historical developments, not merely as interpersonal developments. Social does not reduce to interpersonal; social activity is not merely social interaction. Leont'ev (1978) summarizes Vygotsky's position:

> The analysis of activity comprises the principle method of the scientific study of consciousness. In the study of the forms of *social* consciousness, it is the analysis of social life, the characteristic means of production, and the systems of social relationships. In the study of the *individual* psyche, it is the analysis of the activity of individuals in given social conditions and concrete circumstances that are the lot of them [p. 175].

What is clear from this quotation is the importance of consciousness in the study of human activity and development. Here, then, is another difference between Mead and Vygotsky. Mead believed that the way to study the mind is through the study of behavior, particularly through the study of behavioral acts. Consciousness could not be studied objectively, perhaps could not be studied at all, and certainly was not a necessary component of understanding the behavior of human beings. In summing up the importance of behavioristic psychology, Mead (1964) is very clear about the role of consciousness:

> That is what behavioristic psychology is trying to do, trying to avoid the ambiguity of the term "consciousness." And what is of importance about this psychology is that it carries us back, as I have said, to the act as such. It considers the organism as active. It is out of the interest of the act itself and the relationship of thought to the act itself that . . . pragmatism arises [p. 82].

For Mead, social interaction as the basis of individual development leads to the rejection of consciousness as a key to the development of self and to the primacy of the interaction of the moment, the "social act."

At the theoretical level, Vygotsky's ideas are compelling, challenging, and different from those of Mead. One can see the importance of history in his conception of the social as well as in his discussion of methods. However, it is unfortunate that Vygotsky is explicit about this on the theoretical level only. How in fact to study verbal thought or communication historically is unanswered; there is no clear description of methods given, nor does Vygotsky's experimental work unequivocally illustrate historical materialism. Perhaps it is simply that he did not live long enough to attain such a goal. Vygotsky (1978) viewed the creation of a truly historical science of psychology as a monumental task:

> I don't want to discover the nature of mind by patching together a lot of quotations. I want to find out how science has to be built, to approach the study of the mind having learned the whole of Marx's *method.* . . . In order to create such an enabling theory-method in the generally accepted scientific manner, it is necessary to discover the essence of the given area of phenomena, the laws according to which they change, their qualitative and quantitative characteristics, their causes. It is necessary to formulate the categories and concepts that are specifically relevant to them — in other words, to create one's own *Capital* [p. 8].

It is partially due to the scope and difficulty of the task that Vygotsky's followers in the West (and to a lesser extent, in the Soviet Union) have failed to develop a truly dialectical approach to psychology. Their fundamental paradigm is not a historical one, but a perceptual one based on observable interactions. Thus, Vygotsky and Mead are seen as saying the same thing at times, and research in the tradition of one seems consistent with the work in the other because on one level this is true. When Mead (1964) says: "Language does not simply symbolize a situation or object which is already there in advance; it makes possible the existence or the appearance of that situation or object, for it is a part of the mechanism whereby that situation or object is created [p. 165]," there is no argument with Vygotsky. On a perceptual level, dealing with what is there for the moment, this is a dynamic and reflexive statement about language. But it is not a dialectical one. The statement treats language as a particular, not as located historically and socioculturally. Vygotsky insisted on this, but gave few clues as to how to do it. Without guidelines from him (or from anyone else in Western social science), we fall back on seeing similarities and doing what we know how to do.

Wertsch goes further than most in attempting something more than a pragmatic analysis of mother-child interaction. He tries to trace the transition from inter- to intrapsychological functioning. He is concerned not only with how particular linguistic forms function *in communication,* but more important, with their role in the complexity of developments of which they are a part, including the increasing coherence between mother's and child's definition of task, the child's growing ability to self-regulate his or her behavior (including learning to act in a goal-directed manner and learning new particular skills), and the increasing symmetry of the mother-child relationship within this task setting, as the child becomes able to play a more active, and even leading role. In this, Wertsch is following in the footsteps of Vygotsky more so than in those of Mead. His concern is with more than the particular "social act," the moment-to-moment transitions in social interaction. His attempt to treat the "language-game" as neither cognitive nor social but as a complex human activity embedded in a particular social relationship is a beginning step toward understanding what language is. But ultimately, his work is still bound to the perceptual, to what can be observed, what is dynamically undergoing change. The cultural, historical conditions under which this mother-child interaction takes place are not addressed. The very categories used to perceive, to understand, and to explain (the categories of the participants as well as of the analyst) are also undergoing change, but are not themselves subject to inquiry.

A useful metaphor to explain the crucial difference between the pragmatists and the dialectical materialists comes from Vygotsky. In discussing methodology, he emphasizes the importance of the search for method in psychology. Vygotsky (1978) states that method is "simultaneously prerequisite and product, the tool and the result of study [p. 65]." The concept of tool was an important one for Vygotsky and for Soviet psychology in general. Psychological tools are elements of culture developed by human beings for the mastery of one's own mental processes. Vygotsky did not mean this merely as a useful analogy, but rather as a specific proposal for the scientific study of mind, that is, as a means of analysis for uncovering the sociohistorical determinism of psychological development. The sign is one of the most important psychological tools, for the sign system (speech) makes possible the transition from the interpsychological to the intrapsychological.

Vygotsky's colleague, A. R. Luria, extended the ideas Vygotsky had been developing concerning the influence of psychological tools on the development of the child to an investigation of a population of people undergoing radical social change. In the 1930s, Luria went to Central Asia to study the effects of socialist reconstruction on the illiterate peasants of Uzbekistan (Luria, 1976). He attempted an analysis of the sociohistorical shaping of mental processes. What changes in consciousness, in cognitive organization, accompanied the changes from peasant agriculture to collective farming? Luria (1976) wrote:

> The appearance of a new economic system brought with it new forms of social activity; the collective evaluation of work plans, the recognition and correction of shortcomings, and the allocation of economic functions. Naturally the

socioeconomic life of these regions underwent a complete transformation. The radical changes in social class structure were accompanied by new cultural shifts [p. 13].

Luria conducted extensive observations and "naturalistic" experiments to determine the effects of such changes on different population groups, men, women, the still illiterate, and the newly literate. His study is a classic in the cross-historical tradition and has been closely followed by Scribner and Cole (1979) in their study of literacy's effects on the Vai of Liberia.

Luria's approach begins with the view of psychological tools, language in particular, as a historically specific "tool and result" of human activity. The effect of language and other psychological tools on transforming both societal conditions and the consciousness of individuals was at the heart of his work.

In an examination of conceptions of meaning and explanation in capitalist society, Hood and Newman (1979) extended Vygotsky's concept of tool and result to language (in a formulation I am confident he would agree with): "Meaning for both Wittgenstein and Vygotsky must be understood therefore as not simply socially *based* or as reducible to social fact but as a social condition of society itself. It is perhaps *the* classical example of 'tool and result' [p. 78]."

How do others view language? Most of the authors discussed here recognize this dual role of language, even if they do not state it so clearly. However, what is the specific relationship between tool and result? The importance of the relationship posited is central to understanding the difference between the communicationists and the others. In keeping with Vygotsky's dialectical role of language, Wertsch (1980a) writes that "we need to develop an analysis of language which is concerned with its purposes — specifically, its role in structuring the cognitive and social reality of the group and in facilitating goal directed interaction [p. 5]." In other words, Wertsch views language as a vehicle for learning about the world, and one of the things to be learned about the world is language itself. Through social interaction, through the specific linguistic forms used by mother and child in the course of constructing a puzzle, the child simultaneously becomes integrated into the communicative setting and comes to understand the "strategic task setting." The dialectical role of speech is that it plays a part in defining the task setting; this activity redefines the situation, and in turn, speech is redefined. Language is viewed as both tool and result of interpersonal and intrapersonal psychological functioning.

The communicationists, on the other hand, generally equate the tool and result aspects of language, phrasing it in some cases as a tool, in other cases as result. For example, in his Foreword to Lock's book, Bruner (1978) states the position put forth by the authors: "Language is an instrument for fulfilling various communicative functions. And communicative functions themselves exist as constituents in still broader patterns of social interaction [p. vii]."

On the level of a theory of action, upon which the communicationist position is based, language can be seen as tool and result. It is both an instrument to fulfill communicative functions and "the power to create shared understandings with other people" (Newson, 1978, p. 31). These characteristics are united in the unit of action because language and our knowledge of it are seen as cognitive, perceptual, and ahistorical. This omits the historical processes by which language came to fulfill such functions for the individuals in question and society in general, the relationship between them, and the relationship of these processes to the "still broader patterns of social interaction." Such questions are not primary for the communicationists, nor for pragmatists in general. They take motion, or action, as primary—the ways in which people act to create shared meanings and communicate.

Within a theory of activity, however, as opposed to a theory of action, the tool and result metaphor takes on different meaning. The dialectical, historical view holds that tool and result are not identical, are not united. Rather, they are seen as simultaneous characteristics (in this case) of language that are historically intertwined and related in particular ways to human activity *of all kinds* (interpersonal communication and social organizations, e.g., classes of people in motion, families, political groupings, etc.). Communication is not just a social fact; it is not a given. Rather, it itself needs to be explained from the point of view of the totality of society and of one's life.

From Vygotsky and other Soviet psychologists have come the seeds of a radically different way of understanding human development. There has been a tendency to equate the Soviet concept of activity with the pragmatist's concept of action. This is another misreading, I believe, of the Soviet work, a misreading that is easily done and easily understandable for the reasons already discussed (pp. 358–359). One relevant question here is how to account for qualitative change. Qualitative change means something more than sudden or massive quantitative change. According to Vygotsky, at certain points in development (revolutionary periods) the very nature of development itself changes. For example, Vygotsky (1978) contrasts the differences in memory of older and younger children. The difference is not how much can be remembered or even kinds of information can be remembered; the change is a qualitative one:

> The memory of older children is not only different from the memory of younger children; it also plays a different role in the older child's cognitive activity . . . Our analysis suggests that thinking in the very young child is in many respects determined by his memory, and is certainly not the same thing as the thinking of the more mature child . . . *For the young child, to think means to recall; but for the adolescent, to recall means to think* [pp. 50–51].

This recognition of qualitative change has ramifications for the analyst, for to recognize qualitative change means we must also recognize that the principles that explained development up to this point no longer have explanatory value by themselves. We must develop a new set of principles.

Marxist science attempts to account for qualitative change and to develop new principles, but this is not what the pragmatic methods of the communicationists are about. Indeed, one of the primary goals is to substantiate their hypotheses concerning continuity between prelinguistic and linguistic behaviors. They do not choose to deal with qualitative change, as they do not deal with history. (Recall Trevarthen & Hubley's findings of qualitative change in the infant's behavior at 9 months — "secondary intersubjectivity." Their way of dealing with this change was to reduce it to brain maturation and an innate "need for sharing." Such a reductionist explanation of qualitative changes in development is a common response; the other is ignoring it or doing away with it through a theory of continuity, or quantitive change). This difference between a dynamic and a dialectical view of development can also be seen in how the communicationists deal with the "transition" from prelinguistic to linguistic behaviors. For them, the change is evolutionary; gestures show all the rudiments of language (Lock), and talking is nothing more than verbal pointing (Clark). There is no mention of the transformation of consciousness, of the organization of behavior that occurs through participation in socio-cultural practice to which Vygotsky repeatedly referred.

Vygotsky's (1962) comment from about 50 years ago (– 1936) seems particularly apt:

> Child psychology does not want to know about the sudden, violent and revolutionary changes which appear throughout the course of child development and are so often met in the history of cultural development. To the naive observer, revolution and evolution do not appear to coincide. For him historical development continues only by proceeding along a straight path. When a revolution, the rupture of the historical fabric, or a leap occurs the naive observer sees nothing but catastrophe, gaps, and precipices. For him, historical progression stops at this point until it alights anew on a straight and smooth path.

> The scientific observer, on the other hand, considers revolution and evolution as two mutually connected forms of development which assume each other. The scientific observer sees the sharp changes in the child's development which occur simultaneously with other, similar changes as the determining point in the whole line of development [pp. 5-6].

HISTORY AS SOCIAL

What would a historical approach to language development be? Unfortunately, we do not know the answer, but for good reason. This question has underlying it other questions: What is history? How does one "do history"? The three questions are intertwined, and we need to develop ways of understanding and methods of analysis that are the "tool and result" of these questions. I can only hint at some of the characteristics a historical, dialectical approach would have. The starting point is to heed Vygotsky's advice on how to "discover the nature of mind [p. 8]." By creating one's own *Capital,* I take Vygotsky to mean using the method exemplified in *Capital.* This method, as first articulated by Marx in his 1844 writings (in particular in "Estranged Labor"), puts forth the notion that understanding is the dialectical relationship between: (1) the explanation of the phenomena under study, that is, the process of comprehension employing the categories of the existing society; and (2) the explication of the meanings of these categories, that is, the process of comprehending the categories of existing society in terms of the sociohistorical forces of which they are a reflection. For example, in a discussion of the development of the language of causality, Hood, Fiess, and Aron (1982) hypothesize about the kinds of things children learn through exchanges with adults:

> . . . one of the things being taught is a particular way of making sense of the world, one that, of course, conforms to the norms, customs, and ideology of our society. It is important to delineate substantively what these norms are. But that is not all. In our view, the important fact to be recognized is not that language activities such as these teach particular norms, but that they teach that there are such things as norms. The very way we use language treats the contents of it as somehow separate, independent, and pre-existent. So, children learn through discourse about causality that there are *things* to be explained, as if such things existed independently of their being explained.

This, in part, is what is meant by a dialectical, historical approach to the study of communication and language. And it is this method that is so difficult to employ, antithetical as it is to the tradition of Western science and philosophy. As applied to language development research, we can make a number of suggestions following from this. First of all, unlike the communicationist, the cognitive, and the behaviorist approaches, a dialectical approach does not presuppose that language is neutral. Rather, language and, more generally, ways of communicating must be seen as the products of sociohistorical conditions. What needs to be explained are not just the social contexts causing mother and child to relate in a particular way, but the history of these events shared by mother and child, the history of the language used in creating these shared events, and the relationship between them.

Thus, extending Vygotsky, we view language not as a window to cognition, as a reflection of reality, nor as a means of communication. Rather, language is a uniquely historical activity; by virtue of the many language activities we engage in, human beings are historical beings. What do we mean by "historical beings"? We are historical in that we have the capacity for self-consciously asking how we know what we know, understand what we understand, and mean what we mean. Vygotsky's claim that higher psychological processes are internalized social functions does not merely reverse the order of the traditional Western explanation of development. It leads to a qualitatively different methodology. For, if one begins with the premise that development proceeds from the individual and the inner to the social and the outer, one never has to engage the question of self-consciousness. Understanding is little more than a sharing of like minds. Becoming social means being able to communicate, learning the conventions and norms of one's society, which, it is presumed, exist independently of the activity of their being communicated. It avoids the fact that one of the things we learn when we are learning norms and conventions is that there *are* norms and conventions, that in communicating we are learning that we are communicators, and that in explaining we are learning how we learn to explain. When children learn language they are learning about themselves as historical beings in the sense that they become aware of what it means to be a speaker (a producer of speech). In studying how language develops, then, we are not asking how children acquire a mental capacity or develop communicative competence, but how children become self-conscious, historical beings.

In part, doing history is identifying contradictions. Many approaches to communication identify contradictions of one sort or another. For example, the pragmatist-therapists have advanced the discipline of psychotherapy by identifying contradictions in communnication and developing the concept of the paradox in psychology (e.g., Bateson, 1972; Watzlawick, Beavin, & Jackson, 1967). For a historical dialectical science, however, contradictions "in the world," not only in the language or in communicative interactions, need to be identified. A primary contradiction in the world that we need to recognize is the contradiction between what there is to be understood and our capacity to understand it at any given moment. The communicationists conflate the two, substituting a single unit (i.e., action) for the dichotomy implicit in this conflation. For them, communication, or social interaction, has become an ontological unit; it is the "stuff" of which the world is made.

I believe this change to be of great significance. The pragmatism of Mead and others was an epistemology, a way of understanding the world. It has been changed by many in the social sciences, the communicationists among them, to an ontology, to a statement of what there is in the world to be understood. And, the infant epistemologist of Chomsky's universe is now for them the infant ontologist.

This is a large change, but we are not very much closer to having an understanding of the emergence of communication and the development of language, of their relationship to the social world we live in, nor of how to bring about necessary changes to insure better conditions of child development. Although the studies discussed here make fascinating reading — their data are seductive and their discussions provocative — there is nowhere to go with them except to do more of the same. One is left wondering where it will lead.

What the communicationists have done, in essence, is incorporate a perceptual model as a tool to understand social facts and translate this perceptual model into a social theory. They have indeed succeeded in formulating another way of looking at things; they have given us an alternative to the cognitive view of the emergence of communication and language. The problem with this approach is not with the particulars of this "other" view, but with the enterprise itself. Is that what social scientists should be doing at this time in our history? More and more frequently, we are faced with the failure of new theories and "ways of seeing" to explain and to alter present problems and contradictions of human society — questions of development, learning, mental illness, violence, alienation, to name a few. Although theirs is a science about activity and is clearly an advance over a science about passivity (e.g., innatist, behaviorist, and information-processing theories), it is not a science *that is itself* activity. Devising other "ways of seeing" ultimately leaves the question of what is to be done to policy makers, asserting (even if by omission) that science is neutral. Leaving questions of morals aside, it is becoming increasingly clear that scientific neutrality is an impediment to good science except under the most stable of social periods. The critical problems facing contemporary society attests to the frightening instability of our times and the necessity for a science that in its very activity incorporates social change. We very much need to create own *Capital*.

ACKNOWLEDGMENTS

I wish to express thanks to Fred Newman and Janet Wootten for their invaluable criticism and support during the formulation of the ideas and writing of this paper. In addition, I have benefited greatly from suggestions on a first draft by Lois Bloom, John Dore, John Gliedman, Ray McDermott, Peggy Miller, Lorraine Rocissano, Bambi Schieffelin, and Jim Wertsch. The ideas presented here have been further developed in a recent article (Holzman & Newman, in press).

REFERENCES

Bates, E. *Language and context: The acquisition of pragmatics.* New York: Academic Press, 1976.

Bateson, G. *Steps to an ecology of mind.* New York: Ballatine, 1972.

Bloom, L. *Language development: Form and function in emerging grammars.* Cambridge, Mass.: MIT Press, 1970.

Brown, R. *A first language, the early stages.* Cambridge, Mass.: Harvard University Press, 1973.

Bruner, J. The ontogenesis of speech acts. *Journal of Child Language,* 1976, *2,* 1–19.

Bruner, J. Foreword. In A. Lock (Ed.), *Action, gesture and symbol: The emergence of language.* London: Academic Press, 1978.

Clark, R. A. The transition from action to gesture. In A. Lock (Ed.), *Action, gesture and symbol: The emergence of language.* London: Academic Press, 1978.

Cole, M., Hood, L., & McDermott, R. P. *Ecological niche-picking: Ecological invalidity as an axiom of experimental cognitive psychology* (Rockefeller University Working Paper #4). 1978.

Dore, J. Holophrases, speech acts, and language universals. *Journal of Child Language,* 1975, *2,* 21–40.

Dore, J. Variation in preschool children's conversational performances. In K. E. Nelson (Ed.), *Children's language* (Vol. 1). New York: Gardner Press, 1978.

Flavell, J. H. Metacognitive aspects of problem solving. In L. B. Resnick (Ed.), *The nature of intelligence.* Hillsdale, N.J.: Lawrence Erlbaum Associates, 1976.

Harris, A. Social dialectics and language: Mother and child construct the discourse. *Human Development,* 1975, *18,* 80–96.

Hood, L., Fiess, K., & Aron, J. Growing up explained: Vygotskians look at the language of causality. In C. Brainerd & M. Pressley (Eds.), *Verbal processes in children.* New York: Springer-Verlag, 1982.

Hood, L., McDermott, R. P., & Cole, M. "Let's try to make it a nice day" — Some not so simple ways. *Discourse Processes,* 1980, *3,* 155–168.

Hood, L. & Newman, F. (Eds.). *The practice of method: An introduction to the foundations of social therapy.* New York: The New York Institute for Social Therapy and Research, 1979.

Holzman, L., & Newman, F. Language and thought about history. To appear in M. Hickmann (Ed.), *Social and functional approaches to language and thought.* New York: Academic Press, in press.

Kol'tsova, V. A. Experimental study of cognitive activity in communication (with specific reference to concept formation). *Soviet Psychology,* 1978, *17,* 23–38.

Kreutzer, M. A., Leonard, C., & Flavell, J. H. An interview study of children's knowledge about memory. *Monographs of the Society for Research in Child Development,* 1975, *159.*

Leont'ev, A. N. *Activity, consciousness and personality.* Englewood Cliffs, N.J.: Prentice-Hall, 1978.

Levitan, K. The best path to man. A report from a children's home. *Soviet Psychology,* 1979, *18,* 3–66.

Lock, A. (Ed.). *Action, gesture and symbol: The emergence of language.* London: Academic Press, 1978. (a)

Lock, A. The emergence of language. In A. Lock (Ed.), *Action, gesture and symbol: The emergence of language.* London: Academic Press, 1978. (b)

Lomov, B. F. Psychological processes and communication. *Soviet Psychology,* 1978, *17,* 3–22.

Luria, A. R. *Cognitive development: Its cultural and social foundations.* Cambridge, Mass.: Harvard University Press, 1976.

McNamee, G. D. The social interaction origins of narrative skills. *Quarterly Newsletter of the Laboratory of Comparative Human Cognition,* 1979, *1,* 63–68.

Mead, G. H. *Mind, self and society.* Chicago: University of Chicago Press, 1934.

Mead, G. H. *G. H. Mead on social psychology* (A. Strauss, Ed.). Chicago: University of Chicago Press, 1964.

Newson, J. Dialogue and development. In A. Lock (Ed.), *Action, gesture and symbol: The emergence of language.* London: Academic Press, 1978.

Richards, M. P. M. *The integration of a child into a social world.* Cambridge: Cambridge University Press, 1974.

Scribner, S., & Cole, M. Literacy without schooling: Testing for intellectual effects. *Harvard Educational Review,* 1978, *48,* 448–461.

Trevarthen, C., & Hubley, P. Secondary intersubjectivity: Confidence, confiding and acts of meaning in the first year. In A. Lock (Ed.), *Action, gesture and symbol: The emergence of language.* London: Academic Press, 1978.

Vygotsky, L. S. *Izbrannye psikhologicheskie issledovaniya.* [Selected psychological investigations]. Moscow: Nauka, 1956.

Vygotsky, L. S. *Thought and language.* Cambridge, Mass.: MIT Press, 1962.

Vygotsky, L. S. Development of the higher mental functions. In *Psychological Research on the USSR,* Moscow: Progress Publishers, 1966.

Vygotsky, L. S. *Mind in society.* Cambridge, Mass.: Harvard University Press, 1978.

Vygotsky, L. S. The genesis of higher mental functions. In J. Wertsch (Ed.), *The concept of activity in Soviet psychology.* New York: Sharpe, 1981. (Originally published in Russian, 1960.)

Watzlawick, P., Beavin, J., & Jackson, D. *Pragmatics of human communication: A study of interactional patterns, pathologies, and paradoxes.* New York: Norton, 1967.

Wertsch, J. V. From social interaction to higher psychological process: A clarification and application of Vygotsky's theory. *Human Development,* 1979, *22,* 1–22.

Wertsch, J. V. Adult-child interaction as a source of self-regulation in children. In S. R. Yussen (Ed.), *The development of reflection.* New York: Academic Press, 1980. (a)

Wertsch, J. V. *Semiotic mechanisms in joining cognitive activity.* Paper presented at the US-USSR Conference on the Theory of Activity. Institute of Psychology, USSR Academic of Sciences, Moscow, March 1980. (b)

Wertsch, J. (Ed.). *The concept of activity in Soviet psychology.* New York: Sharpe, 1981.

Wertsch, J. V., Dowley, G., Budwig, N., & McLane, J. The adult-child dyad as a problem solving system. *Child Development,* in press.

Wood, D., Bruner, J. S., & Ross, G. The role of tutoring in problem solving. *Journal of Child Psychology and Psychiatry,* 1976, *17,* 89–100.

Wozniak, R. H. Dialecticism and structuralism: The philsophical foundation of Soviet psychology and Piagetian cognitive developmental theory. In K. Riegel & G. Rosenwald (Eds.), *Structure and transformation: Developmental and historical aspects* (Vol. 3). New York: Wiley, 1975.

Zukow, P. G., & Reilly, J., & Greenfield, P. M. Making the absent present: Facilitating the transition from sensorimotor to linguistic communication. In K. E. Nelson (Ed.), *Children's language,* (Vol. 3). Hillsdale, N.J.: Lawrence Erlbaum Associates, 1982.

12

Beyond Communicative Adequacy: From Piecemeal Knowledge to an Integrated System in the Child's Acquisition of Language

Melissa Bowerman
Max-Planck Institute for Psycholinguistics
Berg en Dalseweg 79
Nijmegen, The Netherlands

When I began observing and recording the language development of my two daughters in the early 1970s, many of the major landmarks in the acquisition of English were well known: the stage of one-word utterances, the onset of short telegraphic sentences, overextensions of words to inappropriate referents, inflectional overregularizations, and so on. My purpose in collecting data was therefore not so much exploratory as to establish a rich, fine-grained data base for investigating known problems such as the scope and nature of the categories underlying early word combinations. As the children passed the initial stages of vocabulary acquisition and syntactic development, however, I began to notice phenomena I had not been looking for: the onset, at periodic intervals in the age range of about 2 to 5 years, of various kinds of errors in word choice and/or syntactic structure. This took place long after my earlier observations had led me to assume that the forms in question had already been mastered. Some types of errors occurred relatively frequently, others relatively infrequently. Whether frequent or infrequent, however, they were recurrent and systematic. Moreover, as I realized when I began listening with a freshly sensitized ear, the errors were not unique to my home-grown subjects but in fact turn up repeatedly in the speech of other English-speaking children of comparable ages.

At first I thought of these errors as intriguing but isolated oddities in the development of English. The more I have puzzled about them, however, the more I have become convinced that their modest initial appearance is deceptive. To account for them adequately in fact requires positing acquisitional processes of considerable theoretical significance. My goal in this chapter is to outline some of these processes and discuss their implications.

The chapter is organized as follows. The first section considers very briefly the kinds of processes that can be inferred to underlie errors that do not set in until after a period of correct usage (hereafter "late" errors). It is argued that the existence of such errors necessitates a careful examination of the question of what it means to "acquire" a piece of linguistic information. In particular, acquisition often seems to be a more extended process than we have envisioned. It may continue long after fully adequate communication has been achieved with respect to a given form, and it sometimes involves covert shifts in the way children have organized linguistic information and related it to other parts of their developing grammar.

The ongoing organization and reorganization of linguistic knowledge is a fascinating phenomenon in its own right (see Bowerman, 1982b). It takes on added significance, however, when we consider its implications for two complex, interrelated issues of the greatest current theoretical importance: the roles played in language acquisition by *meaning* and the child's *intention to communicate*. I therefore defer the discussion of some particular error types until after the second and third sections, in which I summarize a currently influential model of how linguistic forms, meaning, and communication are interrelated in the acquisition of language, point out some challenging problems for this model, and suggest that the notion of "meaning" in language must be reconceptualized before we can hope to solve these problems. In the fourth section, evidence from several types of late errors is marshalled in support of these arguments. A brief concluding section follows.

WHAT CAUSES LATE ERRORS?

Little explicit attention has been paid in the child language literature to the general phenomenon of errors that set in only after a period of correct usage. Nevertheless, every student of language development is well acquainted with one such sequence, the onset of inflectional overregulations (e.g., *goed, foots*) only after the child has been using the correct irregular forms (*went, feet*) for a while (Cazden, 1968; Ervin, 1964). The accepted interpretation of this sequence is that children start out by learning lexical items, both inflected and uninflected, regular and irregular, as independent items. Cazden (1968) refers to these as "stored fragments . . . which are somehow tagged liberally for semantic information on the verbal and nonverbal context [p. 437]." Later children begin to compare forms and to discover regular relationships — statable as rules — holding among subsets of them.[1] At this point they begin to apply the rules too broadly, and irregular forms are regularized. When the irregular forms later reassert themselves, these forms presumably no longer function as isolates, but rather take their place in the system as exceptional counterparts to their noninflected partners.

This account of the acquisition of inflected forms contains an important insight, namely, that what appears to be "the same" linguistic behavior at two stages of the child's development may in fact be supported by very different kinds of linguistic knowledge: piecemeal fragments of information about particular forms and how to use them at an earlier time, and a system that interrelates and integrates these fragments later on. Because of this ambiguity of surface behaviors (which, it should be noted, is also found in children's approaches to nonlinguistic cognitive tasks; cf. Karmiloff-Smith & Inhelder, 1974/75; Strauss, 1982), researchers have wisely tended to exercise caution in crediting children with full adult knowledge of the forms they produce. Usually, however, if a child is found to be producing a word, inflection, or pattern for sentence construction with semantic accuracy and at least moderate frequency and reasonable flexibility with respect to nonlinguistic and/or surrounding linguistic context, we have been willing to conclude that the form has been "acquired," and we do not look for further development. After all, if the child's use of the form is virtually indistinguishable from that of the adult, what remains to be done?

Indeed, in some linguistic domains, perhaps nothing. But in other domains, children apparently do not stop at the point where outwardly adultlike behavior has been achieved. Rather, they go on analyzing the elements of their existing repertoires and discovering further relationships and regularities. The result is the gradual transformation of a loose collection of independent linguistic elements, routines, and relatively small sets of interrelated items into a tighter, more structured system that integrates more items and sets of items on the basis of increasingly abstract, overarching rules and relationships. This process is largely covert; the child continues for the most part to speak as before. But, just as in the familiar domain of inflectional morphology, the evidence that it is taking place lies in the occasional error.

What kinds of reorganizational processes do late errors signal? What are the bases for systematization? Most of the errors I have studied seem to reflect changes in the connections the child has previously established between linguistic forms and categories of meaning. This is what makes late errors so

---

[1]Terms like "compare," "discover," "recognize," "perceive," and "grasp" imply conscious awareness. However, for lack of better terms, they are used in this paper to designate cognitive processes assumed to be wholly unconscious.

relevant to the problem of how meaning and form are interrelated in the acquisition of language, an issue to which we now turn before going on to discuss the implications of some specific error types.

THE PRIMACY OF MEANING IN CURRENT THINKING ABOUT LANGUAGE DEVELOPMENT

In the following discussion, the terms "form" and "meaning" should be construed broadly. Form includes not only surface segments of the language such as words, inflections, and derivational morphemes, but also more abstract constructs such as part-of-speech categories, contrastive patterns of word order or intonation, grammatical functions like subject and direct object, and so on. Meaning should be taken to include not only those notions traditionally considered "semantic" (or "ideational" or "propositional"), but also at least some "pragmatic" notions such as "topic" (the focus here is on the former, however).[2]

In an earlier era, no causal or facilitative role was ascribed to meaning in the acquisition of linguistic forms. The meanings encoded by or correlated with the distribution of particular forms were either largely ignored in studies of language development (especially in the case of syntax) or considered to emerge in the child as a direct consequence of the learning of language. A striking shift has taken place over the last decade, however. Meaning, far from being considered irrelevant to or determined by language acquisition, is now commonly seen as the key to the whole process.[3]

According to this more recent view, children possess powerful cognitive skills that enable them to structure and interpret their experiences on a nonlinguistic basis, that is, to develop notions of agency, spatial location, causality, possession, and so on. When language starts to come in, it does not introduce new meanings to the child. Rather, it is used to express only those meanings the child has already formulated independently of language.

---

[2]Many investigators have used the term "function" for the joint set of semantic and pragmatic concepts I am calling "meaning." I avoid the term "function" in this chapter because it seems subtly biased toward a view against which I wish to raise objections: that the semantic and pragmatic distinctions that figure in a language (e.g., that covary with or have consequences of various sorts for the selection and combination of linguistic forms) have a very direct relationship with the realization of speakers' communicative goals.

[3]The sketch given here of a currently prevalent way of viewing language acquisition is perhaps not embraced without qualification by any one investigator. The approach, as a sort of general Zeitgeist of the field, has been building up gradually and developing more coherence on the basis of converging arguments and bits of evidence presented over the last 14 years or so by many researchers. Some influential works contributing to its early development include, for example, Bloom, 1970; Bowerman, 1973; Brown, 1973; Clark, 1973, 1976; Nelson, 1974; Schlesinger, 1971; Slobin, 1973.

How are specific linguistic forms acquired? The hypothesis we are considering states that new forms are matched to, or "map onto," preestablished concepts or categories of meaning. These meanings may not be isomorphic with the adult meanings identified with the forms in question; the point is simply that each form is matched to some preestablished meaning, whatever it might be. Once the mapping has taken place, the meaning category guides the child's initial generalizations of the form to novel contexts; that is, the child uses the form only in connection with the meaning that he or she has identified with it. A sketch illustrating this general approach to the developmental relationship between form and meaning is presented in Fig. 12.1, along with some representative hypotheses about specific form-meaning matches in English-speaking children.

What is the motor that drives this mapping process? Here is where communication enters the picture. If language acquisition is seen primarily as a process of mapping linguistic forms onto preestablished meanings, it is a plausible step to the hypothesis that new forms enter children's repertoires in response to their desire or intention to express their meanings. This view is sometimes implicit in the literature, discernible, for example, in the inter-

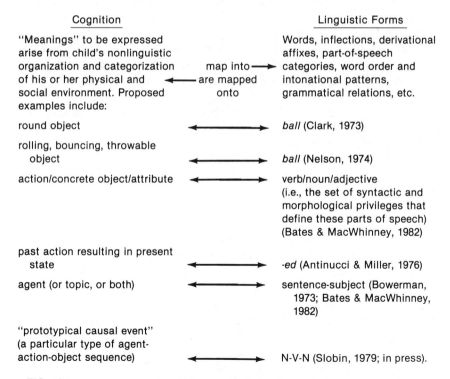

FIG. 12.1   "Forms map onto preestablished meanings" model of language acquisition.

changeable use of the terms "meaning" (or "semantic/pragmatic function") and "communicative intention." More explicit proposals have also been advanced (e.g., Bates and MacWhinney's, 1982, view of the child's linguistic progress as a series of solutions to communicative problems). The general idea is that the development of new or more differentiated meanings is always in advance of children's knowledge of the conventional linguistic devices for expressing them. At first they "make do" with whatever nonlinguistic means (e.g., gestures, eye contact) and linguistic devices are available to them. But the "push" from the mounting complexity of their communicative intentions leads them to seek and master ever more elaborate linguistic devices that will allow them to express these intentions more satisfactorily.

SOME PROBLEMS WITH EXPLAINING GRAMMATICAL DEVELOPMENT BY REFERENCE TO LANGUAGE-INDEPENDENT MEANINGS AND THE DESIRE TO COMMUNICATE THEM

The model that has just been sketched is attractive in part because it invokes and interrelates in an internally coherent way a number of themes that have become important in the study of language development (and language more generally) over the last decade, such as meaning, communication, and the way language structure may reflect both nonlinguistic conceptual predispositions and the requirements of a communication system that must be processed in a linearly organized, temporally fading medium. Despite its appeal, however, many serious problems arise when we begin to look closely at some of the model's assumptions and predictions. I consider questions about formal structure only briefly, and then go more deeply into the problem of meaning.

Form

Are new forms always and necessarily matched to preestablished categories of meaning, or is the child in fact capable of dealing with formal structure without support from meaning? Some of the most interesting test cases for this question are those in which forms of the adult language do correlate with categories of meaning, but only partially. For example, many nouns name concrete objects, but there are nouns that do not, such as *justice* and *kick* (as in *a kick in the ribs*). Likewise, the part-of-speech categories "verb" and "adjective" coincide to some extent with the semantic categories "words for actions" and "words for qualities" (attributes, states), respectively, but many verbs do not denote actions, and many adjectives do not designate qualities. And, to take a third example, many sentence-subjects name an agent who performs an action (*JOHN walked*), but others do not (*JOHN received a present; THIS TENT sleeps five*).

Some investigators working within the framework sketched in Fig. 12.1 have suggested that children exploit partial correlations like these to crack into the formal system; that is, they start out assuming a closer match between a form and its correlated meaning than is actually the case (e.g., Bates & MacWhinney, 1982). If this hypothesis is accurate, children should at first use a given form only in the context of its associated meaning. For instance, they should treat as a verb only words naming actions (where "treat as a verb" would include, e.g., affixing with verb inflections). Once having achieved a working knowledge of a form, however, children would begin to extend its use to other contexts where it is also appropriate but where the associated meaning is absent. This transition could occur gradually, for example, with extension moving from core or prototypical instances of the meaning to "less good exemplars" or metaphorically related meanings, and finally to non-exemplars (cf. Slobin, 1979).

Some aspects of language development that are incompatible with this general approach have been pointed out by Maratsos and Chalkley (1980). These investigators note, for example, that the hypothesis predicts that children should make certain kinds of errors in the early stages of learning about part-of-speech distinctions. Thus, when adjectives of the adult language denote actions or behaviors rather than enduring qualities or states, children should initially treat these words syntactically as verbs. They might, for instance, say *He CAREFULLED the toy* (= was careful with the toy) and *She NASTIED me* (= was nasty to me). Conversely, adult verbs that refer to qualities or states rather than to actions should receive adjectival treatment, for example, *She IS LIKE of him* (= likes him; cf. *is fond of him*); *He IS REMEMBER (of) the movie* (= remembers the movie). Such errors do not seem to occur, however. From this and related evidence, Maratsos and Chalkley conclude that children must be capable of learning forms — even those that correlate partially with categories of meaning — without semantic mediation.

Some experimental evidence that such learning indeed is possible has been presented by Karmiloff-Smith (1979a). The formal domain explored by Karmiloff-Smith was the French gender system, in which masculine and feminine gender correlate, although imperfectly, with sex of referent (in the case of animate referents). Karmiloff-Smith elicited speech from French-speaking children about novel pictured male or female creatures, which she introduced with nonsense species names in contexts free of overt indications of gender. She found that the children's first systematic strategy for assigning gender to the novel nouns had nothing to do with sex of referent, but was based instead on a completely nonsemantic criterion — albeit one that is in fact more reliably predictive of gender in French — the phonological properties of the nouns.

Meaning

So far I have considered only the question of whether formal knowledge is invariably or necessarily acquired with the help of meaning. The answer apparently is no. But there are still more complex problems with the hypothesis that the child proceeds by mapping the formal devices of language only onto already available concepts that strive for expression. Specifically, the hypothesis assumes a relationship between meaning in language and prelinguistic thought, on the one hand, and between meaning in language and communicative intentions, on the other, that is implausibly direct, given considerations of the following kinds.

1. Selectivity in the Obligatory Mapping of Meanings

Slobin (1979) discusses at length one reason why language cannot be taken as a direct mapping of thought. This is that languages are *selective* in what they encode, pulling out certain meaning distinctions for obligatory marking and ignoring others that the speaker is presumably equally capable of entertaining. Not only are languages selective, but they are selective in different ways. English speakers, for example, must constantly indicate whether the referents of the nouns in their sentences are indefinite (*a*) or definite (*the*); Finnish, however, lacks articles, and the marking of (in)definiteness is optional. Navaho sentences with verbs of motion or location require attention to the characteristics of the located or moving object(s) (e.g., whether it is roundish, flat and flexible, or a collection of entities) because the appropriate classification must be marked on the verb (Allan, 1977). Some languages distinguish only between one and more than one (cf. English *dog* vs. *dogs*), others require a three-way classification (one, two, more than two), and still others do not require number to be indicated at all.[4] This kind of variation in obligatory marking means, argues Slobin (1979), that the child needs to learn not only *how* to encode meanings but also *which* meanings to encode: "the child learner needs to determine which subset of notions receives formal marking in his or her native language [p. 7]."

2. Selectivity and the "Intention to Communicate."

Selectivity and variability in which out of all the potential meaning contrasts are obligatorily encoded by a particular language also create problems for the view that progress in the acquisition of linguistic forms is motivated

---

[4]Recall that the issue here is not what a language *can* encode but what it *must* encode. English, for example, can indicate two entities, as opposed to one or more than two, by the optional use of *two* _____. However, the *grammar* of English *requires* a choice between two contrasting forms of the noun, which distinguish only between one and more than one.

by the desire to communicate. As noted earlier, this model makes no explicit distinction between "meaning" and "the (elements of the) message the speaker wishes to communicate." And indeed, it is only when the two are equated that it makes sense to see the child's acquisition of new forms as driven by an ever-unfolding desire to communicate more, or more effectively. But the effort to make this approach work in the face of significant cross-linguistic variability in what meanings are obligatorily encoded commits us to an assumption that is surely absurd: that language-learning children not only make, without encouragement from language, every meaning distinction that could possibly be relevant in the structure of a natural language, but also that they are spontaneously interested in communicating them all. That is, children must entertain these meanings with sufficient explicitness and with enough desire to convey them to their conversational partners to activate in them a search for some suitable linguistic device with which to encode them.

It is only when we limit our attention to our native language that the equation between meaning and communicative intentions might seem tempting. This is because we are either unaware of the meaning distinctions marked obligatorily in our language or we take them so much for granted that it is easy to imagine that what we say somehow reflects communicative intentions that we generate independently of language. But the obligatory distinctions of other languages often seem exotic and difficult. Consider, for example: (1) the distinction between whether a past event is known by direct experience versus by inference or hearsay, essential to the choice between alternative past tense markers in Turkish (Aksu, 1978); (2) the obligatory four-way classification of nouns in sentences of Toba, a language of Argentina, according to whether the objects to which they refer are in view, out of view, coming into view, or going out of view, and furthermore, if they are in view, according to whether they are spatially nonextended (e.g., a fruit), extended vertically (e.g., a fruit still hanging, or a tree), or extended horizontally (e.g., a table) (Klein, 1979). Can such meanings really struggle for expression in the developing minds of all children, including those in our own living rooms? It seems far more plausible that children learn through experience with their local language that certain meanings must be encoded, whether they are spontaneously interested in communicating them or not (see Bowerman, 1976; Schlesinger, 1977).

3. Backgrounded Meanings

Reasons for rejecting the equation between "meaning" and "communicative intention" or "what the child wants to express" go still deeper than the problem of cross-linguistic differences with respect to which meanings are encoded. It is not impossible that, after experience with language, the Turkish speaker's intended message comes to include information about how a past event is known and the Toba speaker begins to feel that it is important to specify the visibility, shape, and orientation of the objects referred to. This would not account for how the child learns the relevant forms in the first place, but it would at least allow us to preserve the belief that "message" and "meaning" are somehow isomorphic in the mature speaker. But meaning is woven into the structure of language in other more subtle ways. In particular, the speaker must control a wide variety of meaning distinctions that govern the applicability or behavior of various linguistic forms but that do not *in themselves* constitute any part of the message to be communicated.

The clearest illustrations of such backgrounded meanings involve what Whorf (1956) termed "covert categories" or "cryptotypes." Cryptotypes, like many other more obvious meanings, involve the classification of the objects, events, relationships, and so forth to which the speaker refers into contrasting categories. Unlike "overt" meaning categories, however, they are not given an explicit formal marker in the sentences in which they figure (an example of an explicit marker for an overt category is -s for plurality in English). Instead, they make their presence felt only indirectly, through what Whorf termed their "reactances," or the constraints they place on the way other forms behave.

Cryptotypic meanings, argued Whorf, typically involve subtle and elusive notions that are difficult to express precisely but that can be apprehended in an intuitive sort of way. One interesting example in English, to which I return in a later section, involves the class of verbs to which reversative *un-* can be prefixed.[5] As Whorf (1956) pointed out, almost all these verbs (with only a few exceptions, now archaic or semiarchaic) denote "centripetal" actions involving "covering, enclosing, and surface-attachment": "Hence we say 'uncover, uncoil, undress, unfasten, unfold, unlock, unroll, untangle, untie, unwind', but not 'unbreak, undry, unhang, unheat, unlift, unmelt, unopen, unpress, unspill' [p. 71]."

A second covert meaning distinction of English, this time involving lexical appropriateness rather than a derivational process, is the contrast between flexible objects extended in one versus two dimensions. This contrast affects the relative acceptability of collocations of the verbs *fold* with potential direct objects; compare, for example, *fold a blanket/handkerchief/shirt* with ?*fold a string/thread/shoelace.*

As a third example, we may refer to the covert meaning invoked by Zwicky (1968) to account for the contrast between verbs that take a marked infinitive in their complement, for example, *persuade/want/plan* (*to go* . . .), and

---

[5]This prefix should be distinguished from the *un-* prefixed to adjectives and past participles functioning as adjectives (*unkind, unbroken*), which has a different meaning (roughly, *not*) and imposes fewer restrictions on the base form.

those that take a present participle, for example, *find/imagine/avoid* (*going ...*). According to Zwicky's (1968) analysis, "Verbs in the former class ... refer to a time preceding the (not necessarily realized) state described by the complement, while verbs in the latter class ... do not imply such a sequence [p. 97]." Some verbs may have both senses, with the consequence that they may take either complement.

Speakers rarely, if ever, have conscious awareness of the covert meaning categories of their language, and it is implausible that these meanings figure explicitly as part of their "communicative intentions" when they produce sentences over which such meanings exert an influence (either by allowing or by blocking certain combinations of forms). Nevertheless, speakers must be credited with controlling such meanings. Among other sources of evidence, we can cite their ability to give firm and relatively consistent judgments about what combinations are and are not acceptable (Zwicky, 1968), even though they cannot ordinarily explicate the bases upon which such judgments are made (at least not without after-the-fact analysis of their own judgments).

Covert categories illustrate in a particularly clear way that "meaning" in language cannot be directly identified with "communicative intentions." But the same point can also be made by reference to more familiar meanings. Consider, for example, "roundness." It is often observed that young children extend the word *ball* to novel referents on the basis of round shape (Clark, 1973). But when the child says *ball* while pointing out or requesting a ball or other round object, does the roundness of the object constitute (part of) the meaning he or she wishes to communicate? This seems unlikely. Roundness plays an important role in the choice of word, but the message itself revolves around the child's desire that the listener should attend to and perhaps act in a certain way on the intended referent. Of course, eventually the child will come to produce utterances in which the communication of roundness is clearly a goal in and of itself as in *Give me the round block* (*not the square one*). But it is interesting to note that many of the criteria used by children in their earliest classifications of objects and events (as reflected in their extensions of words to novel referents) are apparently not yet under conscious control (e.g., are not used to guide behavior in sorting tasks), and hence are probably not yet candidate elements of an intended message.[6]

To summarize, the notion of "meaning in language" is not exhausted by an explication of "communicative intentions." A speaker's communicative intentions at the moment of speech can be described as a representation of the objects, events, attributes, relationships, and the like that he or she plans to

---

[6]See Campbell (1979, pp. 434–435) on this point and his chapter as a whole for relevant discussion of the tendency in studies of language and language development to confuse conscious and unconscious processes (e.g., the distinction between linguistic contents of which speakers have some awareness and those of which they do not).

talk about, along with subsidiary information about what is more important, what is less important, and so on. But the speaker's selection and combination of particular linguistic forms with which to express these intentions are guided by meanings that are not being consciously entertained at that moment and, in many cases, that are never consciously entertained at all. The view of language acquisition as a process of mapping linguistic forms onto preestablished meanings that the speaker wants to express or communicate is ill-suited to explaining this use of backgrounded meanings in the service of other more explicit meanings. Yet this ability is inherent to the knowledge and use of language from first words on, and no theory of language acquisition can be considered adequate unless it accounts for it (see Bowerman, 1983, for further discussion).

4. What are the Child's Units of Meaning?

Language does not offer a unique symbol for every discriminably different stimulus. Instead, it functions in terms of categories, or groups of stimuli that are treated as equivalent. The ability to categorize is one of the most basic cognitive capacities and does not in itself depend on language. Nevertheless, the hypothesis that language acquisition proceeds by a process of mapping linguistic forms onto preestablished meanings — by which is understood *categories* of meaning, such as agency, possession and plurality — raises the question of whether children's nonlinguistic experiences lead them to divide up the world either to the extent to which language requires, or into just the kinds of chunks or units needed. This is a complex issue that cannot be considered in detail here (see Bowerman, 1976; Schlesinger, 1977, for further discussion). For present purposes, I consider only two problems: the breadth of the units and their combinatorial structure.

With respect to category breadth, the basic question concerns the range of items that will be treated similarly (e.g., called by the same word or covered by the same inflection). Is *doggie* used as a label for the house pet, for all small dogs, all dogs, or all four-legged creatures? Does *-ed* represent only past events with a lingering aftermath (e.g., *spilled*) or past events in general? It is well recognized that the breadth of the category that a child associates with a particular form may narrow or broaden over time. Consonant with the hypothesis that forms are initially mapped onto meanings established independently of language, the assumption is typically that nonlinguistic biases for categorizing in certain ways will exert their maximum influence early in the history of the child's use of a form, with category boundaries being adjusted later, where necessary, to the requirements of the specific language being learned (e.g., Slobin, in press). However, we shall see that there is also evidence for the use of *language-specific* categories at first, followed only later by influence from categorizational principles not specifically called for by the language being learned.

The second aspect of categorization with special relevance for the hypothesis that language maps onto preestablished concepts concerns combinatorial structure. By this I mean how the language breaks down complex events into smaller conceptual chunks and assigns these chunks to words or other forms. Talmy (1975, 1976, in press) shows that languages differ systematically in the kinds of semantic configurations to which single-word verbs are attached. Consider, for example, events in which one entity moves with respect to another entity along a certain path and in a certain manner. English has many verbs that "conflate" or combine the notion of movement with the notion of manner; in sentences with these verbs, information about path is expressed with a separate word, a preposition. For example, in *John HOPPED/ ROLLED/STUMBLED/SWAM into/out of/across the cave, hopped* (etc.) means something like "move (along) in a hopping manner/while hopping." The verbs of Romance languages, in contrast, typically conflate motion with path; manner, if it is expressed at all, is encoded by a separate word. This pattern is suggested by the following possible but uncolloquial English sentences: *John ENTERED (= moved into)/EXITED from (= moved out of)/TRAVERSED (= moved across) the cave (while) hopping/rolling/ stumbling/swimming.*

When the notion of causality is added to notions of motion and path, additional patterned cross-linguistic differences can be identified. Slobin (1979), for example, contrasts the verb in the English sentence *Mummy get out telephone* (a 2-year-old's request for his mother to remove a telephone from a cupboard) with the verb in its Turkish equivalent, *Anne telefonu çıkar* ('Mother telephone get-out') in the following way: "the Turkish verb, *çık,* combines change of location and direction in one word [as suggested by the gloss 'to move out of a container'], leaving it to a grammatical suffix [-*ar*] to encode causal agency; the English verb, *get,* combines change of state and causal agency in one word, leaving it to a locative particle, *out,* to encode directionality [p. 5]."

These examples show interesting differences among languages with respect to which combinations of elements are typically treated as units and which elements are handled as additional specifications. But even within languages, there are often alternative ways to distribute elements of meaning across a set of syntactically organized morphemes. Compare, for example, *The news saddened me* with *The news made me sad; I bicycled/flew/walked to work* with *I went to work by bicycle/by airplane/on foot; I went across the field hopping (on one foot)* with *I crossed the field hopping* with *I hopped across the field.*

These cross-linguistic and within-language options for the way meaning is packaged raise perplexing questions for the hypothesis that forms map onto preestablished meanings, especially given the common corollary assumption that children initially prefer a one-to-one mapping between underlying meanings and surface forms (cf. Slobin's, 1973, Operating Principle, "Underlying semantic relations should be marked overtly and clearly"). Does the meaning mapped into English *go in* and French *entrer*, or into English *go down* and French *descendre*, consist of two conceptual units — motion and path — or one? If two units, then English-speaking children would presumably find the mapping process easier than their French-speaking counterparts, because the latter would be stymied in their efforts to give overt marking to each of the two meaning components. If one unit, on the other hand, then English, by "unnaturally" splitting the conceptual package into two pieces, complicates things for the child who must learn it. (Analogous arguments can be constructed for the case represented by English *get out* vs. Turkish *çıkar*.) Given the lack of evidence for selective difficulties with the learning of words for everyday meanings such as "going in," "going down," and "getting out," it is more likely that the child's nonlinguistic conception of these meanings is neutral between the alternative linguistic analyses (i.e., it maps equally readily into either one). If this is the case, however, we cannot argue that forms map in one-to-one fashion directly onto preestablished categories of meanings. We must instead postulate an intermediate step in which the semantic categories required by the structure of the language being learned are constructed out of the resources provided by nonlinguistic cognition.

AN ALTERNATIVE APPROACH TO MEANING

The various considerations that have been raised — variability in the way different languages select meanings for obligatory encoding, the role of backgrounded meanings that guide the speaker's selection and combination of forms but that are not in themselves part of the intended message, and cross-linguistic differences in the makeup of the categories to which forms are attached — suggest that the model of the developmental relationship between form and meaning sketched in Fig. 12.1 not only oversimplifies the problem but is in certain critical respects simply wrong. Specifically, there is no room in the model for an account of how children acquire the *meaning structure* of their language. In Fig. 12.1, meaning is sacrificed to form; that is, the explanation of how linguistic forms are acquired is bought by granting the child for free, courtesy of nonlinguistic cognitive development, the meanings they encode. The price we pay for this explanation is too high. I certainly do not dispute that we need to take into account the contribution to language development of the child's nonlinguistic abilities, but at the same time, we must recognize that the way in which a particular language structures meaning is just as much a part of that language as its formal devices; in other words, it is equally part of what the child must *learn*.

In Fig. 12.2, I sketch informally how the model of Fig. 12.1 must be altered to take account of this. Note in particular that meaning (including both se-

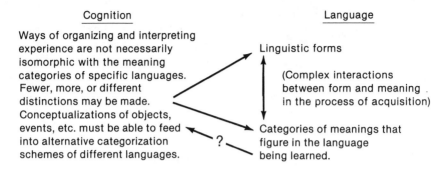

FIG. 12.2   Proposed alternative to Fig. 12.1: An interactional model of the relationship between form and meaning in language acquisition.

mantics and "pragmatic" categories of various sorts that I have not dealt with here, e.g., distinctions of age, rank, setting, etc. that are relevant to the choice between linguistic variants in concrete situations) has been promoted out of cognition into the domain of language proper. New forms can still be mapped directly onto meanings already given by nonlinguistic cognition, as in Fig. 12.1; however, the child can also develop or notice meanings as a consequence of observing the way linguistic forms are used.[7] Whether or how such meaning categories, once established, affect nonlinguistic ways of categorizing and mentally representing events is still an open question (as shown by the question mark).

EVIDENCE FROM LATE ERRORS FOR THE DEVELOPMENT, REORGANIZATION, AND SYSTEMATIZATION OF FORM-MEANING RELATIONSHIPS IN THE COURSE OF LANGUAGE ACQUISITION

So far, arguments for a model such as is proposed in Fig. 12.2 have been based primarily on theoretical considerations. But late errors provide one important kind of empirical support. In particular, they indicate that the initial

---

[7]My wording here is intentially vague in order to sidestep the difficult and controversial issue of whether conceptual distinctions can be learned "from scratch" on the basis of very general cognitive abilities or whether they must be innately present in the child. The case for the latter alternative has been advanced most strongly by Fodor (1975), who argues that concept learning, as a process of inductive extrapolation, presupposes an extremely rich internal language in which hypotheses can be posed about the classes (of objects, events, etc.) across which perceived regularities hold. If Fodor's approach is correct, the basic explanatory problems faced by developmental cognitive psychologists are somewhat different than they have typically been envisioned, but there is still much to account for (e.g., how more complex concepts get built up through the combination of simpler ones, how certain concepts come to have increased salience over other competing possible ways to group stimuli, why concepts appear to emerge in a developmental order).

matches children make between forms and meanings are relatively frag-
mented and context-bound.[8] These matches are serviceable, however; in fact
children can often achieve quite adult-like usage patterns without doing
more. Nevertheless, they do do more: Elements of the existing repertoire are
gradually reworked into form-meaning relationships that are increasingly
abstract and removed from the original contexts of learning, both in response
to subtle regularities across forms within the language being learned and in
response to nonlinguistic categorizational predispositions. The result is a
highly abstract system that reflects both language-specific structuring principles and more general cognitive biases that played little or no role in the initial
"acquisition" of the forms in question.

Examples of three different genres of late errors are given in support of this
claim. Data come primarily from my daughters, Christy and Eva, with occasional comparable examples from other children.[9]

Learning Semantic Categories that Govern/Correlate with the Applicability of Linguistic Forms

As discussed earlier, the hypothesis that forms map onto preestablished
meanings holds that children exploit correlations between categories of
meaning and linguistic forms in order to learn about those forms. (Thus, for
example, "if it is a word that names an action, you can add to it *-ed, -ing,*
etc.") Another possibility, however, is that children learn the morphological
and/or syntactic handling of individual words piecemeal, and only later,
after they already have excellent control over these words, discover that items
that behave alike morphologically or syntactically may also share an abstract
meaning. (Thus, "if it is a word that can take *-ed, -ing,* etc., it is likely to name
an action.") This is how Brown (1957), in a more Whorfian era, interpreted
the ability of preschoolers to guess the referent (action, discrete object, or
substance) of novel verbs, count nouns, and mass nouns. Several kinds of
late errors support the hypothesis that recognition of abstract form-meaning
correspondences often takes place quite late, long after the child is capable of
using exemplars of the form fluently (with each exemplar presumably
mapped onto a "smaller," less abstract meaning).

---

[8]See Karmiloff-Smith (1979a) for a similar view, which also derives support from certain kinds
of late errors, in this case made by French-speaking children in experimental settings.

[9]The language development of Christy and Eva was followed closely from the time of first
words (about 12 months) with daily diary notes and periodic taping of spontaneous speech. Most
of the reported errors were recorded by hand, always immediately after they were produced.
Each error type is also represented in my records by examples gathered from a number of other
less extensively studied children in comparable age ranges. I am grateful to Mabel Rice for data
from Mindy, reported in Table 12.1, and to Charlotte Ruder for data from Scott, reported in
Table 12.3.

Verbs Prefixable with Un-

One example of a form-meaning correspondence that may often be recognized only late involves the covert category associated with reversative *un*-prefixation, discussed earlier. Children learn many legitimate *un-* verbs (e.g., *untie, unbuckle, unfasten*) and use them appropriately for at least 1 to 2 years before they show signs of having analyzed them into two components. Evidence that the analysis has taken place is that the child starts to produce novel reversative verbs prefixed with *un-*. Although some children appear to limit their coinages to verbs of the appropriate semantic category right from the start of productivity, others clearly do not (Bowerman, 1982b).

Christy's production of novel verbs prefixed with *un-* went through two distinct stages. At first, *un-* was prefixed indiscriminately to verbs of a wide variety of semantic types including, as in the first of the following examples, those having meanings directly *opposite* to the covert category of actions of "covering, enclosing, and surface attachment." For example:

1. C, 4;5   (C has just asked why pliers are on table)[10]
    M: I've been using them for straightening the wire.
    C: And *unstraighting* it? (*unstraightening* = bending)
2. C, 4;7   (C is very angry with M for denying a request)
    C: I hate you! And I'll never *unhate* you or nothing!
    M: You'll never unhate me?
    C: I'll never like you.

Similar examples are: *uncome* (= stop coming); *undizzying* (= becoming not dizzy).

After many months, however, *un-* prefixation gradually became limited to verbs of the "right" semantic type, as in these examples:

3. C, 5;1   (M is working on a strap of C's backpack)
    M: Seems like one of these has been shortened, somehow.
    C: Then *unshorten* it. (= lengthen)
4. C, 5;1   (C has stepped on a toy road sign shaped like a triangle, squashing the angles out of it)
    I *unbended* this with [= by] stepping on it. (= straightened)
5. C, 7;11 (C taking a stocking down from the fireplace)
    I'm gonna *unhang* it.

Other late coinages involving verbs of the right semantic category, by both Christy and Eva, include *unbury* (= reverse action of enclosing by burial),

[10]Age given in years; months. In this and subsequent examples, C = Christy, E = Eva, M = Mommy, D = Daddy.

uncapture (= release), *unsqueeze* (= loosen), *untight* (*untighten* = loosen).
See Bowerman (1982b) for further examples and discussion.

Notice that all these examples are errors from the adult point of view. But
the later ones are more sophisticated, for they show that the child has done
further analysis of the semantic characteristics of the set of "real" verbs prefixed with *un-* that she has learned from other speakers. A critical challenge
for those who invoke "communicative need" to account for change and progress in language development is to explain why children "bother" to identify
this kind of correspondence between a form and an abstract meaning, given
that: (1) they do not need it in order to learn or use the *un*-verbs in the English
lexicon;[11] (2) it is unlikely that adult reaction to coinages selectively encour-
ages errors such as those in examples 3–5, but discourages those like 1 and 2.
Apparently children are sensitive to structure and regularity in language regardless of whether the detection of it wins them any communicative advantage, either immediately or in the long run.

Talking About Manner of Causation

A second piece of evidence for children's formulation of abstract categories of meaning that correlate with linguistic forms involves the expression of
causal relations. Consider phrases such as *pull your socks up, cut the string
off, chop the tree down, eat your cereal allgone,* and *wipe the table dry.* Children begin to produce simple sentences containing such phrases as early as 2
years, and do so with enough flexibility that there can be no thought of
"unanalyzed units" — that is, they vary the noun phrases naming the objects
acted upon and also combine (for example) *pull* not only with *up* but also
with *down, out, in,* and so on, as the context demands, and *up* (etc.) not only
with *pull* but also with *push, pound,* and so on. To all outward appearances,
they have excellent control over sentences like these. In the case of Christy
and Eva, therefore, I was startled when well over a year later, sentences such
as those shown in Table 12.1 started to occur (similar examples from other
children are also included).

In the linguistic literature concerning sentences of this sort, two basic types
of analysis predominate. One interprets phrases like *pull up* and *chop down*
as two-part verbs; sentences containing them are considered simple (i.e.,
composed of a single proposition) (e.g., Chomsky, 1962). According to the
other analysis, in contrast, such sentences are complex: At an underlying
level they consist of two separate propositions, one specifying a causing event
(e.g., [(You) pull (on) your socks]; [Daddy chops (on) the tree]) and the other
specifying a change of state or change of location that results from this event

---

[11]Recall that children may already have been using a number of them quite appropriately for a
long time — about 3 years in Christy's case — before showing signs of recognizing that they have a
semantic coherence.

TABLE 12.1
Errors in the Expression of Cause and Effect Relations

1. C 3;8 I *pulled* it *unstapled.* (after pulling a stapled book apart)
2. E 6;0 His doggie *bited* him *untied.* (telling about a TV show in which a dog bites a rope, freeing its master)
3. E 3;9 A gorilla captured my fingers. I'll *capture* his whole head *off.* His hands too. (as she plays with rubber band around fingers)
4. Andrea 4;3 When you get to her, you *catch* her *off.* (while on a park merry-go-round with doll next to her; wants a friend standing nearby to remove doll when doll comes around to her)
5. C 6;2 It's hard not to knock them down 'cause whenever I breathe I *breathe* them *down.* (having trouble setting up a paper village)
6. Mindy 5;6 Are you *washing* me *blind*? (as mommy wipes corners of her eyes)

Similarly: *I'm patting her wet* (by patting her, cause her to become wet); *Feels like you're combing me baldheaded* (by combing [my hair], cause me to become bald-headed); *I'm gonna jump it down* (by jumping on it, cause it to go down); *Don't drive off my feet* (by driving over my feet, cause them to come off); *Untie it off* (by untying it, cause it to come off); *She choked me backwards to the chair* (by choking me, caused me to move backwards to the chair).

Note. From Bowerman (1977, 1982b).

(e.g., [your socks come up]; [the tree falls down]) (Fillmore, 1971; Talmy, 1976). The causing event and resulting event can be quite diverse; that is, many unusual combinations are acceptable in adult speech, such as *The locusts ate the prairie brown and bare* (from a Laura Ingalls Wilder book). "Two-part" verbs like *pull up* are simply very common combinations.

When, following the second analysis, we think of so-called two-part verbs as reflecting a much larger pattern of juxtaposing a causing event with a resulting change of state or of location, we see that the early appearance of productivity with these forms in child speech is misleading. This productivity is in fact limited to types of combinations of causing events and resulting events that children often hear described with sentences of this structural pattern in adult speech. Novel sentences can be produced on the basis of knowledge of particular verb-result complement pairs. But the onset of errors like those in Table 12.1 indicates that the child has gone beyond this piecemeal approach and now recognizes an overarching pattern, a way in which these various sentences are similar both in terms of their abstract semantic configuration and their syntactic structure. Only now is the child for the first time in a position to create truly novel exemplars cut to the same pattern. Many of the new combinations are in fact perfectly grammatical (e.g., *Don't hug me off my chair,* where it is unlikely the child has ever heard a sentence encoding an event in which *hugging* was an action that caused the hugged entity to come *off* something). But others, such as those in Table 12.1, violate certain constraints on how freely the pattern can be realized (see Bowerman, 1977, 1982b, for discussion).

More on the Expansion of Existing Meanings

The two examples just discussed indicate that the child can come to recognize that diverse "small" meanings she has thus far treated independently from one another share a more abstract class meaning and that this class meaning correlates with a certain morphological or syntactic treatment. In these cases, the evidence that the child controls the class meanings is that she *overregularizes*; that is, she applies the formal treatment to words or configurations of forms that instantiate the class meaning but that for one reason or another are exceptions to the treatment.[12] The process of building class meanings that encompass hitherto separate, less abstract meanings can produce symptoms other than overregularization, however. In particular, it appears to be implicated in the onset of semantically based word substitutions. These are errors in which the speaker, instead of using the form that is semantically called for, produces another form with a different but related meaning (Bowerman, 1978, 1982c).

Substitutions of semantically related words are relatively common in adult speech, for instance, *I really LIKE to — HATE to get up in the morning; Not Thackeray but someone who wrote BELOW Thackeray — BEFORE Thackeray* (Fromkin, 1971; Fay & Cutler, 1977). It has been proposed that these errors occur because of a breakdown in the process of sentence production (Fromkin, 1973; Laver, 1973; Nooteboom, 1969). According to this hypothesis, the speaker's plan to talk about something activates a set of candidate lexical items and syntactic arrangements, together with their associated phonology. At this point, more lexical items may be activated than will be ultimately selected. In this case, the speaker must implicitly evaluate competing items and select the one that is optimal, rejecting the rest. Ordinarily this goes smoothly, but occasionally there is a minor lapse and a semantically inappropriate competitor slips through in place of the conventional choice.

In Christy's and Eva's speech, substitution errors involving certain relational words such as verbs, prepositions, adjectives, locative particles, and the prefex *un-* were recurrent (see Table 12.2). The onset of errors like these was preceded by a period ranging from a few weeks up to 2 years during which both the "target" word (or morpheme) and its replacement (substitutions were often reciprocal) were used productively in semantically appropriate contexts and never interchanged. This sequence suggests a process by which initially independent words draw together in meaning, such that mean-

---

[12]Notice, however, that the effects of the discovery of the class meaning are different in the two cases. For *pull up* and the like, the discovery leads to greater productivity than existed previously (as in the case of inflectional overregularizations, e.g., *foots*); for *un-,* however, the result is a *restriction* of a previously more indiscriminate productivity.

TABLE 12.2
Some Genres of Recurrent Semantic Substitution Errors

Make/Let

1. C 3;6   But usually puppets *make*–let people put their hands in.
   (disagreeing with M's use of the word *puppet* for dolls with toilet-paper roll bodies)
2. C 3;9   *Make* me watch it. (begging D to let her watch a TV show)
3. C 3;6   I don't want to go to bed yet. Don't *let* me go to bed.
   (after M has told her she must go to bed)
4. C 3;8   How come you always *let* me wear those?
   (as M puts C's shoes on; she had wanted another pair)

Put/Give

5. C 3;4   You *put* the pink one to me.
   (request for M to give her the pink one of two cups)
6. E 2;4   We're *putting* our things to you.
   (to D, after M has told C and E that it's time to "give" D their Father's Day presents)
7. C 4;1   Whenever Eva doesn't need her towel she *gives* it on my table and when I'm done with it I give it back to her.
8. E 2;7   *Give* some ice in here, Mommy. Put some ice in here, Mommy.
   (pointing to ice crusher)

Spatial Words/Temporal Words

9. E 3;9   Can I have any reading *behind* the dinner?
   (= will you read to me *after* dinner?)
10. E 4;10   Today we'll be packing 'cause tomorrow there won't be enough *space* to pack.
    (= *time*; the day before the family is to leave on a trip early in the morning)
11. C 7;2   Do we have *room* before we go to bed for another reading?
    (= *time*; M has been reading aloud in the evening; just finished book)

Verb + Particle/Un- + Verb

12. C 5;6   . . . so I had to *untake* the sewing.
    (= *take* the sewing/stitches *out*; telling about sewing project at school)
(Similarly: *unpull* [pants] = *pull* pants *down*; *unget* [a knot] = *get* a knot *out*)
13. C 4;5   (Wants to move electric humidifier): I'll get it after it's *plugged out*.
    (Shortly after): Mommy, can I unplug it?
(Similarly: *tuck* [a blanket] *out* = *untuck*; *tangle out* = *untangle*; *hook out* = *unhook*)

Note. From Bowerman (1978, 1982b, 1982c).

ing representations that previously activated only one word now activate one or more other words as well.

In virtually all cases of recurrent substitutions, the "target" element and its replacement can be seen as alternative realizations of a more abstract meaning, that is, as sister meanings taxonomically subordinate to the same superordinate concept.[13] For example, *make* and *let* both specify causation, but differ in the precise nature of that causation (roughly, active vs. passive or "permissive"). *Put* and *give* both specify an act in which an agent causes something to change location, but they differ in whether the new location is animate or not. *Behind* and *after* specify analogous positions in a sequence, but in the spatial and temporal domains, respectively. And two-part verbs with *off/out/down/apart* and so on, like verbs prefixed with *un-*, all specify actions involving the separation or spreading out of parts.

What leads to competition between forms whose meanings are taxonomically related at a higher level of abstraction, when both the existence of separate forms and the child's own past history of correct usage would seem to predict that the individual meanings associated with the forms should remain apart? This is too complex a question to discuss fully here (see Bowerman, 1982c, 1983). However, it is intriguing to note that even though the meanings involved are formally distinguished in English by the use of separate morphemes, their close semantic relationship is attested to by the fact that they are often treated as equivalent in the formal structure of other languages. For example, some languages do not formally mark the distinction between animate and inanimate goals that is observed in *give* versus *put* (Lyons, 1967), and some languages create causative verbs with a morpheme that is indeterminate in meaning between active causation (*make*) and permissive causation (*let*) (Comrie, 1976).

In some cases, there may be no languages that encode with a single form the meanings that substitution errors indicate are similar for children beyond a certain age. Nevertheless, there may still be corroborative cross-linguistic evidence that the meanings are closely related: Often the semantic domain defined by the substitutions (i.e., the class meaning shared by the competing forms) is "divided up" by different languages in ways that suggest an underlying coherence masked by a somewhat arbitrary language specificity in assigning subparts of the domain to different formal classes. The domain of "acts of separation" provides a good example. English shares with Dutch certain cognate formal devices for encoding such acts and often uses them similarly: e.g., English *UNload* and *cut OFF* vs. the Dutch equivalents *ONTladen*

---

[13]The superordinate semantic category that subsumes the more specific meanings of two or more words that substitute for each other may in many cases be best described as having a "family resemblance" structure (Rosch & Mervis, 1975), that is, definable in terms of a set of recurring semantic elements, not all of which are reflected in each submeaning.

and *AFknippen, (knip AF)*. However, sometimes these devices cross over unpredictably; e.g., English *undress, unpack,* and *unhook* vs. Dutch *kleed uit* 'dress out,' *pak uit* 'pack out,' and *haak af/uit* 'hook off/out'; and English *slip out* vs. Dutch *ontglippen* 'unslip'. (Compare these crossovers with errors 12 and 13 in Table 12.2.)

Cross-linguistic evidence of these types indicates that children's recurrent substitution errors may arise from deep-seated cognitive predispositions toward recognizing certain kinds of similarities among events or relationships, regardless of whether these events or relationships are formally treated as equivalent by the lexicon, morphology, or syntax of the language they are learning. This might at first glance appear to support the notion that linguistic forms map onto meanings that are worked out independently of language. But notice that the effect of the classificational biases reflected in the substitution errors I have discussed is *not* observed in the *earliest* stages of language acquisition. To the contrary, in these cases, the child starts out following the very specific form-meaning mappings exemplified in her local language. Only much later, long after she is using the forms in question fluently, is she apparently influenced by more general, nonlinguistic categorizational tendencies. The existence of such sequences, along with evidence for the converse, more expected process whereby "universal" categories of meaning are reflected in children's earliest uses of forms (Slobin, 1979, in press; Bowerman, 1983), indicates that there is a complex interplay in language development between the effects of nonlinguistic cognition and experience with the language being learned.

Breaking Down Global Meanings

In the two immediately preceding sections, I have considered some late errors that seem to reflect processes by which the child formulates class meanings that subsume smaller, previously independent meanings. There is also evidence for a somewhat complementary process of change: the splitting apart of meanings that have functioned earlier in the child's system as unitary conceptual packages.

The relevant errors are of two related types. In *overexplicit marking,* children move from a period in which they routinely encode a given idea with the same word an adult would use to a later period in which they occasionally, or in some cases often, express this meaning with a set of forms that in essence "decompose" it into two or more smaller units, each with its own explicit formal marker. Karmiloff-Smith (1979b) has observed this phenomenon in French-speaking children; one interesting example is the occasional replacement of appropriate noun phrases such as *mes voitures,* 'my cars,' by clumsy paraphrases such as *toutes les miennes de voitures,* 'all (totality) the (plurality, definite reference) mine (first person possessive; plurality of possessed items) of cars,' in which the several elements of meaning that are implicit in *mes* are spelled out in detail. Examples from my own data (Bowerman, 1982c) include the replacement in the child's speech of contextually appropriate, single-word causative verbs like *drop, put,* and *break* by periphrastic forms (e.g., *I drop it → I make it fall; Would you put my shoe on → Would you make my shoe come on?*). Here, a complex causative meaning has been split into two conceptual components. One is an abstract notion of causation, marked with *make* (or sometimes *get*); the other is the caused event or state of affairs itself, usually encoded with an intransitive verb or an adjective.

The second type of error suggesting the breakdown of meanings that initially form a single conceptual unit involves *redundant marking*. Again, there is first a period in which the child uses the conventionally appropriate word for a given notion. This is followed by a period in which he or she occasionally or often adds to this same word another morpheme, which encodes separately an element of meaning that, from the adult point of view, is already incorporated into the original form. Some examples of redundancies that followed initially correct usage are shown in Table 12.3.

The precise cause of overexplicit and redundant marking in child speech is unclear. Karmiloff-Smith (1979b) proposes that such errors reflect children's efforts to come to grips with meaning distinctions to which they have become newly sensitive by giving each distinction its own "external handle." This explanation invokes the principle of one-to-one marking; that is, it assumes that there is push from within to give a separate marker to each unit of meaning (of which the speaker is aware) until a later point when the child can go back to "allow[ing] one external marker to convey several pieces of information" (Karmiloff-Smith, 1979b, p. 112).

An alternative explanation (Bowerman, 1981) links the errors to the semantic substitutions discussed earlier. Errors such as the use of *put* where *give* is needed were described in terms of the competition at the moment of speech between two lexical items, both of which are "activated" by the meaning the child is attempting to encode. In the case of overexplicitness, the competition is not between two lexical items but rather between a lexical and a syntactic way to accomplish approximately the same thing; the syntactic method happens to win out in a context in which the lexical variant is preferred by adults (the converse error, use of a single word where a syntactic construction is needed, also occurs, cf. Bowerman, 1982a). Redundant marking results when two simultaneously activated forms, one a word and the other usually a bound morpheme, are inappropriately combined within the boundaries of a single sentence. (These errors are thus similar to lexical "blends" involving semantically similar words, such as *intertwingled,* from *intertwined* and *mingled.*)

Regardless of which explanation is preferable — a cognitive "push" to mark each meaning element separately versus competition between alternative

TABLE 12.3
Some Genres of Redundant Marking

Un- + Verb (Single Word or Two-Part) that Already Encodes a Reversative Act of Separation (Bowerman, 1981, 1982b)

1. C 4;11   Will you *unopen* this? (= *open*; wants D to take lid off styrofoam cooler because she can't)
2. Scott 5;2 How do you *unbreak* this? (= *break*; trying to pull sheet of stamps apart)
3. E 3;5   How do I *untake* this *off*? (= *take* this *off*; trying to get out of swimsuit)
4. E 4;7   (holding up chain of glued paper strips)
           E: I know how you take these apart. *Unsplit* them and put 'em on.
           M: How do you unsplit them?
           E: Like this. (pulling a link apart)

Enchoative -en with Verb that Already Encodes Change of State (Bowerman, 1982a)

5. E 3;6   It *smoothens* the water out. (stroking wet stomach with washrag in tub)
6. E 4;11   Julie, will you *closen* the yellow so I can use it? (painting with a friend; worried that yellow paint will dry out if not kept closed)
7. C 6;0   First they look like they're wet and then they *fluffen* out. (of newly hatched chicks)
8. Matthew, Will you *straightenen* this out, please? (handing adult a scrunched-up
    3;4   paper cup; note double marking with *-en*)

Turkish: Causative Suffix Added to Verb that is Already Causative (Slobin & Aksu, in press)

9. Adult: *Kim kes - ti onu?*
          who cut-past it-accusative
   Child   *Ben kes -tir- dim*
   2;3   I cut-causative-past
          Intended meaning: "I cut (it)."
          Literal meaning: "I had (someone) cut (it)."

forms with closely related meanings (perhaps both will be needed to account for the full range of errors) — it is important in the present context to note that both accounts postulate the *breakdown* of meanings that are initially matched to given forms in a more global way. This is an explicit part of Karmiloff-Smith's proposal. And the "competition" account also appears to require it, for the following reason. Before morphological devices or certain syntactic patterns (e.g., the periphrastic causative) can become productive, they must be associated with meanings that are independent of particular lexical items. That is, they must be conceptually "free" enough to combine with the meanings contributed by the variety of lexical items with which they can be juxtaposed. (Thus, for example, Turkish *-tir* and English *make* add "causation" to the meaning of the verbs with which they combine; English *un-* and *-en* add "reversal" and "transition into a new state," respectively.) It is, moreover, reasonable to assume that speakers do not make creative use of such a device or pattern in the course of speech production unless they are actively entertaining the meaning to which it is linked. This means that in order for competition to occur at the moment of speech between a single lexical item and a productive syntactic or morphological device, the meaning associated with the lexical item must have, as a subelement or feature with considerable conceptual independence from the rest of the meaning package, the meaning that is associated with the device. Otherwise, the device would not simultaneously be activated. The initial absence of errors of redundancy and overexplicitness, often until long after the relevant productive devices are already part of the child's repertoire, suggests that the requisite conceptual partitioning of a word's meaning is often achieved only after a period in which the meaning is represented in a more global, "unanalyzed" way.

CONCLUSION

The error types discussed in the preceding sections show some of the ways in which the relationship between forms and meanings can change in the course of language development: matches between individual words or phrases and their specific meanings can "join up" as common instances of a match between a more abstract form and a more abstract class meaning; class meanings can develop to interconnect previously independent forms even in the absence of a shared, abstract "matching" form; and the meanings initially matched to words as unanalyzed wholes can subsequently be broken down or reanalyzed into a set of conceptually independent components.

These changes take place after the child would ordinarily have been credited with having "acquired" the forms in question. This indicates that achieving fluent, productive use of a form and achieving adult-like knowledge of its structure are not necessarily isomorphic. Young children know what to do with particular words or groups of words, and they know many syntactic and morphological patterns, but they have not yet recognized many of the deeper relationships and regularities of the language they are learning. To judge from the time of onset of errors of various types, the work of discovering these systematicities occupies the child during most of the preschool years and even beyond.

Evidence for the reorganization and progressive deepening of linguistic knowledge has implications for several theoretical issues. Two that have been considered in this paper are the role of communication and the role of meaning in the acquisition of language. With respect to communication, I have argued that the currently prevalent invocation of "communicative need" to account for the child's linguistic progress is insufficient. How can it explain the child's further analyses of linguistic forms that are already well under control for purposes of everyday communication (see also Karmiloff-Smith, 1979a, 1979b), especially when the primary behavioral evidence of these analyses is the onset of errors where there were none before? The onset of late errors is also difficult to square with other interpretations of the driving force behind progress in language acquisition, such as parental correction and reinforcement or children's perception of a mismatch between the predictions of their own mental grammars and adult speech. This is because both of these explanations predict and can interpret only change in which children go from *incorrect* to *correct* usage, not, as in the case of late errors, change in the reverse direction (Bowerman, 1982c).

What shall we conclude from this? Over a decade ago, Brown (1973) discussed the question of whether linguistic progress comes about through selection pressures of various kinds and, in light of the lack of positive evidence, proposed "a radically different possibility . . . that children work out rules for the speech they hear, passing from levels of lesser to greater complexity, simply because the human species is programmed at a certain period in its life to operate in this fashion on linguistic input [p. 412]." I believe that the evidence presented in this paper strongly supports this general conclusion and would add only the qualification that it is not yet clear whether there is a "critical period" for analyses of the types discussed in this paper.[14]

With respect to meaning, I have pointed out some difficulties with the currently prevalent view that language acquisition is a process of mapping linguistic forms onto meanings already worked out on a nonlinguistic basis. This view is certainly well justified in emphasizing the importance to language acquisition of the child's cognitive development and conceptual predispositions, but it is deficient in its implicit assumption that "meaning in language" is isomorphic with what the child knows on a nonlinguistic basis (and wants to communicate). Meaning in language is undeniably dependent on nonlinguistic cognition, but it is at the same time a highly structured and conventionalized system. This means that children cannot afford to prejudge what meaning categories will be important any more than they can afford to prejudge the formal linguistic devices with which they will have to deal. Both are equally a part of what children must learn. Because forms and meanings are often intricately interrelated, with each one defining the boundaries of the other, we can expect that the transformation of children's knowledge of the world into the categories of meaning that figure in their local language involves complex interactions between linguistic input and nonlinguistic biases and constraints. And indeed this is precisely what late errors suggest. How this process takes place is an aspect of language development that we have

---

[14]For evidence that there indeed is a critical period at least for the decomposition of lexical items into patterned sets of semantic/morphological components, see Newport (1981). Newport reports that errors indicating sensitivity to sublexical semantic structure in speakers of American Sign Language occur almost exclusively among those who have acquired ASL as a native language. Older learners, in contrast, acquire and retain signs as "frozen," unanalyzed units.

barely begun to explore, however. I hope the coming years will see more attention paid to this fascinating puzzle.

ACKNOWLEDGMENTS

This chapter is a revised and expanded version of a paper by the same title delivered as the Keynote Address to the Thirteenth Annual Stanford Child Language Research Forum (April 14, 1981). The research reported here was supported by Grant HD00870 from NICHHD and by a Fellowship from the Netherlands Institute for Advanced Study in the Humanities and Social Sciences, Wassenaar, The Netherlands. In developing these ideas, I have benefited greatly from discussions in the last few years with many colleagues, including in particular Robin Campbell, Eve Clark, Dedre Gentner, Mike Maratsos, Dan Slobin, and Leonard Talmy.

REFERENCES

Aksu, A. *Aspect and modality in the child's acquisition of the Turkish past tense.* Unpublished doctoral dissertation, University of California at Berkeley, 1978.

Allan, K. Classifiers. *Language,* 1977, *53,* 285–311.

Antinucci, F., & Miller, R. How children talk about what happened. *Journal of Child Language,* 1976, *3,* 167–189.

Bates, E., & MacWhinney, B. Functionalist approaches to grammar. In E. Wanner & L. R. Gleitman (Eds.), *Language acquisition: The state of the art.* Cambridge, England: Cambridge University Press, 1982.

Bloom, L. *Language development: Form and function in emerging grammars.* Cambridge, Mass.: MIT Press, 1970.

Bowerman, M. *Early syntactic development: A cross-linguistic study, with special reference to Finnish.* Cambridge, England: Cambridge University Press, 1973.

Bowerman, M. Semantic factors in the acquisition of rules for word use and sentence construction. In D. Morehead & A. Morehead (Eds.), *Directions in normal and deficient child language.* Baltimore: University Park Press, 1976.

Bowerman, M. The acquisition of rules governing "possible lexical items": Evidence from spontaneous speech errors. *Papers and Reports on Child Language Development* (Stanford University Department of Linguistics), 1977, *13,* 148–156.

Bowerman, M. Systematizing semantic knowledge: Changes over time in the child's organization of word meaning. *Child Development,* 1978, *48,* 977–987.

Bowerman, M. The child's expression of meaning: Expanding relationships among lexicon, syntax, and morphology. In H. Winitz (Ed.), *Native language and foreign language acquisition.* New York: New York Academy of Sciences, 1981.

Bowerman, M. Evaluating competing linguistic models with language acquisition data: Implications of developmental errors with causative verbs. *Quaderni di Semantica,* 1982, *3,* 5–66. (a)

Bowerman, M. Reorganizational processes in lexical and syntactic development. In E. Wanner & L. R. Gleitman (Eds.), *Language acquisition: The state of the art.* Cambridge, England: Cambridge University Press, 1982. (b)

Bowerman, M. Starting to talk worse: Clues to language acquisition from children's late speech errors. In S. Strauss (Ed.), *U-shaped behavioral growth.* New York: Academic Press, 1982. (c)

Bowerman, M. Hidden meanings: The role of covert conceptual structures in children's development of language. In D. R. Rogers & J. A. Sloboda (Eds.), *The acquisition of symbolic skills.* New York: Plenum Press, 1983.

Brown, R. Linguistic determinism and the part of speech. *Journal of Abnormal and Social Psychology,* 1957, *55,* 1–5.

Brown, R. *A first language.* Cambridge, Mass.: Harvard University Press, 1973.

Campbell, R. Cognitive development and child language. In P. Fletcher & M. Garman (Eds.), *Language acquisition.* Cambridge, England: Cambridge University Press, 1979.

Cazden, C. B. The acquisition of noun and verb inflections. *Child Development,* 1968, *39,* 433–448.

Chomsky, N. A transformational approach to syntax. In A. A. Hill (Ed.), *Proceedings of the Third Texas Conference on Problems in English.* Austin: University of Texas Press, 1962.

Clark, E. V. What's in a word? On the child's acquisition of semantics in his first language. In T. E. Moore (Ed.), *Cognitive development and the acquisition of language.* New York: Academic Press, 1973.

Clark, E. V. Universal categories: On the semantics of classifiers and children's early word meanings. In A. Juilland (Ed.), *Linguistic studies presented to Joseph Greenberg.* Saratoga, Calif.: Anma Libri, 1976.

Comrie, B. The syntax of causative constructions: Cross-language similarities and divergences. In M. Shibatani (Ed.), *Syntax and semantics, Vol. 6: The grammar of causative constructions.* New York: Academic Press, 1976.

Ervin, S. Imitation and structural change in children's language. In E. H. Lenneberg (Ed.), *New directions in the study of language.* Cambridge, Mass.: MIT Press, 1964.

Fay, D., & Cutler, A. Malapropisms and the structure of the mental lexicon. *Linguistic Inquiry,* 1977, *8,* 505–520.

Fillmore, C. Some problems for case grammar. In R. J. O'Brien (Ed.), *Georgetown University Round Table on Languages and Linguistics 1971.* Washington, D.C.: Georgetown University Press, 1971.

Fodor, J. A. *The language of thought.* New York: Crowell, 1975.

Fromkin, V. A. The non-anomalous nature of anomalous utterances. *Language,* 1971, *47,* 27–52.

Fromkin, V. A. (Ed.). *Speech errors as linguistic evidence.* The Hague: Mouton, 1973.

Karmiloff-Smith, A. *A functional approach to child language.* Cambridge, England: Cambridge University Press, 1979. (a)

Karmiloff-Smith, A. Micro- and macrodevelopmental changes in language acquisition and other representational systems. *Cognitive Science,* 1979, *3,* 91–118. (b)

Karmiloff-Smith, A., & Inhelder, B. If you want to get ahead, get a theory. *Cognition,* 1974–1975, *3,* 195–212.

Klein, H. E. M. Noun classifiers in Toba. In M. Mathiot (Ed.), *Ethnolinguistics: Boas, Sapir and Whorf revisited.* The Hague: Mouton, 1979.

Laver, J. D. M. The detection and correction of slips of the tongue. In V. A. Fromkin (Ed.), *Speech errors as linguistic evidence.* The Hague: Mouton, 1973.

Lyons, J. A note on possessive, existential, and locative sentences. *Foundations of Language,* 1967, *3,* 390–396.

Maratsos, M., & Chalkley, M. The internal language of children's syntax. In K. E. Nelson (Ed.), *Children's language* (Vol. 2). New York: Gardner Press, 1980.

Nelson, K. Concept, word, and sentence: Interrelations in acquisition and development. *Psychological Review,* 1974, *81,* 267–285.

Newport, E. Constraints on structure: Evidence from American Sign Language and language learning. In W. A. Collins (Ed.), *Minnesota Symposium on Child Psychology* (Vol. 14). Hillsdale, N.J.: Lawrence Erlbaum Associates, 1981.

Nooteboom, S. G. The tongue slips into patterns. In A. G. Sciarone, A. J. Van Essen, & A. A. Van Raad (Eds.), *Nomen: Leyden studies in linguistics and phonetics*. The Hague: Mouton, 1969.

Rosch, E., & Mervis, C. B. Family resemblances: Studies in the internal structure of categories. *Cognitive Psychology,* 1975, *7,* 573–605.

Schlesinger, I. M. The production of utterances and language acquisition. In D. I. Slobin (Ed.), *The ontogenesis of grammar*. New York: Academic Press, 1971.

Schlesinger, I. M. The role of cognitive development and linguistic input in language acquisition. *Journal of Child Language,* 1977, *4,* 153–169.

Slobin, D. I. Cognitive prerequisites for the development of grammar. In C. A. Ferguson & D. I. Slobin (Eds.), *Studies of child language development*. New York: Holt, Rinehart & Winston, 1973.

Slobin, D. I. *The role of language in language acquisition*. Unpublished manuscript, University of California at Berkeley, 1979.

Slobin, D. I. Crosslinguistic evidence for the language-making capacity. In D. I. Slobin (Ed.), *The crosslinguistic study of language acquisition*. Hillsdale, NJ: Lawrence Erlbaum Associates, in press.

Slobin, D. I., & Aksu, A. The acquisition of Turkish. In D. I. Slobin (Ed.), *The crosslinguistic study of language acquisition*. Hillsdale, NJ: Lawrence Erlbaum Associates, in press.

Strauss, S. (Ed.). *U-shaped behavioral growth*. New York: Academic Press, 1982.

Talmy, L. Semantics and syntax of motion. In J. P. Kimball (Ed.), *Semantics and syntax* (Vol. 4). New York: Academic Press, 1975.

Talmy, L. Semantic causative types. In M. Shibatani (Ed.), *Syntax and semantics, Vol. 6: The grammar of causative constructions*. New York: Academic Press, 1976.

Talmy, L. Lexicalization patterns: Semantic structure in lexical forms. In T. Shopen (Ed.), *Language typology and syntactic field work*. Cambridge, England: Cambridge University Press, in press.

Whorf, B. L. *Language, thought, and reality* (J. B. Carroll, Ed.). Cambridge, MA: MIT Press, 1956.

Zwicky, A. M. Naturalness arguments in syntax. In B. J. Darden, C.-J. N. Bailey, & A. Davison (Eds.), *Papers of the Chicago Linguistic Society,* 1968, *4.*

13

Language Learnability and Children's Language: A Multifaceted Approach

Steven Pinker
Massachusetts Institute of Technology

Titles are often revealing, and the title of this volume, *Children's Language,* is no exception. In the 1960s and early 1970s most volumes on this topic would probably have been called some variant of *Language Acquisition.* The change in nomenclature, I think, reflects a profound shift in the definition of the field and in the goals its researchers set. In the early 1960s, there was a serious hope that by studying language development in children, one could illuminate the process whereby the child induced the structure of the language of his or her community. For a number of reasons, including a lack of consensus on the form of adult linguistic knowledge and the realization that children's linguistic behavior is determined in part by a variety of nonlinguistic causes, this goal seems far less attainable today. I think many researchers were forced to conclude that if there is no straightforward way to examine children's language and thereby discover how he or she learns the syntax of the adult language, perhaps one can set the more tractable goal of studying the child's language in its own right. Hence the name change.

Though this shift in research emphasis may seem to be a reasonable display of humility in the face of a profound scientific puzzle, and though the new emphasis has raised many fascinating questions on its own, it has led to a somewhat odd asymmetry between developmental psycholinguistics and other branches of cognitive science. This can best be shown by an analogy from cognitive psychology. In a well-known experimental paradigm, subjects are given short lists of digits to memorize and then must quickly decide whether a new "probe" digit is or is not in the memorized list (Sternberg, 1966). Subjects tend to give the right answer in the task 95% of the time or more, and they take proportionally more time to make the decision for longer memorized lists. A plausible theory about what goes on in the subjects' minds as they solve the task (e.g., Sternberg, 1966) is that they store the list in short-term memory, encode the probe digit, compare the probe serially with each element in the list, then respond "yes" if a match occurs and "no" otherwise. This accounts for both empirical findings about subjects' performance: (1) their correctness (because of the exhaustiveness of the search) and (2) their linear increase in reaction time with increasing list length (because of the seriality of the search). There are many variants of this model, but all of them address these two facts. However, a model that accounted only for the reaction time data without accounting for the more basic fact that subjects could perform the task errorlessly to begin with would not be taken seriously (e.g., a model in which only a random sample of items drawn from the list, but proportional in size to it, was scanned). No one in cognitive psychology questions that the subject's success at solving the task is a more fundamental datum than the second-order patterns of performance, like reaction time or serial position effects.

Contrast this situation with language acquisition/children's language. The child, too, is engaged in a computational task — inducing the rules of an entire language on the basis of sentences and other information comprising a small subset of that language — and the child, too, virtually always succeeds in that task. Furthermore, there are second-order patterns of data that might help decide what goes on in the child's mind as he or she solves the task: order of acquisition, over- and undergeneralizations, comprehension errors, and so on. However, unlike cognitive psychology, the concerted research efforts in the field of language acquisition address themselves virtually exclusively to the second-order patterns of data (acquisition order, errors, etc.), ignoring the gross empirical fact that all children successfully learn to speak English (or Japanese, or Warlpiri, etc.) on the basis of sentences addressed to them. The presupposition that this is the primary fact in need of explanation does not seem to hold as strongly, if it holds at all.

In this paper, I describe a research program in language acquisition that has a different emphasis than most. Rather than examining various stages of children's language from the outset and trying to derive implications for the process of acquisition, I began by first considering the empirical fact that the child is ultimately successful at acquiring a language. This led me to consider models of *language learnability:* how, in principle, it may be possible to acquire the rules of an unknown language on the basis of sentences or other relevant inputs to a language learner. Many of the existing models I considered from the mathematical linguistics and computer science literature (Pinker, 1979) were not even remotely plausible as models of human children (though two very significant exceptions are Anderson's, 1977, Language Acquisition System and, especially, Wexler & Culicover's, 1980, Degree-2 Theory; see Pinker, 1979, 1981c, for reviews). I devised a new set of procedures that took sentences and certain semantic information as input and yielded as output a set of grammatical rules (Pinker, 1982). These procedures were designed primarily to meet the requirement of sufficiency at learning grammatical rules, but they also were kept psychologically plausible in the following ways: (1) the mechanisms did not require any sort of input information that was plainly unavailable to the child (e.g., parental feedback contingent on the syntactic well-formedness of the child's utterances); (2) they did not require vast numbers of inputs to learn a rule; (3) they did not engage in generating hypotheses without regard to the input data and only then testing the hypotheses; (4) they were meant to be executed during the left-to-right processing of input sentences; (5) they created rules in a format that had some degree of independent linguistic, psycholinguistic, and computational motivation (see Bresnan, 1982).

Once a basic framework for an acquisition model had been sketched out, it raised many empirical and theoretical questions, and these questions have become the focus of a multifaceted research program that is the subject of this chapter. Children's language enters into several of these questions directly, and into all of them indirectly, though what distinguishes this research program from most in developmental psycholinguistics is its use of children's language as a means rather than an end and its multidisciplinary approach, drawing on computer science and linguistics as much as on experimental or observational studies of the child's behavior. Among the questions raised by the proposed acquisition mechanisms are the following:

1. How adaptable are the proposed acquisition mechanisms to the acquisition of languages other than English or, for that matter, to the acquisition of non-Indo-European languages? This question is best answered by examining the properties of languages that are very different from English and determining the sorts of input data that a child could use to select the appropriate rules (Pinker, 1984; Walsh, 1981).

2. Is there any way of establishing that the formal properties of the grammatical rules whose acquisition we are concerned with make the languages they define learnable in principle? This question may be addressed using elementary combinatorics and mathematical linguistics to establish whether the linguistic rules guarantee that a set of languages will have certain properties conducive to learnability, such as containing only a finite number of possible languages. At the same time, one must examine relevant linguistic evidence to ascertain whether the various assumptions about language that were used in support of the learnability proof are empirically justifiable (Pinker, 1981b, 1982, in preparation).

3. Does the model provide accounts for the wealth of data about children's language development that have been gathered over the past 20 years? Answering this requires examining data from developmental psycholinguistics

relevant to the acquisition of particular constructions, deriving corresponding predictions from the model, altering the model if necessary, comparing
the accounts from the model with others in the literature, and judging
whether modifications inspired by discrepant data are well motivated within
the model—that is, consistent with the general form of its mechanisms, appli-
cable to other developmental data, or useful in accounting for the acquisition
of other rules or other languages (Pinker, 1984).

4. Can the model raise testable new research questions about children's
linguistic development? The ability of a theory to inspire the gathering of
data whose possible interpretations are laid out before they are gathered is a
major asset. We have used the theory to pose empirical questions and have
conducted experiments with children and analyzed transcripts of children's
speech in order to answer them (eg., Lebeaux & Pinker, 1981; Wilson,
Pinker, Zaanen, & Lebeaux, 1981).

5. Does the theory raise testable questions about the acquisition-relevant
input to the child? Although the study of parental speech to children has
grown in the past decade, few of the studies examine how various properties
of parental speech interact with specific acquisition mechanisms to affect the
course of learning (Newport, Gleitman, & Gleitman, 1977, is a notable exception; see also de Paulo & Bonvillian, 1978; Furrow, Nelson, & Benedict,
1979; Gleitman, Newport, & Gleitman, 1984; Hoff-Ginsberg & Shatz, 1982;
Nelson, 1977, 1980; Nelson, Carskaddon, & Bonvillian, 1973; Snow &
Ferguson, 1977, for a sample of debate in this area). The learning mechanisms of the model make some fairly specific demands on early parental input and also predict that certain detailed syntactic properties of parental
speech at various stages may affect the rapidity of acquisition of particular
rules by the child. We have examined transcripts of parental speech (Pinker &
Hochberg, in preparation) with an eye toward testing the assumptions of the
model and describing the acquisition-relevant syntactic properties of parental speech.

6. Do the mechanisms of the theory accomplish the tasks that they were
designed to accomplish? Very often, algorithms that look good individually
on paper make a hash of their task when they are actually set in motion on
real-world inputs. A rudimentary computer simulation of the acquisition
model has been implemented (Walsh, 1981), and it has shown some of the
proposals of the model to be adequate, others to be in need of revision.

In this chapter, I hope to outline the acquisition model briefly and then
give an overview on selected aspects of five of these six projects, which together comprise the "multifaceted approach" mentioned in the title. (For reasons of space, I will not discuss (2), concerning formal properties of the target grammars, and instead refer the reader to Pinker 1982, in preparation).

Each discussion is necessarily highly selective, and in each case, I refer the reader to more detailed presentations. The chapter is a progress report on these activities as of 1982, and most are only in their very early stages (especially (5) and (6)). Furthermore, many of the empirical conclusions I offer are highly tentative, and many of the theoretical proposals will turn out to be wrong in a number of ways. But I present the project as a case study of how learnability theory, computer simulation, linguistic theory, and developmental psycholinguistics might be made to mesh in an attempt to provide a unified account of language acquisition.

A SKETCH OF THE ACQUISITION MODEL

A model of learning must specify precisely at least three things: (1) what is learned; (2) what inputs are used to learn it; and (3) how it is learned. I discuss each in turn very briefly (see Pinker, 1982, 1984, for more detailed presentations).

What Is Learned

I assume that the child learns a rule system of the sort described by Bresnan and Kaplan in their theory of Lexical Functional Grammar (LFG) (Bresnan, 1978, 1982; Kaplan & Bresnan, 1982). An LFG generates two structures for every well-formed sentence in the language: a *constituent structure* (or c-structure) and a *functional structure* (or f-structure). A c-structure is similar to a surface structure or phrase marker tree, as in the Standard Theory of transformational grammar (Chomsky, 1965), with two important differences. First, all c-structures are generated directly by phrase structure rewrite rules rather than being derived by the application of transformations to a deep structure tree. This means that every type of phrase (e.g., active, passive, dative, dative passive, etc.) will be generated directly by phrase structure rules (though alternative expansions of the same category used in different constructions can be collapsed with the use of the standard abbreviatory conventions of parentheses, asterisks, and braces). Second, major constituents in the phrase structure tree are annotated with the names of the grammmatical relations (alternatively, "grammatical functions") they bear to larger constituents they are parts of. This is illustrated in 13.1, a c-structure for the sentence *Sam asked Phil to kiss Jean,* in which the NP dominating *Sam* is annotated as the subject of the sentence, the NPs dominating *Phil* and *Jean* are annotated as the objects of their respective VPs, and the VP dominating *kiss Jean* is annotated as the verb phrase complement of the main verb phrase.

13.1.

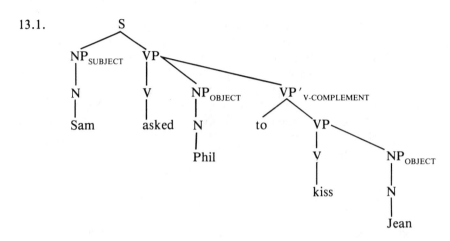

The c-structure 13.1 was generated by the *annotated phrase structure rules* listed in 13.2.

13.2.   S   →   NP_SUBJECT   VP

         NP   →   (det)   N

         VP   →   V   (NP)_OBJECT   (VP')_V-COMPLEMENT

         VP'   →   (to)   VP

The second structure underlying a sentence, the f-structure, is an explicit compilation of all the grammatical information relevant to the semantic interpretation of the sentence. It is generated by the annotated phrase structure rules and the *lexical entries* for each morpheme in the sentence, acting in concert. The f-structure corresponding to 13.1 is presented as 13.3.

13.3.
$$\begin{bmatrix} \text{PREDICATE} & \text{"ask (SUBJECT, OBJECT, V-COMPLEMENT)"} \\ \text{TENSE} & \text{past} \\ \text{SUBJECT} & \text{(PREDICATE "Sam")} \\ \text{OBJECT} & \text{(PREDICATE "Phil")} \\ \text{V-COMPLEMENT} & \begin{bmatrix} \text{PREDICATE "kiss (SUBJECT, OBJECT)"} \\ \text{SUBJECT ( )} \\ \text{OBJECT (PREDICATE "Jean")} \end{bmatrix} \end{bmatrix}$$

The lexical entries that participated in the generation of 13.3 are listed in 13.4.

13.4. Sam: N: PREDICATE = "Sam"
       Phil: N: PREDICATE = "Phil"
       Jean: N: PREDICATE = "Jean"
       asked: V: PREDICATE = "ask (SUBJECT, OBJECT,
                     V-COMPLEMENT)"
                     TENSE = past
                     OBJECT = V-COMPLEMENT'S SUBJECT
       kiss: V: PREDICATE = "kiss (SUBJECT,
                     OBJECT)"

The heart of the f-structure is its PREDICATE entry, which conveys the predicate-argument relations (the "who did what to whom" information) expressed by the sentence. The predicate statement is taken from the lexical entry of the main verb. In the notation, the particular semantic relation signified by the verb (e.g., eating vs. hitting) is symbolized simply as the name of the word, printed in lower case within quotes ("ask"). (This is simply a surrogate for a semantic representation, to be specified by a theory of word meaning.) The arguments of the predicate are individuated by places separated by commas within the parentheses (for *ask*, the first place corresponds to the asker, the second to the asked, and the third to the favor asked). In the PREDICATE statement, each place is filled with the name of the grammatical function that labels the particular argument in the c-structure tree. In this case, the first slot within parentheses, corresponding to the asker, is filled by the function SUBJECT, indicating that the constituent labeled SUBJECT in the tree (in this case, the NP dominating *Sam*) stands for the first argument (the asker) of the relation *ask*. The other functions similarly indicate where to look in the c-structure tree to find the second and third arguments of *ask*. Grammatical functions, then, act as links between surface structure positions and the semantic or logical arguments of a predicate by virtue of being mentioned in two locations within the grammar: in the appropriate slot of the lexical entry for a multiargument predicate and as an annotation to a constituent in a phrase structure rule.

Within the f-structure, the functions label the various arguments of the verb, each one enclosed in its own set of square brackets. The f-structure also contains the grammatically encoded semantic features of the words of the sentence such as the tense and aspect of verbs and the gender, number, person, and so on of the noun phrases. These, too, are taken from the lexical entries for the various words and are entered in the appropriate places within the f-structure (see Kaplan & Bresnan, 1982, for a more complete account of the mechanics of the grammar).

The f-structure, with the help of lexically encoded information, also lists the arguments and predicate argument relations that are not encoded explicitly in the c-structure. In this case, the argument *Phil* is both the object of the verb *ask* and the subject of the verb *kiss*. It is a property of the verb *ask* that its object can also serve as a subject of an embedded complement (as opposed to, say, *John informed Mary to leave Bill; John promised Mary to leave Bill*), and this is encoded in the functional equation OBJECT = V-COMPLEMENT'S SUBJECT annotated to the lexical entry for *ask*. In the f-structure, this coreference is expressed by the SUBJECT f-substructure within the V-COMPLEMENT f-substructure and by the dashed line linking it to the OBJECT f-substructure one level up.

Because there are no transformations within an LFG, every verb that can appear in different surface structures (specifically, within surface structures with different sets of grammatical functions) must have more than one lexical entry, one for each structure. Thus the passive version of 13.1 will have the surface structure shown in 13.5 and the f-structure in 13.6, constructed from the passive lexical entry for *ask* shown in 13.7 (I ignore the auxiliary in the f-structure for brevity's sake).

13.5.

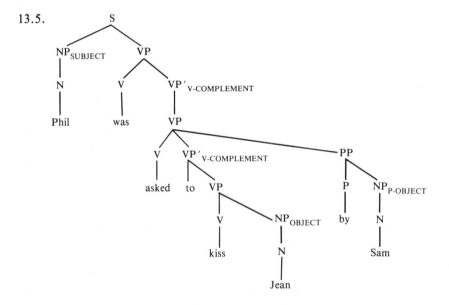

13.6.
$$
\left[
\begin{array}{l}
\text{PREDICATE} \qquad \text{``ask (BY-OBJECT, SUBJECT,} \\
\qquad\qquad\qquad\qquad \text{V-COMPLEMENT)''} \\
\text{TENSE} \quad \text{PAST} \\
\text{SUBJECT (PREDICATE ``Phil'')} \text{---------} \\
\text{BY-OBJECT} \qquad\qquad \text{(PREDICATE ``Sam'')} \\
\text{V-COMPLEMENT.} \left[
\begin{array}{l}
\text{SUBJECT (\qquad) ----} \\
\text{PREDICATE ``kiss (SUBJECT, OBJECT)''} \\
\text{OBJECT (PREDICATE ``Jean'')}
\end{array}
\right]
\end{array}
\right]
$$

13.7.   ask: V: PREDICATE = "ask (BY-OBJECT, SUBJECT,
                              V-COMPLEMENT)"
                     PARTICIPLE = PASSIVE
                     SUBJECT = V-COMPLEMENT'S SUBJECT

As can be seen, the number of places within the argument structure of the predicate of *ask* is the same as before, as is the semantic role of the argument corresponding to each place. What differentiates the passive entry from the active entry is the set of grammatical functions that encode the arguments: SUBJECT and OBJECT encoding the asker and asked, respectively, in the active version versus BY-OBJECT and SUBJECT in the passive version.

The fact that most active verbs have passive counterparts is captured by a lexical rule, which, applied to the active lexical entry, generates a passive entry corresponding to it. Once the passive entry is created, it alone is invoked in its passive sentence; the active entry plays no role. The passive lexical rule shown in 13.8 replaces each mention of OBJECT in a lexical entry by SUBJECT and each mention of SUBJECT by BY-OBJECT. Another part of the rule indicates the change in morphology by adding the equation specifying that the verb is a passive participle.

13.8.   OBJECT   ↦   SUBJECT
        SUBJECT   ↦   BY-OBJECT
        ↦PARTICIPLE = PASSIVE

The theory also has mechanisms for the "long-distance" binding of traces to their antecedents found in relative clauses, wh–questions, and *tough*-movement sentences, but these are beyond the scope of this chapter (see Bresnan, 1982; Kaplan & Bresnan, 1982, for details).

Input

Along with Macnamara (1972), Wexler and Culicover (1980), and many others (see Pinker, 1979), I assume that in many cases in which the child hears an adult sentence, he or she can infer the meaning of the sentence from the nonlinguistic context in which it is uttered and the meanings of some of its individual content words. Thus, the input to the acquisition mechanisms can be treated as a set of pairs, each consisting of a sentence (I assume for convenience that segmentation has already been accomplished) and its inferred meaning, where "meaning" includes: (1) the meanings of the individual content words in the sentence or at least their classification into broad semantic categories such as "thing," "action," "place," "manner," "person," and so on (it is assumed that children at first process only those sentences, or those parts of sentences, whose word meanings they already know); (2) the links between predicates and their arguments, including a classification of arguments into broad thematic categories such as "agent-of-action," "theme-of-action," "propositional argument," and so on; and (3) the grammatically relevant semantic features of the referents of the sentence (e.g., the sex, number, animacy, humanness of the referent objects, and the tense, aspect, modality, etc. of the referent events). This information can be encoded into a generalized f-structure representation described in Pinker (1982, 1984). It also seems reasonable to assume that the child's attentional abilities filter the input sentences so that the beginning, end, stressed, and familiar words of a sentence are most likely to be entered as input into the acquisition mechanisms.

How It Is Learned

The core of the acquisition model is a set of procedures that try to build a phrase marker or tree for an incoming string of words. When a listener already has a full set of grammatical rules, this is simply the ordinary process of syntactic parsing that occurs during sentence comprehension. But for the child, no rules exist at first, and so the parsing process must appeal to procedures other than the consultation of rules to complete the parse. After the parse is complete (or in some cases, while it is in progress), new rules can be coined and added to the child's grammar depending on how the parse was accomplished. I have used two principles of parsing or tree building that can go on before the necessary adult rules have been learned and that, by hypothesis, are what result in the learning of those rules. I present each principle in turn, followed by examples of how the procedures actually operate. I do not state the exact conditions and actions of each procedure in full, but refer the reader to Pinker (1982, 1984) where these procedures are listed explicitly.

Before stating the principles, I should point out that the general form of the learning procedures is highly nativist; that is, the procedures are designed to acquire linguistic rules in certain a priori formats. Specifically, there are procedures designed to acquire annotated phrase structure rules, lexical entries, lexical rules, control equations, and so on, and in each case, the general form of the rule need not be learned, only its particular realization in a given language. In the limited space available here it may be best to justify this assumption by what Fodor (1975) has called the Lyndon Johnson argument, based on the late President's rebuttal "I'm the only President you've got." At the time of this writing, I know of no psychologically plausible and computationally precise syntax acquisition procedure that is not nativist in significant ways (see Pinker, 1979, for a review and arguments). Indeed, Anderson (1976) and Wexler (Wexler & Culicover, 1980), working within radically different pretheoretical and methodological frameworks, both claimed to be forced to a highly nativist stance as a result of their efforts at devising precise language learnability models (though see Anderson, 1983, for a more recent assessment, and Pinker, 1984, for a detailed discussion of nativism in language acquisition theories).

The first principle of acquisition is motivated by the problem of applying the innate procedures to the input data in the appropriate way. Sentences are acoustic objects, and the universal, possibly innate properties of syntax do not pertain to the acoustic properties of sentences (e.g., nouns do not have any universal serial position, stress, pronunciation, etc.). A child must determine the syntactically relevant properties of the acoustic input in order for his or her acquisition mechanisms to apply to the right parts of the input. Based on proposals by Macnamara (1982) and Grimshaw (1981), I have assumed that the child treats the presence of certain *perceptual* or *cognitive* properties and relations holding among word referents (which are available under the hypothesis that semantic input is available and that word meanings are learned before syntax) as clues or evidence for positing certain *grammatical* categories and relations in the input sentence. The acquisition mechanisms can thus be triggered by elements that are more directly "in" the input. Some of the correspondences between perceptual entities and the grammatical entities they cause the child to posit are listed in Table 13.1.

Observe that the proposal that the child uses semantic notions as clues to syntactic categories and relations is related to, but somewhat different from de Villiers' (1981) proposal that examples of grammatical relations with certain semantic properties constitute the prototypical instances of those relations. De Villiers discusses the possibility that agents of actions may be the "best" members of the set of possible grammatical subjects in a language in the same way that a robin is psychologically the "best" example or prototype of the class of birds (as opposed to, say, a penguin; see Rosch, 1973). The consequence of this, she suggests, is that any syntactic rule applying to subjects in general will always apply to agentive subjects, but may or may not apply to nonagentive subjects, even if the child learns the rule in question from nonagentive subjects in the input. This proposal differs from my "semantic bootstrapping hypothesis" in the following ways:

1. It is relevant to the stage at which some rules involving subjects have already been acquired (otherwise the child could not generalize from a nonprototypical to a prototypical subject — they must both be recognized as being subjects first). In contrast, my proposal is designed to account for the acquisition of the first rules involving subjects.

2. My proposal, unlike de Villiers', does not give any special status to agentive subjects in the rule system acquired. Their only role is in helping the child to recognize subjects in the input. The subject symbols in the rules so acquired are not semantically delineated; agentive subjects are like any other subjects. (One exception is in the acquisition of lexical rules, for which I incorporate a proposal not unlike that of de Villiers; see Pinker, 1984.)

TABLE 13.1

Syntax-Semantics Correspondences That May Be Useful in Language Acquisition:
A First Approximation

Grammatical Element or Relation	Perceptual/Semantic Element or Relation
Syntactic Categories	
Noun	Name of Person or Thing
Verb	Action or Change of State
Adjective	Perceptible Physical Property
Preposition	Spatial Relation, Direction, or Path
Grammatical Functions	
Subject	Agent of Action; Cause; Subject of a Predication
Object	Patient of Action; Theme (if there is an agent)
Oblique (e.g., prepositional) Object	Location; Source; Goal
Complement	Complete Proposition serving as an argument within another proposition
Cases	
Nominative or Ergative	Agent of Transitive Action
Accusative or Absolutive	Patient of Transitive Action
Nominative or Absolutive	Actor of Intransitive Action
Tree Relations	
Sister of X	Argument of predicate denoted by X
Sister of X'	Restrictive modifier of predicate denoted by X
Sister of X''	Appositive modifier of predicate denoted by X

Note. I have adopted Jackendoff's (1977) X-bar formulation of phrase structure rules whereby X can stand for N, V, Adj, or P; X' stands for NP, VP, AP, or PP; and X'' and X''' stand for more superordinate versions of NP, VP, etc. According to Jackendoff, all categories are initially introduced into trees as X''' and are composed of a "head" consisting of the same category with one fewer bar (e.g., a noun, N, is the head of a noun phrase, N'), plus a number of "specifiers" (determiners, complementizers, etc.) and "complements" (major phrases such as AP and VP within a mother phrase, e.g. an AP within an NP). The correspondences between tree relations and logical relations is also borrowed from Jackendoff (1977). Note also that the thematic correlates of grammatical relations do not apply across the board, but only to "basic" structures in the sense of Keenan (1976). See Pinker (1984) for discussion.

The assumption that semantics is used as an early clue or inductive basis for syntax allows one to show how the acquisition mechanisms can get started on their first inputs. Let us consider the simple example shown in 13.9, in which 13.9a is the string of words the child hears and 13.9b is an encoding of the inferred meaning of the sentence in an f-structure notation. Because I assume that the child exploits correspondences between thematic relations (agent and patient) and grammatical functions (subject and object), the child can build this f-structure, even though it is primarily a grammatical representation, before learning any syntactic rules.

13.9a.   Sentence: The dog bit the cat.

13.9b.   F-structure:

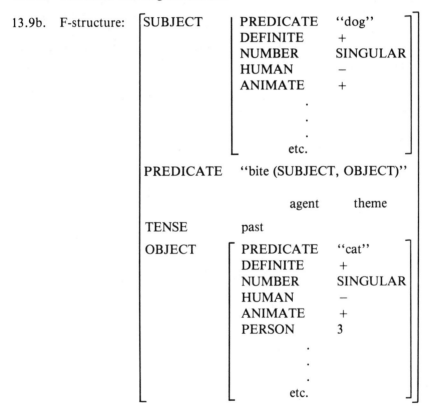

In this example, I assume that the entire word string was encoded intact and that the meaning of each word is already known (see Pinker, 1982, 1984, for an account of how the meaning of words like *the* can be acquired independently of knowing any phrase structure rules). The first thing the child does is create lexical category nodes for each word in the sentence, using the correspondences between perceptual categories and syntactic categories assumed earlier (here I also assume that the canonical category for a word signaling definiteness in discourse is *determiner*). The result is 13.10.

13.10.   det   N   V   det   N
            | | | | |
           the   dog   bit   the   cat

The next task is to deduce how that sequence of lexical categories is grouped into phrases. In principle, this could be done in an infinite number of ways. However, because of the constraints inherent in *X*-bar theory, which I assume to be built into the child's acquisition mechanisms, the child has no choice but to posit the maximal projections of each of the major lexical categories, and so will end up with 13.11. (To prevent clutter, I assume that the maximal projection of a category *X* is *X″*, not *X‴*, except for V, where the maximal projection V‴ corresponds to the sentence or S-node in more traditional notations (see Jackendoff, 1977).

13.11.

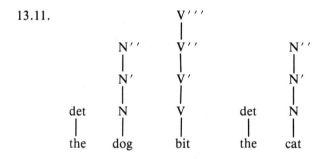

Each constituent is linked to its appropriate f-structure, so the child can see that *the dog* is the agent argument of the predicate *bit,* hence, by hypothesis, the subject argument. Subjects of main verbs, I assume, are universally daughters of the root S-node (V‴ here), so the child makes the corresponding attachment, resulting in 13.12.

13.12.

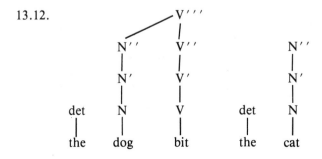

The child's f-structure similarly indicates that the two determiners *the* express the definiteness of the first and last noun phrases, respectively, and that the phrase *the cat* is an argument (the object argument, by hypothesis) of the predicate expressed by *bit*. Using the provision of *X*-bar theory that specifies that determiners are attached as daughters of the maximal projection of the word they modify (Jackendoff, 1977), the child attaches the two instances of *the* to their corresponding N″s and, using the provision specifying that argument phrases are attached as sisters of the words representing the predicates they are arguments of (Jackendoff, 1977), attaches the object noun phrase *the cat* as a daughter of V′. This completes the tree, resulting in 13.13.

13.13.

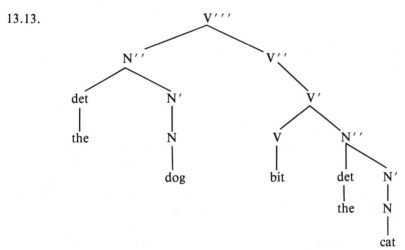

Again using f-structure information, the child annotates maximal projections of words with the grammatical functions that relate them to predicates, yielding 13.14.

13.14.

One usually derives trees using phrase structure rules, but given only a tree, as is the case for our child at this moment, one can just as easily derive the phrase structure rules (and lexical entries) that generate it (13.15).

13.15. $V''' \rightarrow N''_{\text{SUBJECT}}$ V'' (analogous to $S \rightarrow NP_{\text{SUBJECT}}$ VP)

$N'' \rightarrow$ det N'

$N' \rightarrow N$ (analogous to NP$\rightarrow$det N)

$V'' \rightarrow V'$

$V' \rightarrow V N''_{\text{OBJECT}}$ (analogous to VP$\rightarrow$V NP$_{\text{OBJECT}}$)

the:det:DEFINITE $= +$

dog:N:PREDICATE $=$ "dog"

cat:N:PREDICATE $=$ "cat"

bit:V:PREDICATE $=$ "bite (SUBJECT, OBJECT)"

The child has, with a single (string/f-structure) pair, induced five phrase structure rules complete with functional annotations and lexical entries for each word.

This success is attributable in large part to the assumed canonical semantics-syntax correlations that, luckily, held in this example. What about cases in which these correlations do not hold? These correlations will certainly not hold in general in adult speech (e.g., in the sentence *the scandal drove the party from office*). If they did, we would not even have to posit syntactic categories in the adult grammar: *Thing* and *action* and *agent* and *patient* would obviate the need for N and V and SUBJECT and OBJECT. Because these *are* needed in the adult grammar, we have to account for how the child learns nouns that are not things, subjects that are not agents, and so on. Happily, it seems that these noncanonical cases will be encountered later than the more canonical sentences (Pinker & Hochberg, in preparation). Therefore, it can be argued, the child can use the rules acquired from the canonical cases to analyze the noncanonical cases. This is done by attempting as far as possible to parse the sentence using existing rules (just as adults do in normal comprehension) and invoking the semantics-driven acquisition procedures when some part of the sentence cannot be parsed in this way (of course, for the very first sentence, no part is parsable). If there is some portion of the sentence that cannot be parsed (e.g., if there are no lexical entries for the words) and the semantics-driven procedures cannot apply (e.g., if the words do not signify actions, things, etc.), then, I propose, the parse is completed by building the tree top-down and labeling the as yet unknown elements in a way that makes this possible.

To be specific, consider the example sentence *the scandal drove the party from office.* Because the content words are abstract, the procedure used in the last example will not be triggered. However, the child will know the categorization for the word *the,* and thus can begin to parse the sentence with his or her existing rules, starting with 13.16.

13.16.   det
          |
          the scandal drove . . .

The only rule in the child's current grammar introducing determiners is N″→det N′, so the child can confidently build part of the tree subtended by *the* (13.17).

13.17.

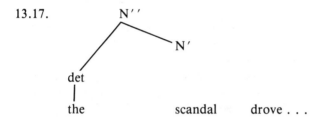

N′ expands only to N in the current grammar, justifying the next stage of the parse, shown in 13.18.

13.18.

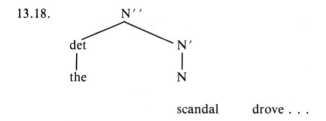

Normally, the parse would grind to a halt at this point, because *scandal* has no category label in the lexicon. But because the grammar allows only one possible category in this position, N, the learning procedure declares that the categorization of the unknown word is just that category and makes the corresponding entry to the lexicon (13.19):

13.19.   scandal N: PREDICATE = "scandal"

Now that there is a complete noun phrase at the beginning of the sentence, the learner can continue the parsing process, using the previously learned rule introducing N'' ($V''' \rightarrow N''_{\text{SUBJECT}} V''$) and V ($V'' \rightarrow V'$ and $V' \rightarrow V \; N''_{\text{OBJECT}}$) to build an additional portion of the tree (13.20).

13.20.

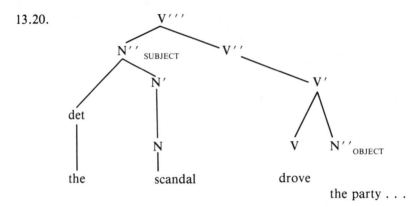

the party . . .

To complete the partial parse, the learner must hypothesize that *drove* is a verb and also that its first two abstract arguments (the "impetus" and the "affected," respectively) are expressed syntactically by the functions SUBJECT and OBJECT (because these functions are annotated to the NPs that dominate its arguments in the tree). The function for the third argument (the "new direction") could similarly be deduced if the rules $V' \rightarrow V(N''_{\text{OBJECT}})$ (PP) and $P' \rightarrow P \; N''_{\text{P-OBJECT}}$ had been acquired from semantically transparent cases like *put* ("P-OBJECT," or prepositional object, will be the function given to directions, paths, or spatial goals). This would result in the lexical entry in 13.21.

13.21. drive V: PREDICATE = "drive (SUBJECT, OBJECT, P-OBJECT)."

Continuing with these procedures, the learner can parse the rest of the sentence and make the corresponding additions to the grammar and lexicon. I call this parse-driven learning procedure *structure-dependent distributional learning*. Presumably, inflections and morphology, once learned from canonical cases, can also be used to identify the category membership of otherwise inscrutable words.

Note that this notion of distributional learning is related to, but distinct in several ways from, the acquisition theory of Maratsos and Chalkley (1980). Maratsos and Chalkley eschew grammatical categories in favor of a procedure that records the correlations among the positional, inflectional, and semantic properties of words. Grammatical categories are then implicit in the obtained patterns of intercorrelations, and the learner can generalize that a new word observed to have one property in a correlated set may be assigned the other properties in that set as well. In Pinker (1984) I point out that without some innate specification of which properties the child should correlate with which other ones, Maratsos and Chalkley's learner would be forced to examine an astronomical number of correlations (e.g., in the sentence *the black cat chased the mouse into the bathtub,* the child might record large numbers of irrelevant local co-occurrences, such as that the word *into* appears in a sentence containing the word *black* and also appears as the third-to-last word in the sentence). Furthermore, most of these properties and their intercorrelations are not linguistically significant in any natural language, a fact that intensifies the wastefulness of the learner's tasks under the model and that itself cries out for explanation. Finally, the absence of explicit syntactic category labels in the rule system attained by the model forces the adult in effect to process an entire correlation matrix every time a member of a category is used, violating an important principle of efficient computational design (Marr & Nishihara's, 1978, "principle of explicit naming").

In contrast, the theory outlined here (and defended in Pinker, 1984) holds that:

1. There is an innately specified "family resemblance structure" (Rosch & Mervis, 1975) for each major grammatical category and relation, specifying a small number of grammatical properties subsets of which the category can assume in various languages.

2. These properties are not such easily detectable but linguistically irrelevant properties as adjacency in the string or serial position, but refer to phrase structure geometry, agreement, control, anaphora, extractability, and so on.

3. Most of these properties are not detectable by themselves in the input by a linguistically novice infant (e.g., no child can deduce that an unknown word in the input must be a verb on account of its "agreeing with its subject" before he or she has learned what a subject is in the target language, and vice versa).

4. Most categories and relations have a canonical semantic property among the correlated properties in the innate family resemblance structure (e.g., thing for noun, agent of action in basic structures for subject), and detection of such properties requires no prior syntactic learning.

5. The child can use the relevant semantic properties of the first words to identify their category membership and coin the first phrase structure and affixational rules. Following that the appropriate distributional tests relevant to defining new category exemplars are specified by the nonsemantic properties of that category, drawn from the family resemblance structure; therefore only the a priori relevant distributional contexts need be examined.

Thus, in comparison with Maratsos and Chalkley, I attribute greater roles to innate patterns of potential correlation among grammatical properties and to canonical semantic properties of grammatical categories and relations. Furthermore, the correlated properties, those that define the distributional contexts used to make generalizations about newly heard words, are more abstract in my model (hence, require some prior learning). However, my proposals are similar to those of Maratsos and Chalkley in that we both suppose that the rule system acquired (which should not be confused with the means of acquiring it) is a formal system defining classes in terms of their syntactic privileges of occurrence, rather than a system defining the behavior of classes that can be antecedently well defined by their semantic properties (see Pinker, 1984, Chap. 2, for further discussion).

EXTENDING THE ACQUISITION MECHANISMS

The procedures whose operation was exemplified in the previous section work nicely for the inputs provided in those examples, but of course, the child cannot be assured of receiving just those inputs. The procedures as used have a moderate degree of cross-linguistic generality—they will learn any constituent order permitted by X-bar theory, and additional mechanisms discussed in Pinker (1982, 1984) will acquire case and agreement markers in languages that signal grammatical relations with those devices. However, it is unclear how the mechanisms would perform on inputs from languages that are radically different from English. The child has no way of knowing in advance which sort of language he or she is to be faced with, and presumably, there is a single set of acquisition mechanisms that work for all languages; hence, assuring that the acquisition mechanisms will be maximally general is a high priority in developing the theory. In this section, I summarize the mechanisms designed to acquire phrase structure rules in more detail, and sketch out the sort of modifications that would be needed to get the mechanisms to produce the right outputs for a certain class of non-Indo-European languages.

The procedures used in the previous section to acquire phrase structure rules are divided into seven "subroutines" (see Pinker, 1982, 1984, for a more detailed listing):

P1. Build as complete a tree for the string as possible by parsing it with existing annotated phrase structure rules and existing lexical entries.

P2. For the parts of the sentence that do not yet subtend branches of the tree, label the words with the lexical categories that are flagged by the semantic properties of the word meaning (e.g., noun for thing, verb for action, etc.). Build a branch extending each lexical category upward to its maximal projection (i.e., X''' according to Jackendoff's formulation of X-bar theory; I used X'' for simplicity in the previous section).

P3. Connect the SUBJECT noun phrase as the daughter of the root S-node (the maximal projection of the main verb of the sentence).

P4. Connect the remaining branches according to the information in the input semantic representation and the X-bar principles (e.g., functional argument = sister of X, restrictive modifier = sister of X', nonrestrictive modifier = sister of X''). If the desired connection is impossible without crossing branches, connect the complement one node higher than the specified node.

P5. Annotate the maximally projected node of each noun phrase with the grammatical function determined for that argument by its thematic relation to the head (SUBJECT = agent, etc.). If a head of a constituent is marked for case (Pinker, 1982, 1984, describes a procedure for the acquisition of case markers), append the equation CASE $= n$ to the phrase, where n is the indicated case, also determined originally by its thematic relation to the verb.

P6. Create annotated phrase structure rules corresponding to the tree fit onto the sentence, according to the usual conventions relating trees to rewrite rules.

P7. Collapse new and old expansions of a category (i.e., the right-hand side of a phrase structure rule) as follows ("symbol" refers here to a category together with the annotation indicating its grammatical function): (1) asterisk any symbol that appears twice in succession in an expansion in one rule (thus, $VP \rightarrow V\ PP\ PP$ becomes $VP \rightarrow V\ PP^*$); (2) if a sequence of symbols in one expansion is properly contained within another expansion, combine the two expansions, putting parentheses around the symbols not contained in the smaller expansion (thus, $VP \rightarrow V$ and $VP \rightarrow V\ NP$ are collapsed into $VP \rightarrow V$ (NP)); (3) if two expansions are identical except for one symbol that differs between them, collapse the expressions by placing the noncommon symbols within braces (thus, $VP \rightarrow V\ NP$ and $VP \rightarrow V\ PP$ are collapsed into $VP \rightarrow V$ $\{{NP \atop PP}\}$); (4) if two symbols appear in braces in one rule and successively in the other (with the rest of the expansions identical), discard the braces and retain the symbols in the correct sequence, each within a pair of parentheses (thus, $VP \rightarrow V$ $\{{NP \atop PP}\}$ and $VP \rightarrow V\ NP\ PP$ are collapsed into $VP \rightarrow V\ (NP)\ (PP)$).

These procedures will create a different phrase structure rule for each order of constituents within a phrase that the child hears (subject then to the collapsing procedure, P7). As mentioned, one would want the procedures to create rules that are more appropriate to languages with various degrees of free word order, such as Japanese or Warlpiri. This involves two steps: indicating the freedom of order of a set of constituents within a phrase and, for languages like Warlpiri (see Hale, 1981), "flattening" the hierarchical structure of the tree so that all maximal constituents are daughters of S. Interestingly, Walsh (1981) points out that the existing procedures will already flatten the tree where necessary, thanks to the last subprocedure of P4, originally designed to handle VSO languages like Irish. If a Warlpiri child hears an adjacent adjective-noun pair, he or she will coin a NP rule generating the adjective and noun as daughters of NP. But then, when he or she hears a sentence in which the adjective and its head noun are separated by, say, a verb, and the inferred f-structure indicates that the adjective indeed modifies that noun, it will be impossible to attach the AP as a daughter of NP without crossing branches. Procedure P4, applied recursively, will attach it as a daughter of S, and P6 will then coin a rule generating AP as a daughter of S. This will give the child a set of "flat" phrase structure rules for languages that require them, using sentences with "tangled" trees as the necessary evidence.

It remains, then, to coin rules allowing n constituents to appear in any of $n!$ orders. A modification of the collapsing procedures (P7) along the lines suggested by Lapointe (1980) perhaps could accomplish this. Roughly, P7 should be modified so that when it encounters categories with the same category label but different functions (e.g., two NP symbols with different case annotations) in one order in one rule and in the other order in another rule, it should collapse the two symbols into a single asterisked symbol bearing the disjunction of the former individual annotations. Thus, for a hypothetical language resembling Japanese, rules 13.22a and 13.22b would be collapsed to form 13.22c.

13.22a.   S → NP$_{\text{SUBJECT}}$ NP$_{\text{OBJECT}}$ V

13.22b.   S → NP$_{\text{OBJECT}}$ NP$_{\text{SUBJECT}}$ V

13.22c.   S → NP*$_{\text{OBJECT}}$ V
                              or
                          SUBJECT

Kaplan and Bresnan's (1982) formal conditions on the consistency, coherence, and completeness of f-structures will rule out the ungrammatical sentences (e.g., with no subject or two subjects) that 13.23c would otherwise generate. When an indirect object then appears in at least two positions relative to the subject and object, it too will be collapsed into rule 13.23c, allowing the child to generate all six orders of subject, object, and indirect object after having heard four (of course, it remains an empirical question whether children do generalize in this way rather than coining each of the six expansions upon hearing them exemplified in parental speech). Finally, P7 should be modified to collapse adjacent categories that appear in different orders in different rules if those categories fall into the same "natural class," in Chomsky's (1970) and Jackendoff's (1977) sense (i.e., if, like adjectives and nouns, they share a syntactic feature such as $+ N$, an abstract feature not to be confused with the category "noun"). This is done by replacing the two symbols with an asterisked variable X or Y, annotated with the feature shared by the formerly distinct categories. Thus, in some hypothetical free constituent order language, 13.23a and 13.23b would be collapsed to form 13.23c.

13.23a.   S → V   NP*   AP*

13.23b.   S → V   AP*   NP*

13.23c.   S → V   XP*
                     [+N]

These sorts of procedures, with suitable refinements perhaps along the lines of Lapointe (1980), seem to be a promising way to modify the P rules to acquire free constituent order rules (see Pinker, 1984, for a more complete presentation, and for empirical evidence that children use procedures of this general sort).

ACCOUNTING FOR EXISTING DATA ON CHILDREN'S LANGUAGE

In the past decade, there have appeared hundreds of studies on children's syntactic development, but because no general theory of language acquisition has existed to provide explanations of the data, the accounts have tended to be ad hoc and unconstrained (Atkinson, 1982; Pinker, 1979). I have argued (Pinker, 1984) that a learnability theory of the sort presented here is an ideal source of constraints on accounts of children's language. The most explanatory accounts of the child's linguistic knowledge at a given stage would have, I argued, the following properties: (1) the account would be embedded in a theory of acquisition showing how the child reached that stage based on the inputs processed until then; (2) the acquisition theory that the specific account was embedded in would show how the child would progress from that stage to full adult competence, also on the basis of inputs that the child would subsequently encounter; and (3) the account would implicate only those properties of nonlinguistic cognitive mechanisms that had independent motivation from studies of adult or child cognition. I saw this as the first step toward providing systematic and motivated accounts of the wealth of data on children's language and tried to follow that strategy in examining five classes of syntactic rules for which abundant developmental data had been gathered:

phrase structure rules, grammatical morphemes, control and complementation, auxiliaries, and lexical entries and productive lexicosyntactic alternations (e.g., dative, passive, and causative). Here I outline a single example from an early draft of that book to give the reader the flavor of how accounts of that sort were justified.

The example concerns errors in coordinating the tense of an auxiliary element with the tense of the main verb in a sentence. In English, when there is an auxiliary or sequence of auxiliaries (e.g., in questions and negations), the first element of the auxiliary must be tensed, and the affixation of all the other auxiliaries and of the main verb is determined by the element immediately preceding it. Some of the particular patterns that hold in English are listed in 13.24.

13.24a.   John is leaving/ *leave/ *left/ *leaves

13.24b.   John leaves/ *leaving/ *leave

13.24c.   John might have been being left by his wife when we
          interrupted him last Thursday.

Rather than employing an affix-hopping transformation (Chomsky, 1957), LFG treats auxiliaries as complement-taking verbs that impose constraints on their complements much like so-called "raising" and "equi" verbs (see Bresnan, 1982). Lexical entries for the four different auxiliary elements (modal, progressive *be,* perfect *have,* and passive *be*) are shown in 13.26, and a tree for a simple auxiliary structure, generated recursively by the rules VP → V VP′$_{V-COMPLEMENT}$ and VP′ → (COMPLEMENTIZER) VP, is shown in 13.25. (As before, I ignore the semantics of these words by the simple expedient of listing the word itself in the PREDICATE statement. I also ignore the complement verbs' status as participles and instead simply list their affixes directly.)

13.25.   might: V: PREDICATE = "might (V-COMPLEMENT)"

              SUBJECT = V-COMPLEMENT'S SUBJECT

              V-COMPLEMENT'S TENSE = −

              AUXILIARY = +

         have: V: PREDICATE = "have (V-COMPLEMENT)"

              SUBJECT = V-COMPLEMENT'S SUBJECT

              V-COMPLEMENT'S AFFIX = *-en*

              AUXILIARY = +

be: V: PREDICATE = "be (V-COMPLEMENT)"

SUBJECT = V-COMPLEMENT'S SUBJECT

V-COMPLEMENT'S AFFIX = *-ing*

AUXILIARY = +

be: V: PREDICATE = "be (V-COMPLEMENT)"

SUBJECT = V-COMPLEMENT'S SUBJECT

V-COMPLEMENT'S AFFIX = *-en*

AUXILIARY = +

13.26.

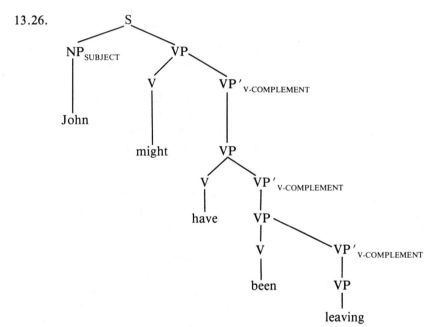

Because auxiliaries are treated here as complement-taking verbs, the learning procedures for auxiliaries are essentially the same as those for complement-taking verbs like *seem* and *ask* outlined in Pinker (1982, 1984). These procedures are triggered when the meaning of a particular auxiliary verb is learned and when the inflection on the complement verb is isolated; in particular, when a verb takes as one of its arguments an entire proposition and that proposition appears in the sentence without its subject. A modal, like *can,* fulfills this requirement because its argument is the entire proposition whose possibility is being asserted, and the subject of that proposition is "missing" in that it does not appear contiguously with that proposition (i.e., *can* intervenes). In addition, there is a subprocedure, triggered by the same condition, that acquires the co-occurrence restrictions between matrix verbs and the affixation of their complements. This subprocedure, which is the focus of the discussion to follow, is listed in 13.27.

13.27.   Add equations of the following form to the lexical entry of the complement-taking verb:

$$\text{V-COMPLEMENT'S } X = Y$$

where X is: TENSE if the embedded verb is either tensed or infinitival, specifying Y to be + or − accordingly.

AFFIX if the embedded verb is a participle, specifying Y to be the affix of the verb.

COMPLEMENTIZER in all cases, specifying Y to be whatever word happens to be found in complementizer position (e.g., when the child hears *I want to go* he adds the equation *V-COMPLEMENT'S COMPLEMENTIZER = to* to the lexical entry for *want*). If no word is found in complementizer position, define Y to be ϕ.

When *can* triggers this procedure, the constraint that its complement verb must be untensed is entered as an equation appended to its lexical entry. Similar conditions will, I assume, lead to the acquisition of entries for *have* and the *be*'s.

This account predicts error-free performance of auxiliaries as soon as the meaning of the words and the segmentation of affixes from stems are accomplished. Problems for the theory arise when there is some systematic error pattern that appears not to be the result of the mere absence of some yet to be learned rule. In the case of auxiliaries, there have been many reports of children overmarking or mismarking the tense of main verbs when auxiliaries are present. Some examples, taken mainly from Kuczaj (1976), are reproduced in 13.28.

13.28.   a.   Does it rolls?

b.   What are you did?

c.   Can you broke those?

d.   I did fell when I got blood.

e.   What's that is?

Several accounts of these errors may be found in the literature (e.g., Hurford, 1975; Erreich, Valian, & Winzemer, 1980), but there are numerous problems with these accounts (Kuczaj, 1976; Maratsos & Kuczaj, 1978; Prideaux, 1976), and no existing account addresses all the data. Here I present part of an account that attempts to remedy some of the deficiencies of its predecessors.

In LFG, fronted auxiliary verbs are simply base generated in an alternative expansion of S such as 13.29.

13.29. $S \rightarrow (V)_{AUX = +}$ $NP_{SUBJECT}$ VP_{TENSE}

As mentioned, the co-occurrence restrictions among auxiliaries and their complement verbs are enforced by equations such as $V - COMPLEMENT'S$ $TENSE = -$ appended to the lexical entries for auxiliary verbs. Errors like 13.28, I claim, are the result of a violation of these restrictions (i.e. those found in 13.25.) Evidence that the errors are due to a failure to apply these constraints, rather than to the misapplication of a transformation specific to auxiliaries, can be found in the fact that children also make overtensing errors when there is a complement-taking verb that is not an auxiliary, such as in *let it rolls* (Pinker, 1984). But that still leaves open the question of why children fail to apply these constraining equations. Three possibilities suggest themselves: (1) the auxiliary and complement verb were not recognized as a verb-complement structure; (2) the tense (or other inflection or participle form) of the particular embedded verb was not identified or recognized as such; (3) the equation failed to be applied in the on-line production of the sentence for performance reasons; or (4) the equation was not learned to begin with. Possibility 1 seems implausible because the children who made these errors placed the auxiliary and complement verb in their correct positions, and the elements of their utterances seemed to be composed in a semantically appropriate way, given their contexts. Rather, it seems to be just the formal constraint equation that was missing or misapplied, and as we see later, we are forced to conclude that (2), (3), and (4) each provide part of the explanation as to why.

First, Maratsos and Kuczaj (1978) point out that the majority of errors such as 13.28 occur when the complement verb has an irregular tensed form. That is, errors of the form *did I broke it?* are more common than those of the form *did I fixed it?* Presumably, this is because *broke* is not analyzed as *break* + *ed* or *break* + *past tense* at this stage, a hypothesis supported by Kuczaj's (1981) observations of inflected irregular forms like *broked* and *wenting*. Of course, if *broke* does not contribute a TENSE feature to the complement it appears in, the equation *V-COMPLEMENT'S TENSE* = − (forbidding the complement to define any tense) will not be prevented from selecting that word as he or she speaks. However, this cannot be the whole story, because overtensing errors also occur with regular tensed forms, though less often.

A second notable fact about overtensing errors is that they occur far more frequently (though not exclusively) in questions and negations than in simple declaratives (Maratsos & Kuczaj, 1978). That is, errors like *can you broke those?* and *you cannot broke those* are more frequent than errors like *you can broke those*. This seems to support Maratsos and Kuczaj's hypothesis that transient "slip of the tongue" errors, independent of the child's linguistic knowledge, are in part responsible for overtensing errors. During sentence production, when the first auxiliary is uttered, its lexical entry must be activated and the constraining equations in the entry must be kept active so that all subsequent word and rule choices may be kept consistent with those equations. Because these activated equations constitute a short-term memory representation, it is reasonable to suppose that information in it begins to decay as soon as it is activated. The longer the interval between activating the equation and using it to constrain a word choice, the more likely it is that the equation will have decayed by the time the word choice must be made. A noun phrase or negation element interposed between the auxiliary and the complement verb may have just that effect; the equation V-COMPLEMENT'S TENSE $= -$ may be inaccessible by the time the embedded verb is chosen, and so nothing may prevent a tensed form from being chosen. Hence, there will be more overtensing errors for negatives and questions.

The final observation relevant to this discussion is that overtensing errors occur far more often with a *do* form as the auxiliary than with other auxiliaries such as *be* or the modals. Pinker (1984) presents data showing that this is not an artifact of the overall greater frequency of *do* in the child's speech. Because both *do* and the other auxiliaries appear with complement verbs with either regular or irregular tensed forms, because both types appear in the same position in questions, and because they appear in the same position in negations, neither of the aforementioned accounts can explain this difference.

Presumably, the difference between *do* and other auxiliaries may be traced to the different degree of strength or accessibility of the constraining equation *V-COMPLEMENT'S TENSE* $= -$ appended to *do* versus the other auxiliaries (I say "accessibility" rather than "presence" because no child makes overtensing errors anywhere near 100% of the time). It is possible that this difference is due to the semantics of *do* as opposed to the other auxiliaries, making its lexical entry harder to learn in general. However, other aspects of its use (e.g., its position, the position of its complement, and its situational appropriateness) are intact, suggesting that something else about *do* makes the constraining equation particularly hard to consolidate into the lexical entry.

Again, the left-to-right nature of sentence processing, which I assume affects both the comprehension and the acquisition process, may provide an answer. *Do,* unlike other modals, hardly ever appears adjacent to its complement verb (except for the relatively infrequent emphatic construction as in *I DID eat it!*). Procedure 13.27 (which coins constraining equations) must keep the lexical entry for the auxiliary "open" or activated while it waits for the complement verb, which appears later in the sentence. When the procedure finds the verb, it then must analyze it so that it can complete the right hand side of the equation *V-COMPLEMENT'S TENSE = ?.* If the open lexical entry, or the as yet uncompleted constraining equation, decays before the verb is found, nothing can be added to the entry. The more often this occurs, the less often the equation will be strengthened and the weaker the equation will be. For auxiliaries other than *do,* part of the time the auxiliary will be adjacent to the main verb (and hence will still probably be active when the complement verb is analyzed), and part of the time it will be fronted or separated by a negation element (and hence will be more decayed when the verb is found). *Do,* however, appears almost exclusively in the more decay-prone fronted position, and so its constraining equation will not reach criterion strength as quickly even if the total number of exposures is the same as for other auxiliaries. With a weaker equation in its entry, tensed forms are less likely to be ruled out during sentence production, and overtensing errors will be more likely. (A similar account will explain why discontinuous elements that constrain each other will be harder to learn, which Slobin, 1973, 1984, shows is a widespread acquisition pattern. The present example, however, allows one to begin to tease apart the effects of disconuity on production versus acquisition. More directly, Mulford and Morgan (1983) present evidence that the relative proximity between two mutually constraining words in Icelandic determines how easily the child can use the constraining relation in acquisition.)

The foregoing is an example of how an explicit acquisition device can assist in the formulation of mechanistic accounts of phenomena previously reported in the literature (see also Chapter 7 of Pinker, 1984, for a more complete account, and for supporting data). New questions are addressed in the next section.

RAISING NEW QUESTIONS ABOUT CHILDREN'S SPEECH

One of the tests of any theory is how well it generates empirical research questions. This is especially important in a field as complex as language acquisition, where there are countless studies one could perform with children, but few that speak directly to theoretical issues about the acquisition of language. When designing acquisition models, there are often points at which several alternative algorithms could do the desired task, but it is not clear which algorithm would best correspond to what the human child does. It is at such points that an experiment with children or an analysis of transcripts of children's speech is especially informative — before the experiment is conducted, the theoretical significance of its possible outcomes is established. In collaboration with several colleagues and students, I have begun to test several questions about language development relevant to the mechanisms of the model, and in this section, I discuss one such set of experiments (Lebeaux and Pinker, 1981; Wilson, Pinker, Zaenen, and Lebeaux, 1981).

The set of experiments from which the present example is taken is addressed to the issue of the learning of verb subcategorizations. Verbs are subcategorized as to whether they appear alone (intransitive verbs, e.g., *sleep*), with an object (transitive verbs, e.g., *hit*), with an object and an indirect object (bitransitive verbs, e.g., *give* in *give me a break*), with an object and a prepositional object (e.g., *donate*), and so on. The learning mechanisms discussed in the first section enter a verb into the lexicon when the verb appears in a sentence that can be parsed using a combination of existing phrase structure rules and the semantically inferred categories and relations discussed in that section. The child defines the subcategorization of a new verb by its logical predicate-argument structure (thus determining the number of places the predicate will have) and by the function labels in the parse tree for the words representing each argument (thus determining the grammatical function encoding each argument). Hence, after the sentence *the dog bites the cat* has been parsed, the entry *bite* (SUBJECT, OBJECT) will be added to the lexicon (SUBJECT and OBJECT coming from the thematic relations of *bite*'s arguments, via the labels on the branches subtended by *dog* and *cat*). Similarly, for the sentence *the scandal drove the party from office,* the entry *drive* (SUBJECT, OBJECT, P-OBJECT) will be added to the lexicon, with the functions SUBJECT and so on again coming from the labels on the appropriate branches, this time thanks to the rules having been learned earlier.

One might ask why the procedures wait until a sentence has been parsed before adding a verb to the lexicon. After all, for a verb like *kiss,* SUBJECT and OBJECT functions are posited on the basis of the corresponding arguments being an agent and a patient, respectively. As that is the information used to label the branches of the tree to begin with, why look at the branches to find out the functions in a lexical entry? Why not just enter the thematically inferred functions directly, when the verb and its arguments are perceived? The answer is that often the "default," semantically based functions for a verb's arguments are not necessarily the correct arguments for a particular verb. Passive entries for verbs, with patient subjects, are the most obvious examples, but verbs like *receive, sustain,* and *undergo* also have nonstandard encodings of their arguments. There are also verbs that logically take two arguments, but grammatically take one (e.g., *eat* as in *John ate*), where the null symbol ϕ represents an unexpressed argument in the lexical entry *eat* (SUBJECT, ϕ). And there are verbs like *justify,* where there are no clues whatsoever from the semantic roles of its arguments as to the grammatical functions that English uses to express those arguments. In all these cases, it is imperative to allow the input sentence to confirm or modify the "default" or semantically induced grammatical encoding of a verb's arguments before that verb is entered into the lexicon.

The theory as presented thus far predicts that children will store a verb and the syntactic context (in terms of grammatical functions) that it is subcategorized to appear in *only* when that verb is encountered in that particular context in an input sentence. There is an alternative, however: children may also be sensitive to the sets of related contexts that verbs systematically appear in; for example, most verbs subcategorized to appear in passive contexts, such as *eat* (by-OBJECT, SUBJECT), have counterparts that can appear in active contexts, such as *eat* (SUBJECT, OBJECT). In the theory of LFG, lexical rules like Passive can generate a passive lexical entry given an active entry as input (or vice-versa). Now, if children induce and then apply lexical rules, they should be able to add a particular verb subcategorization to their lexicon even if they have never heard that verb in that particular context. For example, they could hear a verb in an active context, postulate an active subcategorization for that verb, apply the passive lexical rule to the subcategorization yielding a passive subcategorization, and add both subcategorizations to their lexicon, even though they have never heard the verb in a passive context. (Pinker, 1982, describes a procedure whereby a passive rule could have been learned to begin with.) Thus, it remains an empirical question whether children who use passives at all actually have the ability to induce a lexical rule and apply it to one lexical entry to yield a new one, or whether verb subcategorizations are entered into the lexicon one-by-one as they are encountered in the relevant contexts (for some additional theoretical issues surrounding this question see Baker, 1977; Maratsos, 1978; Maratsos & Chalkley, 1980; Pinker, 1982, 1984).

A related question, also tested in the experiment to be described, is whether the formulation of lexical rules found in LFG is the correct characterization of the rules children use (if indeed they use such rules, as previously discussed). It has been suggested (Maratsos, Kuczaj, Fox, & Chalkley, 1979) that children's passive rule does not manipulate symbols for grammatical relations such as SUBJECT and OBJECT, but manipulates thematic or semantic relations such as agent and patient directly. In a similar vein, de Villiers (1980) proposes that agents may be "better" triggers for rules like passivization than nonagent subjects. In the current theory, thematic relations are used to infer the presence of various grammatical relations in an input sentence, but the rules themselves are all couched in terms of grammatical relations, as in the adult grammar. Thus, if children use productive lexical rules at all, it is still an open question whether those rules should refer to symbols such as SUBJECT and OBJECT or to the thematic roles that were used to find those grammatical relations to begin with.

Although there have been many studies on children's comprehension of passive sentences (e.g., Bever, 1970; de Villiers & de Villiers, 1973; Maratsos, 1974; Maratsos et al., 1979), in such studies one has no control over which verbs the child has heard in which context before he or she enters the lab; hence, the question at hand cannot be answered in such experiments. For example, de Villiers (1980; see also Leonard, 1975) selected children who initially failed to comprehend concrete passive sentences, and exposed them to a series of passivized experiential or action verbs. These children then used the passive to describe pictures, even passivizing action verbs when their exposure had been limited to experiential verbs. However, we cannot interpret this as evidence for productivity, because the action verbs were all common and the child could have heard their passivized versions before entering the lab. The training could simply have increased the strengths of the passive forms and the child's willingness to focus the patient in his or her speech.

Instead, it is necessary to control children's access to the verbs to be tested by making up novel verbs and teaching them to the child then and there under controlled circumstances. This is what Wilson et al. (1981) did for verbs subcategorized for different versions of the dative alternation and what Lebeaux and Pinker (1981) did for active versus passive verbs. Lebeaux and I made up verbs such as *kale* and *gump,* meaning either to leap-frog over, to nuzzle someone's neck with one's nose, to view with binoculars, or to hear through an ear trumpet. Using small animal toys, we demonstrated one of the actions to 4-year-old children and described the action using one of the novel verbs. Half the time the action was described in the active voice and half the time in the passive voice. Then the child was shown the same action two more times, using different animals, and asked to describe what was happening each time. We tried to induce the child to describe one action using the active voice and the other action using the passive voice. Our inducement consisted of asking the question *what is happening with the X?* with *X* being either the agent/experiencer or the patient/object of experience. In such cases, there is a strong bias, at least among adults, to begin the declarative answer with the entity mentioned in the question. Finally, we asked the children to act out, with the toys at hand, active and passive sentences containing the new verb. By using both production and comprehension tests, we hoped to obtain converging evidence on children's acquisition of subcategorization, minimizing possible effects specific to comprehension or production tasks. Each child was taught all four actions, two in the active voice and two in the passive, and was tested for the production and comprehension of the active and passive versions of each verb. One of the active verbs represented an action, and one a sensory act (likewise for the passive verbs). Order and pairing of actions with nonsense syllables were counterbalanced.

The alternative mechanisms just sketched make different predictions about the outcomes of the experiment. If the first view is correct and children enter verb subcategorizations *only* after parsing a sentence containing the verb in the appropriate context, then children should describe a new action in the active voice only when they were presented initially with the active version of that verb. Similarly, they should comprehend active sentences only when presented initially with the active version of that verb (likewise for the production and comprehension of passive verbs, which should occur only when a passive version of the verb was taught). On the other hand, if preschool children have already abstracted a passive rule and can use it to generate a passive entry from an active one and vice versa, then the children should comprehend and produce *all* the actions presented, regardless of teaching condition. Finally, if children have a lexical rule that applies only to causal agents or animate actions, but not to grammatical subjects in general, we might expect them to comprehend and produce the untaught voice only for the two action verbs, not for the two sensory verbs.

The comprehension results are straightforward: With the exception of one child, all children ($n = 16$) acted out all the sentences perfectly. In the production task, performance was also excellent, as the following table listing percentages of correct sentences produced shows.

			Voice taught	
			active	passive
ACTION VERBS		active	.94	.84
	voice produced			
		passive	.59	.62
PERCEPTION VERBS		active	.97	.88
	voice produced			
		passive	.69	.94

Clearly, these results rule out the first hypothesis that children learn verb subcategorizations only upon hearing the verb exemplified in the relevant syntactic context. Even in the least productive case (producing passive action verbs when the active was taught), children produced verbs in entirely novel contexts 59% of the time and comprehended them close to 100% of the time. Nor does the third hypothesis, that children add new lexical entries using only a thematically based rule, receive support from these data because our children were equally likely to generalize verbs to new voices when the verb referred to an action or to a perceptual act. (It is, of course, possible that the children may have conceived of the experiencer of the sensory verbs as some sort of agent; but Loren Ann Frost and I have found evidence for productivity in children even when the verbs denote static spatial relations such as relations similar to *suspend* and *contain*.) It appears that 4-year-olds, who have just acquired the ability to comprehend passive sentences reliably (Bever, 1970), have also abstracted a general rule capturing the relation between the active and the passive voice and can apply this rule to enter new subcategorizations for a verb, subcategorizations not evident from the immediate context that the verb was heard to appear in. Any model of the acquisition of subcategorization must therefore contain mechanisms that coin and apply productive rules as well as those that coin subcategorizations from direct positive evidence.

RAISING QUESTIONS ABOUT PARENTAL SPEECH

Because children learn the syntax of a language on the basis of sentences addressed to them by caregivers or peers, it is important to determine the properties of that input and how those properties affect the operation of the acquisition mechanisms. Though many special properties of parental speech have been documented (e.g., its brevity, clarity, higher pitch, simplicity along certain dimensions, reference to immediate context, etc.; see Snow & Ferguson, 1977), it is not clear what the functions of these properties are with respect to acquisition. Some may help, others may hinder, still others may have no effect at all (see Nelson, 1980; Newport et al., 1977; Pinker, 1979; Wexler & Culicover, 1980). The problem with arguments concerning possible functions of the properties of parental speech is that unless one knows the nature of the device that the input is put into, one cannot make sound claims about what the effects of those properties are likely to be. Indeed, different acquisition algorithms are affected in very different ways by various input parameters (Pinker, 1979).

Once one has a theory about the learning mechanisms, however, one can examine those properties of parental speech that would have clear effects on the operation of those mechanisms. As in the case of using the model to raise questions about children's speech (see the preceding section), using the model to raise questions about parental speech assures one that the results of the investigation will be theoretically relevant beforehand. Hochberg and I have begun an extensive investigation of that sort (Pinker & Hochberg, in preparation), and I report some preliminary results of one part of that investigation here.

Recall that the acquisition mechanism bootstrapped its way into learning phrase structure rules by assuming that syntax and semantics would correspond in early parental speech in predictable ways: that things and people would be referred to using nouns, actions using verbs, agents using subjects, patients using objects, and so on. This raises the important question of the extent to which early parental speech follows these correspondences. If it does not, the acquisition mechanisms would yield incorrect rules. For example, if parents uttered many sentences like *the slapping of John was a disgrace,* the learning mechanism would interpret *slapping* as a verb because it refers to an action and falsely infer that English sentences begin with a verb. Inasmuch as children do not seem to make such dramatic errors (see Maratsos and Chalkley, 1980; Pinker, 1982), either such sentences must be rare in early speech to children or the assumptions that the learning theory is based on are incorrect.

Hochberg and I tested the assumptions by analyzing transcripts of parent-child dialogue gathered by Brown and his colleagues (Brown, 1973) in the 1960s. We focused on the parents' side of the dialogue in the samples of about 700 child utterances that formed the basis of Brown's Stage I (when the child first combined words into strings) and Stage V (when word order, inflections, coordination, embedding, and auxiliaries had all been largely mastered). We assigned each word of a major syntactic category (N, V, A, P) into one of a number of semantic classes: thing, person, location, action, disposition, epistemic relation, physical property, direction, path, emotion, and many others. We also assigned each instance of a grammatical relation (subject, object, indirect object, various prepositional objects) into one of a number of thematic relations: agent of action, experiencer, patient, goal, theme, beneficiary, and so forth. Care was taken to define each semantic/thematic category in a manner independent of its syntactic expression when devising the coding scheme and to consider each word or relation as being eligible to fall into any semantic class when applying the scheme to the parents' speech. The acquisition model would be made more plausible if most physical object names were found to be nouns, most action names verbs, most physical properties adjectives, most agents subjects, most patients objects, and so on. Presumably, as the child develops and the basic structure of the language is laid down, it would be less important for these correspondences to hold, and so they might be smaller in the Stage V sample than in the Stage I sample. Incidentally, such a trend need not imply any "fine tuning" of the parents' speech to their children's linguistic level; it may be that as the child matures, one can discuss more abstract topics with him or her, and hence the syntax-semantics correspondences weaken in parental speech as a byproduct.

Our results largely confirm the general predictions (though the differences between Stages I and V were equivocal). In Stage I, approximately 88% of all actions were referred to using verbs, and 73% of the verbs consisted either of the predicate *be* (36%) or a physical action (37%). All other categories (epistemic, disposition, possession, etc.) split the remaining verbs, with no category accounting for more than 7% of the verbs. Approximately 51% of the nouns in Stage I (including pronouns) referred to physical objects (declining to 34% in Stage V), and another 39% referred to people; virtually 100% of the things and people were labeled using nouns. Approximately 35% of the adjectives (other than possessive pronouns) referred to physical properties, rising to 44% by Stage V, with virtually 100% of the physical properties referred to using adjectives. About 64% of the prepositions (including the proprepositions *where, there,* and *here*) referred to spatial relations, declining slightly at Stage V; virtually 100% of the spatial relations were expressed as prepositions (assuming that words like *there* and *downstairs,* which substitute for entire PPs, are to be considered preopositions; if not, the figure declines to 72% for Stage I and 78% for Stage V). Note that the second percentage listed in each pair is the one relevant to the semantic bootstrapping hypothesis. If the child hears a noun that is not a name of a person or thing, no harm is done as long as the meaning of the noun does not correspond to some other syntactic category. It is only when a name for a person or thing is not a noun that trouble ensues.

Grammatical relations also correlate highly with thematic relations: 100% of the agents were expressed as subjects (i.e., there was not a single full passive in the sample), and 25% of the Stage I subjects were agents, another 21% were experiencers, and 10% were intransitive actors (both of which may also be semantic clues to subjecthood that the learning mechanism could exploit). Of the remaining 44% of the subjects, incidentally, 41% were the subjects of copula sentences. When an instrument of an action was mentioned, it was introduced with the preposition *with* 78% of the time and used as a subject only 2% of the time in Stage I (changing to 59% and 27% in Stage V, respectively). In addition, some 85% of patients were referred to as grammatical objects in Stage I, increasing to 89% in Stage V.

All in all, we see that a vast majority of the relevant putative semantic triggers (thing, action, agent, patient, etc.) quite reliably correlate in parental speech with the syntactic element that they are supposed to trigger in the learner. This implies that our learner is unlikely to be led astray by noncanonical pairings of syntax and semantics (e.g., a noun encoding an action). Furthermore, a plurality, and often a majority, of the instances of the syntactic categories to be induced are in fact used by the parent to convey the semantic element that the child, by hypothesis, uses to induce the category. This implies that the child can use a large part of the input directed at him or her without having to filter out vast numbers of uninformative exemplars. Of course, the cross-individual and cross-cultural generality of these conclusions must still be established, but this investigation tentatively sustains the hope that the proposed acquisition mechanisms will yield valid outputs. It also shows in general how one can study properties of parental speech that have clear implications for learnability issues.

COMPUTER SIMULATION OF LANGUAGE ACQUISITION

Computer simulation serves many purposes in cognitive science: to force the theorist to be explicit, to check the internal consistency of a theory, to generate empirical predictions, and to spell out alternatives for the as yet unspecified parts of the theory (see Kosslyn, Pinker, Smith, & Shwartz, 1979, for a more detailed discussion of the role of simulation in cognitive psychology). Walsh (1981) has implemented and described a LISP program called Lexical-Interpretive Acquirer (LIA), which instantiates a subset of the acquisition mechanisms proposed in Pinker (1982). These mechanisms learn annotated phrase structure rules, control equations, lexical entries, and lexical rules, and make higher order generalizations based on these rules by collapsing phrase structure rules and by applying the lexical rules to learned lexical entries, yielding new lexical entries. Walsh's simulation performed all these tasks successfully, which is no surprise given that this is what the program was designed to do (garbage in, garbage out, a critic might say). The simulation effort becomes interesting when it forces the theorist to reexamine the underlying theory or raises additional empirical and theoretical research issues. Here I discuss one such issue: how the learner compares the alternative phrase structure rules expanding a given category, where each rule has been originally derived from a different input sentence, and collapses them into a single rule.

Collapsed rules by convention contain parentheses indicating optional categories, asterisks indicating iterable categories, and braces indicating a set of categories, one of which must be chosen in that position. An example is the rule expanding English verb phrases, listed in 13.30.

13.30.

$$VP \rightarrow V \quad (NP)_{OBJECT} \left(\left\{ \begin{array}{c} NP_{N\text{-}COMPLEMENT} \\ VP'_{V\text{-}COMPLEMENT} \\ S'_{S\text{-}COMPLEMENT} \end{array} \right\} \right) (PP^*)_{ADJUNCT}$$

An example of a sentence generated in part by this rule is *Mary told Sam that Bill fibbed at the party*.

The various subprocedures of P7, listed earlier, take a phrase structure rule coined by procedures P1–P6 on the basis of the current input sentence and attempt to collapse it with any existing rules that have the same symbol on the left-hand side. For example, a new rule (13.31) may be collapsed with an old rule (13.32) to yield 13.33; a new rule (13.34) will be merged with an old rule (13.35) to yield 13.36.

13.31.   VP → V   NP

13.32.   VP → V

13.33.   VP → V   (NP)

13.34.   VP → V   NP   VP′

13.35.   VP → V   NP   AP′

13.36.   VP → V   NP $\begin{cases} VP' \\ AP' \end{cases}$

In implementing the procedures in P7 and in testing them with rules other than those I had in mind when first proposing them, Walsh found several possibilities that fell through the cracks and would be ignored by the existing procedures. Consider 13.37 and 13.38, one of which may be considered "old," the other "new":

13.37.   VP → V (NP) (VP′)

13.38.   VP → V (VP′) (PP)

An astute learning mechanism should notice that these two rules may be collapsed, yielding 13.39.

13.39.   VP → V (NP) (VP′) (PP)

Note that this rule can generate a sequence V NP VP′ PP, whch neither 13.37 nor 13.38 could generate by itself. However, Walsh discovered during his simulation effort that proceduure P7(2) would not accomplish this collapsing, because neither rule is properly contained within the other. One modification of the collapsing procedure that he found would alleviate this problem is to have it merge two rules if the immediate neighbors of a symbol appearing in only one rule appear in the same relative order, without that symbol, in the other rule.

Walsh also discovered flaws in the procedure that handles the case in which two constituents first appear singly in the same position (leading them to be collapsed within braces as in 13.40), and then appear in a certain order (as in 13.41).

13.40.

$$VP \rightarrow V \quad \left\{ \begin{array}{c} NP \\ AP' \end{array} \right\}$$

13.41. $VP \rightarrow V \quad NP \quad AP'$

Procedure P7(4) retains information about the relative order of the two constituents by replacing 13.40 with 13.42.

13.42. $VP \rightarrow V \quad (NP) \quad (AP')$

However, Walsh showed that certain input orders of various phrases could befuddle the procedure, especially when three distinct constituents are encounted singly in the same position before any two are encountered in some order. For example, if the child first has 13.40 and then coins 13.43, P7(3) will collapse them to yield 13.44.

13.43. $VP \rightarrow V \quad S'$

13.44. $VP \rightarrow V \quad \left\{ \begin{array}{c} NP \\ AP' \\ S \end{array} \right\}$

At this point, encountering a sentence leading to 13.41 would leave the procedure stymied as to how to encode the information that NP precedes AP', while still retaining the information that S' can occur in the same position and leaving open until future sentences are encountered how S' might be ordered with respect to NP and AP'. Walsh's simulation solves this problem by creating 13.43 and retaining 13.44 whenever it encounters information about the relative ordering of two out of three braced constituents. (Another possibility would be to create the single rule, 13.45, under those circumstances.)

13.45

$$VP \rightarrow V \quad \left\{ \begin{array}{cc} (NP) & (AP') \\ & (S') \end{array} \right\}$$

It is important to realize that these collapsing procedures do not simply have the function of making the grammar more parsimonious or elegant. Rather, collapsing two or more rules often enables the learner to generalize beyond the input constituent orders and produce or comprehend novel sequences of constituents. For example, collapsing 13.46 with 13.47 and collapsing the result of that merger with 13.48 yields 13.49, which allows the learner to utter the sequence V AP' PP even though that sequence has never been heard in the input.

13.46.   VP → V   NP

13.47.   VP → V   AP'

13.48.   VP → V   NP PP

13.49.

$$VP \rightarrow V \quad \left\{ \begin{matrix} NP \\ AP' \end{matrix} \right\} \quad (PP)$$

This raises a number of research questions. First, is there a valid cross-linguistic procedure that will make only sound generalizations about how to collapse individual phrase structure rules (cf. p. 13–28)? Second, do children in fact make the generalizations that the collapsing procedures make available (cf. p. 13–48)? This, perhaps could be tested by teaching children novel non-English constituent orders (e.g., *this is a box square, this is a box wiggle,* and *this is a box fuzzy on,* each with a semantically appropriate referent object) and seeing whether they make the same generalizations that LIA's collapsing procedures would (e.g., *this is a box wiggle on*). Third, in what order to parents utter the alternative phrase structure expansions of a category, and do the frequent orders exemplify the straightforward or the difficult cases for the collapsing procedures (cf. the section entitled Raising Questions About Parental Speech)?

Walsh (1981) discovered a number of other deficiences of the acquisition procedures in their original formulation, including certain redundant procedures, certain misordered procedures, and certain insufficiently general procedures, which space limitations prevent me from describing here. However, I hope this section demonstrates how useful computer simulation can be in testing the consistency and power of a putative acquisition mechanism and in raising new research questions concerning its human instantiation.

CONCLUSION

Theories of perception commonly distinguish between "bottom-up" and "top-down" mechanisms. Roughly, bottom-up procedures are said to analyze the sensory data and compute from them a description of the scene in the external world; top-down procedures are said to begin with constraints about the probable structure of the external world and generate hypotheses about the sensory data that are then tested against them. A scientist studying the process of language acquisition is, in a sense, a perceiver; he or she attempts to describe the acquisition process using data about adults' and children's language as a guide. And here, too, there are bottom-up and top-down approaches, the former examining the data and using them to formulate hypotheses about the underlying acquisition mechanisms, the latter formulating hypotheses about mechanisms that are in principle sufficient to accomplish acquisition and then testing them against the rest of the data. Obviously, the approach I have outlined in this chapter is a top-down approach, and I have adopted it for the same reason that many perception theorists find top-down models compelling: The data (sense data in their case, experimental/observational data in ours) are consistent with too many descriptions of the entities that generated them for an observer to choose one uniquely. The bottom-up approach to language acquisition has been the dominant one in psychology for 20 years, and though our knowledge about the course of language development has increased exponentially in that interval, we are not appreciably closer to understanding how languages are acquired than we were at the beginning. Perhaps language acquisition is simply too complicated for that unidisciplinary, bottom-up approach to succeed. In this chapter, I hope to have shown that a top-down approach, combining studies from theoretical linguistics, language typology, mathematical linguistics, computer science, and empirical studies of children and their parents, deserves a crack at the problem.

ACKNOWLEDGMENTS

I am grateful to my collaborators on this probject, without whom I would have nothing to write about: Joan Bresnan, Loren Ann Frost, Jane Grimshaw, Judy Hochberg, Ronald Kaplan, David Lebeaux, Karin Stromswold, Rick Walsh, Ronald Wilson, and Ani Zaanen. I have also benefited from the encouragement and comments of Dan Slobin, Roger Brown, Tom Wasow, and Eve Clark. All can be expected to disagree with one or more of the claims made in this chapter. This research was supported by NSF grants BNS 81–14917, 82–16546, 82–19450, and NIH grant 1 R01 HD 1381–01 and was conducted in part while I was a consultant at the Cognitive and Instructional Sciences Group at the Xerox Palo Alto Research Centers.

REFERENCES

Anderson, J. R. *Language, memory, and thought.* Hillsdale, N.J.: Lawrence Erlbaum Associates, 1976.

Anderson, J. R. Induction of augmented transition networks. *Cognitive Science,* 1977, *1,* 125–157.

Anderson, J. R. *The architecture of cognition.* Cambridge, MA: Harvard University Press, 1983.

Atkinson, M. *Explanations in the study of child language acquisition.* Cambridge: Cambridge University Press, 1982.

Baker, C. L. Syntactic theory and the projection problem. *Linguistic Inquiry,* 1979, *10,* 533–581.

Bever, T. G. The cognitive basis for linguistic structures. In J. R. Hayes (Ed.), *Cognition and the development of language.* New York: Wiley, 1970.

Bresnan, J. W. A realistic transformational grammar. In M. Halle, J. Bresnan, & G. Miller (Eds.), *Linguistic theory and psychological reality.* Cambridge, MA: MIT Press, 1978.

Bresnan, J. W. (Ed.). *The mental representation of grammatical relations.* Cambridge, MA: MIT Press, 1982.

Brown, R. *A first language: The early stages.* Cambridge, MA: Harvard University Press, 1973.

Chomsky, N. *Syntactic structures.* The Hague: Mouton, 1957.

Chomsky, N. *Aspects of the theory of syntax.* Cambridge, MA: MIT Press, 1965.

Chomsky, N. Remarks on nominalization. In R. Jacobs & P. Rosenbaum (Eds.), *Readings in English transformational grammar.* Waltham, MA: Ginn, 1970.

Chomsky, N. *Lectures on government and binding.* Dordrecht, Holland: Foris Publications, 1981.

dePaulo, B., & Bonvillian, J. The effect on language development of the special characteristics of speech addressed to children. *Journal of Psycholinguistic Research,* 1978, *7,* 189–212.

deVilliers, J. The process of rule learning in child speech: A new look. In K. E. Nelson (Ed.), *Children's language* (Vol. 2). New York: Gardner Press, 1981.

deVilliers, J., & deVilliers, P. Development of the use of word order in comprehension. *Journal of Psycholinguistic Research,* 1973, *2,* 331–341.

Erreich, A., Valian, V., & Winzemer, J. Aspects of a theory of language acquisition. *Journal of Child Language,* 1980, *1,* 157–179.

Fodor, J. A. *The language of thought.* New York: Thomas Crowell, 1975.

Furrow, D., Nelson, K., & Benedict, H. Mothers' speech to children and syntactic development: Some simple relationships. *Journal of Child Language,* 1979, *6,* 423–442.

Gleitman, L. R., Newport, E. L., & Gleitman, H. *The current status of the motherese hypothesis. Journal of Child Language,* 1984, *11,* 43–79.

Grimshaw, J. Form, function, and the language acquisition device. In C. L. Baker & J. McCarthy (Eds.), *The logical problem of language acquisition.* Cambridge, MA: MIT Press, 1981.

Hale, K. On the position of Walbiri in a typology of the base. Bloomington: Indiana University Linguistics Club, 1981.

Hoff-Ginsberg, E., & Shatz, M. Linguistic input and the child's acquisition of language. *Psychological Bulletin,* 1982, *92,* 3–26.

Hurford, J. R. A child and the English question formation rule. *Journal of Child Language,* 1975, *1,* 299–301.

Jackendoff, R. S. *X-bar syntax: A study of phrase structure.* Cambridge, MA: MIT Press, 1977.

Kaplan, R. M., & Bresnan, J. W. Lexical functional grammar: A formal system for grammatical representation. In J. W. Bresnan (Ed.), *The mental representation of grammatical relations.* Cambridge, MA: MIT Press, 1982.

Keenan, E. O. Towards a universal definition of "subject." In C. Li (Ed.), *Subject and Topic.* New York: Academic Press, 1976.

Kosslyn, S. M., Pinker, S., Smith, G. E., & Shwartz, S. P. On the demystification of mental imagery. *Behavioral and Brain Sciences,* 1979, *2,* 535–548.

Kuczaj, S. A. II. Arguments against Hurford's auxiliary copying rule. *Journal of Child Language,* 1976, *3,* 423–427.

Kuczaj, S. A. II. More on children's initial failure to relate specific acquisitions. *Journal of Child Language,* 1981, *8,* 485–488.

Lapointe, S. *A theory of grammatical agreement.* Unpublished doctoral dissertation, University of Massachusetts, Amherst, 1980.

Lebeaux, D., & Pinker, S. *The acquisition of the passive.* Paper presented at the Boston University Conference on Language Development, October 1981.

Leonard, L. B. The role of nonlinguistic stimuli and semantic relations in children's acquisition of grammatical utterances. *Journal of Experimental Child Psychology,* 1975, *19,* 346–357.

Macnamara, J. Cognitive basis of language learning in infants. *Psychological Review,* 1972, *79,* 1–13.

Macnamara, J. *Names for things.* Cambridge, MA: MIT Press/Bradford Books, 1982.

Maratsos, M. Children who get worse at understanding the passive: A replication of Bever. *Journal of Psycholinguistic Research,* 1974, *3,* 65–74.

Maratsos, M. P. New models in linguistics and language acquisition. In M. Halle, J. Bresnan, & G. Miller (Eds.), *Linguistic theory and psychological reality.* Cambridge, MA: MIT Press, 1978.

Maratsos, M., & Chalkley, M. The internal language of children's syntax: The ontogenesis and representation of syntactic categories. In K. E. Nelson (Ed.), *Children's language* (Vol. 2). New York: Gardner Press, 1980.

Maratsos, M. P., & Kuczaj, S. A. II. Against the transformationalist account: A simpler analysis of auxiliary overmarkings. *Journal of Child Language,* 1978, *5,* 337–345.

Maratsos, M. P., Kuczaj, S. A. II, Fox D., & Chalkley, M. Some empirical studies in the acquisition of transformational relations: Passives, negatives, and the past tense. In W. A. Collins (Ed.), *The Minnesota Symposia on Child Psychology* (Vol. 12). Hillsdale, N.J.: Lawrence Erlbaum Associates, 1979.

Marr, D., & Nishihara, H. K. Representation and recognition of the spatial organization of three-dimensional shapes. *Proceedings of the Royal Society,* 1978, *200,* 269–294.

Mulford, R., & Morgan, J. L. The role of "local cues" in assigning gender to new nouns in Icelandic. Paper presented at the Boston University Conference on Language Development, October 1983.

Nelson, K. E. Facilitating children's syntax. *Developmental Psychology,* 1977, *13,* 101–107.

Nelson, K. E. Theories of the child's acquisition of syntax: A look at rare events and at necessary, catalytic, and irrelevant components of mother-child conversation. *Annals of the New York Academy of Sciences,* 1980, *345,* 45–67.

Nelson, K. E., Carskaddon, G., & Bonvillian, J. Syntax acquisition: Impact of experimental variation in adult verbal interaction with the child. *Child Development,* 1973, *44,* 497–504.

Newport, E., Gleitman, L., & Gleitman, H. Mother, please, I'd rather do it myself: Some effects and non-effects of maternal speech to children. In C. Ferguson & C. Snow (Eds.), *Talking to children.* New York: Cambridge University Press, 1977.

Pinker, S. Formal models of language learning. *Cognition,* 1979, *1,* 217–283.

Pinker, S. What is a language, that a child may learn it, and a child, that he may learn a language? A review of K. Wexler and P. Culicover's "Formal Principles of Language Acquisition." *Journal of Mathematical Psychology,* 1981, *23,* 90–97. (a)

Pinker, S. *Crucial properties of the learnability proof for Lexical Functional Grammar.* Paper presented to the Sloan Foundation Workshop on Nontransformational Syntax. Stanford University, June 1981. (b)

Pinker, S. A theory of the acquisition of lexical interpretive grammars. In J. Bresnan (Ed.), *The mental representation of grammatical relations.* Cambridge, MA: MIT Press, 1982.

Pinker, S. *Language learnability and language development.* Cambridge, MA: Harvard University Press, 1984.

Pinker, S. On establishing the cardinality of the set of natural languages: A reply to Pullum. Manuscript in preparation.

Pinker, S., & Hochberg, J. *Syntactic and semantic properties of parental speech to children.* Manuscript in preparation.

Prideaux, G. A functional analysis of English question acquisition: A response to Hurford. *Journal of Child Language,* 1976, *3,* 417–422.

Rosch, E. On the internal structure of perceptual and semantic categories. In T. E. Moore (Ed.), *Cognitive development and the acquisition of language.* New York: Academic Press, 1973.

Rosch, E., & Mervis, C. B. Family resemblances: Studies in the internal structure of categories. *Cognitive Psychology,* 1975, *7,* 573–605.

Slobin, D. I. Cognitive prerequisites for the development of grammar. In C. Ferguson & D. I. Slobin (Eds.), *Studies of child language development.* New York: Holt, Rinehart & Winston, 1973.

Slobin, D. I. Universal and particular in the acquisition of language. In L. Gleitman & E. Wanner (Eds.), *Language acquisition: The state of the art.* Cambridge: Cambridge University Press, 1982.

Slobin, D. I. Crosslinguistic evidence for the language-making capacity. In D. I. Slobin (Ed.), *The crosslinguistic study of language acquisition.* Hillsdale, N.J.: Lawrence Erlbaum Associates, in press.

Snow, C. E., & Ferguson, C. A. (Eds.). *Talking to children.* Cambridge: Cambridge University Press, 1977.

Sternberg, S. High speech scanning in human memory. *Science,* 1966, 153, 652–654.

Walsh, R. W. *A computer model for the acquisition of lexical interpretive grammar.* Unpublished bachelor's thesis, Harvard University, 1981.

Wexler, K., & Culicover P. *Formal principles of language acquisition.* Cambridge, MA: MIT Press, 1980.

Wilson, R., Pinker, S., Zaenen, A., & Lebeaux, D. *Productivity and the dative alternation.* Paper presented at the Boston University Conference on Language Development, October 1981.

Author Index

Darcy, N. T., 320, 321, *343*
Darley, F., 300, *318*
De Avila, E. A., 330, *343*
Delattre, P., 8, *32*
Denes, P., 6, 27, *31*
Denninger, M., 251, *289*
de Paulo, 402, *440*
de Villiers, J., 409, 430, *440*
de Villiers, P., 409, 430, *440*
Diaz, R. M., 319, 320, 341, *343*
Di Johnson, A., 161, *193*
Dixon, D., 78, *127*
Dixon, R. M. W., 223, *243*
Dooling, R. J., 10, *32*
Dore, J., 271, 272, 274, *288,* 346, *366*
Dowley, G., 350, *367*
Duchan, J., 230, *243*
Duncan, S. E., 320, *343*
Dunn, L., 334, *343*
Durost, W. N., 167, *193*

E

Earl, N., 122, *126*
Eamon, D. B., 140, *155*
Edwards, M., 301, *316*
Eiler, R. E., 8, 21–26, 29, *31, 32*
Eimas, P. D., 9–12, 16, 17, 20, 21, 23–25, *32*
Elder, J. L., 65, *75*
Elkind, D., 82, 89, *125*
El'konin, D. B., 227, *243*
Ellis, R., 249, 250, 251, 253, 255, 286, *289*
Epstein, I., 321, *343*
Erreich, A., 425, *440*
Ervin, S., 230, *244,* 255, *289,* 370, *397*
Evatt, R., 299, *318*

F

Farr, R., 143, *155*
Farwell, C., 292, *316*
Fay, D., 79, 80, *125,* 388, *397*
Feifel, H., 82, 83, 116, *125*
Fein, G., 61, 63, 65, 67, 69, 70, 71, 73, *75,* 78, *125*
Feiss, K., 363, *366*
Feldman, C., 327, *343*
Feldman, H., 197, 205, 206, 207, *244*
Fenson, L., 63, *75*
Ferguson, C. A., 37, 42, *55, 56,* 139, *157,* 292, 315, *316,* 402, 432, *442*

Ferrier, L. J., 35, 37, 40, *55*
Fey, M., 295, *317*
Fillmore, C., 100, *125,* 211, 223, *244,* 387, *397*
Fischer, K. W., 63, 71, *76*
Fishman, J. A, 341, *343*
Flavell, J. H., 349, *366*
Fleisher, L. S., 151, *155*
Fodor, J. A., 137, *155,* 383, *397,* 408, *440*
Folger, K. M., 69, *75*
Folger, M., 293, 297, *317, 318*
Fowler, H. N., 138, *155*
Fox, D., 429, *441*
Fraser, C., 230, *243*
Fremgen, A., 79, 80, *125*
Frishberg, N., 207, *244*
Frisina, D. R., 161, *194*
Fromkin, V. A., 388, *397*
Fujimura, O., 1, *32*
Fukuda, T., 321, *343*
Furrow, D., 250, 251, 253, *289,* 402, *440*

G

Gajzago, C., 280, *289*
Gallivan, J., 105–114, 117, *125*
Garnes, S., 137, *155*
Garnica, O. K., 37, *55,* 97, *125*
Garvey, C., 65, *75*
Gavin, 8, *31, 32*
Geers, A. E., 137, *155*
Gelman, R., 95, *125,* 293, *316*
Gentile, A., 182, *193*
Gentner, D., 95–97, 119, *125,* 294, 311, *316*
Gibson, E. J., 146, *155*
Gleitman, H., 241, *245,* 250, *289,* 402, *440, 441*
Gleitman, L., 197, 241, 244, *245,* 250, *289,* 402, *440, 441*
Goldin-Meadow, S., 95, *125,* 197–199, 201, 205, 206, 215, 229, 233, 236, 238, 240, *244,* 293, 294, 298, 312, *316*
Goldman, S. R., 148, *156*
Golinkoff, R. M., 130, 133, 136, 146, *155,* 230, *244*
Golomb, C., 65, *75*
Goodman, N., 79, *125*
Goodnow, J., 81, *124*
Goodwin, M., 160, 161, *194, 195*
Grabo, R. P., 320, *343*
Gray, W., 85, *127*
Greenfield, P. M., 236, *244,* 348, *367*
Griffiths, N. L., 167, *193*

Rosch, E. H., 85, 87, 116, 127, 390, *398,* 409, 417, 442
Rosen, R., 169, *193*
Rosenblatt, D., 63, *76*
Rosenthal, R., 330, *344*
Ross, G., 349, *366*
Rowan, L., 304, *317*
Roy, C., 40, *55*
Rubin, A. D., 134, *157*
Rumelhart, D. E., 132, *157*
Rutter, M., 129, 144, 145, *157, 158*
Ryan, E. B., 133, 151, 153, *157*
Ryan, J., 296, *318*
Ryan, M. L., 37, 42, 49, 54, *56*

S

Sachs, J., 242, *245*
Saer, D. J., 320, 321, *344*
Sag, I., 135, *157*
Sag, J. A., 35, *56*
Saltz, E., 78, 79, *127*
Samuels, S. J., 130, 132, *156, 157*
Sandoval, J., 325, *344*
Sartre, J., 139, *157*
Schery, T., 309, *317*
Schieffelin, B., 248, *289*
Schlesinger, I. M., 236, *245,* 372, 377, 380, *398*
Schmitt, P. J., 169, 175, 187, *194*
Scholes, R. J., 135, 136, *157*
Schreiber, P., 135, *156*
Schultz, M. C., 37, *55*
Schvaneveldt, R., 148, 149, *157*
Schwartz, R., 291-295, 297, 299, 304, 310, 314, *317, 318*
Schwartz, S. P., 435, *440*
Scribner, S., 348, 360, *367*
Seligman, M., 95, *125,* 293, *316*
Semelar, T., 148, *157*
Shallert, D. L., 139, 140, *157*
Shatz, M., 402, *440*
Shen, M., 327, *343*
Shibamoto, J., 292, *318*
Shore, C., 69, *75*
Silverstein, M., 223, *245*
Simmons, A., 161, *194*
Simon, H. A., 132, 153, *156*
Simond, A. J., 334, *344*
Sinclair, H., 63, *76*
Sinclair, J. M., 139, *157*
Siqueland, E. R., 9, *32*

Slobin, D. I., 372, 373, 375, 376, 380-382, 391, *398,* 427, *442*
Smilansky, S., 65, *76*
Smiley, S. S., 140, *154*
Smith, B., 14, *32*
Smith, C. S., 227, *245*
Smith, E. E., 81, 87, *127*
Smith, F., 148, *157*
Smith, G. E., 435, *440*
Snow, C. E., 139, 143, *155, 157,* 258, *289,* 402, 432, *442*
Snyder, L., 69, *75*
Sorenson, J. M., 135, 136, *155, 157*
Spencer, H., 131, 132, *157*
Spieker, S., 37, *56*
Spiro, R. J., 133, 139, *157*
Stambak, M., 63, *76*
Stanley, J. C., 143, 145, 148, 153, *154*
Stanovich, K. E., 148, *157, 158*
Stark, R., 300, *318*
Steiner, V., 299, *318*
Stern, D. N., 1
Stern, S., 37, *56*
Stern, W., 70, *76,* 78, *127*
Sternberg, S., 399, 400, *442*
Stevens, K. N., 9, 24, *32*
Stevenson, E., 161, *194*
Stoel, C., 301, *316*
Stokoe, W. C., 203, 204, *245*
Stork, L., 65, *75*
Strange, W., 1, *32*
Straight, H., 295, *318*
Strauss, S., 371, *398*
Streeter, L. A., 8, 11, 12, 16-21, 23-25, 27, *32, 33*
Strohner, H., 175, 187, *194*
Stuckless, E. R., 161, *195*
Summerfield, Q. A., 8, 9, *33*
Sutton-Smith, B., 64, *76*
Swain, M., 330, 332, *342, 344*
Swartz, K., 82, 89, *127*
Syrdal-Lasky, A., 8, *32*

T

Tackeff, J., 230, *243*
Tallal, P., 300, *318*
Talmy, L., 381, 387, *398*
Tanouye, E., 294, *318*
Tavuchis, N., 89, *125*
Taylor, D. M., 341, *343*
Taylor, E. A., 141, *157*

Subject Index